Linux

THIRD EDITION

Tim Parker

SAMS

Unleashed

Copyright © 1998 by Sams Publishing

International Standard Book Number: 0-672-31372-3

Library of Congress Catalog Card Number: 98-85650

Printed in the United States of America

00   99   98   4   3   2   1

Trademarks

Warning and Disclaimer

EXECUTIVE EDITOR
Jeff Koch

ACQUISITIONS EDITOR
Jane Brownlow

DEVELOPMENT EDITOR
Mark Cierzniak

MANAGING EDITOR
Sarah Kearns

PROJECT EDITOR
Mike La Bonne

COPY EDITOR
Suzanne Rose

INDEXER
Cheryl A. Jackson

TECHNICAL EDITORS
Eric Richardson
Sriranga Veeraraghaven
Jan Walter

SOFTWARE DEVELOPMENT SPECIALIST
Jack Belbot

PRODUCTION
Terri Edwards
Brad Lenser
Donna Martin

Overview

Contents

About the Author

Dr. Tim Parker has written more than 40 books covering many aspects of the computer business. He is the technical editor of *SCO World Magazine*, as well as a frequent contributor to dozens of magazines, including *UNIX Review*, *Canadian Computer Reseller*, *UNIQUE: The UNIX Systems Information Source*, *Windows NT Systems*, and others. Dr. Parker is the most widely published UNIX author in the world. When not putting up with temperamental computers, he spends his time flying, diving, and riding his favorite motorcycle.

Dedication

This one is for Yvonne. What more can I say? *Amor vincit omnia.*

Acknowledgments

As with the previous versions of Linux Unleashed, this book has been superbly managed by the fine folks at Sams. Both **Jane Brownlow** and **Mark Cierzniak** worked with me to produce another tome we are all proud of. Thanks to the technical reviewers who took the time to make excellent suggestions for improvements and to the copy editors who made sure every sentence made sense. Without all these people working under very tight deadlines, we would have a much weaker book.

Thanks to the staff at **Caldera** for providing not only multiple versions of their Linux distribution, but also several applications for inclusion. Thanks also to **Lone Star** and **Cactus** for their Lone-Tar product. On a personal level, thanks to **my parents** for tolerating yet another few months when I couldn't visit. Thanks to "**the boys**" for the delightful deviations on Thursday nights. Finally, thanks to **Yvonne** for understanding why I had to, yet again, spend my mornings, days, and evenings in front of my computers instead of with her.

Tell Us What You Think!

As the reader of this book, *you* are our most important critic and commentator. We value your opinion and want to know what we're doing right, what we could do better, what areas you'd like to see us publish in, and any other words of wisdom you're willing to pass our way.

As the Executive Editor for the Operating Systems team at Macmillan Computer Publishing, I welcome your comments. You can fax, email, or write me directly to let me know what you did or didn't like about this book—as well as what we can do to make our books stronger.

Please note that I cannot help you with technical problems related to the topic of this book, and that due to the high volume of mail I receive, I might not be able to reply to every message.

When you write, please be sure to include this book's title and author's name, as well as your name and phone or fax number. I will carefully review your comments and share them with the author and editors who worked on the book.

Fax:	317-581-4663
Email:	opsys@mcp.com
Mail:	Executive Editor
	Operating Systems
	Macmillan Computer Publishing
	201 West 103rd Street
	Indianapolis, IN 46290 USA

Introduction

The phenomenal popularity of Linux has taken us by surprise. When we started to write the first edition of *Linux Unleashed* way back in 1994, we had no idea that Linux was going to take the world by storm. Oh sure, we knew Linux was a great operating system. We knew Linux was a superb way to play with UNIX on your PC. We knew experimenters and programmers would fall in love with Linux. But we didn't expect to be writing so many revisions of the book. This is, to date, the fifth *Linux Unleashed* book we've written, two of which were specifically aimed at RedHat and SlackWare versions, while this series has covered all versions. On top of that, my *Linux System Administrator's Survival Guide* (also published by Sams) has been in demand for the past three years.

Why is Linux so popular? Part of the reason has to be its ready availability both in terms of price (free or at a very low price) and accessibility (hundreds of Web and FTP sites, thousands of CD-ROMs in bookstores). Another part of the popularity has to be its attraction as a UNIX system. Whatever our friends in Redmond say, UNIX always has been more powerful than Windows (recent versions of Windows won't even run on an 80386!). This trend is bound to continue, because UNIX simply makes better use of the fast processors we use today. Multitasking and multithreading were invented for UNIX. Windows is just catching up now.

Yet another reason for the popularity of Linux is the number of applications available. Cruise any of the Web sites that offer Linux applications and you'll be overwhelmed. And these applications are not trivial games or half-hearted attempts to provide basic functionality to Linux. The applications are professionally done, full featured, and rival those selling for big bucks on any other operating system. Linux is also popular because of its support mechanism. Got a problem? Post a note on Usenet's Linux newsgroups and you'll have answers fast. Finally, Linux is popular because it's just plain fun to play with. What more can you ask of an operating system?

We've added quite a bit of new material to this edition of *Linux Unleashed*. We received a lot of suggestions by email that we took to heart and worked into better descriptions of installation and configuration, as well as some new application chapters. We've rewritten many chapters from scratch to make them more readable. The result, we hope, is a book you'll enjoy reading from start to finish.

Introduction

IN THIS PART

Introduction to Linux

by Tim Parker

IN THIS CHAPTER

CHAPTER 1

You've seen dozens of books about it. You've read magazine articles about it. There are Usenet newsgroups with hundred of messages a day, CD-ROMs of Linux archives sold by the thousands, and even more Windows users wandering around trying to figure out what to make of this Linux phenomenon. Despite the popularity of this operating system, there are still thousands, if not millions, of users who are curious about Linux but are afraid to take the first steps: installing and playing with the system. That's what this book is intended to help with. We'll guide you step-by-step through the installation procedure, show you how to use Linux, and generally introduce you to this wonderful world of UNIX.

Before we start, though, a quick word on pronouncing "Linux." There are two schools of thought about the *i* sound in "Linux"; because Linux is similar to UNIX and was originally developed by a programmer with the first name Linus, many assume that the long *i,* as in "line-ucks," is the correct pronunciation. On the other hand, Linux was actually developed to replace a UNIX workalike called Minix (with a short *i*), so the rest of the Linux community calls the operating system "lih-nicks." Which is correct? The original developers use the latter pronunciation, while most North Americans prefer the former. Choose whichever you prefer. Either way, we know what you mean.

What Is Linux?

Linux, for those who haven't figured it out by now, is a freely distributed multitasking multiuser operating system that behaves like UNIX. Linux was designed specifically for the PC (Intel CPU) platform and takes advantage of its architecture to give you performance similar to high-end UNIX workstations. A number of ports of Linux to other hardware platforms have also appeared, and they work much like the PC version that we'll concentrate on here.

To begin, let's look at the Linux operating system as a package. When you install Linux, what do you get? Here's a quick list, most of which is expanded in future chapters.

Linux's Kernel

Linux is a complete multitasking, multiuser operating system that behaves like the UNIX operating system in terms of kernel behavior and peripheral support. Linux has all the features of UNIX, plus several recent extensions that add new versatility to Linux. All source code for Linux and its utilities is freely available.

The Linux kernel was originally developed for the Intel 80386 CPU's protected mode. The 80386 was originally designed with multitasking in mind (despite the fact that most

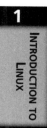

of the Intel CPUs are used with single-tasking DOS), and Linux makes good use of the advanced features built into the CPU's instruction set. Memory management is especially strong with the 80386 (compared to earlier CPUs). A floating point emulation routine allows Linux to function on machines that do not have math coprocessors.

Linux allows shared executables, so that if more than one copy of a particular application is loaded (either by one user running several identical tasks or several users running the same task), all the tasks can share the same memory. This process, called copy-on-write pages, makes for much more efficient use of RAM.

The Linux kernel also supports *demand paging*, which means that only the sections of a program that are necessary are read into RAM. To further optimize memory usage, Linux uses a unified memory pool. This enables all free memory on the system to be used as disk cache, effectively speeding access to frequently used programs and data. As memory usage increases, the amount of cache is automatically adjusted.

To support large memory requirements when only small amounts of physical RAM are available, Linux supports *swap space*. Swap space (which is somewhat of a misnomer) allows pages of memory to be written to a reserved area of a disk and treated as an extension of physical memory. By moving pages back and forth between the swap space and RAM, Linux can effectively behave as if it had much more physical RAM than it does, albeit at the cost of some speed due to the hard drive's slower access.

Linux uses *dynamically shared libraries* extensively. Dynamically shared libraries use a common library section for many different applications, effectively reducing the size of each application. Linux does allow full library linking (called *statically linked libraries*) for portability to machines that may not have the dynamic libraries.

To make Linux widely acceptable, it supports a number of different file systems, including those compatible with DOS and OS/2. Linux's own file system, called `ext2fs`, is designed for optimal use of the disk.

Linux is ideally suited for application development and experimentation with new languages. As part of the distribution software there are several different compilers, including C, C++, Fortran, Pascal, LISP, Ada, BASIC, and Smalltalk. Many of the Linux compilers, tools, debuggers, and editors are from the Free Software Foundation's GNU project.

GNU Software

GNU (a recursive acronym for *Gnu's Not UNIX*) was developed by the Free Software Foundation (FSF) to provide royalty-free software to programmers and developers. Since it was created, many programmer packages and toolkits have been developed and assigned to FSF for distribution. Most of the GNU software mirrors commercially available software (which usually has a hefty licensing fee attached), and in many cases is an improvement.

Linux includes many GNU utilities, including the languages mentioned earlier, debuggers, compiler tools, and more. Text processing, print utilities, and other GNU tools are also included with most Linux distributions.

X

X (sometimes called X Window) is a graphical user interface designed at MIT to provide portable GUI applications across different platforms. The version of X supplied with Linux is called XFree86, and is a direct port of the standard X11R5 system to 80386-based architectures. XFree86 has been enhanced to provide compatibility with some other GUIs, including Open Look.

XFree86 supports several different video cards at a number of resolutions, offering a high-resolution graphical interface. Any X application can be recompiled to run properly under Linux, and a number of games, utilities, and add-on applications have been developed and supplied as part of the X system.

The XFree86 system also includes application development libraries, tools, and utilities. This allows programmers to write applications specifically for X without having to invest in expensive software development kits or libraries.

DOS and Windows Interface

Because Linux is designed for PC machines, it made sense to provide some compatibility with Microsoft MS-DOS as part of the operating system. Linux provides a DOS emulator as part of the distribution system, which allows many DOS applications to be executed directly from within Linux. Don't expect complete portability of DOS applications, though, as some are written to access peripherals or disk drives in a manner that Linux can't cope with. The WINE project has developed a Microsoft Windows emulator for Linux. This enables Windows applications to be run from within Linux, too. A better approach, called WABI, is available at additional cost. WABI lets Linux run Windows applications under X.

Linux does allow you to transfer files seamlessly between DOS and the Linux file system, accessing the DOS partitions on a hard disk directly, if so configured. This makes it easy to move files and applications back and forth between the two operating systems.

TCP/IP

TCP/IP (Transmission Control Protocol/Internet Protocol) is the primary networking system used by UNIX and Linux. TCP/IP is a full family of protocols that were developed for the Internet, and you must use TCP/IP when you venture out onto the Internet. If you want to interconnect with other UNIX machines, you will probably have to use TCP/IP as well.

The Linux TCP/IP implementation provides all the networking software and drivers usually associated with a commercial UNIX TCP/IP package. With it you can create your own local area network, attach to existing Ethernet LANs, or connect to the Internet.

Networking is a strong feature of Linux and will be dealt with in considerable detail later in this book. You don't have to network your Linux system, of course, but a network is cheap and simple to install and is a fantastic method for transferring files between systems. You can network over modems, too, so you can have your friends' Linux machines on a network.

Linux's History

Linux was developed as a freely distributable version of UNIX. UNIX is the most widely used operating system in the world and has long been the standard for high-performance workstations and larger servers. UNIX, first developed in 1965, has a strong programmer-oriented user group that supports the operating system.

Because UNIX is a commercial product, though, it must be purchased for each platform it will run on. Licensing fees for UNIX versions for PC machines range from a few hundred to several thousand dollars. In an attempt to make UNIX widely available for no cost to those who want to experiment with it, a number of public domain UNIX systems have been developed over the years.

One of the early UNIX workalikes was Minix, written by Andy Tanenbaum. Although not full-featured, Minix provided a small operating system that could be used on PC machines. To expand on Minix, a number of users started developing an enhanced and more fully featured operating system that would take advantage of the 80386 CPU's architecture. One of the primary developers of this system, which became known as Linux, was Linus Torvalds of the University of Helsinki who released an early version of Linux in 1991. A first commercial "almost bug-free" release was unleashed to the programming community in March 1992.

Soon, many programmers were working on Linux, and as the challenge and excitement of producing a growing UNIX workalike caught on, Linux grew at a remarkable rate. It continues to grow as programmers adapt features and programs that were originally written as commercial UNIX products to Linux. New versions of Linux or its utilities are appearing at an astounding rate. It is not unusual to see a new release every week, even. As the number of developers working on Linux grew, the entire UNIX workalike operating system was eventually completed, if not perfected, and now includes all the tools you will find in a commercial UNIX product.

To avoid any charges for Linux whatsoever, the Linux developers do not use any code from other UNIX systems. There are no licensing fees involved with the Linux operating system and part of its mandate is to be made freely available. Some companies have undertaken the task of assembling and testing versions of Linux, which they package on a CD-ROM for a (usually) minimal price.

What Linux Can Do for You

Why should you bother with Linux? That's a fair question and one that is difficult to answer. If you're curious about UNIX or other operating systems, then Linux gives you a great environment to experiment with at a very reasonable—if not free—cost. If you need more power from your hardware than Windows or DOS gives you, then Linux is the operating system that can give it to you. If you need a robust, reliable server for your company Internet or World Wide Web services, Linux can do that just fine and very inexpensively. But, if you don't want to learn something new, don't want to leverage your existing hardware, and like the frequent crashes involved with Windows, then forget about Linux!

Learning UNIX Through Linux

Let's get one thing clear right from the start. Even though Linux is not called UNIX, it is a complete UNIX implementation. It conforms to many of the same standards as off-the-shelf, genuine, dyed-in-the-wool UNIX (in fact, better than many commercial UNIX versions), and it would be very difficult for even a veteran UNIX user to know whether they were working with Linux or UNIX without using tools that specify the identity of the system. Why isn't Linux called UNIX? Copyright reasons.

Because Linux is UNIX in all but name, it's a great way to learn UNIX. Not only can Linux run on most PCs that are sitting around your basement (try that with most commercial UNIX versions today; most of them need a Pentium or fast 80486), it is a fraction of the cost of a full-blown UNIX. Anything you learn with Linux is directly transferable to a

UNIX platform. Applications you write under Linux can usually be recompiled under UNIX and work perfectly.

Having said all that, Linux is an obvious way to learn the joys of UNIX. UNIX is one of the most powerful operating systems available and is commonly used by large corporations and other companies focusing on research and development. The reason is simple: UNIX puts the most power at a developer's fingertips. It's also the best way to network a bunch of machines. While you may not need to know UNIX now, you never know what will come up in the future. It looks great on your résumé, too.

Running a Business

You really can run a business on a system using Linux. UNIX is the most widely used business operating system, so it makes sense that Linux can do the same, too. It's entirely feasible for you to use a set of networked Linux servers connected to any other type of client machine (Windows, DOS, Macintosh, or other UNIX workstations) to control your entire business.

In the early days of Linux development, this was considered risky because the operating system just wasn't stable enough. Companies can't afford a server that crashes repeatedly. Since then, Linux has matured, become more robust, and offers all the features except the very high security classifications that commercial UNIX offers. It's not uncommon for a Linux system to go years without requiring a shutdown or a lockup (although you should occasionally reboot Linux systems to clean out temporary file directories and logs). That's something that very few other operating systems can claim. (How often has your Windows system crashed in the last couple of months?)

The real difference between using Linux or commercial UNIX for your business comes down to two issues: Linux is cheaper, but commercial UNIX has better technical support. Obviously, if money is no object for your business (at least in the thousand-dollar range that a complete commercial UNIX platform costs), then the first issue is not applicable. Technical support is important, especially for businesses, so it is often useful to pay for commercial UNIX versions for this feature alone. Having said that, it's also true that you'll usually get better technical support for Linux over the Internet than commercial UNIX help lines offer!

Internet Servers

Linux is ideally suited for running a Web server, FTP server, or email service to your home, office, or organization. Most of this is because of the UNIX heritage. All these services first appeared under UNIX, and the operating system is ideally suited to these tasks. Linux can be easily configured to work as an Internet server, as you will see in Chapter 47, "Setting Up an Internet Site."

Is Linux better than Windows NT, UNIX, or Macintosh for use as an Internet server? Perhaps better is not the word. It's certainly not any worse and costs less than all the others. Plus, Linux has a ton of public domain software available to help support Internet services, and there's lots of experience using Linux for small ISPs that you can draw on.

What You Need to Run Linux

The Linux operating system is attractive to many users because it offers a UNIX workstation environment on old and new Intel-based machines alike. The hardware requirements are not very demanding, unless you want to get into application development and extensive GUI use. You've got an old 80386 sitting in the basement? Why not convert it into a Linux platform. It'll run just fine. Ready to upgrade your older 80486 or early Pentium and just can't throw it away when the new machine arrives? A perfect Linux platform awaits you.

This chapter looks at the basic hardware necessary for Linux installation. The minimum requirements are discussed, as is support for most peripherals. Expanding your system with new hardware is covered later in this book in the system administration section.

Minimum System Requirements

Because Linux was mostly developed by PC users, the hardware support built into the operating system is fairly typical for a PC. There are few esoteric devices that have drivers, unless a programmer took the time to write one and then released it to the Linux community. There is also a scarcity of third-party vendors offering hardware accessories (such as multiport boards) for Linux, although this is slowly changing as Linux use becomes widespread.

The minimum system requirements for Linux is an 80386SX or better, 2MB RAM or more, floppy disk drive, a hard drive with 40MB or more, and a video card and monitor. Having said that, most users' systems are better equipped. To get realistic performance from a non-GUI (character-based) Linux installation, you need an 80386 with 8MB RAM. If you want to run X or Motif, a fast 80486 or Pentium with 16MB RAM is plenty.

Let's look at each of the component parts of a Linux system in a little more detail.

Motherboard Requirements

The hardware required to set up a Linux system mirrors a typical PC installation. It starts with the motherboard, which should be an Intel 80386 or later (or one of the Intel workalikes such as AMD). Remarkably, Linux will run even on a slow 80386SX, although "slow" is the operative word whenever you try to do anything on these old systems.

For application development work, though, an 80486DX or later is recommended because of the high CPU usage of the compiler and linker. The same is true of X users, since X is a notorious CPU hog. You can compile applications on an 80386, just as you can run X on one, but the performance can sometimes deteriorate to the point of annoyance.

Linux can make use of a floating point unit if you have one (they are built into the DX and Pentium series chips). If an FPU is not installed, Linux will provide a memory-based emulator that has reasonable performance. Either Intel or workalike add-on FPUs are supported, although some problems have been reported with third-party floating point units, such as the Weitek chip.

Linux supports ISA (Industry Standard Architecture), EISA (Extended Industry Standard Architecture), and PCI (Peripheral Component Interconnet) motherboards, but not MCA (IBM's MicroChannel Architecture). VESA Local Bus motherboards, which allow peripheral cards direct access to the motherboard components, are also supported if you have one of these earlier units lying around.

RAM requirements vary depending on the size of the Linux system you want to run. A minimum Linux system executes quite well in 2MB, although there is a great deal of swapping involved. 4MB of RAM should be considered an effective minimum, with more memory resulting in faster performance. For development work and X users, 8MB is a good working minimum (although X functions with 4MB with a lot of swapping). Reasonable performance requires 16MB to avoid swapping.

Linux systems that will have more than one user should increase the amount of RAM. Each user's load dictates the amount of RAM required. For example, 8MB easily supports two users, even both running X. With a third-party multiport board supporting eight users, 16MB RAM is a good choice, although they cannot run X. For X users, a good rule of thumb is 4MB per user minimum, unless the Linux machine can offload the X processing to the user's machine in a client-server layout.

Linux uses all the available RAM in your machine. It does not impose any architectural limitations on memory as DOS and some other operating systems do. Any available memory is completely used.

To extend the amount of physical RAM on a system, a Linux swap partition is recommended. The swap space is used as a slower extension of actual memory, where data can be exchanged with physical RAM. Even with RAM-heavy systems, a swap space should be created. The size of the swap space depends on the amount of RAM on the system, the number of users, and the typical usage.

Hard Disks

Linux can run completely from a floppy with no hard disk, although it doesn't offer a truly useful environment. Linux is designed primarily for hard disk use and supports all the common hard disk controller systems including IDE (Integrated Drive Electronics), EIDE (Extended Integrated Drive Electronics), ESDI (Enhanced Small Device Interface), RLL (Run Length Limited), and SCSI (Small Computer System Interface). Linux supports the older 8-bit original PC controllers, although most of today's controllers are 16-bit AT or PCI designs.

Linux is not choosy about the manufacturer and type of hard disk. As a rule, if DOS can handle the drive, so can Linux. This applies to all but SCSI drives, which require special handling. However, Linux is still restricted by older PC BIOS versions which impose limitations on the number of sectors, heads, and cylinders. There is an effective 1,024KB size limit on drives with these older BIOS chips, and even some smaller drives can't be handled properly by Linux or DOS because of BIOS problems. Some device drivers now make these drives accessible to DOS and Linux but you have to root around to find the correct driver. If you can't find the proper driver and have one of the older BIOS chips, the BIOS will step the drive down in capacity to one of the acceptable formats, effectively removing disk space from use (for example, your brand new 8GB drive may be only a 1GB to your machine, wasting 7GB of disk space). Occasionally, you can solve these BIOS limitations by replacing the BIOS itself, although upgrades for older machines are seldom available.

SCSI devices are supported by Linux for most standard devices, but there are many different SCSI controllers and protocols on the market and not all work well with Linux. Linux does support the most common SCSI controllers, though. Some other controllers are supported with enhanced BIOS chips on the PC motherboard. A size limitation on the SCSI drives is still imposed by older BIOS versions, so a 2GB drive has only 1GB available to Linux and DOS. Other UNIX systems, such as SCO UNIX, can use the rest of the drive in most cases.

The size of disk space required by Linux depends on the parts of the operating system that are installed. A minimum effective system should be considered as 20MB, which gives enough room for the basic utilities but not X. If you want to load the entire basic

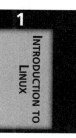

Linux system, including development tools and X, you should provide at least 250MB just for the files. On top of these values, add whatever space is required for your personal files and temporary storage by Linux. A good rule of thumb is to double the space requirements.

On top of the user space, remember to leave room for the swap space. Although the swap space size depends on the purpose and use of the system, a good number to use is 40MB to 64MB.

More than one drive can be used, although a Linux partition should be placed on the first drive. If you need it, DOS and Windows must be loaded on the first drive, as well, because partitions can be placed on other drives if necessary. The number of drives supported depend on the drive controller and BIOS. IDE systems are usually limited to two drives, while EIDE can handle four drives. ESDI and RLL controllers are usually limited to two drives. SCSI controllers can handle up to seven drives per controller (15 with the newer SCSI standards), and several controllers can be located in a single system. SCSI is the most versatile (and also the most expensive) system.

Because hard disks are now inexpensive, obtaining large-capacity drives is relatively easy. Linux can share a disk with up to three other operating systems (and even more with a few tricks), so if you plan to load DOS, Windows 95, and Linux, for example, allocate enough space for each operating system when loaded.

Video System

Linux can use almost any video card that works without special drivers under DOS and Windows. This includes CGA, EGA, VGA, and Super VGA, as well as Hercules video cards. Some enhanced resolution cards are also supported under Linux, such as the Cirrus Logic, Diamond, ATI, and Trident cards. Since there are hundreds of video cards available, though, there are not enough drivers for all models and special video modes available. Because most cards support default VGA and SVGA modes, these can be used in almost every case.

X imposes its own video card requirements, which require bitmap capabilities of a high-resolution card. Although X can run on a VGA or SVGA system, for optimum results a high-resolution card is required. For this reason, make sure that a video driver is available for Linux before purchasing a new video card or that it is compatible with an older card that works with a driver already in existence.

Mouse

Linux doesn't use the mouse for character-based sessions, but it is necessary for X. Linux handles practically every type of mouse and trackball that has DOS or Windows drivers. This includes the Microsoft, Logitech, Mouse Systems, and other vendors as well as compatibles. The bus and serial-port mouse are both supported.

Some other pointing devices such as pens, as well as some joysticks used for cursor movement, are supported.

Tape Drives

Any SCSI tape drive that has a controller recognized by Linux is usable. There are other tape drives that use a proprietary interface which requires a dedicated hardware card. In most cases, if the IRQ, DMA, and memory address can be configured into Linux, the tape drive will be accessible.

Some QIC and similar small-cartridge drives are becoming popular, driven either by the floppy controller card or the parallel port. Drivers for some of these tape drives are available, although not all are supported. Since many of these small QIC drives rely on proprietary compression schemes to boost data density on tapes, you may not be able to write more than the raw cartridge capacity to these drives.

CD-ROM

Because most CD-ROMs use either a SCSI or EIDE interface, you will need either a SCSI or EIDE controller card. Older CD-ROM drives used to be driven by a variety of cards, such as sound boards. For these, you need a suitable Linux driver. SCSI-based CD-ROM drives will be recognized and supported by Linux as long as the SCSI controller card is recognized.

Linux can't read all formats of CD-ROMs. At present, it handles only ISO-9660 format file systems. Although ISO-9660 is widely used, not all CD-ROMs are written using it so don't be surprised if a DOS or Macintosh CD-ROM cannot be mounted properly.

Removable Media

Removable media support in Linux depends on the type of interface used by the media. Most SCSI-based systems (such as Iomega's Jaz and SCSI ZIP drives, as well as SyQuest SCSI cartridges) can be used, although the changing of media while a file system is loaded is seldom properly supported. Iomega's Bernoulli systems and LaserSafe Pro magneto-optical cartridge systems can all be used with Linux without special drivers,

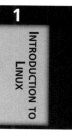

as long as the cartridges can be formatted. Some other magneto-optical and removable magnetic media systems will also function properly.

Some removable media requires special drivers, especially those which do not use SCSI but rely on a dedicated hardware card. There is very limited support in Linux for these devices; what is there is mostly provided by programmers who have written a driver for their own use and then made it public domain.

Printers

Practically all parallel and serial port printers are widely supported as nonintelligent devices. Some drivers are available for specific popular printers, such as the Hewlett-Packard LaserJets and DeskJets, although there are many printers that do not have dedicated drivers yet. If no driver exists for your printer, it will behave as an ASCII-only device.

You can often program your own interface to nonsupported printers by writing a translation table or device driver.

Modems

Linux supports most serial asynchronous modems, as well as some synchronous devices. Support for ISDN modems is also available as well. As a general rule, if DOS and Windows can use the modem, so can Linux.

Linux supports all baud rates, including the newer compression schemes such as 56K systems with some driver installation. More than one modem is supported on the system. Indeed, you can hang as many modems off a Linux system as you have serial ports.

Terminals

Linux supports character-based terminals connected through a serial port or a multiport card. Most existing character-based terminals can be used, and any terminal for which you have the control codes can be added. Graphics terminals, in the UNIX sense, use simple ASCII graphic characters and are not X-capable.

X terminals are supported although not all X terminals work properly. X terminals typically need a high-speed connection to properly display graphics (either through a serial port or from a network port). A PC running X client software can function as an X terminal, as well.

Multiport Cards

Some UNIX-based multiport cards will work with Linux because drivers have been released either by the vendor or users. Before purchasing a multiport card, though, check the availability of drivers. Some multiport cards offer expansion parallel ports as well as serial ports, and these will also need drivers.

Some multiport cards can be connected through a SCSI controller card instead of built as a dedicated card that plugs into an expansion slot. Even SCSI-based expansion cards will need a driver for Linux to use them properly. Network-based multiport cards, including remote access servers, often work without special drivers because each port on the card behaves like a network device.

Network Cards

Since Linux is a UNIX system, its primary network protocol is TCP/IP. Other protocols can be used with Linux, but because TCP/IP is included with each Linux software package and is the default network protocol, it is the most widely used. TCP/IP's role as the protocol of the Internet also makes it popular. TCP/IP is usually used over Ethernet networks, so most networking systems in Linux are designed around Ethernet.

Many Ethernet network interface cards (NICs, also called network adapters) are available. The most popular Ethernet cards from 3Com, Novell, Western Digital, Hewlett-Packard, and Intel all work cleanly with Linux. Many compatible Ethernet NICs from other vendors also function properly.

Copyrights

Just because Linux is distributed free, it doesn't mean the software is not copyrighted. Linux is copyrighted under the GNU General Public License (GPL) which is known in the programming community as a "copyleft" instead of "copyright" because it allows you to redistribute the Linux software to anyone who wants it, along with the complete source code. However, the original owner of the components retains the copyrights to the software.

There is no warranty of any kind with Linux. Even if you buy the Linux software from someone and pay them for maintenance, you cannot ever deal with the Linux programmers themselves. They make no statement of functionality at all. If Linux destroys all your accounting data, for example, it's tough luck. You assume the risk. However, it's also true that Linux has proven itself very stable and there are no incidents of serious data damage that were not caused by user error! Another way of looking at the issue is

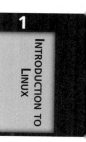

that if you are going to trust your business to Linux, you may be better off buying a commercial UNIX system that does have a warranty.

According to the GNU GPL, you can even sell Linux, if someone is willing to pay for it. You can modify any of the code and repackage it as you want. However, you do not own the software and cannot claim copyright, even if you have modified the source code. One condition imposed by the GNU GPL is that you must provide all source code with the system if you sell it for profit, so others can further modify and sell it, too.

There are no royalties of shareware fees paid to the authors and developers of Linux. For the most part, they provide the software to end users simply for the true love of programming and to share their code with other programmers who appreciate it.

Getting Help

Linux does not have a telephone support line. In one sense, you are on your own when you install Linux. On the other hand, there are many thousands of Linux users who are willing to help everyone from neophyte to experienced programmer. All you have to know is where to look for help. There are two sources: written documentation and the user community.

The first exposure most people get to Linux is the Linux INFO-SHEET, a relatively short ASCII document that is available from Usenet, BBSs, and many user groups. The INFO-SHEET is a quick summary of Linux and is posted at regular intervals to the Linux newsgroups on Usenet.

The Linux Documentation Project was created to provide a complete set of public domain documentation for Linux. From a few rough installation notes a couple of years ago, the documentation has expanded to include almost a thousand pages, some very good, some not. The following primary documents are currently available or soon to be released:

- Linux Installation—how to install and configure Linux
- Linux User's Guide—a guide for first-time users
- Linux System Administrator's Guide—a guide to various aspects of system administration
- Linux Network Administration Guide—setting up and using networks
- Linux Kernel Hacker's Guide—a guide to modifying the Linux kernel

As well as these primary documents, there are about a dozen smaller guides to specific or esoteric aspects of Linux. These smaller guides are called "How to" documents.

Together, they form a growing document suite that covers practically every aspect of Linux. Not all the documents are up-to-date, as changes to the operating system have occurred since they were first written.

The Linux documents have been written by several different people, so the styles and layout are not consistent. However, these documents are available with most distributions of the software. A bound printed copy of the documentation set of the Linux Documentation Project is available, published by Linux Systems Labs.

A number of Frequently Asked Questions (FAQ) files are available through the Linux newsgroups on Usenet and as part of the distribution set. The FAQs tend to be quick problem-solving items, designed to save you from thumbing through many pages of online documentation. One FAQ called the META-FAQ is available and provides basic information about Linux, where to get it, and the documentation that goes with it. It, too, is regularly posted to newsgroups.

There is a file called the Linux Software Map (LSM) that contains a list of many of the components in Linux. Unfortunately, the LSM is incomplete and lacks considerable chunks of data. However, it is a good starting point if you want to see what is included with Linux. The LSM is updated at intervals and can be obtained from Usenet, from a Linux FTP site, or with many distribution sets.

Finally, there are the Linux mailing lists, available to anyone with email to the Internet (or forwarded by someone with access). Information on the Linux mailing lists (there are quite a few) is available from Usenet newsgroups or BBSs.

Usenet Newsgroups

Linux newsgroups on Usenet are a useful forum for information and answers to questions about Linux. There are several different newsgroups about Linux, and you should use your newsreader software to search for all newsgroups with the work "linux" in the title. Many online services such as CompuServe and Delphi allow access to the newsgroups, and some have their own forums for Linux users. Bulletin Board Systems (BBSs) dedicated to Linux in whole or in part are also appearing, and many excerpt the Usenet conversations for the BBS users who do not have access to Usenet.

Usenet is a collection of discussion groups (called "newsgroups") available to Internet users. There are over 10,000 newsgroups generating hundred of megabytes of traffic every day. Of all these newsgroups (which cover every conceivable topic), several are dedicated to Linux.

You can access Usenet newsgroups through newsreader software that accesses either the Internet or a local site that does (called a newsfeed). Alternatively, most online services such as CompuServe, America Online, and Delphi also offer access to Usenet as part of their service (sometimes at an additional cost).

Usenet newsgroups are divided into three categories: primary newsgroups that are readily available to all users; local newsgroups with a limited distribution (usually based on geography); and alternate newsgroups that may not be handled by all news servers due to the relaxed rules of etiquette on them. The primary newsgroups of interest to Linux users when this book was written are:

- `comp.os.linux.admin`—deals with administering Linux systems
- `comp.os.linux.advocacy`—proponents of the Linux system sound off
- `comp.os.linux.announce`—announcements important to the Linux community (a moderated newsgroup, meaning someone approves the postings before you get to see them)
- `comp.os.linux.answers`—questions and answers to problems about Linux
- `comp.os.linux.development`—ongoing work on Linux in general
- `comp.os.linux.development.apps`—ongoing work on Linux applications
- `comp.os.linux.development.system`—ongoing work on the Linux operating system
- `comp.os.linux.hardware`—issues with Linux and hardware support
- `comp.os.linux.help`—questions and advice about Linux
- `comp.os.linux.misc`—Linux-specific topics not covered by other groups
- `comp.os.linux.networking`—Linux networking issues
- `comp.os.linux.setup`—setup and installation problems with Linux

These primary newsgroups should be available at all Usenet sites unless the system administrator filters them out for some reason. The other Linux newsgroups tend to change frequently, primarily because they are either regional or populated with highly opinionated users. The `.alt` (alternate) newsgroups are particularly bad for this. One `.alt` newsgroups in operation when this book was written is

        `alt.uu.comp.os.linux.questions`

If you have access to Usenet, regularly scan the newsgroup additions and deletions to check for new Linux newsgroups or existing groups that have folded. Notices about newsgroup changes are usually posted to all existing groups, but every now and then one gets through without fanfare. Online services that provide access to Usenet usually maintain lists of all active newsgroups which can be searched quickly.

The traffic on most of these Linux newsgroups deal with problems and issues of installing, configuring, administering, or using the operating system. There is a lot of valuable information that passes through the newsgroups quickly, so check them regularly. The most interesting messages that deal with a specific subject (called a "thread") are often collected and stored as an archive for access through an FTP site.

What's in This Book?

This book is intended to guide you through the installation and configuration of Linux, setting up and using the system from a system administration point of view, and take you step-by-step from being a neophyte to UNIX and Linux to a proficient user. Throughout this book, we touch on a lot of material, some in a considerable amount of depth, other subjects with just a superficial treatment to give you an idea of the subject and what Linux can do.

What this book is not is an all-inclusive reference. There's no way for any book under 10,000 pages to tell you everything you need to know. We can't hope to teach you things such as C or C++ programming, for example, although we can show you how to set up your environment and use the included compilers. There's no way we can walk you through every problem or issue that can arise in the next few years of using Linux, either, but we can give you enough of a background and the appropriate tools to deal with the issues. We also let you know where to go to get answers.

So, enjoy working with Linux and this book. We've tried very hard to make it a pleasant read, and hope you learn a lot. Above all, have fun. Linux is a great operating system!

Summary

Now that we've covered the basics of Linux, we can move on to looking at the types of Linux that are available, installing the system of your choice, and getting to know the operating system. The rest of this section of the book deals with installation and basic configuration. The following section then leads you into using Linux. If you've already installed your operating system, you can skip ahead to the "Getting to Know Linux" section. Otherwise, read the next few chapters to help you get the system installed correctly.

The following chapters will be helpful if you want to learn how to:

Install Linux, see Chapter 3, "Installing Linux."

Use Linux, see Part II, starting with Chapter 6, "Getting Started."

Install the X software package, see Chapter 22, "Installing and Configuring XFree86."

Administer your Linux system, start with Chapter 32, "System Administration Basics."

Types of Linux

by Tim Parker

CHAPTER 2

This chapter covers a couple of subjects that you will need to know about prior to installing Linux. If you do not already have Linux available to install or if you want to obtain a different version than the one you have, the first part of this chapter explains where and how to get Linux. The rest of the chapter explains which disk sets are necessary to install Linux and what each disk set does. You'll need to know this information when you add features to your Linux system.

There are a lot of different versions of Linux available on the market: There's Slackware, Red Hat, Caldera, SLS (Softlanding Linux System), TAMU (Texas A&M University), Yggdrasil, and about a dozen others. There are differences between the versions—some significant, others not. The version that is best for you is difficult to predict ahead of time. A lot of the differences you'll find in versions of Linux are little items that add up: better installation routines and administration tools, technical support, better hardware drivers, and so on. While you can mix and match to some extent, most people choose one version and stick with it. While you can always reload another version of Linux, there should be very good reasons to do so before you bother.

Where to Get Linux

Linux is readily (and freely) available for you if you know where to look. Since Linux is distributed without a central organization controlling it (as with commercial UNIX versions), there is no single responsible party to keep Linux updated and easily available. It is completely up to you to find a source of the software and to make sure the version you receive has all the components you need. You also have to be careful choosing versions because many distributors such as book and computer superstores often stock several different versions (often from the same Linux distributor), some of which may not be very recent.

There are several ways you can obtain a copy of Linux. Choose whichever method is most convenient or economical for you, depending on your priorities. The most common method of obtaining a complete set of Linux binaries and utilities is through a CD-ROM such as the one that accompanies this book or in a packaged multi-CD set from a distributor such as Workgroup Solutions. Alternatives to purchasing a CD-ROM include downloading from FTP sites and Bulletin Board Systems (BBSs), most of which offer free copies (although you absorb download time charges, if any). You can also get a copy of Linux mailed to you from some sources.

The method you choose to obtain a copy of Linux also dictates to some extent how complete the software set will be. CD-ROM versions, for example, usually have every piece of Linux software available included on the disk, while some BBSs and FTP sites only offer a basic distribution that is enough to install and use as a basic system. The small systems, for example, may not include all the available language compilers and X software.

CD-ROM Linux

There are over a dozen different manufacturers and distributors offering CD-ROM–based versions of Linux as this book is being written. The packages differ in the release number of the Linux software that is included on the disk, as well as the amount of bundled material included with the operating system. You can purchase single and double CD-ROM packages that include most of the software, or four and six CD-ROM collections that include a ton of support material, Usenet threads, auxiliary documentation, and alternate kernel builds.

Most distributions include much of the same basic products but differ in how they are organized. There's also a big difference in the value of added features from each distributor, such as new installation documents and utilities or system administration tools. Since most Linux distributions are available for well under $100 even for the 6-disk sets, choose the set of software and release of Linux that best suits you.

Check the disks you buy to make sure you have the most recent release of the Linux kernel (compare version numbers among CD-ROMs available) as well as all the add-ons that you want. Cover sheet copy on most CD-ROMs gives you a general idea of the release number (such as Slackware 3.4 or Red Hat 5.0) and the included software (such as XFree86, compilers, and so on). It can sometimes be hard to identify the contents from the sparse identification on the cover of some CD-ROM collections, so you may find yourself unwittingly purchasing outdated or incomplete material. Luckily, Linux CD-ROMs tend to be inexpensive.

A few vendors have dressed up their Linux collections with added utilities or boot disks that make installation much easier. The addition of precompiled games, applications, and user utilities makes these CD-ROMs a little more attractive. Typically, the vendors charge a little more for these versions, but often you get a well-written manual and sometimes technical support as well for the few extra dollars. Caldera is a good example of a popular premium package (although "premium" is a false term here, since Caldera's software tends to cost less than some of the larger shareware CD-ROM collections).

FTP Sites

The File Transfer Protocol (FTP) is a widely used Internet protocol (part of the TCP/IP family) that lets you transfer files from remote machines. There are several anonymous FTP sites that distribute Linux software (anonymous means you don't need an account on the remote machine to access the files; you log in as "guest" or "anonymous" and use your name or email address as a password). If you have access to the Internet, either directly or through an online service provider like CompuServe or America Online, you can access these Linux distribution sites.

To use FTP, you must be on a machine that supports TCP/IP. This can be your existing PC running a DOS or Windows package or a UNIX or Linux workstation, either of which is connected to an Internet service that gives you FTP capabilities. Both ends of an FTP connection must be running a program that provides FTP services, although it's a safe bet that if the system you are dialing into is an FTP site, they are running FTP! To download a file from a remote system, you must start your FTP software and instruct it to connect to the FTP software running on the remote machine.

The Internet has many FTP archive sites. These are machines designed to allow anyone to connect to them and download software. In many cases, FTP archive sites mirror each other so that they have exactly the same software. You connect to the site that is easiest to get to or gives you the best response speed. The most commonly used FTP site for Linux software is sunsite.unc.edu. The archives at sunsite contain a comprehensive list of available Linux software and older kernels, drivers, and utilities. Many of the CD-ROM collections you can buy in a store are simply copies of the contents of sunsite. If you're looking for Linux through FTP, sunsite.unc.edu is one of the best places to start.

Using FTP to Connect and Download Files

Using FTP to connect to a Linux FTP site is quite easy (assuming you have access to the Internet, of course). You can start FTP with the name of the remote system you want to connect to or enter it after starting FTP (the former is easier). If you are directly connected to the Internet, enter the ftp command with the name of the remote site, such as:

```
ftp sunsite.unc.edu
```

In this case, we're using a command-line interface, although there are some very useful GUI-based FTP clients, such as those with Windows X client packages. Using this type of interface is a lot friendlier than command-line FTP because it mirrors the Windows Explorer interface. You simply select the files you want on the remote machine and drag them to a folder on your machine. Packages like eXceed can be used to access your Linux X server from other machines on a local area network.

If you are using an online service such as CompuServe or Delphi, usually you must access their Internet service area and invoke FTP from there. Most online services let you enter the name of the FTP site at a prompt. A few services place limitations on the amount of traffic you can transfer, so downloading Linux may be bothersome with these services unless you like being hit with high surcharges.

Since many people use command-line-based FTP to obtain their Linux software, that's the version we'll use in this section. You can start FTP after you have connected to the Internet through your ISP. If you are using a Windows machine, a DOS window is often the easiest way to connect. Open a DOS window and enter the name of the server you want to reach on the ftp command line.

Once you issue the FTP command, your system attempts to connect to the remote machine. When it completes the connection successfully, the remote machine prompts you for a user ID. You must have a valid user ID and password for that system unless it supports anonymous FTP (which all Linux FTP sites do). When you first connect and before you log in, a message usually displays informing you that anonymous FTP is supported on the remote system. For example, the login below for the Linux FTP archive site sunsite.unc.edu immediately tells you anonymous login is acceptable:

```
ftp sunsite.unc.edu
331 Guest login ok, send your complete e-mail address as password.
Enter username (default: anonymous): anonymous
Enter password [tparker@tpci.com]:
¦FTP¦ Open
230-                WELCOME to UNC and SUN's anonymous ftp server
230-                      University of North Carolina
230-                    Office FOR Information Technology
230-                          SunSITE.unc.edu
230 Guest login ok, access restrictions apply.
FTP>
```

The login for an anonymous FTP site is usually "guest" or "anonymous." The login message usually tells you which is used or you can try both. The remote machine will prompt you for a password in most cases. You don't have to supply one with some systems, while others ask for your username or email address. This is used for tracking purposes only and has no security problems associated with it (unless you don't have a password on your local account!).

After the login process is finished and you have supplied the login and password, you then see the prompt "FTP>." This indicates the system is ready to accept FTP commands. Some systems display a short message when you log in which contains instructions for downloading files as well as any restrictions that are placed on you as an anonymous FTP user. Other information may be displayed about the location of useful files. For example, you may see messages like this one from the FTP site sunsite.unc.edu:

```
To get a binary file, type:  BINARY and then: GET "File.Name" newfilename
To get a text file, type:    ASCII  and then: GET "File.Name" newfilename
```

```
Names MUST match upper, lower case exactly. Use the "quotes" as shown.
To get a directory, type: DIR. To change directory, type: CD "Dir.Name"
To read a short text file, type: GET "File.Name" TT
For more, type HELP or see FAQ in gopher.
To quit, type EXIT or Control-Z.

230-  If you email to info@sunsite.unc.edu you will be sent help
➥information
230-  about how to use the different services sunsite provides.
230-  We use the Wuarchive experimental ftpd. if you "get"
➥<directory>.tar.Z
230-  or <file>.Z it will compress and/or tar it on the fly. Using ".gz"
➥instead
230-  of ".Z" will use the GNU zip (/pub/gnu/gzip*) instead, a superior
230-  compression method.
```

Once you are on the remote system, you can use Linux (UNIX) commands to display file contents and move around directories. To display the contents of a directory, use the command ls or the DOS equivalent dir. To change to a subdirectory, use the cd <dir> command. To return to the parent directory (the one above the current directory), use the command cd ... Unlike Linux, there are no keyboard shortcuts available with FTP so you have to type in the names of files or directories in their entirety (and correctly).

As you move through the directories and find a file you want to move to your system, use the FTP get command, as in:

```
get "file1.txt"
```

The commands get (download) and put (upload) are relative to your home machine, not to the remote. When you issue a get command, you are telling your system's FTP software to get a file from the remote machine. A put commands tells FTP to put a file from your local machine onto the remote machine. It is important to remember which command moves in which direction or you could accidentally overwrite files.

The quotation marks around filenames are optional for most versions of FTP, but they do provide specific characters to the remote version (preventing shell expansion). This can prevent error messages from FTP or accidental transfers of many files instead of just one, so quotation marks are a useful practice to employ.

When you issue a get command, the remote system transfers data to your local machine and displays a status message when it is completed. There is no indication of progress during transmission of a large file, so be patient. This is a sample transcript of a get command:

```
FTP> get "file1.txt"
200 PORT command successful.
150 BINARY data connection for FILE1.TXT (27534 bytes)
226 BINARY Transfer complete.
27534 bytes received in 2.35 seconds (12 Kbytes/s).
```

FTP provides two modes of file transfer: ASCII (7 bit characters) and Binary (8 bit characters). Some systems automatically switch between the two, although it is a good idea to manually set the mode to ensure you don't waste time. You must download all Linux distribution files in Binary mode. To set FTP in binary transfer mode (for any executable file), type the command

```
binary
```

You can toggle back to ASCII mode with the command ASCII. If you transfer a binary file in ASCII mode, it will not be executable. Transferring an ASCII file in Binary mode does not affect the contents of the file, so Binary is a good default transfer mode.

> **TIP**
>
> If there are many files you want to transfer all at once and don't want to bother typing each file's name, use the mget command. Simply type mget and a wildcard, and an FTP prompt appears asking if it should transfer each file matching that name. For example, let's say "mget *" matches all the files in the directory; you'll be asked whether you want to get each one. To suppress the questions and force a transfer of each file that matches your wildcard, do so by entering the command prompt. This turns off the prompts and transfers all the matching files one after another.

To quit FTP, type the command quit or exit. Both commands close your session on the remote machine, then terminate FTP on your local machine.

Keep in mind that the Linux archives are quite sizable, and transferring even a small distribution can take a while with asynchronous modems. If you use a slow modem (9,600 baud or less), you may want to consider an alternative method since your connection will have to remain in place for many hours. Some remote sites limit the amount of time you can stay connected.

Linux FTP Archive Sites

The list of Linux FTP archive sites changes slowly, but the sites listed below were all valid and accessible as this book went to press. Many of these sites are mirror sites, providing exactly the same content as the primary sites. The primary sites (also called home sites) for the Linux FTP archives are `tsx-11.mit.edu`, `sunsite.unc.edu`, and `nic.funet.fi`. Home sites are where most of the new software loads begin. The majority of sites on the previous list mirrors one of these three sites.

The site nearest you can be found by using the country identifier at the end of the site name (uk=United Kingdom, fr=France, and so on). Most versions of FTP allow either the machine name or the IP address to be used, although if the name cannot be interpreted by the local Internet gateway, the IP address is the best addressing method. Make sure you enter the four components of the IP address correctly. Table 2.1 shows the sites that were good sources of Linux material as this book went to press.

TABLE 2.1. LINUX FTP SITES AND THEIR IP ADDRESSES.

Site name	IP address	Directory
`tsx-11.mit.edu`	18.172.1.2	/pub/linux
`sunsite.unc.edu`	152.2.22.81	/pub/Linux
`nic.funet.fi`	128.214.6.100	/pub/OS/Linux
`ftp.mcc.ac.uk`	130.88.200.7	/pub/linux
`fgbl.fgb.mw.tu-muenchen.de`	129.187.200.1	/pub/linux
`ftp.infdrrnatik.twmuenchen.de`	131.159.0.110	/pub/Linux
`ftp.dfv.rwth-aachen.de`	137.226.4.105	/pub/linux
`ftp.informatik.rwth-aachen.de`	137.226.112.172	/pub/Linux
`ftp.ibp.fr`	132.227.60.2	/pub/linux
`kirk.bu.oz.au`	131.244.1.1	/pub/OS/Linux
`ftp.uu.net`	137.39.1.9	/systems/unix/ linux
`wuarchive.wustl.edu`	128.252.135.4	/systems/linux
`ftp.win.tue.nl`	131.155.70.100	/pub/linux
`ftp.stack.urc.tue.nl`	131.155.2.71	/pub/linux
`ftp.ibr.cs.tu-bs.de`	134.169.34.15	/pub/os/linux
`ftp.denet.dk`	129.142.6.74	/pub/OS/linux

If you encounter difficulties connecting to one site, try another. If difficulties persist, there may be a problem with your access to the Internet.

World Wide Web

Everyone is using the World Wide Web (WWW) and you can use it to obtain a copy of Linux from one of several different Web sites. The primary FTP site offers Web access through the URL:

```
http://sunsite.unc.edu/mdw/linux.html
```

You can use any Web client software, such as Mosaic or Netscape, to access the Web site and use the menu-driven system to download a copy of the Linux files. Most Linux Web sites also offer documentation files.

There are many different Linux support Web sites on the Internet now, too many to list. Use your favorite search engine (such as yahoo.com or altavista.digital.com) and use the keyword Linux. You'll get an overwhelming list of matches. You can usually narrow the search with keywords like "binaries" or a specific version (such as "Slackware").

Email

If you don't have access to a Linux distribution site through the Internet's FTP or Web services, you can still get the files transferred to you if you have email. This is an alternative for those using online systems which allow Internet mail but do not allow direct access to FTP sites and for some corporate systems that do not allow you to dial out directly to reach FTP sites but can transfer email. To get Linux by email from an FTP site, you can use the site's ftpmail utility.

All of the sites mentioned above in the Linux FTP site list support ftpmail. To get complete instructions on using ftpmail, all you need to do is send an email message to ftpmail login at one of the sites (for example, address your email to ftpmail@sunsite.unc.edu). The body of the email message should have only the word "help" in it. Any other comments may cause the ftpmail utility to incorrectly process your request. For this reason, you may want to suppress any signature files that are automatically appended to your email.

Upon receiving your request, ftpmail will send you instructions about how to use the service. In most cases you embed the FTP commands you want executed at the remote site as the body of your mail message. For example, to get a directory listing of the Linux directory, send a mail message with the body:

```
open sunsite.unc.edu
cd /pub/Linux
ls
quit
```

The `ftpmail` utility at the remote site processes the commands as if they were typed directly into FTP. To transfer a file to yourself through email, send the following mail message:

```
open sunsite.unc.edu
cd /pub/Linux
binary
get README
quit
```

This sends you the file README via email. The ftpmail system is slower than FTP since you must wait for the email to make its way to the target machine, be processed by the remote system's `ftpmail` utility, format a reply, then send the return message back to you. Still, ftpmail does provide a useful access method for those without FTP connections and an easy way to check the contents of the Linux directories on several machines without having to log in to them. This can be useful when you want to occasionally check for updates to the software.

One caution: The files you want to transfer may exceed your mail system's maximum file size limits. Some mail systems break the files into smaller chunks and allow you to reassemble them when you receive them, but some email systems impose a small size limit on email making it impractical to use ftpmail to get large files like the complete Linux software distribution.

Bulletin Board Systems (BBSs)

There are hundreds of Bulletin Board Systems (BBSs) around the world that now provide access to the Linux distribution software and support Linux discussion groups. Some BBSs regularly download new Linux releases from the FTP home sites, while others rely on the BBSs' users to update the software.

Any list of BBSs with Linux software would be lengthy and out of date quickly, so the best method to obtain this information is to obtain a list of current BBS sites from Zane Healy, who maintains a complete list of BBSs offering Linux material. To obtain the BBS list, send email requesting the Linux list to `healyzh@holonet.net`. If you don't have access to email, try a few local bulletin board systems and post messages asking for local sites that offer Linux software or ask someone with Internet access to post email for you. Many BBSs will also have the list, although the accuracy of the list may vary.

What's a Linux Release?

A Linux release has two meanings to most users. The first meaning has to do with the vendor or distributor that provides Linux. For example, both Slackware and Red Hat are Linux releases. As mentioned earlier in this chapter, the differences between some releases are subtle, but there are differences.

The second meaning of release has to do with the version of Linux you use. For example, Slackware 2.3 and Slackware 2.4 are both releases of Linux. More properly, these should be *versions* of the same release (Slackware), but the term release has been used for every new set of kernels and tools provided by Linux since the very early days. It's somewhat confusing when someone asks you which release of Linux you're using because you're not sure if they mean the vendor or version, so most people beat the problem by providing both ("I'm running Slackware 2.0.33," for example).

Do you need to have the very latest version of a Linux release? Most likely not. The differences between most version increases are typically small, especially for incremental releases such as 2.3 to 2.4. Unless there is some feature or driver support that you really want with the latest version, it's seldom worth the bother of upgrading. There are much more important differences between major version upgrades, such as from the 1.X series to 2.X series kernels. Major kernel upgrades are almost always worth installing, although you may have to reinstall everything from scratch with major version updates.

> **NOTE**
>
> Avoid the common trap of upgrading your system every time a new release of Linux is available. Some people have to be running the very latest version of each software package on their system, but the effects of moving from 2.0.33 to 2.0.34 are most likely undetectable on most systems. The real motivation for upgrading should be for better performance, drivers for hardware, or major version upgrades. If you do catch "versionitis," you're going to spend more time upgrading each component of your system than working (or playing) with it. Often, you'll end up reloading your entire system as well.

Linux Releases and Disk Sets

A release is a collection of Linux software sufficient to install and run the entire operating system. The release is made up of a number of collections of software, called disk sets (even though they may not come on disks). Most Linux systems have a number of disk sets included when you obtain the distribution software.

Although most of the CD-ROMs and FTP sites have the same software, a few label the disk sets differently. To illustrate the disk sets available with Linux, one of the more popular CD-ROM versions, Slackware, can be used as an example. The current set of disk sets available with the Slackware Linux distribution is:

- Disk Set A—the base system. This contains the kernel and a set of basic utilities including shell, editor, and user utilities. Disk Set A is the only disk set that fits on a single high-density floppy. This lets you install and run Linux even from a floppy disk!

- Disk Set AP—Linux applications, including many different editors, all the standard UNIX command utilities, man pages, and GNU add-ons like GhostScript.

- Disk Set D—program development. This disk set includes the GNU languages, development utilities, libraries, and compiler tools. There is also a lot of source code for libraries used to customize the Linux kernel.

- Disk Set E—GNU emacs editor.

- Disk Set F—FAQ (Frequently Asked Questions) files and other Linux help files.

- Disk Set I—documentation files for the GNU software.

- Disk Set IV—Interviews libraries, include files, and documentation. Interviews is a C++ GUI development package.

- Disk Set N—networking software. This disk set includes the TCP/IP protocol set, UUCP, mail utilities, news system, and several utilities.

- Disk Set OI—ParcPlace Object Builder and Object Interface Library. These are commercial development packages made available to Linux developers by ParcPlace.

- Disk Set OO—Object Oriented Programming (OOP) tools including the GNU Smalltalk compiler and the Smalltalk Interface to X (STX).

- Disk Set Q—source files for the Linux kernel and boot images.

- Disk Set T—the TeX and LaTeX2 test formatting systems. TeX is widely used for typesetting.

- Disk Set TCL—Tcl language set, including Tcl, Tk, TclX, and utilities.

- Disk Set Y—games collection.

- Disk Set X—XFree86 including the X system and several window managers.

- Disk Set XAP—applications for X, including file managers, GhostView, some libraries, games, and utilities.

- Disk Set XD—X development kit including X libraries, server link kit, and PEX support. This disk set is necessary if you are going to develop X-based applications.

- Disk Set XV—window manager for X. This disk set includes the XView libraries and the Open Look window managers. These can be used instead of the window manager included in Disk Set X.

Although Disk Set A lets you install a Linux system from a floppy, for a full installation (hard disk-based with standard utilities), you should have Disk Sets A, AP, D, and F. This collection gives you a character-based Linux system. If you want to run X, you will also need Disk Sets X and XAP. Programmers will need to load the development Disk Sets (D and XD, for X applications).

Updating Existing Linux Systems

If you've already got Linux up and running, it may be time to upgrade your system. In most cases, upgrading a running system is as easy as copying the new software into a directory and rebuilding your kernel to link in your existing drivers. In some cases, upgrading the system means loading everything from scratch (usually necessary only with a major version change or a change in Linux vendor).

Most Linux versions that you buy are not intended to upgrade existing software automatically (as Windows versions do, for example). Instead, you are often expected to back up everything on your disks, install the new version, and then restore the files from your backup. Luckily, usually all you have to do is copy a few kernel files over to your existing directory structure and recompile to upgrade most kernels. We will deal with upgrading existing systems in more detail in the next chapter.

Summary

In this chapter we've looked at what makes up a Linux release, where you can get Linux software, and information about the disk sets that make up Linux as a whole. Now you can get your software ready for the next step, which is installing and configuring Linux. Here's a list of chapters with related information about:

How to install Linux, see Chapter 3, "Installing Linux" and Chapter 5, "Wrapping Up the Installation."

How to use Linux, see Part II, including Chapter 6, "Getting Started," and Chapter 11, "bash."

How to install and configure the X server system, see Chapter 22, "Installing and Configuring XFree86."

System administration issues, see the chapters in Part VI including Chapter 32, "System Administration Basics."

Installing Linux

by Tim Parker

CHAPTER 3

Working with Linux

You have probably already installed Linux. Even so, you may not be happy with the installation, either because of poor organization or because you were experimenting with it and would like to try again with a better configuration. This chapter looks at the issues you should address when you install Linux for the first time (or reinstall it, as the case may be), and how to update your existing Linux installation with new software releases.

Bear in mind that this chapter takes a general approach to installing Linux using three of the popular versions of Linux: Slackware, Red Hat, and OpenLinux (which is based on Slackware). Depending on the version of Linux you are installing and the release version, your prompts and choices may be different. Luckily, much will be easy to figure out as all versions of Linux tend to have straightforward prompts once you get to the package installation routines.

The process for installing Linux is straightforward, although there are lots of little problems scattered throughout that can cause hassles. Don't believe the "easy installation" claims on many packages of the distribution software! Several steps still require patience, experimentation, and a knowledge of what is going on before Linux will install painlessly. The essential steps for installing Linux follow:

- Create boot and root disks for Linux.
- Partition the hard disk.
- Boot Linux from a floppy.
- Create a swap file.
- Create a Linux filesystem.
- Install the Linux software.
- Configure the kernel.
- Set the boot process.
- Reboot into Linux from your hard disk.

We look at each of these steps in a little more detail. The process is very similar for installing from a CD-ROM and from a disk (which may have come from an FTP site, for example). Because CD-ROM is the most common form of installation, we use that process as an example in this chapter.

If you are installing from floppy and have downloaded the distribution files (or copied them from a CD-ROM), you need a DOS-formatted floppy for each disk in the distribution disk set. You can use standard DOS copy commands to copy the disk set files to the floppy, one floppy for each file in the distribution set. The files are all numbered so you know which floppy is in which set, and what their order should be.

Floppyless Installation

If your hard disk already has an operating system like DOS, or one that produces a DOS window like Windows, you can try installing directly from the CD-ROM. Boot into your existing operating system, change to the CD-ROM drive, and look for a single executable program with either a .COM or .EXE extension. Some Red Hat Linux versions, for example, have an executable called RED HAT that takes care of the installation process for you. If that's the case, issue the following command at the DOS prompt (or whatever the executable is called):

```
RED HAT
```

You are asked a series of questions by the program to help it determine the best images for the boot kernel. You can also provide any special startup installation commands during this stage.

> **TIP**
>
> Do not run the floppyless installation process from inside a Windows 3.1, Windows 95, or OS/2 session. Boot your system into DOS or DOS mode and run it from there.

The floppyless installation routine guides you through the kernel determination process by displaying all possible choices on menus and prompting you for your answers. The process is intuitive and can be used by anyone who knows the type of hardware installed on their system. If you are not sure about the hardware, you can still try the floppyless installation; the worst that can happen is that you will have to try again with different settings.

If there are some hardware configuration issues the installation process detects, it may offer advice on setting parameters or making changes. These bits of advice are, for the most part, just that: advice. You don't have to heed the advice if you don't want. In some cases, the advice makes a lot of sense (such as resolving IRQ conflicts), in which case you should take care of the issue. (There's a table of commonly used IRQs later in this chapter.)

Boot and Root Disks

Even if you are installing from CD-ROM, you still need two high-capacity floppies (either 1.2MB or 1.44MB). These are the boot and root floppies. The *boot* floppy holds the kernel that is used to start Linux the first time, leading to your installation. The *root* floppy holds a small filesystem that includes utilities needed for the installation. The two disks together form a complete and very small implementation of Linux. There is enough of a system on the two floppies to actually play with Linux, although many of the utilities are missing.

> ## TIP
>
> If you have a recent system, you may not need boot and root floppies at all. Current BIOS versions allow booting from the CD-ROM drive, especially when the system is all SCSI-based. Some IDE-based CD-ROM systems allow booting from the CD-ROM drive, too. If your system supports CD-ROM booting, you need only insert the Linux CD and reboot the system. The CD software automatically selects the correct boot and root images to use.

In most cases, the boot and root floppies are copied from existing files that are called "images." The *image* is a precompiled version of the system that you duplicate onto the floppies, eliminating the need to start from scratch. CD-ROM and FTP distributions have directories for several boot and root images, depending on the hardware on your system. You must select the image that matches your hardware as much as possible, copy them to the disks, and start your system with the disks.

You can do most of these steps from DOS, although you can't use the DOS copy command to create the boot and root floppies. The floppies must be created with a utility that ignores the DOS formatting. This utility, commonly called RAWRITE.EXE, is included with most Linux software distributions.

Selecting a Boot Kernel and Root Image

CD-ROMs usually have directories under the root directory called bootdsks.144 and rootdsks.144 (for 3.5-inch 1.44MB floppies) and bootdsks.12 and rootdsks.12 (for 5.25-inch 1.2MB floppies) that contain the boot and root images, respectively. You should run DOS either from a floppy or a partition on your hard disk to examine the CD-ROM. If you are copying your files from an FTP site, you can select the boot and root images you need while connected to the remote FTP machine and transfer only the images you need to your local machine.

The types of boot kernels usually available are described in a file in the kernel image directories. The images are named to reflect the hardware for which they have drivers installed into the kernel. For example, the kernel image "scsi" has drivers in the kernel for SCSI-based systems, and if you are on a PC that has a SCSI controller, hard disk, and CD-ROM, this is the image you want to copy to your boot floppy.

The number of boot images available is quite wide. The primary images available from most CD-ROMs and FTP sites, and the hardware they are designed to handle, are as follows:

- *aztech.* IDE and SCSI hard disk drivers, and Aztech non-IDE CD-ROM support. This includes Aztech, Okana, Orchid, and Wearnes non-IDE CD-ROM drives.
- *bare.* IDE hard disk drivers only (no CD-ROM support).
- *cdu31a.* IDE and SCSI hard disk drivers, with a Sony CDU31 or Sony CDU33a CD-ROM drive.
- *cdu535.* IDE and SCSI hard disk drivers, with a Sony 535 or Sony 531 CD-ROM drive.
- *idecd.* IDE and SCSI hard disk drivers, with IDE or ATAPI CD-ROM drive. This driver works with IDE-based CD-ROM drives.
- *mitsumi.* IDE and SCSI hard disk drivers, with a Mitsumi CD-ROM drive.
- *net.* IDE hard disk drivers and Ethernet network card drivers.
- *sbpcd.* IDE and SCSI hard disk drivers with Sound Blaster Pro or Panasonic CD-ROM drivers. This is for CD-ROM drives run off a Sound Blaster card (as supplied in many Sound Blaster multimedia kits).
- *scsi.* IDE and SCSI hard drivers with SCSI peripherals (CD-ROM drives).
- *scsinet1.* IDE and SCSI hard disk drivers, SCSI CD-ROM driver, and Ethernet drivers for networking. The SCSI drivers support Adaptec 152X, 1542, 1740, 274x, and 284x adapters, Buslogic adapters, EATA-DMA adapters (such as DPT, NEC, and AT&T cards), Seagate ST-02 adapters, and Future Domain TCC-8xx and 16xx adapters. SCSI adapters compatible with any of these cards will also work.
- *scsinet2.* IDE and SCSI hard disk drivers, SCSI CD-ROM driver, and Ethernet drivers for networking. The SCSI drivers support NCR5380-based adapters, NCR 53C7 and 8xx adapters, Always IN2000 adapter, Pro Audio Spectrum 16 adapter,

Qlogic adapter, Trantor T128, T128F, and T228 adapters, Ultrastor adapters, and the 7000 FASST adapters. Compatibles of any of these cards should also work.

- *xt.* IDE and IBM PC-XT-compatible hard disk drivers.

With some distributions, an extension is added to the kernel image name to indicate the floppy type. For example, if the kernel image is for a 1.44MB floppy, it will have the filetype ".144" as part of the name. Similarly, a filetype of ".12" indicates a 1.2MB image. You cannot interchange these images, or the disk will be useless (in other words you cannot load a .12 image onto a 1.44MB disk). Most distributions don't bother with this convention because the files are in the appropriate directories for the disk size.

There are fewer choices for the root floppy image. Most distributions include four basic images, although a few more esoteric images also appear from time to time. The basic root floppy images are as follows:

- *color.* Offers a full-screen color-based installation script for installing Linux.
- *tape.* Designed to support Linux installation from a cartridge tape. This kernel was still not functioning properly at the time of writing.
- *tty.* A dumb terminal installation version with no color or graphics.
- *umsdos.* Used to install UMSDOS, which allows you to install Linux into an existing MS-DOS partition. The installation script creates the subdirectories it needs. UMSDOS is not as efficient or fast as a dedicated Linux partition, but you can retain your current disk partitions.

Each of the root images has the disk size as part of its name (color144 and color12, for example).

If you obtained your boot and root images from an FTP or BBR site, the files may be compressed and archived. If they are, they will end with the filetype .gz. Before you can install the images to a floppy, they must be uncompressed with the gzip utility.

TIP

The color root image is a lot more attractive than the tty image and can make the Linux installation a bit friendlier. However, the color image is intolerant of typing errors and doesn't always proceed smoothly. It's worth a try, in most cases, unless you know exactly how you want to install Linux. The color process tends to require much more user interaction, clicking on OK buttons at many stages.

After you have determined which of the boot and root images you want to use (if you are not sure, pick the boot image that most closely matches your hardware configuration and the color or tty root image), you can create the boot and root floppies. If you choose the boot and root images incorrectly, don't worry. The most that can happen is that you won't be able to install Linux, and you can start the process again.

Creating the Boot and Root Floppies

You can create the boot and root floppies either from DOS or from UNIX (or Linux). If you don't run DOS yet and don't have a DOS boot disk, you must use another machine to create the two floppies. Because the DOS-based floppy creation is the most common, we deal with it first.

To create the boot and root floppies, you must use a utility program to write the image to disk. If your image files are compressed (they will have a .gz extension), they must first be uncompressed with the gzip utility (which usually resides in the /bin or /usr/bin directories, part of your path by default with most Linux installations). If you are working from CD-ROM, you must copy the files to a DOS hard disk because you can't write the uncompressed image to the CD-ROM. Even if you start with uncompressed files, it may be easier to copy the images to a temporary DOS directory because it will save you the hassle of worrying about directory pathnames.

To uncompress a .gx file, issue the following command, where `filename` is the name of the compressed file (including the .gz extension):

```
gzip -d <filename>
```

The `-d` option tells gzip to decompress the file. After it is completed, the .gz file is erased and only the uncompressed file remains (with the same filename, less the .gz extension). You should uncompress the boot and root images. For example, you could issue these commands to uncompress the scsi.144 and color144 images.:

```
gzip -d scsi.gz
gzip -d color144.gz
```

These images can now be written to the high-density floppies. The two floppies don't have to be blank because the RAWRITE utility doesn't respect DOS formatting conventions. RAWRITE is usually included in CD-ROM Linux distributions in one of the top directories. The two floppies must be high density, though. You can mix types (in other words, you can use a 1.2MB boot and 1.44MB root floppy) with some distributions of Linux, although it's not recommended for most systems. It is a lot easier to keep everything the same disk size. The disks must be formatted using DOS' format program. The boot disk must be the correct size for your system's boot floppy drive (A: in DOS terms).

3

INSTALLING LINUX

To write the images to the two floppies, you need the RAWRITE utility and two DOS-formatted floppies. RAWRITE is a DOS program that writes the images, block-by-block, to the floppy. To use the RAWRITE program, simply enter its name. RAWRITE prompts you for the name of the file to copy and the destination drive letter. RAWRITE then copies the images. Once completed, the disk cannot be read by DOS. Label the disks as the boot and root floppies, for convenience.

If you have access to a UNIX or Linux system, you can create the boot disks from within that operating system. You need to put the two image files on the UNIX or Linux system and use the dd utility to copy them to floppy. First, make sure the images are uncompressed (no .gz extension). If they are not, uncompress them with the UNIX gunzip utility (a GNU utility that you may have to obtain from another source, if it's not included with your distribution).

To uncompress files in UNIX or Linux, issue this command, where `filename` is the name of the image file, with its .gz extension:

```
gunzip <filename>
```

The gunzip utility erases the compressed file and leaves an uncompressed version in its place.

To copy the images to a floppy, you need to know the device name of the floppy within the operating system. For most systems, the first floppy drive is /dev/fd0 and the second floppy drive is /dev/fd1. (Some systems treat the floppy drives as raw devices, which have the names /dev/rfd0 and /dev/rfd1.) Copy the image files to the floppy with this command, where `filename` is the name of the uncompressed image:

```
dd if=<filename> of=/dev/fd0 obs=18k
```

The `dd` command converts file formats. The `if` and `of` parts of the command indicate the input and output filenames or devices. The `obs` portion of the command indicates the output block size (in this case, 18KB).

For example, to copy the scsi and color144 images to the first floppy (3.5-inch 1.44MB), issue these two commands:

```
dd if=scsi of=/dev/fd0 obs=18k
dd if=color144 of=/dev/fd0 obs=18k
```

The two floppies are now ready to boot a minimum Linux system for you.

The Installation Routine: A Quick Guide

This section gives you a quick overview of the installation routine used by many versions of Linux (the model used for this section is Red Hat, but the same applies to most others). This section can be used by those with experience with Linux or very simple hardware setups. If you run into any problems during the installation process, check the more detailed sections later in this chapter.

Once you have successfully loaded your boot and root images either from disk or CD-ROM, you are launched into the installation routine. The Red Hat Linux distribution has a very useful menu-driven installation routine that is much more forgiving of errors than many other Linux versions. For the most part, you need only read the screens and make logical choices to have the installation process continue properly. Many of the steps are automated and occur without your intervention.

If something happens with the automated installation routine that causes an error, a warning on the screen is displayed, and you are dropped into a manual installation routine. This can be used just as easily as the automated routine; it simply takes a little longer. Again, menu-driven options make the process painless.

You can probably install Linux on your system based entirely on the automated installation routine. If this is the case, you can move on to other chapters in this book. The rest of this chapter covers some of the most important steps in setting up and installing a Linux system in more detail. If you encounter problems during the installation or want to make changes to your configuration, you can check the respective sections later in this chapter. For the moment, we take a quick look at each of the steps in the automated installation process.

Choosing Text or Graphics Installation

Red Hat Linux gives you two choices for installation: text-based or X-based. If you have installed Linux before or are familiar with operating systems, you can use either with equal confidence. The graphical interface installation using X is a more visually pleasant process and is a neat aspect of Red Hat Linux.

On the other hand, the text-based installation process is more traditional and familiar to veteran Linux users. If you are unsure of how to use X or of your system configuration with respect to mouse and video card, you should stay with the text-based installation. It guides you through each step with full descriptions on the screen.

Setting Up Your Hard Drive

If you have not set Linux up on your system before or you need to allocate partitions for Linux on your system, you need to use a disk partitioning scheme. Red Hat Linux gives you a choice of two disk partitioning utilities: fdisk and cfdisk. The fdisk utility is similar to the DOS fdisk program. It is covered in more detail in the section "Installing the Linux Partitions" later in this chapter.

The cfdisk utility is similar to fdisk except full-screen. Many people find cfdisk easier to use than fdisk because it uses simple mnemonic commands to perform each function. The choice of partitioning utility is entirely up to you; they both do the same job.

If you have set new partitions on your hard disk for Linux, you must reboot your system to make them effective (don't forget to write the partition table to disk when you exit either fdisk or cfdisk!). After a reboot, start the installation process again either from your boot floppies or the CD-ROM, and the new disk partitions will be recognized by Linux.

Formatting the Partitions

After the disk partitions are set, Red Hat tries to detect your swap partition. The installation routine displays a window listing the device names of all your swap partitions. To format the swap partition, choose one of the partitions listed (or the only entry if you set up only one swap partition) and choose Yes from the menu to start the formatting. The process takes about a minute, depending on the size of the swap partition.

After the swap partition has been formatted and made available to the kernel, the installation routine detects any Linux data partitions. These are displayed with the option to format them. For a new installation, you should format the Linux partition using this screen.

Setting Up Ethernet

During the swap and Linux data formatting process, Red Hat asks whether you want to install Ethernet now. If you have an Ethernet card in your machine and want to set it up while the installation process is running, you can do so. If you don't have an Ethernet card or want to delay the installation for later, that's fine, too, and you skip a few steps.

If you elect to set up Ethernet now, you are asked for a machine name and a domain name. After that, you are prompted for the IP address of your machine and the subnet mask (which is generated automatically and probably doesn't need changing). A few other configuration settings (such as whether you are using a gateway and NFS server) might be displayed. Again, the default settings are fine for almost every system.

You are asked if your machine uses a gateway. If you use a separate machine to access the Internet or another network, answer yes. If you are not planning to use the machine as a gateway, answer no. If you use a gateway, you are asked for its identification.

You also are asked whether this machine is to use a nameserver. If your network has a DNS (Domain Name System) server that performs IP address conversions, answer Yes and supply its identification. Otherwise, answer No. You can always add a nameserver later after the system is up and running.

Setting Up the Mouse

After a message about the Metro-X server supplied with Red Hat Linux and a selection of the type of graphics card to use (if in doubt, select standard VGA or SVGA), you are asked for the type of mouse attached to your system. (The mouse is not tied to Metro-X specifically; this is just the way the installation routine works.) Select the entry that matches the type of mouse you use, or one that is compatible with your mouse. You are then asked to which device your mouse is attached. In most cases, the mouse is attached to COM1 (/dev/ttyS0) or COM2 (/dev/ttyS1). Select the proper entry. If you are not sure which port your mouse uses, select COM1—it is the most common configuration.

Configuring X

If you have selected the X-based installation routine, Red Hat Linux tries to determine your video system so it can start X. If you are using the text-based installation routine, this process is skipped for now.

In most cases Red Hat Linux tries to set up the X system by checking the type of video card you have. You will probably see a message asking whether you want the installation routine to *autoprobe*, which means it tries to determine the type of video card and video chipset installed on your machine. If you have a particular reason for not autoprobing (some video cards hang if they are sent the wrong sequence), you must supply the configuration information manually. If you are unsure of whether autoprobing should be allowed, let it try. The worst that can happen (usually) is that the system will hang, and you will have to reboot.

After autoprobing, the installation routine displays the type of video chipset it found and the amount of memory it thinks is on the card. For most systems, accept the defaults unless you know exactly what type of chipset and onboard RAM you have.

After answering all the questions properly, X starts, and you can see the X-based installation procedure.

Selecting Packages to Install

Whether you are using X or a text-based installation, a screen appears that lists all the packages on the Linux CD-ROM. You can select which packages are to be installed during the setup process. You can install as many or as few of these packages as you want. You can delay the installation of many of them until later if you want.

After selecting the packages to be installed, you can see a message asking whether you want to have individual package contents displayed for selection. This lets you select only portions of the more generic packages for installation. If you select this option, you must wait by your screen and provide input at regular intervals. If you want Linux to install all the components in a package, answer No to this prompt, and you can leave the system to install by itself.

After you have selected the packages to be installed, Red Hat's installation routine starts installing the software. You can see status messages on the screen as the process goes along.

Using LILO

After the installation process has formatted the drive partitions and copied all the software packages you selected to the data partition, you are asked whether you want to run LILO to set up the boot system for this drive. If you have a disk drive devoted only to Linux or it is a split DOS/Linux drive, you can run LILO and set the drive to boot into either operating system.

If you are running another operating system, such as UNIX or OS/2, you may elect not to use LILO and create a boot floppy instead. LILO is covered in much more detail in Chapter 4, "Using LILO."

Partitioning the Hard Disk

Hard disks are divided into *partitions*, or areas dedicated to an operating system. A hard disk can have up to four primary partitions, with some partitions being further divided into more logical drives by the operating system software. A more complete discussion of partitions is in Chapter 4.

If you are running Linux from a DOS partition using the UMSDOS root image, you don't have to worry about repartitioning your drives. Your existing drive's partitions are used. However, since UMSDOS is a poor filesystem compared to Linux, you probably want to create your own Linux partitions. Check the later section "Using UMSDOS," for information on setting up UMSDOS.

Linux really requires two partitions: one for the Linux swap space, and one for the Linux software filesystem itself. The swap space is used as an extension of your machine's physical RAM and can be quite small. The Linux filesystem partitions tend to be quite large because they must hold all the Linux software. You can have several Linux file-system partitions, although one must be designated as the boot partition (where the kernel and primary utilities are located).

If you are using an existing hard disk that has an operating system already installed on it, you must repartition your hard disk to make room for Linux. This tends to be a destructive process, meaning that anything on your hard disk will be destroyed. Make backups of your existing data if you want to keep it!

Partitioning of a hard disk is done with the `fdisk` utility. If you have used `fdisk` in DOS, the Linux version does the same task, although the menus are completely different (and much more complicated). Many PC-based UNIX systems also use `fdisk` to partition hard drives.

> **TIP**
>
> A DOS utility called FIPS sometimes allows nondestructive changes to your partitions, assuming no data is on the areas that are to be repartitioned. FIPS is available from many sources, including most of the Linux FTP sites and on some Linux CD-ROMs. However, you should make backups, just in case.

You must decide how much space to allocate to the different partitions before you start because changing your mind later means destroying all the data you have saved to disk. The Linux swap space partition size depends on the amount of RAM in your system, the number of users you expect, and the type of development you will do.

If you are going to maintain a DOS partition on the same disk, you must balance the disk space requirements of both operating systems against your total disk capacity. A mini-mum Linux filesystem partition will be about 20MB, although closer to 100MB is need-ed for a full X-based installation.

Linux Swap Space Partition

How big should the swap space partition be? There's no single size that works for all installations, unfortunately. Generally, since the swap space is used as an extension of physical RAM, the more RAM you have, the less swap space is required. You can add the amount of swap space and the amount of RAM together to get the amount of RAM Linux will use. For example, if you have 8MB of RAM on your machine's motherboard and a 16MB swap space partition, Linux will behave as though you had 24MB RAM total.

Linux uses the swap space by moving pages of physical RAM to the swap space when it doesn't need that page at the moment, and vice versa when it needs the memory page. So why not make a very large swap space and let Linux think it's in heaven? Because the swap space is much slower in access time than RAM, and there is a point where the size of the swap space acts against your Linux system's efficiency, instead of for it.

Swap space may not even be needed if you have lots of RAM. For example, if you have 16MB of physical RAM and don't intend to do any application development or run X, you won't make much use of the swap space because Linux can fit everything it needs in the 16MB. (You still should have a small swap space, just in case.)

If you are running X, developing applications, or running memory-hog applications, such as databases, swap space is crucial even if you have lots of physical RAM. Even 16MB RAM is not enough for X, so you need swap space.

A good rule is to create a swap space with the maximum size limit of 16MB. Unless you have a very small-capacity hard disk, this won't be a major drain on your resources, and it gives Linux plenty to work with. If you don't want to allocate this much space, a good rule is to have a total of 16MB RAM (swap space plus physical RAM). Don't eliminate the swap space completely, though, unless you have a lot of RAM. At a minimum, set up a 4MB swap space. Running out of RAM can cause Linux to lock up or crash, which isn't a pretty sight!

Setting Up Partitions

Because the versions of `fdisk` in DOS, OS/2, UNIX, and Linux all differ, we won't bother explaining all the steps. The `fdisk` utility is very easy to use, so if you have used PC machines for a while, this will not be a problem for you. Remember that `fdisk` destroys existing data on your disk! You can set up your Linux disk partitions either from DOS or from within Linux. It really doesn't matter which approach you use, although the DOS `fdisk` program is a little easier to use than Linux's. If you are using DOS's `fdisk` to repartition a DOS area on your drives, you might as well use it to set up the Linux swap space and filesystem partitions, too.

To set up partitions for Linux, remove any existing partitions first (unless you want to keep them as they are). If you intend to use DOS on the same system as Linux, DOS should be the first partition on the disk so it can boot. (There are a few ways to get by this using LILO, but it is still a good rule to leave DOS as the first partition.) If you are keeping an existing DOS partition, leave at the first partition as DOS.

You should create a DOS boot disk, which can reformat and transfer the DOS kernel to the hard drive, regardless of whether you are leaving an existing DOS partition or creating a new one. To create the boot disk, use this DOS command (assuming A: is the drive the disk is in):

```
format a: /s
```

The /s option transfers the operating system kernel. Next, copy the utilities FDISK, FORMAT, SYS, and CHKDSK to the boot floppy. You should also copy an editor, such as EDIT, as well as your existing CONFIG.SYS and AUTOEXEC.BAT files (although you could rename them). This disk lets you format any new DOS partitions. Alternatively, if you are starting from scratch with a new DOS partition, you can simply reload DOS from the original disks when you're ready to format the DOS partition.

If you are removing an existing DOS partition and re-creating a smaller one (as you would if your entire disk were DOS before Linux came into your life), follow these steps (after making a backup of your DOS data):

1. Remove the existing DOS partition.
2. Create a new primary DOS partition as the first partition.
3. Make the DOS partition active.
4. Reboot the system from your boot floppy (or DOS disks).
5. Format the DOS partition and transfer the DOS kernel (COMMAND.COM).
6. Restore your backup files to the DOS partition (this can be done at any time).

Next, set up the Linux swap space partition by creating a partition of the proper size. You can do this step either from DOS or when you have booted Linux from the boot and root floppies. For the sake of this chapter, it is assumed that you are setting up the partitions from DOS, although the process is the same either way.

Most versions of fdisk allow you to enter the size of the partition in megabytes, with the utility calculating the sector numbers that apply to it. Set the size of the Linux swap space to whatever size you decided, to a maximum of 16MB. Don't make the partition active or format it! You can set up the swap space partition in an extended disk partition, but a primary partition is a better choice if your disk can support it.

Finally, create the Linux filesystem partition to be whatever size you want, or the rest of the disk if that's the only partition missing. Again, don't activate or format the partition. When you are running the Linux installation routine, you will identify and format the swap space and filesystem partitions properly.

Using UMSDOS

UMSDOS enables you to use an existing DOS partition to house your Linux system (not all versions of Linux support UMSDOS; in fact, most recent versions do not but older versions do). Because you are forcing Linux to use the DOS disk layout, you suffer some performance limitations compared to creating a dedicated Linux partition. On the other hand, UMSDOS lets you keep your disk drive the way it is, preventing the hassle of repartitioning and reformatting your drive. It is also a fast and easy way to install Linux if you only want to experiment for a while before installing a full system.

It is important to realize that UMSDOS does not let you run DOS and Linux at the same time. UMSDOS (UNIX in MS-DOS) only creates the Linux filesystem under the DOS formatted partition, although it is modified to allow long filenames, Linux file permissions, and more. When you start the system, you still have to choose between booting Linux or DOS as the operating system. If you start DOS, you can't use the extended Linux filenames, although you are able to snoop around the directories. Filenames may not make much sense because of the contraction from long Linux filenames to DOS-compatible filenames, though.

The only limitation about UMSDOS, as we've already mentioned, is that the DOS filesystem is not designed as well as the Linux filesystem, and this causes some performance degradation. This isn't really a major problem because most people do not notice the difference unless they are running a file-intensive application, such as X or compiling programs. You can always start with UMSDOS, and if you decide you like Linux enough, you can back up the Linux data and repartition the drive to create a true Linux filesystem.

If you want to use UMSDOS, you have to perform a few extra steps when setting up the disk. You must still create the boot and root disks, although you need a root image that supports UMSDOS. Most distributions have the root images umsds144 and umsds12 for this purpose.

When you boot Linux and it asks which partition to use for the filesystem, specify the DOS partition. UMSDOS then initializes the filesystem for you. After that, the procedure for installing the rest of Linux is the same as a dedicated Linux partition.

Installing the Linux Partitions

The Linux installation process starts when you boot your system from the boot floppy. After the kernel has loaded, you are prompted to remove the boot floppy and insert the root floppy. When the root filesystem has been read, you are either sent directly to an installation script or presented with the login prompt. Log in as root. No password is required because none has been added to the system.

The first step is to set up the disk partitions using `fdisk`, if you haven't already done so. If you have more than one hard drive, you can place your Linux partitions on either drive. If you are planning to keep a DOS partition, though, make sure it is the first partition on the first drive. Linux isn't so picky. If you want to boot Linux cleanly, place a Linux filesystem on the first drive. You can also create Linux filesystems on the second drive. Linux swap partitions can be on either drive, although it is a good idea to keep it on the first drive with the first filesystem.

Linux's `fdisk`

Linux's `fdisk` program is different from the one in DOS, so you should check the menus frequently to determine the proper commands. You invoke Linux's `fdisk` in the same manner as DOS's. If you don't specify a drive, `fdisk` assumes the first one in the system. Otherwise, you can specifically indicate which disk drive to partition by giving the device name on the command line, as in the following, which invokes `fdisk` for the second drive:

```
fdisk /dev/hdb
```

If your system has IDE, ESDI, or RLL drives, the first is /dev/hda and the second /dev/hdb. SCSI drives are /dev/sda, /dev/sdb, and so on. Because seven SCSI drives can be supported on a single controller, you could have up to /dev/hdg. (You can go even higher with another controller card, but few Linux systems require this!)

WARNING

You should not use Linux's `fdisk` utility to create partitions for operating systems other than Linux. If, for example, you want a DOS partition on your disk, create it with DOS's `fdisk`. Linux does not write the partition table properly for other operating systems!

As mentioned earlier, Linux's `fdisk` commands are different than the `fdisk` commands for DOS. Essentially, the commands you need to run Linux's `fdisk` utility are as follows:

- `d`   Deletes an existing partition
- `l`   Lists all known partition types
- `n`   Creates a new partition
- `p`   Displays the current partition table
- `q`   Quits `fdisk` without saving changes
- `t`   Changes a partition's type code
- `v`   Verifies the partition table
- `w`   Writes current partition table to disk and exits

The process for setting up a partition is to first examine the partition table to make sure any existing partitions are correct. If you have a DOS partition on your drive, it should show in the partition table. If you created Linux swap and filesystem partitions when you were in DOS's `fdisk`, they should appear in the partition table, too, although the partitions types will be incorrect.

Setting Up Linux Partitions

To create the Linux swap space, use the `n` command and give the starting sector number. Usually, this is immediately after any existing DOS partition (or other operating systems you have installed). Linux's `fdisk` lets you specify the size of the partition either by supplying an end sector number or by giving a size in megabytes. The latter is much easier to work with, so just enter the size in megabytes that you want to set your Linux swap space partition to be (remember there is a maximum of 16MB for the swap space size). The format is usually +XXM, where XX is the number of megabytes (such as +16MB). You can also specify kilobytes, but you don't want to create a swap partition that is less than 1MB.

> **TIP**
>
> Most older PC BIOSs cannot handle more than 1,024 cylinders on a disk drive. You may not be able to create DOS or Linux partitions or filesystems that go beyond the 1,023rd cylinder (numbering starts at zero). Some other operating systems, such as SCO UNIX, enable you to use anything beyond the 1,024 limit. Linux can use partitions beyond the 1,024 limit, but can't boot from them. If you have a disk drive that has more than 1,023 cylinders, make sure your primary Linux partition ends before 1,023. You can create extra partitions following that cylinder and mount them as second filesystems.

The `fdisk` program asks you whether you want to create a primary or an extended partition. If you are creating a primary partition, it wants the number (one to four—remember a DOS partition has to be number 1 to boot). In most cases, you should create only primary partitions, unless you have a large disk drive. Extended partitions can be used to add logical drives inside them, as DOS creates logical drives. In Linux, extended partitions are not the same as extended filesystems!

After you have created the Linux partition, you should assign its type. Some versions of `fdisk` prompt for this right away; others let you select the option to assign filesystem types from the `fdisk` menu. In either case, the letter 1 displays all known filesystem types. Choose the one that designates a Linux swap space (number 82) and check the partition table. Your Linux swap space partition should have the correct size and partition type displayed. Actually, Linux doesn't care about the partition type numbers and ignores them completely. Some other operating systems do note them, however, so it's a good practice to label them correctly to prevent future problems. It also helps you keep the partition table nicely organized.

Next, create your primary Linux filesystem partition in the same manner. If you want to use the rest of the disk drive for that partition, you can enter the end sector number of your drive (Linux's `fdisk` tells you the range you can use). This would be the usual default if your hard drive has a DOS, Linux swap space, and Linux filesystem partition on it. After you have created the Linux filesystem, you should identify its filetype as 82, which is a "Linux native" type.

You should note somewhere the size of the swap space and filesystem partitions, in blocks, because you will need this information later. You can read this straight from the partition table.

After you've created the Linux partitions and are satisfied with the partition table layout, save and exit `fdisk`. If you don't save the information, you must repeat the process.

Enabling the Swap Space for Installation

Linux' installation routine requires a good chunk of RAM to proceed. If you have 4MB of RAM or less, you will have problems installing Linux unless you have the kernel use the swap space. (If you have only 4MB or less of RAM in your system, you should have a swap space of at least 8MB, and preferably 16MB.) If you try to install Linux and get memory error messages, it's because there is not enough RAM, and the swap space is needed.

> **TIP**
>
> If you've turned the swap space on and still get error messages when you try to install Linux, you need either more physical RAM or a larger swap space. It's better to increase the swap space and install Linux now than it is to have to redo it later. To increase the size of a swap space partition, you may have to remove the existing Linux partitions and re-create them with `fdisk`.

If you have a small amount of RAM, you should enable the swap space to help the installation process. Even if you have lots of RAM, there's no reason not to enable the swap space now, anyway. To enable the swap space, issue the following command, in which `partition` is the name of the partition, and `size` is the size of the partition in blocks:

`mkswap -c partition size`

You may have noted this number earlier when setting up the partition table. If not, you can start `fdisk` again and read the size in blocks from the partition table display.

For example, if you have set up the Linux swap space on partition /dev/hda2 (the second primary partition on the first non-SCSI drive) and it has a size of 13,565 blocks, you would issue the following command:

`mkswap -c /dev/hda2 13565`

The `-c` option tells the `mkswap` utility to check for bad blocks in the partition. If this option is on, it will take a little longer to create the swap partition, but a bad block in the swap partition can cause your entire system to crash, so it's worth the delay. If `mkswap` finds any errors in the swap space, it will generate an error message. However, since `mkswap` flags bad blocks to be left alone, you can ignore the messages unless there are a considerable number of them, in which case your hard drive has too many bad blocks!

When the swap partition has been formatted, you enable the Linux swap space partition with the command swapon. Usually, you must specify the partition, although some versions can figure the partition out automatically from the partition table. It never hurts to be explicit, though. To enable the swap partition just formatted, enter the command

`swapon /dev/hda2`

Repeat the `format` and `swapon` commands for each swap partition if you created more than one. As soon as the `swapon` command is executed, the Linux kernel starts to use the new swap space as an extension of the physical RAM.

Creating the Linux Filesystem Partition

After you have a swap space configured and working, you can set up the Linux file-system. This step may be automated by some Linux installation scripts, or you may have to execute it yourself. Either way, this section explains what is going on.

You have already allocated the partition table to support a Linux filesystem. Now you can create the filesystem with the `mkfs` (`make filesystem`) command. The exact format of the command depends on the type of filesystem you are setting up. The most popular filesystem (for reasons of speed and flexibility) is called the Second Extended filesystem (which has nothing to do with extended partitions on a hard disk). To create a Second Extended filesystem, issue this command, in which `partition` is the device name and `size` is the size of the partition in blocks (taken from the partition display in `fdisk`):

```
mke2fs -c <partition> <size>
```

For example, to create a filesystem in /dev/hda3, which is 162,344 blocks in size, the command would be

```
mke2fs -c /dev/hda3 162344
```

When specifying the size of a partition, make sure you use blocks and not sectors or cylinders. Using the wrong value results in errors or only a fraction of your partition being used.

The `mke2fs` utility checks the partition for bad blocks (the `-c` option), then set the filesystem up properly in that partition. If you are setting up a large partition, the disk check can take a few minutes, but you should not ignore it unless you know your disk is good.

The other filesystems available to Linux are the Xia filesystem, the Extended filesystem, and the Minix filesystem. The Xia filesystem is good, but not as popular as the Second Extended. The Extended filesystem is an older version of Second Extended, while the Minix filesystem is compatible with the old Minix operating system (which Linux was written to replace). You can create these filesystems with the following commands:

- Extended—`mkefs`
- Minix—`mkfs`
- Xia—`mkxfs`

All three commands take the same arguments as the Second Extended filesystem command. The Minix filesystem is limited to 64MB.

None of the `mkfs` commands format the filesystem, but simply set it up. You are prompted for a filesystem format during the installation process.

Installing Linux

After the partitions are created and formatted, and the filesystems have been created, you can install the Linux software. This step may be automated, depending on the installation procedure included with your Linux distribution. Most versions of Linux include a utility called `setup`, which installs the software for you. From the Linux prompt, type the command:

```
setup
```

If you are running the color root image, you will get graphical full-screen windows for the installation process. Other root images use character-based installation messages. Either way accomplishes the same task, and many users who install Linux frequently avoid the color root image because it can take a little longer to answer all the questions the script poses, and some keyboard typing errors are difficult to correct easily.

Whichever root image you choose, it is a good idea to read each screen carefully. Many choices are presented to you during the installation, and although the default choices are correct for most people, you should make sure each time.

The setup installation script asks for several pieces of information. You have the option of letting Linux install everything without your prompting except when Disk Sets change, but this should be used only if you know exactly what is going on your disk. If you are installing Linux for the first time or want to choose the software to be installed by examining descriptions of each package, use the verbose options to show all messages and let you control the process.

You are also asked for the source of the software. If you have a CD-ROM, it should have been activated during the boot process if the drivers were correct for your hardware. Select the CD-ROM option. You may be asked to further narrow down the type of CD-ROM you have on your system. Choose the correct entry (or the one nearest it) and hope for the best! If you are installing from another disk drive partition (such as another Linux partition or a DOS partition), provide the full device and path names.

You are prompted for the target of the installation. This is where you want the software to be installed. The newly created Linux partition is probably the location you want, so enter the partition name. You might be asked whether you want to format that partition, and you should answer yes. (Running `mkfs` or its variants does not format the partition for you.)

Finally, Linux displays a list of the Disk Sets you can install. Choose the ones you want. Some setup versions let you further refine the list of utilities when the Disk Set is installed. As a last step, verify the information, then let Linux install itself. Watch for messages and prompts, and follow any onscreen instructions. If you are installing from floppy, you are prompted at intervals to change to the next disk in the Disk Set.

At the end of the installation routine, you may be prompted whether you want to create a boot disk. This boot disk allows you to bring the system up at any time, especially if the normal boot process fails. It is a good idea to create a boot disk. This disk is not the same as the boot floppy you made to start the installation (which is useful only when you reinstall from scratch).

Setting the Boot Process

The last step in the Linux installation is setting the boot device. Most of the time, Linux is booted by a utility called LILO (Linux Loader). LILO can boot your system in several different ways, depending on whether you want to use your system with another operating system or not. Most of the time, you will want LILO to boot your system into Linux with the option to load DOS (if you have it on your system).

The LILO screens explain most of the choices quite well, but LILO has a few quirks to it. That's why there's a complete chapter on it next, which explains what LILO does and how to make it behave properly. For now, if you are impatient, follow the defaults, but don't let LILO overwrite your hard disk's Master Boot Record. Doing so can cause a bit of a hassle when you want to boot DOS. You can, however, let LILO write a boot sector to your Linux partition, and then use fdisk to make either DOS or Linux active.

If you're not too sure what to do with LILO, ignore it for now. You have a boot floppy that lets you start your machine, and when you better understand LILO, you can set it up the way you want.

As a last step in the installation process, reboot your machine and let Linux boot from the boot floppy or from LILO, if you installed it. If all boots properly, you can continue to use Linux as you normally would. If you experienced problems booting, watch error messages and check the installation process to see which part went screwy. As long as you have your boot disk, you should be able to get into Linux without a problem.

Viewing Installed Software Files

When Linux is up and running, you might want to install or remove Disk Sets and other software. You can also check that components of a Disk Set have been properly installed.

There are a few different utilities available for this task, but the most common is called `pkgtool`.

When you enter the `pkgtool` command name at the shell prompt, you are presented with a menu that lets you install new software, remove existing software, or view installed files in a package.

To view the contents of a package, select View from the main `pkgtool` menu, then choose the name of the package from the list presented. The list should include all the Disk Set tools you have installed, as well as any additional software installed after the first installation. Selecting a tool name sends `pkgtool` to check all the files that should be in the software and report its success.

Sometimes the list of software in a package can take a while to appear. Be patient. The list `pkgtool` presents usually has a brief description of the tool and a list of all the files in the installation.

Troubleshooting

Many different problems can occur while setting up and installing a Linux system, although most of them are self-explanatory from error messages. A few commonly encountered problems can be easily dealt with, though, so we'll look at them briefly.

Software Installation

You may encounter a few errors when installing Linux. If you get the message `device full`, it means you have run out of disk space and need to either break up the installation into several partitions or install fewer components. If you haven't installed the basic system, you need more disk space. You must delete your partitions and start the installation process again, allocating more to Linux.

Errors such as `read error`, `file not found` and `tar: read error` are indicative of a problem with either the disk medium you are installing from or an incomplete Disk Set. These problems usually occur with floppies and tend to indicate a bad disk. All you can do in most cases is replace the disk with a new one.

Hard Disk and Disk Controller

When Linux boots it displays a few messages, one of the most important being a partition check. You will see messages like this:

```
Partition check:
hda: hda1 hda2 hda3
hdb: hdb1 hdb2
```

In this example, the first non-SCSI disk has three partitions and the second disk has two. Your system's output will probably be different, of course. If you don't see any partition information, either the hard disk controller is not recognized properly or the disk drives themselves are not accessible. These problems have a number of potential causes, including the obvious:

- Check the cables inside the computer. The hard disk cable should run from the adapter card to each drive's connector. Make sure the cables are connected in the proper manner (the red strip on the cable is at pin 1 on the connector).

- Check that the power connector is attached to each disk drive. Without power, your drive won't spin up, and Linux can't touch it.

- Check the partition table to make sure you created a Linux partition properly.

After that, if the drive is not working properly with Linux but works okay when you boot DOS, it is probably a kernel driver for the hard disk that is at fault. Some IDE drives, for example, are not as well-behaved (not conforming to the IDE standards) as others, and your IDE kernel driver might not be able to talk to your drives. Try using a different kernel image and see whether the problem solves itself. If you are using a SCSI kernel and adapter and the drives are not recognized, use the utilities that came with the SCSI adapter card to force a check of the hard drives. They may have a SCSI ID set incorrectly.

Device Conflicts

One of the most common problems is when hardware is not recognized properly. This can happen to a CD-ROM, a network card, and even a hard disk. This is usually caused by a conflict in the IRQ (interrupt), DMA (Direct Memory Address), or I/O address settings. When two devices have the same settings on any one of the three characteristics, Linux and the BIOS may not be able to communicate with the device properly.

A symptom of this problem may be Linux hanging when it tries to find a specific device, as explained on the boot messages. When Linux boots up, it generates verbose messages on the console that explain what it is doing. If you see a message that it is trying to connect to the network card, for example, and it never gets past that point, chances are that the network card has a conflict with another device. (Totally failed cards are very rare and don't usually stop the boot process because Linux ignores devices it can't access. The problem with a working card with conflicting settings is that Linux is getting messages from two devices that don't act the same.)

To check for conflicts, you should run a diagnostic utility under DOS, such as MSD or Norton Info. These can show you the current IRQ, DMA, and I/O addresses and pinpoint any conflicts. They can also be used for finding available settings.

3

INSTALLING LINUX

Alternatively, you should check the settings of every device in your system for conflicts. Usually, network cards conflict with sound boards, non-SCSI tape driver cards, video cards, and similar add-on cards. Most cards use DIPs or jumpers to set these parameters, so check them against the documentation. To help isolate the problem, remove cards that are not necessary, such as a sound card, and see whether the boot process moves past the device that caused the hangup.

Another problem that can occur is with SCSI devices (and a few others, although much rarer), which must have specific settings in the kernel image. Some kernels were compiled with settings that are default values for adapters or disk drives, and if the settings have been changed, the kernel hangs. This is often the case with special-purpose kernels that have been developed for nonmainstream adapters. To check for this type of problem, investigate any documentation that came with the kernel image.

The most common devices in a PC (COM ports, parallel ports, and floppies) and their IRQ, DMA, and I/O addresses are shown in Table 3.1. These are the default values for a PC, but they may be changed by users. Because only two COM ports (serial ports) are usually supported by DOS, they share IRQ values. The I/O addresses are different, though. Both floppy disks share the same I/O addresses, IRQ, and DMA.

TABLE 3.1. COMMON DEVICES IN A PC AND THEIR IRQ, DMA, AND I/O ADDRESSES.

Device	IRQ	DMA	I/O address (hex)
COM 1 (/dev/ttyS0)	4	N/A	3F8
COM 2 (/dev/ttyS1)	3	N/A	2F8
COM 3 (/dev/ttyS2)	4	N/A	3E8
COM 4 (/dev/ttys3)	3	N/A	2E8
LPT 1 (/dev/lp0)	7	N/A	378-37F
LPT 2 (/dev/lp1)	5	N/A	278-27F
Floppy A (/dev/fd0)	6	2	3F0-3F7
Floppy B (/dev/fd1)	6	2	3F0-3F7

Network cards, SCSI adapters, sound boards, video cards, and other peripherals all must have unique IRQ, DMA, and I/O addresses, which can be difficult to arrange with a fully loaded system. For more information on available values, check your device or card installation manual for recommended values and potential conflicts.

SCSI Problems

SCSI is one of the most versatile interfaces, and it pays for that versatility in potential problems. Linux is usually good about reporting problems with SCSI devices, although the error messages may leave you wondering about the real cause of the problem.

Table 3.2 lists many of the common SCSI errors and their probable causes. Find the message that closely matches the error message Linux displays in this table to determine your corrective steps.

TABLE 3.2. COMMON SCSI ERRORS AND THEIR PROBABLE CAUSES.

Error	Cause
SCSI device at all possible IDs	One or more devices is at the same SCSI ID as the controller. Check and change device IDs. Controllers should be ID 7.
Sense errors	Probably caused by bad termination. Check that both ends of the SCSI chain are terminated. If that is not the problem, the cable is likely at fault.
Timeout errors	Usually caused by a DMA, IRQ, or I/O address conflict. See the previous section for more information.
SCSI adapter not detected	The BIOS is disabled or the SCSI adapter is not recognized by the kernel. Check the drivers.
Cylinders beyond 1024	Your disk has more than 1,024 cylinders, which the PC BIOS can't handle. Linux can use more than 1,024 cylinders, but it can't boot from a partition that extends across that cylinder boundary.
CD-ROM drive not recognized	Some CD-ROMs require a CD in the drive to be recognized properly. Insert a CD and reboot.

Booting Linux

If you have installed Linux and the system won't boot properly from your hard disk, it may be a problem with LILO or with the partitions. If you created a boot floppy, boot from that. If that boots without a problem, check the partition table by executing fdisk. Make sure the Linux partition is active. If it is and you still can't boot from the hard disk, boot from the floppy and run LILO again to configure the boot sector. See Chapter 4 for more information on LILO.

A problem sometimes occurs when Linux can't find the main Linux partition. Boot from the floppy and hold down the Shift or Control key. This produces a menu that allows you to specify the boot device explicitly. This problem can usually be corrected with LILO.

Summary

Much of this chapter was familiar to you if you have installed Linux before, although some users really don't know what was going on during the automated installation script. Knowing the process and staying on top of it helps to prevent problems with the Linux installation.

The next step is using LILO to configure the boot system properly, a commonly misunderstood and misused process. The next chapter looks at LILO. For more information related to the subject of installation and associated subjects, you can jump to other chapters:

To learn how to use your new Linux system, read Part II, starting with Chapter 6, "Getting Started."

To learn about installing and configuring X so you can use a graphical interface, see Chapter 22, "Installing and Configuring XFree86."

To learn how to manage your system, read Part VI, starting with Chapter 32, "System Administration Basics."

Using LILO

by Kamran Husain

CHAPTER 4

IN THIS CHAPTER

LILO (which means *LInux LOader*) is the boot loader used by Linux to load the operating system kernel. LILO is versatile: It can boot Linux kernels from any type of file system, including floppy disk as well as from other operating systems.

This chapter looks at LILO, the way hard disks are laid out with Linux, the boot process, and the most common boot processes and the interactions of LILO with each. This should help you install and use LILO efficiently and effectively.

There are several versions of LILO available. Most current versions support one of two different directory structures. The more traditional (and older) structure resides in the /etc/lilo directory. The newer structure has files scattered in several directories including /etc, /sbin, and /boot. Because the older /etc/lilo structure is the most common, it is used for examples in this chapter. If you are using the new structure (check for the existence of /etc/lilo), substitute the new pathnames as necessary.

Installing LILO

Most systems have LILO already installed and configured. If your system already has LILO installed, you can skip this section unless you want to update your version.

A quick installation procedure is available with most versions of Linux to install a minimum set of files required for LILO. This is described in the file QuickInst.old or QuickInst.new, in some versions of Linux (but not all). The QuickInst routines can be used only for a first-time LILO installation or to replace an existing LILO set. They should not be used for updates as any existing configuration information is overwritten.

> **NOTE**
>
> Before LILO can be compiled for use, the kernel has to be configured by executing makeconfig. All kernel header files must be in the directory /usr/include/linux for LILO to compile properly. The LILO installation and compilation process should be run from a Bourne shell (or complete compatible). Problems have been reported with versions of the Korn shell when LILO is compiled, so use /bin/sh or /bin/bash.

A full installation of LILO requires that all the files in the LILO distribution archive (usually called lilo.xxx.tar.gz where xxx is the version number) are extracted into a directory other than /etc/lilo. (This is because the installation will fail if the final destination is the same as the source directory.) After the distribution files are located in a temporary directory, follow these steps:

1. Check the `Makefile` for valid configuration information (see the later "LILO Makefile" section).

2. Compile LILO. If you want to use the older `/etc/lilo` directory structure, issue the first command that follows. If you want to use the new directory structure, issue the second command.

   ```
   make -f Makefile.old

   make -f Makefile.new
   ```

3. Copy all the LILO files to the target directory with one of the following commands, depending on whether the new or old directory structure is selected:

   ```
   make -f Makefile.old install

   make -f Makefile.new install
   ```

4. Check the `lilo` directories. You should see the following files: `any_d.b`, `boot.b`, `chain.b`, `disktab`, `lilo`, `os2_d.b`.

If the files do not exist or errors are generated in the process, restart the installation. You should check the `Makefile` for accurate information. After LILO has been installed properly, you can use it to install a boot process.

Handling Disk Problems

Some systems may have difficulty with hard disks that do not allow the disk parameters (heads, sectors per track, and cylinders) to be read. If error messages about "bad geometry" are generated or the LILO installation fails with disk errors, the disk parameters are a likely source of trouble. This is especially true with SCSI disks and hard disks with a capacity of 1GB or more.

In this case, the disk parameters must be manually entered into the file `disktab`. This is discussed in more detail in the section "Disk Parameter Table" later in this chapter. Edit the `disktab` file as explained to include the disk parameters, then follow these steps to test the new LILO configuration by copying it to a floppy disk and booting from it:

1. Open the LILO directory (usually `/etc/lilo`).

2. Execute the following command to copy the LILO configuration to the floppy. Substitute the kernel image name after the "image" parameter. (If you don't want to overwrite an existing map file on your system, add the `-m` option to the `lilo` command using another map filename to write to.)

   ```
   echo image=kernel_name ¦ ./lilo -C - -b /dev/fd0 -v -v -v
   ```

3. Reboot your system from the floppy disk.

4

USING LILO

If the configuration is correct, LILO reads the floppy for the boot loader, then loads the kernel from the hard disk. If everything boots properly and you can move around the file system, the disk parameters are correct. If you can't access the hard disk file system, the parameters are incorrect and should be re-entered.

LILO Makefile

The LILO Makefile supplied with the LILO installation files is valid for most installations, although you should carefully check all the entries. LILO uses either Makefile or another file called /etc/lilo/config.defines. If the config.defines file exists, Makefile is ignored. For most purposes, editing the Makefile is sufficient, although if you plan to use LILO a lot, the config.defines file is a better alternative because it isn't overwritten with new versions of LILO.

There are a number of parameters that should be checked in the Makefile before you go on. Table 4.1 summarizes these parameters and explains what they do.

TABLE 4.1. LILO Makefile PARAMETERS.

Parameter	Meaning
IGNORECASE	Makes image names not case sensitive. Active by default.
NO1STDIAG	Does not generate diagnostic messages when read errors are encountered in the boot loader. Disabled by default.
NOINSTDEF	If the install option is omitted from the command line, don't install a new boot sector. Instead, modify the old one. Disabled by default.
ONE_SHOT	Disables the command line timeout if any key is pressed. Disabled by default.
READONLY	Prevents overwriting of the default command line sector of the map file. Disabled by default.

Updating LILO

If you want to update an existing version of LILO with a newer one, the process is the same as a first-time installation except that existing configuration files are renamed to .old automatically. For example, chain.b is renamed to chain.old. If the new version of LILO behaves properly, the .old files can be deleted.

Whenever you update the version of LILO, you must update the boot sector to add the new locations and map file format. To update the boot sector, simply run LILO.

Linux and Hard Disk Layouts

To understand how LILO works, it is necessary to understand how a hard disk is laid out. You probably already know that a hard disk is essentially a set of concentric tracks, radiating out from the center of the disk platter. Each track is divided into a number of sectors.

Hard disks are identified by the number of platters (or, more accurately, the number of heads: The number of platters can be greater than the number of heads because one or more surfaces—typically the top and bottom—might not be used for data storage), the number of tracks per inch of disk platter (measured radially), and the number of sectors per track. The capacity of each sector leads to the total capacity of the disk by multiplying the number of sectors per track, the number of tracks, and the number of platters with heads.

Linux is usually integrally tied with DOS, so it is useful to look at the way DOS uses a hard disk. A single-purpose (single DOS operating system, for example) hard disk (and most floppy disks) have a boot sector followed by a data area that includes an administrative block.

The boot sector is the first sector on the hard disk and is read when the system starts to load the operating system. The boot sector essentially contains a bootstrap to direct the machine to the startup routines.

The administrative block is usually part of the data area, although it is commonly not accessible directly by users. The administrative area contains the administrative tables that show file locations in terms of head/track/sector. DOS uses the File Allocation Table (FAT), while UNIX and Linux use the superblock or i-node tables. The administrative table is not usually read until the boot process has been started.

The data area is used to store files (including the operating system startup code). Each file on the hard disk will have an entry in the administrative block that indicates the file-name and physical location on the hard disk. Other information is usually also stored in the administrative block (such as owner, permissions, date and time, and so on, depending on the operating system).

When there is lots of space on a hard disk, you will probably want to install more than one partition (probably supporting more than one operating system, such as providing both DOS and Linux on the same disk). You can create up to four "primary" partitions on a DOS disk.

A partition table is written to the first sector (boot sector) of each hard disk (not each platter) that contains the details of the partition table. This sector is sometimes called the *Master Boot Record* or MBR. The only difference between a Master Boot Record and a boot sector is that the MBR contains partition information. Hard drives have boot sectors usually called MBRs whereas floppies have boot sectors with no MBR, although the two terms are used interchangeably. A partition table is written to the start of each extended partition, when they exist on a hard disk. Linux boot sectors are created by a program called the *map installer*.

When several partitions are used on a hard disk, they are referred to by Linux as /dev/hda1, /dev/hda2, and so on. Extended partitions would be numbered /dev/hda5, /dev/hda6, and so on (because only four primary partitions are allowed). The entire hard disk is called /dev/hda. A second hard disk would be /dev/hdb (with partitions /dev/hdb1, /dev/hdb2, and so on). Other letters in the disk names may be used, depending on the type of hard disk and its adapter. For example, a SCSI hard disk may be called /dev/sda1 instead of /dev/had (used for IDE and EIDE drives).

The Boot Sector

To understand the Linux boot process, a look at the DOS boot sector is necessary. Figure 4.1 shows the DOS boot sector layout. The program code is the bootstrap to the operating system. The disk parameters include the File Allocation Table (FAT).

The LILO boot sector is similar to the DOS boot sector, except the disk parameter section is not used and the boundaries between code sections are different. The Linux boot sector layout is shown in Figure 4.2. The differences between the two boot sectors can cause a problem for DOS if the Linux LILO boot sector is written to a DOS disk's Master Boot Record because DOS won't be able to load properly.

The magic number referred to in both boot sector layouts is a two-byte number used by some operating systems to verify that the sector read is the boot sector.

FIGURE 4.1.
The DOS boot sector layout.

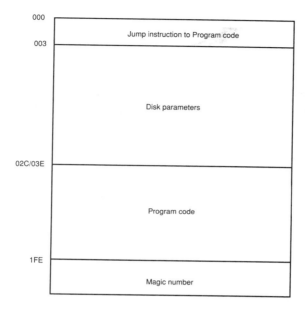

FIGURE 4.2.
The Linux LILO boot sector layout.

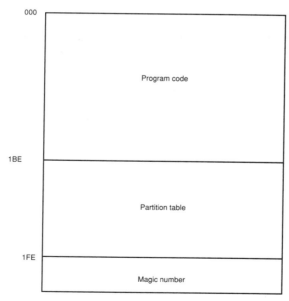

The Linux LILO boot sector can, in theory, be used to boot DOS because the partition table area of the boot record can contain the DOS' FAT file, but in practice the boot process usually fails. It is much better to use a boot sector written to the Linux partition.

> **WARNING**
>
> Because the DOS and Linux LILO boot sectors differ, you should install DOS before Linux. This will make sure that the DOS boot sector is written to the hard disk. If you install Linux first and the Linux LILO boot sector is written to the hard disk, DOS cannot boot.

The LILO boot sector can be saved on a boot floppy, on the Master Boot Record of the hard disk, on the boot sector of the Linux partition, or in the boot sector of an extended partition. It cannot be stored in any non-Linux partition or on any hard disk other than the first.

Note that although DOS cannot handle a boot sector in an extended partition, Linux can through extensions to `fdisk` or a utility program called `activate`.

> **WARNING**
>
> A common problem with LILO is that it will write a LILO boot sector anywhere, even into locations that cannot be accessed by the operating system. Make sure you are writing your LILO boot sector to a valid location. If you have already installed Linux and are making changes, keep a boot floppy at hand.

The Boot Process

During the boot process, the boot sector is read to obtain the bootstrap for the operating system. In the case of DOS, the Master Boot Record or boot sector is read, then COMMAND.COM is loaded. COMMAND.COM is the DOS operating system kernel.

Although usually set up when the Linux installation process is followed, you may want to alter the boot system used by Linux. There are several approaches that can be used depending on your requirements and machine hard drive configuration. We can look at a few of the typical configuration examples to show how the boot process can be modified.

Dedicated Linux Hard Disk

With a dedicated Linux installation or a Linux boot by default (and despite other operating systems on the hard disk), the Master Boot Record can be replaced with the Linux LILO boot sector. LILO will then boot straight into Linux from the Master Boot Record without touching partition boot sectors. In some cases, though, you may have to explicitly specify the boot sector. In other words, at the `boot:` prompt you may have to specify `boot=/dev/hda` (or whichever device holds the modified Master Boot Record) if the default values do not work.

> **WARNING**
>
> If you replace the Master Book Record with LILO for a dedicate Linux system and then later remove Linux, you will have to low-level format the hard drive or restore the old MBR before the drive can be used by another operating system such as DOS.

To install LILO as a dedicated Linux boot, follow these steps:

1. Boot Linux as usual. Make sure you have a boot floppy disk in case of problems.
2. Copy your existing Master Boot Record to a floppy in case of problems. The command to copy the MBR from the main drive (`/dev/hda`) to a floppy using 512 character blocks (the default) is

   ```
   dd if=/dev/hda of=/fd/MBR bs=512 count=1
   ```

3. Use the setup or LILO installation program to copy LILO into the boot sector, setting LILO in the Master Boot Record.
4. Reboot the machine to boot from the Master Boot Record.

Your machine should load Linux automatically. If Linux does not boot, use your boot floppy to start Linux and either repeat the process or restore the original Master Boot Record from the floppy using the following command:

```
dd if=/fd/MBR of=/dev/hda bs=446 count=1
```

Using BOOTACTV

A slight modification of the last boot process is replacing the MBR with a utility called BOOTACTV which prompts for the partition to boot from. This requires a non-DOS–compatible copy of the boot sector to be written, so it should be used only when Linux will be the dominant operating system and when LILO is not booting the other operating systems properly.

When in place, the Master Boot Record holds a copy of BOOTACTV. When booted, BOOTACTV allows you to make a choice of which operating system to boot. BOOTACTV can then read a boot sector from a partition to load that operating system.

To install BOOTACTV, follow these steps:

1. Boot Linux as usual. Make sure you have a boot floppy disk in case of problems.

2. Copy your existing Master Boot Record to a floppy disk in case of problems. The command to copy the MBR from the main drive (/dev/hda) to a floppy using 512 character blocks (the default) is

   ```
   dd if=/dev/hda of=/fd/MBR bs=512 count=1
   ```

3. Use the setup or LILO installation program to copy LILO into the boot sector of the Linux partition (*not* the Master Boot Record).

4. Install BOOTACTV into the Master Boot Record. The BOOTACTV utility is usually called bootactv.bin and should be in the current directory when you install it into the MBR with the following command:

   ```
   dd if=bootactv.bin of=/dev/hda bs=446 count=1
   ```

5. Reboot the machine to boot BOOTACTV from the Master Boot Record.

Your machine should load BOOTACTV and allow you to boot any other operating system on a partition. If Linux or another operating system does not boot, use your boot floppy disk to start Linux. If only Linux doesn't boot, the boot sector LILO for the Linux partition is not working and can be rewritten using the setup or LILO configuration utilities. If none of the partitions will boot, remove BOOTACTV by replacing the old Master Boot Record with the following command:

```
dd if=/fd/MBR of=/dev/hda bs=446 count=1
```

You can also reinstall the Master Boot Record from within DOS, if you have a DOS boot floppy. When in DOS, issue the following command:

```
fdisk /mbr
```

TIP

If you don't want to alter your Master Boot Record but have more than one partition dedicated to Linux, you can install BOOTACTV on one of the partition's boot sectors and use the fdisk utility to toggle the active partition. However, if the hard disk is repartitioned or the file systems are altered in size, the boot sector has to be rewritten. To write BOOTACTV to the fourth primary hard disk partition, for example, copy the existing MBR to the partition's boot sector, then install BOOTACTV with the following commands:

```
dd if=/dev/hda of=/dev/hda4 bs=512 count=1
dd if=bootactv.bin of=/dev/hda4 bs=446 count=1
```

DOS and Linux

Most Linux installations coexist with DOS and use the DOS Master Boot Record. In this case, the MBR is read and the active partition (set by fdisk) is booted automatically. This is one of the safest installation methods because no changes to the DOS-installed Master Boot Record are performed, and it is easy to remove or reconfigure partitions at any time without worrying about compatibility with the MBR.

> **NOTE**
>
> Later versions of DOS (6.00 or higher) overwrite an existing MBR if installed after Linux. This makes it impossible to boot Linux from the MBR, although DOS will boot. Fix the problem by running LILO again or by making the Linux partition active.

The active partition can be changed at any time using the fdisk utility or the Linux utility activate. The setup program within Linux can usually change the boot partition, too. Only one partition on a hard disk can be active at a time. Some operating systems, including Linux, let you change your mind about which operating system to boot after the active partition has been read, assuming a delay was built into the boot process. Linux, for example, can display the boot: prompt and wait for a reply or a timeout to occur before starting to boot Linux.

To use this approach for Linux, simply install LILO into the boot sector of the Linux partition. To make it bootable, run fdisk and set that partition number as the active partition. Rebooting the machine will boot into the active partition.

When Linux is replaced or removed, the boot sector of the new operating system overwrites the Linux partition's boot sector, requiring no changes to the MBR.

4

USING LILO

Using BOOTLIN

With the Linux BOOTLIN configuration, which is also a common form of installation, no changes to the Master Boot Record are made. During the boot process, the Master Boot Record is read, and then a decision about which operating system to load is made. This decision is usually based on a user prompt. Essentially, this is the same as a normal DOS boot except the program BOOTLIN is invoked in either the CONFIG.SYS or AUTOEXEC.BAT files. This can then execute a program that lets you choose the operating system to load. The program BOOT.SYS, for example, may be used to present a menu that lets you choose between a Linux and DOS boot.

To install BOOTLIN in your DOS partition, follow these steps:

1. Boot Linux. Make sure you have a boot floppy disk in case of problems.
2. Place a copy of the Linux kernel in your DOS partition either through DOS or with one of the Linux Mtools. You only have to copy the kernel file into the home directory (or any subdirectory) of the DOS partition. This can even be done from a floppy.
3. Copy BOOT.SYS and BOOTLIN.SYS to the DOS partition, using the same process as the Linux kernel.
4. Add both the BOOT.SYS and BOOTLIN.SYS files to your CONFIG.SYS file.
5. Make sure DOS is the active partition and reboot the machine.

When DOS starts, the BOOT device driver should give you the option of booting DOS or Linux. If you have problems, simply remove the BOOT.SYS and BOOTLIN.SYS files from the CONFIG.SYS file and you are back to normal.

Using the BOOT.SYS program has a useful advantage: No boot sectors are altered to support several operating systems. This can make it easy to load and to remove operating systems from a hard disk. Both the Master Boot Record with active partition and BOOT.SYS approaches can be employed together so that the hard disk starts to boot whichever operating system has the active flag, then pauses and waits for confirmation from the user (or a timeout to occur). In this case, no changes to the Master Boot Record need to be made.

Boot Parameters

Regardless of which boot process you use, when Linux is booting, LILO pauses momentarily to check that the Shift, Control, and Alt keys are not pressed and that CapsLock and ScrollLock are set. If none of the keys are pressed and the locks are on, LILO displays the boot: prompt. At this point, LILO is waiting for the name of the boot image to be entered or if a timeout or Enter is pressed, the default boot image is loaded. The boot image is the kernel of whichever operating system is to be loaded, including DOS.

If you want to boot an image other than the default, you can enter its name at the `boot:` prompt. To obtain a list of all known boot images, enter a question mark or hit the Tab key (depending on the image and keyboard setting). The default boot image name is located in the file `/etc/rc` or /etc/lilo.conf (depending on the version of Linux) on the line that reads

```
BOOT_IMAGE=
```

You can specify parameters for the kernel from the `boot:` prompt, too. You specify a parameter by entering it after the `boot:` prompt. Unless overridden, the parameters are used by the default image when it boots. Valid parameters differ a little depending on the version of Linux, but most versions support the following parameters:

- `no387`   Disables any onboard floating-point unit (FPU).
- `root`   Boots from a device specified after the root parameter, such as `root=/dev/ sda1`. The root command requires a hexadecimal device number of the full path name of the device.
- `ro`   Mounts the root file system as read-only.
- `rw`   Mounts the root file system as read-write.
- `single`   Boots the Linux system into single user (system administrator) mode.

The root parameter allows a hexadecimal device number to be used. The device numbers are assigned depending on the type of device. For floppy drives, the numbers are assigned starting with 200, so `/dev/fd0` is 200, `/dev/fd1` is 201, `/dev/fd2` is 202, and so on. Hard disks have numbers assigned depending on the type of device. For most hard disks, the numbers start at 301 (not 300 because there is no `/dev/hd0`): `/dev/hda1` is 301, `/dev/hda2` is 302, and so on. When a second hard drive is used, the numbers jump to 340: `/dev/hdb1` is 341, `/dev/hdb2` is 342, and so on. For `/dev/sda` devices, numbering starts at 801: `/dev/sda1` is 801, `/dev/sda2` is 802, and so on. The second hard drive starts at 811: `/dev/sdb1` is 811, `/dev/sdb2` is 812, and so on. Because floppy and hard drives are usually the only devices that can act as a boot device, these numbers should suffice for all occurrences except removable media.

4

USING LILO

Parameters can be combined if separated by a space. For example, at the `boot:` prompt the following line boots the kernel called `image5` located on the device `/dev/hda2`:

```
image5 root=/dev/hda2 single ro
```

The file system will be mounted as a read-only device. Single-user mode only will be invoked.

The Map Installer

The *map installer* is the program that updates the boot sector and creates the map file. The map installer is usually the file /etc/lilo/lilo. Whenever the map installer is running, it checks for errors in the boot sector. If an error is detected, no changes to the boot sector are written and the installer terminates.

When a boot sector is successfully updated by the map installer, the old boot sector contents are copied into the directory /etc/lilo with the name boot.hex_num where hex_num is the hexadecimal device number of the partition that was rewritten. (The hexadecimal device numbers were mentioned in the previous section.) When the map installer writes to a partition's boot sector, the old copy of the boot sector is stored in a file with the name part.hex_num. Again, hex_num is the number of the device.

The map installer behavior can be modified by command-line parameters supplied when the installer is invoked or by entries in the configuration file /etc/lilo/config. Many of the options can be given both on the command line and in the configuration file. Before looking at the execution of the map installer and boot examples, we should look at the configuration options.

Map Installer Command-line Syntax

The LILO map installer utility accepts a number of options on the command line. Many of the command-line options are mirrored by configuration variables, discussed in the next section. Allowed options are shown in Table 4.2.

TABLE 4.2. OPTIONS THAT THE MAP INSTALLER ALLOWS.

Option	Meaning
b dev	Uses dev as the boot device. If no value is specified, the default device given by the boot configuration variable is used.
c	Turns compact on, merging read requests for adjacent sectors into one request to reduce load time. Often used for boot floppies. The compact configuration variable can also be used to specify this option.
C file	Uses file as the configuration file. If no file is specified, /etc/lilo/config is used as the default.
d secs	The number of tenths of seconds to wait before booting the first image. Also can be specified in the configuration variable delay.
f file	Uses file as the name of the disk parameter table (called disktab). If a filename is omitted, the file /etc/lilo/disktab is used.

Option	Meaning
i sector	Installs the kernel as the new boot sector. Can be read from the `install` configuration variable.
I name	Displays the path of the name kernel image file. If no matching name is found, an error is generated. The option "v" can be added after the name to verify the existence of the image file. This option uses the BOOT_IMAGE environment variable.
l	Generates linear sector addresses instead of the default `sector/head/cylinder` addresses. Can also be specified with the configuration variable `linear`.
m file	Uses `file` as the location of the map file. If no filename is given, `/etc/lilo/map` is used.
P fix	Allows LILO to adjust `sector/head/cylinder` addresses using the table file. Also specified with the `fix table` configuration variable.
P ignore	Overrides correction of `sector/head/cylinder` addresses. Also specified with the `ignore table` configuration variable.
q	Displays the currently mapped files.
r dir	Performs a `chroot` command on `dir` before continuing. This is necessary if the root file system is mounted in a different location from the map installer command. Because the current directory is changed with this command, use absolute pathnames for all files.
R words	Stores words in the map file for use by the boot loader. The words are parameters used by the boot process as part of the default command line. The first word must be the name of the boot image.
s file	Copies the original boot sector to file instead of `/etc/lilo/boot.hex_num`.
S file	Same as s but overwrites the old file if it exists.
t	Performs a test by executing the entire installation process except writing the map file and boot sector. Ideally used with the v option to verify accurate behavior of the map installer.
u dev	Restores the backup copy of the boot sector for `dev`. If no device is specified, the default value is used or, failing a valid value, the current root device. The backup copy is checked for a time stamp before the write is completed.
U dev	Same as u except no check for the time stamp.
v level	Uses the verbose output level specified to display messages.
V	Displays the version number of the map installer, then exits.

4

USING LILO

Map Installer Configuration File Options

Configuration options for the map installer can be stored in the file `/etc/lilo/config`. The file consists of sets of parameter-value pairs, although some options do not need a value. Whitespace can be used between parameters, the equal sign, and the value. Comments can be included by starting the line with a pound sign. A newline character terminates the comment.

As a rule, variable names are not case sensitive, whereas values usually are. It is good practice, though, to keep all entries lowercase (as is UNIX convention).

The options shown in Table 4.3 can be put into the map installer configuration file `/etc/lilo/config`.

TABLE 4.3. MAP INSTALLATION OPTIONS.

Option	Meaning
alias=name	Allows an image to be called by the string name as well as its normal filename.
append=string	Appends string to the command line passed to the kernel. Mostly used to pass boot parameters about hardware devices that are not automatically detected by the kernel.
backup=file	Copies the original boot sector to file instead of `/etc/lilo/boot.hex_num`. Can also be a device (like `/dev/null`).
boot=dev	Specifies the device that contains the boot sector. If no name is specified, the currently mounted root partition is used.
compact	Merges read requests for adjacent sectors into a single read request, reducing the load time and file size. This is commonly used with floppy disks.
delay=secs	Gives the delay in tenths of a second to wait before booting the image. If no delay is given, boot is immediate.
disktab=file	Gives the name of the disk parameter table. If no filename is given, `/etc/lilo/disktab` is used.
fix-table	Lets LILO adjust `sector/head/cylinder` addresses. Usually used with operating systems that may change these addresses. LILO will readjust incorrect entries if `fix-table` is specified.
force-backup=file	Similar to `backup`, but overwrites any existing file. If `force-backup` is used in the configuration options, any backup option is ignored.
install=sector	Installs the image in the specified boot sector. If no value is given, `/etc/lilo/boot.b` is used.
label=name	Renames an image to the alternate string name.

Option	*Meaning*
linear	Generates linear sectors instead of sector/head/cylinder addresses. Linear addresses are independent of disk geometry and are translated in real time. Linear boot disks may not be portable.
literal=string	Similar to the append variable but removes any other options, using only those specified in string.
map=file	File is the map file location. If no value is given, /etc/lilo/map is used.
message=file	Uses the file contents as a message displayed before the boot: prompt. The message cannot be larger than 64Kb. If the message is changed or moved, the map file must be rebuilt.
optional	Makes an image optional. If the image's file can't be located, it is not booted. This is useful for testing new kernels.
password=password	Sets a password for all images. If the option that is restricted exists, a password is required only to boot the image the configuration file refers to.
prompt	Forces the boot: prompt without checking for any keypresses. Usually combined with timeout to force unattended reboots.
ramdisk=size	Sets the optional RAM disk to size. Setting equal to zero suppresses the RAM disk.
read-only	Mounts the root file system as read-only.
read-write	Mounts the root file system as read-write.
restricted	Relaxes password protection.
root=dev	Specifies the device to be mounted as the root file system. If the value current is used, the root device is the device on which the root file system is currently mounted (unless changed with the -r command-line option).
serial=parms	Sets a serial line for control, initializing the line and accepting input from it (as well as the console). The format of the parameters is port, baud_rate, parity, bits. When serial is set, the delay value is set to 20 automatically, unless overridden.
timeout=secs	Sets the number of tenths of seconds to wait for keyboard input before loading the image. Also used to specify password input time-outs. Default value is infinite.
verbose=level	Displays progress messages. The higher the level, the more messages. If the -v command line option is also included, the higher level is used.

4

USING LILO

continues

TABLE 4.3. CONTINUED

Option	Meaning
vga=mode	Sets the VGA text mode for use during booting. Valid values are normal (80×25 text mode); extended or ext (80×50 text mode); ask (prompt for the mode during boot); and any valid text mode value. To obtain a list of available modes, boot with the parameter vga=ask and press Enter when asked for a value. Case is not important in the values of the vga option.

If any parameter is not specified either on the command line or in the configuration file, default values are used. Some values are also maintained within the kernel image (such as ramdisk, root, and vga).

Boot Images

LILO can boot a kernel image from several locations, such as a regular file on the root file system or any other mounted file system, from a block device such as a floppy disk, or from the boot sector of another partition or disk. The type of boot is dictated by entries in a configuration file.

Boot image configuration files can have several variables defined, all of which have been mentioned previously. Valid configuration file variables are alias, label, optional, password, ramdisk, read-only, read-write, restricted, root, and vga.

To boot a kernel image from a file, all that is necessary in the configuration file is the name of the image. For example, the following line boots the image called linux_main:

```
image=/linux_main
```

To boot an image from another device, the sectors that must be read on that device have to be specified. There are several methods of providing the sector information. The starting sector must be provided, but you can then either specify a number of sectors to be read (start+length) or the end sector number (start-finish). If only one number is provided (the start sector), only that sector is read.

For example, the contents of this configuration file boot the kernel from the floppy disk, starting at sector 1 and reading the next 512 sectors:

```
image=/dev/fd0
     range=1+512
```

More than one configuration can be specified for an image because LILO stores values in an image descriptor file and not in the image itself. For example, a configuration file can contain the following entries:

```
image=/linux_main
     label=linux-hda1
     root=/dev/hda1
image=/linux_main
     label=linux-hda3
     root=/dev/hda3
image=/linux_main
     label=linux-flop
     root=/dev/fd0
```

This code has three configurations for the same Linux kernel (linux_main) but has different root devices with three different alternate names. The boot devices for the image are /dev/hda1, /dev/hda3, and /dev/fd0, respectively. Whitespace in the configuration file is ignored, so the indentations are for ease of reading only.

Disk Parameter Table

LILO is usually able to obtain information about the hard disks and floppy disks on the system by reading the kernel. On some systems, though, this isn't possible (this is especially the case with some SCSI adapters and adapters that do not behave as IDE or SCSI "normal" devices). When LILO can't obtain the disk parameter information, it generates an error message about "bad geometry."

The disk parameters can be physically read by LILO from the file /etc/lilo/disktab. When the disktab file exists, it takes precedence over any autodetected values. The disktab file contains the device number (hexadecimal), its BIOS code, and the disk geometry. A sample disktab file could have the following entries:

```
# /etc/lilo/disktab - LILO disk paramter table
#
# Dev. num   BIOS code   Secs/track   Heads/cyl   Cyls   Part. Offset
#
     0x800       0x80        32           64       1714       0
     0x801       0x80        32           64       1714       1001
```

This shows a SCSI disk with two partitions. The first partition /dev/sda1 has a device number 800, and the second partition /dev/sda2 has the device number 801. Both partitions have the BIOS code 80. Both the device number and BIOS code have to be given in hex format, hence the leading "0x." The disk has 32 sectors per track, 64 heads per cylinder, and 1,714 cylinders. Because both partitions are on the same disk, these parameters will be the same.

The partition offset is an optional field. The first partition starts at offset 0, and the second at offset 1001 (the number of sectors from the start of the disk). The partition offsets need only be explicitly given when the kernel cannot obtain that information. Most hard disks (including removable and optical disks) don't need the partition offsets, but CD-ROMs sometimes do.

> **TIP**
>
> When filling in the `/etc/lilo/disktab` file, you don't have to have the details exactly right. Most systems remap the drive parameters to 32 sectors per track and 64 heads, whether those numbers are correct or not. (This is a BIOS action.) The number of cylinders must be at least equal to or higher than the number of actual cylinders to avoid truncation of the disk space that the operating system recognizes.

Some BIOS versions do not allow disks exceeding certain values. This is usually a problem with IDE and SCSI controller cards that are designed for DOS systems with relatively small (<1 GB) disk drives and earlier BIOS versions. Device drivers allow some high-capacity drives to be used, although some systems will have a problem accessing files beyond the 1 GB limit.

Removing or Disabling LILO

To prevent LILO from booting the system, the boot sector must be disabled (by using `fdisk` to change the active partition) or removed completely. Most versions of LILO can be quickly disabled with the following command:

```
/etc/lilo/lilo -u
```

If you are using the newer directory structure, substitute the pathname as necessary.

When removing a LILO boot sector in the Master Boot Record of the disk, the MBR must be replaced with another record. If you want to replace the MBR with a DOS MBR from a booted DOS disk, enter the following command:

```
fdisk /mbr
```

Because backup copies of the boot sector are created whenever LILO creates a new version, the older versions of the boot sector can be copied back in place (assuming they are still available). For example, to restore the Master Boot Record saved in a file called `boot.0800` (800 is the device number of a SCSI drive), issue the following command:

```
dd if=/etc/lilo/boot.0800 of=/dev/sda bs=446 count=1
```

If you are using another device, substitute the name of the saved boot file and the device name.

Troubleshooting LILO

LILO displays error messages when it can't function properly. These error messages should be sufficient to identify the problem. The most common error messages and their solutions are shown in Table 4.4.

TABLE 4.4. LILO ERROR MESSAGES.

Message	*Solution*
Can't put the boot sector on logical partition X	LILO attempted to put the boot sector on the correct root file system on a logical partition. MBRs can only boot primary partitions by default. Override with the `-b` option and an explicit boot partition value or use the configuration `variable boot=device`.
Got bad geometry	The disk controller (mostly SCSI) doesn't support automatic geometry detection. Use the file `/etc/lilo/disktab` to provide the disk parameters.
Invalid partition table, entry X	The `sector/head/cylinder` and linear addresses of the first sector of the partition don't match. This usually occurs when an operating system creates partitions not aligned to tracks. Try the `fix table` option.
First sector doesn't have a valid boot signature	The first sector of the device doesn't seem to be a valid boot sector. Check the device name or rerun LILO to install the boot sector.
Cylinder number of too big	A file is located beyond the 1,024th cylinder which LILO can't access because of BIOS limitations.
XXX doesn't have a valid LILO signature	XXX was located but isn't a valid LILO entry. If XXX is the boot sector, you should use the `-I` option or the `install` option to install the LILO boot sector.
XXX has an invalid stage code	The entry at XXX is corrupted. Rerun LILO.
Kernel XXX is too big	The kernel is larger than 512 Kb, which LILO can't handle. Remove some unused drivers and recompile the kernel.
Partition entry not found	The partition is not in the partition table.
Sorry, don't know how to handle device XXX	LILO can't determine the disk parameters. Use the file `/etc/lilo/disktab` to specify them.

4

USING LILO

Summary

This chapter includes all the information you need to install and use LILO to create your boot sectors for Linux. LILO is quite versatile and can handle several different configurations with ease. It allows you to tailor your installation to boot the best way for your use.

Although LILO is used only when first setting up your Linux system and after kernel changes, you should know the basics of its operation so you know what is happening to your hard disks and their boot sectors. This is especially true when you use other operating systems on the same system. From here, you may want to jump ahead to other chapters:

> To start using your Linux system, read Chapter 6, "Getting Started."
>
> To configure X so you can work with a GUI instead of character-based terminals, see Chapter 22, "Installing and Configuring XFree86."
>
> To administer your newly installed Linux system, see Chapter 32, "System Administration Basics."

Wrapping Up the Installation

by Tim Parker

IN THIS CHAPTER

CHAPTER 5

Now that you've installed Linux and configured LILO to boot your system the way you want it to, everything should be working just fine. Unfortunately, computer operating systems have a way of not working properly, despite your doing everything you should. This chapter deals with a couple of issues: checking out your system to make sure it is installed and working properly, and using the package installation tools to add new software to your system. We wrap up the chapter with a look at using multiple CD-ROM drives on your system.

Booting Linux

If you worked through the last two chapters, you have installed Linux (most likely from a CD-ROM) and LILO. Your system should reboot into Linux (or give you the option of booting Linux, depending on how you set your system up) when you do a cold restart (power off, then back on). If it doesn't, the most likely cause of problems is LILO.

The usual culprit is that the Master Boot Record or the boot partition did not have the Linux boot instructions written to them. The LILO chapter explains how to correct this problem.

Your system will often boot into Linux properly, but some of your devices won't be working properly. It is very rare for hard drives, floppies, and CD-ROMs not to be recognized because these are all detected and configured during the installation process. However, sound cards, network cards, external SCSI devices, and peripherals such as printers and scanners are sometimes not found after a system reboot. This is most often a configuration problem in which the kernel does not know how to communicate with the device properly.

Emergency Boot Procedure

What happens if you've installed Linux, used LILO (or maybe forgot), and rebooted the machine? Either you booted into another operating system on the disk or got the dreaded "No OS" message from the machine's BIOS. Do you have to start all over again? Luckily, no. If you have the boot and root disks you created when you first installed Linux, you're safe.

Boot the system off the install (boot) disk. The system gives you the familiar boot: prompt. The way to tell the Linux boot disk to load off the hard disk where your installed kernel is, instead of off the disks and start again, is to specify the location of the kernel. This is usually done with the partition name, such as /dev/hda1 for the first partition on the disk. The command to boot from this partition would be typed at the boot prompt like this:

```
boot ro root=/dev/hda1
```

This tells LILO to find the kernel to boot from on that partition. You should use the proper partition name, of course, and a Linux kernel must be there to read.

After you have booted the system from floppy, run LILO to set up the boot sequence the way you want it.

Using dmesg

If you have devices that are not recognized properly after booting, you should check the boot messages your system generates. You can see all the messages by typing the command dmesg at the shell prompt. If a device is not recognized properly, you will see one or more lines in the dmesg output about that device. For example, if your network card is not properly detected you may see messages like this:

```
loading device 'eth0'...
ne.c:v1.10 9/23/94 Donald Becker (becker@cesdis.gsfc.nasa.gov)
NE*000 ethercard probe at 0x300: 00 00 6e 24 1e 3e
eth0: NE2000 not found at 0x300
eth0 not loaded
```

As was mentioned, this error almost always occurs because you provided the wrong configuration information. In the case of the network card above, the IO address on the card was 330H not 300H. Running the setup utility again lets you change these parameters.

Changing Disk Partitions

Whether your system had Windows or DOS on before Linux, or maybe just has Linux now, in the future you may want to modify the layout of the disk drivers to allow other operating systems to be loaded. If you want to modify your partitions' sizes, there are several commercial products (such as PartitionMagic from PowerQuest Corporation) that can do the job, but there's also a tool we've looked at in earlier chapters that works just fine under DOS and Windows—FIPS. FIPS lets you size existing partitions without requiring a full backup-reformat-restore operation.

You've already seen how to run FIPS from the DOS or Windows prompt. Prior to running FIPS, you should defragment your file system using one of the utilities included with DOS or Windows for that task, and then run FIPS to create new partitions or remove existing ones.

If you've installed Linux, you're not out of luck: You can boot off a floppy disk and use the Linux CD-ROM to run FIPS, or copy FIPS to your boot floppy when in Linux. You can use this technique to convert an all-Linux disk to a shared Linux-Windows disk. You should not run FIPS from the Linux directory, even under an emulator software package such as Wabi because the results are not predictable.

Installing Additional Software

So your Linux system is up and running, but you want more software? There are several sources of additional software you can load on your system, including CD-ROMs, WWW pages, and FTP sites. You can also purchase software from vendors. In some cases, software includes an installation utility that needs to be run to install the package properly. Commercial software is usually like this, as you will see in Part VIII of this book when we look at some commercial applications.

For other applications, especially those that come in the disk sets that most CD-ROM versions of Linux include, you must use a package tool such as `installpkg`, `pkgtool`, or `pkgadd`. The name of the tool differs considerably, depending on your version and release of Linux, so you should check the documentation that came with your system for the exact name and actions necessary to add software. As an example of the process, we can look at two different tools. The first is RPM (Red Hat Package Manager), and the second is `installpkg` (which is available with many versions of Linux).

RPM

RPM is not restricted to Red Hat Linux; it has appeared in several different versions of Linux. RPM is a character-based system that allows you to build, install, query, verify, update, and uninstall software packages. (A software package in Linux terms consists of an archive of files and information about that package, such as the package name, version number, and a brief description.) RPM has ten modes of operation, each with a different set of options. This can make RPM a little confusing to work with, although most of the uses are straightforward. RPM's modes and their purposes are shown in Table 5.1.

TABLE 5.1. RPM's MODES AND WHAT THEY ARE USED FOR.

Mode name	Command line	Used for
Build	`rpm -[blt]O`	Build a package
Fix permissions	`rpm --setperms`	Fix the permissions on a package
Install	`rpm -i`	Adding new software

Mode name	Command line	Used for
Query	rpm -q	Check to see what packages and files are installed
Rebuild Database	rpm --rebuilddb	Rebuild the package database
Set owners and groups	rpm --setugids	Set the owner and group of a package
Show RC	rpm --showrc	
Signature check	rpm --checksig	Check the package to ensure there are no errors
Uninstall	rpm -e	Remove a package
Verify	rpm -Vl-yl --verify	Verify that a package is installed properly (all files installed)

We won't bother with a lot of detail about all these options because most are self-explanatory and covered in the documentation, but a few common-usage examples will help you become more familiar with RPM. To install software with RPM, you need to specify the package name that you want to install. The syntax of the install command is as follows:

```
rpm -i [install-options] <package_filename>
```

There are dozens of installation options possible, most of which don't do very much except modify the behavior of RPM slightly. A few of the more useful installation options for RPM are

- allfiles. Installs or upgrades all the files in the package.
- force. The same as using replacepkgs, replacefiles, and oldpackage together.
- h or --hash. Displays 50 hash marks as the package archive is unpacked to show the system is working (use with the -v option for a nicely formatted status display).
- includedocs. Installs documentation files (usually done by default).
- ignoreos. Forces installation or upgrading if the operating systems of the RPM and the host are not the same.
- keep-temps. Keeps temporary files created during the installation process, useful for debugging installation problems.
- percent. Displays progress percentages as files are unpacked (intended to make RPM easy to run from scripts).

- `quiet`. Displays a minimal set of messages (but all error messages).
- `replacefiles`. Installs the package even if new files replace files from already installed packages.
- `replacepkgs`. Installs the package(s) even if they are already installed.
- `test`. Does not install but checks for conflicts.

Check the man page for a full list of options. The packagee name to be added is usually given as a complete path, although a URL is also possible with many versions of RPM. To install a package called Xgames, the command would be given like this:

```
rpm -i /mnt/cdrom/col/install/Xgames.rpm
```

In this case, the package is called Xgames.rpm, and the full path to the package is given (this one is on a CD-ROM in the col—collections—directory).

The verify mode of the RPM command is handy for making certain that all portions of a package have been installed and still exist on your system. This is sometimes necessary after installing other packages that may overwrite part of an existing package. When you verify a package, RPM compares information about the installed files in the package with information about the files taken from the original package and stored in the RPM database. Among other things, verifying compares the filename, size, check sum, permissions, type, owner, and group of each file. Any discrepancies in the comparison are displayed on the screen.

To use the verify mode of RPM, use the command with the -w option and the package name. RPM will use one of these eight characters to show a failure of one of the tests:

- 5   MD5 sum (checksum)
- S   File size incorrect
- L   Symbolic link incorrect
- T   Time incorrect
- D   Device incorrect
- U   User owner incorrect
- G   Group owner incorrect
- M   Mode incorrect (includes permissions and file types)

If you find errors in a package, it is usually easiest to reinstall the package.

installpkg

The `installpkg` utility is a hold-over from UNIX, where it has been around for years. The `installpkg` utility can be used to install a package in much the same way as RPM. The command to install the package Xgames would be

```
installpkg /usr/col/Xgames
```

By default `installpkg` looks for packages with `.tgz` file extensions. If you have a different extension and know that `installpkg` can handle it, specify the full package name including the extension on the command line. In the case of the above command, the `installpkg` tool extracts any files in the package `/usr/col/Xgames.tgz`, unpacking them as it goes.

The directory used by `installpkg` as the base for its installation is the current one, so in the case of the above example, whatever directory we are in when we issue the `installpkg` command is where the Xgames package is installed.

Other Installation Commands

Many versions of Linux have bundled their own package management system. These can be either character-based, like `installpkg` and RPM, or graphical. A good example of such a tool is LISA (Linux Installation and System Administration), a tool bundled with Caldera OpenLinux (a Slackware release) and some other versions of Linux. LISA can be run from the character terminal or from X terminals. LISA offers a menu-driven interface that prevents you having to worry about all the command-line options that bog down RPM and `installpkg`.

When you start LISA, the opening menu lets you select either system administration tasks or package management (see Figure 5.1). Keyboard arrow keys move between the selections.

FIGURE 5.1.
LISA's menu-driven interface is much more friendly than a command line.

From the main menu, choose the Software Package Administration option, and a new menu appears that lets you examine packages already installed or add new packages, as shown in Figure 5.2.

FIGURE 5.2.

LISA lets you examine packages already installed or add new packages.

If you choose to examine available packages, LISA shows a list of the default packages Linux knows about. Figure 5.3 shows the main list of available packages. Further information about the files in each package can be obtained from each package choice. You can add other packages by inserting media (such as a CD-ROM or providing a pathname) and having LISA examine the new package options. From there, you can choose which packages to install, and LISA takes care of the rest, just as RPM and `installpkg` did.

FIGURE 5.3.

The primary distribution packages accompanying this version of Linux.

Multiple CD-ROM Devices

In theory, there is no real limit to the number of CD-ROM devices your Linux system can handle. As long as there are device numbers (major and minor device numbers are discussed in Chapter 33, "Devices"), then the device is legal. So why would anyone want more than one CD-ROM device on his system? There are a number of reasons: CD-ROM changers, CD-ROM writers, and CD-ROM libraries are all common. We can look at each of these in turn.

CD Changers

One of the most common reasons for multiple CD-ROM devices is that a CD-ROM changer is being used. A CD-ROM changer allows you to have three, six, or some other number of CDs inside the changer body, but only one CD-ROM is actually used by the read mechanism at a time. A good example of a popular CD-ROM changer is the NEC Multispin series, both internal and external devices allowing multiple CD-ROMs to be inserted into the changer and individually accessed with either front-panel buttons or software commands.

When configured on a Windows system, CD-ROM changers usually set up a different drive letter for each of the CD-ROMs possible in the changer. For example, when a six-disk NEC Multispin is installed under Windows 95, the devices are numbered from the last hard drive up; so if you have a single hard drive `C:`, the CD-ROMs would be `D:` through `I:`. You can't read two of the CD-ROM drives at the same time, but changing drive letters in Windows changes the loaded CD-ROM in the changer.

Linux works with changers in one of two ways: You can configure the changer as a single CD-ROM drive and use the front-panel buttons to manually change disks, or you can set up different devices for each CD-ROM. The choice is yours, not Linux's. Of the two, the former is easier but the latter gives you more flexibility. Because Linux doesn't like you changing CD-ROMs after they have been mounted, you really should unmount the CD-ROM before changing CDs whichever option you choose. To configure a changer for more than one CD-ROM device, follow the same procedure as a single CD-ROM but increment the device number (`/dev/cd0`, `/dev/cd1`, `/dev/cd2`, and so on). Only one of these devices can be linked to `/dev/cdrom` at a time.

CD Writers

CD writers are another reason to install multiple CD-ROM drives on your Linux system. CD write devices enable you to burn your own CD-ROMs, usually in a one-shot method, although CD rewritable devices are slowly becoming more reasonably priced. Although the manufacturers of the CD writers (such as Hewlett-Packard's SureStore series) do not directly support Linux, there are some drivers available for Linux, mostly developed by other users.

A CD writer can be used as a read-only standard CD-ROM device under Linux with no special configuration. Since most CD writer devices are SCSI based, the configuration as a SCSI CD-ROM is simple. If you do want to configure it as a writable device, you need one of the previously mentioned drivers, usually available at FTP sites. Because copying CD-ROMs is one of the most prevalent uses of a CD writer, you will often configure the CD writer as a second device (/dev/cd1) after the first, normal CD-ROM (/dev/cd0). You can have both IDE and SCSI CD-ROM devices active at the same time.

CD Libraries

Finally, a common use for multiple CD-ROM devices is to act as a library subsystem. Suppose you have a large amount of data that must be accessed over a network, or you've got reference material you want to offer through the Internet. Whatever the reason, there are many arguments for using multiple CD-ROM drives instead of high-capacity hard drives to offer material (not the least of which is cost).

Configuring multiple CD-ROMs in this case is simple: Set up the devices in order (/dev/cd0, /dev/cd1, and so on) and mount each CD-ROM in the proper location on the Linux file system. Users accessing the server are steered to the proper CD-ROM drive because of the mounting.

Changing CDs

Whenever a CD-ROM is to be made available to the system, it is mounted on the file system with a command like this:

```
mount type device mount_point
```

type is any special instruction that applies to the CD-ROM (such as USO9660 file system or read-only), device is the device name, and mount_point is where the CD-ROM contents are to be placed in the Linux file system. For example, to mount an ISO9660 (which is the standard for CD-ROM contents) CD on the first CD device /dev/cd0 to the mount point /usr/cdrom, you would issue this command:

```
mount -t ISO9660 /dev/cd0 /usr/cdrom
```

From then on, all queries to the /usr/cdrom directory and its subdirectories are steered to the CD-ROM and its contents. When you want to change the CD to another one, you should not just eject the first and insert the second (in fact, many CD-ROM drives will not allow you to do this if the disk is in use). Instead, you have to unmount the CD with the umount command, specifying either the mount point or the device. One of these two commands would unmount the CD-ROM mounted with the preceding command:

```
umount /dev/cd0
umount /usr/cdrom
```

Both commands accomplish the same task.

Summary

This chapter has looked at a few issues, including using the package management tools to add new software to your system and using multiple CD-ROM drives. This chapter rounds out the installation section of this book. From here, we move on to look at how you can use the Linux system you've just installed. You may want to bounce around and look up other useful information, instead of continuing on in sequence.

To learn how to install sound cards and use them in conjunction with your system for multimedia applications, see Chapter 21, "Multimedia Linux."

To learn how to install and configure XFree86, the X server that provides you with a GUI interface to Linux, see Chapter 22, "Installing and Configuring XFree86."

To learn about CD-ROM devices, major and minor device numbers, and how to add new devices such as multiple CD-ROMs, see Chapter 33, "Devices."

Getting to Know Linux

IN THIS PART

CHAPTER 6

Getting Started

by Ed Treijs and Tim Parker

IN THIS CHAPTER

Starting and Stopping Your Linux System

The startup phase of Linux depends on the configuration of LILO that you chose during your Linux installation. In the simplest case, Linux starts automatically from your hard drive or from a boot floppy disk. If your system has multiple versions of Linux or other operating systems installed, you will have to enter a boot string to start Linux.

When your Linux system starts up, you see quite a few Linux initialization messages scroll across the screen. These are system messages that indicate the hardware that Linux recognizes and configures, as well as all the software drivers it loads when starting up. When Linux completes its startup sequence, you should see a prompt similar to this one:

```
darkstar login:
```

You will probably see another name before the login prompt, which in most versions of Linux is set when you install the software. Some Linux systems also show the current version number of the software when the login prompt is displayed, like this:

```
Welcome to Linux 1.2.13darkstar login:
```

Don't worry if your prompt doesn't look exactly like this because each version of Linux does it a bit differently. You will get some sort of a prompt—such as a dollar sign—with every version, though.

> **WARNING**
>
> A Linux system must always be shut down properly. Improper shutdown, usually caused by simply turning off your system at the power switch, can cause serious damage to your Linux filesystem! When you are finished using your Linux system, you must shut it down properly as described in the next section. If you start to boot up Linux and then change your mind, you should let the system start up fully and then follow the shutdown procedure. You risk losing files or your entire system if you fail to follow this advice!

You already know how to start Linux, but it is even more important to know how to shut down the system properly. Like many multiuser systems such as UNIX and Windows NT, if Linux is not powered down properly, damage to individual files or the entire filesystem can result. This is caused by Linux keeping more current versions of the disk's table of contents (known as the I-node table) in memory in order to speed disk access. When you shut down the system properly, the memory version of the I-node table is written to disk prior to the system halting. If you power down without writing the memory version of the I-node table to disk, the disk's contents may not be correct and files may be lost. Also, since Linux is continually using the disk drives even when you are not using the system, it's possible that a disk write-protect could get interrupted when you power off manually. Shutting down the system properly causes all disk writes to cease.

The easiest way to ensure a proper shutdown is to press the Ctrl+ Alt+Delete keys simultaneously. (This is the famous Ctrl+Alt+Delete "three-finger salute" used in DOS and Windows.) Pressing `Ctrl+Alt+Delete` causes a number of advisory messages and Linux shutdown messages to be displayed. When the Linux shutdown procedure has finished, your monitor shows either the initial "power-on" screen or a shutdown message before turning your computer off. Since the shutdown process takes Linux only a few seconds, this is not time-consuming. It's fast and easy, and maintains your system's integrity.

One quick warning: If any users are logged in to your Linux system when you do the `Ctrl+Alt+Delete` sequence, they will be logged off rather forcefully and possibly lose whatever they were working on. Use the `Ctrl+Alt+Delete` sequence with care, and try to tell everyone to log off if they are using the system. You can use the `who` command to find out who is logged in (see "The `who` Command" section found later in this chapter).

Linux Shutdown Commands

There are several other ways to shut down the system, but the `Ctrl+Alt+Delete` sequence is probably the easiest. A number of other commands can activate the shutdown process, but they vary, depending on the version of Linux you are using. Commonly used commands are `shutdown`, `haltsys`, and `fasthalt`. Experiment with your particular Linux version to find out which commands are supported.

The second most commonly used method of shutting down Linux (aside from `Ctrl+Alt+ Delete`) is none other than the `shutdown` command. The syntax usually allows you to specify several parameters, such as the amount of time before Linux shuts down and whether to reboot immediately. Practically every Linux version of `shutdown` requires an argument that indicates the number of seconds to wait before starting the shutdown procedure. For example, the command:

```
shutdown -t45
```

tells Linux to wait 45 seconds before starting the shutdown process. The time argument often requires the `-t` option ahead of it, but some versions assume any number is the number of seconds. If you want to start the shutdown process immediately, you can set the number of seconds to zero or on some systems type the word **now**:

```
shutdown now
```

An -r option tells Linux to reboot after shutting down. This can be handy when you want to load new configuration information such as device drivers. There are several other options supported by shutdown. Usually, you can find them by simply typing **shut-down** with no arguments and checking the error message that appears. Alternatively, the main page will have a list of supported options, too.

The fasthalt and haltsys commands are left over from other versions of UNIX but have been implemented in some Linux releases. Both commands do as their names imply and quickly shut the system down.

What's This About "Logging In"?

After you boot the system, Linux waits for a login. A login is simply the name that you supply to Linux to identify yourself to the operating system. Linux keeps track of which names are permitted to log in to the system and allows only valid users to have access. All others are refused access.

Every login name on the system is unique and typically, a password is assigned to each one. This secret password is like the identification number you use with your bank card to prove that you are who you say you are. Also, the things you can do with your login—the login's privileges—are controlled by Linux; different logins have different levels of privileges. Some logins can do anything they want to the system, while others may not be able to do very much. The system administrator (or whoever creates the login) assigns these privileges.

WARNING

Usually, login names reflect a person's real name. On larger systems, login names are usually composed of the first and last names, such as tparker or rmaclean. Smaller systems tend to be less formal, so you may simply have first names or first name and an initial, such as tim, timp, or tjp. Some administrators base login names on something else entirely, such as wizard or goblin, but these tend to have very little meaning to others outside the single machine.

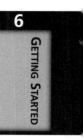

Although you can't have two identically named logins on your system, you can easily create logins for users with the same (real) name by changing one or two characters. So the login names `suej` and `suek`, for example, are treated by Linux as completely separate logins.

Conversely, there is no reason that one person (for instance, you) can't have two, three, or a dozen login names. In fact, because you will be the system administrator of your Linux system, you will have one or more administrative logins and one or more regular user logins.

At the login prompt, type your name, your dog's name, or any other random name that occurs to you. None of these are valid logins (at least not yet). The system asks you for a password; it doesn't matter what you type, so simply press Enter or type a random string of characters. Because the logins are not valid on the system, Linux won't let you in. It displays the message `Login incorrect` to tell you that either the name or the password you entered is not valid.

Most likely, the only valid login on your Linux system after installation is the most powerful and dangerous login Linux offers: `root`. In the section "Creating a New Login" that appears later in this chapter, we will create a safe login for you to use. This safe login can have your name, your dog's name, or whatever you choose. Some versions of Linux prompt you to create a user login during the installation procedure, so you have two logins (`root` and a username) that you can use.

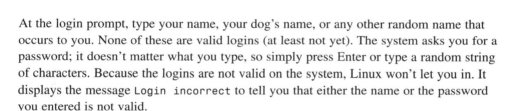

WARNING

Why does Linux bother asking for a password even when the login name is not valid? It's because Linux uses a program called `login` that's instructed to get your login and password first, then check the list of valid users. The login program then displays a message that shows if you are denied access or it lets you through to the next program that starts your user session.

Why You Should Not Use the `root` Login

You will have to use the `root` login from time to time. Some things simply cannot be done on the Linux system without logging in as `root`. You should not, however, use the `root` login as your regular user login. This is especially true if you are exploring the system, poking around and trying out new commands that may not do what you thought they would. You could cause damage to your operating system installation and have to reinstall from scratch.

Linux, as you already know, is a multiuser, multitasking operating system. Multiuser means that several people can be using Linux at the same time (of course, you have to add some additional terminals to your system, or it will get very crowded around the keyboard). Multitasking means that Linux can do more than one thing at a time. For example, you can spell-check a document while downloading information from a remote system. (Multiuser implies multitasking, because all users must be able to do their own work at the same time.) Linux, therefore, is very good at juggling all of these tasks, keeping them from interfering with one another and providing safeguards so that you cannot damage the system or another user's work.

> **WARNING**
>
> The root login does not restrict you in any way. This means that with one simple command, issued either on purpose or by accident, you can destroy your entire Linux installation. For this reason, use the root login only when necessary. Avoid experimenting with commands whenever you log in as root.

When you log in as root, you *become* the system. The root login is also sometimes called the *superuser* login and with good reason. To use an analogy, instead of being simply a passenger on an airplane, you suddenly have all the power and responsibility of the flight crew, the mechanics, and the cabin crew. "Hmm, what does this do?" becomes an extremely dangerous phrase when logged in as root.

One of the oldest stories in UNIX lore tells of new users who log in as root and, in ten keystrokes, destroy their system completely and irrevocably. But if you're careful to follow the steps given here, and stop and take a moment to think about the commands you are giving, none of the "How many new users does it take to nuke a system?" jokes will apply to you!

> **NOTE**
>
> System administrator is another term you will see often. A system administrator is the actual person who sets up and maintains the Linux system. The amount of work involved in system administration varies from system to system. A full-time system administrator may be required in an office that has several powerful

machines with many users, peripheral units such as printers and tape drives, and are connected to a network. Your Linux system will most likely not require that level of dedication!

System administration, because it deals with sensitive matters such as creating or deleting logins, requires superuser privileges. These privileges are provided by the root login. So, the system administrator is an actual person wielding superuser powers gained by logging in as root.

Your First Login

In spite of all the warnings about using the root login, let's log in as root. Because root is the only authorized login on a newly installed Linux system with permission to create other accounts, this is unavoidable. Also, we will be performing a couple of important procedures that require root privileges. However, after this first login, we will create a user ID that can prevent accidental damage to the operating system.

At the login prompt

```
darkstar login:
```

type

```
root
```

and press the Enter key. When you installed Linux, you may have been asked for a password for the root login or the subject simply may not have come up. If the latter is the case, the root login has no password, so you are not prompted for one. If you did assign a password during installation, type the password at the prompt and press Enter. Don't forget your root password—if you do, you must reinstall the entire system.

TIP

Linux is *case-sensitive* (as are all UNIX versions). A capital R is, to Linux, a completely different letter from a lowercase r. When you type Linux commands, you must use the proper case or Linux will not understand them. The majority of Linux commands are typed in lowercase. This includes the login root; if you type Root or rOoT, Linux will reject the login. The passwords pepper, Pepper, and PEPPER are all different to Linux, too.

continues

There is one curious exception, though. If you type the login IN ALL CAPITALS, the system will accept it—but from then on, everything on your screen will be in capital letters! This is caused by an operating system code left over from the early days when some terminals had only uppercase letters. Although these terminals are no longer in use, the login program retains this historical curiosity. We advise you not to use capital letters, though, because the system looks very strange when you use it in this mode.

If you mistype your login or your password, Linux will deny you access. Try again. Because you are on the main console, you can try as many times as you want (or until your fingers get sore). Some systems can lock out a terminal after a number of failed login attempts, but the main system console is almost always left for unlimited attempts.

After you have logged in as root, the system starts up a user session for you. At this point, you should see something similar to the following on your screen:

```
darkstar login: root
Last login: Sun Dec 11 17:26:18 on tty1
Linux 1.2.13 (POSIX).
You have mail.

If it's Tuesday, this must be someone else's fortune.
darkstar:~#
```

Some systems won't tell you anything at all when you successfully log in, and all you see is a line with the pound character. In the case of the preceding system, Linux tells you when the login for this user was last used (this information may not appear the very first time you log in), and then provides some version information. Linux also tells you that this login has a mail message waiting to be read. Finally, if games were installed on your system, Linux may give you a witty saying or aphorism (generated by a program called fortune). You may see some combination of the preceding or something entirely different. Linux vendors have customized their systems so much that it's hard to predict what you'll see when you log in.

If your system does show it, it is always good practice to scan the line that starts with Last login and check that the time given is correct. This is especially important if your Linux system is accessed by other users or is connected to other systems through modems or a network. If the time given does not look right, it could be that someone is

using your login to break into your system or using your username without your permission. To prevent this, change the password. (We'll show you how to change your password soon.)

Let's read the mail message that's waiting for us later, after taking care of some important steps. (If you're curious, on most systems the mail message is sent by the installation procedure when the operating system is installed and concerns registration matters for Linux.)

Your "fortune" is chosen randomly from a long list, so don't expect to see the one shown in the previous example. If you didn't install the games package during the Linux installation routine, you won't see a fortune. You can install the games package at any time if you really want this feature.

The final line you see on the screen (with the pound sign at the end) is the system prompt. This prompt tells you that Linux is waiting for you to type in your commands—it's prompting you for input. The system prompt

```
darkstar:~#
```

also displays some additional useful information which helps you figure out where you are

- `darkstar` is the system name.
- The ~ character indicates your location in the file system (explained in Chapter 8, "Using the File System").
- The # character usually indicates that you're logged in as `root` (although the $ sign is used in some operating systems and makes it difficult to quickly ascertain whether you are logged in as `root` or a regular user). According to UNIX conventions, regular user prompts are either % or $, depending on the shell, while # is reserved for `root`. These symbols are called shell prompts because they are used by the shell to prompt you for commands.

Passwords

In Linux (and just about all other UNIX systems), the superuser login name is `root`. No matter how humble or huge the system, if you can log in as `root`, the system is wide open for you to do whatever you want. Obviously, letting just anyone log in as `root` is unacceptable because it exposes the system to potentially serious damage.

To prevent unauthorized access, the `root` login should always have a password, and that password should be *secure*. You may have noticed that Linux may not have asked for a `root` password on your system. That is because, on installation, the `root` password is set to the *null string*, which is a word with no characters. With `root` and any other login, Linux does not usually bother asking for the password if it's the null string. On the other hand, if you were asked to set a `root` password during installation, you will have to enter it at the password prompt.

The null string is the least secure password there is because anyone who knows a valid username (such as `root`) can access the system. It is up to you to change the password. Linux lets you choose what the new password will be and accepts it without complaint. Unfortunately, this can lead to a false sense of security.

It is common knowledge that in the past users often chose passwords that they could easily remember: their dog's name, their birthday, their hometown, their spouse's name, and so on. The problem is that these passwords were also easy to break, either through guessing or by more sophisticated means. This led some system administrators to insist on difficult-to-break, randomly picked passwords (such as `S8t6WLk`). People could not remember these passwords at all, so they wrote them down and placed them on their desks. Others who were trying to break into the system would find the passwords and gain use of that login.

For this reason, system administrators recommend you choose a password that is not a personal identifier and is not a single word that can be looked up in the dictionary. This is because some password-cracking routines simply scan through a large dictionary, checking each word. Try mixing letters and numbers together. For example, instead of choosing the password `pepper`, try `pep4per`. It's very difficult for a password-cracking routine to get all the possible combinations of every word mixed with a number in a dictionary.

The best passwords are ones with combinations of upper- and lowercase letters and numbers that are still easy to remember. `Fri13th`, `22Skidoo`, and `2Qt4U` are just a few examples. These hard-to-guess passwords are known as *strong* passwords, while easy-to-guess ones are called *weak*.

For the best security, passwords should be changed every so often. Many system administrators recommend once every two or three months as reasonable. This guards against dictionary-based guessing attacks and also minimizes damage when the password has been broken but nothing has been done with it yet.

NOTE

Don't leave your terminal unattended while you're logged in. The idly malicious may take the opportunity to make some changes to your files or send a nasty mail message to people you'd hate to alienate. Always log out or lock your terminal when you leave. Of course, if your system is in the basement or spare bedroom and there's no one else in the house, and you're not networked or connected to a modem that's online, then you don't have to worry too much about break-ins or malicious damage. Still, logging off when you leave your desk is a good habit to cultivate and prepares you for when you go live to the rest of the world through the World Wide Web and the Internet.

Of course, the amount of system security you require depends on how much access there is to your system and the sensitivity of the information found on it. The root password should always be a good, secure one. If nothing else, it will discourage you from casually logging on as root, especially if you leave your user logins with null passwords.

If you are using Linux at home for experimenting, much of the security worries mentioned previously may seem silly. However, it doesn't ever hurt to use good security, and the practice can be carried over to larger UNIX systems at work.

We change or assign a password for the root login (or any other login, for that matter) using the Linux command passwd. The spelling of the command has its history in the development of UNIX when long commands, such as password, were avoided due to the number of characters that had to be typed. Only someone logged in as root can change the root login (no other login has such privileges), but the root login can change any other login password. A user can almost always change their own login password, unless the system administrator has prevented that action.

To change the root password at the system prompt, login in as root (if you haven't already) and type the command passwd. You will see the following messages:

```
darkstar:~# passwd
Changing password for root
Enter new password:
```

At the prompt, type your new, secure password. What you type is not displayed on the screen. This keeps anyone looking over your shoulder (called "shoulder surfing") from reading the password you've just entered.

> **WARNING**
>
> Make sure you type the password slowly and carefully. If any other user's password is lost or forgotten, it can be reset by the root login. But, if the root password is lost or forgotten, you must reinstall Linux.

Because it's so important that passwords are entered correctly, the system double-checks the spelling of the password for you by asking you to type it again:

```
Retype new password:
```

Again, what you type is not displayed on the screen. If your two password entries match, you see the following:

```
Password changed.
darkstar:~#
```

The password is now changed in the system's configuration files. The change is effective immediately, and your old password is discarded.

If the two password entries you typed do not match completely (remember, case is important), Linux gives you a message similar to this one:

```
You misspelled it. Password not changed.
```

and changes are not made to the password. You need to start over with the passwd command from the beginning.

> **TIP**
>
> If you want to leave a program right away and return to the shell prompt, try Ctrl+C (hold the Ctrl key and press C; this is sometimes written as ^C). This usually terminates whatever program you're in (usually without ill effects) and redisplays the shell prompt. For example, if you're starting to change your password and haven't thought of a good one, pressing Ctrl+C when Linux is asking for your new password terminates the routine and your old password is kept.

Creating a New Login

Now that you have assigned a password for the root account, the next step is to create a login with which you can safely explore the Linux system and try out some of the basic commands covered in the following chapters. Some Linux systems ask you to create a

user account when you are installing the system, but most don't. Even if you did create a user login during installation, you'll probably want to add more for friends, family, or for you to use for other purposes.

Linux has a utility called `adduser` which simplifies and automates the task of adding a new user to the system. (This isn't how they did it in the good old days. You should be glad—in the past, files had to be manually edited to add users and all their associated information, a tedious and error-prone process.)

To create a user, at the shell prompt type the command `adduser`:

```
darkstar:~# adduser
Adding a new user. The username should be not exceed 8 characters
in length, or you many run into problems later.

Enter login name for new account (^C to quit):
```

The prompts on your system may be slightly different, but they all approach the task of adding a user login the same way. Some Linux versions have full-screen utilities for the same task or make a utility available under a graphical windowing system that is a lot more attractive, but the bottom line is that the same information is required and must be entered by you.

Login names are used by all valid system users. You can create a login for yourself that you will use permanently, or you can create a temporary login for exploring the system and remove it later. Unlike some multiuser systems such as Windows NT, you can create and delete logins as often as you want, even reusing the same login name over and over again.

The key to every account is the login name. Login names can be made of any character or number string you want, although in general you should limit the length of the name to eight characters (which allows portability over networks and the Internet). Typically, login names bear a resemblance to the user's real name, so that Joe Smith's login name may be `joe`, `jsmith`, or `joes`. It's a good idea to keep a consistent naming principle, especially if you are going to have several users on your system (you'll be surprised how many friends want accounts on your Linux system!).

With some versions of Linux, you have to specify the login name that you're trying to create on the same line as `adduser`:

```
adduser joes
```

If your system requires this, you'll see an error message when you try to use the `adduser` command by itself.

At the `adduser` prompt, enter the login name that you want to create. It is advisable to use all lowercase letters to avoid confusion. Do not exceed the eight-character limit at this point. (Although a mixed case login can be useful for confusing people trying to hack into your system, it causes problems when your system tries to talk to others over a network.)

For our sample user account in this chapter, let's create the user `fido`. (After all, as the joke goes, "On the Internet, no one knows if you're a dog!") Of course, you can substitute your choice on the screen in place of `fido` (unless you really like our login name).

```
Enter login name for new account (^C to quit): fido
Editing information for new user [fido]
Full Name:
```

After entering the login name, a status message from the `adduser` utility usually appears, followed by a set of questions about the new user and the type of environment to present the account with when the user logs in. (The exact order of questions may be different, but usually most of the same information is requested.)

In the example previously shown, the `adduser` routine is waiting for the user's real name. At this prompt, type the full name of the user. Uppercase, lowercase, mixed case, and spaces are fine. This information is not mandatory but is used by the system for some other tasks. Other users can also identify you with this name when you are on a network.

```
Full Name: Fido Dog
GID [100]:
```

The system is waiting for you to provide a GID or *Group ID*, which is discussed in more detail in Chapter 35, "Users and Logins." The last part of the prompt, [100], means that it's suggesting a GID of 100. This is the default choice and is good for most systems unless you are part of a larger network which has a naming policy in effect. For most users, the default is a great way to start and you can always change it later if you need to.

> **TIP**
>
> In this `adduser` utility and many other Linux programs, default choices are presented in square brackets. Simply press the Enter key to accept the default, or type the new value if you don't want to accept the default value.
>
> Sometimes (as you will see later in the `adduser` utility) you are given two choices—usually y for yes and n for no—separated by a / or ¦ character. The uppercase letter is the default choice which you can select by pressing Enter. The other choice must be typed explicitly. In the following examples, yes is always the default choice: [Y/n], [Y¦n], [Yn].

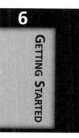

After the Group ID has been given, the `adduser` program wants even more information:

```
GID [100]:
Checking for an available UID after 100
First unused uid is 101
UID [101]:
```

The `adduser` utility does not echo your Group ID choice to the screen if you simply press Enter. This can be a little disconcerting if you're not used to it, especially if you look back and try to figure out what you've done. If you don't see anything, the default value is used. Most Linux commands don't echo what you have done, so this is a good time to get used to it.

The `adduser` utility now asks for a User ID or UID. In this case, Linux suggests a default value of 101. Again, the default is fine in this case, so simply press Enter. You can pick any number that isn't already in use, but there's not much point in changing either the GID or UID unless you have specific organizational reasons to do so.

> **NOTE**
>
> The User ID is used by Linux whenever it is referring to something you have done. The operating system is designed to use a number rather than the full login name because it takes up less room and is easier to manipulate. The User ID is important and each login on the system has its own unique number. By convention, UIDs of less than 100 (500 on some versions) are special system UIDs; root's UID is 0. Regular users get UIDs starting at 100 (or 500).

> **NOTE**
>
> A few versions of Linux, such as Caldera's OpenLinux, don't bother asking you any questions at all when you use the `adduser` command. The `adduser` routine just finds the next GID and UID and assumes default values for all the rest of the information, too. While this is fast and easy, it does make configuring a login with nonstandard characteristics a bit more difficult.

The `adduser` utility then shows two more prompts asking for the user's home directory and the shell:

```
Home Directory [/home/fido]:
Shell [/bin/bash]:
```

Choose the default values for Home Directory and Shell. You'll see more about directories in Chapter 9, "File and Directory Permissions," and look at different shells in Chapter 11, "bash," Chapter 12, "pdksh," and Chapter 13, "tcsh." The default values are suitable for most user IDs.

As a last step, the adduser program asks for a password for the new user. At the prompt, enter a suitable password. If you press Enter without typing anything else, the password is set to the same string as the login or a null password, depending on the version of Linux. These two approaches are not recommended, however, because they are easy to guess. Even a simple password is better than none.

```
Password [fido]:

Information for new user [fido]:
Home directory: [/home/fido] Shell: [/bin/bash]
uid: [501] gid: [100]

Is this correct? [y/N]:
```

The adduser program now verifies that you are happy with all the information you have entered. If you are, type y for yes, and press Enter. The default value (shown by the capital letter) is N for no. If you choose the default, you are telling the script that the information displayed is not correct, and you have to start the whole process over again.

When you answer y to the question Is this correct?, the adduser program creates the new user's directory and adds the user information to the system configuration files. You may see the following information appear on the screen as the adduser utility does its work. When the utility has finished, you see the Linux shell prompt again:

```
Adding login [fido] and making directory [/home/fido]

Adding the files from the /etc/skel directory:
./.kermrc -> /home/fido/./.kermrc
./.less -> /home/fido/./.less
./.lessrc -> /home/fido/./.lessrc
./.term -> /home/fido/./.term
./.term/termrc -> /home/fido/./.term/termrc
darkstar:~#
```

We will look at how to remove unwanted users from your /etc/passwd file in Chapter 35, "Users and Logins."

Logging Out

Now that you have created a new user, you can use it in the next couple of chapters to explore Linux. To finish with your session as `root`, log out of the system by typing **logout**:

```
darkstar:~# logout

Welcome to Linux 1.2.13
darkstar login:
```

You see the login prompt display again. At this point, you can log back in as `root` or as the new user you have just created.

Some systems allow you to log out with the `Ctrl+D` sequence. If the shell you are using supports `Ctrl+D` as a logout command, the login prompt reappears. Otherwise, you may see a message such as this:

```
Use "logout" to leave the shell.
```

If you have used other UNIX systems before, you may be used to using `Ctrl+D` to log out. The default shell used by Linux does not support `Ctrl+D` unless the key mappings are changed to allow it. Some versions of Linux also allow the logoff command to be used with most shells.

Trying Out Your New Login

Now you can try out your new login. We can also look at some of the interesting features and capabilities of Linux.

At the login prompt, type the login name you have just created. If you were conscientious and assigned a nonzero-length password to your new login, enter the password when prompted.

You should now see the following (or something similar to it):

```
darkstar login: fido
Password:
Last login: Sun Dec 11 19:14:22 on tty1
Linux 1.2.13 (POSIX).

Quiet!  I hear a hacker....
darkstar:~$
```

The messages for the most part are the same as when you logged in as root. Some systems don't show you anything except the shell prompt, but you can change that. Note that your prompt looks different from the root prompt or the pound sign. The $ prompt indicates that you are a regular user running under the bash shell (which was the default choice presented by the adduser program). Also, there is no You have mail message (because you have no mail).

> **NOTE**
>
> Linux can be configured to automatically mail a message to all new users. This can be a greeting or can give system information and etiquette.

To see an example of the difference between the root login and a regular user login, type **adduser** at the shell prompt and press Enter.

```
darkstar:~$ adduser
bash: adduser: command not found
```

The message you get looks somewhat cryptic. However, it has a typical Linux error message structure, so it's worth making a little effort now to understand it.

Linux Error Messages

First of all, in the error message shown previously there's quite a bit of information. The program that is giving you the message is your shell, bash. It therefore announces itself with bash:, somewhat like the character in a play script. Next is the shell's "monologue." Being the "strong and silent" type of character, bash's monologue is very terse and to the point. It declares the program that is causing problems (adduser) and the specific problem with this program: the command (adduser) can't be found.

If the error message were expanded into real English, it would read something like this: "Hi, I'm bash. You know that adduser command you gave me? I looked everywhere for adduser but I couldn't find it, so I couldn't perform whatever actions adduser would have specified." With time, you will get quite good at understanding Linux error message grammar.

Search Paths

Why can root find adduser, but an ordinary user cannot? Linux has many directories, and each directory can hold many files (one of which can be the elusive adduser). In theory, Linux could go search through the entire file system until it found adduser. But if root accidentally mistyped adduser as aduser, Linux would have to rummage through every nook and cranny before finally giving up. This could take many seconds and cause needless wear and tear on your hard drive (not to mention drive you nuts while every file was searched every time you typed anything).

Therefore, Linux has *search paths* for finding commands (which we discuss in more detail in Chapter 8). Usually, only a small part of the entire Linux file system is on the search path along which Linux searches. Because root makes use of many system administration programs such as adduser, the directories that hold these programs are in root's search path. Ordinary users do not have system administration directories in their search path.

> **TIP**
>
> Linux search paths are very similar to those you may be aware of for DOS or Windows. The syntax for the paths and the way the directories are written are different but the approach is the same.

There is a way around this problem of not finding a file which is not in your search path, though. If you explicitly tell Linux where a file is located, then it doesn't have to look through its search path. As it happens, adduser is found on most Linux systems in the /sbin directory. Try running /sbin/adduser.

```
darkstar:~$ /sbin/adduser
bash: /sbin/adduser: Permission denied
```

This time, bash could find adduser (because you told it exactly where to look) but discovered that an ordinary user does not have permission to run adduser. As you can see, Linux limits the actions of logins to their privilege level and only root (at least at this point) can run adduser. (We'll talk about privileges in Chapter 9.)

The who Command

A very simple Linux command, which is also one of the most commonly used when you learn more about working with the shell and shell programming, is the who command. This simple command does one task: It shows you who is logged in at the moment. The who command is unusual in Linux because it takes no arguments. You use it by itself on the command line. Here's a sample command and its output:

```
$ who
tparker     tty02        May 18 18:29
root        tty01        May 15 15:18
```

```
root        tty03        May 15 15:17
bills       ttyp0        May 18 18:29
ychow       ttyp1        May 25 17:31
```

The who command shows you three columns of information for each user that is on the system. First it shows the login that the user is employing. The second column shows the terminal the user is using (this is a device name, something we'll look at in more detail in Chapter 33, "Devices"). The third column shows the time that the user logged in.

If a user is logged in on more than one terminal or virtual terminal (we'll discuss virtual terminals in the next section), then each login is displayed. In the preceding output, you can see root is logged in twice on two different terminals.

The output of who is generated every time you run the command, so if a user logs off, the output from who is accurate from the moment you issue the command.

Virtual Terminals

Linux, as mentioned earlier, is a multiuser, multitasking system. This means that more than one login can access the system at the same time and that each login can be doing one or more different things all at the same time. A serious multiuser system has several terminals (consisting of a keyboard and a display screen) wired or networked to the main computer unit.

Although you probably don't have any terminals attached to your system, you can still log in several times under the same or different login names using your single keyboard and screen. This magic is performed by using *virtual terminals* which allow your single screen and keyboard to act like a dozen different terminals, each identified by one of the function keys located at the top of your keyboard.

As an example, press Alt+F2. When you do, everything on your screen should disappear, to be replaced by the following:

```
Welcome to Linux 1.2.13
darkstar login:
```

Log in with your "regular" login (not root). When the shell prompt is displayed, type who at the prompt and press Enter. You should see something similar to the following:

```
darkstar:~$ who
fido        tty2         Dec 14 01:42
fido        tty1         Dec 14 01:40
```

When you run the Linux command who, your screen displays the names of all logins currently logged into the system, where they are logged in from, and when they logged in. (Your login name appears, of course, instead of fido in the preceding example.)

By convention, tty1 is the main console screen. It is the "normal" screen that appears after Linux has started up (unless you start up with a windowing interface), so you don't have to do anything special to get it. If you have switched to any other virtual consoles, you can return to tty1 by pressing Alt+F1.

So you want to know how many virtual screens are active on your system? Try going through all the Alt+F*n* keys. Alternatively, on some systems you can scroll through the virtual screens by using the Alt+right arrow combination to move up through the screens or Alt+left arrow to move down. Most Linux systems start with either six, ten, or twelve virtual consoles defined. You can change this number, but you'll probably never use more than three or four, so the default is fine.

Why bother with virtual consoles? Quite often you find yourself doing something—perhaps in a long and complicated program—and realize that you should have done something else first. Simply flip to another virtual terminal and do whatever it is. It's as if you have two terminals running at the same time.

Another handy use of virtual terminals is when, through experimentation or otherwise, your screen locks up or starts displaying strange symbols when you hit a key. From a different virtual terminal, you can try to troubleshoot the problem or restart the system, if necessary.

Linux also comes with a very powerful multitasking windowing environment called X. Installing and running X window systems is described later in this book (see Chapter 22, "Installing and Configuring XFree86").

Commands and Programs

"Run the who command" and "Run who" are much more common ways of saying "Type **who** at the prompt and press Enter." We use the shorter expressions wherever their meaning is clear. Sometimes people familiar with Linux drop the word "run" so that one user might tell another, "I tried who but didn't see anything unusual." It's understood by the context that when they "tried who," they actually "ran" it.

Something else you may notice if you are reading carefully is that there seems to be both Linux *programs* and Linux *commands*. A command is that which you type at the shell prompt. For this reason, the combination of the shell prompt and what you type after it is often called a *command line*. When you press the Enter key, Linux takes the command you've entered and tries to perform it. The Linux system has built-in responses to some commands; for other commands, it finds the appropriately named program on your hard disk and executes that program.

In the strictest sense, then, the command is what you type, and the program is what performs your command. However, very simple programs with straightforward results, such as who, are often referred to as commands, although there is actually a who program on your hard disk. More complicated programs, usually interactive ones such as adduser or open-ended ones such as a text editor, are called programs in the more traditional sense. So you might hear one experienced user tell another, "The adduser program worked fine. I tried the who command 15 minutes later and the new user had logged in already."

Summary

In this chapter, we assigned a password to the root login and created a new user ID to be used in the next few chapters. We learned some useful Linux terminology tips that will serve us well in the future. At this point, you can either ensure that you have logged out of all virtual terminals or simply move on to the next chapters.

There are a number of chapters that explain in detail what we've just covered, and you may want to read them right now for more information:

To learn more about Linux commands you'll use on a regular basis, see Chapter 7, "Basic Linux Commands."

To learn more about the Bourne Again Shell that you use by default, see Chapter 11.

And to learn more about file permissions and the way they affect which files you can read, see Chapter 9.

Basic Linux Commands

by Ed Treijs and Tim Parker

How Linux Commands Work

Most Linux commands are very flexible. When you enter a Linux command, there are several ways to tailor the basic command to your specific needs. We will look at the two main ways used to modify the effect of a command:

- Specifying or redirecting a command's input and output
- Using command options

A simple way to picture what a Linux command does is to imagine that it's a black box that is part of an assembly line. Items come down a conveyor belt, enter the black box, get processed in some way, come out of the black box, and are taken away on another conveyor belt. Command options let you fine-tune the basic process happening inside the black box. Command redirection lets you specify which conveyor belt will supply the black box with items and which conveyor belt will take away the resulting products. This analogy seems simple, but is a surprisingly effective way of understanding some complex concepts of UNIX and Linux.

Once you understand how redirection and command options work, you will be able to (at least in principle) use any Linux or UNIX command. This is because UNIX is based on a few simple design principles. The most important of these principles for our purposes is that commands are simple and single-purpose, as well as flexible about where they get information from and where to put it when they've finished. All Linux commands, therefore, should work in consistent ways. Of course, UNIX has evolved over the 35 years or so it has been around, and design principles can sometimes get buried under all the changes. But they still make up the foundation, so that UNIX-based systems such as Linux are surprisingly coherent and consistent in how they work.

TIP

Pressing Ctrl+U at any point, right up to before you press Enter, lets you clear everything you've typed on the command line. You can use this whenever you spot an error at the very beginning of your typing or when you decide you don't want to run a particular command after all. You can also use the Backspace key to "back up" by erasing characters (in fact, it can be almost a reflex action), but it's usually faster to just erase the whole command line and start again. Alternatively, you can use the Ctrl+C sequence to cancel whatever you are typing and display a new shell prompt.

Perhaps the most powerful keys to use at the command prompt are the arrow keys in those versions of the shell that support them. The left and right arrows move the cursor non-destructively. If you make a typo early in the line, you can left-arrow your way to the character and type in a correction. Additionally, the up and down arrows enable you to jump through a list of the last several commands used (similar to DOS's **DOSKEY** utility).

Command Options

You can use command options to fine-tune the actions of a Linux command. Quite often, a Linux command does almost—but not quite—what you want it to do. Instead of making you learn a second command, Linux lets you modify the basic, or default, actions of the command by using options. A simple example is when you want to sort a list of names into order. Linux has a sort command that can do that for you, but maybe you want to reverse the order of sorting so Z comes before A. Instead of having a backward sort command, a single letter option reverses the sort order. Some commands have many options, some have a few.

The **ls** command is an excellent, and useful, example of a command that has a great many options. The **ls** command lists the files found on the Linux system's hard drive. This sounds simple enough, doesn't it? Try entering the following command:

```
darkstar:~$ ls
darkstar:~$
```

Well, nothing much seems to happen in this case, and most systems respond like this if you're using a brand-new user login.

Now try typing **ls -a**. Type it exactly as shown. The space between **ls** and **-a** is necessary, and there must be no space between the **-** and the **a**.

```
darkstar:~$ ls -a
./              .bash_history  .kermrc        .lessrc
```

Here you have modified what **ls** does by adding a command option—in this case, **-a**. By default, **ls** lists only files whose names don't begin with a period. However, **-a** tells **ls** to list all files, even ones that begin with a period. (These are usually special files created for you by Linux. Because Linux can't hide files the way some operating systems can, it treats any file starting with a period as a special configuration file that doesn't appear with the usual list commands.) At present, all the files in your directory start with a period, so **ls** by itself does not list any files; you must add **-a** to see all of the files you have at present.

The `ls` command has many more options. You can use more than one option at a time. For example, try typing `ls -al`:

```
darkstar:~$ ls -al
total 10
drwxr-xr-x   3 fido      users         1024 Dec 21 22:11 ./
drwxr-xr-x   6 root      root          1024 Dec 14 01:39 ../
-rw-r--r--   1 fido      users          333 Dec 21 22:11 .bash_history
-rw-r--r--   1 fido      users          163 Dec  7 14:31 .kermrc
-rw-r--r--   1 fido      users           34 Jun  6  1993 .less
-rw-r--r--   1 fido      users          114 Nov 23  1993 .lessrc
drwxr-xr-x   2 fido      users         1024 Dec  7 13:36 .term/
```

You now get a listing with many more details about the files. (These will be explained in Chapter 8, "Using the File System.") The `1` option can be used by itself; `ls -1` gives detailed descriptions of files that don't begin with a period. Sometimes filenames are so long they don't fit on a single line; Linux simply wraps the remainder to the next line.

> **NOTE**
>
> Strictly speaking, the hyphen (-) is not part of the command option. The hyphen simply tells Linux to understand each letter immediately following it as a command option. There *must* be a space before the hyphen, and there *must not* be a space between the hyphen and the letter or letters making up the command option. There *must* be a space after the command option if anything else is to be entered on the command line after it.
>
> You can type more than one command option after the hyphen, as we did with `ls -al`. In this case, we are specifying both the `a` and the `1` options. The order in which you specify options usually doesn't matter; `ls -al` gives the same results as `ls -1a`. Combining options doesn't work with all Linux commands; it works only with those that use a single letter to specify each option.
>
> Multiple options can also be specified individually, with each option preceded by a hyphen and separated from other options by spaces—for example, `ls -a -1`. This is usually done only when a particular option requires a further parameter.

By default, `ls` lists files in alphabetical order. Sometimes you may be more interested in when a file was created or last modified. The `t` option tells `ls` to sort files by date instead of alphabetically by filename, showing the newest files first. Therefore, when you enter `ls -alt`, you see the following:

```
darkstar:~$ ls -alt
total 10
drwxr-xr-x   3 fido      users         1024 Jan  2 13:48 ./
-rw-r--r--   1 fido      users          333 Dec 21 22:11 .bash_history
```

```
drwxr-xr-x   6 root      root        1024 Dec 14 01:39 ../
-rw-r--r--   1 fido      users        163 Dec  7 14:31 .kermrc
drwxr-xr-x   2 fido      users       1024 Dec  7 13:36 .term/
-rw-r--r--   1 fido      users       3016 May 13  1994 .emacs
-rw-r--r--   1 fido      users        114 Nov 23  1993 .lessrc
-rw-r--r--   1 fido      users         34 Jun  6  1993 .less
```

The **r** option tells **ls** to produce a reverse output. This is often used with the **t** option. The following is an example of what displays when you enter **ls -altr**:

```
darkstar:~$ ls -altr
total 10
-rw-r--r--   1 fido      users         34 Jun  6  1993 .less
-rw-r--r--   1 fido      users        114 Nov 23  1993 .lessrc
-rw-r--r--   1 fido      users       3016 May 13  1994 .emacs
drwxr-xr-x   2 fido      users       1024 Dec  7 13:36 .term/
-rw-r--r--   1 fido      users        163 Dec  7 14:31 .kermrc
drwxr-xr-x   6 root      root        1024 Dec 14 01:39 ../
-rw-r--r--   1 fido      users        333 Dec 21 22:11 .bash_history
drwxr-xr-x   3 fido      users       1024 Jan  2 13:48 ./
```

Many other options can be used with **ls**, although you have just worked with the most commonly used ones. The important thing to remember is that you can usually customize a Linux command by using one or more command options.

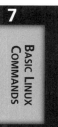

7

BASIC LINUX
COMMANDS

NOTE

With the basic Linux commands, case is important! For instance, **ls** has an **R** option (*recursive:* show files in subdirectories, too) which gives much different results from the **r** option.

TIP

You can think of **a** as the "all files" option, **l** as the "long list" option, **t** as the "sort by time" option, **r** as the "reverse sort" option, and so on. In fact, most options in Linux are *mnemonic*—the option letter stands for a word or phrase. Some option letters mean the same thing in many different Linux commands. For instance, **v** often means *verbose*—in other words, "Give me lots of detail."

However, do not assume that on an unfamiliar command certain options will work in the "usual" way! For instance, **r** is the recursive option for many Linux commands; however, in the case of **ls**, reverse sort is more commonly used, and therefore it gets the easier-to-type lowercase *r*, while recursive is left with the capital *R*. It might seem like not much extra effort to press the Shift key to get the capital letter, but try typing a string of four or five options, one of which is capitalized!

Other Parameters

Linux commands often use parameters that are not actual command options. These parameters, such as filenames or directories, are *not* preceded by a hyphen.

For instance, by default **ls** lists the files in your current directory. You can, however, tell **ls** to list the files in any other directory simply by adding the directory to the command line. For instance, **ls /bin** lists everything in the **/bin** directory. This can be combined with command options, so that **ls -l /bin** gives you detailed listings of the files in **/bin**. Try this. You will be impressed by the number of files in the **/bin** directory!

You can also specify **ls** to list information about any particular file by entering its filename. For instance, **ls -la .lessrc** displays detailed information only about the **.lessrc** file. If the file doesn't exist, Linux doesn't show anything.

Input and Output Redirection

Many Linux commands let you specify which file or directory they are to act upon, as we saw earlier with the example **ls -l /bin**.

You can also "pipe" the output from a command so that it becomes another command's input. This is done by typing two or more commands separated by the ¦ character. (This character normally is found on the same key as the \ character. You must hold the Shift key or you get \ instead of ¦). The ¦ character means "Use the output from the previous command as the input for the next command." Therefore, typing **command_1¦command_2** does both commands, one after the other, before giving you the results.

Using our assembly-line metaphor, items are being processed through two black boxes instead of just one. When we use piping, it's like hooking up the first command's output conveyor belt to become the input conveyor belt for the second command.

> **TIP**
>
> Although Linux doesn't care whether ¦ is set off by spaces, if **command_1 ¦ command_2** is easier for you to read and understand than **command_1¦command_2**, by all means use spaces around ¦.

You may have noticed that the output of **ls -l /bin** is many lines long, so that much of the information scrolls off the screen before you can read it. You can pipe this output to a

formatting program called **more**, which displays information in screen-sized chunks.
When you enter **ls -l /bin ¦ more**, you see the following:

```
darkstar:~$ ls -l /bin ¦ more
total 1611
-rwxr-xr-x   1 root      bin           1248 Sep 17 04:25 arch*
-rwxr-xr-x   1 root      bin         295940 Sep  5 01:45 bash*
-rwxr-xr-x   1 root      bin           4840 Nov 24  1993 cat*
-rwxr-xr-x   1 root      bin           9220 Jul 20 12:06 chgrp*
-rwxr-xr-x   1 root      bin          13316 Jul 20 12:06 chmod*
-rwxr-xr-x   1 root      bin          13316 Jul 20 12:06 chown*
lrwxrwxrwx   1 root      root            17 Dec  7 13:37 compress ->
/usr/bin/comp
ress*
-rwxr-xr-x   1 root      bin          21508 Jul 20 12:06 cp*
-rwxr-xr-x   1 root      bin          41988 May  1  1994 cpio*
lrwxrwxrwx   1 root      root             4 Dec  7 13:40 csh -> tcsh*
-rwxr-xr-x   1 root      bin           5192 Nov 24  1993 cut*
-rwxr-xr-x   1 root      bin          19872 Mar 23  1994 date*
-rwxr-xr-x   1 root      bin          17412 Jul 20 12:06 dd*
-rwxr-xr-x   1 root      bin          13316 Jul 20 12:06 df*
-rwxr-xr-x   1 root      bin          66564 Jun  9  1994 dialog*
-rwxr-xr-x   1 root      bin           1752 Sep 17 04:25 dmesg*
lrwxrwxrwx   1 root      root             8 Dec  7 13:37 dnsdomainname ->
hostname
*
-rwxr-xr-x   1 root      bin          13316 Jul 20 12:06 du*
-rwxr-xr-x   1 root      bin           3312 Mar 23  1994 echo*
-rwxr-xr-x   1 root      bin          36684 May  4  1994 ed*
-rwxr-xr-x   1 root      bin            326 Mar 23  1994 false*
--More--
```

The **--More--** at the bottom of the screen tells you that there's more text to come. To go
to the next screen of text, press the Spacebar. Every time you press the Spacebar, **more**
displays another screen full of text. When the last screen with text has been displayed,
more returns you to the Linux prompt.

> **TIP**
>
> The **more** command can do many other things. For instance, to move back one
> screen at a time, press **b** for "back." (Not all versions of **more** support the **b**
> option.) Another useful command is **q** for "quit." This lets you leave immediate-
> ly, without having to go through all the remaining screens of text. Ctrl+C does
> the same thing.
>
> While in **more**, press **h** for "help." This lists the commands available within **more**.

> **NOTE**
>
> Linux sometimes includes the command **less** instead of **more**. One difference you will notice is that, unlike **more**, **less** requires you to type **q** to return to the command line, even if you're at the end of the text to be displayed. This may seem cumbersome, but it prevents you from accidentally exiting the program by pressing the Spacebar once too often.
>
> The name **less** is a play on **more**. Originally, **less** was designed to have many features that **more** lacked. The version of **more** included in most Linux system has most of these features, however.
>
> The Linux **man** program, discussed later, uses **less** to display text. Most other UNIX systems use **more** by default. Don't get confused. Just remember to press **q** to exit from **less**!

Another thing you can do in Linux is send output to a file instead of the screen. There are many different reasons why you might want to do this. Perhaps you want to save a "snapshot" of a command's output as it was at a certain time or maybe you want to save a command's output for further examination. You might also want to save the output from a command that takes a very long time to run, and so on.

To send output to a file, use the > symbol (found above the period on your keyboard). For instance, you can place the output of the **ls -l /bin** command into a file called **output** by typing **ls -l /bin > output**. Again, spaces around > are optional and not strictly necessary, but they do make the command much more readable.

If you now enter an **ls** or **ls -l command**, you will see that you've created a new file called **output** in your own directory.

To view the contents of a file, you can again use the **more** command. Just specify the name of the file you want to look at. In this case, type **more output**.

> **WARNING**
>
> Be careful! When you use >, you completely overwrite the previous contents of the file from which you specify to take the output (if that file existed). For example, if we already have a file called **output** in our directory, its old contents will be completely replaced by the output from **ls -l /bin**. Linux *will not* warn you that you are about to do this!

> Be particularly careful if you're not in your usual directory or if you're logged in as **root**. You could, for instance, accidentally clobber a Linux program by mistake. It's a good idea to check whether the output file already exists before using >. In our example, we could have typed **ls -l output** beforehand. If no information is displayed, the file does not exist.

You can specify that you want to add your output to the end of the file, rather than replace the file's contents, by using >>. Type **who >> output** to add the output of the **who** command to the end of the text already in the file **output**.

You can examine the results by using either **more** or **less** and paging through to the end of the file or by using the Linux command **tail**, which displays the last few lines of the specified file. In this case, type **tail output** to see the last few lines of the file **output**. Try using **tail**!

7

BASIC LINUX
COMMANDS

Notational Conventions Used to Describe Linux Commands

There is a set of accepted notational conventions used to describe, in a concise and consistent way, the correct syntax for any given Linux command. This specifies what options or parameters you must use, what options or parameters you can or cannot use, and so on. Sometimes this set of conventions is used to give a complete and exhaustive listing of a command's syntax, showing every possible command and parameter. Sometimes it is used to make a particular example more general and the command's basic usage clearer. You'll run into these notations in manuals, man pages, and other sources of information.

If you remember the following five basic rules, you will be able, in principle, to understand the syntax of any Linux or UNIX command.

Six Basic Rules of Linux Notation

1. Any text standing by itself, and not within [], <>, or {}, must be typed exactly as shown.

2. Any text within square brackets ([]) is optional. You can type it or not type it. For instance, the syntax **ls [-l]** means you must type **ls** (per the first rule), while adding **-l** is optional but not necessary. Do not type the square brackets themselves! In our example, type **ls** or **ls -l**. Do not type **ls [-l]** .

3. Angle brackets (<>) and the text within them must be replaced by appropriate text (usually a name or value). The text within the brackets usually indicates the nature of the replacement. For instance, the syntax **more** `<filename>` means that you should replace *<filename>* with the name of the file you want to examine using **more**. If you want to look at the file **output**, type **more output**. Remember, do not use the angle brackets when you actually type the command!

4. Curly braces (**{}**) indicate that you must choose one of the values given within the braces. The values are separated by ¦ (which in this case means *or*, not *pipe!*). For example, the syntax **command** `-{a¦b}` means you must enter either **command -a** or **command -b**.

5. An ellipsis (**...**) means "and so on." They are normally used with parameters such as filenames, which is described later.

6. The sixth basic rule states that the brackets can be combined as necessary. For instance, you don't have to type a filename with the **more** command which would be indicated as **more** `[<filename>]`. The outer set of square brackets makes the entire parameter optional. If you do decide to use the parameter, replace the inner set of angle brackets with the appropriate value. Because the **more** command enables one or more filenames to be specified, the syntax becomes **more** `[<file-name> ...]`. The ellipsis means you can have as many *<filenames>* as you want, such as **more output1 output2 output3**.

Online Help Available in Linux

Linux has help facilities available online. If you forget the exact use of a command, which option means what, or if you're looking for the right command to use, the answer might be available straight from Linux. The two help facilities we will try out are the **bash** shell's **help** command and the **man** command, which is available on almost all UNIX systems, including Linux.

The Linux Man Pages

The "man" in "man pages" stands for "manual." (As usual, the creators of UNIX shortened a long but descriptive word to a shorter, cryptic one!) Typing **man** `<command>` lets you view the manual pages dealing with a particular command.

Try typing **man passwd** to see what the Linux manual has to say about the **passwd** command.

The general layout of a man page is as follows:

```
COMMAND(1)                 Linux Programmer's Manual                COMMAND(1)

NAME
       command - summary of what command does

SYNOPSIS
       <complete syntax of command in the standard Linux form>

DESCRIPTION
       More verbose explanation of what "command" does.

OPTIONS
       Lists each available option with description of what it does

FILES
       lists files used by, or related to, command

SEE ALSO
       command_cousin(1), command_spouse(1), etc.

BUGS
       There are bugs in Linux commands??

AUTHOR
       J. S. Goobly (goobly@hurdly-gurdly.boondocks)

Linux 1.0                      22 June 1994                              1
```

The man page for **passwd** is actually quite understandable. Be warned, however, that man pages are often written in a very formal and stylized way that sometimes bears little resemblance to English. This is done not to baffle people, but to cram a great deal of information into as short a description as possible. For example, try entering **man ls**. Notice how many options are available for **ls** and how long it takes to explain them.

Although it can take practice (and careful reading!) to understand man pages, once you get used to them the first thing you'll do when you encounter an unfamiliar command is call up the man page for that command.

Finding Keywords in Man Pages

Sometimes you know what you want to do, but you don't know which command you should use to do it. Use the keyword option by typing **man -k** *<keyword>***,** and the **man** program returns the name of every command whose **name** entry (which includes a very brief description) contains that keyword.

For instance, you can search on **manual**:

```
darkstar:~$ man -k manual
man (1)                   - Format and display the online manual pages
whereis (1)               - Locate binary, manual, and or source for program
xman (1)                  - Manual page display program for the X Window System
```

You have to be careful to specify your keyword properly, though! Using **directory** as your keyword isn't too bad, for example, but using **file** gives you many more entries than you will want to wade through.

> **NOTE**
>
> You may have noticed that commands seem to be followed by numbers in brackets, usually **(1)**. This refers to the manual section. Back in the days when UNIX manuals came in printed, bound volumes, normal commands were in Section 1, files used by administrators were in Section 5, programming routines were described in Section 3, and so on. Therefore, some man pages are not about commands at all, but rather about files or system calls used in Linux!
>
> If a particular entry shows up in more than one section, **man** will show you the lowest-numbered entry by default. You can see higher-numbered entries by specifying the section number. For instance, Section 5 has a manual entry on the **passwd** file. To see this rather than the manual entry for the **passwd** command, type **man 5 passwd**.
>
> In general, **man** *<n> <entry>* will find the man page for *<entry>* in Section *<n>*.

The bash Shell help Facility

When you type a command at the prompt, the shell program takes what you've written, interprets it as necessary, and passes the result to the Linux operating system. Linux then performs the actions requested of it. Many Linux commands require Linux to find and start up a new program. However, the shell itself can perform a number of functions.

These functions can be simple, often-used commands, so that the overhead of starting up separate programs is eliminated or they can be facilities that make the shell environment friendlier and more useful. One of these facilities is the **help** command, which provides information on the built-in functions of the **bash** shell.

Type **help** at the prompt. You will see at least some of the following:

```
GNU bash, version 1.14.15(1)
Shell commands that are defined internally. Type 'help' to see this list.
Type 'help name' to find out more about the function 'name'.
Use 'info bash' to find out more about the shell in general.

A star (*) next to a name means that the command is disabled.

%[DIGITS ¦ WORD] [&]                . [filename]
:                                   [ arg... ]
alias [ name[=value] ... ]          bg [job_spec]
bind [-lvd] [-m keymap] [-f filena  break [n]
builtin [shell-builtin [arg ...]]   case WORD in [PATTERN [¦ PATTERN].
cd [dir]                            command [-pVv] [command [arg ...]]
continue [n]                        declare [-[frxi]] name[=value] ...
dirs [-l]                           echo [-neE] [arg ...]
enable [-n] [name ...]              eval [arg ...]
exec [ [-] file [redirection ...]]  exit [n]
export [-n] [-f] [name ...] or exp  fc [-e name] [-nlr] [first] [last
fg [job_spec]                       for NAME [in WORDS ... ;] do COMMA
function NAME { COMMANDS ; } or NA   getopts optstring name [arg]
hash [-r] [name ...]                help [pattern ...]
history [n] [ [-awrn] [filename]]   if COMMANDS; then COMMANDS; [elif
jobs [-lnp] [jobspec ...] ¦ jobs -  kill [-s sigspec ¦ -sigspec] [pid
let arg [arg ...]                   local name[=value] ...
logout                              popd [+n ¦ -n]
pushd [dir ¦ +n ¦ -n]               pwd
read [-r] [name ...]                readonly [-n] [-f] [name ...] or r
return [n]                          select NAME [in WORDS ... ;] do CO
set [--abefhknotuvxldHCP] [-o opti  shift [n]
source filename                     suspend [-f]
test [expr]                         times
trap [arg] [signal_spec]            type [-all] [-type ¦ -path] [name
typeset [-[frxi]] name[=value] ...  ulimit [-SHacdmstfpnuv [limit]]
umask [-S] [mode]                   unalias [-a] [name ...]
unset [-f] [-v] [name ...]          until COMMANDS; do COMMANDS; done
variables - Some variable names an  wait [n]
while COMMANDS; do COMMANDS; done   { COMMANDS }
```

You will have to pipe the output of **help** to **more** (**help ¦ more**) to keep the first part from scrolling off your screen.

Wildcards: * and ?

In many a late-night card game, jokers are shuffled into the deck. The jokers are *wild-cards* that can become any card of your choice. This is obviously very useful! Linux also has wildcards. They are more useful than jokers in a card game.

Linux has several wildcards. Wildcards are used as a convenient and powerful shortcut when specifying files (or directories) that a command is to operate on. We will briefly look at the two most popular wildcards: * and ?. (There are quite a few more wildcards supported by Linux, but they are seldom used and would only complicate the issue at this point.)

The most commonly used wildcard is *, which stands in for any combination of one or more characters. For example, `c*` matches all filenames that begin with c. You can see this for yourself by typing `ls /bin/c*`. What happens if you type `ls /bin/c*t` at the command line? How about `ls /bin/*t` at the command line?

The ? wildcard is more restrictive than *. It stands in only for any *one* character. You can see this by comparing `ls/bin/d*` with `ls/bin/d?`.

> **NOTE**
>
> Wildcards can only be used to match filenames and directory names. You can't, for example, type **pass*** at the Linux prompt and expect Linux to run the **pass-wd** program for you.

> **WARNING**
>
> Be very careful when using wildcards with dangerous commands, such as the ones used to permanently delete files! A good check is to run `ls` with the wildcards you plan to use and examine the resulting list of files to see whether the wildcard combination did what you expected it to do. Also double-check that you typed everything correctly *before* pressing the Enter key!

Environment Variables

When you log in, Linux keeps a number of useful data items in the background ready for the system to use. The actual data is held in something called an *environment variable*, whose name is often descriptive or mnemonic. In fact, this is no different from the way you and I remember things. We know that there is always a piece of information called "day of the week" (the environment variable); however, we change the data in this variable, from Monday to Tuesday to Wednesday, and so on, as days go by.

To see the list of *exported* environment variables, type **env**. A typical output is from the **env** command looks like this:

```
$ env
FMHOME=/frame
HOME=/usr/tparker
HUSHLOGIN=FALSE
HZ=100
LOGNAME=tparker
MAIL=/usr/spool/mail/tparker
PATH=:/frame/bin:/bin:/usr/bin:/usr/tparker/bin:.
SHELL=/bin/sh
TERM=ansi
TZ=EST5EDT
```

7

BASIC LINUX COMMANDS

The environment variable's name is on the left and the value held by the variable is on the right. The word "exported" is used here to mean something special; when an environment variable is exported, it is available to every program and utility on the system that you start. It stays available until you log off. You can define variables that are effective only for a single program or that don't have the same effect as exported variables.

The most important variable to note is the **PATH**, the value of which is your *search path*. As we will see in the next chapter, when you type a command, Linux searches every place listed in your search path for that command.

A longer list of environment variables, consisting of several new variables in addition to the ones shown earlier, is displayed by the command **set**. Here's the output from the set command on the same system as the preceding one:

```
$ set
FMHOME=/frame
HOME=/usr/tparker
HUSHLOGIN=FALSE
HZ=100
IFS=

LOGNAME=tparker
MAIL=/usr/spool/mail/tparker
MAILCHECK=600
OPTIND=1
PATH=:/frame/bin:/bin:/usr/bin:/usr/tparker/bin:.
PS1=$
PS2=>
SHELL=/bin/sh
TERM=ansi
TZ=EST5EDT
```

The new variables that appear on the list are local: They have not been marked for export. For more information on exporting variables, see Chapter 10. You can think of local variables as items of information needed for only a certain time or location. For instance, remembering the variable "what-floor-am-I-on" becomes an unnecessary piece of information after you leave the building! You may see the same output for both the **set** and **env** commands in some cases, but they actually do report slightly different things.

Processes and How to Terminate Them

In the previous chapter, we learned about the **who** command, which shows you the login names of everyone who is logged into the system. The **who** program actually gets its information from the Linux system, which maintains and updates the list of the system's current users.

In fact, Linux keeps much more detailed records about what is happening on the system than just who is logged in. Because Linux is a multitasking system in which many programs or program threads may be running simultaneously, Linux keeps track of individual tasks or *processes*. Every time you enter a command, that's a process. Whenever the system does anything, that, too, is a process. Essentially, everything that Linux does is called a process, and there can be dozens of processes running at the same time.

The Process Status Command: ps

To find out what processes are running, we use the **ps** command. "ps" stands for "process status," not the "post script" you might write at the end of a letter. Remember that **ps**, like all Linux commands, is lowercase.

Typing **ps** by itself gives you a concise listing of your own processes. When you don't specify any options to **ps**, that's the default behavior, listing your own processes:

```
darkstar:~$ ps
  PID TTY STAT   TIME COMMAND
   41 v01 S      0:00 -bash
  134 v01 R      0:00 ps
```

The information in the first column, headed **PID**, is important. This is the Process ID number, a unique number assigned to each process and which Linux uses to identify that particular process. You must know a process's PID to be able to kill it. Every process on the system has a PID, and the numbers range from 0 to 65,565 then restart from the beginning, making sure each number is used only once at any one time. Linux uses numbers instead of names for each process because it's faster and easier that way.

The **TTY** column shows you which terminal the process was started from. You will see your own terminal listed when you try the **ps** command.

The **STAT** column give the status of the process. The two most common entries in the status column are **S** for *sleeping* and **R** for *running*. A sleeping process is one that isn't currently active. However, don't be misled. A sleeping process might just be taking a very brief catnap! In fact, a process can switch between sleeping and running many times every second.

The **TIME** column shows the amount of system time used by the process. Clearly, neither of our processes is taking up any appreciable system time! That's often the case with modern machines, as most processes execute so quickly that the time column scarcely moves above a single digit.

Finally, the **NAME** column contains the name of the program you're running. This is usually the command you type at the command line. However, sometimes the command you enter starts one or more processes, called *children*, and in this case, you'll see these additional processes show up as well, without ever having typed them yourself. Your **login** shell will have a - before it, as in **-bash** in the previous example. This helps to distinguish this *primary* shell from any other shells you may enter from it. These will not have the - in front.

7

BASIC LINUX
COMMANDS

> **NOTE**
>
> If you are logged in as **root**, you see a list of *all* processes on the system. This is because the **root** username, being the superuser, owns everything that happens on the Linux system.
>
> If you are an "ordinary" user, but have also logged in on another terminal (including another virtual terminal you have selected by pressing Alt+F*n* as discussed in Chapter 6, "Getting Started"), you see the processes you are running on the other terminal (or terminals), as well.
>
> Don't be worried if you see slightly different columns of information when you use **ps**. The output tends to vary a little bit, especially with options in use, with different versions of Linux. The basic information is much the same, though.

One useful option with **ps** is **u**. Although it stands for "user," it actually adds quite a few more columns of information in addition to just the username:

```
darkstar:~$ ps -u
USER        PID %CPU %MEM SIZE  RSS TTY STAT START   TIME COMMAND
fido         41  0.1  6.8  364  472 v01 S    23:19   0:01 -bash
fido        138  0.0  3.3   72  228 v01 R    23:34   0:00 ps -u
```

In addition to the username in the **USER** column, other interesting new items include **%CPU** which displays the percentage of your computer's processing power that is being used by the process, and **%MEM** which displays the percentage of your computer's memory that is being used by the process.

If you want to see all processes running on the system and not just the processes started by your own username, you can use the **a** command option. (The **root** login sees every-one's processes automatically and does not have to use **a**, so **root** can get the following output by simply typing **ps**.)

```
darkstar:~$ ps -a
PID TTY STAT  TIME COMMAND
  62 v03 S    0:00 /sbin/agetty 38400 tty3
  63 v04 S    0:00 /sbin/agetty 38400 tty4
  64 v05 S    0:00 /sbin/agetty 38400 tty5
  65 v06 S    0:00 /sbin/agetty 38400 tty6
 330 v02 S    0:00 -bash
 217 v01 S    0:00 -bash
 217 v01 S    0:00 ps -a
```

As you can see, quite a few "other" processes are happening on the system! In fact, most of the processes we see here are running whether or not anyone is actually logged into the Linux system. All the processes listed as running on **tty psf** are actually system processes and are started every time you boot up the Linux system. Processes of the form **/sbin/agetty 38400 tty6** are login processes running on a particular terminal waiting for your login.

It can be useful to combine the **a** and **u** options (if you're not **root**).

```
darkstar:~$ ps -au
USER        PID %CPU %MEM SIZE  RSS TTY STAT START   TIME COMMAND
root         72  0.0  3.6  390  532 v01 S    17:55   0:01 -bash
root         74  0.0  1.5   41  224 v03 S    17:55   0:00 /sbin/agetty
38400 tty3
root         75  0.0  1.5   41  224 v04 S    17:55   0:00 /sbin/agetty
38400 tty4
root         76  0.0  1.5   41  224 v05 S    17:55   0:00 /sbin/agetty
38400 tty5
root         77  0.0  1.5   41  224 v06 S    17:55   0:00 /sbin/agetty
38400 tty6
```

```
root          78  0.0  1.5   56  228 s00 S    17:55   0:00 gpm -t mman
root          98  0.0  1.5   41  224 v02 S    18:02   0:00 /sbin/agetty
38400 tty2
root         108 18.8  3.6  384  528 pp0 S    18:27   0:01 -bash
```

A more technical **1** option can sometimes be useful:

```
darkstar:~$ ps -l
 F   UID   PID  PPID PRI NI SIZE  RSS WCHAN      STAT TTY    TIME COMMAND
 0   501    41     1  15  0  364  472 114d9c      S   v01   0:00 -bash
 0   501   121    41  29  0   64  208 0           R   v01   0:00 ps -l
```

The interesting information is in the **PPID** column. PPID stands for "Parent Process ID"—in other words, the process that started the particular process. Notice that the **ps -1** command was started by **-bash**, the **login** shell. In other words, **ps -1** was started from the command line. Notice also that the PPID for the login shell is PID **1**. If you check the output from **ps -au** previously, you can see that the process with PID of **1** is **init**. The **init** process is the one that spawns, or starts, all other processes. If **init** dies, the system crashes!

> **NOTE**
>
> The Linux **ps** command has some quirks when it comes to options. First of all, the dash before the options is not necessary. In the earlier example, **ps 1** would work the same as **ps -1**. Because most Linux commands *do* require the use of dashes with their command options and other versions of UNIX *might* require dashes when using **ps**, it's best to use the dash anyway.
>
> Second, the order in which you enter the options does matter, especially if you try to combine the **1** and **u** options! Try typing **ps -lu**, and then **ps -ul**. This behavior is not covered in the **ps** man page. The moral is twofold: First, use the minimum possible number of command options. Second, the man pages are, alas, not always correct and complete.

The Process Termination Command: `kill`

Although these processes are usually well-behaved and well-managed by Linux, sometimes they may go out of control. This can happen if a program hits a bug or a flaw in its internal code or supplied data or if you accidentally enter the wrong command or command option.

Being able to identify these errant processes and then being able to terminate or *kill* them is an essential piece of knowledge for *all* Linux users. (Obviously, the world was a less kind and gentle place when the **kill** command was developed and named.) When you are your own system administrator, as in our case, it's doubly important to be able to kill processes that have gone awry or locked up!

The **kill** command is used to terminate processes that can't be stopped by other means.

> **NOTE**
>
> Before going through the following procedure, if it's a program that you're stuck in, make sure you can't stop or exit it by pressing Ctrl+C or some other key combination like **q**.

1. Switch to another virtual console and log in as **root**.

2. Run **ps -u** and identify the offending process. Note the process ID (PID) number for that process. You will use its PID in the next step.

3. Use the **kill** program by typing **kill <*PID*>,** where *PID* is the Process ID you want to kill. Make sure that you have correctly identified the offending process! As **root**, you can kill any user process, including the wrong one if you misread or mistype the PID.

4. Verify that the process has been killed by using **ps -u** again. You can type **ps -u <*PID*>,** which shows you the status of only the specified PID. If there's a null result and you're just given the Linux prompt again, the PID is dead, so go to step 8. However, it's best to look at the complete **ps -u** list if it's not too long. Sometimes the offending process reappears with a new PID! If that is the case, go to step 6.

5. If the process is still alive and has the same PID, use **kill**'s **9** option. Type **kill -9 <*PID*>.** Check it in the same way as in step 4. If this does not kill the process, go to step 7. If the process is now dead, go to step 8.

6. If the offending process has reappeared with a new PID, that means that it's being created automatically by some other process. The only thing to do now is to kill the parent process, which is the true offender! You may also have to kill the parent process when **kill -9** does not work.

7. Use **ps -l** to identify the troublesome process's PPID. This is the PID of the parent process. You should check the parent's identity more closely by typing **ps -u <*Parent PID*>** before going ahead and killing it as described in step 3, using the PID of the *parent* in the **kill** command. You should follow through with step 4 and, if necessary, step 5, making sure the parent process has been killed.

8. The process is killed. Remember to log off. Do not leave **root** logged in on virtual consoles because you may forget that the **root** logins are there.

> **NOTE**
>
> Sometimes processes are simply unkillable! In this case, your best bet is shutting down the Linux system and rebooting.

Linux keeps ordinary users (as opposed to **root**) from killing other users' processes (maliciously or otherwise). For instance, if you are an ordinary user and try to kill the **init** process, which always has PID=1, you will see a message similar to this one:

```
darkstar:~$ kill 1
kill:  (1) - Not owner
```

Actually, not even **root** can kill the **init** process, although there is no error message. The **init** process is one of those "unkillable" processes discussed earlier because it's such a key process. That's all for the best!

Becoming Someone Else: The su Command

Usually, when you want to temporarily become a different user, you simply switch to another virtual terminal, log in as the other user, log out when you're done, and return to your "home" virtual terminal. However, there are times when this is impractical or inconvenient. Perhaps all your virtual terminals are busy already, or perhaps you're in a situation (such as logged on via a telephone and modem) in which you don't have virtual terminals available.

In these cases, you can use the **su** command. "su" stands for "super user." If you type **su** by itself, you will be prompted for the **root** password. If you successfully enter the **root** password, you will see the **root #** prompt and have all of **root**'s privileges.

You can also become any other user by typing **su** *<username>*. If you are **root** when you type **su** *<username>*, you are not asked for that user's password since in principle you could change the user's password or examine all the user's files from the **root** login anyway. If you are an "ordinary" user trying to change to another ordinary user, you will be asked to enter the password of the user you are trying to become.

> **NOTE**
>
> Although **su** grants you all the privileges you would get if you logged on as that user, be aware that you won't inherit that login's exact environment or run that login's startup files (if any). This means that **su** is not really suited to doing extended work, and it's quite unsuitable for troubleshooting problems with that login.

The grep Command

"What on earth does **grep** mean?" you ask. This is a fair question. **grep** must be the quintessential UNIX acronym because it's impossible to understand even when it's spelled out in full! **grep** stands for *Global Regular Expression Parser*. You will understand the use of this command right away, but when "Global Regular Expression Parser" becomes a comfortable phrase in itself, you should probably consider taking a vacation.

What **grep** does, essentially, is find and display lines in a file that contain a pattern that you specify. In other words, it's a tool that checks for substrings.

There are two basic ways to use **grep**. The first use of **grep** is to filter the output of other commands. The general syntax is *<command>* ¦ **grep** *<pattern>*. For instance, if you want to see every actively running process on the system, type **ps -a** ¦ **grep R**. In this application, **grep** passes on only those lines that contain the pattern (in this case, the single letter) R. Note that if someone were running a program called **Resting**, it would show up even if its status were **S** for sleeping because **grep** would match the R in **Resting**. An easy way around this problem is to type **grep " R "**, which explicitly tells **grep** to search for an R with a space on each side. You must use quotes whenever you search for a pattern that contains one or more blank spaces.

The second use of **grep** is to search for lines that contain a specified pattern in a specified file. The syntax here is **grep** *<pattern>* *<filename>*. Be careful. It's easy to specify the filename first and the pattern second by mistake! Again, you should be as specific as you can with the pattern to be matched, in order to avoid "false" matches.

Summary

By this point, you should have tried enough different Linux commands to start getting familiar (if not yet entirely comfortable) with typical Linux usage conventions.

It is important that you be able to use the man pages provided online by Linux. A very good exercise at this point is to pull up man pages for all the commands we have looked at in the past two chapters: **login**, **passwd**, **who**, **adduser**, and so on. If any of the commands listed under "See also:" look interesting, by all means take a look at their man pages, too!

In Chapter 8, we head out from "home" and poke around in the Linux file system. As system administrators, we should know what our hard drives contain! For instance, there are special "administrator-only" directories crammed with goodies.

Several more "essential" commands are also introduced. By the end of the next chapter, you will have seen and tried most of the important "user" Linux commands and had a taste of some of the "administrator" commands. If you are interested in other related subjects, you can jump to the following chapters:

> Working with the editors that come with Linux is discussed in Chapter 16, "Text Editors: vi and emacs."
>
> Configuring X so you can use a GUI is discussed in Chapter 22, "Installing and Configuring XFree86."
>
> Programming under Linux is discussed in Part V, starting with Chapter 25, "gawk."

Using the File System

by Ed Treijs and Tim Parker

In This Chapter

Chapter 8

To understand how Linux works and to use the system beyond a superficial level, you must be familiar with the Linux notion of files and the file system into which they are organized. If you've worked with another operating system such as DOS or Windows, you've already seen these concepts because both operating systems base their approach for files, directories, and file systems on UNIX. As you will see, there is a lot more flexibility in the way UNIX and Linux handle file systems than the rather strict and limited way both DOS and Windows manage them.

Files: An Overview

The most basic concept of a file—and one you may already be familiar with from other computer systems—defines a *file* as a distinct chunk of information that is found on your hard drive. *Distinct* means that there are many separate files, each with its own particular contents. To keep files from getting confused with one another, every file must have a unique identity. In Linux, you identify each file by its name and location. In each location or *directory,* there can be only one file by a particular name. So, for instance, if you create a file called **novel**, and you get a second great idea, either you will have to call it something different, such as **novel2**, or put it in a different directory to prevent *overwriting* the contents already in your original **novel**.

Common Types of Files

Files can contain various types of information. The following three types will become the most familiar to you on a Linux system:

- User data: Information that you create and update. The simplest user data is plain text or numbers. You will learn to create these simple files later in this chapter. More complicated user data files might have to be *interpreted* by another program to make sense. For instance, a spreadsheet file looks like gibberish if you look at it directly. To work with a spreadsheet, you have to start the spreadsheet program and read in the spreadsheet file.

- System data: Information, often in plain text form, that is read and used by the Linux system—to keep track of which users are allowed on the system, for example. As a system administrator, you are responsible for changing system data files. For instance, when you create a new user, you modify the file **/etc/passwd**, which contains the user information. Ordinary users of the system are usually not concerned with system data files, except for their private startup files.

- Executable files: These files contain instructions that your computer can perform. This set of instructions is often called a *program*. When you tell the computer to perform them, you're telling it to *execute* the instructions given to it. To human eyes, executable files contain meaningless gibberish—obviously your computer doesn't think the way you do! Creating or modifying executable files takes special tools. You learn how to use these programming tools in Part V, "Linux for Programmers."

While we have decided there are three different types of files, it's important for you to realize that there is no difference between the type of files as far as the Linux file system is concerned. Each file is a chunk of data on the disk drives that contains information. What is inside each file is irrelevant to Linux until you try to use the file. The **bash** shell that we've been using, for example, can run any executable file, but may not be able to figure out what kind of data is in the user or system data files. The contents of the file are relevant only to the application that uses them, not to Linux as an operating system. The only exception to this general statement are the system data files that Linux uses when starting and running the system. In this case, Linux knows how to read the contents of the files itself.

Filenames

Linux allows filenames to be up to 256 characters long. These characters can be lower- and uppercase letters, numbers, and other characters, usually the hyphen (-), the underscore (_), and the period (.). While Linux allows you to use 256 characters in a filename, there are two things to bear in mind.

First, not all the characters are significant. If you have two filenames both 250 characters long which differ only in the last (250th) character, to Linux the files have the same name. This is because Linux takes only the first 32 or 64 characters of the filename (depending on the version of Linux) as significant. The rest of the filename is there for your convenience, and Linux keeps track of the information, but usually doesn't consider the rest of the characters after the 33rd or 65th as important for its own uses.

Secondly, remember that you have to type all those long names. Sure, you can call a file by a name 256 characters long, but you also have to type it when you want access to the file (unless you use metacharacters or wildcards). Common sense indicates you should use reasonably short, descriptive filenames. If your file contains statistical data for January, you can call the file **Jan_stats** or simply *data_Jan*, which is a heck of a lot easier to type than the filename **statistical_data_for_January**. There's nothing to stop you using the long name, though.

Filenames don't normally include reserved *metacharacters* such as the asterisk, question mark, backslash, and space because these all have meaning to the shell. We met some

8

USING THE FILE SYSTEM

metacharacters when we discussed wildcards in the previous chapter. Other metacharacters will be introduced in the Linux shell chapters. (It is possible to create files that have metacharacters in them but they tend to pose problems for the operating system and applications.)

Directories: An Overview

Linux, like many other computer systems, organizes files into *directories*. You can think of directories as file folders and their contents as the files. However, there is one absolutely crucial difference between the Linux file system and an office filing system. In the office, file folders usually don't contain other file folders. In Linux, file folders *can* contain other file folders. In fact, there is no Linux "filing cabinet"—just a huge file folder that holds some files and other folders. These folders contain files and possibly other folders in turn, and so on.

Parent Directories and Subdirectories

Imagine a scenario in which you have a directory, A, that contains another directory, B. Directory B is then a *subdirectory* of directory A, and directory A is the *parent directory* of directory B. You will see these terms often, both in this book and elsewhere.

With Linux, there is no real limit to the number of directories and subdirectories you have on your system. The same applies for the number of files. As long as there is space on the hard drive, Linux will be able to save files and directories. A directory can have an unlimited number of subdirectories, and they themselves can have an unlimited number of subdirectories, and so on. Each directory and subdirectory can have an unlimited number of files. The key to understanding the way Linux organizes files and directories is recognizing that there is only one top-level directory, from which all others are subdirectories.

The Root Directory

In Linux, the directory that holds all the other directories is called the *root directory*. This is the ultimate parent directory; every other directory is some level of subdirectory. The root directory has a special symbol, /, which is used to show it is the top level. You'll see how all other subdirectories branch off from the root directory in the next few sections.

From the root directory, the whole structure of directory upon directory springs and grows like some electronic elm tree. This is called a *tree structure* because, from the single *root* directory, directories and subdirectories branch off like tree limbs. You'll also hear this called a hierarchical directory structure because there is a hierarchy of levels of directories, with the highest level as the root directory.

Just a quick word about file systems. You'll see the words file system used throughout this book. That's because UNIX has always referred to directory structures as file systems. There's quite a bit of history behind it, but all the directories on your Linux system are your system's file system. That's where Linux stores the files.

How Directories Are Named

Directories are named just like files, and they can contain upper- and lowercase letters, numbers, and characters such as **-**, **.**, and **_**. Essentially, to Linux a directory name is a file because it makes no distinction between the two. You can name directories the same, as long as they are not in the same parent directory (to prevent having two directories called "data" under the same parent directory), but you can have any number of directories called "data" in your file system as long as they don't share parents.

The slash (**/**) character is used to show files or directories within other directories. For instance, **usr/bin** means that **bin** is found in the **usr** directory. Note that you can't tell from this example whether **bin** is a file or a directory, although you know that **usr** must be a directory because it holds another item—namely, the directory **bin**. When you see **usr/bin/grep**, you know that both **usr** and **bin** must be directories, but again, you can't be sure about **grep**. The **ls** program often shows directories followed by a backslash (sometimes this requires the -F option)—for example, to show that fido is a directory, **ls** shows it as **fido/**. This notation implies that you could have, for instance, **fido/file**; therefore, **fido** must be a directory.

As mentioned earlier, the root directory is shown simply by the symbol / rather than mentioned by name. It's very easy to tell when / is used to separate directories and when it's used to signify the root directory. If / has no name *before* it, it stands for the root directory. For example, **/usr** means that the **usr** subdirectory is found in the root directory, and **/usr/bin** means that **bin** is found in the **usr** directory and that **usr** is a subdirectory of the root directory. Remember, by definition the root directory cannot be a subdirectory.

The Home Directory

Linux provides each user with his or her own directory called the *home* directory. Within this home directory, users can store their own files and create subdirectories. Users generally have complete control over what's found in their home directories. Because there are usually no Linux system files or files belonging to other users in your home directory, you can create, name, move, and delete files and directories as you see fit.

WARNING

Your home directory does not provide privacy! Normally, any user can go into another's home directory and read (and copy!) the files stored there (although he can't delete or change the files). When Linux creates your home directory, it in effect provides you with an open office cubicle whose desk and filing cabinet drawers are unlocked.

You *must* lock up everything you want to keep private. (This topic is covered in Chapter 9, "File and Directory Permissions.") It is generally considered rude or nosy to poke around in someone else's home directory, just as it's rude or nosy to poke around in someone's office while they're away from their desk, but the world is full of nosy and rude people so you must take precautions!

Note that anyone logged in as root can read and manipulate *all* the files on the system, including files that users have locked up. If you can't trust the system administrator (who usually has the root password), don't use the system!

The location of a user's home directory is specified by Linux and can't be changed by the user. This is both to keep things tidy and to preserve system security. The location of your home directory depends on which version of Linux you're using and how the system installed itself, but usually it is something like /**home**/**tim** or /**usr**/**tim**, where "tim" is the login name. When you log into the system, you are placed in your home directory by default.

Navigating the Linux File System

Fortunately, navigating the Linux file system is simple. There are only two commands to be learned, and one of them has absolutely no options or parameters!

The pwd Command: Where Am I?

Type **pwd** at the Linux command prompt. You see

```
darkstar:~$ pwd
/home/fido
darkstar:~$
```

This tells you that you're currently in the directory /**home**/**fido**. (If you are logged in under a different username, you will see that name in place of **fido**.) This is your home directory. As we mentioned earlier, when you log in, Linux always places you in your home directory.

The letters "pwd" stand for "print working directory." Again, a command's name or function has been cut down to a few easy-to-type characters. (You will often see the term *current directory* used in place of *working directory*.)

You might be wondering what "working directory" or "being in a directory" really means. It simply means that Linux commands, by default, perform their actions in your working directory. For instance, when you run **ls**, you are shown only the files in your working directory. If you want to create or remove files, they will be created or removed in your working directory. You can change your working directory with the **cd** command, as you'll see in a moment.

Absolute and Relative Filenames

If you specify only the name of a file, Linux looks for that file in your working directory. For example, **more myfile** lets you read the contents of the file **myfile**. But **myfile** must be in your current working directory or the **more** command can't find it.

Sometimes you want to specify a file that isn't in your current directory. In this case, you must then specify the name of the directory the file is in, as well as the name of the file itself. If, for example, your current directory has a subdirectory called **novel** which contains a file called **chapter_1**, you could type **more novel/chapter_1** which tells **more** that it should look in the subdirectory **novel** for the file **chapter_1**. This is called a *relative filename*. You are specifying the location of **chapter_1** *relative* to where you are now, in the subdirectory **novel**, which in turn is found in your current directory. If you have changed your working directory, the relative filename will no longer work.

Two special directory specifications are "." and "..". The single period "." always stands for the directory you are currently in, and ".." stands for the parent directory of your current directory. (You will see how "." and ".." are used later in this chapter.) Any filename that includes "." or ".." is, by definition, a relative filename.

A filename that is valid from any location is called an *absolute filename*. Absolute filenames always begin with /, signifying the root directory. So if you specify a filename as **/home/fido/novel/chapter_1**, there is no doubt as to where the file is located. Every file on your system has a unique absolute filename. You can use the absolute filename to figure out what Linux is doing when you specify a filename. In the example just mentioned, Linux will start in the root directory / and look for a subdirectory called **home**. Linux makes **/home** the current directory temporarily and looks for a directory called **fido**, then makes that current, looks for **novel** and makes that current. Once in novel, Linux looks for a file or directory called chapter_1. You can read the absolute filename like a road map, telling you how to navigate the Linux file system.

Someone else on the system might also have a directory called **novel** in his or her home directory. Perhaps it even contains a file called **chapter_1**. In this case, you can't distinguish the two files by using the relative filename **novel/chapter_1**. However, the absolute filenames *will* be different—for instance, **/home/fido/novel/chapter_1** as opposed to **/home/mary/novel/chapter_1**. The **novel** subdirectory in **/home/fido** is *not* the same subdirectory as the **novel** directory in **/home/mary**! The two are in quite separate locations and only coincidentally do they share the same name. The two files will have completely different contents, too.

Going Places: The `cd` Command

The **cd** (change directory) command lets you change your working directory. You can think of it as moving to another directory. If you've worked with DOS or the DOS prompt in Windows, you've seen this command before (yes, it was swiped from UNIX!).

The syntax of the **cd** command is

```
cd <directory>
```

There must be a space between **cd** and the directory specification. You should specify only one directory name to be changed into. The directory specification can be an absolute or relative one. For instance, type **cd ..** followed by **pwd:**

```
darkstar:~$ pwd
darkstar:/home$ /home/fido
darkstar:~$ cd ..
darkstar:/home$ pwd
/home
darkstar:/home$ cd ..
darkstar:/$ pwd
/
darkstar:/$ cd ..
darkstar:/$ pwd
/
```

As you can see in the preceding example, we started in **/home/fido** (that's the absolute path name) and then moved up one directory level with the **..** command. That put us in **/home**. Another move to the parent and we're in the root directory. We can't go any higher than the root directory because there is no parent directory for the root directory. Typing **cd ..** when in the root directory simply leaves you in the root directory.

Note that the Linux command prompt usually shows you which directory you are currently in, so you don't have to type **pwd** all the time. (We'll continue to use **pwd** for clarity.) Not all Linux systems do show your current directory in the shell prompt because the system administrator may have customized the prompt for you.

Let's suppose you want to go into a subdirectory of your home directory. We can **cd** back to your home directory and then **cd** into a subdirectory called **book**:

```
darkstar:/$ cd /home/fido
darkstar:~$ pwd
darkstar:/home$ /home/fido
darkstar:~$ cd book
darkstar:~/book$ pwd
/home/fido/book
```

In this case, we used **cd** to get back **home** (verified with the **pwd** command), then told Linux to make the subdirectory book our current directory. We know the directory book is below our home directory, so we used relative filenames to move into it. We could have specified the absolute pathname, too, but this was much easier. To avoid any confusion or mistakes, use the absolute directory names when using the **cd** command:

```
darkstar:/$ cd /usr/bin
darkstar:/usr/bin$ pwd
/usr/bin
```

When you type an absolute directory name, you go to that directory, no matter where you started from. When you type **cd ..**, where you end up depends on where you started.

To see the effect of changing your working directory, type **ls**. The list of files is so long that the first part scrolls off your screen. The **ls** command shows you the contents of your current directory (as always), but now your current directory is **/usr/bin**, which contains many more files than your home directory.

There's No Place Like Home

Here's a handy trick that many UNIX and Linux users don't use. Type **cd** without any directory specification:

```
darkstar:/usr/bin$ cd
darkstar:~$ pwd
/home/fido
```

Typing **cd** by itself always returns you to your home directory, no matter where you are when you type **cd**. When exploring the file system, you sometimes wind up deep in a blind alley of subdirectories. Type **cd** to quickly return home or type **cd /** to return to the root directory.

The ~ in your prompt is another special character. It stands for your home directory. There's no reason to type **cd ~** when **cd** works just as well, and is much easier to type! A tilde (~) by itself indicates your own home directory.

Linux also uses the ~ symbol to mean the parent directory of user directories. When you type **cd** *~<user>*, you move to that user's home directory. This is a very useful trick, especially on large systems with many users and more complicated directory structures than the simple /**home**/*<user>* on your Linux system.

When you're changing to a distant directory, it's often a good idea to take several steps. If you mistype a very long directory specification, you will have to retype the entire specification. Sometimes it may not even be clear why **cd** gave you an error! Taking a number of shorter steps means less retyping in case of an error. Consider this example:

```
darkstar:~$ cd /usr/docs/faq/unix
bash: /usr/docs/faq/unix: No such file or directory
```

You're pretty sure that this path is correct. Let's change directories one step at a time:

```
darkstar:~$ cd /usr
darkstar:/usr$ cd docs
bash: docs: No such file or directory
```

There's a problem with **docs**. The directory is actually named **doc**:

```
darkstar:/usr$ ls
bin/   doc/   games/   info/   man/   sbin/   spool/
darkstar:/usr$ cd doc
darkstar:/usr/doc$ cd faq/unix
darkstar:/usr/doc/faq/unix$ pwd
/usr/doc/faq/unix
```

Creating and Deleting Files

Linux has many ways to create and delete files. In fact, some of the ways are so easy to perform that you have to be careful not to accidentally overwrite or erase files!

WARNING

Go through the following sections very carefully. You should be logged in as your "ordinary" username, *not* as root! Only when you're absolutely sure you understand these sections thoroughly should you use these commands while logged in as root.

There is no "unerase" command in Linux! Be *sure* you know what you're doing!

Return to your home directory by typing **cd**. Make sure you're in your /**home**/*<user>* directory by running **pwd**.

In the last chapter, you created a file by typing **ls -l** /**bin** > **output**. Remember, the > symbol means "redirect all output to the following filename." Note that the file **output** didn't exist before you entered this command. When you redirect to a file, Linux automatically creates the file if it doesn't already exist.

What if you want to type text into a file rather than some command's output? The quick and dirty way is to use the command **cat**.

cat: That Useful Feline

The **cat** command is one of the simplest, yet most useful, commands in Linux. (It certainly does more than any living feline!) The **cat** command basically takes all input and outputs it to a file or other source such as the screen. By default, **cat** takes its input from the keyboard and outputs it to the screen. Type **cat** at the command line:

```
darkstar:~$ cat
```

The cursor moves down to the next line, but nothing else seems to happen. Now **cat** is waiting for some input so type a few short lines:

```
hello
hello
what
what
asdf
asdf
```

Everything you type is repeated onscreen as soon as you press Enter!

How do you get out of this? At the start of a line, type ^**D** (Ctrl+D). (In other words, hold the Ctrl key and press D.) If you're not at the beginning of a line, you have to type ^**D** twice. ^**D** is the Linux "end of file" character. When a program such as **cat** encounters a ^**D**, it assumes that it has finished with the current file, and it goes on to the next one. In this case, if you type ^**D** by itself on an empty line, there is no next file to go on to, and **cat** exits.

In this simple exercise, **cat** accepted input from the keyboard and displayed it back to you on the screen. Not a very useful command so far, is it? Fortunately, there's a lot more flexibility to **cat**.

> **NOTE**
>
> When you say that a program *exits,* you mean that it has finished running and that you are back at the Linux command prompt. It may seem odd to talk about the *program* exiting when, from your point of view as a user, you have exited the program. This turn of phrase goes back to the early days of UNIX, when it was coined by the people who were programming the system. They looked at things from the program's point of view, not the user's!

So how do you use **cat** to create a file? Simple! You redirect the output of **cat** from the screen to a file:

```
darkstar:~$ cat > newfile
Hello world
Here's some text
```

You can type as much as you want. When you are finished, press ^**D** by itself on a line; you are back at the Linux prompt. Instead of showing you each line as you typed it on the screen, **cat** has redirected it to a file called **newfile**.

Now you want to look at the contents of **newfile**. You can use the **more** or **less** commands, but instead, let's use **cat**. Yes, you can use **cat** to look at files simply by providing it with a filename:

```
darkstar:~$ cat newfile
Hello world
Here's some text
darkstar:~$
```

Cool! You can also add to the end of the file by using **>>**. Whenever you use **>>**, whether with **cat** or any other command, the output is always *appended* to the specified file. (Note that the ^**D** character does not appear onscreen. It's shown in the examples for clarity.)

```
darkstar:~$ cat >> newfile
Some more lines
^D
darkstar:~$ cat newfile
Hello world
Here's some text
Some more lines
darkstar:~$
```

To discover what **cat** actually stands for, let's create another file.

```
darkstar:~$ cat > anotherfile
Different text
```

```
^D
darkstar:~$
```

Now, try this:

```
darkstar:~$ cat newfile anotherfile> thirdfile
darkstar:~$ cat thirdfile
Hello world
Here's some text
Some more lines
Different text
darkstar:~$
```

cat stands for *concatenate*; **cat** takes all the specified inputs and regurgitates them in a single lump. We've concatenated newfile and anotherfile together into thirdfile. This by itself would not be very interesting, but combine it with the various forms of input and output redirection available in Linux and you have a powerful and useful tool.

Sometimes you want to change just one line of a file, or perhaps you are creating a large and complicated file and don't want to rely on **cat** (which doesn't allow you to correct errors). For this, you should use one of the editing programs available in Linux. They are discussed in Chapter 16, "Text Editors: vi and emacs."

Creating Directories

To create a new directory, use the **mkdir** command. The syntax is **mkdir <name>**, where <name> is replaced by whatever you want the directory to be called. This creates a subdirectory with the specified name in your current directory:

```
darkstar:~$ ls
anotherfile    newfile      thirdfile
darkstar:~$ mkdir newdir
darkstar:~$ ls
anotherfile    /newdir        newfile        thirdfile
```

8

USING THE FILE
SYSTEM

TIP

The mkdir command is already familiar to you if you have used MS-DOS systems. In MS-DOS, you can abbreviate mkdir as md. You might think that md would work in Linux, because, after all, most of the commands we've seen have extremely concise names. However, Linux doesn't recognize md; it insists on the full mkdir.

If you frequently switch between Linux and MS-DOS, you may want to use mkdir for both systems. However, be warned that you could start typing other Linux commands in MS-DOS—for example, typing ls instead of dir!

The `mkdir` command creates an entry for that subdirectory in Linux's table of all files and directories, which is called the I-node table. When Linux creates a directory name, it doesn't actually write anything to the disk drive because a directory name has no physical contents until you save a file to it. Directories are used by Linux as a convenience for the user.

You can use both relative and absolute pathnames with `mkdir`, for example:

```
$ pwd
/usr/tparker/temp
$ ls
$ mkdir book1
$ ls
book1
$ mkdir /usr/tparker/temp/book2
$ ls
book1
book2
```

In the first case we've used relative names to create a directory called **book1** under the current directory. In the second example, we've used absolute addressing to create **book2** in the same location. We can use whichever format is more convenient. Both methods accomplish the same result.

Moving and Copying Files

You often need to move or copy files. The **mv** command moves files (which is the same as renaming them) and the **cp** command copies files. The syntax for the two commands is similar:

```
mv <source> <destination>
cp <source> <destination>
```

As you can see, **mv** and **cp** are very simple commands. Here's an example:

```
darkstar:~$ ls
anotherfile    /newdir        newfile        thirdfile
darkstar:~$ mv anotherfile movedfile
darkstar:~$ ls
movedfile      /newdir        newfile        thirdfile
darkstar:~$ cp thirdfile xyz
darkstar:~$ ls
anotherfile    /newdir        newfile        thirdfile      xyz
```

You can use **cat** (or **more** or **less**) at any time to verify that **anotherfile** became **movedfile** and that the contents of file **xyz** are identical to the contents of **thirdfile**.

It can get more confusing if you're moving or copying files from one directory to another. This is because a file's *real* name includes its absolute path—for instance, **/home/fido/newfile**. However, Linux lets you leave off parts of the file's name because it's more convenient to refer to **newfile** rather than **/home/fido/newfile**.

For example, suppose you want to move **newfile** from your current directory into the **newdir** subdirectory. If you want the file to keep the same name, you can type

```
darkstar:~$ mv newfile newdir/newfile
```

However, it's much more common to type

```
darkstar:~$ mv newfile newdir
```

primarily because it's a little shorter. In this case, because you have typed a directory name for the destination, Linux assumes that you want the file to be placed in the specified directory with the same name as the existing file.

You can also use **cd** to change to the directory you want to move the file to:

```
darkstar:~$ cd newdir
darkstar:~newdir$ copy ../newfile .
```

This example is a bit less intuitive than the first two. You specify that the source is **../newfile** which means "the file **newfile** in the current directory's parent directory." The destination you simply specify as ".", which is short for "the current directory." In other words, you're telling **mv** to "go up one level, grab **newfile**, and move it to right here." Because this is less intuitive, you might find yourself automatically *pushing* a file from your current directory to another directory rather than *pulling* a file from another directory into your current directory.

You can also change the name of the file while moving or copying it to another directory by specifying the new name you want. The following is just one possible way:

```
darkstar:~$ cp newfile newdir/anothername
```

This creates a copy of **newfile** in the directory **newdir** and names the copied file **anothername**.

8

USING THE FILE
SYSTEM

> ### WARNING
>
> When moving or copying files between directories, you should always double-check that the file's destination directory exists and verify the directory's name. Otherwise, the results of your command can be unexpected, as the following two examples show.
>
> If in the example just shown, let's say you mistyped newdir as mv newfile mewdir—you wind up with a file called mewdir in your current directory and no file newfile in the newdir subdirectory!
>
> Another way you get an unexpected result is to type cp newfile newdir if you didn't realize that the directory newdir already existed. In this case, you are expecting to create an identical file called newdir in your current directory. What you are actually doing is creating a copy of newfile, called newfile, in the subdirectory newdir.

The **mv** command is much more efficient than the **cp** command. When you use **mv**, the file's contents are not moved at all; rather, Linux makes a note that the file is to be found elsewhere within the file system's structure of directories.

When you use **cp**, you are actually making a second physical copy of your file and placing it on your disk. This can be slower (although for small files, you won't notice any difference), and it causes a bit more wear and tear on your computer. Don't make copies of files when all you really want to do is move them!

Moving and Copying with Wildcards

If you have 20 files in a directory, and you want to copy them to another directory, it would be very tedious to use the **cp** command on each one. Fortunately, you can use the wildcards * and ? to copy more than one file at a time.

If you want to move or copy *all* files in a directory, use the wildcard *:

```
darkstar:~$ cp * /tmp
```

This command copies every file in your current directory to the directory /**tmp**.

You can use * along with other characters to match only certain files. For instance, suppose you have a directory that contains the files **book1**, **book_idea**, **book-chapter-1**, and **poem.book**. To copy just the first three files, you can type **cp book* /tmp**. When you type **book***, you are asking Linux to match all files whose names start with **book**. In this case, **poem.book** does not start with **book**, so there is no way **book*** can match it. (Note that if your filename were **book.poem**, **book*** would match it.)

As you saw at the outset, **mv** and **cp** are very simple commands. It's specifying the files that is the complicated part! If things still seem confusing, don't worry. Even experts sometimes mess up "simple" moves and copies. Follow the examples and try any different ways you can think of. There is a definite logic as to how the files to be moved and copied should be specified. It takes a while to become familiar with this logic, and you will probably have to practice a while before these things become intuitive.

Moving Directories

To move a directory, use the **mv** command. The syntax is **mv** *<directory>* *<destination>*. In the following example, let's move the **newdir** subdirectory found in your current directory to the **/tmp** directory:

```
darkstar:~$ mvdir newdir /tmp
darkstar:~$ cd /tmp
darkstar:/tmp$ ls
/newdir
```

The directory **newdir** is now a subdirectory of **/tmp**.

When you move a directory, all its files and subdirectories go with it.

You can use the **mv** command to rename a directory without moving it. For example, if you want to rename the directory **newdir** to **olddir** without copying it, the command

```
mv newdir olddir
```

does the task. All the files in **newdir** now are under **olddir**.

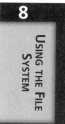

Removing Files and Directories

Now that you know how to create files and directories, it's time to learn how to undo your handiwork.

To remove (or delete) a file, use the **rm** command (**rm** is a very terse spelling of *remove*). The syntax is **rm** *<filename>*. For example, the command:

```
darkstar:~$ rm dead_duck
```

removes the file **dead_duck** from your current directory.

```
darkstar:~$ rm /tmp/dead_duck
```

removes the file **dead_duck** from the **/tmp** directory.

You can use wildcards with the **rm** command, just as with all other Linux commands. This can cause you a lot of problems when you type the command at the wrong location.

For example, the command

```
darkstar:~$ rm *
```

removes all files from your current directory. There's no way to undelete the files, so if you issued this command by accident, you're out of luck. The moral of the story is to be very careful when using wildcards with the **rm** command!

You can combine wildcards and directory paths. For example, the command

```
darkstar:~$ rm /tmp/*duck
```

removes all files ending in **duck** from the **/tmp** directory.

As soon as a file is removed, it is *gone!* Always think about what you're doing before you remove a file. You can use one of the following options to keep out of trouble when using wildcards:

- Run **ls** using the same file specification you use with the **rm** command. For instance:

```
darkstar:~$ ls *duck
dead_duck    guiduck    lame-duck
:~$ rm *duck
```

In this case, you *thought* you wanted to remove all files that matched ***duck**. To verify that this indeed was the case, all the ***duck** files were listed (wildcards work the same way with all commands). The listing looked okay, so you went ahead and removed the files.

- Use the **i** (interactive) option with **rm**:

```
darkstar:~$ rm -i *duck
rm: remove 'dead_duck'? y
rm: remove 'guiduck'? n
rm: remove 'lame-duck'? y
darkstar:~$
```

When you use **rm -i**, the command goes through the list of files to be deleted one by one, prompting you for the okay to remove the file. If you type **y** or **Y**, **rm** removes the file. If you type any other character, **rm** does not remove it. The only disadvantage of using this interactive mode is that it can be very tedious when the list of files to be removed is long.

Removing Directories

The **rm** command works primarily with files. If you try to delete a directory with **rm**, an error message displays. The command normally used to remove (delete) directories is **rmdir**. The syntax is **rmdir** *<directory>*.

Before you can remove a directory, it must be empty (the directory can't hold any files or subdirectories). Otherwise, you see

```
rmdir: <directory>: Directory not empty
```

This is as close to a safety feature as you will see in Linux!

This one might baffle you:

```
darkstar:/home$ ls
fido/     root/    zippy/
darkstar:/home$ ls zippy
core      kazoo       stuff
darkstar:/home$ rm zippy/*
darkstar:/home/zippy$ ls zippy
darkstar:/home$ rmdir zippy
rmdir: zippy: Directory not empty
darkstar:~$
```

The reason for the **Directory not empty** message is that files starting with . are usually special system files that are usually hidden from the user. To list files whose names start with ., you have to use **ls -a**. To delete these files, use **rm .***:

```
darkstar:/home$ ls -a zippy
./   ../    .bashrc     .profile
darkstar:/home$ rm zippy/.*
rm: cannot remove '.' or '..'
darkstar:/home$ ls -a zippy
./   ../
darkstar:/home$ rmdir zippy
darkstar:/home$ ls
fido/    root/
darkstar:~$
```

You will most often come across this situation in a system administrator role.

Sometimes you want to remove a directory with many layers of subdirectories. Emptying and then deleting all the subdirectories one by one is very tedious. Linux offers a way to remove a directory and all the files and subdirectories it contains in one easy step. This is the **r** (recursive) option of the **rm** command. The syntax is **rm -r** *<directory>*. The directory and all its contents are removed.

> ### WARNING
>
> You should use `rm -r` only when you absolutely have to. To paraphrase an old saying, "It's only a shortcut until you make a mistake." For example, if you're logged in as `root`, the following command removes all files from your hard disk, and then it's "Hello, installation procedure" time (do *not* type the following command!):
>
> ```
> rm -r /
> ```
>
> Believe it or not, people do this all too often. Don't join the club!

Fear of Compression: The Zipless File

Most Linux files are stored on the installation CD-ROM in compressed form. This allows more information to be stored. If you work with DOS or Windows, you may have seen utilities that ZIP files into a larger library. Utilities such as PKZIP and WINZIP are very popular in those operating systems. The same type of technique has been used by UNIX for decades, although a different name and compression technique are used.

When you install Linux, the installation program uncompresses many of the files it transfers to your hard drive. However, if you look, you will be able to find compressed files!

Any file ending in .gz—for example, **squashed.gz**—is a compressed file. To uncompress this particular type of file, type **gunzip** *<file>*. For this example, type **gunzip squashed.gz**. The **gunzip** program creates an uncompressed file and removes the .gz extension. Therefore, you wind up with a normal file called **squashed**. To compress a file, use the **gzip** command. Typing **gzip squashed** compresses **squashed** and renames it **squashed.gz**.

Another type of compressed file you may see ends with the extension .zip. Use **unzip** to uncompress these files. To create files of this type, use **zip**.

There's a couple of other compression systems used by Linux. These provide compressed files ending with .Z or .z (the two are not produced by the same compression tool).

Important Directories in the Linux File System

Most of the directories that hold Linux system files are "standard." Other UNIX systems will have identical directories with similar contents. This section summarizes some of the more important directories on your Linux system.

/

This is the root directory. It holds the actual Linux program, as well as subdirectories. Do not clutter this directory with your files!

/home

This directory holds users' home directories. In other UNIX systems, this can be the /usr or /u directory.

/bin

This directory holds many of the basic Linux programs. **bin** stands for *binaries*, files that are executable and which hold text only computers can understand.

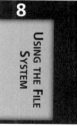

/usr

This directory holds many other user-oriented directories. Some of the most important are described in the following sections. Other directories found in /usr include

docs	Various documents, including useful Linux information
man	The man pages accessed by typing **man** *<command>*
games	The fun stuff!

/usr/bin

This directory holds user-oriented Linux programs.

/usr/spool

This directory has several subdirectories. **mail** holds mail files, **spool** holds files to be printed, and **uucp** holds files copied between Linux machines.

/dev

Linux treats *everything* as a file! The /**dev** directory holds *devices*. These are special files that serve as gateways to physical computer components. For instance, if you copy to /**dev**/**fd0**, you're actually sending data to the system's floppy disk. Your terminal is one of the /**dev**/**tty** files. Partitions on the hard drive are of the form /**dev**/**hd0**. Even the system's memory is a device!

A famous device is /**dev**/**null**. This is sometimes called the *bit bucket*. All information sent to /**dev**/**null** vanishes—it's thrown into the trash.

/usr/sbin

This directory holds system administration files. You must be the **root** user to run most of these commands.

/sbin

This directory holds system files that are usually run automatically by the Linux system.

/etc

This directory and its subdirectories hold many of the Linux configuration files. These files are usually text, and they can be edited to change the system's configuration (if you know what you're doing!).

Summary

You should now feel more comfortable working in Linux. Understanding and being able to navigate the Linux file system is very important because Linux simply consists of some files organized in a fairly standard way.

You still may find yourself stumped by certain file or directory problems. Remember that the online man pages can assist you. Linux gives you a lot of flexibility in creating files, specifying absolute or relative names, and setting permissions. Don't be afraid to experiment (as an ordinary user, in your home directory). There are too many different ways to perform tasks to list or exhaustively describe here. Don't cling to rigid recipes written on a piece of paper. You learn by trying!

Check out Chapters 9, "File and Directory Permissions," and 10, "GNU Project Utilities," through Chapter 13, "tcsh," especially if you want to create programs or macros from system command files or to learn more about the built-in user interface features in Linux shells. Chapter 16 also has very useful information about editing text files.

After you are familiar with shells and get some practice manipulating files and directories, you can move on to the advanced topics in Part III, "Editing, Typesetting, and More," through Part VIII, "Advanced Programming Topics," of this book. If you are interested in other subjects, you can jump to them from here:

> Working with the editors that come with Linux is discussed in Chapter 16, "Text Editors: vi and emacs."

> Configuring X so you can use a GUI is discussed in Chapter 22, "Installing and Configuring XFree86."

> Administering your Linux system is discussed in Part VI, starting with Chapter 32, "System Administration Basics."

File and Directory Permissions

by Tim Parker

IN THIS CHAPTER

CHAPTER 9

If there's one subject that tends to confuse newcomers to UNIX and Linux, it's working with file permissions. This subject is confusing because it has rarely been properly explained. After you understand what is going on and what the file permission commands do, you'll readily understand this subject. Take your time working through this material and you should find it fairly clear and easy to grasp.

You already saw that when you perform a long directory listing with the `ls -l` command, there's a lot of information displayed other than the filename. For example, look at this long directory listing:

```
-rwxr-xr-x   2 tparker   group        4512 May  9 09:20 book1
-rwxr-xr-x   2 tparker   group        5727 May  9 09:20 book
```

There are seven fields of data in this directory listing. From left to right they are:

- A set of permissions (which we'll explain shortly)
- The number of links (we'll worry about that in another chapter)
- The user ID that owns the files (in this case, `tparker`)
- The group that owns the files (in this case, `group`)
- The size of the file in bytes
- The date and time the file was created
- The name of the file

In this chapter we're going to concentrate on the permissions, owner, and group of the file.

Every Linux file and directory has an owner and group, as well as a set of permissions. You can change the permissions and ownership of your files and directories to provide greater or lesser access. File permissions also determine whether a file can be executed as a command or not.

File and Directory Ownership

When you create a file, you are that file's owner by default, and your login appears in the third column of the directory listing. Whatever group you are in when the file is created is placed in the fourth column. (We haven't talked about groups yet, but they are simply a number of user IDs that have a similar group name for common access to files and directories.) Being the file's owner gives you the privilege of changing the file's permissions or ownership. Of course, once you change the ownership to another user, you will probably not be able to change the ownership or permissions anymore.

Users and Ownership

File *owners* are set up by the system during installation. Linux system files are owned by IDs such as root, uucp, and bin. Do not change the ownership of these files, even if you are logged in as root. That's because the permissions are set correctly when Linux installs the software, and if you change them, you may prevent the system from accessing the file properly.

> **TIP**
>
> Although it's sometimes tempting to change ownerships of system files, this can cause real problems for utilities that don't run as root and need to read those files. In most cases if you change the ownership or the permissions of a system file, the utilities that use that file will lock up or terminate. Change ownership of files only when you know they are user files!

You can use the chown (change ownership) command to change the ownership of a file. The syntax of the chown command is

```
chown <owner> <filename>.
```

owner indicates where to insert the user ID that will own the file, and filename indicates the name of the file that you are setting ownership for. You can use wildcards with the chown command to indicate a number of files at once.

In the following example, you change the ownership of the file myfile to the login bill:

```
darkstar:~$ ls -l myfile
-rw-r--r--   1 fido      users          114 Dec  7 14:31 myfile
darkstar:~$ chown bill myfile
darkstar:~$ ls -l myfile
-rw-r--r--   1 bill      users          114 Dec  7 14:31 myfile
```

Before you can change the login of the file owner, Linux checks to confirm that it exists. After you have changed the ownership of the file, you may not be able to do anything else with the file, so be careful. To make any further changes to the file myfile or to chown it back to fido, you must use either su or log in as bill and use the chown command to set you back to the owner.

9

FILE AND DIRECTORY PERMISSIONS

> **NOTE**
>
> Although Linux shows you the login name that owns the files and directories, it really keeps track of this information through the user ID number (such as 101). Linux prefers numbers to characters because they are easier to manipulate.

> **NOTE**
>
> It is possible to have files owned by a user who doesn't exist. This usually occurs when the system administrator deletes a user. All the files that user ID owns are still tagged with that ownership because Linux doesn't scan the filesystem and change these names when a user is deleted. In the case of a file owner that doesn't exist, root is usually the only login that can change the ownership.

Groups

Files (and users) also belong to *groups*. Groups are normally used in larger installations, and it may be that you never have to worry about them. But remember that groups are a convenient way of providing access to files for more than one user but not to every user on the system. For instance, users working on a special project could all belong to the group project. Files used by the whole group would also belong to the group project, giving those users special access.

Groups are typically used for logical groups of users. The example above uses a project as the grouping, but groups can be used for different departments, types of users (administrator, accounting, programmers, and so on), or for locations on a large network.

You are a member of one group at all times. When you log in you are placed in your default group, which is set when root creates your user account. You can belong to many different groups, but you can be logged in to only one group at a time. To change the group you are a member of, use the newgrp command. For example, if you are a member of a group called users and also a group called programmers, and you need to change to the programmers group because they have special access to a compiler, issue this command:

```
newgrp programmers
```

Linux does not tell you which group you're in. Usually the only way to find out which group is active is to save a file and then look at the permissions. If you try to change to another group that you don't belong to with newgrp, Linux will give you a friendly warning like this one:

```
newgrp programmers
newgrp: Sorry
```

Changing Group Ownership

You've already seen how to change the ownership of a file. You might also want to change the group owner. To change the ownership of a group, you don't have to belong to the group, but you must own the file. Before you can begin, Linux first checks that the group exists.

The chgrp command is used to change the group the file belongs to. It works just like chown:

```
chgrp <group> <filename>
```

For example, to change the ownership of the file book to a group called editors, issue this command:

```
$ l book*
-rwxr-xr-x   2 tparker   group        4512 May  9 09:20 book
$ chgrp editors book
$ l book*
-rwxr-xr-x   2 tparker   editors       4512 May  9 09:20 book
```

You can use wildcards with both chown and chgrp, as the following example shows:

```
$ l book*
-rwxr-xr-x   2 tparker   group        4512 May  9 09:20 book1
-rwxr-xr-x   2 tparker   group        4625 May  9 09:21 book2
-rwxr-xr-x   2 tparker   group        7834 May  9 09:22 book3
$ chown bills book*
$ l book*
-rwxr-xr-x   2 bills    group        4512 May  9 09:20 book1
-rwxr-xr-x   2 bills    group        4625 May  9 09:21 book2
-rwxr-xr-x   2 bills    group        7834 May  9 09:22 book3
$ chgrp editors book*
$ l book*
-rwxr-xr-x   2 bills    editors       4512 May  9 09:20 book1
-rwxr-xr-x   2 bills    editors       4625 May  9 09:21 book2
-rwxr-xr-x   2 bills    editors       7834 May  9 09:22 book3
```

Notice that the chgrp and chown commands don't affect anything else about the file, such as the date and time it was created or the permissions in the first field.

9

FILE AND
DIRECTORY
PERMISSIONS

File Permissions

Since the early days, UNIX has tried to set up a flexible, powerful, yet simple set of file access permissions that balances security with convenience. The approach UNIX (and hence Linux) takes is simple. It sets only three different types of access (called permissions) that you may have on a file or directory. These are read, write, and execute permissions.

Having read permission to a file enables you to look at the file's contents. In the case of a directory, read permission lets you list the directory's contents using ls.

Write permission enables you to modify (or delete) the file, even if you are not the owner. In the case of a directory, you must have write permission in order to create, move, or delete files in that directory.

Execute permission enables you to execute the file by typing its name. This has no effect if the contents of the file can't be understood by an application. For example, having execute permission on a file that has statistical data in it won't allow you to run it. On the other hand, if the file is a statistical analysis program, it needs execute permission for it to run. With directories, execute permission enables you to cd into them.

So, we have three types of permissions: read, write, and execute. UNIX separates all users on the system into three categories based on the ownership of the file or directory. There is one set of permissions (read, write, and execute) for the owner, another set (read, write, and execute) for anyone in the group that owns the file, and a third set (read, write, and execute) for everyone else on the system (called other or world). The three sets of permissions are written one after another in a consistent format. The permissions are always in order of read, write, and execute; first for owner, then for group, then for other.

That's nine bits of information to indicate the permissions of the file or directory. These bits always appear in a block of ten and are the first thing you see in a long directory listing. The first character is special and indicates whether the entry is a file or directory (there are a few other valid values, but we won't bother with them now). For a concrete example, let's look at the long directory listing for myfile again:

```
-rw-r--r--   1 fido      users          163 Dec  7 14:31 myfile
```

The first character of the permissions is -, which indicates that it's an ordinary file. If this were a directory, the first character would be d. The next nine characters are broken into three groups of three, giving permissions for owner, group, and other. Each triplet gives read, write, and execute permissions, always in that order. Permission to read is signified by an r in the first position, permission to write is shown by a w in the second position, and permission to execute is shown by an x in the third position. If a particular permission is absent, its space is filled by -.

In the case of myfile, the owner has rw-, which means read and write permissions. This file cannot be executed by typing myfile at the Linux prompt since there is no execute permission. The group permissions are r--, which means that members of the group users can read the file but cannot change it or execute it. Likewise, the permissions for all others are r--, or read-only.

UMASK Settings

When you create a file (such as with redirection), how does Linux know which file permissions to assign? The answer is that a variable called the UMASK (user file creation mask) contains the instructions for every file you create. The system administrator can set the UMASK setting for any user or for the entire set of users on the whole system. You can change your own UMASK setting, but not that of others (unless you are logged in as root).

The value of UMASK can be shown at any time by typing the command umask (lowercase to distinguish it from the environment variable UMASK) at the shell prompt:

```
$ umask
022
```

You may have four numbers instead of three, but the first one doesn't mean anything so simply ignore it. What do the numbers mean? They are a set of octal numbers which indicate the user, group, and other permissions. The valid set of numbers in the umask command are shown in Table 9.1.

TABLE 9.1. OCTAL VALUES USED BY UMASK AND THEIR MEANINGS.

Octal number	Permissions granted
0	Read and write (and execute for directories)
1	Read and write
2	Read (and execute for directories)
3	Read
4	Write (and execute for directories)
5	Write
6	Execute for directories only
7	No permissions

In the UMASK setting of 022 shown earlier, the simple translation, according to this table, is that the user has read and write permissions (and execute for directories), while group and other have read-only (and execute for directories). This corresponds to the following directory block:

rw-r--r--

The column regarding execute for directories shows that if you were to create a directory with this UMASK setting, the permissions would include execute (which allows cd to be used to change that directory). The permission block for a directory created with this set of umask values would be as follows:

rwxr-xr-x

Note that there is no way to automatically assign execute permission to a file using the file creation mask. This was done intentionally so that you, the system administrator, have to manually set the execute permission on a file.

To change your UMASK setting, specify the three new values you want to use. For example, the setting 077 removes all permissions for group and other:

```
$ umask
0022
$ who > file1
$ ls -l
total 2
-rw-r--r--   1 tparker   group           37 May  9 11:18 file1
$ umask 077
$ who > file2
$ ls -l
total 4
-rw-r--r--   1 tparker   group           37 May  9 11:18 file1
-rw-------   1 tparker   group           37 May  9 11:18 file2
```

Notice that the permissions of file2 have set no access for members of the group or for the other users on the system. Only the owner has access to this file. Your UMASK setting is in effect until you log out.

Changing File Permissions

You will probably be happy with the default permissions on your files for a while. Eventually, though, you will want to change them, either to add execute permission to a program that you own (so you can run it) or to let others have better or more restrictive access. To change file permissions, UNIX uses the chmod (change mode of a file) command.

The syntax of the `chmod` command is

```
chmod <specification> file.
```

There are two ways to write the permission specification. One is by using the numeric coding system for permissions (called *absolute setting*) or by using letters (called *symbolic setting*). The latter is easier to understand, so let's start with that.

Using symbolic setting of permissions, you specify which of the permissions to change from the four possible sets of u (user), g (group), o (other), or a (all). You can use any combination of these as well, in order to change just group and other permissions and leave user alone. This set of letters is followed by a + to add permissions or a - to remove them. This in turn is followed by the permissions to be added or removed from the letter r (read), w (write), or x (execute), or any combination of the three letters.

The general syntax of this approach is

```
chmod [u¦g¦o][+¦-][r¦w¦x] filename Ö
```

There is no space between the three parts of the symbolic permission section of the command, but there must be a space after `chmod` and before the filename. A few examples make this a little clearer. To add execute permissions for the group and others, type

chmod go+r myfile

To remove read and write permission from user, group, and other use one of the following commands:

```
chmod ugo-rw filename
```

```
chmod a-rw filename
```

A few important notes about changing these permissions: Not all systems support a for all. If they don't, you will have to specify ugo, as shown in the preceding example. You can specify as many files as you want on the command line, either by listing them one after another separated by spaces or by using wildcards. Finally, when you change permissions using this method, it doesn't matter whether a permission was on or off when the command started because the `chmod` command overrides those permissions. However, if you don't specify a particular set of permissions (user, group, or other), those permissions are not touched. For example, look at the following commands:

```
$ l
total 4
-rwxrwxrwx   1 tparker   group          37 May  9 11:18 file1
-rw-------   1 tparker   group          37 May  9 11:18 file2
$ chmod go-rw file*
$ l
```

9

FILE AND
DIRECTORY
PERMISSIONS

```
total 4
-rwx--x--x   1 tparker   group        37 May  9 11:18 file1
-rw-------   1 tparker   group        37 May  9 11:18 file2
```

The chmod command changes the permissions of file1 as requested, leaving the user permissions alone. Since file2 didn't have read or write permissions to start with, the command didn't change the permissions at all. The command did run properly, however.

NOTE

Anyone who has permission to read a file can also copy that file. When a file gets copied, the copy is owned by the person doing the copying. He or she can then change ownership and permissions, edit the file, and so on.

WARNING

Don't assume that a no-write permission makes a file safe!

Removing write permission from a file doesn't prevent the file from being deleted. It does prevent it from being accidentally deleted because Linux asks whether you want to override the file permissions. You have to answer y or the file is not deleted.

The other way to change permissions is to use an absolute setting. In this method, you specify exactly which permissions you want the user, group, and other permissions to be. This is done through a set of octal numbers which, perversely, are the opposite of those you saw in the umask command. The values allowed are

0 or ---: no permissions

1 or --x: execute

2 or -w-: write-only

3 or -wx: write and execute

4 or r--: read-only

5 or r-x: read and execute

6 or rw-: read and write

7 or rwx: read, write, and execute

You must specify which of these eight numbers applies for user, group, and other. For example, to set a file to the default permissions of read and write for user, read-only for group and other, use the setting 644. Here are a few examples of using chmod with octal absolute settings:

```
darkstar:~$ ls -l myfile
-rw-r--r--   1 fido     users          114 Dec  7 14:31 myfile
darkstar:~$ chmod 345 myfile
darkstar:~$ ls -l myfile
--wxr--r-x   1 fido     users          114 Dec  7 14:31 myfile
darkstar:~$ chmod 701 myfile
darkstar:~$ ls -l myfile
-rwx-----x   1 root     users          114 Dec  7 14:31 myfile
```

This method of using octal numbers has the advantage of specifying the permissions in an absolute, rather than relative, fashion. Also, it's easier to tell someone "Change permissions on the file to 755," than to say "Change permissions on the file to read-write-execute, read-execute, read-execute."

The primary problem with octal addressing is that it's difficult to learn all the combinations unless you do it often. And, if all you want to do is add a single permission, such as execute for user or write for group, you still have to figure out all the values instead of using simpler symbolic notation.

The method you use with chmod tends to depend on your experience with Linux. As you use the system more, you'll find you start using octal addressing more often but still revert to symbolic every now and then for simple changes.

Changing Directory Permissions

You change directory permissions with chmod exactly the same way you do with files. Linux treats directories exactly the same as files, so the approach makes sense. Remember that if a directory doesn't have execute permissions, you can't cd to it, so giving or removing execute permission on a directory can have important implications for users.

WARNING

Any user who has write permission in a directory can delete files in that directory, whether or not that user owns or has write privileges to those files.

Most directories, therefore, have permissions set to drwxr-xr-x. This ensures that only the directory's owner can create or delete files in that directory.

It is especially dangerous to give write permission to all users for directories!

You can change directory permissions with octal or symbolic modes, as the following examples show:

```
$ mkdir bigdir
$ ls -l
total 2
drwxr-xr-x   2 tparker   group          512 May   9 12:10 bigdir
$ chmod go+w bigdir
$ ls -l
total 2
drwxrwxrwx   2 tparker   group          512 May   9 12:10 bigdir
$ chmod 755 bigdir
$ ls -l
total 2
drwxr-xr-x   2 tparker   group          512 May   9 12:10 bigdir
```

Use whichever method you find the most convenient.

TIP

If you're familiar with the binary system, think of rwx as a three-digit binary number to make calculating absolute addressing values easier. If permission is allowed, the corresponding digit is 1. If permission is denied, the digit is 0. So r-x would be the binary number 101, which is 4+0+1, or 5. --x would be 001, which is 0+0+1, which is 1, and so on.

Summary

You should now be more comfortable changing file and directory permissions, as well as the owner and group. As we mentioned at the start of this chapter, this is the subject that confuses most Linux users; we hope that by going slowly you've grasped the ideas behind these commands. You can now move on to the next few chapters, which talk about shells and shell utilities in more detail. For more information, see the following chapters:

The Bourne Again Shell, your default interface to Linux, is discussed in Chapter 11, "bash."

The built-in shell programming commands for extending the power of your interface are examined in Chapter 14, "Shell Programming."

Text editors to create a file is described in Chapter 16, "Text Editors: vi and emacs."

The X interface is discussed in Chapter 22, "Installing and Configuring XFree86."

GNU Project Utilities

by Peter MacKinnon

IN THIS CHAPTER

The GNU project, administered by the Free Software Foundation (FSF), seeks to provide software (in the form of source code) that is freely available to anyone who wants to use it. The project has a lengthy manifesto that explains the motivation behind this libertarian undertaking (for which we should all be thankful, since GNU has some of the best software around!). One of the key ideas within this manifesto is that high-quality software is an intrinsic human right, just as is the air that we breathe. Although GNU software is freely distributed, it is not public domain and is protected by the GNU General Public License. The main purpose behind the license is to keep GNU software free.

For more information on the FSF, you can write to them at

Free Software Foundation
675 Massachusetts Avenue
Cambridge, MA 02139

You can also request copies of the *GNU Bulletin* by sending e-mail to `gnu@prep.ai.mit.edu`.

The distribution of Linux on this book's CD-ROM comes with virtually all of the GNU programs that are currently available. They are archived using the `tar` program and compressed using the GNU `gzip` utility. `gzip` tends to compress better than the standard UNIX compression utility, `compress`. Files compressed with `gzip` end with a `.gz` suffix, whereas `compress` files end in `.Z`. However, `gzip` can uncompress `compress` files as well as its own.

Each of these compressed files has a version number included in its filename so that you can determine which version is most current. After you decompress and un-`tar` the GNU file, the program can be compiled and installed on your system. Most of the files come with their own makefile. Most of the programs are refinements of standard Linux utilities, such as `make` and `bc`.

GNU Software Currently Available

So much software is developed by or made available through the Free Software Foundation that each program cannot be described in detail. The following sections have brief descriptions of the GNU utilities and programs that are included with this distribution of Linux. They are summaries based on the descriptions of the programs as supplied by GNU.

acm

acm is a multiplayer aerial combat game designed for the X window system that can be played in a LAN environment. Players engage in simulated air-to-air combat against one another using missiles and cannons.

Autoconf

Autoconf generates shell scripts that can automatically configure source code packages (such as those for GNU). Autoconf creates a script for a software package from a file that lists the operating system features that the package can utilize. Autoconf requires GNU m4 to generate the required macro calls for its operation.

bash

The shell called bash is an enhancement of the Bourne shell (thus the name, which stands for Bourne Again Shell). It offers many of the extensions found in csh and ksh. The bash shell also has job control, csh-style command history, and command-line editing with Emacs and vi modes built in. See Chapter 11, "bash."

bc

bc is an algebraic language that can be used interactively from a shell command line or with input files. GNU bc has a C-like syntax with several extensions, including multi-character variable names, an else statement, and full Boolean expressions. Unlike standard bc, GNU bc does not require the separate dc program, which is another GNU calculator utility.

BFD

The *Binary File Descriptor* (BFD) library allows a program that operates on object files (such as ld or gdb) to support many different formats efficiently. BFD provides a portable interface, so that only BFD needs to know the details of a particular format. One result is that all programs using BFD support formats such as a.out (default C executable) and COFF.

Binutils

Binutils includes a collection of development programs, including ar, c++filt, demangle, gprof, ld, nlmconv, objcopy, objdump, ranlib, size, strings, and strip.

`Binutils` Version 2 is completely rewritten to use the BFD library. The GNU linker `ld` emits source-line numbered error messages for multiply defined symbols and undefined references. `nlmconv` converts object files into Novell NetWare Loadable Modules (NLM). The `objdump` program can display data such as symbols from any file format understood by BFD.

Bison

`Bison` is an upwardly compatible replacement for the parser generator `yacc`. `Bison` takes a description of tokens in the form of a grammar and generates a parser in the form of a C program.

GNU C Compiler

Version 2 of the GNU C Compiler (`gcc`) supports three languages: C, C++, and Objective-C. The language selected depends on the source file suffix or a compiler option. The runtime support required by Objective-C programs is now distributed with `gcc`. The GNU C Compiler is a portable optimizing compiler that supports full ANSI C, traditional C, and GNU C extensions. GNU C has been extended to support features such as nested functions and nonlocal `goto` statements. Also, `gcc` can generate object files and debugging information in a variety of formats. See Chapter 27, "Programming in C," for more detailed information about C language support.

GNU C Library

The GNU C library supports ANSI C and adds some extensions of its own. For example, the GNU `stdio` library lets you define new kinds of streams and your own `printf` formats.

GNU C++ Library

The GNU C++ library (`libg++`) is an extensive collection of C++ classes, a new `iostream` library for input/output routines, and support tools for use with `g++`. Among the classes supported are multiple-precision integers and rational numbers, complex numbers, and arbitrary-length strings. Prototype files also exist for generating common container classes.

Calc

Calc is a desk calculator and mathematical tool that is used within GNU Emacs. Calc can be used as a basic calculator, but it provides additional features including choice of algebraic or Reverse Polish Notation (RPN), logarithmic functions, trigonometric and financial functions, complex numbers, vectors, matrices, dates, times, infinities, sets, algebraic simplification, differentiation, and integration.

GNU Chess

GNU Chess pits you against the computer in a full game of chess. It has regular-terminal, curses (a full-screen interface library for C), and X-terminal interfaces. GNU Chess implements many specialized features, including sophisticated heuristics that will challenge your best Bobby Fischer moves.

CLISP

CLISP is an implementation of Common Lisp, the list-processing language that is widely used in artificial-intelligence applications. CLISP includes an interpreter and a byte compiler and has user interfaces in English and German that can be chosen at compile time.

GNU Common Lisp

GNU Common Lisp (gcl) has a compiler and interpreter for Common Lisp. It is highly portable, extremely efficient, and has a source-level Lisp debugger for interpreted code. gcl also has profiling tools and an Xlib interface.

cpio

cpio is a program that copies file archives to and from tape or disk. It can also be used to copy files into a larger archive file or to other directories.

CVS

The Concurrent Version System (CVS) manages software revision and release control in a multideveloper, multidirectory, multigroup environment. It works in conjunction with RCS, another source code control program.

dc

dc is an RPN calculator that can be used interactively or with input files.

DejaGnu

DejaGnu is a framework for writing scripts to test any program. It includes the embeddable scripting language Tcl and its derivative expect, which runs scripts that can simulate user input.

Diffutils

The Diffutils package contains the file-comparison programs diff, diff3, sdiff, and cmp. GNU diff compares files showing line-by-line changes in several formats and is more efficient than its traditional version.

ecc

ecc is an error-correction checking program that uses the Reed-Solomon algorithm. It can correct a total of three byte errors in a block of 255 bytes and can detect more severe errors.

ed

ed is the standard line-based text editor.

Elib

This is a small library of Emacs Lisp functions, including routines for using doubly linked lists.

GNU Emacs

GNU Emacs is the second implementation of this highly popular editor developed by Richard Stallman. It integrates Lisp for writing extensions and provides an interface to X. In addition to its own powerful command set, Emacs has extensions that emulate other popular editors such as vi and EDT (DEC's VMS editor). For more information on Emacs, refer to Chapter 16, "Text Editors: vi and emacs."

GNU Emacs 19

Emacs 19 is a richer version of the Emacs editor with extensive support for the X window system. It includes an interface to the X resource manager, has X toolkit support, has good RCS support, and includes many updated libraries. Emacs 19 from the FSF works equally well on character-based terminals as it does under X.

es

es is a shell based on rc that has an exception system and supports functions that return values other than just numbers. It works well interactively or in scripts, particularly because its quoting rules are simpler than the C and Bourne shells.

Fileutils

Fileutils is a GNU collection of standard (and not-so-standard) Linux file utilities, including chgrp, chmod, chown, cp, dd, df, dir, du, install, ln, ls, mkdir, mkfifo, mknod, mv, mvdir, rm, rmdir, touch, and vdir.

find

find is a program that can be used both interactively and in shell scripts to find files given certain criteria and then execute operations (such as rm) on them. This program includes xargs, which applies a command to a list of files.

finger

finger displays information about one or more Linux users. GNU finger supports a single host that can act as the finger server host in sites that have multiple hosts. This host collects information about who is logged into other hosts at that site. Thus, a query to any machine at another site returns complete information about any user at that site. Here's some sample output from a finger command:

```
# finger tparker@tpci.com
Login: tparker                        Name: Tim Parker
Directory: /usr/tparker               Shell: /bin/sh
On since Sat Jun  6 11:33 on tty02, idle 51 days 21:22 (messages off)
On since Sun Jun  7 15:42 on ttyp0, idle 0:02
On since Sat Jun  6 11:33 on ttyp1, idle 21 days 10:01
Mail last read Tue Jun 16 18:38:48 1998
```

10

GNU PROJECT
UTILITIES

As you can see, this version of `finger` (output differs a little depending on the operating system and version) shows the /etc/passwd details (login, comment line, home directory, and shell) as well as some session information.

flex

`flex` is a replacement for the `lex` scanner generator. The `flex` program generates more efficient scanners than does `lex`. The `flex` program also has the advantage that it generates C code. Scanners are used to identify tokens from input.

Fontutils

The `Fontutils` create fonts for use with `Ghostscript` or `TeX`. They also contain general conversion programs and other utilities. Some of the programs in `Fontutils` include `bpltobzr`, `bzrto`, `charspace`, `fontconvert`, `gsrenderfont`, `imageto`, `imgrotate`, `limn`, and `xbfe`.

gas

`gas` is the GNU assembler that converts assembly code into object files. Native assembly works for many systems, including Linux.

gawk

`gawk` is upwardly compatible with the `awk` program, which uses pattern-matching to modify files. It also provides several useful extensions not found in other `awk` implementations (`awk`, `nawk`), such as functions to convert the case of a matched string. For more detailed information, see Chapter 25, "gawk."

gdb

`gdb` is a debugger with a command-line user interface. Object files and symbol tables are read using the BFD library, which allows a single copy of `gdb` to debug programs of multiple-object file formats. Other new features include command-language improvements, remote debugging over serial lines or TCP/IP, and *watchpoints* (breakpoints triggered when the value of an expression changes). An X version of `gdb` called `xxgdb` also is available.

gdbm

The `gdbm` library is the GNU replacement for the traditional `dbm` and `ndbm` database libraries. It implements a database using lookup by hash tables.

Ghostscript

Ghostscript is GNU's PostScript-compatible graphics language. It accepts commands in PostScript and executes them by writing directly to a printer, drawing in an X window, or writing to a file that you can print later (or to a bitmap file that you can edit with other graphics programs).

Ghostscript includes a graphics library that can be called from C. This allows client programs to use Ghostscript's features without having to know the PostScript language. For more information, consult Chapter 24, "Ghostscript."

Ghostview

Ghostview is used as an X-based previewer for multipage files that are interpreted by Ghostscript.

gmp

GNU mp (gmp) is an extensive library for arbitrary precision arithmetic on signed integers and rational numbers.

GNats

GNU's A Tracking System is a problem-reporting system. It uses the model of a central site or organization that receives problem reports and administers their resolution by electronic mail. Although it is used primarily as a software bug-tracking system, it could also be used for handling system-administration issues, project management, and a variety of other applications.

GNU Graphics

GNU Graphics is a set of programs that produces plots from ASCII or binary data. It supports output to PostScript and the X window system, has shell scripts examples using graph and plot, and features a statistics toolkit.

GNU Shogi

Shogi is a Japanese game similar to chess, with the exception that captured pieces can be returned to play. GNU Shogi is based on the implementation of GNU Chess; it implements the same features and uses similar heuristics. As a new feature, sequences of partial board patterns can be introduced in order to help the program play a good order of moves toward specific opening patterns. There are both character- and X-display interfaces.

gnuplot

gnuplot is an interactive program for plotting mathematical expressions and data. It handles both curves (two-dimensional) and surfaces (three-dimensional).

GnuGo

GnuGo plays the game of Go (also known as Wei-Chi).

gperf

gperf is a utility to generate "perfect" hash tables. There are implementations of gperf for C and C++ that generate hash functions for both languages.

grep

This package contains GNU grep, egrep, and fgrep. These utilities, which search files for regular expressions, execute much faster than do their traditional counterparts.

Groff

Groff is a document-formatting system that includes drivers for PostScript, TeX dvi format, as well as implementations of eqn, nroff, pic, refer, tbl, troff, and the man, ms, and mm macros. Written in C++, these programs can be compiled with GNU C++ Version 2.5 or later.

gzip

gzip can expand LZW-compressed files, but uses a different algorithm for compression that generally produces better results than the traditional compress program. It also uncompresses files compressed with the pack program.

hp2xx

GNU hp2xx reads HPGL files, decomposes all drawing commands into elementary vectors, and converts them into a variety of vector (including encapsulated PostScript, Metafont, various special TeX-related formats, and simplified HPGL) and raster output formats (including PBM, PCX, and HP-PCL).

indent

GNU `indent` formats C source code according to the GNU coding standards but, optionally, can also use the BSD default, K&R, and other formats. It is also possible to define your own format. `indent` can handle C++ comments.

Ispell

`Ispell` is an interactive spell checker that suggests other words with similar spelling as replacements for unrecognized words. `Ispell` can use system and personal dictionaries, and standalone and GNU `Emacs` interfaces are also available.

m4

GNU `m4` is an implementation of the traditional macroprocessor for C. It has some extensions for handling more than nine positional parameters to macros, including files, running shell commands, and performing arithmetic.

make

GNU `make` adds extensions to the traditional program that is used to manage dependencies between related files. GNU extensions include long options, parallel compilation, flexible implicit pattern rules, conditional execution, and powerful-text manipulation functions. Recent versions have improved error reporting and added support for the popular += syntax to append more text to a variable's definition. For further information about `make`, please see Chapter 56, "Source Code Control."

mtools

`mtools` is a set of public-domain programs that allow Linux systems to read, write, and manipulate files on an MS-DOS file system (usually a disk).

MULE

`MULE` is a MULtilingual Enhancement to GNU `Emacs` 18. It can handle many character sets at once, including Japanese, Chinese, Korean, Vietnamese, Thai, Greek, the ISO Latin-1 through Latin-5 character sets, Ukrainian, Russian, and other Cyrillic alphabets. A text buffer in `MULE` can contain a mixture of characters from these languages. To input any of these characters, you can use various input methods provided by `MULE` itself.

NetFax

`NetFax` is a freely available fax-spooling system that provides Group 3 fax transmission and reception services for a networked Linux system. It requires a fax modem that accepts Class 2 fax commands.

NetHack

NetHack is a display-oriented adventure game that supports both ASCII and X displays.

NIH Class Library

The NIH Class Library is a portable collection of C++ classes, similar to those in Smalltalk-80, that has been developed by Keith Gorlen of the National Institutes of Health (NIH) using the C++ programming language.

nvi

nvi is a free implementation of the vi text editor. It has enhancements over vi including split screens with multiple buffers, the capability to handle eight-bit data, infinite file and line lengths, tag stacks, infinite undo, and extended regular expressions.

Octave

Octave is a high-level language that is primarily intended for numerical computations. It provides a convenient command-line interface for solving linear and nonlinear problems numerically.

Octave does arithmetic for real and complex scalars and matrices, solves sets of nonlinear algebraic equations, integrates functions over finite and infinite intervals, and integrates systems of ordinary differential and differential-algebraic equations.

Oleo

Oleo is a spreadsheet program that supports X displays and character-based terminals. It can output encapsulated PostScript renditions of spreadsheets and uses Emacs-like configurable keybindings. Under X and in PostScript output, Oleo supports variable-width fonts.

p2c

p2c traslates from Pascal code to C. It recognizes many Pascal variants including Turbo, HP, VAX, and ISO, and produces entirely usable C source code. If you are using an older machine with some legacy applications, p2c can be a very handy application because it saves you from having to recode all your old Pascal applications from scratch.

patch

patch is a program that takes the output from diff and applies the resulting differences to the original file in order to generate the modified version. It would be useful for developing a source code control system, if one were so inclined.

PCL

PCL is a free implementation of a large subset of CLOS, the Common Lisp Object System. It runs under CLISP, mentioned earlier.

perl

perl is a programming language developed by Larry Wall that combines the features and capabilities of sed, awk, shell programming, and C, as well as interfaces to system calls and many C library routines. It has become wildly popular for sophisticated applications that are not dependent on complex data structures. A "perl" mode for editing perl code comes with GNU Emacs 19.

ptx

GNU ptx is the GNU version of the traditional permuted index generator. It can handle multiple input files at once, produce TeX-compatible output, and produce readable KWIC (KeyWords In Context) indexes without needing to use the nroff program.

rc

rc is a shell that features C-like syntax (even more so than csh) and better quoting rules than the C and Bourne shells. It can be used interactively or in scripts.

RCS

The Revision Control System (RCS) is used for version control and management of software projects. When used with GNU diff, RCS can handle binary files such as executables and object files. For more information on RCS, please see Chapter 56.

recode

GNU `recode` converts files between character sets and usages. When exact transformations are not possible, it may get rid of any offending characters or revert to approximations. This program recognizes or produces nearly 150 different character sets and is able to transform files between almost any pair.

regex

`regex` is the GNU regular expression library whose routines have been used within many GNU programs. Now it is finally available by itself. A faster version of this library comes with the `sed` editor.

Scheme

`Scheme` is a language that is related to LISP. The chief difference is that `Scheme` can pass functions as arguments to another function, it can return a function as the result of a function call, and functions can be the value of an expression without being defined under a particular name.

screen

`screen` is a terminal multiplexer that runs several separate "screens" (ttys) on a single physical character-based terminal. Each virtual terminal emulates a DEC VT100 plus additional functions. `screen` sessions can be idled and resumed later on a different terminal type.

sed

`sed` is a noninteractive, stream-oriented version of `ed`. It is used frequently in shell scripts and is extremely useful for applying repetitive edits to a collection of files or to create conversion programs. GNU `sed` comes with the `rx` library, which is a faster version of `regex`.

Shellutils

`Shellutils` can be used interactively or in shell scripts and includes the following programs: `basename`, `date`, `dirname`, `echo`, `env`, `expr`, `false`, `groups`, `id`, `nice`, `nohup`, `printenv`, `printf`, `sleep`, `stty`, `su`, `tee`, `test`, `true`, `tty`, `uname`, `who`, `whoami`, and `yes`.

Smalltalk

GNU Smalltalk is an interpreted object-oriented programming language system written in C. Smalltalk itself has become extremely popular among programmers recently and tends to be regarded as a "pure" object-oriented implementation language.

The features of GNU Smalltalk include a binary image save capability, the ability to invoke user-written C code and pass parameters to it, a GNU Emacs editing mode, a version of the X protocol that can be called from within Smalltalk, and automatically loaded per-user initialization files. It implements all of the classes and protocol in Smalltalk-80, except for the graphic user interface (GUI) related classes.

Superopt

Superopt is a function sequence generator that uses a repetitive generate-and-test approach to find the shortest instruction sequence for a given function. The interface is simple: You provide the GNU superoptimizer, gso, a function, a CPU to generate code for, and how many instructions you can accept.

tar

GNU tar is a file-archiving program that includes multivolume support, automatic archive compression/decompression, remote archives, and special features that allow tar to be used for incremental and full backups.

Termcap Library

The GNU Termcap library is a replacement for the libtermcap.a library. It does not place an arbitrary limit on the size of Termcap entries, unlike most other Termcap libraries.

TeX

TeX is a document-formatting system that handles complicated typesetting, including mathematics. It is GNU's standard text formatter. For more information on TeX, please refer to Chapter 19, "TeX and LaTeX."

Texinfo

Texinfo is a set of utilities that generate both printed manuals and online hypertext-style documentation (called "Info"). Programs also exist for reading online Info documents. Version 3 has both GNU Emacs Lisp and standalone programs written in C or shell

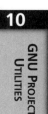

script. The `texinfo` mode for GNU `Emacs` enables easy editing and updating of `Texinfo` files. Programs provided include `makeinfo`, `info`, `texi2dvi`, `texindex`, `tex2patch`, and `fixfonts`.

Textutils

The `Textutils` programs manipulate textual data and include the following traditional programs: `cat`, `cksum`, `comm`, `csplit`, `cut`, `expand`, `fold`, `head`, `join`, `nl`, `od`, `paste`, `pr`, `sort`, `split`, `sum`, `tac`, `tail`, `tr`, `unexpand`, `uniq`, and `wc`.

Tile Forth

`Tile Forth` is a 32-bit implementation of the `Forth-83` standard written in C. Traditionally, Forth implementations are written in assembler to use the underlying hardware as optimally as possible, but this also makes them less portable.

time

`time` is used to report statistics (usually from a shell) about the amount of user, system, and real time used by a process.

tput

`tput` is a portable way for shell scripts to use special terminal capabilities. GNU `tput` uses the `Termcap` database, instead of `Terminfo` as many others do.

UUCP

This version of `UUCP` (UNIX-to-UNIX copy) supports the `f`, `g`, `v` (in all window and packet sizes), `G`, `t`, `e`, Zmodem, and two new bi-directional (`i` and `j`) protocols. If you have a Berkeley sockets library, it can make TCP connections. If you have TLI libraries, it can make TLI connections.

uuencode/uudecode

`uuencode` and `uudecode` are used to transmit binary files over transmission media that support only simple ASCII data. The most common use for these two utilities is on Usenet newsgroups.

wdiff

`wdiff` is another interface to the GNU `diff` program. It compares two files, finding which words have been deleted or added to the first in order to create the second. It has many output formats and interacts well with terminals and programs such as more. wdiff is especially useful when two texts differ only by a few words and paragraphs have been refilled.

Summary

The GNU project provides UNIX-like software freely to everyone, with the provision that it remain free if distributed to others. GNU software can be compiled for many different types of systems, including Linux. Many GNU utilities are improvements of existing Linux counterparts and include new implementations of shells, the C compiler, and a code debugger. Other types of GNU software include games, text editors, calculators, and communication utilities. Each utility can be separately uncompressed, untarred, and compiled itself.

From here, you can read about related subjects:

Using text editors such as vi and Emacs to write your own documents is covered in Chapter 16, "Text Editors: vi and emacs."

Printing your documents out on an attached printer is covered in Chapter 20, "Printing."

Programming with the awk language, useful for managing files and matching patterns is covered in Chapter 25, "gawk."

10

GNU PROJECT
UTILITIES

bash

by Rick McMullin and Tim Parker

IN THIS CHAPTER

CHAPTER 11

This chapter and the two that follow look at the shells available to you under Linux in a little more detail. Most Linux systems come with several shells, including bash, pdksh, and tcsh. We'll start with bash (Bourne Again Shell) because it's the default shell used by Linux and the most popular shell for new users. We'll also look at the most commonly used bash commands and the environment variables bash uses. By the end of this chapter, you should be able to work faster and more efficiently with bash.

Shells in a Nutshell

What is a shell, anyway? It seems to be a word used all the time in Linux, but the exact meaning is vague for many new users (and some veterans). This section explains what a shell program is and why it is so important when using Linux.

What Is a Shell?

The shell is a program used to interface between you (the user) and Linux (or, more accurately, between you and the Linux kernel). Figure 11.1 illustrates the relationship between the user, the shell, and the Linux kernel. Every command you type at a prompt on your screen is interpreted by the shell, then passed to the Linux kernel.

FIGURE 11.1.

The relationship between the user and the shell.

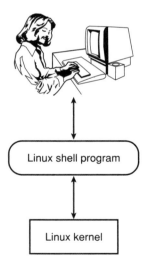

Linux shell program

Linux kernel

> **NOTE**
>
> If you are familiar with MS-DOS, you will recognize this relationship as almost identical to the relationship between a DOS user and the COMMAND.COM program. The only real difference is that in the DOS world, no distinction is made between the COMMAND.COM program and DOS (or to be more accurate, the DOS kernel).

The shell is a command-language interpreter. It has its own set of built-in shell commands. The shell can also make use of all of the Linux utilities and application programs that are available on the system.

Whenever you enter a command it is interpreted by the Linux shell. For example, in earlier chapters when you were introduced to the Linux file- and directory-manipulation commands, all of the sample commands entered at the command prompt were interpreted by whichever Linux shell you were using.

Some of the commands, such as the print working directory (pwd) command, are built into the Linux bash shell. Other commands, such as the copy command (cp) and the remove command (rm), are separate executable programs that exist in one of the directories in the file system. As the user, you don't know (or probably care) if the command is built in to the shell or is a separate program. Figure 11.2 shows how the shell performs this command interpretation.

FIGURE 11.2.

Command interpretation by the shell.

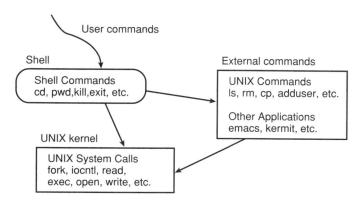

Figure 11.2 illustrates the steps that the shell takes to figure out what to do with user commands. It first checks to see whether the command is one of its own built-in commands (such as cd or pwd). If the command is not one of these built-in items, the shell checks to see if it is an application program. *Application programs* can be utility programs that are part of Linux, such as ls and rm, or they can be application programs that are either purchased commercially, such as xv, or are available as public domain software, such as ghostview.

The shell tries to find these application programs by looking in all of the directories that are in your search path. As we mentioned in an earlier chapter, the *path* is a list of directories where executable programs can be found. If the command that is entered is not an internal shell command and is not an executable file in your path, an error message is displayed similar to this one:

```
$ doit
doit: not found
```

As the last step in running a successful command, the shell's internal commands and all of the application programs are eventually broken down into system calls and passed to the Linux kernel.

Another important aspect of the shell is that it contains a very powerful interpretive programming language. This language is similar in function to the MS-DOS interpreted language, but is much more flexible. The shell programming language supports most of the programming constructs found in high-level languages, such as looping, functions, variables, and arrays.

How the Shell Gets Started

Earlier in this chapter you learned that the shell is the main method through which a user interacts with the Linux kernel. But how does this program get initialized to do so? The shell is started after you successfully log in to the system, and it continues to be the main method of interaction between the user and the kernel until you log out.

Each user on your system has a default shell. The *default shell* for each user is specified in the system password file, called /etc/passwd. The *system password file* contains, among other things, each person's user ID, an encrypted copy of each user's password, and the name of the program to run immediately after a user logs in to the system. The program specified in the password file does not have to be one of the Linux shells, but it almost always is.

The Most Common Shells

Several different kinds of shells are available on Linux and UNIX systems. The most common are the Bourne shell (called sh), the C shell (csh), and the Korn shell (ksh). Each of these three shells has its own advantages and disadvantages.

The *Bourne shell* was written by Steven Bourne. It is the original UNIX shell and is available on every UNIX system in existence. The Bourne shell is considered to be very good for UNIX shell programming, but it does not handle user interaction as well as some of the other shells available.

The *C shell*, written by Bill Joy, is much more responsive to user interaction. It supports features, such as command-line completion, that are not in the Bourne shell. The C shell's programming interface is thought by many not to be as good as that of the Bourne shell but is used by many C programmers because the syntax of its programming language is similar to that of the C language. This is also why it is named the C shell.

The *Korn shell* (ksh) was written by Dave Korn. He took the best features of both the C shell and the Bourne shell and combined them into one that is completely compatible with the Bourne shell. ksh is efficient and has both a good interactive interface and a good programming interface.

> **NOTE**
>
> There are many quality reference books about the Bourne, C, and Korn shells. If you want to use these shells instead of the three shells discussed in this and the next two chapters, you might want to find a good reference book on the particular shell you prefer. Because the shells included with Linux are the ones used by most people, we will concentrate on those.

In addition to these shells, many other shell programs took the basic features from one or more of the existing shells and combined them into a new version. The three newer shells that are discussed in this book are tcsh (an extension of csh), the Bourne Again Shell (bash, an extension of sh), and the Public Domain Korn Shell (pdksh, an extension of ksh). bash is the default shell on most Linux systems.

The Bourne Again Shell

The Bourne Again Shell (bash), as its name implies, is an extension of the Bourne shell. bash is fully backward-compatible with the Bourne shell, but contains many enhancements and extra features that are not present in the Bourne shell. bash also contains many of the best features that exist in the C and Korn shells. bash has a very flexible and powerful programming interface, as well as a user-friendly command interface.

Why use bash instead of sh (the original Bourne shell)? The biggest drawback of the Bourne shell is the way that it handles user input. Typing commands into the Bourne shell can often be very tedious, especially if you are using it on a regular basis and typing in a large number of commands. bash provides several features that make entering commands much easier.

Command-line Completion

Often when you enter commands into bash (or any other shell), the complete text of the command is not necessary in order for the shell to be able to determine what you want it to do. For example, assume that the current working directory contains the following files and subdirectories:

```
News/  bin/   games/     mail/  samplefile  test/
```

If you want to change directories from the current working directory to the test subdirectory, enter the command

```
cd test
```

Although this command works just fine, bash enables you to accomplish the same thing in a slightly different (and faster) way. Since test is the only file in the directory that begins with the letter *t*, bash should be able to figure out what you want to do after you simply type **t**:

```
cd t
```

After the letter is typed, the only thing that you could be referring to is the test subdirectory. To get bash to finish the command for you, press the Tab key:

```
cd t<tab>
```

When you do this, bash finishes the command and displays it on the screen. The command doesn't actually execute until you press the Enter key, which verifies that the command bash comes up with is the command that you really intend.

For short commands like this, you might not see very much value in making use of command-line completion. Using this feature may at first slow you down when typing short commands. After you get used to using command-line completion, though, and when the commands you enter get a little longer, you will wonder how anyone lived without this feature.

So what happens if more than one file in the directory begins with the letter *t*? It would seem that this would cause a problem if you wanted to use command-line completion. Let's see what happens when you have the following directory contents:

```
News/  bin/   mail/       samplefile  test/  tools/ working/
```

Now you have *two* files in the directory that start with the letter t. Assuming that you still want to cd into the test subdirectory, how do you do that using command-line completion? If you type **cd t<tab>** as you did before, bash does not know which subdirectory you want to change to because the information you have given is not unique.

bash then beeps to notify you that it does not have enough information to complete the command. After beeping, bash leaves the command on the screen as it was entered. This enables you to enter more information without retyping what was already typed. In this case, you only need to enter an **e** and press the Tab key again. This gives bash enough information to complete the command on the command line for you to verify:

```
cd test
```

If instead you decide that you want to cd into the tools subdirectory, you can type:

```
cd to<tab>
```

This gives bash enough information to complete the command.

Whenever you press the Tab key while typing a command, bash tries to complete the command for you. If it can't complete the command, it fills in as much as it can and then beeps, notifying you that it needs more information. You can then enter more characters and press the Tab key again, repeating this process until bash displays the desired command.

Wildcards

Another way that bash makes typing commands easier is by enabling users to use wildcards in their commands. The bash shell supports three kinds of wildcards:

> * matches any character and any number of characters.
>
> ? matches any single character.
>
> [...] matches any single character contained within the brackets.

The * wildcard can be used in a manner similar to command-line completion. For example, assume the current directory contains the following files:

```
News/  bin/   games/      mail/  samplefile  test/
```

If you want to cd into the `test` directory, you can type `cd test` or use command-line completion:

```
cd t<tab>
```

This causes `bash` to complete the command for you. Now, there's a third way to do the same thing. Because only one file begins with the letter *t*, you can also change to the directory by using the * wildcard. To do that enter the following command:

```
cd t*
```

The * matches any character and any number of characters, so the shell replaces the `t*` with `test` (the only file in the directory that matches the wildcard pattern).

This only works reliably if there is one file in the directory that begins with the letter *t*. If more than one file in the directory begins with the letter *t*, the shell tries to replace `t*` with the list of filenames in the directory that match the wildcard pattern. The `cd` command `cd`s into the first directory in this list, which is listed alphabetically, and may or may not be the intended file.

A more practical situation in which to use the * wildcard is when you want to execute the same command on multiple files that have similar filenames. For example, assume the current directory contains the following files:

```
ch1.doc    ch2.doc    ch3.doc        chimp  config    mail/  test/
tools/
```

If you want to print all of the files that have a `.doc` extension, you can easily do so by entering the following command:

```
lpr *.doc
```

In this case, `bash` replaces `*.doc` with the names of all of the files in the directory that match that wildcard pattern. After `bash` performs this substitution, the command that is processed is:

```
lpr ch1.doc ch2.doc ch3.doc
```

The `lpr` command can be invoked with the arguments of `ch1.doc`, `ch2.doc`, and `ch3.doc`.

> **NOTE**
>
> Given the directory contents used in the previous example, there are several ways to print all of the files that have a .doc extension. Any of the following commands also work:
>
> ```
> lpr *doc
> lpr *oc
> lpr *c
> ```

The ? wildcard functions in an identical way to the * wildcard except that the ? wildcard only matches a single character. Using the same directory contents shown in the previous example, the ? wildcard can be used to print all of the files with the .doc extension by entering the following command:

```
lpr ch?.doc
```

The [. . .] wildcard enables you to specify certain characters or ranges of characters to match. To print all of the files in the example with the .doc extension using the [. . .] wildcard, enter one of the following two commands:

```
lpr ch[123].doc
```

Using a command to specify a range of characters, enter:

```
lpr ch[1-3].doc
```

Command History

bash also supports command history. This simply means that bash keeps track of a certain number of previous commands that have been entered into the shell. The number of commands is given by a shell variable called HISTSIZE. For more information on HISTSIZE, see the "bash Variables" section later in this chapter.

bash stores the text of the previous commands in a history list. When you log in to your account, the history list is initialized from a history file. The filename of the history file can be set using the HISTFILE bash variable. The default filename for the history file is .bash_history. This file is usually located in your home directory. (Notice that the file begins with a period. This means that the file is hidden and only appears in a directory listing if you use the -a or -A option of the ls command.)

Just storing previous commands into a history file is not all that useful, so bash provides several ways of recalling them. The simplest way of using the history list is with the up- and down-arrow keys, which scroll through the commands that have been previously entered.

Pressing the up-arrow key causes the last command that was entered to appear on the command line. Pressing the up-arrow again puts the command previous to that one on the command line, and so on. If you move up in the command buffer past the command that you want, you can also move down the history list a command at a time by pressing the down-arrow. (This is the same process used by the DOS doskey utility.)

The command displayed on the command line through the history list can be edited, if needed. bash supports a complex set of editing capabilities that are beyond the scope of this book, but there are simple ways of editing the command line for small and easy changes. You can use the left- and right-arrow keys to move along the command line. You can insert text at any point in the command line and delete text by using the Backspace or Delete key. Most users will find these simple editing commands sufficient.

> **NOTE**
>
> The complex set of editing commands that bash offers is similar to the commands used in the emacs and vi text editors.

Another method of using the history file is to display and edit the list using the history and fc (fix command) commands built in to bash. The history command can be invoked using two different methods. The first method uses the command:

```
history [n]
```

When the history command is used with no options, the entire contents of the history list are displayed. The list that is displayed onscreen might resemble the following list:

```
1  mkdir /usr/games/pool
2  cp XpoolTable-1.2.linux.tar.z /usr/games/pool
3  cd /usr/games/pool/
4  ls
5  gunzip XpoolTable-1.2.linux.tar.z
6  tar -xf XpoolTable-1.2.linux.tar
7  ls
8  cd Xpool
```

```
 9   ls
10   xinit
11   exit
12   which zip
13   zip
14   more readme
15   vi readme
16   exit
```

Using the n with the history command causes only the last *n* lines in the history list to be shown. So, for example, history 5 shows only the last five commands.

The second method of using the history command is to modify the contents of the history file or the history list. The command has the following command-line syntax:

```
history [-r¦w¦a¦n] [filename]
```

In this form, the -r option tells the history command to read the contents of the history file and use them as the current history list. The -w option causes the history command to write the current history list to the history file (overwriting what is currently in the file). The -a option appends the current history list to the end of the history file. The -n option causes the lines that are in the history file to be read into the current history list.

All of the options for the second form of the history command can use the filename option as the name of the history file. If no filename is specified, the history command uses the value of the HISTFILE shell variable.

The fc command can be used in two different ways to edit the command history. In the first way, the fc command is entered using the following command-line syntax:

```
fc [-e editor_name] [-n] [-l] [-r] [first] [last]
```

where all options given in braces are optional. The -e *editor name* option is used to specify the text editor to be used for editing the commands. The *first* and *last* options are used to select a range of commands to take out of the history list. *first* and *last* refer either to the number of a command in the history list or to a string that fc will try to find in the history list.

The -n option is used to suppress command numbers when listing the history commands. The -r option lists the matched commands in reverse order. The -l command lists the matched commands to the screen. In all cases—except when the -l command option is used—the matching commands are loaded into a text editor.

> **NOTE**
>
> The text editor used by `fc` is found by taking the value of `editor name` if the `-e editor name` option is used. If this option is not used, `fc` uses the editor specified by the variable `FCEDIT`. If this variable does not exist, `fc` uses the value of the `EDITOR` variable. Finally, if none of these variables exists, the editor that is chosen is `vi`, by default.

Aliases

Another way that `bash` makes life easier for you is by supporting command aliases. *Command aliases* are commands that the user can specify. *Alias commands* are usually abbreviations of other commands, designed to save keystrokes.

For example, if you are entering the following command on a regular basis, you might be inclined to create an alias for it to save yourself some typing:

```
cd /usr/X11/lib/X11/fvwm/sample-configs
```

Instead of typing this command every time you want to go to the `sample-configs` directory, you can create an alias called `goconfig`, which causes the longer command to be executed. To set up an alias like this you must use the `bash alias` command. To create the `goconfig` alias, enter the following command at the `bash` prompt:

```
alias goconfig='cd /usr/X11/lib/X11/fvwm/sample-configs'
```

Now, until you exit from `bash`, the `goconfig` command will cause the original, longer command to be executed as if you had just typed it.

If you decide after you have entered an alias that you do not need it, you can use the `bash unalias` command to delete the alias:

```
unalias goconfig
```

There are a number of useful aliases that most users find helpful. These can be written in a file that executes when you log in to save you from typing them each time. Some aliases that you may want to define are:

- `alias ll='ls -l'`: allows you to get a long directory listing with a two-letter "l" command
- `alias lo='logout'`: gives you a fast way to enter the logout command
- `alias ls='ls -F'`: adds slashes to all directory names to make them easier to see

If you are a DOS user and used to using DOS file commands, you can use the `alias` command to define the following aliases so that Linux behaves like DOS:

- `alias dir='ls'`
- `alias copy='cp'`
- `alias rename='mv'`
- `alias md='mkdir'`
- `alias rd='rmdir'`

> **TIP**
>
> When defining aliases, don't include spaces on either side of the equal sign or the shell can't properly determine what you want to do. Quotation marks are necessary only if the command within them contains spaces or other special characters.

If you enter the `alias` command without any arguments, it displays all of the aliases that are already defined. The following listing illustrates a sample output from the `alias` command:

```
alias dir='ls'
alias ll='ls -l'
alias ls='ls -F'
alias md='mkdir'
alias net='term < /dev/modem > /dev/modem 2> /dev/null&'
alias rd='rmdir'
```

Input Redirection

Input redirection changes the source of input for a command. When a command is entered in bash, the command is expecting some kind of input in order to do its job. Some of the simpler commands must get all of the information they need passed to them on the command line. For example, the rm command requires arguments on the command line. You must tell rm which files are to be deleted on the command line or it issues a prompt telling you to enter rm -h for help.

Other commands require more elaborate input than a simple directory name. The input for these commands can be found in a file. For example, the wc (word count) command counts the number of characters, words, and lines in the input that has been given to it. If you type wc <enter> at the command line, wc will wait for you to tell it what it should be counting and a prompt then appears on the command line asking for more information. Because the prompt is sometimes not easily identifiable, it may not be obvious what is happening. (It may even appear as though bash has died because, although everything you type shows up onscreen, nothing else appears to be happening.)

What is actually occurring is that the wc command is collecting input for itself. If you press Ctrl+D, the results of the wc command are written to the screen. If you enter the wc command with a filename as an argument as shown in the following example, wc returns the number of characters, words, and lines contained in that file:

```
wc test
11 2 1
```

Another way to pass the contents of the test file to wc is to redirect the input of the wc command from the terminal to the test file. This results in the same output. The < symbol is used by bash to mean "redirect the input to the current command from the specified file." So, redirecting wc's input from the terminal to the test file can be done by entering the following command:

```
wc < test
11 2 1
```

Input redirection is not used all that often because most commands that require input from a file have the option to specify a filename on the command line. There are times, however, when you come across a program that does not accept a filename as an input parameter, and yet the input that you want to give exists in a file. Whenever this situation occurs, you can use input redirection to get around the problem.

Output Redirection

Output redirection is more commonly used than input redirection. *Output redirection* enables you to redirect the output from a command into a file, as opposed to having the output displayed onscreen.

There are many situations in which this can be useful. For example, if the output of a command is quite large and does not fit on the screen, you may want to redirect it to a file so that you can view it later using a text editor. There also may be cases where you want to keep the output of a command to show to someone else or to print the results. Finally, output redirection is also useful if you want to use the output from one command as input for another. (There is an easier way to use the output of one command as input to a second command. This is shown in the "Pipes" section.)

Output redirection is done in much the same way as input redirection. Instead of using the < symbol, the > symbol is used.

As an example of output redirection, you can redirect the output of the `ls` command into a file named `directory.out` using the following command:

```
ls > directory.out
```

Pipes

Pipes (often called *pipelines*) are a way to string together a series of commands. This means that the output from the first command in the pipeline is used as the input to the second command in the pipeline. The output from the second command in the pipeline is used as input to the third command in the pipeline, and so on. The output from the last command in the pipeline is the output that actually displays onscreen (or is put into a file if output redirection is specified on the command line).

You can tell `bash` to create a pipeline by typing two or more commands separated by the vertical bar or "pipe" character, ¦. The following example illustrates the use of a pipeline:

```
cat sample.text ¦ grep "High" ¦ wc -l
```

This pipeline takes the output from the `cat` command (which lists the contents of a file) and sends it into the `grep` command. The `grep` command searches for each occurrence of the word "High" in its input. The `grep` command's output then consists of each line in the file that contains the word "High." This output is then sent to the `wc` command. The `wc` command with the `-l` option prints the number of lines contained in its input.

To show the results on a real file, suppose the contents of sample.text appeared as follows:

```
Things to do today:
Low: Go grocery shopping
High: Return movie
High: Clear level 3 in Alien vs. Predator
Medium: Pick up clothes from dry cleaner
```

The pipeline then returns the result 2, indicating that you have two things of importance to complete today:

```
cat sample.text ¦ grep "High" ¦ wc -l
2
```

Prompts

bash has two levels of user prompts. The first level is what you see when bash is waiting for a command to be typed. (This is what you normally see when you are working with bash.)

The default first-level prompt is the % character. If you do not like the % character as the prompt or prefer to customize your prompt, you can do so by setting the value of the PS1 bash variable. For example:

```
PS1="Please enter a command"
```

sets the bash shell prompt to the specified string.

The second level of prompt is displayed when bash is expecting more input from you in order to complete a command. The default for the second-level prompt is >. If you want to change the second-level prompt, you can set the value of the PS2 variable, as in:

```
PS2="I need more information"
```

In addition to displaying static character strings in the command prompts (as in the two preceding examples), you can also use some predefined special characters. These special characters place things such as the current time into the prompt. Table 11.1 lists the most commonly used special character codes.

TABLE 11.1. PROMPT SPECIAL CHARACTER CODES.

Character	Meaning
\!	Displays the history number of this command.
\#	Displays the command number of the current command.
\$	Displays a $ in the prompt unless the user is root. When the user is root, it displays a #.
\\	Displays a backslash.
\d	Displays the current date.
\h	Displays the host name of the computer on which the shell is running.
\n	Prints a newline character. This causes the prompt to span more than one line.
\nnn	Displays the character that corresponds to the octal value of the number nnn.
\s	The name of the shell that is running.
\t	Displays the current time.

Character	Meaning
\u	Displays the username of the current user.
\W	Displays the base name of the current working directory.
\w	Displays the current working directory.

These special characters can be combined into several useful prompts to provide you with information about where you are. (They can be combined in very grotesque ways, too!) Several examples of setting the PS1 prompt follow here:

```
PS1="\t"
```

This causes the prompt to have the following appearance (there is no space after the prompt):

```
02:16:15
```

The prompt string

```
PS1=\t
```

causes the prompt to have the following appearance:

```
t
```

This shows the importance of including the character sequence in quotation marks. The prompt string

```
PS1="\t\\ "
```

causes the prompt to look like this:

```
02:16:30\
```

In this case, there is a space following the prompt because there was a space within the quotation marks.

Job Control

Job control refers to the ability to control the execution behavior of a currently running process. Specifically, you can suspend a running process and cause it to resume running later. bash keeps track of all processes that it starts (as a result of user input) and lets you suspend a running process or restart a suspended one at any time during the life of that process. (For more information on processes, see Chapter 34, "Processes.")

Pressing Ctrl+Z suspends a running process. The bg command restarts a suspended process in the background, whereas the fg command restarts a process in the foreground.

These commands are most often used when a user wants to run a command in the background but accidentally starts it in the foreground. When a command is started in the foreground, it locks the shell from any further user interaction until the command completes execution. This is usually not a problem because most commands take only a few seconds to execute. If the command you are running takes a long time, though, start the command in the background so that you can continue to use bash to enter other commands in the foreground.

For example, if you start the command find / -name "test" > find.out (which scans the entire file system for files named test and stores the results in a file called find.out) in the foreground, your shell may be tied up for many seconds or even minutes, depending on the size of the file system and the number of users on the system. If you issue this command and want to continue executing in the background so you can use the system again, enter the following:

```
control-z
bg
```

This first suspends the find command, then restarts it in the background. The find command continues to execute, and you have bash back again.

Customizing bash

Many ways of customizing bash have already been described in this chapter. Until now, the changes that you made affected only the current bash session. As soon as you quit, all of the customizations will be lost. You can, however, make the customizations more permanent by storing them in a bash initialization file.

You can put any commands that you want to be executed each time bash is started into this initialization file. Commands that are typically found in this file are alias commands and variable initializations.

The bash initialization file is named either .profile or .bash_profile, depending on the version of Linux you are using. For simplicity's sake, we'll assume .profile is used, although you should substitute the name your Linux system uses. Each user who uses bash has a .profile file in his home directory. This file is read by bash each time it starts, and all of the commands contained within it are executed.

Many Linux systems use a default profile file (note the lack of a period before the filename). This file is located in the /etc directory and is read when you start bash. If you want to add your own customizations to bash, you must copy this file into your home directory (if it is not already there) and call it .profile.

NOTE

Some setup programs automatically make a copy of the `.profile` file in your home directory for you when they create your login. However, not all routines do this, so you should check your home directory first. Remember that all files starting with a period are hidden and can only be displayed with the `ls -A` or `ls -a` command.

bash Command Summary

Some of the most useful commands built into the `bash` shell are summarized in Table 11.2.

TABLE 11.2. THE bash COMMANDS WE'VE USED IN THIS CHAPTER.

bash *command*	*What it's used for*
alias	Used to set `bash` aliases (command nicknames that can be defined by the user).
bg	Background command. Forces a suspended process to continue to execute in the background.
cd	Change working directory. This command changes the current working directory to the directory specified as an argument.
exit	Terminates the shell.
export	Causes the value of a variable to be made visible to all subprocesses that belong to the current shell.
fc	Fix command. Used to edit the commands in the current history list.
fg	Foreground command. Forces a suspended process to continue to execute in the foreground.
help	Displays help information for `bash` built-in commands.
history	Brings up a list of the last *n* commands that were entered at the command prompt, where *n* is a configurable variable specifying the number of commands to remember.
Kill	Used to terminate another process.
pwd	Print working directory. Prints the directory in which the user is currently working.
unalias	Used to remove aliases that have been defined using the `alias` command.

bash has many more commands than are listed here, but these are the most frequently used ones. To see the other commands bash offers and for more details of the commands listed, refer to the bash man page (type **man bash**).

bash Variables

There are a lot of variables used by bash. Some of the most useful of these variables, including the variable name and a brief description, are shown in Table 11.3.

TABLE 11.3. THE MOST COMMONLY USED bash VARIABLES.

Variable name	What it's used for
EDITOR, FCEDIT	The default editor for the fc bash command.
HISTFILE	The file used to store the command history.
HISTSIZE	The size of the history list.
HOME	The HOME directory of the current user.
OLDPWD	The previous working directory (the one that was current before the current directory was entered).
PATH	The search path that bash uses when looking for executable files.
PS1	The first-level prompt that is displayed on the command line.
PS2	The second-level prompt that is displayed when a command is expecting more input.
PWD	The current working directory.
SECONDS	The number of seconds that have elapsed since the current bash session was started.

bash has many more variables than are listed here, but the most commonly used ones are shown. To find out the other variables bash offers, call up the man page with the command man bash.

Summary

In this chapter you looked at some of the useful features of the Bourne Again Shell, bash. You have seen how command completion, aliasing, and job control can all combine to make you more productive and efficient when working with bash.

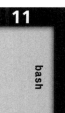

In the next chapter we'll look at another popular Linux shell, the Public Domain Korn Shell (pdksh). It offers many useful features, too, providing you with a choice of shells. If you want to skip ahead to learn about other subjects, feel free:

Learn about shell programming and how you can use it to make your experience with bash more powerful, in Chapter 14, "Shell Programming."

Learn about using editors to create and edit files, in Chapter 16, "Text Editors: vi and emacs."

pdksh

*by Rick McMullin and
Tim Parker*

IN THIS CHAPTER

CHAPTER 12

In the last chapter, you saw the Bourne Again Shell (bash) in some detail. Not everyone wants to use the bash shell, so several other shells are included with most Linux systems. One of them is pdksh, a variation on the Korn shell. We'll also look at how you can customize your copy of pdksh, as well as several of the important commands and variables used by the shell.

The Public Domain Korn Shell (pdksh)

The Korn shell, written by David Korn, was the third mainstream shell written for UNIX (after the Bourne shell and the C shell). Because of this, it incorporates many of the features of the Bourne and C shells together. The Korn shell is not usually distributed with all UNIX versions, so many users don't get to work with it. The Korn shell is important to UNIX users, though, because it builds a lot of the important new features of the C shell into the much older Bourne shell, while remaining completely compatible with sh. Because of the Korn shell's popularity among UNIX users, a version was developed for Linux called the Public Domain Korn Shell, or pdksh.

The current version of the Public Domain Korn Shell does not support all of the features that exist in the commercial version of the Korn shell. It does support most of the main features, however, and adds a few new features of its own.

Command-Line Completion

Often, when you are entering commands at the command line, the complete text of the command is not necessary in order for pdksh to be able to determine what you want to do. Command-line completion enables you to type in a partial command, and then by entering a key sequence, tell pdksh to try to finish the command for you.

pdksh does not default to allow the user to perform command-line completion. You must enter a command to tell pdksh that you want to be able to use command-line completion. In order to enable command-line completion, enter one of the following commands:

```
set -o emacs
set -o vi
```

This causes pdksh to accept command editing that is similar to emacs or vi. Choose the editor that you are most familiar with, and use the basic editor commands for command-line editing.

After the command-line completion function is enabled, you can perform command-line completion by pressing the Esc key twice (when using emacs command-line editing) or by pressing \ (when using vi command-line editing). For example, if your current directory contains the files

```
News/        bin/        games/        mail/        sample.text        test/
```

and you want to edit the file sample.text using the vi text editor, enter the following command:

```
vi sample.text
```

After the "s" is typed, the only file that you can be referring to is sample.text because it is the only file in the current directory that begins with the letter "s". To get pdksh to finish the command when you are using emacs-style command editing, press the Esc key twice after typing **s**:

```
vi s<escape><escape>
```

To get pdksh to finish the command when you are using vi command editing, press the \ key after typing **s**:

```
vi s\
```

Either of these commands causes pdksh to finish the line for you and displays the result on the screen. The command does not execute until you press the Enter key. This is to give you a chance to confirm that the command pdksh displays is the command that you really intend.

If the sample.text file is not the only file in the directory that begins with the letter "s", pdksh completes the command as far as it can and then beeps, indicating that it needs more information to complete the command.

> **NOTE**
>
> The keyboard equivalent of pressing the Esc key is Ctrl+[, usually written as ^[. The caret (^) is the abbreviation for the Ctrl key. Pressing Esc twice using the Ctrl+[sequence would be written as ^[^[. You may see this convention in books or man pages.

Wildcards

The `pdksh` shell makes entering commands easier by enabling the user to use wildcards. `pdksh` supports the same wildcards that `bash` does:

  * matches any character and any number of characters.

  ? matches any single character.

  [...] matches any single character contained within the brackets.

The * wildcard can be used in a way that is similar to command-line completion. For example, if the current directory contains the files

```
News/          bin/          games/          mail/          sample.text          test/
```

and you want to edit the `sample.text` file by using the `vi` text editor, you can perform this task by using the following wildcard:

```
vi s*
```

The * matches any character (and any number of characters), so `pdksh` replaces `s*` with `sample.text` (the only file in the directory that matches the wildcard pattern).

This works reliably if there is only one file in the directory that begins with the letter "s." If more than one file starts with the same letter, the shell tries to replace `s*` with the list of filenames that match the wildcard pattern and runs `vi` on the first file in this list. After you quit editing the first file, the second file in the list is loaded into `vi`, and so on for each file that matches the wildcard pattern. If you intend to edit more than one file, this is fine, but if you only want to edit the `sample.text` file, this command will not work the way you need it to.

A more practical situation in which to use the * wildcard is when you want to execute the same command on multiple files that have similar filenames. For example, assume that the current directory contains the following files:

```
News/          bin/          games/          mail/          sample.text
temp1.out
temp2.out      temp3.out     test/
```

If you want to delete all of the files with an .out extension, you can do it by entering the following command:

```
rm *.out
```

In this case, pdksh replaces *.out with the names of all of the files in the directory that match the wildcard pattern. After pdksh performs this substitution, the following command is processed:

```
rm temp1.out temp2.out temp3.out
```

The rm command is invoked with the arguments of temp1.out, temp2.out, and temp3.out.

The ? wildcard functions in a similar way to the * wildcard, except that the ? wildcard matches only a single character. Assuming the same directory contents as in the previous example, the ? wildcard can be used to delete all of the files with the .out extension by entering the following command:

```
rm temp?.out
```

The [...] wildcard enables you to specify characters or ranges of characters to match. To print all of the files in the previous example that have the .doc extension, enter one of the following two commands:

```
rm temp[123].out
rm temp[1-3].out
```

Command History

The pdksh shell supports a command history in much the same way as bash. The pdksh shell keeps track of the last HISTSIZE commands that have been entered (HISTSIZE is a user-definable pdksh variable).

pdksh stores the text of the last HISTSIZE commands in a history list. When you log in, the history list is initialized from a history file. The filename of the history file can be set using the HISTFILE pdksh variable. The default filename for the history file is .ksh_history which is located in your home directory. Notice that the file begins with a ., meaning that the file is hidden and appears in a directory listing only if you use the -a or -A option of the ls command.

The shell provides several ways of accessing the history list. The simplest way is to scroll through the commands that have been previously entered. In pdksh, this is done differently depending on whether you are using emacs or vi command editing.

If you are using emacs command editing, scroll up through the history list by pressing Ctrl+p and scroll down through the list by pressing Ctrl+n. If you are using vi command-line editing, scroll up through the history list by pressing either the k or - keys, and scroll down through the history list by pressing j or +.

> **NOTE**
>
> When using vi command editing, you must be in command mode for the key commands to work. You enter command mode by pressing the Esc key.

The command that is on the command line can be edited. The pdksh shell supports a complex set of editing capabilities (most of which are beyond the scope of this book). You can use the left- and right-arrow keys to move along the command line. You can insert text at any point and delete text from the command line by using the Backspace or Delete key. Most users should find these simple editing commands sufficient; for those who do not, there are many other more complicated ways of editing the command line.

> **NOTE**
>
> The complex set of editing commands that pdksh offers is similar to the commands contained in the emacs or vi text editors (you can set either emacs or vi emulation by using the set -o emacs or set -o vi commands). If you are familiar with emacs (or vi), these commands will be familiar to you.

Another method of using the history file is to display and edit it using fc (fix command), the built-in pdksh shell command. If you read Chapter 11, "bash," you may remember that bash supports another command called history, which allows you to view and modify the history file. The history command was left out of the pdksh shell because all of its functionality could be provided by the fc command.

> **TIP**
>
> Even though the history command is not built in to pdksh, the command normally still works because it is usually set up as an alias to the fc -l command. For example, the .kshrc file usually contains a line such as alias history='fc -l', which provides behavior almost identical to the history command that is built in to other shells.

The `fc` command is used to edit the command history. It has a number of options, as is illustrated in the following command syntax:

```
fc [-e ename] [-nlr] [first] [last]
```

All options given in braces are optional. The `-e` portion of the command is used to specify the text editor that is to be used for editing the commands in the command history. The first and last options select a range of commands to take out of the history list. First and last can refer either to the number of a command in the history list or to a string that `fc` tries to find in the history list.

The `-n` option suppresses command numbers when listing the `history` commands that match the specified range. The `-r` option lists the matched commands in reverse order. The `-l` command lists the matched commands to the screen. In all cases except for the `-l` option, the matching commands are loaded into a text editor.

The text editor used by `fc` is found by taking the value of `ename` if the `-e` option is used. If this option is not used, `fc` uses the editor specified by the variable `FCEDIT`. If this variable does not exist, `fc` uses the value of the `EDITOR` variable. Finally, if none of these variables exist, the editor chosen is `vi`.

If you enter the `fc` command with no arguments, it loads the last command that was entered into the editor. Remember that when you exit the editor, `fc` attempts to execute any commands that are in the editor.

The easiest way to understand what the `fc` command does is to look at a few examples:

`fc` loads the last command into the default editor.

`fc -l` lists the last 16 commands that were entered.

`fc -l 5 10` lists the commands with the history number between 5 and 10, inclusive.

`fc 6` loads `history` command number 6 into the default editor.

`fc mo` loads into the default editor the most recent command that starts with the string `mo`.

Aliases

Another way `pdksh` makes life easier for you is by supporting command aliases. Command aliases are commands that you can specify and execute. Alias commands are usually abbreviations of other commands.

You tell `pdksh` to execute a Linux command whenever it encounters the alias. For example, if you have a file in your directory that holds a list of things that you must do each day, and you typically edit the file every morning to update it, you could find yourself entering the following command on a regular basis:

```
vi things-to-do-today.txt
```

Because you are entering this command quite often, you may want to create an alias for it to save yourself some typing. So instead of typing this command every time you want to edit the file, you can create an alias called `ttd` that causes the longer command to be executed.

To set up an alias such as this, use the `pdksh` `alias` command. To create the `ttd` alias, enter the following command at the `pdksh` command prompt:

```
alias ttd='vi things-to-do-today.txt'
```

From the time that you enter the `alias` command until the time you exit from `pdksh`, the `ttd` command causes the longer command to be executed. If you decide after you enter an alias that you no longer want that alias, you can use the `pdksh` `unalias` command to delete the alias:

```
unalias ttd
```

After you use the `unalias` command to remove an alias, the alias no longer exists and trying to execute it causes `pdksh` to display `Command not found`.

The following are some aliases that you may want to define:

```
alias ll='ls -l'
alias log='logout'
alias ls='ls -F'
```

If you are a DOS user and you prefer to use DOS file commands, you may also want to define the following aliases:

```
alias dir='ls'
alias copy='cp'
alias rename='mv'
alias md='mkdir'
alias rd='rmdir'
```

If you enter the `alias` command without any arguments, it prints all of the aliases that are already defined to the screen. There is a way to make sure that all of your `alias` commands get executed each time you start `pdksh`. This is done by using an initialization file, which we will discuss later in this chapter in the "Customizing `pdksh`" section.

Input Redirection

Input redirection is used to change the source of input for a command. Typically, when a command is entered in `pdksh`, the command expects some kind of input in order to do its job. Some of the simpler commands must get all of the information that they need passed to them on the command line. The `rm` command, for example, requires you to tell it on the command line which files you want to delete; if you do not specify any files, it issues a prompt telling you to enter `rm -h` for help.

Other commands require more elaborate input than a simple directory name. The input for these commands is typically found in a file. For example, the `wc` (word count) command counts the number of characters, words, and lines in the input that was given to it. If you enter the `wc` command with a filename as an argument, `wc` returns the number of characters, words, and lines that are contained in that file. An example of this is:

```
wc test
11 2 1
```

Another way to accomplish passing the contents of the test file to `wc` as input is to change (or redirect) the input of the `wc` command from the terminal to the test file. This results in the same output. The < character is used by `pdksh` to redirect the input to the current command from the file following the character. So, redirecting `wc`'s input from the terminal to the test file is done by entering the following command:

```
wc < test
11 2 1
```

Input redirection is not used too often because most commands that require input from a file have an option to specify a filename on the command line. There are times, however, when you come across a program that does not accept a filename as an input parameter, and yet the input that you want to give to the command exists in a file. Whenever this situation occurs, you can use input redirection to get around the problem.

Output Redirection

Output redirection is more commonly used than input redirection. Output redirection enables you to redirect the output from a command into a file, as opposed to having the output displayed on the screen.

There are many situations in which this capability can be very useful. For example, if the output of a command is quite large and does not fit on the screen, you may want to redirect it to a file so you can view it later using a text editor. Output redirection is done in much the same way as input redirection. Instead of using the < symbol, the > symbol is used.

To redirect the output of an ls command into a file named `directory.out`, the following command is used:

```
ls > directory.out
```

Pipelines

Pipelines are a way to string together a series of commands. This means that the output from the first command in the pipeline is used as the input to the second command. You can tell pdksh to create a pipeline by typing two or more commands separated by the ¦ character. The following is an example of using a pdksh pipeline:

```
cat test.file | sort | uniq
```

This is a fairly common pipeline. Here, the contents of `test.file` (the output from the cat command) are fed into the input of the sort command. The sort command, without any options, sorts its input alphabetically by the first field in the input. The sorted file is then piped into the uniq command. The uniq command removes any duplicate lines from the input. If `test.file` contains the lines

```
Sample dialog
Hello there
How are you today
Hello there
I am fine
```

the output from the pipeline is the following:

```
Hello there
How are you today
I am fine
Sample dialog
```

All of the lines in the file have been sorted by the first word in the line, and one of the Hello there lines has been removed because of the uniq command.

Shell Prompts

pdksh has three levels of user prompts. The first level is what the user sees when the shell is waiting for a command to be typed. (This is what you normally see when you are working with the shell.) The default prompt is the $ character. If you do not like the dollar sign as the prompt or prefer to customize the prompt, you can do so by setting the value of the PS1 pdksh variable.

To set a variable, give the name and equal sign, and the string you want to set it to. Make sure you do not place any spaces on either side of the equal sign or the shell will not interpret your command properly. For example, the line

```
PS1="! Tell me what to do"
```

sets the shell prompt to the string ! Tell me what to do. The pdksh shell keeps track of how many commands have been entered since it was started. This number is stored into the shell variable called !. When you include the ! in the prompt, it displays the current command number in the prompt. The previous prompt command causes the command number followed by the string Tell me what to do to be displayed on the command line each time pdksh is expecting you to enter a command.

The second level prompt is displayed when pdksh is expecting more input from you in order to complete a command. The default for the second level prompt is >. If you want to change the second level prompt, you can do so by setting the value of the PS2 pdksh variable, as in the following example:

```
PS2=" I need more information"
```

This causes the string I need more information to be displayed on the command line whenever pdksh needs something from you to complete a command.

pdksh does not support the advanced prompt options that bash supports. There is no predefined set of escape codes that you can put in a pdksh prompt variable to display such items as the time or current working directory. You can, however, put other pdksh variables into a prompt variable. For example, the following two prompts are valid:

```
PS1="(LOGNAME) "
PS1='($PW(D) '
```

The first example causes your prompt to be equal to your UNIX username. The second example causes your prompt to be the current working directory. The single quotes are needed here so that the value of the PWD variable does not get assigned to the variable only the first time it is executed. If you use double quotes, the PWD variable is evaluated only when the command is first entered. (The prompt will always be the directory name

of the directory that you are in when you enter the command.) The single quotes cause the value of the PS1 variable to be equal to the current value of the PWD variable. For more information on using these quotes, see Chapter 14, "Shell Programming."

Job Control

Job control is the capability to control the execution behavior of a currently running process. Specifically, you can suspend a running process and cause it to resume running at a later time. The pdksh shell keeps track of all of the processes that it starts, and you can suspend a running process or restart a suspended one at any time during the life of that process.

Pressing the Ctrl+Z key sequence suspends a running process. The bg command restarts a suspended process in the background and the fg command restarts a process in the foreground.

These commands are most often used when a user wants to run a command in the background but accidentally starts it in the foreground. When a command is started in the foreground, it locks the shell from any further user interaction until the command completes execution. This is usually not a problem because most commands take only a few seconds to execute. If the command you are running is going to take a long time, you typically start the command in the background so that you can continue to use pdksh to enter other commands while it completes running.

If you start a command in the foreground that is going to take a long time, your shell may be tied up for several minutes. If you have done this and want to continue executing the command in the background, enter the following:

```
control-z
bg
```

This suspends the command and restarts it in the background. The command continues to execute and you have control of pdksh.

Key Bindings

One useful feature that pdksh supports, which is lacking in the Bourne Again Shell, is *key bindings*. This feature enables you to change the behavior of key combinations for the purpose of command-line editing.

If, for example, you do not like the fact that you have to use the emacs key sequence Ctrl+P to move up in the history buffer, you can change the key sequence for that command to something else. The syntax for doing the key binding is the following:

```
bind <key sequence> <command>
```

This feature effectively enables you to customize pdksh to have the exact feel that you want. One of the most commonly used key bindings is to bind the up, down, left, and right arrows to be used as they are in bash (for scrolling up and down the history list, and for moving left and right along the command line). This binding is typically found in your .kshrc file, which is the startup file for the shell (it is read whenever the shell starts).

The bind commands that are needed to create these bindings are as follows:

```
bind '^[['=prefix-2
bind '^XA'=up-history
bind "^XB'=down-history
bind '^XC'=forward-char
bind '^XD'=backward-char
```

Table 12.1 gives some of the most useful editing commands that you can use for binding keys, along with the default binding and a description of each. You can get a listing of all of the editing commands that pdksh supports by typing the bind command without any arguments.

TABLE 12.1. USEFUL KEY BINDINGS FOR pdksh.

Keystroke	Meaning
abort (^G)	Used to abort another editing command. It is most commonly used to stop a history list search.
backward-char (^B)	Moves the cursor backward one character. This command is often bound to the left arrow key.
backward-word (^[b)	Moves the cursor backward to the beginning of a word.
beginning-of-line (^A)	Moves the cursor to the beginning of the command line.
complete (^[^[)	Tells pdksh to try to complete the current command.
copy-last-arg (^[_)	Causes the last word of the previous command to be inserted at the cursor position.

continues

TABLE 12.1. CONTINUED

Keystroke	Meaning
delete-char-backward (ERASE)	Deletes the character that is to the left of the cursor.
delete-char-forward	Deletes the character to the right of the cursor.
delete-word-backward (^[ERASE)	Deletes the characters to the left of the cursor back to the first white space character that is encountered.
delete-word-forward (^[(d)	Deletes the characters to the right of the cursor up to the first character that occurs after a white space character.
down-history (^N)	Moves down one line in the history list. This command is often bound to the down-arrow key.
end-of-line (^E)	Moves the cursor to the end of the current line.
forward-char (^F)	Moves the cursor forward one character. This command is often bound to the right-arrow key.
forward-word (^[F)	Moves the cursor forward to the end of a word.
kill-line (KILL)	Deletes the current line.
kill-to-eol (^K)	deletes all of the characters to the right of the cursor on the current line.
list (^[?)	Causes pdksh to list all of the possible command names or filenames that can complete the word in which the cursor is currently contained.
search-history (^R)	Searches the history list backward for the first command that contains the inputted characters.
transpose-chars (^T)	Exchanges the two characters on either side of the cursor. If the cursor is at the end of the command line it switches the last two characters on the line.
up-history (^P)	Moves up one command in the history list. This command is often bound to the up-arrow key.

Customizing Your pdksh

Many ways of customizing pdksh have been described in this chapter. Until now, though, the changes that you made only affected the current pdksh session. As soon as you quit pdksh, all of the customizations that you made were lost. However, there is a way of making the customizations more permanent.

This is done by storing all of your customizations in a pdksh initialization file. Users can put commands into this file that they want to be executed each and every time pdksh is started. Examples of commands that are typically found in this file are aliases and initializations of variables (such as the prompts).

In order to set up your customization file, you must tell pdksh where to look for the initialization file. This is different than with bash. The bash shell automatically knows where to look for its customization file. To tell pdksh where to look for the customization file, you need to create a file in your home directory called .profile. This file is read and all of the commands in the file are executed each time you log in to the system.

A sample of the commands that you should place in your .profile file are as follows:

```
export ENV=$HOME/.kshrc
EDITOR=emacs
```

The first line in the .profile file sets the ENV variable. This is the variable that pdksh looks at to find the initialization file that it should use. If you plan to customize pdksh, you should tell pdksh to look for a file in your home directory. The filename .kshrc is often used as the pdksh initialization filename, but you can pick another name if you want.

If you are not planning to customize pdksh, you can set the ENV variable to be equal to the system default pdksh initialization file. This file is in the /etc directory and is called ksh.kshrc.

The second line in the .profile file sets the EDITOR variable. This is used by the .kshrc initialization file to determine what type of command-line editing commands to use for your session. If you prefer to use vi command-line editing, you can set this variable to be equal to vi.

TIP

Instead of copying the file to your home directory, you can create a new file in your home directory that calls the system default file, and then add customizations afterward.

12

pdksh

pdksh Commands

There are a lot of commands available to you in the pdksh shell, but most of them you'll never need. Some of the most useful built-in pdksh commands are shown in Table 12.2.

TABLE **12.2.** USEFUL pdksh COMMANDS AND WHAT THEY DO.

Command	What it does:
.	Reads and executes the contents of the file. (This will be discussed in more detail in Chapter 14.)
alias	Used to set aliases, command nicknames that can be defined by the user.
bg	(Background command) forces a suspended process to continue to execute in the background.
cd	(Change working directory) changes the current working directory to the directory specified.
exit	Terminates the shell.
export	Causes the value of a variable to be made visible to all subprocesses that belong to the current shell.
fc	(Fix command) is used to edit the commands that are in the current history list.
fg	(Foreground command) forces a suspended process to continue to execute in the foreground.
kill	Is used to terminate another process.
pwd	(Print working directory) prints to the screen the directory in which the user is currently working.
unalias	Is used to remove aliases that have previously been defined using the alias command.

pdksh Variables

Some of the most useful pdksh variables are listed in Table 12.3, including the variable name, a short description, and default value (if one exists).

TABLE 12.3. USEFUL pdksh VARIABLES AND WHAT THEY DO.

Variable name	What it is:
EDITOR, FCEDIT	The default editor for the fc bash command.
HISTFILE	The name of the file that is used to store the command history.
HISTSIZE	The size of the history list.
HOME	The HOME directory of the current user.
OLDPWD	The previous working directory (the one that was current before the current directory was entered).
PATH	The search path that bash uses when looking for executable files.
PS1	The first level prompt that is displayed on the command line.
PS2	The second level prompt that is displayed when a command is expecting more input.
PWD	The current working directory.
SECONDS	The number of seconds that have elapsed since the current bash session was started.

Summary

We've looked at many of the features of the Public Domain Korn Shell (pdksh). It is similar to the Bourne Again Shell in many aspects, but it does add some new utilities.

In the next chapter, we look at tcsh, a version of the C shell that is available with Linux. After you have seen the features and the way you use the three shells, you should be able to decide which shell is best for you to use on a regular basis. Of course, you can use any shell at any time by simply typing its name. You may want to learn about other subjects before moving on to the C shell. To:

Learn about shell programming and how you can use it to make your experience with bash more powerful, see Chapter 14, "Shell Programming."

Learn about using editors to create and edit files, see Chapter 16, "Text Editors: vi and emacs."

Learn about using the X GUI, see Chapter 22, "Installing and Configuring XFree86."

CHAPTER 13

tcsh

by Rick McMullin

IN THIS CHAPTER

The last two chapters introduced you to the Bourne Again Shell (bash) and the Public Domain Korn Shell (pdksh). This chapter introduces a third shell, tcsh. In addition to these topics, we will see how you can customize tcsh to suit your tastes. You will also be introduced to several important tcsh commands and variables.

Rounding out the chapter is a section on several neat little features that tcsh provides that are not available in any of the other shell programs we have discussed.

An Introduction to tcsh

tcsh is a modified version of the C shell (csh). It is fully backward-compatible with csh, but it contains many new features that make user interaction much easier. The biggest improvements over the csh are in the areas of command-line editing and history navigation.

Command Completion

Just like pdksh and bash, tcsh supports command-line completion. You invoke command-line completion in tcsh exactly the same way that you do in bash: by pressing the Tab key at any point while you type a command.

When you press the Tab key, tcsh tries to complete the command by matching what has been typed with any file in the directory that the command is referring to. For example, let's say that you type the following command and then press the Tab key:

```
emacs hello
```

Here, tcsh tries to match the letters hello with any file (or subdirectory) in the current directory. If there is a single file in the current directory that begins with the letters hello, tcsh fills in the rest of the filename for you. Now let's see what happens when you type the following command and then press the Tab key:

```
emacs /usr/bin/hello
```

In this case, tcsh will try to match the letters hello with any file in the /usr/bin directory. From these examples, you can see that you must give tcsh something to go on before asking it to complete the command for you.

Another example of using command-line completion is as follows: Assume that the directory that you are currently in contains these files:

```
News/ bin/ mail/ sample.txt testfile ttd.txt
```

If you want to print the `sample.txt` file, type the following command:

```
lpr sample.txt
```

Using command-line completion, you can get away with typing the following command and then pressing the Tab key:

```
lpr s
```

At this point, `tcsh` attempts to complete the command and finds that the only file that can possibly match what was typed so far is the `sample.txt` file. `tcsh` then completes the command by putting the following text on the command line:

```
lpr sample.txt
```

You can now either confirm that this is the intended command by pressing the Enter key, or you can edit the command if it isn't the one that you want. Be careful using these shortcuts with some commands, notably `rm`, as you may end up deleting more files than you intended!

Wildcards

`tcsh` enables you to use wildcards in your commands. It supports the same three wildcards as `bash` and `pdksh`:

* * matches any character or any number of characters.
* ? matches any single character.
* [...] matches any single character contained within the brackets.

The * wildcard can be used to perform some of the same functions as command-line completion. If you enter a command like

```
cd t*
```

and only one subdirectory in the current directory begins with the letter t, this command behaves the same as if you had used command-line completion by pressing the Tab key.

The * matches any character or any number of characters, so the shell replaces the t* with the file in the directory that matches the wildcard pattern.

This works reliably only if there is one file in the directory that starts with the letter "t". If more than one file in the directory starts with the letter "t", the shell tries to replace t* with the list of filenames in the directory that match the wildcard pattern, and the `cd` command makes the first directory in this list the working directory. This ends up being the file that comes first alphabetically and may or may not be the intended file.

13

tcsh

A case that is more suited to using the * wildcard is if you want to perform the same operation on a number of files that have similar filenames. For example, assume the current directory contains the following files:

```
Mail/ atc1.stk atc2.stk bin/ borl.stk cdrom.txt lfi.stk temp/
```

If you want to print both of the files that start with `atc` and end with the `.stk` extension, you can do so by typing

```
lpr a*.stk
```

This command will do the job because there are no other files in the directory that start with the letter "a" and have the `.stk` extension.

Using the `?` wildcard, the following command accomplishes the same thing:

```
lpr atc?.stk
```

Using the `[...]` wildcard, you can enter the following command to get the same files to print:

```
lpr atc[12].stk
```

Command History

The `tcsh` shell provides a mechanism for accessing the command history that is similar to ones provided with `bash` and `pdksh`. The shell remembers the last `history` commands that were entered into the shell (where history is a user-definable `tcsh` variable).

`tcsh` stores the text of the last `history` commands in a history list. When you log in to your account, the history list is initialized from a history file. The default filename for the history file is `.history`, but you can change it using the `histfile` `tcsh` variable. This file is located in your home directory. Notice that the file begins with a period. This means that the file is a hidden file and appears in a directory listing only if you use the `-a` or `-A` options of the `ls` command.

> **NOTE**
>
> In order for the history list to be saved in the history file, make sure that the `savehist` variable is set to the number of commands that you want to save. Refer to the `.login` file listing in the "Customizing `tcsh`" section of this chapter for an example of setting this variable.

The simplest way of using the history list is to use the up- and down-arrow keys to scroll through the commands that were entered earlier. Pressing the up-arrow key causes the last command entered to appear on the command line. Pressing the up-arrow key again puts the command before that on the command line, and so on. If you move up in the command buffer past the command that you want, you can move down the history list one command at a time by pressing the down-arrow key.

The command that is on the command line can be edited. You can use the left- and right-arrow keys to move along the command line, and you can insert text at any point. You can also delete text from the command line by using the Backspace or Delete key. Most users should find these simple editing commands sufficient, but for those who do not, tcsh also supports a wide range of equivalent emacs and vi editing commands. See the "Key Bindings" section of this chapter for more information on vi and emacs command-line editing.

Another method of using the history file is to display and edit the history list using a number of other editing commands that tcsh provides. The history command can be invoked by any one of three different methods. The first method has the following command-line syntax:

```
history [-hr] [n]
```

This form of the history command displays the history list to the screen. The n option is used to specify the number of commands to display. If the n option is not used, the history command displays the entire history list. The -h option causes history to remove the command numbers and timestamps that are usually present in the output of the history command. The -r option tells history to display the commands in reverse order, starting with the most recent command. The following command displays the last five commands that were entered:

```
history 5
```

The second method of invoking the history command is used to modify the contents of the history file or the history list. It has the following command-line syntax:

```
history -S | -L | -M [filename]
```

The -S option writes the history list to a file. The -L option appends a history file to the current history list. The -M option merges the contents of the history file with the current history list and sorts the resulting list by the timestamp contained with each command.

13

tcsh

> **NOTE**
>
> All of the options for the second form of the `history` command use the `filename` option as the name of the history file. If no filename is specified, the `history` command uses the value of the `histfile` variable. If the `histfile` variable isn't set, it uses the `~/.history` (home directory) file.

The `history` command using the `-c` option clears the current history list.

In addition to the `history` command and its options, `tcsh` also contains many history navigation and editing commands. The following commands are used to navigate through the history list:

- `!`*n* re-executes the command with the history number of *n*.
- `!-`*n* re-executes the command that is *n* commands from the end of the history list.
- `!!` re-executes the last command that was entered.
- `!c` re-executes the last command in the history list that begins with the letter c.
- `!?c?` re-executes the last command in the history list that contains the letter c.

The history editing commands enable you to replace words and letters in previously entered commands as well as add words to the end of previously entered commands. More information on these editing commands can be found by referring to the `tcsh` man page. You can view this man page by entering the following command at the shell prompt:

```
man tcsh
```

Aliases

Command aliases are commands that you can specify and execute. Alias commands are usually abbreviations of other Linux commands. You tell `tcsh` to execute a Linux command whenever it encounters the alias. For example, if you enter the following `alias` command:

```
alias ls 'ls -F'
```

the `ls -F` command is substituted for the `ls` command each time the `ls` command is used.

If you decide after you enter an alias that you don't need or want that alias to exist any longer, you can use the `tcsh unalias` command to delete that alias:

```
unalias cd
```

After you use the `unalias` command to remove an alias, the alias no longer exists, and trying to execute that alias causes `tcsh` to return a `command not found` error message.

Some aliases that you may want to define are:

- `alias ll 'ls -l'`
- `alias ls 'ls -F'`

If you are a DOS user and are accustomed to using DOS file commands, you may also want to define the following aliases:

- `alias dir 'ls'`
- `alias copy 'cp'`
- `alias rename 'mv'`
- `alias md 'mkdir'`
- `alias rd 'rmdir'`

13

tcsh

> **NOTE**
>
> When you define aliases, quotation marks are necessary only if the command within them contains spaces or other special characters.

If you enter the `alias` command without any arguments, it prints to the screen all of the aliases that are already defined. The following listing illustrates sample output from the `alias` command:

```
alias ls 'ls -F'
alias dir 'ls'
alias ll 'ls -l'
alias md 'mkdir'
alias rd 'rmdir'
```

Input and Output Redirection

The standard input and output of a command can be redirected using the same syntax that is used by `bash` and `pdksh`. The < character is used for input redirection, and the

> character is used for output redirection. The following command redirects the standard input of the `cat` command to the `.cshrc` file:

```
cat < .cshrc
```

In practice, input redirection isn't used very often because most commands that require input from a file support passing the filename as an argument to the command.

Output redirection is used much more frequently. The following command redirects the standard output of the `cat` command to the file named `cshenv` (which has the effect of storing the contents of the `.cshrc` and `.login` files in one file named `cshenv`):

```
cat .cshrc .login > cshenv
```

> **CAUTION**
>
> The file to which output is being redirected is created if it does not exist and is overwritten without warning if it already exists.

Pipelines

`tcsh` pipelines, just like `bash` and `pdksh` pipelines, are a way to string together a series of Linux commands. This means that the output from the first command in the pipeline is used as the input to the second command in the pipeline. The output from the second command in the pipeline is used as input to the third command in the pipeline, and so on. The output from the last command in the pipeline is the output that the user actually sees. This output is displayed to the screen (or put into a file if output redirection was specified on the command line).

You can tell `tcsh` to create a pipeline by typing two or more commands separated by the | character. The following command illustrates an example of using a `tcsh` pipeline:

```
cat file1 file2 | wc -l
```

The `cat` command in this pipeline appends `file2` to the end of `file1` and passes the resulting file to the `wc` command. The `wc` command prints to the screen the total number of lines contained in the resulting file.

Prompts

tcsh has three levels of user prompts. The first-level prompt is what you see when tcsh is waiting for you to type a command. The default prompt is the % character. This prompt can be customized by assigning a new value to the prompt tcsh variable:

```
set prompt="%t$"
```

This example changes the first-level prompt to the current time followed by a dollar sign.

The second-level prompt is displayed when tcsh is waiting for input when in a while or for loop (used in shell programming, discussed in Chapter 14, "Shell Programming"). The default for the second-level prompt is %R?, where %R is a special character sequence that displays the status of the parser. You can change the second-level prompt by setting the value of the prompt2 tcsh variable. For example:

```
set prompt2="?"
```

changes the second-level prompt to a question mark.

The third-level prompt is used when tcsh displays the corrected command line when automatic spelling correction is in effect. This prompt is set using the prompt3 variable, and it has a default value of CORRECT>%R (y|n|e)?. See the "Correcting Spelling Errors" section that appears later in this chapter for more information on this feature.

tcsh supports special character codes in its prompt variables. These codes are similar to the codes that bash supports in its prompts. The main difference between the two is that the syntax for using them is different. Table 13.1 lists the most commonly used special character codes.

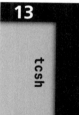

13

tcsh

TABLE 13.1. tcsh PROMPT SPECIAL CHARACTER CODES.

Character code	Meaning
%/	Displays the current working directory.
%h, %!, !	These codes all display the current history number.
%t, %@	These codes both display the time of day.
%n	Displays the username.
%d	Displays the current day of the week.
%w	Displays the current month.
%y	Displays the current year.

The following is an example of setting the prompt variable:

```
set prompt="%h %/"
```

This command sets the prompt to display the history number of the current command, followed by the current working directory.

Job Control

Job control refers to the ability to control the execution behavior of a currently running process. Specifically, you can suspend a running process and cause it to resume running at a later time. tcsh keeps track of all the processes that it starts as a result of user input. You can suspend a running process or restart a suspended one at any time during the life of that process.

Pressing the Ctrl+Z key sequence suspends a running process. The bg command restarts a suspended process in the background, and the fg command restarts a process in the foreground.

These commands are most often used when you want to run a command in the background but accidentally start it in the foreground. When a command is started in the foreground, it locks the shell from any further user interaction until the command completes execution. This is usually not a problem because most commands take only a few seconds to execute. If the command you're running is going to take a long time, you will probably want to start the command in the background so that you can continue to use tcsh to enter other commands.

For example, if you start a command that is going to take a long time in the foreground, such as

```
find / -named "test" > find.out
```

your shell will be tied up for several minutes. If you have done this and want to cause the find command to continue executing in the background, you can enter the following:

```
Ctrl-z
bg
```

This suspends the find command and then restarts it in the background. The find command continues to execute, and you regain control of tcsh.

Key Bindings

Like the pdksh, tcsh provides the ability to change and add key bindings. The tcsh implementation of key bindings is more powerful than the way key bindings are done in pdksh.

With tcsh you can bind to things other than the built-in editor commands. This means that you can bind a key to a UNIX command, for example. tcsh also enables you to bind vi editing commands, whereas pdksh only allows the binding of emacs editing commands.

Key bindings can be very useful, especially if you're using a favorite editor other than emacs or vi. The basic syntax for defining key bindings is

```
bindkey [option] <instring or keyname> <outstring or command>
```

The options that bindkey supports are not discussed in this book. If you want to learn about the bindkey options, refer to the tcsh man page. The basic function of the bindkey command is to bind the key sequence contained in the first argument to the command contained in the second argument.

The following list gives some of the most useful editing commands that you can bind key sequences to, along with the default key binding for that command. You can list all the bindings that are defined in tcsh by typing the bindkey command without any arguments.

- beginning-of-line (^A): Moves the cursor to the beginning of the command line.
- backward-char (^B): Moves the cursor back one character.
- end-of-line (^E): Moves the cursor to the end of the command line.
- forward-char (^F): Moves the cursor forward one character.
- backward-delete-char (^H): Deletes the character to the left of the cursor.
- kill-line (^K): Deletes all of the characters to the right of the cursor.
- clear-screen (^L): Removes all of the text from the shell window.
- down-history (^N): Moves down one command in the history list.
- up-history (^P): Moves up one command in the history list.
- kill-whole-line (^U): Deletes all of the characters on the current line.

All of these commands are the same whether you're in emacs or vi insert mode. tcsh supports many more editing commands than are listed here. To see what these commands are, refer to the tcsh man page.

The following are examples of setting key bindings:

```
bindkey ^W kill-whole-line
bindkey ^S beginning-of-line
```

Other Neat Stuff

tcsh supports several neat features that none of the other shells discussed in this book supports. This section lists a few of the most useful of these extended features.

Correcting Spelling Errors

This feature, which is not available with any of the other shells discussed in this book, is a dream come true for many people (including me). If you're plagued by recurring typos, this feature alone might cause you to use tcsh over any of the other shells. You can tell tcsh to correct spelling errors in a command that you entered, and you can also tell it to automatically try to correct commands that it can't figure out.

The first function isn't quite as useful because you must know that you have made a typing mistake before you actually execute the command. This feature is invoked by pressing Esc+S on the command line before you press Enter.

For example, suppose you want to change to the /usr/X386/X11/bin directory, so you type the following command on the command line:

```
cd /usr/X387/X11/bun
```

If you caught the typing errors before you executed the command (by pressing the Enter key), you can correct the errors by pressing Esc+S. tcsh then tries to correct the spelling of the command and changes the command to read

```
cd /usr/X386/X11/bin
```

You can now press the Enter key, and the command executes just as you wanted. Obviously this command has some limitations because the shell can't (yet) read your mind, but for simple character transpositions or capitalization errors, it works very nicely.

The second method of instructing tcsh to perform spelling corrections on your commands is to set the correct tcsh variable. This variable, depending on what options you use, tells tcsh to try to correct spelling errors in command names or anywhere in the command. The syntax for setting the correct variable is one of the following:

```
set correct=cmd or
set correct=all
```

After you set the correct variable, whenever you enter a command that tcsh doesn't understand, it automatically checks to see if the command has any spelling errors. If it finds possible spelling errors, it gives you the corrected command and asks if the new command is what you intended. For example, if you set the correct variable with the all option and then enter the following command:

```
cd /usr/gmes
```

tcsh would respond with the following prompt on the command line:

```
CORRECT>cd /usr/games (y|n|e)?
```

If you respond to the prompt by pressing the y (yes) key, tcsh executes the corrected command. If you respond to the prompt by pressing the n (no) key, tcsh executes the command that you initially entered, which in turn causes an error message to be displayed.

If you respond to the prompt by pressing the e (edit) key, tcsh puts the command that you entered back on the command line and enables you to edit it.

Precommands

tcsh supports a way of executing a command prior to displaying each command prompt. This is done through the use of a special variable called precmd. If the precmd variable is set, the command that it is set to is executed before the command prompt is displayed onscreen. For example, assume that you set the precmd variable using the following command:

```
alias precmd time
```

After this alias is declared, the time command is always executed before the command prompt is displayed onscreen.

Change Directory Commands

tcsh also supports change directory commands. These commands are executed only when the current directory changes (usually as a result of executing the cd command). This type of command is probably more useful than the precommands just mentioned because there are times when you may want to know something about a directory that you just entered.

This feature is supported in the same way precommands are supported, except that you must provide an alias for a different variable. The variable used for this is cwdcmd. If this variable is aliased to a command, that command is executed each time you change current working directories.

A common use for this variable is to display the current directory to the screen. This can be done by entering the command

```
alias cwdcmd 'pwd'
```

This displays the name of the new directory each time a new directory is entered.

> **WARNING**
>
> You should not put a cd command into cwdcmd. Doing so could cause an infinite loop that will cause you to lose control of tcsh.

Monitoring Logins and Logouts

tcsh provides a mechanism that enables you to watch for any user who logs on or off the system. It does this through a tcsh variable named watch.

The watch variable contains a set of user ID and terminal number pairs. These pairs can contain wildcards and also can contain the word "any," which tells tcsh to match any user or terminal. The syntax for setting the watch variable is

```
set watch=(<user> <terminal>)
```

The *user* in this command refers to a Linux user ID. *terminal* refers to a Linux terminal device number.

Most people use this capability to watch for friends logging on to the system. For example, if you were waiting for a person with the username jules to come to work in the morning, you could set the following watch variable:

```
set watch=(jules any)
```

This command will then inform you when a person with the user ID jules logged in to the system on any terminal. tcsh defaults to checking the defined watches every 10 minutes. If you want to know with greater or lesser frequency, you can change this default by passing the number of minutes to wait between checks as the first parameter to the watch variable. For example, to check every five minutes to see if "jules" has logged in, you would use the following watch variable:

```
set watch=(5 jules any)
```

This does the same thing as the first command, except that it checks every 5 minutes instead of every 10 to see if "jules" has logged in. Be careful using this type of command on a heavily loaded or slow Linux system as you're contributing to the load. If you're using these commands for a short period of time for a particular purpose, that's fine, but don't let them run nonstop or you'll be loading the system for no good reason.

Customizing tcsh

We've shown many ways of customizing tcsh in this chapter. If you simply enter the commands that we have discussed at the command line, the changes you make will be lost every time you log out of the system. This section describes how to store these changes in a file that are executed each time you start tcsh.

> **TIP**
>
> If you make even a small mistake editing the tcsh files, you can cause problems when logging in. For this reason, make safety backup copies before you edit and verify each of your edits carefully before you save the new file.

Two initialization files are important to tcsh. The first is called the login file. The commands in this file are executed when you first log in to Linux. The contents of the default login file are as follows:

```
if ($?prompt) then
#this means that the shell is interactive
  umask 022
  set cdpath = ( /usr/spool )
  set notify
  set history = 100
  set histfile = .history
# The savehist variable is set to tell tcsh to
# save the history list to the history file on
# logout. The value of 25 means that tcsh will
# save the last 25 commands to the history file.
  set savehist = 25
  setenv OPENWINHOME /usr/openwin
  setenv MANPATH /usr/local/man:/usr/man/preformat:/usr/man:/usr/X11/man:
  /usr/openwin/man
setenv MINICOM "-c on"
  setenv HOSTNAME "`cat /etc/HOSTNAME`"
  set path = ( $path /usr/X11/bin /usr/andrew/bin
➥$OPENWINHOME/bin /usr/games . )
endif
# I had problems with the Backspace key installed by 'tset,' but you might
want
```

13

tcsh

```
# to try it anyway, instead of the 'setenv term.....' below it.
# eval `tset -sQ "$term"`
# setenv term  console
if ! $?TERM setenv TERM console
set prompt = "%m:%~%# "
alias ls 'ls -F'
if ( { tty --silent } ) then >& /dev/null
  echo "";fortune;echo ""
endif
```

This file, csh.login, can be found in the /etc directory. If you want to change any of the settings found in csh.login, copy it to your home directory and make the changes you want there.

The other file that tcsh makes use of is cshrc. The commands in this file are executed each time a copy of the tcsh program is run. Examples of the types of commands that usually appear in this file are aliases and variable declarations. This file, csh.cshrc, is also contained in the /etc directory. If you want to make changes to this file, copy it to your home directory and make your changes there.

When you first log in to Linux, tcsh executes the /etc/csh.cshrc file, followed by the /etc/csh.login file. It then checks your home directory to see if you have a personal copy of the csh.cshrc file. This file can be named either .tcshrc or .cshrc. If you have one of these files in your home directory, tcsh executes it next.

tcsh then checks to see if you have your own copy of the csh.login file in your home directory. This file must be named .login. If you do have a .login file in your home directory, it is executed next.

Whenever you start another copy of tcsh after you log in to the system, it executes the commands that are in the /etc/csh.cshrc file and then checks your home directory to see if there is a .tcshrc or a .cshrc file there.

tcsh Command Summary

Here are some of the most useful tcsh commands:

- alias: Used to set and display aliases, command nicknames that can be set by the user.
- bg: Background command. Forces a suspended process to continue running in the background.
- bindkey: Enables users to change the editing actions that are associated with a key sequence.

- **cd**: Changes the current working directory to the directory specified.
- **exit**: Terminates the shell.
- **fg**: Foreground command. Forces a suspended process to continue running in the foreground.
- **history**: Enables users to display and modify the contents of the history list and the history file.
- **kill**: Terminates another process.
- **logout**: Terminates a login shell.
- **set**: Used to set the value of tcsh variables.
- **source**: Reads and executes the contents of a file. This command is discussed in more detail in Chapter 14.
- **unalias**: Used to remove aliases that have been defined using the alias command.

tcsh Variables

Here are some of the most useful tcsh variables:

- **autocorrect**: If this is set, tcsh automatically tries to correct command-line spelling errors.
- **histfile**: The name of the file that is used to store the command history.
- **history**: The size of the history list.
- **home**: The user's home directory.
- **path**: The search path that tcsh uses when looking for executable programs.
- **prompt**: The first-level prompt that displays on the command line.
- **prompt2**: The second-level prompt that displays when a for, foreach, or while loop is expecting input.
- **prompt3**: The third-level prompt that displays when tcsh is attempting to correct a spelling error in a command.
- **savehist**: This variable must be set to the number of history commands that you want to save, if you want tcsh to save the history list when you log out.
- **watch**: Contains a list of user terminal pairs to watch for logins and logouts.

Summary

The last three chapters have presented the fundamental commands and concepts of the three most popular UNIX shells. tcsh is the most feature-rich shell of those presented but that doesn't necessarily mean that it's the best shell for you to use. In the end, this decision will probably be based on your personal preference as opposed to what features are offered.

The next chapter looks at the programming languages that are provided by each of the shells we have discussed. You may want to learn about other subjects before of moving on to the C shell. To learn about:

> Using editors to create and edit files, read Chapter 16, "Text Editors: vi and emacs."
>
> Sending output to your printers under Linux, see Chapter 20, "Printing."

Shell Programming

by Rick McMullin

IN THIS CHAPTER

The last three chapters described how to use the most common Linux shell programs; now let's take a closer look at the powerful interpretive programming languages that these shell programs have built into them.

This chapter describes the fundamentals of shell programming and compares the bash, pdksh, and tcsh programming languages. This chapter covers the following topics:

- Creating and running shell programs
- Using shell variables
- The importance of quotation marks
- The test command
- Conditional statements
- Iteration statements
- Functions

This chapter contains several small examples of shell programs. Each new concept or command that is introduced has some example code that further explains what is being presented.

Creating and Running Shell Programs

At the simplest level, shell programs are just files that contain one or more shell or Linux commands. These programs can be used to simplify repetitive tasks, to replace two or more commands that are always executed together with a single command, to automate the installation of other programs, and to write simple interactive applications.

To create a shell program, you must first create a file using a text editor and put the shell or Linux commands you want to be executed into that file. For example, we'll assume you have a CD-ROM drive mounted on your Linux system. This CD-ROM device is mounted when the system is first started. If you later change the CD in the drive, you must force Linux to read the new directory contents. One way of achieving this is to put the new CD into the drive, unmount the CD-ROM drive using the Linux umount command, and then remount the drive using the Linux mount command. This sequence of steps is shown by the following commands:

```
umount /dev/cdrom
mount -t iso1960 /dev/cdrom /cdrom
```

Instead of typing both of these commands each time you change the CD in your drive, you can create a shell program that will execute both of these commands for you. To do this, put the two commands into a file and name the file remount (or any other name you want).

Several ways of executing the commands are contained in the remount file. One way to accomplish this is to make the file executable. This is done by entering the following command:

```
chmod +x remount
```

This command changes the permissions of the file so that it is now executable. You can now run your new shell program by typing **remount** on the command line.

> **NOTE**
>
> The remount shell program must be in a directory that is in your search path, or the shell will not be able to find the program to execute. Also, if you are using tcsh to write programs, the first line of the shell program must start with a # for tcsh to recognize it as a tcsh program file.

Another way you can execute the shell program is to run the shell that the program was written for and pass the program in as a parameter to the shell. In a tcsh program, this is done by entering the following command:

```
tcsh remount
```

This command starts up a new shell and tells it to execute the commands that are found in the remount file.

A third way of executing the commands in a shell program file is to use the . command (in pdksh and bash) and the source command in tcsh. This command tells the shell to execute all the commands in the file that is passed as an argument to the command. For example, the following command can be used to tell bash or pdksh to execute the commands in the remount file:

```
. remount
```

To do the same thing in tcsh, type the following command:

```
source remount
```

14

SHELL
PROGRAMMING

Another situation in which a simple shell program can save a lot of time is described in the following example. Let's say that you are working on three different files in a directory, and at the end of every day you want to back up those three files onto a floppy disk. To do this, simply type a series of commands similar to the following:

```
mount -t msdos /dev/fd0 /a
cp file1 /a
cp file2 /a
cp file3 /a
```

As stated in the example, one way of doing this is to mount the floppy drive and then type three copy commands, one for each file you want to copy. A simpler way is to put the four commands into a text file called `backup` and then execute the `backup` command when you want to copy the three files onto the floppy drive.

> **NOTE**
>
> You will still have to ensure that the backup shell program is executable and is in a directory that is in your path before you run the command.

Using Variables

As is the case with almost any language, the use of variables is very important in shell programs. You've already seen in the introductory shell chapters some of the ways in which shell variables can be used. Two of the variables introduced were the PATH variable and the PS1 variable. These are examples of built-in shell variables or variables that are defined by the shell program you are using. This section describes how you can create your own variables and use them in simple shell programs.

Assigning a Value to a Variable

In all three of the shells discussed earlier, you can assign a value to a variable simply by typing the variable name followed by an equal sign and the value you want to assign to the variable. For example, if you want to assign a value of 5 to the variable `count`, enter the following command in `bash` or `pdksh`:

```
count=5
```

With `tcsh` you must enter the following command to achieve the same results:

```
set count = 5
```

> **NOTE**
>
> With the bash and pdksh syntax for setting a variable, make sure that there are no spaces on either side of the equal sign. With tcsh, it doesn't matter if there are spaces or not.

Notice that you do not have to declare the variable as you would if you were programming in C or Pascal. This is because the shell language is a nontyped interpretive language. This means that you can use the same variable to store character strings that you use to store integers. You store a character string into a variable in the same way that you store the integer into a variable. For example, to set the variable called "name" to have the value "Garry" use these commands:

```
name=Garry          (for pdksh and bash)
set name = Garry     (for tcsh)
```

Accessing the Value of a Variable

After you have stored a value into a variable, how do you get the value back out? You do this in the shell by preceding the variable name with a dollar sign ($). If you want to print the value stored in the count variable to the screen, you do so by entering the following command:

```
echo $count
```

> **TIP**
>
> If you omit the $ from the preceding command, the echo command displays the word count onscreen.

Positional Parameters and Other Built-In Shell Variables

The shell has knowledge of a special kind of variable called a positional parameter. Positional parameters are used to refer to the parameters that are passed to a shell program on the command line or a shell function by the shell script that invokes the function. When you run a shell program that requires or supports a number of command-line options, each of these options is stored into a positional parameter. The first parameter is

14

SHELL
PROGRAMMING

stored into a variable named 1, the second parameter is stored into a variable named 2, and so forth. These variable names are reserved by the shell so that you can't use them as variables you define. To access the values stored in these variables, you must precede the variable name with a dollar sign ($) just as you do with variables you define.

The following shell program expects to be invoked with two parameters. The program takes the two parameters and prints the second parameter that was typed on the command line first and the first parameter that was typed on the command line second.

```
#program reverse, prints the command line parameters out in reverse #order
echo "$2" "$1"
```

If you invoke this program by entering

```
reverse hello there
```

the program returns the following output:

```
there hello
```

Several other built-in shell variables are important to know about when you are doing a lot of shell programming. Table 14.1 lists these variables and gives a brief description of what each is used for.

TABLE 14.1. BUILT-IN SHELL VARIABLES.

Variable	Use
$#	Stores the number of command-line arguments that are passed to the shell program.
$?	Stores the exit value of the last command that was executed.
$0	Stores the first word of the entered command (the name of the shell program).
$*	Stores all the arguments that are entered on the command line ($1 $2 ...).
"$@"	Stores all the arguments that were entered on the command line, individually quoted ("$1" "$2" ...).

The Importance of Quotation Marks

The use of the different types of quotation marks is very important in shell programming. All three kinds of quotation marks and the backslash character are used by the shell to perform different functions. The double quotation marks (" "), the single quotation marks (' '), and the backslash (\) are all used to hide special characters from the shell. Each of these methods hides varying degrees of special characters from the shell.

The double quotation marks are the least powerful of the three methods. When you surround characters with double quotes, all the whitespace characters are hidden from the shell, but all other special characters are still interpreted by the shell. This type of quoting is most useful when you are assigning strings that contain more than one word to a variable. For example, if you want to assign the string `hello there` to the variable `greeting`, type the following command:

```
greeting="hello there" (for bash and pdksh)
set greeting = "hello there" (for tcsh)
```

This command stores the `hello there` string into the `greeting` variable as one word. If you type this command without using the quotes, you do not get the results that you want. `bash` and `pdksh` will not understand the command and will return an error message. `tcsh` simply assigns the value `hello` to the `greeting` variable and ignores the rest of the command line.

Single quotes are the most powerful form of quoting. They hide all special characters from the shell. This is useful if the command that you enter is intended for a program other than the shell.

Because the single quotes are the most powerful, you can write the `hello there` variable assignment using single quotes. You may not always want to do this. If the string being assigned to the `greeting` variable contains another variable, you have to use the double quotes. For example, if you want to include the name of the user in your greeting, then type the following command:

```
greeting="hello there $LOGNAME" (for bash and pdksh)
set greeting="hello there $LOGNAME" (for tcsh)
```

> **TIP**
>
> Remember that the LOGNAME variable is a shell variable that contains the Linux username of the person who is logged in to the system.

This stores the value `hello there root` into the `greeting` variable if you are logged in to Linux as `root`. If you try to write this command using single quotes, it will not work because the single quotes hide the dollar sign from the shell and the shell doesn't know that it is supposed to perform a variable substitution. The `greeting` variable will be assigned the value `hello there $LOGNAME` if you write the command using single quotes.

Using the backslash is the third way of hiding special characters from the shell. Like the single quotation mark method, the backslash hides all special characters from the shell, but it can hide only one character at a time, as opposed to groups of characters. You can rewrite the greeting example using the backslash instead of double quotation marks using the following command:

```
greeting=hello\ there (for bash and pdksh)
set greeting=hello\ there (for tcsh)
```

In this command, the backslash hides the space character from the shell, and the string `hello there` is assigned to the `greeting` variable.

Backslash quoting is used most often when you want to hide only a single character from the shell. This is usually done when you want to include a special character in a string. For example, if you want to store the price of a box of computer disks into a variable named `disk_price`, use the following command:

```
disk_price=\$5.00 (for bash and pdksh)
set disk_price = \$5.00 (for tcsh)
```

The backslash in this example will hide the dollar sign from the shell. If the backslash were not there, the shell would try to find a variable named 5 and perform a variable substitution on that variable. Assuming that no variable named 5 is defined, the shell assigns a value of `.00` to the `disk_price` variable. This is because the shell substitutes a value of null for the `$5` variable.

> **NOTE**
>
> The `disk_price` example could also have used single quotes to hide the dollar sign from the shell.

The back quotation marks (`` ` ``) perform a different function. They are used when you want to use the results of a command in another command. For example, if you want to set the value of the variable `contents` equal to the list of files in the current directory, type the following command:

```
contents=`ls` (for bash and pdksh)
set contents = `ls` (for tcsh)
```

This command executes the `ls` command and stores the results of the command into the `contents` variable. As you'll see in the upcoming section "Iteration Statements," this feature can be very useful when you want to write a shell program that performs some action on the results of another command.

The `test` Command

In `bash` and `pdksh`, a command called `test` is used to evaluate conditional expressions. You would typically use the `test` command to evaluate a condition that is used in a conditional statement or to evaluate the entrance or exit criteria for an iteration statement. The `test` command has the following syntax:

```
test expression
```

or

```
[ expression ]
```

Several built-in operators can be used with the `test` command. These operators can be classified into four groups: integer operators, string operators, file operators, and logical operators.

The shell integer operators perform similar functions to the string operators except that they act on integer arguments. Table 14.2 lists the `test` command's integer operators.

TABLE 14.2. THE `test` COMMAND'S INTEGER OPERATORS.

Operator	Meaning
int1 -eq int2	Returns True if int1 is equal to int2.
int1 -ge int2	Returns True if int1 is greater than or equal to int2.
int1 -gt int2	Returns True if int1 is greater than int2.
int1 -le int2	Returns True if int1 is less than or equal to int2.
int1 -lt int2	Returns True if int1 is less than int2.
int1 -ne int2	Returns True if int1 is not equal to int2.

The string operators are used to evaluate string expressions. Table 14.3 lists the string operators that are supported by the three shell programming languages.

14

SHELL
PROGRAMMING

TABLE 14.3. THE test COMMAND'S STRING OPERATORS.

Operator	Meaning
str1 = str2	Returns True if str1 is identical to str2.
str1 != str2	Returns True if str1 is not identical to str2.
str	Returns True if str is not null.
-n str	Returns True if the length of str is greater than zero.
-z str	Returns True if the length of str is equal to zero.

The test command's file operators are used to perform functions such as checking to see whether a file exists and checking to see what kind of file is passed as an argument to the test command. Table 14.4 lists the test command's file operators.

TABLE 14.4. THE test COMMAND'S FILE OPERATORS.

Operator	Meaning
-d filename	Returns True if file, filename is a directory.
-f filename	Returns True if file, filename is an ordinary file.
-r filename	Returns True if file, filename can be read by the process.
-s filename	Returns True if file, filename has a nonzero length.
-w filename	Returns True if file, filename can be written by the process.
-x filename	Returns True if file, filename is executable.

The test command's logical operators are used to combine two or more of the integer, string, or file operators or to negate a single integer, string, or file operator. Table 14.5 lists the test command's logical operators.

TABLE 14.5. THE test COMMAND'S LOGICAL OPERATORS.

Command	Meaning
! expr	Returns True if expr is not true.
expr1 -a expr2	Returns True if expr1 and expr2 are true.
expr1 -o expr2	Returns True if expr1 or expr2 is true.

The tcsh Equivalent of the test Command

The tcsh does not have a test command, but it supports the same function using expressions. The expression operators that tcsh supports are almost identical to those supported by the C language. These expressions are used mostly in the `if` and `while` commands, which are covered later in this chapter in the "Conditional Statements" and "Iteration Statements" sections.

The `tcsh` expressions support the same kind of operators as the `bash` and `pdksh` `test` command. These are integer, string, file, and logical expressions. The integer operators supported by `tcsh` expressions are listed in Table 14.6.

TABLE 14.6. THE TCSH EXPRESSION INTEGER OPERATORS.

Operator	Meaning
int1 <= int2	Returns True if int1 is less than or equal to int2.
int1 >= int2	Returns True if int1 is greater than or equal to int2.
int1 < int2	Returns True if int1 is less than int2.
int1 > int2	Returns True if int1 is greater than int2.

The string operators that `tcsh` expressions support are listed in Table 14.7.

TABLE 14.7. THE TCSH EXPRESSION STRING OPERATORS.

Operator	Meaning
str1 == str2	Returns True if str1 is equal to str2.
str1 != str2	Returns True if str1 is not equal to str2.

The file operators that `tcsh` expressions support are listed in Table 14.8.

TABLE 14.8. THE TCSH EXPRESSION FILE OPERATORS.

Operator	Meaning
-r file	Returns True if file is readable.
-w file	Returns True if file is writable.
-x file	Returns True if file is executable.
-e file	Returns True if file exists.
-o file	Returns True if file is owned by the current user.
-z file	Returns True if file is of size 0.
-f file	Returns True if file is a regular file.
-d file	Returns True if file is a directory file.

The logical operators that `tcsh` expressions support are listed in Table 14.9.

TABLE 14.9. THE TCSH EXPRESSION LOGICAL OPERATORS.

Operator	Meaning
exp1 ¦¦ exp2	Returns True if exp1 is true or if exp2 is true.
exp1 && exp2	Returns True if exp1 is true and exp2 is true.
! exp	Returns True if exp is not true.

Conditional Statements

The `bash`, `pdksh`, and `tcsh` each have two forms of conditional statements. These are the `if` statement and the `case` statement. These statements are used to execute different parts of your shell program depending on whether certain conditions are true. As with most statements, the syntax for these statements is slightly different between the different shells.

The `if` Statement

All three shells support nested `if-then-else` statements. These statements provide you with a way of performing complicated conditional tests in your shell programs. The syntax of the `if` statement is the same for `bash` and `pdksh` and is shown here:

```
if [ expression ]
then
        commands
elif [ expression2 ]
then
        commands
else
        commands
fi
```

> **NOTE**
>
> The `elif` and `else` clauses are both optional parts of the `if` statement. Also note that `bash` and `pdksh` use the reverse of the statement name in most of their complex statements to signal the end of the statement. In this statement, the `fi` keyword is used to signal the end of the `if` statement.

The `elif` statement is an abbreviation of `else if`. This statement is executed only if none of the expressions associated with the `if` statement or any `elif` statements before it were true. The commands associated with the `else` statement are executed only if none of the expressions associated with the `if` statement or any of the `elif` statements were true.

In `tcsh`, the `if` statement has two different forms. The first form provides the same function as the `bash` and `pdksh` `if` statement. This form of `if` statement has the following syntax:

```
if (expression1) then
     commands
else if (expression2) then
     commands
else
     commands
endif
```

The second form of `if` statement provided by `tcsh` is a simple version of the first `if` statement. This form of `if` statement evaluates only a single expression. If the expression is true, it executes a single command; if the expression is false, nothing happens. The syntax for this form of `if` statement is the following:

```
if (expression) command
```

This statement can be written using the first form of `if` statement by writing the `if` without any `else` or `else if` clauses. This form just saves a little typing.

The following is an example of a `bash` or `pdksh` `if` statement. This statement checks to see whether there is a `.profile` file in the current directory:

```
if [ -f .profile ]
then
     echo "There is a .profile file in the current directory."
else
     echo "Could not find the .profile file."
fi
```

The same statement written using the `tcsh` syntax is shown here:

```
#
if ( { -f .profile } ) then
     echo "There is a .profile file in the current directory."
else
     echo "Could not find the .profile file."
endif
```

14

SHELL PROGRAMMING

> **NOTE**
>
> Notice that in the tcsh example the first line starts with a #. This is required for tcsh to recognize the file containing the commands as a tcsh script file.

The case Statement

The case statement enables you to compare a pattern with several other patterns and execute a block of code if a match is found. The shell case statement is quite a bit more powerful than the case statement in Pascal or the switch statement in C. This is because in the shell case statement you can compare strings with wildcard characters in them, whereas with the Pascal and C equivalents, you can only compare enumerated types or integer values.

Once again, the syntax for the case statement is identical for bash and pdksh and different for tcsh. The syntax for bash and pdksh is the following:

```
case string1 in
      str1)
            commands;;
      str2)
            commands;;
      *)
            commands;;
esac
```

string1 is compared to str1 and str2. If one of these strings matches string1, all commands up to the double semicolon (;;) are executed. If neither str1 nor str2 matches string1, the commands associated with the asterisk are executed. This is the default case condition because the asterisk matches all strings.

The tcsh equivalent of the bash and pdksh case statement is called the switch statement. This statement's syntax closely follows the C switch statement syntax. Here it is:

```
switch (string1)
      case   str1:
            statements
      breaksw
      case   str2:
            statements
      breaksw
      default:
            statements
      breaksw
endsw
```

This behaves in the same manner as the `bash` and `pdksh` `case` statement. Each string following the keyword `case` is compared with `string1`. If any of these strings matches `string1`, the code follows it until the `breaksw` keyword is executed. If none of the strings match, the code follows the default keyword until the `breaksw` keyword is executed.

The following code is an example of a `bash` or `pdksh` `case` statement. This code checks to see if the first command-line option is `-i` or `-e`. If it is `-i`, the program counts the number of lines in the file specified by the second command-line option that begins with the letter i. If the first option is `-e`, the program counts the number of lines in the file specified by the second command-line option that begins with the letter e. If the first command-line option is not `-i` or `-e`, the program prints a brief error message to the screen.

```
case $1 in
    -i)
        count=`grep ^i $2 | wc -l`
        echo "The number of lines in $2 that start with an i is $count"
        ;;
    -e)
        count=`grep ^e $2 | wc -l`
        echo "The number of lines in $2 that start with an e is $count"
        ;;
    * )
        echo "That option is not recognized"
        ;;
esac
```

The same example written in `tcsh` syntax is shown here:

```
# remember that the first line must start with a # when using tcsh
switch ( $1 )
    case -i | i:
        set count = `grep ^i $2 | wc -l`
        echo "The number of lines in $2 that begin with i is $count"
    breaksw
    case -e | e:
        set count = `grep ^e $2 | wc -l`
        echo "The number of lines in $2 that begin with e is $count"
    breaksw
    default:
        echo "That option is not recognized"
    breaksw
endsw
```

14

SHELL PROGRAMMING

Iteration Statements

The shell languages also provide several iteration or looping statements. The most commonly used of these is the `for` statement. In addition to the `for` loop, there are several others (such as `while` and `until`) but they are all variations of the same approach. The `for` loop is by far the most commonly used in shell programs.

The `for` Statement

The `for` statement executes the commands that are contained within it a specified number of times. `bash` and `pdksh` have two variations of the `for` statement. The `for` statement syntax is the same in both `bash` and `pdksh`.

The first form of `for` statement that `bash` and `pdksh` support has the following syntax:

```
for var1 in list
do
      commands
done
```

In this form, the `for` statement executes once for each item in the list. This list can be a variable that contains several words separated by spaces or it can be a list of values that is typed directly into the statement. Each time through the loop, the variable `var1` is assigned to the current item in the list until the last one is reached.

The second form of `for` statement has the following syntax:

```
for var1
do
      statements
done
```

In this form, the `for` statement executes once for each item in the variable `var1`. When this syntax of the `for` statement is used, the shell program assumes that the `var1` variable contains all the positional parameters that were passed into the shell program on the command line.

Typically, this form of `for` statement is the equivalent of writing the following `for` statement:

```
for var1 in "$@"
do
      statements
done
```

The equivalent of the `for` statement in `tcsh` is called the `foreach` statement. It behaves in the same manner as the `bash` and `pdksh` `for` statement. The syntax of the `foreach` statement is the following:

```
foreach name (list)
     commands
end
```

The following is an example of the `bash` or `pdksh` style of `for` statement. This example takes as command-line options any number of text files. The program reads in each of these files, converts all the letters to uppercase, and then stores the results in a file of the same name but with a `.caps` extension.

```
for file
do
tr a-z A-Z < $file >$file.caps
done
```

The same example written in `tcsh` shell language is shown next:

```
#
foreach file ($*)
   tr a-z A-Z < $file >$file.caps
end
```

The while Statement

Another iteration statement offered by the shell programming language is the `while` statement. This statement causes a block of code to be executed while a provided conditional expression is true. The syntax for the `while` statement in `bash` and `pdksh` is the following:

```
while expression
do
     statements
done
```

The syntax for the `while` statement in `tcsh` is the following:

```
while (expression)
     statements
end
```

The following is an example of the `bash` and `pdksh` style of `while` statement. This program lists the parameters that were passed to the program, along with the parameter number.

```
count=1
while [ -n "$*" ]
do
     echo "This is parameter number $count $1"
     shift
     count=`expr $count + 1`
done
```

As you will see in the section titled "The shift Command," the shift command moves the command-line parameters over one space to the left.

The same program written in the tcsh language is shown next:

```
#
set count = 1
while ( "$*" != "" )
        echo "This is parameter number $count $1"
        shift
        set count = `expr $count + 1`
end
```

The until Statement

The until statement is very similar in syntax and function to the while statement. The only real difference between the two is that the until statement executes its code block while its conditional expression is false, and the while statement executes its code block while its conditional expression is true. The syntax for the until statement in bash and pdksh is

```
until expression
do
        commands
done
```

The same example that was used for the while statement can be used for the until statement. All you have to do to make it work is negate the condition. This is shown in the following code:

```
count=1
until [ -z "$*" ]
do
        echo "This is parameter number $count $1"
        shift
        count=`expr $count + 1`
done
```

The only difference between this example and the while statement example is that the -n test command option (which means that the string has nonzero length) was removed, and the -z test option (which means that the string has zero length) was put in its place.

In practice, the until statement is not very useful because any until statement you write can also be written as a while statement. tcsh does not have an equivalent of the until statement other than rewriting it as a while loop.

The shift Command

bash, pdksh, and tcsh all support a command called shift. The shift command moves the current values stored in the positional parameters one position to the left. For example, if the values of the current positional parameters are

```
$1 = -r   $2 = file1   $3 = file2
```

and you execute the shift command

```
shift
```

the resulting positional parameters are as follows:

```
$1 = file1   $2 = file2
```

You can also move the positional parameters over more than one place by specifying a number with the shift command. The following command will shift the positional parameters two places:

```
shift 2
```

This is a very useful command when you have a shell program that needs to parse command-line options. This is true because options are typically preceded by a hyphen and a letter that indicates what the option is to be used for. Because options are usually processed in a loop of some kind, you often want to skip to the next positional parameter once you have identified which option should be coming next. For example, the following shell program expects two command-line options—one that specifies an input file and one that specifies an output file. The program reads the input file, translates all the characters in the input file into uppercase, then stores the results in the specified output file. The following example was written using bash, pdksh syntax.

```
while [ "$1" ]
do
      if [ "$1" = "-i" ] then
            infile="$2"
            shift 2
      elif [ "$1" = "-o" ]
      then
            outfile="$2"
            shift 2
      else
            echo "Program $0 does not recognize option $1"
      fi
done

tr a-z A-Z nfile $outfile
```

The select Statement

pdksh offers one iteration statement that neither bash nor tcsh provides. This is the select statement. This is actually a very useful statement. It is quite a bit different from the other iteration statements because it does not actually execute a block of shell code repeatedly while a condition is true or false. What the select statement does is enable you to automatically generate simple text menus. The syntax for the select statement is

```
select menuitem [in list_of_items]
do
        commands
done
```

where square brackets are used to enclose the optional part of the statement.

When a select statement is executed, pdksh creates a numbered menu item for each element in the *list_of_items*. This *list_of_items* can be a variable that contains more than one item, such as choice1 choice2, or it can be a list of choices typed in the command. For example:

```
select menuitem in choice1 choice2 choice3
```

If the list_of_items is not provided, the select statement uses the positional parameters just as it does with the for statement.

After the user of the program containing a select statement picks one of the menu items by typing the number associated with it, the select statement stores the value of the selected item in the menuitem variable. The statements contained in the do block can then perform actions on this menu item.

The following example illustrates a potential use for the select statement. This example displays three menu items and when the user chooses one of them, it asks whether that is the intended selection. If the user enters anything other than y or Y, the menu is redisplayed.

```
select menuitem in pick1 pick2 pick3
do
        echo "Are you sure you want to pick $menuitem"
        read res
        if [ $res = "y" -o $res = "Y" ]
        then
                break
        fi
done
```

A few new commands are introduced in this example. The read command is used to get input from the user. It stores anything that the user types into the specified variable. The break command is used to exit a while, until, repeat, select, or for statement.

The repeat Statement

tcsh has an iteration statement that has no equivalent in pdksh or bash. This is the repeat statement. The repeat statement executes a single command a specified number of times. The syntax for the repeat statement is the following:

```
repeat count command
```

The following is an example of the repeat statement. It takes a set of numbers as command-line options and prints that number of periods to the screen. This program acts as a very primitive graphing program.

```
#
foreach num ($*)
      repeat $num echo -n "."
      echo ""
end
```

> **NOTE**
>
> Any repeat statement can be rewritten as a while or for statement. The repeat syntax is just more convenient.

Functions

The shell languages enable you to define your own functions. These functions behave in much the same way as functions you define in C and other programming languages. The main advantage of using functions as opposed to writing all of your shell code in line is for organizational purposes. Code written using functions tends to be much easier to read and maintain and also tends to be smaller, because you can group common code into functions instead of putting it everywhere it is needed. The tcsh shell does not support functions.

The syntax for creating a function in bash and pdksh is the following:

```
fname () {
      shell commands
}
```

pdksh also allows the following syntax:

```
function fname {
      shell commands
}
```

Both of these forms behave in the exact same way.

Once you have defined your function using one of these forms, you can invoke it by entering the following command:

```
fname [parm1 parm2 parm3 ...]
```

Notice that you can pass any number of parameters to your function. When you do pass parameters to a function, it sees those parameters as positional parameters, just as a shell program does when you pass parameters to it on the command line. For example, the following shell program contains several functions, each of which is performing a task associated with one of the command-line options. This example illustrates many of the topics covered in this chapter. It reads all the files that are passed on the command line and—depending on the option that was used—writes the files out in all uppercase letters, writes the files out in all lowercase letters, or prints the files.

```
upper () {
        shift
        for i
        do
                tr a-z A-Z <$1 >$1.out
                rm   $1
                mv $1.out $1
                shift
        done; }

lower () {
        shift
        for i
        do
                tr A-Z a-z <$1 >$1.out
                rm $1
                mv $1.out $1
                shift
        done; }

print () {
        shift
        for i
        do
                lpr $1
                shift
        done; }

usage_error () {
        echo "$1 syntax is $1 <option> <input files>"
        echo ""
        echo "where option is one of the following"
        echo "p  -- to print frame files"
```

```
        echo "u  -- to save as uppercase"
        echo "l  -- to save as lowercase"; }

case $1
in
     p ¦ -p)      print $@;;
     u ¦ -u)          upper $@;;
     l ¦ -l)      lower $@;;
     *)               usage_error $0;;
esac
```

Summary

This chapter introduced you to many of the features of the bash, pdksh, and tcsh programming languages. As you become familiar with using Linux, you will find that you use shell programming languages more and more often.

Even though the shell languages are very powerful and also quite easy to learn, you might run into some situations where shell programs are not suited to the problem you are solving. In these cases, you may want to investigate the possibility of using one of the other languages available under Linux. At this point, there are a lot of other programming languages you may want to look at. To learn more about:

awk, which is useful for handling both search patterns and large columns of numbers, see Chapter 25, "gawk."

Perl, useful for many quick script tasks as well as Web pages, see Chapter 28, "Perl."

Smalltalk/X, which is used to program object-oriented applications under the X GUI, see Chapter 31, "Smalltalk/X."

14

SHELL PROGRAMMING

FTP and Telnet

by Tim Parker

IN THIS CHAPTER

CHAPTER 15

Two of the most useful tools for communicating with other Linux and UNIX systems (or any operating system, for that matter) are FTP (for transferring files) and Telnet (for logging in to other systems). In this chapter we'll look at how you can use both tools, as well as mention TFTP, which is a simplified version of FTP.

FTP

There are two different ways to use FTP and TFTP: through a command line or through a graphical interface. Most Linux systems are restricted to character-based commands unless you find a shareware or commercial GUI product. GUI-based FTP clients are much more common on Windows machines. Both character and GUI versions accomplish exactly the same task (the transfer of files from one machine to another) but do it through a different user interface. We'll concentrate on the character-based versions here because that's what most Linux systems provide.

When it comes to what the function of FTP is and what FTP does, the name essentially says it all: File Transfer Protocol. FTP was developed specifically to provide a method of transferring files from one machine to another without needing complex communications protocols like XMODEM, YMODEM, ZMODEM, or Kermit, as well as removing the need to log in to the remote machine fully. FTP provides a quick method of logging into the remote machine, moving about the file system (subject to permissions, of course), and transferring files either to or from the remote system quickly.

To use FTP to transfer files, the machine you are running (the client) must have FTP client software. Linux and UNIX machines almost always have the FTP client software included as part of their basic distribution system. The other end of the connection—the machine you want to connect to—is called the server, and it must be running a program that accepts incoming FTP requests. This is called the FTP server and usually must be running all the time for FTP connections to work.

Multitasking operating systems like Linux usually have the FTP server program included as part of the basic distribution. In most cases, the server is called "ftpd," which stands for FTP daemon. (A *daemon* is a program that operates in the background while a machine is running.) The ftpd daemon is almost always loaded automatically as part of the Linux boot process, unless the system administrator explicitly removes it.

If you are connecting to a PC (running OS/2, Windows, Windows 95, NetWare, or a similar operating system) or a Macintosh server, chances are the server will not have FTP server software running by default. When these operating systems are installed, they lack most of the TCP/IP services. The system administrator must activate them explicitly. Without the server software running on a PC, you can't connect to the server with your FTP client.

Most TCP/IP packages for PCs and Macintoshes include a server program for FTP that enables other users to connect to that machine. Indeed, most TCP/IP packages have both the FTP client and FTP server software as part of the distribution, enabling you to set your machine up as both a client and a server to others (assuming you want to allow others access to your file system).

Setting Up FTP Server Service

Before we look at how to connect and transfer files from another machine (the server), we should mention how you can set up your machine as an FTP server. You may have to do this on the remote machine, too. Each machine that is to accept transfer requests must have the FTP server software active. This is pretty easy to do, as you will see in a moment. You can also set up your existing machine as an FTP server, allowing other machines on the network to connect into your system and transfer files.

All the clients and server software programs you might need are included as part of the Linux distribution (although it must be installed, of course). It doesn't matter whether you are setting up access-controlled or anonymous FTP services because the basic steps you follow to install and configure the FTP daemon are the same.

The configuration process starts with choosing an FTP site name. You don't really need a site name, although it can make it easier for remote users to find your system, especially if they are using an anonymous login. FTP site names are usually of the general format

```
ftp.domain_name.domain_type
```

where `domain_name` is the domain name (or an alias) of the FTP server's domain, and `domain_type` is the usual DNS extension. For example, if you have an FTP site named

```
ftp.tpci.com
```

it is clear that this is the FTP server for anyone accessing the `tpci.com` domain.

The FTP daemon, called `ftpd`, must be started. Usually, the `inetd` process starts the FTP daemon by watching the TCP command port (channel 21) for an arriving request for a connection. Then it starts `ftpd` to service that request.

> **NOTE**
>
> Make sure that `ftpd` can be started when needed by `inetd` by checking the `inetd` configuration file (usually `/etc/inetd.config`) for a line that looks like this:
>
> ```
> ftp    stream   tcp   nowait   root    /etc/ftpd    ftpd
> ```
>
> If this line doesn't exist, add it. With most Linux and UNIX systems, this line is already in the `inetd` configuration file, although it may be commented out—in which case you should remove the comment symbol.

The `ftp` entry in the `inetd` configuration file tells `inetd` that FTP is to use TCP and that it should spawn `ftpd` every time a new connection is made to the `ftp` port. The `ftpd` daemon can be started with the `-l` option attached, which enables logging. You can ignore this option if you want as long files get quite large, quickly.

If you are going to set up a user-based FTP service where each person accessing your system has a valid login name and password, you must create an account for each user in the `/etc/passwd` file as you would if they were direct users of the Linux system. To set up an anonymous FTP server, you must create a login for the anonymous user ID. This is done in the normal process by adding a user to the `/etc/passwd` file. The login name should be the name you want people to use when they access your system. Usually this name is "anonymous" or "ftp." You need to select a login directory for the anonymous user that can be protected from the rest of the file system. A typical `/etc/passwd` entry looks like this:

```
ftp:*:400:51:Anonymous FTP access:/usr/ftp:/bin/false
```

This sets up the anonymous user with a login of `ftp`. The asterisk password prevents anyone gaining access to the account. The user ID number (400) is unique to the system. The group ID (51) shows the group the `ftp` login belongs to.

For better security, it is a good idea to create a separate group just for the anonymous FTP access (edit the `/etc/group` file to add a new group), then set the FTP user to that group. Only the anonymous FTP user should belong to that group, as it can be used to set file permissions to restrict access and make your system more secure. The login directory in the example above is `/usr/ftp`, although you can choose any directory as long as it belongs to the anonymous FTP user (for security reasons, again). The startup program shown in the above example is `/bin/false`, which helps protect your system from access to accounts and utilities that do not have a strong password protection.

Using FTP

It doesn't matter whether you are on a Linux system, a UNIX machine, a Windows PC, or a Macintosh. When you are ready to use FTP to transfer files, you start a client FTP software package, specify the name of the remote system you want to connect to, then let the two machines establish an FTP session. After you are connected, you can start transferring files.

Character-based FTP is usually started with the name or IP address of the target machine. GUI-based FTP clients usually display a window first, from which you can select a Connect option or the name or IP address of the remote system from a list. If you use a machine name, such as "darkstar" or "superduck," the name must be resolvable into an IP address by your system for FTP to connect.

When FTP successfully connects to the remote machine, you normally must be able to log in with a valid user login and password. Some systems allow an anonymous or guest login. On large networks where a system such as Yellow Pages (YP) or Network Information Services (NIS) is used, logins are usually permitted across the network onto most machines. If YP or NIS is not employed on your LAN, you must be in the valid user file of the remote machine to obtain FTP access (except for anonymous FTP, of course). You can log into the remote with a different user ID from your local machine's login (if there is one). To transfer files from one system to another, you must have proper permissions on both systems.

Here's a very important point: after logging in using FTP, you are not actually on the remote machine. You are still logically on your client machine, and all instructions for file transfers and directory movement are with respect to your local machine and not the remote one. This is the opposite of Telnet, a difference that causes considerable confusion among newcomers to FTP and Telnet.

> **WARNING**
>
> Remember that all references to files and directories are relative to the machine that initiated the FTP session. If you are not careful, you can accidentally overwrite existing files.

Connecting with FTP

You need a login and password to connect to a remote machine (the server), and you have your local machine ready to run FTP (the client). The appearance of the screens and the prompts that you see from the remote machine vary considerably, depending on the operating system and FTP software each system is running.

On a UNIX or Linux system, and many DOS TCP/IP systems, you can start FTP with the name of the remote system or its IP address, the character-based FTP client is started with the IP address of the remote machine, and after a user ID and password are supplied, you're connected.

FTP Commands

Once you have connected to a remote system, you want to move about the directory structure and transfer files. An FTP user has a number of commands available; the most frequently used commands are summarized in Table 15.1. These commands are usually used only with character-based FTP clients, as the GUI-based clients use menu items for these functions.

TABLE 15.1. FTP USER COMMANDS.

FTP Command	Description
ascii	Switch to ASCII transfer mode
binary	Switch to binary transfer mode
cd	Change directory on the server
close	Terminate the connection
del	Delete a file on the server
dir	Display the server directory
get	Fetch a file from the server
hash	Display a pound character for each block transmitted
help	Display help
lcd	Change directory on the client
mget	Fetch several files from the server
mput	Send several files to the server
open	Connect to a server
put	Send a file to the server
pwd	Display the current server directory

FTP Command	*Description*
quote	Supply an FTP command directly
quit	Terminate the FTP session

The primary file transfer commands are get and put. Remember that all commands are relative to the client (the machine you issue the commands on), so a get command moves a file from the server to the client whereas a put command puts a file from the client to the server.

Character-based FTP clients show how this works quite easily. Consider the following example:

```
get autoexec.bat
705 bytes received in 0.1 seconds (0.00 kbytes/s)
```

Here the user has logged in to a remote machine, then issued a get command to transfer the file autoexec.bat from the remote (which is a Windows FTP server) to the local client. As you can see, the FTP client issues a status report showing the size of the file and the amount of time it took to transfer.

The mget and mput commands are similar to get and put, but they transfer more than one file at a time. For example, the command:

```
mget config.*
```

will transfer all the files name config.* from the FTP server to the local client's directory. For each file that matches the pattern, the server prompts to make sure you want to transfer it.

You can move around the remote machine using the cd command to change directories and pwd to print the current directory (these are UNIX commands). Note that if you are on a client UNIX machine, the UNIX / must be used instead of the DOS \ character to indicate directory changes. Again, you have to know the operating system of the remote machine to prevent problems.

File access rights and permissions are always considered by FTP when files are transferred and you move into other directories. If you do not have the proper permissions as set by the server, you can't perform the action, and you will see an error message.

File Transfer Modes

FTP was developed in the early days of TCP/IP, when practically all files were ASCII format. When binaries had to be transferred (a binary defined as any file that did not

15

FTP AND TELNET

have the regular ASCII characters), the mode of the transfer had to be manually changed from ASCII (often called text) to binary. FTP enables file transfers in several formats, which are usually system-dependent. The majority of systems (including UNIX systems) have only two modes: text and binary. Some mainframe installations add support for EBCDIC, while many sites have a local type that is designed for fast transfers between local network machines. (The local type may use 32- or 64-bit words.)

To change the format of the file transfers to allow you to move any file other than a text file, you must first make sure FTP is in binary mode with this command:

```
bin
```

You can return to character mode with the command

```
ascii
```

It's important to be aware of which mode you are in. Linux FTP, by default, usually starts in character (ASCII) mode.

Text transfers use ASCII characters separated by carriage-return and newline characters, whereas binary enables transfer of characters with no conversion or formatting. Binary mode is faster than text and also enables for the transfer of all ASCII values (necessary for non-text files). On most systems FTP starts in text mode, although many system administrators now set FTP to binary mode for their users' convenience. FTP cannot transfer file permissions, as these are not specified as part of the protocol. Some FTP clients and servers can detect the type of file and adjust themselves accordingly. If in doubt, use binary.

Usually there are no keyboard shortcuts (such as pressing the Tab key to fill in names that match) available with FTP. This means you have to type in the name of files or directories in their entirety (and correctly). If you misspell a file or directory name, you will get error messages and have to try again. Luckily, if you are performing the FTP session through an X Window or Windows environment, you can cut and paste lines from earlier in your session.

Anonymous FTP Access

FTP requires a user ID and password to enable file transfer capabilities, but there is a more liberal method of allowing general access to a file or directory called *anonymous FTP.* Anonymous FTP removes the requirement for a login account on the remote machine, usually allowing the login anonymous with a password of either guest or the user's actual login name. The following session shows the use of an anonymous FTP system:

```
tpci> ftp uofo.edu
Connected to uofo.edu.
220 uofo.edu FTP server ready.
Name (uofo:username): anonymous
331 Guest login ok, send userID as password.
Password: tparker
230 Guest login ok, access restrictions apply.
ftp>
```

If the remote system is set to allow anonymous logins, you will sometimes be prompted for a password and then given a warning about access limitations. If there is a file on the remote system you require, a get command will transfer it. Anonymous FTP sites are becoming common, especially with the expanding interest in the Internet.

If anonymous FTP is supported on a remote system, a message usually tells you exactly that. The login shown below is for the Linux FTP archive site called sunsite.unc.edu:

```
ftp sunsite.unc.edu
331 Guest login ok, send your complete e-mail address as password.
Enter username (default: anonymous): anonymous
Enter password [tparker@tpci.com]:
¦FTP¦ Open
230-                  WELCOME to UNC and SUN's anonymous ftp server
230-                         University of North Carolina
230-                     Office FOR Information Technology
230-                             SunSITE.unc.edu
230 Guest login ok, access restrictions apply.
FTP>
```

After the login process is completed, you see the prompt FTP>, indicating the remote system is ready to accept commands.

When you log on to some systems, you may see a short message containing instructions for downloading files, explaining any restrictions that are placed on anonymous FTP users, or information about the location of useful files. For example, you may see messages like this (taken from the Linux FTP site):

```
To get a binary file, type:  BINARY and then: GET "File.Name" newfilename
To get a text file, type:    ASCII  and then: GET "File.Name" newfilename
Names MUST match upper, lower case exactly. Use the "quotes" as shown.
To get a directory, type: DIR. To change directory, type: CD "Dir.Name"
To read a short text file, type: GET "File.Name" TT
For more, type HELP or see FAQ in gopher.
To quit, type EXIT or Control-Z.

230-  If you email to info@sunsite.unc.edu you will be sent help
➥information
230-  about how to use the different services sunsite provides.
```

```
230- We use the Wuarchive experimental ftpd. if you "get"
➥<directory>.tar.Z
230- or <file>.Z it will compress and/or tar it on the fly. Using ".gz"
➥instead
230- of ".Z" will use the GNU zip (/pub/gnu/gzip*) instead, a superior
230- compression method.
```

Most anonymous FTP sites are set to read-only and do not allow you to upload files
(put files) to them. You are usually very restricted regarding where you can go in their
file system, too.

Trivial File Transfer Protocol (TFTP)

The Trivial File Transfer Protocol (TFTP) differs from FTP in two primary ways: it does
not log on to the remote machine and it uses the User Datagram Protocol (UDP) connectionless transport protocol instead of TCP. TFTP is usually not used for file transfers
between machines where FTP can be used instead, although TFTP is useful when a diskless terminal or workstation is involved. Typically, TFTP is used when a file is requested
from a very busy server or when it can be delivered at any time. Using TFTP is much
like using email: you send a message asking for a file, and eventually the file arrives
back on your system.

TFTP handles access and file permissions by imposing restraints of its own. On most
systems a file can be transferred using TFTP only if it is accessible to all users. Because
of lax access regulations, most system administrators impose more control over TFTP or
ban its use altogether.

The main instructions from the TFTP command set are shown in Table 15.2. Although
they appear similar to the FTP command set, they differ in several important aspects
because of the connectionless aspect of the TFTP protocol. Most noticeable is the
connect command, which simply determines the remote's address instead of initiating a
connection.

TABLE 15.2. TFTP'S COMMAND SET.

TFTP Command	Description
binary	Use binary mode for transfers
connect	Determine the remote's address
get	Retrieve a file from the remote
put	Transfer a file to the remote
trace	Display protocol codes
verbose	Display all information

TFTP enables both text and binary transfers. As with both Telnet and FTP, TFTP uses a server process (`tftpd` on a UNIX system) and an executable, usually called `tftp`. Because of the nature of TFTP, Windows and similar PC-based operating systems don't usually support it. In most cases, TFTP is used between UNIX machines.

A sample character-based TFTP session is shown here, with full trace options and binary transfers turned on:

```
> tftp
tftp> connect tpci_hpws4
tftp> trace
Packet tracing on.
tftp> binary
Binary mode on.
tftp> verbose
Verbose mode on.
tftp> status
Connected to tpci_hpws4.
Mode: octet Verbose: on Tracing: on
Rexmt-interval: 5 seconds, Max-timeout: 25 seconds
tftp> get /usr/rmaclean/docs/draft1
getting from tpci_hpws4:/usr/rmaclean/docs/draft1 to /tmp/draft1 [octet]
sent RRQ <file=/usr/rmaclean/docs/draft1, mode=octet>
received DATA <block1, 512 bytes>
send ACK <block=1>
received DATA <block2, 512 bytes>
send ACK <block=3>
received DATA <block4, 128 bytes>
send ACK <block=3>
Received 1152 bytes in 0.2 second 46080 bits/s]
tftp> quit
```

You may have to use TFTP in some cases where network conditions are bad or the server doesn't accept standard FTP. Usually, though, FTP should be your choice of protocol.

Using Telnet

Telnet gives you the capability to log into a remote server and act as though you were physically attached to that machine and all its resources. If the server has a powerful CPU, you can use that CPU instead of your weaker local processor. If the server has some special devices, such as a scanner, CD-writer, or magneto-optical storage device, you can use them. You can also use the remote server's file system.

Using Telnet is quite simple because the protocol takes care of all the configuration and setup processes for you. As part of its startup, Telnet passes a series of messages between the client and server that establish the terminal identifications and special features your terminal allows. All you have to do, really, is tell Telnet which machine you want to log into, then supply the user ID and password.

There are a number of Telnet implementations available for practically every operating system there is. These implementations include commercial products (usually as part of a TCP/IP suite) and public domain or shareware programs that are designed specifically for `telnet` emulation. The choice of a `telnet` program is pretty much a personal one because the programs all do the same task.

Starting `telnet` is a simple matter. If you are at a command prompt, such as on a Linux system, you normally enter the `telnet` command followed by the name of the remote machine you want to log into. You can supply either a name or an IP address for the remote machine, although a name must be resolvable by TCP/IP into an IP address. Some systems may impose security limitations on Telnet, so if you are not sure of access capabilities, check with your system administrator.

The `telnet` command supports a lot of options that can customize the behavior of the service, although they are seldom used in typical Telnet sessions. The options supported tend to change depending on the version of Telnet and the operating system, so you may want to check the documentation supplied with your operating system if you want to modify the default behavior of Telnet. Most people find that the standard application is good enough, with no need for options.

Using Telnet and GUIs

If you want to connect to a remote GUI system and display graphics on your local machine, you need to instruct both ends of the connection how to display graphics. If you are connecting from one Linux machine to another, the process is quite easy because Linux has the capability to redirect windowing output with a minimal of fuss. If you are calling from one UNIX or Linux machine to another running Motif, for example, the first step is to allow the remote machine to open windows on your terminal. This is done with the `xhost` command. The command

```
xhost +
```

instructs Linux to allow a remote machine to open windows on your display. (This is an all-encompassing command, allowing any remote machine to open windows on your terminal. This may not be desired, so you can specify the remote machine name following the plus sign to limit access, if you want.)

After you have established a Telnet connection to the remote GUI-based system, you need to instruct it to open all windows on your local machine. With Linux, you can do this with the DISPLAY environment variable. If you are using the C Shell, issue a command like this:

```
setenv DISPLAY tpciws5:0.0
```

where tpciws5 is the name of your local terminal. The :0.0 portion of the command following your local terminal name must be supplied, or the GUI will not open windows properly. The setenv command is used by the C Shell to set the environment variable DISPLAY used by Motif and X. Under the Bourne and Korn shells, you must change the command to reflect the syntax of those shells.

TN3270 and Others

Depending on the type of system you are logging into, Telnet may not be able to provide proper terminal characteristics for you. This is especially true of machines, such as IBM mainframes and some minicomputers, that require IBM 3270 terminal emulation. The basic Telnet program is unable to provide this capability, so a special version of Telnet called TN3270 is usually supplied with telnet. TN3270 offers proper IBM 3270 terminal emulation. Some TCP/IP suites also include TN5250, which is a higher-capability terminal than the 3270. Both 3270 and 5250 terminals support full color.

TN3270 and TN5250 can be used with any type of server as long as it can emulate those terminal types. You can use TN3270 to obtain color when connected to a smaller UNIX server, for example, whereas Telnet won't provide that capability. Most TN3270 and TN5250 systems enable you to change onscreen fonts and colors at will.

Summary

FTP and Telnet are extremely useful on local area networks where you have many applications residing on different machines. Telnet is very easy to get going, start up, and use. All you need is the remote machine's IP address and a connection (through TCP/IP) to the network. From here, there are a number of related subjects you may want to read about. To learn about:

Setting up X on your Linux systems, see Chapter 22, "Installing and Configuring XFree86."

Administering your system and the processes on it, see Part VI, starting with Chapter 32, "System Administration Basics."

FTP sites that hold Linux binaries, see Appendix A, "Linux FTP Sites and Newsgroups."

15

FTP AND TELNET

Editing, Typesetting, and More

IN THIS PART

Text Editors:
vi and emacs

by Peter MacKinnon

What Are Editors and Why Do I Need One?

A *text editor* is one of the most essential tools provided with the Linux (or virtually any) operating system. With an editor, you can create and modify text files that have a wide variety of applications:

- User files such as .login and .cshrc
- System files
- Shell programs
- Documents
- Mail messages

These are but a few of the many different types of text files that you will use when working with Linux. Basically, editors enable you to insert, delete, move, and search text ranging from individual characters to thousands of lines.

Two of the most popular editors for the Linux system are emacs and vi. These editors are both full-screen text editors; put simply, they use every row and column of your terminal screen to display the textual contents of a file. Both of these editors feature a rich set of commands. The essential commands for manipulating text can be learned reasonably quickly; the more sophisticated commands may take a little longer to master. However, you will likely appreciate this investment as you see how much time these powerful tools can save you.

Choosing one editor over another can be a matter of taste. Both emacs and vi are efficient and can handle virtually any size file. The emacs editor is better suited to complex editing tasks and comes with an online help facility, but for simple editing jobs, either editor is equally good. It comes down to whichever one you feel more comfortable using.

The Editing Functions

Although there are a variety of text editors for Linux that have different interfaces, they all basically do the same things. Any useful text editor should support the following features at a minimum.

Inserting and Deleting Text

The most intrinsic function of a text editor is to allow you to enter and erase characters as you see fit. This also implies that you have complete control over the movement of the cursor and its placement in the text.

Reading and Writing Files

Because you will want to save the text files that you create for future use and reuse, an editor can write your text to an external file. Whenever you need to make changes to your file, an editor can read the file from disk. A nice feature is that text editors are designed to accommodate ASCII-formatted files, so an editor (such as emacs) can read any file written by another editor (such as vi), and vice versa.

Searching Text

Personally scanning line after line of a large file for instances of a particular word is either a great way to improve your powers of concentration or an exercise in self-torture. That is why text editors provide sophisticated search capabilities. These include the use of regular expressions, as well as fixed strings. Remember that regular expressions include metacharacters (such as ., ?, and *) that replace and expand unknown text patterns.

Editors also support search-and-replace functions that allow you to change multiple instances of a string pattern with a single command.

Copying and Moving Text

Because there is no guarantee that the way text is initially typed into a file is the way it should forever remain, editors provide you with the means to copy, cut, and move (or paste) blocks of text. These blocks can range in size from several pages to a single character. The distinction between copying and cutting text is that cutting deletes the selected block of text after it has been copied to a buffer, whereas copying does not.

Editing Buffers

What is a buffer, you ask? *Buffers* are places in the memory of the editing program where text can reside as you make changes to a file. For example, the first time you edit a file, the text you have entered actually exists in a buffer that is written to an external file when you do a save. Buffers can also be used at other times in editing, particularly when it is necessary to temporarily move a block of text to memory as you make changes (in other words, cutting and pasting). Many editors allow you to manage multiple buffers simultaneously.

These editors have many commands that are not fully detailed in this chapter. Before engaging in any long and arduous editing task, consult the man page for the editor you are using. There may be an easier way of doing whatever it is that you want to do. As you gain experience with an editor, you will discover convenient shortcuts and functions to perform your most tedious editing chores.

The `vi` Editor

The `vi` editor is installed with virtually every UNIX system in existence. Because of this, `vi` is considered by many to be the default text editor of the UNIX system (upon which Linux is based). `vi` has two modes of operation and terse commands, both of which make it a somewhat more difficult editor to learn than `emacs`. However, it is a useful editor to learn if `emacs` has not been installed on your Linux system.

Starting `vi`

You invoke `vi` from the command line by typing

```
vi
```

The screen clears and a column of tildes (~) appears in the leftmost column. You are now editing an empty, unnamed file. Whatever text you place in this file will exist in a buffer until you write the contents of the buffer to some named file. The tilde is `vi`'s way of telling you that the line where the tilde appears is empty of text.

`vi` can also be started with a file or a list of files to edit:

```
vi filename1 filename2 filename3 ...
```

Typically, you will probably edit only one file per `vi` session. If you are editing a list of files, `vi` edits each one in the sequence that they appear on the command line.

Alternatively, `vi` can be invoked from the command line as

```
vi +n filename
```

where *n* represents the line number where `vi` will place its cursor in *filename*. This is useful for programmers debugging large source code files who need to quickly jump to a known line containing an error.

Another example is useful in illustrating the vi editor. Enter

```
vi asong
```

at the command line and let's see what happens.

vi modes

At the bottom of the screen in the left corner, you will see

```
"asong" 0 lines, 0 characters
```

The messages that display on this status line tell you what vi is doing or has just done. In this case, vi is telling you that it has opened an empty buffer whose contents are saved (whenever you do a save) to the file asong.

At this moment, you are in the command mode of vi. This is the major conceptual leap required in working with this editor. When editing text, you must remember whether you are in command mode or text mode. In *command mode,* any character sequences that you enter are interpreted as vi commands. In *text mode,* every character you enter is placed in the buffer and displayed as text onscreen.

Four commands are echoed at the bottom of the screen on the status line:

/	Searches forward
?	Searches backward
:	An ex command (ex is a standalone line-based editor used within vi)
!	Invokes a shell command

Each of these types of status-line commands must be entered by pressing Return. This is not true for other types of vi commands, such as the ones that do insertions.

TIP

To find out whether you are in command mode, use the set showmode preference described in the section, "Setting Preferences," later in this chapter.

Inserting Text

So, knowing that you are in command mode, let's insert some text. Basically, there are two commands for entering text on the current line: the letters i and a. These letters in lowercase insert (i) text to the left of the cursor or append (a) text to the right of the cursor. As with many `vi` commands, the uppercase versions of these letters have similar effects with subtle differences: uppercase `I` and `A` insert and append at the beginning and end of the current line, respectively, regardless of the cursor position.

After you type either of these letters, you are placed in input mode. Any text entered after this point is displayed onscreen.

Type an `i` and enter the following:

```
Down I walk<Enter>
by the bay,<Enter>
Where I can<Enter>
hear the water.<Enter>
Down we walk<Enter>
by the bay,<Enter>
My hand held<Enter>
by my daughter.<Enter>
```

To exit from input mode, press Esc. Notice that the letter `i` does not display before you enter the text, meaning that the `i` was correctly interpreted as a command. Also, it is important to note that it is not necessary to press Return after pressing `i` for input mode.

Quitting `vi`

Now that you have some text for your file, let's quit the editor to see the results. The commands used for saving the file and exiting `vi` are slightly different from the `i` and `a` commands used in editing text; you must precede the command with a colon (`:`).

In this case, you want to do a save and exit, which are actually combined in one command. Enter `:` and a colon appears at the bottom left of your screen. `vi` has recognized that you are about to enter an `ex` command, and it will echo the remaining characters of the command after the colon. Type `wq` and press Return. `vi` quickly informs you that it has written the file to disk and tells you how many lines it contains. `vi` exits, and you find yourself back at the shell prompt. Another way to save and exit is to type `ZZ`. The difference between this method and using `wq` is that `ZZ` writes the file to disk only if it has been modified since the last save.

If no changes have been made to the file you opened, you quit `vi` by simply typing `:q`. This does not work if the file has been modified. If you are sure that you don't want to save what you have done, enter `:q!`. This command forces `vi` to quit, regardless of any edits.

To make sure that `vi` saved the file `asong` correctly, use the `cat` command to quickly view the file's contents:

```
% cat asong
Down I walk
```

```
by the bay,
Where I can
hear the water.
Down we walk
by the bay,
My hand held
by my daughter.
%
```

Everything is exactly as you typed it in the file, so no surprises here.

Moving the Cursor

Moving the cursor around in vi essentially involves the following four keys:

h	Moves the cursor one space to the left
j	Moves the cursor down one line
k	Moves the cursor up one line
l	Moves the cursor one space to the right

These keys can perform their operations only when vi is in command mode. For convenience, most implementations of vi map these keys to their directional counterparts on the keyboard arrow keys.

vi enables you to move through a file in bigger "leaps" as well. Below are some commands for scrolling more than one line at a time:

Ctrl+u	Scrolls up a half-screen
Ctrl+d	Scrolls down a half-screen
Ctrl+f	Scrolls down one full screen
Ctrl+b	Scrolls up one full screen

The size of these movements largely depends on the terminal settings.

It is also possible to move the cursor to a specific line in a file. If you want to move to the fifth line, type 10G or :10 while in command mode. G by itself moves the cursor to the end of the file. The cursor does not move if the number given is not applicable (for example, typing :10 in an eight-line file has no effect).

vi also enables you to move the cursor one word at a time. A word is defined as any sequence of non-whitespace characters. To move to the beginning of the next word on the current line, press w. Press b to move the cursor to the beginning of the current or previous word.

Deleting Text

vi has commands for deleting characters, lines, and words. *Deletion* means that the selected text is removed from the screen but is copied into an unnamed text buffer from which it can be retrieved.

To delete a word, use the dw command. If you want to delete the word to the right of the cursor, type dw. You can also delete several words at a time. For example, the command 4dw deletes the next four words on the current line.

Lines can be deleted individually or by specifying a range of lines to delete. To delete the current line, enter dd. The command 4dd deletes four lines (the current line and three below it). dG deletes all lines from the current one to the end of the file.

On the current line, you can delete in either direction: d^ deletes backward to the beginning of the line; d$ (or D) deletes forward to the end of the line.

To delete individual characters, x deletes the character underneath the cursor, and X deletes the character to the left of the cursor. Both of these commands accept a number modifier: For example, 4x deletes the current character and the four characters to the right.

Unwanted changes such as deletions can be immediately undone by the u command. This "rolls back" the last edit made.

Copying and Moving Text

Moving sections of text around in a file basically requires three steps:

1. "Yank" the text into a buffer.
2. Move the cursor to where you want to insert the text.
3. Place the text from the buffer at the new location.

Yanking text means to copy it into either a named or unnamed buffer. The *unnamed buffer* is a temporary storage space in memory that is continually overwritten by successive yanks. vi has 26 named buffers that correspond to each letter of the alphabet.

To yank the current line into the unnamed buffer, the command is yy or Y. These commands can be modified by a number indicating how many lines beneath the cursor are to be yanked. For example, the command

3yy

in your file asong (with the cursor on the top line) yanks the following text into the temporary buffer:

```
Down I walk
by the bay,
Where I can
```

This text can also be yanked into the named buffer a by the following command:

```
"a3yy
```

The double quote (") tells the yank command to overwrite the contents of the named buffer a. If you type a capital A instead of a lowercase a, the three lines are appended to the end of the a buffer. This overwrite-versus-append concept works the same for all the named buffers.

If you move the cursor to the end of the file using the :$ command, you can then paste the contents of the unnamed buffer to the end of the file. This is done using the p command, which pastes the contents of a buffer to the right of the cursor (P pastes to the left of the cursor). The paste command can also specify a named buffer in the same way as the yank command:

```
"ap
```

Yanks can also be performed on words using the command yw. This command can also use named buffers and accepts numeric modifiers.

Searching and Replacing Text

Text searches in vi can be performed in either direction: forward or backward. Searches are always started from the current cursor location and continue from the top or bottom of the file, depending on which direction you use. In other words, searches "word wrap" the file.

You can use your file asong to illustrate searches. To search forward through asong for the word "bay," type

```
/bay
```

and press Return. Notice that this is a status-line command. The command /bay is echoed on the status line and the cursor is moved to the first occurrence it finds in the forward direction of the string "bay." Interested in finding another instance of "bay"? Enter a / character. This command continues the search for "bay" in the forward direction and places the cursor at the next instance of "bay." Each time you enter the / key, vi tries to find an instance of the previous string pattern. When it reaches the end of the file, vi loops back and continues its search at the start of the file.

You can also search backward for strings in vi by using the ? command. It works in exactly the same manner as the / command, but in the opposite direction. Try it out by entering

```
?I
```

in asong, instructing vi to search back for instances of "I." This search can be repeated by typing ?, as you might have suspected. You can continue a search by pressing n, which always continues a search in the same direction as the previous search. However, typing N uses the same search string but in the opposite direction.

As mentioned earlier, searches can be made very powerful through the use of regular expressions. The search command is supplied in the same fashion as described before (/ or ?), but square brackets are added to instruct vi to do a regular expression expansion of the enclosed characters. For example, search forward through asong from the first line for all strings containing the substring "er." Type

```
/[*]er[*]
```

vi's first matching string arrives at "Where." If you type n, vi moves the cursor to "watermelon," and so on. You can also specify collections of characters or ranges of characters to match. Try typing the following:

```
/[a-z]y
```

This command used in asong finds the strings "by" and "my," as well as any word with these strings inside them (such as "bay"). This works because the range of characters given are treated as an enumerated range of ASCII values. Thus, you could also include a range of numbers (for example, 0-9). Now try the following command:

```
/[Mm]y
```

This locates the strings "My" and "my."

In vi, searches without regular expressions find only exact matches of the supplied pattern (including the case of the letters in the pattern). Clearly, regular expressions can be used to enhance many types of searches in which you may not know exactly how a pattern appears in a file.

One of the more common applications of a search is to replace instances of one word (or pattern) with another. This is done with an ex command that starts with a colon. To search the entire asong file for the string "Down" and replace it with the string "Up," type

```
:%s/Down/Up/g
```

The s indicates that this is a search operation, the % means that the entire file is to be searched, "Down" is the pattern to be found, "Up" is the new pattern, and the g tells vi that the search should continue until there are no more pattern matches. Without the g, vi would perform the replacement on only the first match it finds. This command also works with regular expressions appearing in the search pattern and the replacement pattern.

Setting Preferences

vi is *configurable,* which means that you can set options to control your editing environment. These options are initialized with default values that you can modify in vi at any time. vi is configured using the set command. The set command must be preceded by a colon and entered by pressing Return. For example, to display line numbers in the editor, enter

```
:set number
```

The following table describes a few of the more common set commands.

all	Displays a list of all available set options and their current status
errorbells	Sounds the terminal bell when an error occurs
ignorecase	Searches are case-insensitive
number	Displays line numbers in the leftmost column of the screen (these are not written to the file)
showmode	An indicator appears at the bottom right of the screen if you are in input mode, change mode, replace mode, and so on

set commands that do not take a value can be switched off by inserting a "no" as a prefix to the set parameter. For example, the command

```
:set nonumber
```

switches line numbering off. The command

```
:set
```

shows only the options that you have changed.

The settings that you use in a vi session are (unfortunately) lost each time you exit vi. If you do not like the idea of resetting these options each time you use vi, there is an easier way to perform this initialization. Use the vi initialization file called .exrc. vi searches for this file in your home directory each time it is invoked. If it can't find this file, it uses the defaults set within the `vi` program. As you will see in the following example, the `.exrc` file can also be used to define `vi` macros.

A sample `.exrc` file looks something like this:

```
set number
set errorbells
set showmode
```

Note that the colon is not required before a `set` command in an `.exrc` file.

A Summary of Essential Commands

Table 16.1 is a summary of the more essential commands described in this chapter. You should consult the `vi` man page for more details on the many other `vi` commands.

TABLE 16.1. ESSENTIAL `vi` COMMANDS.

Command	What it does
i	Starts inserting text at the cursor
h	Moves the cursor one character to the left
j	Moves the cursor down one line
k	Moves the cursor up one line
l	Moves the cursor one character to the right
Ctrl+f	Scrolls forward one screen
Ctrl+b	Scrolls backward one screen
ndd	Deletes the next *n* lines
nyy	Yanks the next *n* lines into the unnamed buffer
p	Puts the contents of the unnamed buffer to the right of the cursor
u	Undoes the last change
:wq	Writes changes and exits `vi`
:q!	Exits `vi` without saving changes
:set all	Shows all `set` parameters and their values
/string	Searches forward for *string*

The emacs Editor

emacs has become the editor of choice for many users because of its online help facility and its extensive collection of editing commands. For programmers, emacs is especially attractive because it can be configured to format source code for a variety of languages such as C, C++, and Lisp. `emacs` is somewhat easier to learn than `vi`, but it also features a much larger set of commands.

Starting emacs

`emacs` is invoked from the command line by entering

```
emacs
```

To start `emacs` with a file to be edited, enter

```
emacs filename
```

If you start `emacs` with a file, the screen displays the contents starting from the first line. Note the two lines at the bottom of the screen. The first of these lines, known as the *mode line,* displays the name of the file being edited and the part of the file that you are looking at (for example, `TOP`, `20%`, `BOT`). The last line on the screen is the echo line, which `emacs` uses to display system messages and as a prompt for more input.

Control and Meta Keys

You are quite free at this point to start entering text into the edit buffer at the cursor location. However, you're probably wondering, "How do I move the cursor around?" Before explaining this little detail, there are two keys that you should know about: the Control key and the Meta key. The Control key is used in most of the commands for `emacs`, but some use the Meta key instead. Commands in `emacs` consist of combinations of the Control or Meta key followed by some other character. It is necessary to hold the Control key when pressing the next character, whereas the Meta key can be pressed and released before you enter the next character. For the PC, the Meta key is usually the Alt key.

Moving the Cursor

Now that you know about the Control key, we can talk about the cursor-movement commands. The basic ones that you need to remember are

Ctrl+f	Moves the cursor forward one character
Ctrl+b	Moves the cursor back one character
Ctrl+-p	Moves the cursor to the previous line
Ctrl+n	Moves the cursor to the next line
Ctrl+-a	Moves the cursor to the beginning of the line
Ctrl+e	Moves the cursor to the end of the line

Most implementations of emacs conveniently map the first four movement commands to the arrow keys on the keyboard. Let's edit a new file called asong2. Start emacs by entering the following command from the shell:

```
emacs asong2<Enter>
```

Now enter the following text into the buffer:

```
This is a file for edit
And you have to give emacs some credit
It's really quite swell
And all you have to do is spell
emacs works, if you let it!
```

Now use the Ctrl+b command to move back through this lovely piece of poetry. Notice how the cursor jumps to the end of each line after reaching the beginning of the previous line. This works the same way in the opposite direction using the Ctrl+f command.

Another useful way of moving around is by scrolling through a file one screen at a time. The command Ctrl+v moves the cursor forward one screen at a time. The command META+v moves the cursor in the opposite direction.

Like vi, emacs treats a sequence of non-whitespace characters as a word. You can move the cursor forward one word at a time with the META+f command. The META+b command moves back one word.

Quitting emacs

At this time, you can stop editing to save the contents of the buffer to your file asong2. To do this, issue the command sequence Ctrl+x Ctrl+s. As you enter this command, notice how the command displays on the echo line as you type it. To quit emacs and return to the shell, enter the command Ctrl+x Ctrl+c. If you make changes that haven't been saved using Ctrl+x Ctrl+s, emacs will ask for confirmation before quitting.

Deleting Text

You can delete text in several ways. The Backspace (or Delete) key is used to erase the character that precedes the cursor. The command Ctrl+d deletes the character underneath the cursor, and Ctrl+k deletes, or "kills," all characters from the cursor to the end of the line. Words can be deleted also: META+d deletes the word the cursor is currently located over, and META+Del (the Delete key) deletes the word just before the current word.

If you ever find that you have done an edit that you didn't want, simply press Ctrl+x u to undo the previous editing changes.

TIP

Change your mind about a command? Press Ctrl+g to abort the current command operation.

Working with Multiple Files

emacs enables you to edit several files in one session, each contained within its own buffer. To copy an external file into a new buffer, use the Ctrl+x Ctrl+f command. After entering this command, you see the following prompt on the echo line:

```
Find file: ~/
```

emacs is smart when it looks for files. It supports *filename completion,* which means that you can simply type a few characters of a filename, and emacs attempts to match a file (or files) to whatever you have typed so far. To do this, type .log and press the Tab key. emacs expands this to ~/.login, and you can see your .login file in a new buffer by pressing Return. If two or more files match the pattern supplied, pressing the Tab key cycles through them.

After you load a new file into emacs, you can switch between buffers by using the Ctrl+x b command followed by the name of the buffer that you want. The buffer's name is that of the file that was loaded into it. The Ctrl+x b command also uses filename completion, so you can use the Tab key to cycle through your edit buffers after supplying a few relevant characters.

When you finish editing a buffer, instead of saving the contents by using the Ctrl+x Ctrl+s command, you might decide that you do not really want to keep the edits that you made. You can kill the current buffer by entering the command Ctrl+x k. emacs then prompts you for the name of the buffer to kill, but by simply pressing Return, you can kill the current buffer. Next, emacs asks for confirmation to which you can respond by typing yes (if you're sure) and pressing Return.

TIP

Whenever you are working with just two buffers, you can simply press Return after entering the Ctrl+x b command to switch to the other buffer.

Copying and Moving Text

In order to copy and move blocks of text in emacs, you must define the region of text by marking the beginning and end points of the text block. This is done by moving the cursor to where you want the block to begin and marking it using the Ctrl+Space command (in this case, Space means literally pressing the spacebar). The end of the block is defined by wherever you place the cursor after that. To make a copy of the block, enter the command META+w. The text within the block is copied to emacs's internal clipboard from which it can be pasted at another location using the Ctrl+y command. Alternatively, you can cut the block into the clipboard using Ctrl+w instead of META+w. Cutting, of course, deletes the text from its current location.

Let's try out some of these techniques on your buffer asong2. Use the META+< command to jump to the beginning of the buffer. Enter a Ctrl+Space to mark the start of the block and then use Ctrl+n to move down a line. Cut the block to the clipboard using Ctrl+w, move the cursor to the end of the buffer using META+>, and paste it using Ctrl+y. The result is something like this:

```
It's really quite swell
And all you have to do is spell
emacs works, if you let it!
This is a file for edit
And you have to give emacs some credit
```

Searching and Replacing Text

You can search forward and backward through text using the Ctrl+s and Ctrl+r commands, respectively. These commands, like many in emacs, use *command completion*. This is the same concept as filename completion: you supply a few characters, and emacs tries to fill in the rest. In this case, however, emacs moves the cursor to each instance it finds of the string supplied.

As you enter more characters, emacs narrows its search further. When you have found a correct match, press Return or use any of the cursor-movement commands to halt the search.

As with vi, searching in either direction wraps around the beginning or end of the file, depending on in which direction you are searching. However, when emacs reaches the top or bottom of the file, it tells you that the search failed. You can keep searching by pressing Ctrl+s or Ctrl+r accordingly, and emacs will continue using the current string.

To illustrate how searching in emacs works, let's search backward through your file asong2. Enter Ctrl+r and type an s. emacs moves the cursor to the "s" in "works." Next type a w. emacs now tries to find a pattern that matches the string sw. The cursor ends up on the "w" in "swell." You can edit the search string by using the Backspace, or Delete, key. Delete the w and type a p. What happens?

Searches-and-replaces are done by entering the query-replace command. This is qualified by the META-x command, which tells emacs that the text to follow is a full command and not a key combination. After you enter the query-replace command, you are prompted for the string to be found. Enter the string and press Return. emacs then prompts you for the replacement string. After you enter the replacement string, emacs searches for every instance of the first string and, if it finds one, asks if it should be replaced with the second string.

Using Modes with Buffers

emacs is versatile enough to handle many different types of editing chores. It enables you to associate modes to buffers so that you can have text formatting specific to your editing application. If you enter the command Ctrl+x m, emacs enters mail mode that formats a buffer with To: and Subject: fields, as well as a space for the body of the mail message. emacs can even send the mail message for you (by entering Ctrl+c Ctrl+c) after you finish editing it.

emacs also supports modes for many different programming languages, such as C. When a file with the extension .c (C source code) or .h (C header file) is loaded into emacs, the buffer is automatically set to C mode. This mode has knowledge of how C programs are formatted, and pressing the Tab key indents a line correctly based on its place in the program (a for loop within another for loop, as an example).

Online Help in emacs

One of the best features of the emacs editor is that if you ever get stuck or are just plain overwhelmed by it all, help is just a few keystrokes away—and lots of it! If you need a short emacs tutorial, just enter Ctrl+h t. If you need to find out what function a particular key supports, type Ctrl+h k and then press the key. The help option has many different topics. Use Ctrl+h i to load the info documentation reader and read about all the types of help available.

A Summary of Essential Commands

emacs, like the vi editor, has such a rich command set that we can cover only a portion of it in this chapter. Table 16.2 is a summary of the strictly essential commands that you need for basic editing in emacs. The emacs man page should be consulted for a more comprehensive description of the full emacs command set.

TABLE 16.2. ESSENTIAL emacs COMMANDS.

Command	What it does
Ctrl+b	Moves back one character
Ctrl+d	Deletes the current character
Ctrl+f	Moves forward one character
Ctrl+g	Cancels the current command
Ctrl+h	Enters emacs online help
Ctrl+n	Moves forward to the next line
Ctrl+p	Moves back to the previous line
Ctrl+s	Searches forward for a string
Ctrl+v	Scrolls forward one screen
META+v	Scrolls backward one screen
Ctrl+x u	Undoes the last edit
Ctrl+x Ctrl+c	Exits emacs
Ctrl+x Ctrl+s	Saves the buffer to a file

Summary

There are many text editors available for the Linux system. Two of the most popular are vi (which is actually an alias to the elvis editor) and emacs. Both provide basic editing functions such as inserting and deleting text, reading and writing of external files, text searching, and copying and moving text. vi is a full-screen editor that has two modes: command mode and text mode. emacs is an extendable and powerful editor that is highly configurable to suit a variety of editing tasks (such as programming, document writing, and changing user or system files). From here, you can find related material to read. To learn more about

groff, a text formatting utility, read Chapter 17, "groff."

TeX and LaTeX, more flexible text editors and formatters, read Chapter 19, "TeX and LaTeX."

Setting up your system to use the X windowing system, read Chapter 22, "Installing and Configuring XFree86."

groff

by Tim Parker

IN THIS CHAPTER

The groff program is the GNU version of nroff and troff, text-formatting languages that have been used in UNIX for many years. The groff system includes versions of troff, nroff, eqn, tbl, and other UNIX text-formatting utilities. The groff language is used primarily to compile man pages written and stored in groff/nroff format into a form that can be printed or displayed onscreen.

The nroff language was designed to provide text formatting in lineprinters, whereas troff was developed for phototypesetters. The commands in the two languages are identical, although some commands that cannot be processed by a lineprinter are ignored by nroff. In most cases, you don't use nroff or troff directly, but use a macro package to access them.

For the most part, nroff and troff have fallen into disuse with the development of powerful word processors and desktop publishing packages. Their sole remaining use is for formatting man pages, which continue to be used widely.

Both nroff and troff have many commands that you will never require. Therefore, in this chapter we will look at the basic command set necessary for you to use the groff version of the two languages, and how they can be used for man page-specific applications. If you really want to use groff for advanced text formatting, you should pick up a dedicated book on the subject.

Embedding Commands

One aspect of groff that may take a little getting used to is that the way you type lines in the file isn't necessarily the way they will be displayed in the finished output. The groff system runs text lines together as much as possible. For example, the source file

```
This is fine stuff.
It is really interesting and
could keep me busy for hours.
```

covers three lines in the source, but when formatted, it runs together by groff to look like this:

```
This is fine stuff. It is really interesting and could keep me busy for
hours.
```

with line breaks wherever necessary because of the page layout. This has an advantage in that you don't have to worry about making everything look properly formatted within the source. However, the disadvantage is that you don't have an accurate idea of what the output will look like until you see it.

A look at a groff source file shows that it is all ASCII characters which contain the usual text of the displayed output and a set of commands starting with a period, like this:

```
This is a bunch of text that will be displayed.
Here is even more text.
.ps 14
The line above is a groff command, identified by the
period in the first column of the line.
```

Most groff commands are on a line by themselves, although a few can be embedded anywhere on a line. These commands are usually prefaced by a backslash, much as the shell uses the backslash as an escape character. An example of a line with embedded commands is

```
This \fBline\fR has two embedded \fIgroff\fR commands.
```

Although there will be times when you want to use embedded commands, the majority of the commands used will be on a single line, starting with a period.

Controlling Character Appearance

The groff language has a few commands for controlling the way characters look when printed or displayed. These include changing the size and line spacing of characters, as well as controlling fonts.

Sizes and Line Spacing

Character size and line spacing are not usually useful when displaying text onscreen, unless you are using a bitmapped terminal. They are used for printed documents, though. You can change the size of text with the .ps (point size) command:

```
This is the default 10-point size.
.ps 14
This is now in fourteen-point size.
.ps 20
This is a point size of twenty.
.ps 6
And this is a really small point size of six.
```

> **NOTE**
>
> A point is 1/72 of an inch, so a 36-point character size is half an inch high. The 12-point size used most commonly is 1/6-inch high. Different versions of groff support different point sizes, but most versions support 6, 7, 8, 9, 10, 11, 12, 14, 16, 20, 24, 28, and 36 points. If you set a value that is not supported, it is rounded up to the next highest value (to a maximum of 36). The default point size is 10. If you use the .ps command without a value, groff reverts to the previous value.

Within a sentence, the point size can be changed with the line-embedded command \s followed by the point size. For example:

```
This is in 10-point, while \s20this is in twenty,\s10 and back to 10
again.
```

The \s command should be followed by a legal point size. The special command \s0 causes groff to revert to its previous value. Relative changes are also supported, so you can embed commands such as \s+2 and \s-2, although only a single digit can be specified (so you can't change by more than 9 points).

Line spacing is the vertical spacing between lines. Vertical spacing is not tied to point size, so it needs to be adjusted manually. As a general rule, use a vertical spacing about 20 percent larger than the point size. The default vertical spacing is 11.

Line spacing is controlled by the .vs (vertical space) command. In the next example, we change the point size and the vertical spacing to permit the characters to be printed clearly without overlap:

```
This is in normal 10-point, 11 vertical space size.
.ps 12
.vs 14
This is in 12-point with 14 vertical spacing.
```

If you use the .vs command without a value, groff reverts to the previous value.

If you want to force spacing for some reason, such as to separate sections of text, use the .sp (space) command. Used with no argument, .sp gives one blank line. It can also take arguments of i for inches and p for points:

```
This is default 10-point 11 vertical spaced text.
.sp
We have a blank line above this because of the command.
.sp 3.5i
This is three and a half inches below the previous line.
```

You can use fractions in most groff commands, as this example shows.

Fonts

Changing fonts requires the command `.ft` (font type). In the early days of `troff`, only four fonts were supported: Roman, Roman bold, Roman italic, and a set of special characters. Other fonts had to be specially loaded in the phototypesetter. For this reason, `groff` defaults to Roman.

To switch to Roman bold, use the command `.ft B`, while `.ft I` switches, not surprisingly, to Roman italic. To return to the normal Roman font, the command `.ft R` is used, although on most systems, `.ft` by itself will suffice:

```
This is in normal Roman font.
.ft B
This is bold.
.ft I
This is italic.
.ft
This is back to normal Roman font.
```

You can switch fonts with a line-embedded command, too, using `\f` followed by either `I` or `B`, switching back to the normal font with `R`:

```
This is normal, \fBbold\fR and \fIitalics\fR.
```

Since underline wasn't supported on most system printers, underlined text was converted to italic. The underline command `.ux` would italicize the next x lines of text.

Because we now have many more fonts to work with than Roman, we must be able to change fonts within `groff`. The command to change fonts is `.fp` (font physically mounted), which also requires a number to indicate the position the font was mounted in the phototypesetter (old stuff, isn't it?). For example, if Helvetica was mounted in font position three and we referred to it by the font letter `H`, the command

```
.fp 3 H
```

would instruct the phototypesetter to switch to Helvetica in font position three. `groff` still retains these old-style commands.

Indenting and Line Length

The line length is set to default to 6.5 inches within `groff`. To override this value, the `.ll` (line length) command is used with an argument indicating the units. For example, the command

```
.ll 7i
```

switches `groff` to use a seven-inch line length. The maximum length accepted is usually about 7.5 inches, so to use wider paper than that you have to move the left margin over to compensate with the `.po` (page offset) command. The value `.po 0` sets the left margin as far over as possible.

To indent text, you use the `.in` (indent) command. It takes a number and an indicator of the units as arguments, as the following example shows:

```
This is normal stuff.
.in 0.75I
This is indented three-quarters of an inch.
```

To move the right margin to the left so that you can make a distinctive block of text within a normal chunk, use the `.ll` (line length) command shown earlier:

```
This is normal text, and goes on and on.
Even more text that continues the transition.
.in 1i
.ll -1i
This is now indented one inch to the left, and the
right margin is indented one inch from the normal right
margin.  This makes the text stand out a little.
.in -1i
.ll +1i
And this is back to normal.  The block will stand out nicely
amongst all this normal text.
```

Notice that in this example relative movements of plus and minus a value are used to make it easier. This way, we don't have to measure the page. To revert to original values, use the commands `.in` and `.ll` with no arguments, as well.

An indent and line-length change is effective until the next command changes it. Sometimes you want to affect only a single line, though. If you want to indent only a single line, use the `.ti` (temporary indent) command:

```
This is really fine stuff.  You can tell, 'cause I'm
still awake.
.ti 3i
This line is temporarily indented by three inches, but the
next line will be back to normal.
```

Tabs are used to set column output. Usually, tabs are used with `groff` only for unfilled text, which is material that displays in columns. Tab stops are set, by default, every half inch. To override these values, use the `.ta` (tab) command. The command

```
.ta 1i 2i 3i 4i 5i 6i
```

sets the tabs at every inch instead. You can think of the setting of tabs within `groff` much as they are done on a typewriter, from left to right. Tabs are usually set for columns of

numbers or tables, but the groff macro gtbl is much better at this. (You get a look at gtbl in the next chapter.)

Other Character Controls

The groff system has special instructions for controlling the size of individual letters, as well as formulas and special characters such as Greek letters. However, because it is unlikely groff is used for this type of output these days, we'll ignore those capabilities. If you want more information on how to provide these special features, check the groff man pages or consult a good troff book.

Macros

A *macro* is a shorthand notation for a set of commands or strings. Many commands used to write man pages are macros. To give a practical example of a groff macro, suppose we want every paragraph to start with a blank line and a temporary indent of half an inch. The groff commands to do this are

```
.sp
.ti +.5i
```

Instead of typing these two lines every paragraph, we can define a macro of one character (or more) that does it for us.

To define the macro, we use the .de (define) command followed by the name of the macro and the commands. It looks like this, placed somewhere at the top of the source code:

```
.de PP
.sp
.ti +.5I
..
```

The last line with two periods indicates the end of the definition. Now, whenever we use the command .PP, it will be executed as the lines in the macro.

NOTE

Make sure that you don't define a macro with the name of a reserved groff command, or the macro will not be executed.

Using mm

The mm (memorandum macros) package is not really part of nroff or troff, although both can use it. The mm program reads a source file much as groff does and translates it to output. Many of the mm macros are used for man pages. Indeed, many users find the nroff and troff commands too awkward or complicated, whereas mm is fully able to meet all their basic formatting needs.

To add mm commands, use the period in the first column as with groff. The mm macros are usually quite simple and easy to work with. Let's look at the most important of them here.

Paragraphs and Headers

Like groff, mm runs text together when reformatting, regardless of line breaks in the source file. To force a new paragraph, use the .P command. It forces a line break and adds a blank line to the output. Paragraphs are usually formatted so that they are flush left.

Headings are created with the .H command. For example, the command

```
.H This is a Heading
```

creates a break, outputs the heading text in bold, and leaves a bit of a space between the heading and the text that follows it.

There can be seven levels of headings; 1 is the highest and 7 is the lowest. To specify the heading level, add the number as the first argument after the .H command:

```
.H 2 This is a level 2 heading
```

The mm heading macro numbers the headings automatically, although you can suppress the numbering with the .HU (heading unnumbered) command. To reset the numbering (at a section break, for example), use the .nr (number register) command followed by the heading level and the number to use. For example, the command

```
.nr H2 1
```

restarts the numbering of second-level headings at 1.

Lists

Lists are easily created in mm with the .LI (list) command and the .LE (list end) command. This creates a bulleted list. For example, the command

```
.LI
thing 1
.LI
thing 2
.LE
thing 3
```

creates a bulleted list of the three bits of text. You can create a list with dashes instead of bullets using the .DL (dash list) command. The mark list command, .ML, creates a list with the character of your choice.

If you want a numbered list, use the .AL (automatic list) command. Lists with no arguments are created with Arabic numbers. To create an alphabetical list (A, B, C, and so on), use the macro command .AL A. Roman numerals (i, ii, iii, iv, v, and so on) can be used with the .AL I command.

You can nest list types as necessary. For example, the command

```
.AL I
.LI
groff
.AL
.LI
macros
.LI
mm
.LE
.LI
gtbl
.LI
geqn
.LE
```

creates output that looks like this:

```
I.   groff
        1. macros
        2. mm
II.    gtbl
III.   geqn
```

It's important to be careful when terminating each list with an .LE command to ensure that you terminate the proper one. Experimentation and practice help you get the hang of this. You may have noticed that it takes a lot of commands to make a little list!

Font Changes

Changing fonts with mm is quite simple. When working from a period command, the command .B (bold) creates bold text until an .R (restore) command, while .I (italic) does the same until an .R command. If you want to bold or italicize only one word, you can do it after the period command, as this example shows:

```
This is normal text
.B
This is bold.
So is this.
.R
This is normal.
This is a single
.Bbold
word, though.
```

When you change only one word, you don't need an .R command.

Changes can be performed within text in the same manner as with groff:

```
This is an \fIitalics set of words\fR until here.
```

Footnotes

To create a footnote, use the .FS (footnote start) and .FE (footnote end) commands. Every footnote on a single page will be collected and printed at the bottom. Footnotes are automatically numbered unless you specify another character:

```
This is normal text.
.FS
This is a footnote with its proper number in front of it.
.FE
This is more normal text.
.FS *
But this is a footnote marked with an asterisk.
.FE
This is even more normal text.  At the bottom of the page
will be a numbered footnote and an asterisked footnote.
```

You can use any valid character for the optional footnote mark, including special characters supported by groff.

Summary

As you probably expect, there is a lot to both groff and mm that we haven't looked at. Because groff is seldom used these days, we covered only the most important aspects. As mentioned earlier, if you want to learn more about groff or mm, find a good reference book on the subject. From here you can learn more about:

geqn and gtbl for more formatting of text, see Chapter 18, "geqn and gtbl."

TeX and LaTeX, two powerful text formatters, see Chapter 19, "TeX and LaTeX," and Chapter 20, "Printing."

Setting up multimedia capabilities for your Linux system, see Chapter 21, "Multimedia Linux."

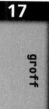

geqn and gtbl

by Tim Parker

CHAPTER 18

Now that you are comfortable with `groff`, you can look at two useful add-ons for `groff`: `geqn` and `gtbl`. In this chapter, you learn the following:

- What are `geqn` and `gtbl`?
- How to create complex equations easily.
- How to format tables for `groff` documents.

In the last chapter, you saw how `groff` is used to produce formatted documents for both screen and printer. Unfortunately, `groff` is not the easiest package to work with for complex problems such as tables and equations, so a set of macros for these tasks was developed.

The utilities `gtbl` and `geqn` are preprocessors which means that you write the source code as usual, but then the `gtbl` and `geqn` programs scan through and replace their specific commands with `groff` commands. Except for these specific commands, no other changes to the text or `groff` commands are performed.

geqn

The `geqn` preprocessor is designed for formatting complex equations and printing special symbols. You need only use `geqn` if you are using `groff` to create a document with these kinds of characters embedded within them.

Although `groff` has enough power to provide simple equations, it is not particularly friendly or powerful enough for more than single-line material. On the other hand, `geqn` is quite easy to work with. Most aspects of `geqn` are designed to look like equivalent English commands or words.

You can quickly move through a set of the important parts of `geqn`. As you will see, it is remarkably easy to work with.

Executing geqn

The `geqn` preprocessor is invoked before the `groff` formatter. Usually, this is accomplished with a simple pipe command:

```
geqn filename | groff
```

This processes *filename* through `geqn`, which converts `geqn` commands to equivalent `groff` commands and then sends the result to `groff` for processing.

The command

```
geqn file1 file2 file3 | groff
```

processes three files and sends them all to `groff`.

Remember that many consoles can't display equations properly because they are not bitmapped and don't have the character set available. You may have to output the results to a printer to see any exercises you try.

Equations

You must tell geqn where equations begin and end by using the commands .EQ (equation start) and .EN (equation end). Within the two commands, anything that is typed is treated as an equation. For example, the command

```
.EQ
b=c*(d+x)
.EN
```

is formatted to the equation

```
b=c*(d+x)
```

If you try that line without the equation indicators, feeding it straight to groff, you don't receive the same output because groff can't interpret the characters properly.

You can number equations, as is often required in technical documents, by placing a number after the .EQ command. For example, the command

```
.EQ 15
b=c*(d+x)
.EN
```

places the number 15 in the left margin next to the equation.

Subscripts and Superscripts

To place superscripts and subscripts in an equation, use the commands sup and sub. The words sup and sub must be surrounded by spaces. For example, the command

```
E=mc sup 2
```

produces Einstein's most famous equation.

To indicate the end of a subscript or superscript and continue with normal characters, use a space or a tilde (~) character. For example, the command

```
x=(z sup 2)+1
```

gives you the finished output

$x=(z^2)+1$

which is probably not what you want. Instead, use one of the following commands:

```
x=(z sup 2 )+1
x=(z sup 2~)+1
```

In these commands, the space or the tilde indicates the end of the superscript. This gives you the following output:

```
x=(z²)+1
```

You can subscript subscripts and superscript superscripts by simply combining the formats:

```
y sub x sub 3
```

You can also produce both subscript and superscript on the same character using the two commands together:

```
x sub y sup 3
```

Because a space is used to indicate the end of a subscript or superscript, this can cause a problem when you want spaces either as part of the equation or to separate words to be converted. To get around this problem, use braces to enclose the subscript or superscript:

```
w sup {x alpha y}
```

This shows that the Greek letters are also available, as they are within `groff`. You can have braces within braces, as well:

```
omega sub { 2 pi r sup { 2 + rho }}
```

Try these commands for yourself and experiment to see the output.

NOTE

While it might seem at first that you'd want Greek letters only for complex equations, the letters are handy for many simple mathematical formulas, too. It's well worth knowing how to generate each of the common letters and what they look like on paper.

Fractions

To create a proper-looking fraction, use the keyword `over`. The `geqn` preprocessor automatically adjusts the length of the line separating the parts. For example, the command

```
a = 2b over {3c alpha}
```

produces an equation with a horizontal line separating the two components, just as if you were writing the equation out on paper.

You can, of course, combine all the other elements of geqn to create more complex-looking equations:

```
{alpha + beta * gamma sup 3} over {3 sub {4 + alpha}}
```

When you are combining sup and sub with over, geqn processes sup and sub first, and then it does over, much as if it were actually writing the equation.

Square Roots

To draw a square root symbol, use the keyword sqrt, and geqn ensures that the square root symbol is properly drawn to enclose all parts of the equation that are indicated as belonging to the square root. Very large square root signs that cover a lot of material on many lines, for example, do not look particularly good when printed. You may want to consider using the superscript 0.5 instead.

You can use sqrt quite easily. For example, the command

```
sqrt a+c - 1 over sqrt {alpha + beta}
```

shows the first square root sign over a+c and the second one over the part in braces.

Summations, Set Theory, and Integrals

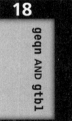

To produce a summation, use the keyword sum and the keywords from and to to show the upper and lower parts of the command. For example, use the command

```
sum from x=1 to x=100 x sup 2
```

to create the formula for summing x squared over the range 1 to 100. If you want to use a special word, use braces:

```
sum from x=1 to {x= inf} x sup 2
```

This is the same command, except summing from 1 to infinity. The braces ensure that the to component is properly interpreted. If no from or to component is specified, they are not printed.

To use integrals, the keyword int is used and can again take a from argument:

```
lim from n=1 xy sup 3 = 9
```

Other reserved words for geqn are used with set theory. You can use the keywords union and inter for the union and intersection of sets.

Brackets, Bars, and Piles

As equations get more complicated, you will need to use more brackets and braces. You can generate brackets ([ ]), braces ({}), and parentheses (( )) as needed using the `left` and `right` commands:

```
left { b over d+1} = left ( alpha over {beta + gamma} )
```

This produces large braces, and parentheses are required to surround the terms. You can nest these, of course, with `geqn` adjusting the sizes properly. Braces are usually bigger than brackets and parentheses.

For floor and ceiling characters, use the `left floor`, `right floor`, `left ceiling`, and `right ceiling` commands. For example:

```
left ceiling x over alpha right ceiling > left floor beta over 2 right
floor
```

draws the equation with the proper vertical bars and ceiling and floor markers.

To create a pile of elements, use the reserved word `pile`. The following example shows the usage best:

```
X = left [ pile { a above b above c } right ]
```

This produces output with the three elements a, b, and c stacked vertically within big braces.

Matrices

To make a matrix requires a little more work. You could probably make a matrix using the `pile` command, but if the elements are not of equal height, they will not line up. For that reason, use the keyword `matrix`. The general format is

```
matrix {
  ccol { elements }
  ccol { elements }
```

in which `ccol` produces centered columns. For left-adjusted columns, use `lcol`; `rcol` produces right-adjusted columns. The elements are specified individually. For example, the command

```
matrix {
  ccol { x sub 1 above y sub 1 }
  ccol { x sub 2 above y sub 2 }
```

produces the matrix

$$x_1 \ x_2$$
$$y_1 \ y_2$$

All matrices must have the same number of elements in each column or geqn can't process the matrix properly.

> **NOTE**
>
> Some mathematical packages allow you to have varying numbers of elements in matrix columns. This is a bad practice because such a table is no longer a real matrix. Each column should have exactly the same number of elements, as should each row.

Quoted Text

Any characters placed within quotation marks are not interpreted by geqn. This is useful for text strings that may contain reserved words, such as the following:

```
italics "beta" = beta + gamma
```

Here, the word beta will appear in italics without being converted to the beta character.

Character Changes

You can change font and point size with geqn in much the same way as with groff. The default setting is usually Roman 10 point. If you want to set bold characters, use the keyword bold; italic sets italic font.

```
x=y bold alpha
```

You can also use the keyword fat, which widens the character (useful for things such as grad characters). These reserved words affect only what immediately follows, so you must use braces if the area to be changed is more than a single block of characters.

```
x=y*2 bold {alpha + gamma}
```

To change the size of characters, use the size keyword:

```
size 16 {alpha + beta}
```

This sets the enclosed text in 16 point size. Incremental changes are acceptable.

To affect the entire equation, you can use the gsize (global size) and gfont (global font) commands at the start of the geqn block:

```
.EQ
gsize 14
gfont H
....
```

This makes it easy to format the equations however you wish.

Using geqn

As you have seen, geqn is quite friendly and easy to use, especially if you are used to writing out equations longhand. You should play around with the system and learn the different features. There are more commands available within geqn, but the main ones have been shown to you. For more information, check the man pages or a good groff book that includes eqn.

gtbl

The gtbl routine is designed to help in the preparation of charts, multicolumn lists, and any other material presented in a tabular format. The gtbl commands are not difficult to work with but can be awkward to learn, so studying examples is the best method.

To use gtbl, two special commands are used to indicate to groff that the area between the two commands is to be processed as gtbl instructions. These two key commands are .TS (table start) and .TE (table end). Commands between these two are processed by gtbl first, which converts the gtbl commands to groff commands; then, the source is passed to groff.

Tables are independent of each other with gtbl, meaning that each must contain all the information for formatting the data within the table and can't rely on a previous format. Tables contain three types of information: text for the table itself, options that control the behavior of gtbl, and formatting commands to lay out the table itself. The general format of a gtbl source code section is as follows:

```
.TS
options;
format.
data
.TE
```

Let's look at the important parts of the gtbl layout first and then see how they are combined to produce finished tables.

Executing gtbl

Because gtbl is a preprocessor, it is invoked on the source file, and then the results are passed to groff. The simplest way to do this is with the command

```
gtbl filename | groff
```

in which the gtbl preprocessor runs against the source in *filename* and then sends the output to groff. If you are processing more than one file at a time, or you need to send the output of gtbl to another preprocessor, such as geqn, you use piping slightly differently. The command

```
gtbl filename | geqn | groff
```

sends the output to geqn and then to groff.

Options

There can be a single line of options after a .TS command that affects the entire table. Any options must follow the .TS command. If more than one option is specified, they must be separated by spaces, commas, or tabs, and terminate in a semicolon. gtbl accepts the following options:

center	Centers the table (default is left-justified).
expand	Makes tables as wide as current line length.
box	Encloses the table in a box.
allbox	Encloses each element of the table in a box.
doublebox	Encloses the table in two boxes.
tab (*n*)	Uses *n* instead of a tab to separate data.
linesize (*n*)	Uses point size *n* for lines or rules.
delim (*mn*)	Uses *m* and *n* as equation delimiters.

When gtbl attempts to lay out a table, it tries to keep the entire table on one page if possible, even if it has to eject the previous page only partially completed. This sometimes causes problems because gtbl can make mistakes estimating the size of the table prior to generating it, especially if there are embedded line commands that affect spacing or point size. To avoid this problem, some users surround the entire table with the display macros .DS (display start) and .DE (display end). You can ignore this for most tables, unless you start embedding commands within the data.

Format

The format section of the table structure indicates how the columns are to be laid out. Each line in the format section corresponds to one line of data in the finished table. If not enough format lines are specified to match all the lines of data, the last format line specified is used for the remainder of the table. This lets you use a specific format for headers and a single format line for the rest of the table. The format section ends with a period.

Each line in the format section contains a keyletter for each column in the table. Keyletters should be separated by spaces or tabs for each column to enhance readability.

18

geqn AND gtbl

Keyletters are case-independent (so you can use upper- or lowercase for the keyletters or a mixture of the two, without affecting the layout). Supported `gtbl` keyletters are as follows:

l	Left-justified entry
r	Right-justified entry
c	Centered entry
n	Numeric entries lined up by units
a	Aligned on left so that widest entry is centered
s	Previous column format applies across rest of column

A sample format section consists of a letter for each column, unless the entry is repeated across the page. A sample format section looks like this:

```
c       s       s
l       n       n .
```

In this sample, the first line of the table is formatted with the first, second, and third columns centered (the s repeats the previous entry). The second and subsequent lines have the first entry left-justified and the next two lined up as numbers. The period ends the format section. If you like, you can put all these format keyletters on a single line, using a comma to separate the lines:

```
c s s, l n n .
```

A table formatted by this set of commands looks like this (with random numbers inserted to show the lineup):

```
        Centered_Title
Entry1  12.23   231.23
Entry2   3.23    45.2
Entry3  45      123.2344
Entry4   3.2      2.3
```

Numeric data is usually aligned so that the decimal places are in a vertical column. However, sometimes you want to override this format by forcing a movement. The special character \& is used to move the decimal point. The special characters disappear when the table is printed. To show the effect of this special character, the following sample shows normal formatting and entries with the special character embedded (the first column is the source input and the second is the generated output):

```
14.5            14.5
13              13
1.253            1.253
3\&1.21         31.21
53.2            53.2
6\&2.23          62.23
```

You can see that the numbers usually line up with the decimal point in a vertical row, except where moved over by the \& characters. Even if a number has no decimal point specified (as in the second line of the example), it is lined up as though one were present after the last digit.

The following are a few additional keyletters that can be used to create special formats and make the tables more attractive:

_	Horizontal line in place of column entry.
=	Double horizontal line in place of column entry.
|	Between column entries, draws a vertical line between columns. Before the first keyletters, draws a line to the left of the table. After the last keyletters, draws a line to the right of the table.
||	Between column entries, draws a double vertical line.
e/E	Sets equal width columns. All columns that have a keyletter followed by e or E are set to the same width.
f/F	Followed by a font name or number, changes the entry to the font specified.
n	Any number following a keyletter. Indicates the amount of separation between columns.
p/P	Followed by a number, changes the point size of the entry to the specified number. Increments acceptable.
t/T	Vertically spanned items begin at the top line. Normally, vertically spanning items (more than one line in the table) are centered in the vertical range.
v/V	Followed by a number, gives vertical line spacing.
w/W	Followed by a number, sets the width.

The order of these characters on the format line is not important, although the spacing between each format identifier must still be respected. Multiple letters can be used. The entry

```
np14w(2.5i)fi
```

sets the numeric entry (n) in italics (fi), with a point size of 14 (p14) and a minimum column width of 2.5 inches (w(2.5i)).

You may need to change the format of a table midway through—for example, to present summaries. If you must change the format, use the .T& (table continue) command.

Data

Data for the table is entered after all the format specifications have been completed. Data for columns is separated by tabs or any other character indicated in the tabs option. Each line of data is one line of the table. Long lines of data can be broken over several lines of source by using the backslash character as the last character in a line.

Any line starting with a period and followed by anything other than a number is assumed to be a groff command and is ignored by the preprocessor. If a single line of the data consists of only underscore or equal sign characters (single and double lines), it is treated as extending the entire width of the table.

You can embed a block of text within a table by using the text commands of T{ (start of text) and }T (end of text). This lets you enter something that can't be easily entered as a string separated by tabs.

Examples

The best way to understand how to use gtbl is to look at some simple examples. Here's a basic table command:

```
.TS
doublebox;
c c c, l l n.
Name        Dept        Phone
Joe         8A          7263
Mike        9F          2635
Peter       2R          2152
Yvonne      2B          2524
.TE
```

All of the entries in the data section are separated by tabs. This produces a table with three columns, the first line of which is centered text. The rest of the table has the first and second columns left-justified and the last column aligned by decimal point (there are none in this case). The entire table is surrounded by two boxes.

A slightly more complex example uses a table title followed by a row of column headings and then the data. Separate each element in the table by a box in this case:

```
.TS
allbox;
c s s
c c c
n n n .
Division Results
East        West        North
15          12          14
```

```
12              12              18
36              15              24
.TE
```

Try typing in these examples, or create your own, to see what effect the different commands have. When you've started using gtbl, it isn't that difficult.

Summary

Although word processors have made utilities such as geqn and gtbl less popular than they used to be, some diehard UNIX people still like to use them. There may be times when you can't produce an equation the way you want with your favorite word processor, so you might have to return to the basics. Also, because word processors capable of fancy formulas tend to be expensive, utilities such as geqn and gtbl are ideal for the occasional user who doesn't want to spend a lot of money on a seldom-used tool. From here, you can learn more about using:

gawk, a handy and quick programming language for advanced users and system administrators, in Chapter 25, "gawk."

Perl, another programming language that is very popular for Web-based scripting in Chapter 28, "Perl."

Smalltalk/X, an X-based implementation of the object-oriented programming language, in Chapter 31, "Smalltalk/X."

CHAPTER 19

TeX and LaTeX

by Peter MacKinnon

IN THIS CHAPTER

TeX (pronounced *tech*) is a text formatting system invented by Donald Knuth. It lets you produce professionally typeset documents by embedding TeX commands within a normal ASCII text file. This text file can then be converted to what is known as a *dvi* (device-independent file), which can be either previewed onscreen using an X Window program called xdvi or converted to a PostScript file for printing.

TeX is a powerful program in that it enables you to define specific typesetting commands (such as font size, page size, or space between lines). It also works as a programming language that enables you to create macros for defining more abstract units of text such as documents, headings, and paragraphs. The benefit of these high-level macros is that they enable you to concentrate on the writing of a document, not the typesetting. The key appeal of TeX for engineers and scientists is that it supports the typesetting of complex mathematical formulas.

Typesetting Versus Writing

The usefulness of a document can be limited by its appearance. Consider two documents: one that is well-organized with clearly defined units of text such as chapters, headings, and paragraphs, and another that has no paragraph breaks and no space between lines. The first document is much more appealing to the reader, whereas the second document is downright painful to read. So, despite the best efforts of an author to create a *magnum opus,* or even a recipe for strawberry jam, the meaning behind the words may get lost in a typographical abyss.

In book publishing, authors aren't usually responsible for anything beyond the genius of their words. They usually leave the design and crafting of the book to a book designer. This person then hands the design template to page layout technicians. TeX performs this book design and typesetting role for you, enabling you, the author, to be your own publisher. It gives you control over the publication of your own material while still allowing you to concentrate on what you're supposed to be writing about!

TeX

A TeX file can be created with any Linux text editor such as vi or emacs. You can enter text into a file called arkana.tex like this:

```
Do you suppose that Alfred Hitchcock would have had as successful a
directing
career if he did not have the considerable talents of actors Cary Grant
and
James Stewart in his most popular films? That's a tough one to answer...
\bye
```

After you save your file, use the TeX program to convert it to a dvi file using this command:

```
$ tex arkana
```

The resulting arkana.dvi file that is created contains your text. This file can be used by different output devices (hence the name) for viewing or printing. For example, if you want to print your dvi file to a PostScript printer, convert it to a ps format, and print it using the dvi2ps utility:

```
$ dvi2ps arkana.ps | lp
```

This assumes that the default printer is PostScript-capable. If you want to just preview how the text looks, use the X application xdvi:

```
$ xdvi arkana.dvi &
```

The tex command also produces a log file entitled arkana.log, containing any error and warning messages, and other information such as the number of pages of output. The beauty of all this indirect representation of TeX output is that the TeX source file and its resulting dvi are very portable, particularly from Linux to its ancestor UNIX.

Simple Text Formatting

Most of the work in creating a TeX document is putting in the words that discuss whatever you're writing about. As shown earlier, it is fairly simple to create an unadorned TeX file: The only special command you used was \bye. This command tells the TeX program that it has reached the end of the document. The \bye command uses one of several characters that TeX treats with special interest, specifically the backslash or *escape* character. Here is the set of special characters that TeX recognizes: \, {, }, ~, #, $, %, ^, &, and the space character. The meaning behind these characters will be discussed as you progress.

One of the main conveniences of TeX is the intelligent way it deals with text. Words are any sequence of characters separated by whitespace characters. The number of whitespace characters between words is immaterial because TeX treats them as one character. Sentences are recognized by the last word preceding a ., ?, !, or :. Paragraphs are distinguished by a blank line following a sentence. Much like the spaces between words, TeX treats excess blank lines as redundant and ignores them. Thus, the text

```
How do you compare
these two terrific leading men? James Stewart had that good-natured,
All-American      charm      mixed
with a surprising element of vulnerability, uncommon
among      other major Hollywood actors.
```

19

TeX and LaTeX

```
Cary Grant, on the other
hand, was versatile     enough to play the villain as well as the suave
hero in many films.
```

is formatted by TeX as follows:

```
How do you compare these two terrific leading men? James Stewart had that
good-natured, All-American charm mixed with a surprising element of
vulnerability, uncommon among other major Hollywood actors.

Cary Grant, on the other hand, was versatile enough to play the villain as
well as the suave hero in many Hitchcock films.
```

You can also insert comments into your TeX file using the % character. Text following a % character is treated as a comment and not made part of the TeX output. The text

```
From her% Nothing to do with Hitchcock
% ...nothing at all
e to there
```

is formatted as

```
From here to there
```

TeX has several commands for manipulating paragraphs. The \par command starts a new paragraph, which has the same effect as inserting a blank line.

```
From here \par to there
```

The preceding line is formatted as follows:

```
From here
to there
```

The \noindent command tells TeX not to indent the paragraph:

```
I grew up on Newcastle Street.

\noindent That was close to Hazlehurst.
```

This is output as follows:

```
        I grew up on Newcastle Street.
That was close to Hazlehurst.
```

You can also use the escape character before a space in order to force the insertion of an extra space:

```
I think that I need an extra\ \ \ space or two.
I'm sure       of it.
```

This becomes

```
I think that I need an extra    space or two.
I'm sure of it.
```

Fonts

Fonts are representations of characters that share similar size and style. The default font that TeX uses is roman. You can override this by using the internal names that TeX associates with fonts that are externally loaded. You can also add new font definitions. The definitions that TeX knows about by default are: \rm (roman), \tt (typewriter), \bf (bold), \sl (slanted), and \it (italic). TeX continues using whatever font was last specified (including the default) until it is instructed to do otherwise. Therefore, the text

```
This is roman, but I think I will switch to \tt typewriter for a while;
then again, maybe \it italic would be nice. Now back to \rm roman.
```

appears as follows:

This is roman, but I think I will switch to typewriter for a while; *then again, maybe italic would be nice.* Now back to roman.

You can add a font and change its size using a command like this:

```
\font \fontname=auxiliary font
```

To use a 12-point roman font, redefine the \rm definition to use the cmr12 auxiliary font, like this:

```
\font\rm=cmr12
We are changing from this font \rm to that font.
```

This formats as follows:

We are changing from this font to that font.

Fonts have up to 256 different symbols including the standard numeric, uppercase, and lowercase character symbols that you use most frequently. Symbols that are not represented on a standard keyboard can be accessed using the \char command. This command uses the integer that follows it as a character code index into a font's character table. For example, the text

```
TeX would interpret \char 37 as a comment symbol
but it would not
care about a \char 43 sign.
```

is processed by TeX as follows:

```
TeX would interpret % as a comment symbol but it would not
care about a + sign.
```

Controlling Spacing

You've seen how you can insert individual extra spaces in TeX files. Now, let's examine how you can have more control over the spacing of larger portions of text. TeX has a series of commands that recognize the following units of measurement:

Unit	Meaning
em	Approximately the width of the character M, depending on the font in use
in	Inches
pt	Points (1 inch equals 72.27 points)
mm	Millimeters (1 inch equals 25.4 millimeters)

These units are used with decimal numbers to specify the amount of spacing that you need. The \hskip command can insert a horizontal space on a line, like this:

```
\tt From here \hskip 0.5in to there
```

This produces the following output:

```
From here      to there
```

You can also supply a negative number, which moves the text following the \hskip command to the left (the negative direction). The \hfil command distributes horizontal space in a paragraph when space is available. The interesting thing about the \hfil command is the fact that TeX inserts one implicitly for each paragraph. Bearing this detail in mind, you can use this command to flush text left or right, or center it on a line, like this:

```
\noindent \hfil Some centered text. \par
```

This is output as follows:

```
                    Some centered text.
```

The \vskip command can insert a vertical space between paragraphs using a given unit of measurement (much like \hskip). The command

```
\vskip 40mm
```

places a vertical space of 40 millimeters between its preceding and succeeding paragraphs. TeX also provides vertical skipping commands in convenient units: \smallskip, \medskip, and \bigskip.

The vertical equivalent of \hfil is the \vfill command, which can distribute vertical spaces between paragraphs when extra space (nontext) is available. TeX assumes an implicit \vfill command at the end of a document.

You can also explicitly add line breaks and page breaks to your document with the \break command. If this command appears within a paragraph, TeX inserts a line break. If it appears between paragraphs, a page break is inserted. Conversely, you can specify points in your document where you want the text to be kept together and not broken across lines or pages. This is done by using the \nobreak command.

Page Layout

A page is composed of a header, footer, and body. The header and footer contain information such as chapter title, section heading, and page number. The body is where the main information in your document appears. By changing how this information is ordered in your TeX document, you are actually designing the look of the finished product.

The \headline and \footline commands both take arguments that specify their content. The format of these commands is as follows:

```
\headline={parameters}
```

The parameters could be a list of things such as a page number command and an \hfil command:

```
\headline={\hfil \the\pageno}
\footline={\hfil}
```

This pair of commands creates a right-justified page number and a blank footer on each page.

You can change the size of the text box that TeX uses for paragraphs by using the \hsize command. For instance, the text

```
\hsize=2in
This text is 2 inches wide but we could choose to make it wider or
thinner.
```

produces the following:

```
          This text is 2 inches wide but
          we could choose to make it
          wider or thinner.
```

Margins can be adjusted inward or outward using the \leftskip and \rightskip commands, respectively. By providing positive values to these commands, they move the margin inward, depending on which side you specify (left or right). As you may expect, negative values have the opposite effect: They move the margins outward. Indentation is controlled similarly by using the \parindent command.

19

TeX and LaTeX

The \baselineskip and \parskip commands control the regular vertical spacing between lines and paragraphs, as in the following:

```
\baselineskip=0.15in
\parskip=0.3in
```

Baseline refers to the distance between the bottoms of characters (such as an *i*) on consecutive lines.

Using Groups

Normally, TeX continues using such things as fonts and text styles until you explicitly change the format. The grouping features of TeX enable you to define changes that are local to particular sections of text. The formatting originally specified is then restored after the group has been processed.

There are two ways to specify how text is grouped. One is to use the \begingroup and \endgroup command pair. The other is to use the braces { and }. Although both of these perform grouping roles, braces are also used to specify parameters to commands and, as such, must be used with care.

As an illustration of the use of groups in TeX, the text

```
Let's see \begingroup \it how {\bf this grouping stuff} really
works \endgroup, shall we?
```

produces the following:

```
Let's see how this grouping stuff really
works, shall we?
```

You may have noted from the example that, in fact, groups can contain other groups.

Mathematical Symbols

One of the most powerful features of TeX is its capability to generate correct mathematical notation for formulas with convenient commands. This is one of the key reasons behind TeX's popularity among engineers and scientists.

TeX distinguishes between formulas that must appear within regular text (inline formulas) and those that must appear on their own line (displayed formulas). You must use the $ symbol to denote inline formulas, as in

```
The equation $2+3=x$ must evaluate to $x=5$.
```

which is generated as the following:

```
The equation 2+3=x must evaluate to x=5.
```

However, displayed formulas are denoted using two consecutive $ symbols, as in

```
The equation $$2+3=x$$ must evaluate to $$x=5$$.
```

which produces the following:

```
     The equation
```

$$2+3=x$$

```
must evaluate to
```

$$x=5.$$

Table 19.1 shows some of the math symbols that TeX can generate, their associated commands, and their meaning.

TABLE 19.1. SOME OF THE MATH SYMBOLS THAT TeX CAN GENERATE.

Symbol	TeX *Command*	Meaning
[185]	\pi	Pi
[183]	\sum	Sum
{	\{	Open bracket
}	\}	Close bracket
[186]	\int	Integral
[178]	\leq	Less than or equal to
[179]	\geq	Greater than or equal to
[173]	\neq	Not equal to
[165]	\bullet	Bullet
[201]	\ldots	Horizontal ellipses
[215]	\diamond	Diamond
[198]	\Delta	Delta

TeX uses particular fonts for the formulas it produces. These can be overridden in the usual fashion, but the changes are applicable only to letters and digits.

Using Figures in Your Document

Figures that are drawn outside of TeX can be inserted into their own space. This space "floats." In other words, TeX knows that it must keep track of the figure space as the text around it is added or deleted. This flexibility means that you, the writer, need not worry about exactly where in the document your figures will appear.

To insert a figure that must appear at the top of a page, use the following command:

```
\topinsert figure \endinsert
```

Here, *figure* can be an external reference or an internal definition. TeX tries to place the figure at the top of the next page with sufficient space.

You can also tell TeX that you want a figure to appear on its own page by using this command:

```
\pageinsert figure \endinsert
```

Macros

Macros have made TeX a highly extendible system. They essentially enable you to create new commands by associating existing commands and text sequences to a macro name. After they are defined, these macros can be used in other parts of your document to replace repetitive pieces of text, or to encapsulate abstract operations.

A macro is defined once, using the following format:

```
\def macroname {new text}
```

In this case, *macroname* is a name or TeX command preceded by a backslash character. Any reference to this macro name is replaced by the new text throughout the document. For example, the macro definition

```
\def\brg{burger}
Ham\brg, cheese\brg, lim\brg.
```

is output as follows:

```
Hamburger, cheeseburger, limburger.
```

Macros can refer to other macros, as in

```
\def\tig{a tigger }
\def\wond{a wonderful thing }
\def\pooh{\wond is \tig cause \tig is \wond}
\pooh\par
```

which produces the following:

```
a wonderful thing is a tigger cause a tigger is a wonderful thing
```

> **WARNING**
>
> You must be careful of recursive macro definitions: macros that refer to their own names within their definition. Such macro definitions cause TeX to continuously (and vainly) evaluate the macro, leading to an infinite loop. The following is an example of this:
>
> ```
> \def\itself{\itself}
> \itself
> ```

TeX macros have the added feature of being able to accept parameters when expanded, if a list of formal parameters has been specified in the macro definition. To create a macro using parameters, you would use this format:

```
\def macroname (list of formal parameters) {new text}
```

Here, the list of parameters is specified as #1, #1#2, #1#2#3, and so on. This is a powerful aspect of macros because it can change the output of an expanded macro based on the parameter in use. For example, the code

```
\def\parm#1{This is the #1 time I'll say this.}
\parm{first}
\parm{second}
\parm{last}
```

produces the following:

```
This is the first time I'll say this.
This is the second time I'll say this.
This is the last time I'll say this.
```

Each parameter that is used must be passed separately by enclosing it in braces, as in

```
\def\family#1#2{My #1 is #2.}
\family{wife}{Cindy}
\family{sister}{Sheila}
\family{father}{Myles}
```

which makes the following output:

```
My wife is Cindy.
My sister is Sheila.
My father is Myles.
```

OK - tjp

You must specify an appropriate number of parameters in your macro definition. The macro definition

```
\def\mistake#1{This is wrong because of #2.}
```

is incorrect because it refers to a second parameter that is not specified in the formal parameter list.

Macros can be redefined in your document, but you should be aware that only the most recent definition will be applied. Also, macros defined within groups are valid only within the scope of the group.

Macro definitions can be nested one within another, as in the following:

```
\def\hey{Hey\def\hey{hey}}
\hey, \hey, \hey.
```

This has the following output:

```
Hey, hey, hey.
```

As with many topics within this book, we have examined only some of the highlights of TeX. There is much more to learn but, having covered the basics regarding macros, you can now look at the most popular extension of TeX, which uses macros to enhance the creation of documents. This extension is LaTeX.

LaTeX: An Enhancement of TeX

LaTeX is a collection of macros that build on the capabilities of TeX and provide a higher level of abstraction for the creation of documents. It is essentially a style library that encourages uniform formatting and typesetting across documents. LaTeX macros shift the emphasis away from the details of things such as "set text to 8-point slanted" to concepts that writers identify more readily with, such as the emphasis of a word or phrase. Thus, LaTeX macros have names that are more representative of the way writers *think* when they are writing.

Because LaTeX is an extension of TeX, you'll find it easy to become quickly productive in LaTeX, assuming that you have some experience in TeX. Whitespace and spacing between paragraphs are handled in the same manner as in TeX. The special characters in TeX are the same in LaTeX, and comments are denoted using the % character.

The key differences between TeX and LaTeX become apparent as you learn more about the macros that define the layout of your document in a convenient fashion.

Defining a **LaTeX** Document

Every LaTeX document begins with the \documentclass command. The parameter passed to this command specifies what kind of document you want to write. The basic document classes are described in Table 19.2.

TABLE 19.2. DOCUMENT CLASSES.

Document Class	Description
article	Used for short reports, reference cards, presentations, scientific journals, and so on.
book	Used for complete books.
report	Used for reports having several chapters, theses, and so on.

To create a very basic LaTeX document, simply place some words between the two commands \begin{document} and \end{document}. The text that precedes the \begin{document} command is called the *preamble*, and the text that comes after is known as the *body*. So, you can create a very simple document such as the following:

```
\documentclass{article}
\begin{document}
What a small document this is.
\end{document}
```

To process this document (which you will edit in a file called gloves.tex), use the following command:

```
% latex gloves
```

This produces a dvi file and a log file in the same manner used by TeX. The dvi file can either be converted to PostScript, or viewed directly using xdvi.

You can specify options with the type of document in the \documentclass command using the following format:

```
\documentclass[option]{document class}
```

These options relate to the physical structure of the document. Some of the more common ones are listed in Table 19.3.

19

TeX and LaTeX

TABLE 19.3. `\documentclass` OPTIONS.

Option	Description
10pt, 11pt, 12pt	The default font for the document, which is `10pt` if not otherwise stated.
fleqn	Displays formulas as left-justified instead of centered.
leqno	Numbers formulas on the left side.
letterpaper, a4 paper	The paper size, which is `letterpaper` by default.
openright, openany	Starts the first page of a chapter on the right side, or on the next available page.
titlepage, notitlepage	Does or does not start a new page after the title.
twocolumn	Splits each page into two columns (useful for newsletters).
twoside, oneside	Generates double- or single-sided output.

Some of the differences between document classes are encapsulated by the defaults that they use for the options mentioned. For instance, articles and reports are single-sided by default, whereas books are not. Articles do not use the options for title pages and starting right-sided chapters because they do not understand what a chapter is. Thus, the document classes in LaTeX are smart enough to do the kind of layout that you expect for the type of document you need.

Packages

LaTeX also has the `\usepackage` command, which enables you to extend the capabilities of LaTeX even further by using an external *package* of features. The format is as follows:

`\usepackage{package name}`

package name can be any of several available packages. For instance, the doc package is used for the documentation of LaTeX programs, and the makeidx package provides support for the production of indexes.

You can also control what page styles LaTeX applies to your document by using the `\pagestyle` command. Table 19.4 describes the basic page styles available.

TABLE 19.4. PAGE STYLES.

Style	Description
empty	Sets the header and footers to be empty.
headings	Prints the current chapter heading and page number on each page with an empty footer.
plain	Prints the page number centered in the footer (the default page style).

You can also vary page styles in your document using the \thispagestyle command. This applies the supplied page style to the current page only.

Using Special Characters

LaTeX supports the use of international characters, such as umlauts (··) and circumflexes (^). These characters are generated using a command variant on the letter itself. For example, the text

```
What a na\"\i ve fj\o rd you are!
```

produces the following:

What a naïve fjörd you are!

International spacing can also be applied using the \frenchspacing command. This command tells LaTeX not to insert the usual extra space after a period.

Putting Structure into a LaTeX Document

LaTeX has commands that make it easy to enhance your document structurally, thus making it easier for the reader to digest. For the article document class, the commands are as follows:

\section

\subsection

\subsubsection

\paragraph

\subparagraph, and

\appendix.

These commands, with the exception of \appendix, accept titles as arguments, and are declared before the body of text that they represent. LaTeX takes care of the rest; it sets the appropriate spacing between sections, section numbering, and title font. The \appendix command uses alphabetic increments in order to number succeeding appendix sections.

For the report and book classes, there are two additional commands: \part and \chapter. The \part command enables you to insert a section without affecting the

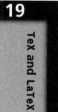

numbering sequence of the chapters. You can suppress the appearance of a section in the table of contents by inserting a * character in the section command, as in the following:

```
\section*{I don't want to know about it}
```

You probably want to add a title to your document. This is done by specifying the arguments to the title commands and then calling the \maketitle command:

```
...
\title{Confessions of a LaTeX Enthusiast}
\author{Me}
\date
\begin{document}
\maketitle
...
```

To insert a table of contents in your document, issue the \tableofcontents command (big surprise) at the point where you want the table to appear. When you process your document with LaTeX, it needs two passes: one to make note of all the section numbers, and the other to build the table of contents from the information it collected in the first pass.

Adding Other Structural Elements

You can add cross-references to your document, which tie associated elements such as text, figures, and tables to text in other parts of your document. Use the \label command to set a point that you want to refer to, and give it an argument that is any name you choose. This name can then be referred to by the \ref and \pageref commands to generate a cross-reference containing the section number and page number that the section title appears on.

You can easily add footnotes using the \footnote command, which accepts the text of the footnote as an argument.

The structure of a document can be enhanced by controlling the presentation of the text that appears between section titles. This can be easily managed by using LaTeX environments. Environments are specified by bounding a portion of text with \begin and \end commands, and passing an environment name to each command, as in the following:

```
\begin{hostileenvironment}
Looks like we're surrounded, said Custer.
\end{hostileenvironment}
```

LaTeX has many predefined environments for practical applications, as described in Table 19.5.

TABLE 19.5. PREDEFINED ENVIRONMENTS.

Environment	Description
center	Centers text.
description	Used to present descriptive paragraphs.
enumerate	Used for numbered or bulleted lists.
flushleft	Paragraphs are left-aligned.
flushright	Paragraphs are right-aligned.
itemize	Used for simple lists.
quote	Used to quote single paragraphs.
quotation	Used for longer quotes that span several paragraphs.
tabular	Typesets tables with optional row and column separators.
verbatim	Produces typed text. Useful for representing programming code, for example.
verse	Used to control the linebreaks in poems.

Working with Figures and Tables

LaTeX also supports the variable placement (or "floating") of figures and tables in a document using the table and figure environments. A figure could be specified as follows:

```
\begin{figure}[!hbp]
\makebox[\textwidth]{\framebox[2in]{\rule{0pt}{2in}}}
\end{figure}
```

The options passed to the \begin{figure} command are placement specifiers that indicate your preferences for the location of the figure. LaTeX has to juggle the placement of floating figures and tables in a document by using these preferences, as well as internal guidelines such as the maximum number of floats allowed per page. In this example, you told LaTeX to keep the figure with its adjacent text (h), at the bottom of the next applicable page (b), or, failing that, on a special page with other floating figures (p). The ! character overrides LaTeX's best intentions for placing the figure, which may not necessarily jibe with what you are saying with the other placement specifiers.

Tables and figures can be labeled using the \caption command, which must be issued within the table or figure environment.

These are just some of the basics for using LaTeX, but hopefully they are sufficient to give you a place to start on the road to making your documents more visually appealing. You have probably noticed that LaTeX is somewhat easier to work with than TeX itself, because it hides much detail from you as an author.

19

TeX and LaTeX

VirTeX and IniTeX

Two other TeX-related programs work together but perform slightly different roles. The IniTeX program is used to create a TeX format (.fmt) file containing font definitions and macros. The VirTeX program can then quickly load this precompiled format file, much more quickly than TeX can. The command to use a format file is as follows:

```
$ virtex \&myformat sometexfile
```

The & character is necessary for VirTeX to recognize that it is loading a format file first; the & must be escaped using the \ character so as not to confuse the shell. The difference between VirTeX and IniTeX is that VirTeX can't be used to create TeX format files, but it executes much faster.

Summary

TeX is a document-formatting system for Linux that enables authors to produce their own high-quality publications. It produces documents that are portable among output devices such as printers or displays. TeX supports many typographical features and is particularly well-suited to the formatting of correct mathematical notation. It has macros that can be used to enhance the power of its basic command set. LaTeX, one of the most popular extensions to TeX, uses sophisticated macros to help you organize and typeset your documents based on its contents. From here, you can learn about:

Using gawk, a handy and quick programming language for advanced users and system administrators, in Chapter 25, "gawk."

Using Perl, another programming language that is very popular for Web-based scripting in Chapter 28, "Perl."

Using Smalltalk/X, an X-based implementation of the object-oriented programming language, in Chapter 31, "Smalltalk/X."

Printing

by Tim Parker

CHAPTER 20

In previous chapters you've seen a little about printing, and we'll be covering the subject from the system administrator's point of view in a later chapter. However, it is worth taking some time to look at how you can print files under Linux, what devices are available to you, how to set up printers, and some of the eccentricities of the Linux printing system.

It's worth remembering that many of the printing routines used in Linux are inherited from 30 years of UNIX. In the early days, a printer on every desktop was unheard of. In most cases, a single printer or printer pool was used for everyone on a large network. UNIX's printing routines were written with this model in mind, and although it has been upgraded and adapted to our systems today, many anachronisms are still found in the print routines.

Setting Up a Printer

In most cases Linux's installation routine will have asked you if you wanted to set up a printer when you installed the operating system. At that point you usually had a list of printer models to choose from, and Linux asked for the port your printer is attached to. If you chose to configure a printer at that point, it should be working properly. If you skipped that installation option or didn't get to choose it (some versions of Linux don't bother asking), you must configure the printer manually.

There are two pieces of information you need to have before configuring a printer. The first is to know the type of printer you are using (the full name, as well as any compatible models, if possible). The reason you need to know compatible model names is simple: Linux knows about very few printers. If you just bought a brand new state-of-the-art printer that came with Windows drivers, that's great for Windows. Linux can't use those drivers, and you can bet that the printer manufacturer didn't bother including a CD with Linux drivers on it! Fortunately, most printers you buy today are compatible with an older model that Linux does know about. For example, the newest Hewlett-Packard laserjet series does not have Linux drivers, but all the newest models are backward compatible with older laserjet models, and so work with the older Linux drivers. You may not get all the features of the new printer, but at least you can use the device!

The other piece of information you need to configure your printer is the port it is on. Printers tend to be available in three different connection types: parallel port, serial port, and network port. You know the parallel and serial ports from your Windows and DOS world, but network ports tend to be used only on larger systems. Parallel ports are the easiest because the communications parameters for parallel ports are unchanging. You only need to know whether you are using the first or second parallel port on your PC (most PCs only have a single parallel port: LPT1).

Serial port printers are common and require an RS-232 cable. You need to know not only the port number (COM1, COM2, and so on), but also the speed at which the printer communicates and how many bits it uses. You'll often see things like 9600 baud, 8 bits. You must configure the printer and the serial port to run at the same speed, or you'll get garbage, or worse, nothing, from your printer.

Network ports are actually easier to configure than serial ports. Each printer on the network has an IP address, and all you need to tell Linux is where the printer is and what kind of driver to use.

Port Names

Linux uses different names for its devices than DOS and Windows. We'll be looking at the device names and how they are used in more detail in Chapter 33, "Devices," so we'll keep it simple here. A DOS LPT1 port is called /dev/lp0 in Linux, and LPT2 is called /dev/lp1. The /dev part of the name indicates to the system where to get information about that device, and the lp0 and lp1 indicate that these devices are parallel ports. Linux numbers everything starting with 0, so the second port is lp1.

The same applies for serial ports. A DOS COM1 port is know to Linux as /dev/ttyS0, COM2 is /dev/ttyS1, COM3 is /dev/ttyS2, and COM4 is /dev/ttyS3. Linux allows many serial ports, and the naming convention changes with many multiport cards, but it's safe to use /dev/ttyS0 and /dev/ttyS1 for your COM1 and COM2 ports because most PCs have these two serial ports on their motherboards.

> **TIP**
>
> Each serial port on a Linux system actually has two names. For example, COM1 is known as both /dev/ttyS0 and /dev/ttycua0. The second format is used for bidirectional devices such as modems. Don't use the /dev/cua* devices for printers.

Printer Drivers

Every printer on the Linux system must have a printer driver. The printer driver essentially tells Linux how to send instructions to that printer. It'll have things like "to eject a page, do this" and "to change color to red, do this" as a series of instruction codes.

Linux has a series of printer drivers included with it, and more are available from Web and FTP sites. You need to find a printer driver intended for your printer or one of the printers that it is compatible with. If you use a noncompatible printer driver, then you may get all kinds of strange behavior from your printer!

Linux reads all the information about a printer and how to talk to it from a file called /etc/printcap. The /etc/printcap file is quite large and is usually set so that only root can modify it. Each entry in the /etc/printcap file describes how to do different things to your printer. Some Linux systems prevent any kind of access to the /etc/printcap file and insist you use a tool to modify it. For example, Figure 20.1 shows the output from a RedHat 5.0 system when you try to use more to display the contents of the /etc/printcap file. In this case, RedHat wants you to use the X-based print tool to modify the /etc/printcap file. Not all versions of Linux are this careful and let you modify (and screw up) the file to your heart's content.

FIGURE 20.1.

Some systems don't let you browse the /etc/printcap file.

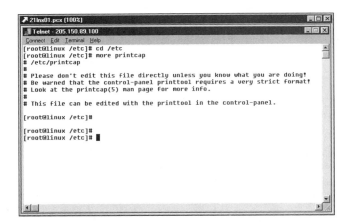

You could edit the /etc/printcap file with all your printer's codes (which is how we used to do it in the old days) but that's slow, awkward, and prone to errors. Instead, it's better to look for a compatible driver for your printer and let that take care of the problems for you.

Apart from the driver that tells Linux how to talk to your printer, there are other devices that may be involved every time you print something. This typically occurs when your printer uses a page descriptor language (PDL) such as PCL or PostScript. When a PDL is involved in printing, your application or the shell sends your data to be printed to the PDL first, which acts like a filter to convert the data to the proper format for printing. This formatted data is then sent to the printer using the printer driver.

If you have a printer that can handle many different PDLs, you could potentially have more than one filter involved. Each filter system is set up separately for a printer. For example, if you have a Hewlett-Packard LaserJet that handles both PCL and PostScript, you may have one printer defined that use the PCL filter, then the LaserJet device driver, and another printer defined that uses the PostScript filter and then the same LaserJet device driver. Both printers use the same device driver and port, which is fine for Linux. It lets you define as many printers as you want, in any combination of ports and filters. When you send something to the printer, your command tells Linux which printer definition (filter, device driver and port) to use. Some printers, notably older dot matrix and daisywheel printers, do not need filters, and these accept data straight from the application to the device driver.

Linux Print Commands

Because Linux is based on UNIX, several print commands and utilities may be used on your version. The most common print commands are `lpr`, `lpd`, and `lpc`. These three print utilities are all slightly different, and configuring them to work properly can often be more troublesome than configuring the rest of the Linux system!

When you print a file (from Emacs or a word processor, for example), the print utilities are invoked. They copy the data to be printed to a spool directory and store the contents in a file. This is done for two reasons: It frees up your application right away so you can continue working (you don't have to wait for the printing to finish before you can go on), and it allows the Linux utilities to manage print requests by priority, types of printers, forms required, and other properties. The spool directory is usually /usr/spool/lp or /var/spool/lp, although some Linux versions use other directory paths. Typically there is a separate subdirectory for each printer defined on the system, such as /usr/spool/lp/laserjet and /usr/spool/lp/bubblejet, for a system with two printers defined.

Whenever you submit a print request, Linux responds with a print request ID number. This is sometimes suppressed by applications but usually shown when you print from a command line. The command to print a file from the shell prompt is usually the `lp` command followed by the filename or a wildcard, such as the following:

```
lp file1.txt
```

When this command is executed, the system returns the print request ID number:

```
request id is hplj-307 (1 file)
```

In this case, the request ID number is hplj_307, which tells you the printer's name (hplj) and that this is the 307th print request that printer has handled since the counter started at zero. The total number after the request ID shows how many files are to be printed (in this case, one). If wildcards had been used, this number may be different, as shown in this example:

```
lp text*.doc
request id is hplj_308 (12 files)
```

In this case, even though we have printed 12 files, only one print request ID number is assigned to that bunch. This is normal: Linux's printing utilities treat each individual print request (no matter how many files or pages are involved) as a single request.

After an application has submitted a print request and the data has been copied to the spool directory, a printer daemon looks at the directory contents and arranges to print the files in order. This print daemon is running all the time and simply looks at the spool directories checking for new arrivals. When one comes in, the daemon checks that the destination printer is available and then sends the data to the printer. If the printer is busy or not available for some other reason, the daemon holds the print request until it can be queued. The printer daemon can also prioritize print requests if instructed to by users.

Many useful commands let you see what you've queued to the printers and what the print request IDs are, and they let you manage the queue a little. The system administrator can manage any print request and the queues, but users can usually only manage their own print requests. Several commands supported by Linux versions do much the same thing, so check your own system to see which commands are provided.

To find out all the print requests that are in the print queue (stored in the spool directory), you can use the `lpq` command. When run, `lpq` shows the files in the printer and their current location in the queue. This lets you judge how long it will take for your jobs to print. Some systems allow the `lpstat` command to show the same thing. If you have nothing in the queue, `lpstat` won't show you anything. It only shows your requests unless you use the `-t` option, in which case `lpstat` shows the entire print queue, as well as status messages about each printer the system knows about. Many Linux systems use the `lpc` command to show current status of all printers.

To remove a print request from the queue, most Linux systems use the `lprm` command followed by the print request ID number, such as the following:

```
lprm hplj-307
```

Some systems allow you to use the cancel command in the same way:

```
cancel hplj-307
```

You will often get a message back from the system telling you that the print job has been canceled or rm-ed from the queue:

```
request "hplj-307" canceled
```

Summary

In this chapter you've seen how Linux handles printers and device drivers, as well as how filters are involved. Linux has scripts that install printers for you automatically, so going through the tedious and troublesome procedure of manually installing a printer, setting up the queues, and checking file and directory permissions will be skipped. From here, there are a number of chapters you may want to read to learn more:

To learn about the Ghostscript and Ghostview utilities which substitute for PostScript on Linux, read Chapter 24, "Ghostscript."

To learn more about devices and device drivers, see Chapter 33, "Devices."

To learn more about using printers on networks, see Chapter 37, "Networking."

Multimedia Linux

by Tim Parker

IN THIS CHAPTER

CHAPTER 21

One of the limitations of the first few versions of Linux was its lack of support of sound cards, joysticks, and other multimedia input and output routines. The last few releases of Linux have seen a major change in this aspect, though, and now Linux can be as fully capable of multimedia as Windows 98 can. This chapter looks at how you can configure your Linux system for multimedia applications.

Sound Cards

A sound card does more than play a few beeps and prerecorded sounds when you open windows, do something wrong, or close down your system. A sound card is ideal for playing games, where it can generate both music and sound effects. It can be used to record sounds and voice to a file, and play it back later. A sound card can let you play an audio CD in your CD-ROM player, so you can listen to music as you work. And a sound card can act as an interface to some devices, such as a CD-ROM or SCSI device chain.

All sound cards work digitally: They use discrete chunks of data to tell the sound card chips what tone to generate, how loud to make it, and other parameters that define sound. Sound cards can generate these chunks of data at different rates; the faster and with more detail they are generated, the better the sound seems to our ears. As an example, most CDs sample data at the rate of 44.1 thousand samples per second, with 16 bits used for each sample. If you work out the math, that means that in an hour there are about 600 megabytes of data to produce CD-quality sound. Many sound cards from a few years ago couldn't handle this amount of data. Instead, they used 8 bits of data per sample, and sampled at rates as low as 8 thousand samples per second. The difference between the two is clearly audible if you listen on a decent stereo, but harder to differentiate when you listen through small, cheap PC speakers.

Sound files today are available in a wide variety of formats. Each format differs in the sampling rate, the number of bits per sample, whether a compression algorithm is used, and the number of channels used (mono is one channel, stereo is two, and so on). The most common forms are summarized in Table 21.1.

Table 21.1. Common sound file format characteristics.

File extension	Channels	Sample size	Sample rate	Comments
.au	2	8 bit	8 KHz	Sun UNIX format
.mod	2	8 bit	varies depending on algorithm	
.raw	2	8 bit	22 KHz	

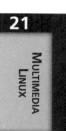

File extension	Channels	Sample size	Sample rate	Comments
.voc	1	8 bit	22KHz	
.wav	1	8 bit	22KHz	
.wav	2	16 bit	44KHz	

A number of sound card drivers are included with current versions of Linux. These all have drivers for Linux written by owners of the cards, who are experienced with device driver programming and made the effort to support their cards. Kindly, they make the drivers available to everyone who uses Linux. (You can't use the drivers that came with your sound card because they are usually DOS- or Windows-specific, and the architecture of the operating systems is not interchangeable.) Even if you do not have a Linux driver for your specific card, it may be supported through a compatible card driver. For example, many sound cards are SoundBlaster-compatible, so a SoundBlaster driver may work (but then again, may not).

Using the PC Speaker

So you don't have a sound card yet. You're not completely out of luck. A driver is available for the small speaker built into practically every PC box. While this may sound as though it won't be much good, the driver manages to elicit surprisingly good 16-bit stereo sound from the tiny device, allowing you to play games like Doom. If you're handy with wiring, you can also string a pair of wires to an external speaker instead of the internal, although you have to remember the amplifier on the motherboard is very low power. If you want to use the PC speaker driver, you have to download it because there are few versions of Linux that include it as part of the distribution.

> **Tip**
>
> To obtain the latest version of the PC speaker driver for Linux, check the FTP site ftp.informatik.hu-berlin.de/pub/os/linux/hu-sound or one of the Linux FTP archives listed in Appendix A, "Linux FTP Sites and Newsgroups." The most recent version of the driver when this chapter was written was 0.9.

Included with the PC speaker driver is a set of instructions that guide you through the installation and configuration procedure. A sample file included with the distribution package lets you test the speaker to make sure it is behaving properly.

Configuring a Sound Card

Some versions of Linux come with a routine that can link in support for your sound card. Usually you choose the type of sound card from a menu during the installation procedure, and the install routine takes care of the rest for you. If that's the case, then the sound card should be properly working and you can skip this section. If your version of Linux didn't ask about sound cards when it installed or your sound card is not working properly, you will have to go through the installation and configuration routine described here.

NOTE

Some CD-ROMs of Linux software include sound card configuration routines that can't be accessed until the operating system installation has been completed. Red Hat 5.0, for example, includes the utility sndconfig which can configure most SoundBlaster and compatible cards for you. Check your CD-ROM documentation to see which (if any) utilities have been provided for you.

The first step to setting up a sound card for Linux is to install the card itself. This is done by following the instructions that come with the sound card. There are no special steps that you must follow to configure a sound card for Linux, other than making sure the IRQ (interrupt), DMA (direct memory address), and I/O address are unique (which is necessary under DOS and Windows). If you installed the sound card already, you can obtain these settings from your Control Panel or other utilities. Some older sound cards use jumpers or DIP switches to establish these parameters. Whichever way they are set, you need to note them for your configuration under Linux.

TIP

If you are using a sound card that supports Plug and Play, you should install it under Windows or DOS first because Linux doesn't have the ability to set the parameters for these cards in most cases. After installing the card under Windows or DOS, use the Control Panel or similar utility to display the settings chosen for the sound card and note them. You'll need to enter these values when setting up the card under Linux.

If you are going to configure Linux sound cards, disable the PNP option in your system's BIOS because it can cause configuration information on the Plug and Play cards to be reset to default values or to be changed entirely. Usually the BIOS has an option something like "PNP OS?" with the setting of Yes by default. Set this option to No for best results with Linux.

After installing the sound card, you need to link the proper sound card device driver into the kernel. If you haven't worked with the kernel before, it's not a scary process. You most likely didn't have to link your kernel when you installed Linux, as most distributions come with prebuilt kernels which lack the sound card support. You need to recompile all the drivers (including the sound card driver) into a brand new kernel.

If you downloaded a device driver for your sound card from a Web or FTP site, chances are good that there is a README file of some sort with the driver itself. Make sure you read this file for any requirements the driver has (such as specific DMA or I/O addresses) and any special steps required during the recompilation of the kernel.

Every version of Linux has slightly different kernel recompile routines, but in general the steps are simple:

1. Log in as `root`
2. `cd` to `/usr/src/linux`
3. Enter the command `make config`

Alternatively, some versions of Linux have an X-based utility to rebuild the kernel. For those systems, open a window and cd to the proper directory, then use the command `make xconfig`.

You must always be `root` when rebuilding the kernel; otherwise you won't have access to the directories and utilities necessary to compile the kernel. Most versions of Linux keep the `makefile` for the recompile in `/usr/src/linux`, but if your version is different you should check the documentation or README files that came with your software.

When you run the config routine, it asks you a series of questions about whether you want to include certain components, as shown in Figure 21.1. In most cases, you will want to accept the defaults unless you know otherwise. One good example is when config asks whether you want to include a sound card (which is usually toward the end of a long list of questions). You should select yes. The config routine then asks a whole bunch of questions about which sound card to include, as shown in Figure 21.2.

FIGURE 21.1.

The config routine asks if you want to include components in your recompilation of the Linux kernel.

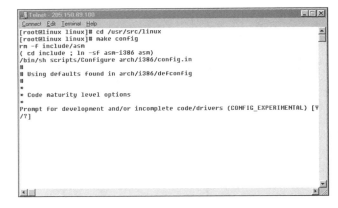

FIGURE 21.2.

The config routine asks a lot of questions about which sound card you want to support.

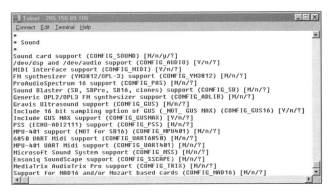

When you are asked for each type of sound card, answer N to the ones you know you are not using and Y to the one you want. Don't let Linux guess your card, as it invariably guesses wrong.

NOTE

If you had a sound card preconfigured in the kernel, config will ask you if you want to use it with a question like this:

Old configuration exists in /etc/soundconf. Use it [Y/n]?

If you had a working sound card before, then answer Y. If your card did not work, then answer N.

After going through what may seem like a very long list of sound cards, you are asked some more generic questions that apply to many cards, such as

```
/dev/dsp and /dev/audio support [N/y]?
```

You should answer Y for this as the two devices mentioned are commonly used by sound card utilities. You are also asked if you want to use MIDI interface device support and FM synthesizer support:

```
MIDI interface support [N/y]
FM synthesis (YM2813/OPL-3) support [N/y]
```

If your card has a MIDI interface you should answer Y to the first. Many cards use a Yamaha FM synthesis chip to generate sound, in which case you should answer Y to the second (some cards support both MIDI and FM synthesis).

The last part of the sound card questions deal with the IRQ, DMA, and I/O address of the card. You should enter the values that you noted earlier for your sound card:

```
I/O base for SB
The default value is 220
Enter the value: 200

SoundBlaster IRQ
The default value is 7
Enter the value: 5

SoundBlaster DMA
The default value is 1
Enter the value: 1
```

You may be asked even more questions, depending on the sound card and the driver. Enter the values carefully since an error means you have to start the whole config process again.

To wrap up the sound card configuration routine, you'll be asked whether you want to save the details:

```
The sound card has been configured.
Save copy of this configuration in /etc/soundconf [Y/n]
```

Go ahead and save the configuration to prevent hassles whenever you rebuild your kernel in the future.

After a few more prompts about components to be compiled into the new kernel, the system starts the compilation process. Some systems have extra steps involved here, depending on how LILO is configured on your machine. The compilation can take anywhere from a couple of minutes to thirty minutes, depending on the speed of your machine and the number of components that have to be compiled.

You're not finished yet! After recompiling the kernel you have to configure the device files properly. Again, this process might be explained in a README that came with your sound card drivers. Rather than do the device file configuration manually, a better approach is to look for the `Readme.linux` file that is usually stored in the `/usr/src/linux/drivers/sound` directory. The bottom of this file contains a short shell script that can do the device file settings painlessly for you. Cut these lines out and paste them into another file, make it executable, then run the script. After the kernel is recompiled and the device files configured, you can reboot the machine.

The script that should be run (cut from the `Readme.linux` file) looks like this (superfluous comment lines have been removed for clarity):

```
#!/bin/sh
AUDIOPERMS=622
# Create the devices

#       Mixer devices

if [ -e /dev/mixer ]; then
        rm -f /dev/mixer
fi

if [ -e /dev/mixer0 ]; then
        rm -f /dev/mixer0
fi

mknod -m 666 /dev/mixer0 c 14 0
ln -sf /dev/mixer0 /dev/mixer
if [ -e /dev/mixer1 ]; then
        rm -f /dev/mixer1
fi
mknod -m 666 /dev/mixer1 c 14 16


#       Sequencer       (14, 1)
#
if [ -e /dev/sequencer ]; then
        rm -f /dev/sequencer
fi
mknod -m 666 /dev/sequencer c 14 1

if [ -e /dev/patmgr0 ]; then
        rm -f /dev/patmgr0
fi
mknod -m 666 /dev/patmgr0 c 14 17
if [ -e /dev/patmgr1 ]; then
        rm -f /dev/patmgr1
fi
mknod -m 666 /dev/patmgr1 c 14 33
```

```
#       music    (14, 8)
        #
        if [ -e /dev/music ]; then
                rm -f /dev/music
        fi

        mknod -m 666 /dev/music c 14 8
        if [ -e /dev/sequencer2 ]; then
                rm -f /dev/sequencer2
        fi
        ln -s /dev/music /dev/sequencer2

#       Midi devices

if [ -e /dev/midi ]; then
        rm -f /dev/midi          # Old name. Don't use it
fi
        if [ -e /dev/midi00 ]; then
                rm -f /dev/midi00
        fi
        mknod -m 666 /dev/midi00 c 14 2
ln -sf /dev/midi00 /dev/midi

        if [ -e /dev/midi01 ]; then
                rm -f /dev/midi01
        fi
        mknod -m 666 /dev/midi01 c 14 18

        if [ -e /dev/midi02 ]; then
                rm -f /dev/midi02
        fi
        mknod -m 666 /dev/midi02 c 14 34

        if [ -e /dev/midi03 ]; then
                rm -f /dev/midi03
        fi
        mknod -m 666 /dev/midi03 c 14 50

#       DSP              (14, 3)

if [ -e /dev/dsp ]; then
        rm -f /dev/dsp
fi
if [ -e /dev/dsp0 ]; then
        rm -f /dev/dsp0
fi
mknod -m $AUDIOPERMS /dev/dsp0 c 14 3
ln -s /dev/dsp0 /dev/dsp

#       DSPW             (14, 5)
```

```
if [ -e /dev/dspW ]; then
        rm -f /dev/dspW
fi
if [ -e /dev/dspW0 ]; then
        rm -f /dev/dspW0
fi
mknod -m $AUDIOPERMS /dev/dspW0 c 14 5
ln -s /dev/dspW0 /dev/dspW

if [ -e /dev/dspW1 ]; then
        rm -f /dev/dspW1
fi
mknod -m $AUDIOPERMS /dev/dspW1 c 14 37
#       SPARC compatible /dev/audio     (14, 4)
#
if [ -e /dev/audio ]; then
        rm -f /dev/audio
fi
if [ -e /dev/audio0 ]; then
        rm -f /dev/audio0
fi
mknod -m $AUDIOPERMS /dev/audio0 c 14 4
ln -s /dev/audio0 /dev/audio


#       DSP1            (14, 19) /dev/dsp for the second soundcard.
#                                Also the SB emulation part of the
#                                PAS16 card.

if [ -e /dev/dsp1 ]; then
        rm -f /dev/dsp1
fi
mknod -m $AUDIOPERMS /dev/dsp1 c 14 19
#       SPARC audio1    (14, 20)
#                                /dev/audio for the second soundcard.
#                                Also the SB emulation part of the
#                                PAS16 card.

if [ -e /dev/audio1 ]; then
        rm -f /dev/audio1
fi
mknod -m $AUDIOPERMS /dev/audio1 c 14 20

#       /dev/sndstat    (14,6)  For debugging purposes

if [ -e /dev/sndstat ]; then
        rm -f /dev/sndstat
fi
mknod -m 666 /dev/sndstat c 14 6
exit 0
```

Troubleshooting the Installation and Configuration

As with any device, there can be problems that need to be corrected after installing and configuring your sound card. Of course, your system may be working perfectly, in which case you can skip this section.

If after compiling the new kernel you have no sound card support and there are no messages during the boot sequence about sound cards, chances are high that you're not booting off the new kernel. The following command displays the details of the kernel that booted.

```
uname -a
```

Check the time and date to see if it coincides with the recompilation. If not, you may have to use LILO to install the new kernel on your boot device, or repeat the entire recompilation process again.

> **TIP**
>
> The /proc/version file on most Linux systems contains the same information as the uname -a command. You can use either to check the version of the kernel.

Assuming the version of the kernel is the one you just compiled, you need to check that the sound card is linked into the kernel itself. The file /proc/devices lists the character and block mode devices the kernel includes. Look for an entry for "sound" (usually number 14). If it's not there, the sound card components were not linked into this kernel and you need to redo the config routine.

If the /proc/devices file looks okay and you saw a message during the boot sequence about the sound card (you can replay all those messages using either the dmesg command or by looking at the /var/adm/messages file), chances are you're using a "compatible" card that isn't very compatible. This is common with SoundBlaster-compatible cards, where the drivers for the real card don't find the compatible card. Check the README files with the driver to see if there's any mention of your specific card and problems with it, and check the manufacturer's Web or FTP site.

Another way to check the status of your sound card installation is to look at the file /dev/sndstat. If you don't find this file, you haven't run the sound card installation script from the end of the file /usr/src/linux/drivers/sound/Readme.Linux. Cut the script from the file, make it executable, and run it. Then you should find a file called `/dev/sndstat` generated for you.

There are several error messages you may see in `/dev/sndstat` that help you determine the problem with your sound card. Table 21.2 shows the most common messages, the reason they are generated, and a possible solution. In each case the error message is preceded by the device name.

TABLE 21.2. `/dev/sndstat` ERROR MESSAGES.

Error message	Reason generated and solution
No such device	The kernel does not contain the sound card drivers. Rebuild the kernel.
No such device or address	The sound card driver couldn't find the sound card at the configuration you specified. Check the configuration settings.

Applications for Sound Cards

There are quite a number of applications that work with your sound card, depending on what you want to do. Most of these applications are available from FTP sites or may be included with your CD-ROM Linux distribution. To check whether the files are on your system or your CD-ROM, use the `find` command to look for the executable program's name.

We're not going to look at each application that is available for Linux because there are several dozen. Instead, we'll pick a few representative examples. Checking out the FTP sites will show you all the others that are available.

vplay, vrec, splay, and srec

The `vplay` utility and its three partners are a suite of sound tools called `snd-util` developed by Hannu Savolainen and Michael Beck. These are straightforward sound recording and playback utilities developed in the early stages of Linux, but work well even today if you are willing to use a command-line interface instead of a fancy GUI. The `srec` tool records sounds and `splay` replays them. (To record, you need either a microphone or other input device such as a feed from a CD.)

> **TIP**
>
> The easiest source of the `snd-util` 3.0 package (the current version as this book
> went to press) is through FTP:
>
> `ftp.sunsite.unc.edu/pub/Linux/apps/sound/snd-util-3.0.tar.gz`

The `srec` utility lets you specify the amount of time to record, as well as the sampling
rate. Sound is stored in the raw file format (`.raw` file extension). To record a twenty
second sample of sound using a 21KHz sampling rate and store the output in the file
`sample.raw`, use this command:

```
srec -t 20 -s 21000 sample.raw
```

To replay the sound just recorded, you need the `splay` utility and must specify both the
filename and the sampling rate:

```
splay -s 21000 sample.raw
```

If you choose the wrong sampling rate you'll notice right away since the sound will not
resemble the original.

The `vplay` and `vrec` commands are based on `splay` and `srec` respectively, but add the
ability to save files in `.wav` format and `.voc` format (used by SoundBlaster cards).

WAVplay

WAVplay is a graphical sound recording and playback utility developed by Andre
Fuechsel. WAVplay lets you see the sound wave as it is recorded and played back. You
can alter the sampling speed and the number of bits per sample by clicking on options on
the GUI. Both stereo and mono signals can be recorded. WAVplay only records `.wav`
files.

> **TIP**
>
> The latest version of WAVplay is 2.1 and can be retrieved from the FTP site:
>
> `ftp.sunsite.unc.edu/pub/Linux/apps/sound/players/wavplay021w1.tar.z`

Sound Studio

Sound Studio was written by Paul Sharpe. It is an X-based application that provides practically every tool you could want to use with sound recording and playback. Sound Studio allows you to record, edit, and play back several formats of sound files. Written in Tcl/Tk for Linux (along with some C code), Sound Studio shows what can be done with this operating system.

> **TIP**
>
> The latest version of Sound Studio is 0.21 and can be retrieved from the FTP site:
>
> `ftp.sunsite.unc.edu/pub/Linux/apps/sound/players/studio.0.1.tgz`

MiXViews

MiXViews is similar to Sound Studio in that it is X-based, but was developed on UNIX workstations and ported to Linux. The author is Douglas Scott. MiXViews allows for recording and playback of sound files in most formats. You can use MiXViews to edit sound waves on the screen. Unlike the other tools mentioned here, MiXViews extends the power of the sound card by allowing filtering, scaling, and mixing of sounds.

> **TIP**
>
> The latest version of MiXViews can be retrieved from the FTP site:
>
> `ftp.ccmrc.ucsb.edut/pub/MixViews`

Joysticks

Some games are a lot more fun when played with a joystick instead of the mouse and keyboard. Since a joystick port is built into most computers (either on the motherboard or on a multifunction board with serial or parallel ports), it would be nice to take advantage of the port. Unfortunately, a joystick driver is not built in to Linux. Fortunately, there are several joystick drivers that have been released. Of course, a joystick is only useful for playing those games that support this device. A game that doesn't support the joystick will probably not be playable with one.

> **TIP**
>
> The latest version of the Linux joystick driver was 0.8.0 at press time. This driver can be retrieved from most FTP sites listed in the Appendix and from the FTP site:
>
> ```
> ftp.sunsite.unc.edu/pub/Linux/kernel/patches/console/joystick-
> 0.8.0.tar.gz
> ```

The joystick driver is distributed as a loadable kernel module so you need the module utility to install it. The module utility is included with most versions of Linux. A loadable module allows the device driver to be loaded and unloaded as needed by the application, saving system resources and avoiding a kernel rebuild.

To install the joystick driver, unpack the distribution using `tar` and `gunzip`, checking that the header file `joystick.h` has the correct information in it (most joysticks work on I/O address 201). Then compiling the driver and using a script file included with the driver, create the device files. After that, loading the module makes the joystick available to you (and Doom!). Most versions of the joystick driver include a utility to test the driver to make sure it is working properly.

Summary

In this chapter we've looked at installing and configuring both a sound card and a joystick. Since you already have a CD-ROM working on your system, you're all set to use practically any of the multimedia applications that are now available for Linux. From here, you may want to read about some related topics such as:

Learn how to install X so you can work with the X-based sound file applications in Chapter 22, "Installing and Configuring XFree86."

Learn about Wabi which lets you run Windows applications under X in Chapter 23, "Wabi."

Learn about rebuilding the kernel to include your sound card drivers in Chapter 57, "Working with the Kernel."

GUIs

IN THIS PART

Installing and Configuring XFree86

by Tim Parker

In This Chapter

Most Linux users want to use the X graphical user interface (GUI) distributed as part of the system. The version of X supplied with most Linux software packages is XFree86, which is an implementation of the X Window system developed at MIT. XFree86 is available for several different PC UNIX versions, including Linux, and has been expanded over the more traditional X system to include the wide variety of hardware that is used in PC machines.

There are at least two major releases of XFree86 available with Linux. Some distributions have the slightly older version 2.X, although most now offer the latest 3.X releases. In this chapter, we will look at installing and preliminary configuration of both XFree86 versions, although most of the examples will use the XFree86 3.X versions.

> **TIP**
>
> It is important that you understand the complete XFree86 installation process before you actually install your software. In some cases, you can cause damage to hardware and the Linux software already installed if you select inappropriate drivers!

What Is XFree86?

XFree86 is a public domain version of the X11 windowing system developed by MIT and now copyright to the MIT Consortium. In keeping with the desire of the developers of Linux to have no copyright code that requires licensing as part of the operating system, XFree86 was developed specifically for the PC architecture. XFree86 works with many PC-based UNIX systems including Linux, although it is not limited to Linux.

There are several versions of XFree86 available, all based on different releases of X. The most commonly used Linux version of XFree86 is release 2.X, which is based on X11 Release 5 (shortened to X11R5 for convenience). The latest versions of XFree86 are release 3.X, which are based on X11 Release 6 (X11R6), the most current version of the X Window system. Bug fixes and minor changes in utilities are often available as incremental version numbers. These can be obtained and loaded over a release of the same number. For example, if you have loaded XFree86 v2.1 and obtain the fix release 2.1.1, it must be loaded over 2.1 and not by itself. The bug fix releases do not contain the complete system—only the updates.

> **WARNING**
>
> Do not use XFree86 version 2.0! It has several critical bugs. Instead, use at least version 2.1 or 2.1.1. Earlier versions (in the 1.X series) are nowhere near as "talented," stable, and capable as the 2.X and 3.X series, so avoid the earliest releases, too.

A bit of terminology: The official name of the GUI is X. It is often also called X Window or X Windows, although these uses are greatly discouraged. (The latter version smacks of Microsoft's MS-Windows product.) For the most part, the terms X, X11, XFree86, and X Window can be used interchangeably, but avoid X Windows. It's a sure method of annoying veteran UNIX users and showing yourself to be either a beginner or boorish!

A few problems arose in the early days of the XFree86 development, primarily because of a lack of information from the official X Consortium (which controls the standards of X). To solve the problem, the XFree86 Project Inc. was founded and became a member of the X Consortium and was thereby granted access to information about new releases well before they were available to the general public. XFree86 is now a trademark of the XFree86 Project Inc.

Many Linux versions of XFree86 contain directories and references to a product called X386. X386 was an earlier version of X11R5 for the PC architecture, and XFree86 retains many of the X386 naming conventions for directories and files. However, X386 and XFree86 are different products and have no connection (other than naming conventions).

XFree86 requires at least 8MB of RAM in your machine to operate and a virtual memory of at least 16MB. In other words, with an 8MB RAM machine, you would need a swap space of at least 8MB, although more is highly recommended. If you have 16MB of RAM, you don't need the swap space although it should be used for safety's sake, especially if you plan on running memory-hogging applications. If you plan on using X a lot, set up your system to have 32MB of virtual RAM for best performance (preferably at least 16MB RAM and the rest swap space).

Version 2.X of XFree86 can be tweaked to run in 4MB of RAM, although it is a slow process (both tweaking and running) and hence is not recommended. XFree86 version 3.X does not run properly in 4MB (although it can, with a lot of effort, be shoehorned in but then runs so slow as to be useless). XFree86 version 3.X does run in 8MB RAM, although 16MB is preferable. Again, a total of at least 16MB virtual memory is recommended, with 32MB preferable.

XFree86 Software Distribution

Most XFree86 distributions are provided as part of the software on a Linux CD-ROM or disk set. Since CD-ROM is the most common form of distribution, we'll use it as the example throughout this chapter. However, the instructions do apply equally for disk distributions and software packages obtained from an FTP or BBS site.

Typically, the XFree86 software is located in a set of directories called x1, x2, x3, and so on. The Slackware distribution has directories running up to x14, for example. Other distributions may differ in the number of directories. There are also XFree86 applications stored in a set of directories called xap1, xap2, and so on. The software is usually supplied in gzipped format. The contents of each directory are usually displayed in a text file, naming the files and summarizing their purposes.

Before you install the XFree86 software, first verify that it will work with your existing Linux software. XFree86 releases have a dependency on certain versions of the Linux kernel, the C library (libc), and the ld.so version. A file in the distribution directories should explain the lowest version number of each of these three items that is necessary to run XFree86. Alternatively, if you obtained the XFree86 software packaged with a Linux release, it is in most cases compatible and you can skip the verification stage.

The XFree86 software can be installed manually by unzipping each file, then extracting the files in the archive. The files must then be properly loaded into the final directories. This can be a very tedious and lengthy process and should be avoided except by true masochists or those who want to know exactly what is going on. Instead, use the installation routines that are supplied by the Linux vendor, such as setup.

The directories used by XFree86 version 2.X tend to mirror those used by the X386 software product. For most Linux systems, the primary directory is /usr/X386. To be consistent with software packages and utilities that expect a more common X11R5, X11R6, or X11 directory, Linux generally uses links between the X386 directory and the others as necessary. These links are often created by the Linux installation routine.

> **TIP**
>
> XFree86 version 3.X abandons the /usr/X386 directory convention in favor of the more common X location /usr/X11R6. When upgrading an installation of XFree86 version 2.X to version 3.X, keep in mind the change of directory names and either change links or remove the old /usr/X386 versions completely. Make sure your path is changed, too.

> **NOTE**
>
> To simplify the directory structure for XFree86, links are usually created to a directory called /usr/X11 which can be linked to /usr/X386 and /usr/X11R6. Check your directory structure to determined which links are in place on your system. Also check your PATH environment variable to see which directory is in the search path (if one has been added at all).

Choosing an X Server

Before installing XFree86, you must decide which type of server to use. The XFree86 servers are drivers for the video system (because X is a GUI, it makes extensive use of the video card in your system). Choosing the wrong type of server for your video card can cause your entire system to behave erratically (and in some cases damage your video card or monitor!). Be sure that the server matches your hardware.

There are several drivers available in most XFree86 distribution sets, and the names of the files tend to indicate the video card they are designed for. For example, you may encounter the following server files in most XFree86 versions:

- XF86_Mono   Monochrome video card (generic)
- XF86_VGA16   16-color VGA video card (generic)
- XF86_SVGA   Color SVGA video card (generic)
- XF86_S3   Accelerated server for S3-based video cards
- XF86_Mach8   Accelerated server for Mach8 video cards
- XF86_Mach32   Accelerated server for Mach32 video cards
- XF86_8514   Accelerated server for 8514/A video cards

The generic indications in the preceding list mean that the server has no card-specific instructions, whereas the other servers have card-specific video card requirements. For example, the XF86_S3 server can be used only with video cards using the S3 chipset. Check with your video card documentation (or use a diagnostic utility program) to determine your video card's chipset. Your distribution version of XFree86 probably has other specific server versions, so check the documentation for compatibility details.

The generic server drivers work with most cards that provide VGA and SVGA support. However, because the generic driver provides only the basic VGA and SVGA video instructions, any fancy features or extra power your video card may have will not be used. That's why the card-specific servers were developed: They let you use the full capabilities of fancy video cards.

> **WARNING**
>
> Installing an X server with the wrong specific video card driver can cause damage to your system! If you are not sure of the video card chipset, use a generic driver. Most video cards can handle VGA and SVGA generic drivers without a problem. If you're not sure, use generic!

Most distributions of XFree86 have a default configuration of a standard VGA system prewritten into the configuration files. You can use this default setting without worrying about other configuration items in some cases, but it is better to check the configuration files manually before running XFree86 for the first time.

The server name to be used by XFree86 is changed by modifying the symbolic link to the file called X under the XFree86 bin directory (such as /usr/X386/bin/X or /usr/X11R6/bin/X). You can change the server at any time by creating a new link to the required server file. For example, if you want to use the SVGA server when your system is currently configured for the VGA server, issue the following commands:

```
rm /usr/X11R6/bin/X
ln -s /usr/X11R6/bin/XF86_SVA /usr/X11R6/bin/X
```

The first line removes the current link and the second adds the link between XF86_SVGA and X. The directory names for the XFree86 base directory may change, depending on the version of XFree86 you are running (although if they are linked together, it won't matter which you change).

Installing XFree86 Manually

As mentioned earlier in this section, you can install XFree86 without using the installation scripts. In some cases, you will want to do this if you have to perform installation across directories or place the files in directories other than their default values. Some users like to manually install XFree86 so they know what is happening at each step: It's a great way to learn the intricacies of the X operating system (although it can be a long operation).

To manually install the XFree86 distribution software, you must extract the files into the proper directories using the gzip command. The general process is quite simple:

- Log in as root. You must install XFree86 as the superuser.
- Create the directory /usr/X386. This directory may already exist on your system because it is created by some Linux installation scripts.

- Change to the /usr/X386 directory.

- For each file in the distribution set, use the gzip utility to extract and install the contents. The general format of the command follows:

```
qzip -dc tarfile | tar xvof -
```

- Repeat the process for each file in the XFree86 product set. You will have to change to each distribution directory manually (on a CD-ROM or different disk, for example), and use gzip on each archive file in that directory.

The tar utility flags shown in the preceding command line ensure that the original ownership of the files is preserved and that the output is displayed on the screen for you. After all the XFree86 files have been installed into the correct directories, you can continue with the configuration process.

Installing XFree86 Using a Script

Most users want to automate the installation process. It is faster, requires less interaction from the user, and is much less prone to errors. For this reason, most XFree86 distribution releases either include an installation script or use the Linux setup program.

When installing using the Linux setup script (or similar utility) supplied with Linux distributions, you are usually prompted as to whether you want to install XFree86 during the initial Linux installation. If you answered affirmatively to this question, the binaries for XFree86 will already be installed. If you didn't get prompted for XFree86 installation, it may have been installed automatically. Check the directories /usr/X386/bin or /usr/X11R6/bin for files. If there are a large number of files in either directory, XFree86 was installed for you.

Just because XFree86 was installed from the distribution media automatically doesn't mean you can use it immediately. You should still go through the configuration process by using the ConfigFX86 or fx86config utilities or manually edit the Xconfig or XF86Config file (depending on the version of XFree86). Most automated installations include default VGA or SVGA preconfigured files, but it's still a good idea to check the contents of the Xconfig or XF86Config file before you try to run XFree86.

Path Environment Variable

It is important to put the XFree86 binary directory in your path, controlled by an environment variable PATH or path (depending on the shell). The location of the variable's definition depends on the type of shell you are using, and the login you generally use to run XFree86. In general, you should simply add either /usr/X386/bin (XFree86 version 2.X) or /usr/X11R6/bin (XFree86 version 3.X) to the path definition statement.

For example, if you use bash for most purposes, a .profile file is read when you log in to set environment variables. If you log in as a user other than root, the .profile file is kept in your home directory. If you use the root login, the .profile may be kept in the root directory or you may be using the default system .profile kept in the file /etc/profile (note the lack of a period when the file is in /etc: This is a convention used to show it is a globally available .profile).

If it isn't already in the path, add the XFree86 bin directory to the path or PATH variable definition. A .profile file for bash may have the following line after adding the XFree86 directory:

```
PATH="/sbin:/usr/bin:/bin:/usr/X11/bin:/usr/openwin/bin"
```

For C shell users (including tcsh) other than root, the syntax is a little different. The startup file .login or csh.login contains a line defining the path. Adding the XFree86 directory is a matter of tacking it in to the definition:

```
set path = ( /sbin /usr/bin /bin /usr/X11/bin /usr/openwin/bin . )
```

Of course, your exact path definition lines will probably differ, but as long as you add the XFree86 bin directory to the path, then log out and back in, the binaries should be found properly by the shell.

Configuring XFree86

Before you can run XFree86, some configuration information should be specified. This is the part that tends to frustrate newcomers to XFree86, as it can be a convoluted process to get your configuration files exactly right and allow XFree86 to execute properly. Hopefully, a few simple step-by-step instructions will streamline the process.

There is a utility called either ConfigFX86 or fx86config provided with many distributions of Linux and XFree86 that simplify the entire XFree86 installation process, but only if you have one of the supported graphics cards. A list of cards supported by ConfigFX86 and fx86config is usually included in the Hardware HOWTO file provided with the Linux distribution software. If you can't find the HOWTO file, it can be obtained from most FTP and BBS locations. Make sure the version of the file corresponds to the Linux version you are running. More details about ConfigFX86 and fx86config are provided in the later section "Using ConfigFX86 and fx86config." (You can, in some cases, provide enough information for ConfigFX86 and fx86config to use your unlisted video card for the installation. This is discussed in the following section.)

If you don't have the Hardware HOWTO file or your video card is not listed and you don't want to use a generic driver, then you must manually configure XFree86. Even if you use the `ConfigXF86` or `fx86config` script to install XFree86, you may still have to make manual modifications to tweak your installation.

Most of the configuration details for XFree86 version 2.X are contained in a file called `Xconfig`, whereas XFree86 version 3.X uses a file called `XF86Config` or `Xconfig`, depending on the version. The bare-bones instructions for setting up an `Xconfig` or `XF86Config` file are spread out over several text files included with the XFree86 distribution set. In most cases, you should check the `README`, `VideoModes.doc`, `README.Config`, and `README.Linux` files. That's not all: You also have to read the man pages for `Xconfig`, `XF86Config` `XFree86`, and `XFree86kbd`. Finally, you should check the man pages for the server version you are running, if one is provided. (It's a good idea to print out the man pages for easier reference.)

There are a few items of information you need to properly complete the `Xconfig` or `FX86Config` file. Before you start configuring XFree86, take a moment to note the following details:

- The XFree86 server to be used.
- The type of mouse on your system and the port it is connected to.
- Your video card's brand name and chipset. If you're not sure of the chipset, either consult your documentation or use a utility program such as `SuperProbe` (Linux) or `MSD` (DOS).
- Your video monitor brand name and model number, as well as the size of the monitor. It also helps to know the maximum horizontal and vertical scan frequencies, usually available from the monitor's documentation.
- The type of keyboard you will be using if not the U.S. generic type. Most users have the U.S. type, although some countries have customized keyboards that require different key mappings.

If you don't know some of the information and don't have an easy way (such as a utility program) to find out, you should check the documentation that comes with XFree86. Many distributions contain a directory such as `/usr/X11/lib/X11/doc` (usually linked to `/usr/X386/lib/X11/doc` or `/usr/X11R6/lib/X11/doc`) that contains a number of files describing many cards and monitors supported by XFree86 and the essential configuration information (such as monitor scan rates, which are always difficult to determine because you invariably can't remember where you placed the manual).

When you've noted all this configuration information, you are ready to start configuring XFree86. This all begins with the `Xconfig` or `XF86Config` file.

22

INSTALLING AND CONFIGURING XFREE86

Where to Put `Xconfig` or `XF86Config`

The `Xconfig` or `XF86Config` file can be located in several places on the Linux file system. Usually, it resides in the `/usr/X386/lib/X11` directory, which is also where a sample `Xconfig` or `XF86Config` file is often found. If you have easy access to the `/usr/X386/lib/X11` directory, it's the best place for the `Xconfig` or `XF86Config` file. (Formally, the file is referenced in `/usr/X11R6/lib/X11` or `/etc`, but because `/usr/X386` is linked to `/usr/X11R6`, the two directories point to the same place. You may run into the X11R6 directory referenced in documentation, but as long as the link to the X386 directory is in place, you can use either.)

> **NOTE**
>
> Unless you are manually installing configuration information, don't worry about whether you should be using `Xconfig` or `XF86Config`. Automated installation scripts will use the proper file. If you are performing a manual configuration, use `XConfig` for XFree86 version 2.X and `XFConfig` for XFree86 version 3.X.

If you can't use `/usr/X386/lib/X11` (maybe it's read-only or on a remote server) or don't want to because you need a customized version of the `Xconfig` file, the file can also be placed in the `/etc` directory or in your home directory. If the `Xconfig` file is in your home directory, it will apply only to your sessions and any configuration information will not be valid for other users. The `/etc` directory location for the XFree86 `Xconfig` file means the configuration information is applicable to all users.

You can also put the `Xconfig` file in the directory `/usr/X386/lib/X11` specific to a particular host machine. To do this, the `Xconfig` filename is appended with the name of the host machine. For example, the file `Xconfig.merlin` will apply the configuration information only to users logging in from the machine "merlin."

The Linux convention for the `Xconfig` file is to place it in the `/etc` directory. Because this is not the usual location for XFree86 installations, a link must be created to the `/etc/Xconfig` file to `/usr/X386/lib/X11` or your home directory. This allows XFree86 to find the `Xconfig` file properly.

SuperProbe

`SuperProbe` is a utility that attempts to determine the type of video card (and the amount of video RAM installed on that card) in many PC systems. It works on ISA, EISA, and VLB (local bus) architectures, but not on MCA or PCI architectures (although

SuperProbe versions for these systems may be available by the time you read this book). If you already know which video card you have, then SuperProbe is of little use to you.

SuperProbe attempts to identify video cards by probing for certain known unique registers on each video card it knows about. This has one drawback: Some instructions executed by SuperProbe can cause your machine to lock up! Although it is unlikely damage will occur because of SuperProbe, the file system will have to be cleaned up if the machine must be reset. For this reason, make sure you are the only user on the machine. A backup of your system is also highly advisable.

> **TIP**
>
> Running SuperProbe by itself is almost guaranteed to lock up any machine, so use it with care and follow the instructions in this section for giving SuperProbe a basic idea of the testing it should do.

SuperProbe is included as part of the XFree86 distribution set with many CD-ROMs and can be obtained from FTP and BBS sites that offer Linux software. SuperProbe is not exclusive to Linux but can run under several other PC UNIX systems. A man page is available for SuperProbe.

SuperProbe uses a number of command-line options to specify its behavior. Although the exact options change with each new release of the software, the basic options of interest to you are limited to a few:

- `-bios` specifies the video card BIOS' address, normally set to C0000. If you should set your BIOS address to some other value, it will be specified with this option.

- `-info` displays a list of all video cards SuperProbe knows about and the names of the cards as recognized by SuperProbe.

- `-no_16` disables 16-bit testing. Used only for old, 8-bit video cards.

- `-no_bios` disables testing of the video card BIOS and assumes the card is an EGA, VGA, SVGA, or later type. If your video card is new, this is a useful option for preventing many BIOS-caused system freezes.

- `-no_dac` disables testing for a RAMDAC type. This can be used with VGA and SVGA cards to prevent potential freezes.

- `-no_mem` skips the testing for the amount of video RAM installed on the video card.

- `-order` specifies the order in which chipsets should be tested. This is useful if you think you know the types of chipsets, but want confirmation. Alternatively, if you suspect the video card has one of a few chipsets, you can list just those.

- `-verbose` displays information on the screen as to the actions and results of `SuperProbe`. A useful option that should be used in all cases to show progress and potential problems.

One of the first steps to take is to display a list of all the video cards `SuperProbe` knows about. Issue the following command:

```
SuperProbe -info
```

and you see a list that shows the cards, chipsets, and RAMDACs that `SuperProbe` can recognize. Note that the utility name `SuperProbe` is mixed case, with uppercase *S* and *P*. This is unusual for a Linux system and may take experienced UNIX and Linux users a moment to get used to.

If you have an older 8-bit card, you can determine the chipset with the following command:

```
SuperProbe -no16 -verbose
```

If you have a 16-bit (or higher) card which you suspect to be an S3, Cirrus Logic, or Tseng chipset, for example, you can use the -order option to simplify testing (and prevent potential problems):

```
SuperProbe -order S3,Cirrus,Tseng -verbose
```

There are no spaces between chipsets specified after the order option. The verbose option lets you see what is going on. It is advisable to narrow the search for a chipset in this way to prevent lockups. Even if you know exactly which video card is in your system, don't assume `SuperProbe` will function properly. `SuperProbe` has an annoying habit of hanging up a system because of conflicts with other cards or devices. Use it with care.

Using `ConfigFX86` and `fx86config`

`ConfigFX86` and `fx86config` use simple interfaces to let you select supported video cards and video monitors. If your video card is supported by the `ConfigFX86` or `fx86config` utility (check the Hardware HOWTO and XFree86 README files), you can use the `ConfigFX86` and `fx86config` installation routine to simplify the configuration process enormously. If it is provided with your XFree86 distribution, `ConfigFX86` and `fx86config` will be located in the directory `/usr/X386/bin`. `ConfigFX86` was written by Stephen Zwaska.

There is documentation available for ConfigFX86 and fx86config, usually placed in /usr/X386/bin with the executable file. Some versions of Linux and XFree86 don't supply the documents, though. The documentation is often supplied in multiple formats. There is an ASCII version called ConfigFX86.txt and a PostScript version called ConfigFX86.ps (or the fx86config versions).

When you run either ConfigFX86 or fx86config, you are shown some general information, then prompted for the information you gathered earlier about your system. In most cases, you are shown a list of supported values and asked to choose one. Following through these choices in order provides the utility with the proper information to build your Xconfig file.

The xf86config utility, for example, asks for your mouse type, whether you want to enable special features for the mouse (such as the middle button on a three-button mouse), the device the mouse is attached to, horizontal and vertical sync ranges of your monitor, a name for your monitor, the chipset used by your video card, the server to run, the location of the file linked to the server, the amount of RAM installed on your video card, whether you want a clockchip setting, and the resolutions the video card supports in order. After you have answered all the questions, xf86config asks whether the utility should create the XF86config file.

After the XF86Config or Xconfig file is created using the script, you should resist the temptation to start up X immediately. Instead, take the time to examine the file manually to prevent any chance of damage to your hardware from an incorrect setting. The following section on manually configuring the Xconfig or XF86Config file explains all the settings. After you're sure everything is fine, launch X with the command startx.

The Xconfig and XF86Config Files in Detail

If you are manually entering your configuration information into the Xconfig or XF86Config files, you need to know how the files are laid out and how to enter your specific details. All versions of XFree86 have at least one sample configuration file, usually called Xconfig.eg or XF86Config.eg located in the lib directory. You should use this file as a template for creating your own configuration file. Copy the example file to a new file without the .eg extension and make the changes described as follows.

The `Xconfig` and `XF86Config` files are not short, but there are lots of comments scattered throughout. The format of the configuration files is a set of sections for each aspect of the XFree86 configuration. The general order of sections is as follows:

- Pathnames to binaries and screen fonts
- Keyboard information
- Mouse information
- Server file
- Video information

Let's look at each section in a little more detail. If you have run the automated configuration file generator utilities such as `xf86config` or `XF86Config`, check the entries in the generated file. If you are manually editing the file, proceed slowly and methodically to prevent errors.

> **NOTE**
>
> The code excerpts shown in the rest of this section are from the `XF86Config` file created by XFree86 version 3.X because it is the latest version and usually included with new software distributions. The `Xconfig` file for XFree86 version 2.X is similar and you should have no problem following the same procedures by examining the `Xconfig` file.

Notice that each section in the `Xconfig` or `XF86Config` file starts with the keyword "section" followed by the name of the section. The section is terminated with the keyword "EndSection." This makes it easier to find the sections you want to work with. Comments in the file all start with a pound sign.

Pathnames

In most cases, the pathnames provided in the configuration files do not need changing unless you installed XFree86 in a directory other than the default value. The paths used by XFree86 for screen fonts and other files are given in a section of the configuration file that looks like this:

```
Section "Files"

# The location of the RGB database. Note, this is the name of the
# file minus the extension (like ".txt" or ".db"). There is normally
# no need to change the default.

    RgbPath      "/usr/X11R6/lib/X11/rgb"
```

```
# Multiple FontPath entries are allowed (which are concatenated together),
# as well as specifying multiple comma-separated entries in one FontPath
# command (or a combination of both methods)

    FontPath        "/usr/X11R6/lib/X11/fonts/misc/"
    FontPath        "/usr/X11R6/lib/X11/fonts/Type1/"
    FontPath        "/usr/X11R6/lib/X11/fonts/Speedo/"
    FontPath        "/usr/X11R6/lib/X11/fonts/75dpi/"
FontPath     "/usr/X11R6/lib/X11/fonts/100dpi/"

EndSection
```

The preceding code defines the search paths for the screen fonts and RGB database. If you installed XFree86 into the default directories or let the installation routines proceed with default values, you should not have to change anything here.

Note that the directories referenced in this XF86Config file follow the formal naming conventions for X, using /usr/X11R6. However, because these are linked to /usr/X11, /usr/X386, and potentially other directories in most installations, the link can be followed to the target file. Make sure to verify that the directories actually do point to the screen fonts by going into each directory in turn and examining the files they contain. If the directory doesn't exist or is empty, XFree86 won't be able to load the fonts properly and will crash or generate error messages.

If you add new fonts to your XFree86 installation, they should go in one of the font directories specified in the XF86Config file.

Keyboard Settings

In most installations, the keyboard setting defaults to a U.S. 101-key keyboard with standard key mappings. This will be valid for most computer systems. A few tweaks to the file will help simplify your life, though, so the keyboard section shouldn't be completely ignored. The following code shows the keyboard section from the FX86Config file:

```
Section "Keyboard"

    Protocol        "Standard"

# when using XQUEUE, comment out the above line, and uncomment the
# following line

#    Protocol        "Xqueue"

    AutoRepeat      500 5

# Let the server do the NumLock processing. This should only be required
# when using pre-R6 clients
#    ServerNumLock
```

```
# Specify which keyboard LEDs can be user-controlled (eg, with xset(1))
#     Xleds       1 2 3
# To set the LeftAlt to Meta, RightAlt key to ModeShift,
# RightCtl key to Compose, and ScrollLock key to ModeLock:

#     LeftAlt     Meta
#     RightAlt    ModeShift
#     RightCtl    Compose
#     ScrollLock  ModeLock

EndSection
```

The Protocol should be left as "standard." The Xqueue line is commented out and should remain that way unless you implement an Xqueue for XFree86. The autorepeat setting tells XFree86 how long to wait for a key to be pressed before generating multiple keystrokes (for example, if you depress the "x" key for more than a certain number of milliseconds, it starts printing multiple x's).

ServerNumLock controls whether the NumLock key is on or off when XFree86 starts up. The ServerNumLock option is commented out by default in most sample configuration files. If you are running XFree86 version 2.X (or earlier), it is a good idea to uncomment the line. This helps tailor your keyboard for better operation under XFree86. With XFree86 version 3.X, you can leave it commented out because the server will handle the NumLock behavior.

In theory, you can use the Xleds setting to permit programming of the LED buttons on most keyboards (for Num Lock, Caps Lock, and Scroll Lock). Leave it commented as the LEDs are not used for much user feedback.

The rest of the section controls how the Alt, Ctrl, and Shift keys behave. Some UNIX applications expect special keystrokes called "meta" keys, composed of holding a special key while another key is pressed (such as Ctrl+C in DOS or UNIX). These entries let you control which keys are interpreted as Alt, Meta, Control, and ModeLock. Most installations have no problem with all these lines commented out because the number of Linux applications that need special keystrokes is very small (and those are in limited distribution).

You can use XFree86 to translate keystrokes to international characters automatically. In most cases, the keyboard layout is read by XFree86 from the kernel, although you can override this setting. The X11 standards allow only four key tables to be modified, much fewer than Linux.

Mouse Definition

XFree86 uses the mouse heavily, so you must specify the type of mouse on the system and how it is connected. XFree86 supports most popular mouse versions, and any types not directly supported can usually be used in emulation of one of the more popular types such as Microsoft or Logitech. The mouse section of the XF86Config file is labeled as "pointer" (from pointing device) and looks like this:

```
Section "Pointer"

    Protocol    "Microsoft"
    Device      "/dev/mouse"

# When using XQUEUE, comment out the above two lines, and uncomment
# the following line.

#     Protocol    "Xqueue"

# Baudrate and SampleRate are only for some Logitech mice

#     BaudRate    9600
#     SampleRate  150

# Emulate3Buttons is an option for 2-button Microsoft mice

#     Emulate3Buttons

# ChordMiddle is an option for some 3-button Logitech mice

#     ChordMiddle

EndSection
```

The Protocol section is the name of the mouse or the emulation to use. The names of supported mouse systems are listed in the Xconfig or XF86Config man page, so if you use a mouse from a vendor other than Microsoft or Logitech, check the man page or other supplied documentation to find the name of the protocol to specify. Another method of identifying the type of mouse is to watch the startup messages when Linux boots: It will often identify the type of mouse.

The Microsoft mouse inevitably uses the Microsoft protocol. Many Logitech mouse devices are Microsoft-compatible, whereas newer versions use the MouseMan protocol. Dexxa and many other mouse device vendors emulate the Microsoft mouse, so the Microsoft protocol can be used.

The Device entry specifies the port the mouse is attached to, using Linux device terminology. In most cases, the entry /dev/mouse is sufficient, as the Linux installation procedure will have configured the mouse already. If you are using a mouse configured on the PS/2 port of IBM PS/2 models, use the PS/2 device driver and not a serial port device driver. Valid device drivers are listed in the man page or the documentation files accompanying XFree86, but most versions support the following devices:

- /dev/mouse: to use the Linux default mouse driver
- /dev/inportbm: Microsoft bus mouse only
- /dev/logibm: Logitech bus mouse only
- /dev/psaux: PS/2 port mouse

A bus mouse requires a specific IRQ to be set in both XFree86 and the kernel. Make sure the IRQ is the same in both places.

As with the keyboard, there is an option for Xqueue users. Because most XFree86 installations don't use Xqueue, leave this line commented out. The baud rate and sampling rate lines, as the comment indicates, are for some older Logitech mouse devices. Most mouse devices will not need these lines, so keep them commented out. If your mouse does not work without these settings, try 9600 baud, followed by 1200 baud if that doesn't work. Some earlier versions of XFree86 liked to have a baud rate specified, but try it without an entry first.

The Emulate3Buttons option is useful if you have a two-button mouse. When active, Emulate3Buttons allows you to simulate the press of a middle button by pressing both the left and right mouse buttons simultaneously. Many Linux (and UNIX) applications make use of three buttons on the mouse, so this is a useful option for Microsoft and compatible mouse users.

Finally, the ChordMiddle option is used with some Logitech mouse models. If you use the Logitech driver, try the mouse under XFree86 without this option turned on. If the mouse doesn't behave properly, try uncommenting this line. Most Logitech mouse devices don't need ChordMiddle turned on.

Monitor Model

Setting the monitor properly is an important step in configuring XFree86, and one that is easy to mess up. If some of the settings are incorrect, damage can occur to the monitor, so take care! Patience and common sense will help, although the monitor's operations manual is a much better source of information.

If you are unsure about any settings, select the most basic level until you can get more information. For example, if you're not sure whether your monitor supports high resolutions, stick with VGA or SVGA until you can get confirmation.

The monitor section in the XF86Config file is broken into smaller subsections for convenience. We can look at the subsections in a little more detail. The first section asks for information about the monitor type and model number. This subsection looks like this:

```
Section "Monitor"

    Identifier     "Generic Monitor"
    VendorName     "Unknown"
    ModelName      "Unknown"
```

The entries in this section are text strings only and have no real configuration value for XFree86. The only time they are used is when the text strings are echoed back to you when XFree86 starts up or a utility displays configuration information. You can enter the proper values for these items to make XFree86 a little more friendly to work with.

The next subsection deals with the horizontal bandwidth of the monitor. This is an important section, and you should try to find the actual values for your monitor. Some settings for specific brands are listed in the documentation accompanying XFree86, especially in the documents `Monitors` and `VideoModes.doc`. Check your distribution directories for any specification document files. If you can't find specific values for these settings, use the lowest setting as a default, unless you know your monitor is capable of higher values. The bandwidth section looks like this:

```
# Bandwidth is in MHz unless units are specified

    Bandwidth      25.2

# HorizSync is in kHz unless units are specified.
# HorizSync may be a comma separated list of discrete values, or a
# comma separated list of ranges of values.
# NOTE: THE VALUES HERE ARE EXAMPLES ONLY. REFER TO YOUR MONITOR'S
# USER MANUAL FOR THE CORRECT NUMBERS.

    HorizSync   31.5 # typical for a single frequency fixed-sync monitor

#   HorizSync    30-64         # multisync
#   HorizSync    31.5, 35.2    # multiple fixed sync frequencies
#   HorizSync 15-25, 30-50  # multiple ranges of sync frequencies
```

The bandwidth settings have good comments next to them, as shown in the preceding code. If you were installing a multisync monitor, for example, you could comment out the 31.5K Hz line and uncomment the 30-64 KHz line.

The vertical refresh rate is set in another subsection and is as critical to your monitor's good health as the bandwidth. Again, check the documentation for more information. The vertical refresh subsection code looks like this:

```
# VertRefresh is in Hz unless units are specified.
# VertRefresh may be a comma separated list of discrete values, or a
# comma separated list of ranges of values.
# NOTE: THE VALUES HERE ARE EXAMPLES ONLY. REFER TO YOUR MONITOR'S
# USER MANUAL FOR THE CORRECT NUMBERS.
```

22

INSTALLING AND
CONFIGURING
XFREE86

```
    VertRefresh 60  # typical for a single frequency fixed-sync monitor

#   VertRefresh    50-100        # multisync
#   VertRefresh    60, 65        # multiple fixed sync frequencies
#   VertRefresh    40-50, 80-100 # multiple ranges of sync frequencies
```

The comments in the file help out again, showing you the most common settings. These can be used as a guide but you should check your documentation for specifics.

Setting the video modes correctly is very important, as too high a video resolution may cause snow, a blank screen, or a system crash. The SuperProbe utility discussed earlier can help determine supported video modes, although most monitors have a good list of supported modes in their documentation. The XFree86 Monitors file also lists many popular monitors and their modes. The subsection for setting the video modes is as follows:

```
# Modes can be specified in two formats. A compact one-line format, or
# a multi-line format.

# A generic VGA 640x480 mode (hsync = 31.5kHz, refresh = 60Hz)
# These two are equivalent

#    ModeLine "640x480" 25.175 640 664 760 800 480 491 493 525

     Mode "640x480"
        DotClock     25.175
        HTimings     640 664 760 800
        VTimings     480 491 493 525
     EndMode

# These two are equivalent

#    ModeLine "1024x768i" 45 1024 1048 1208 1264 768 776 784 817 Interlace

     Mode "1024x768i"
        DotClock     45
        HTimings     1024 1048 1208 1264
        VTimings     768 776 784 817
        Flags        "Interlace"
     EndMode
```

The preceding examples show a standard VGA (640×480) resolution and a high (1,024×768) resolution. You can modify these entries to match your specific resolution requirements. As you can see from the preceding code, you need to know the dot clock and horizontal and vertical timings for your monitor and video card. Check the documentation! Note that you can specify all the details for the modes on a single line, but the more verbose listings are easier to read and work with.

Video Cards

The next subsection of the XF86Config file deals with the video card your system uses. You can have several cards defined with different resolutions, or simply enter the one that you will use the most. For example, the following subsection has a VGA and SVGA generic driver defined:

```
Section "Device"
    Identifier      "Generic VGA"
    VendorName      "Unknown"
    BoardName       "Unknown"
    Chipset      "generic"
    VideoRam     256
    Clocks      25.2 28.3
EndSection

Section "Device"
    # SVGA server auto-detected chipset
    Identifier      "Generic SVGA"
    VendorName      "Unknown"
    BoardName       "Unknown"
EndSection
```

The Identifier, VendorName, BoardName, and optional Chipset entries are strings and are used only for identification purposes. The VideoRam (the amount of RAM on the video board) and Clocks entries are used to specify any particular behavior for your card. These should be carefully checked to verify the information, as illegal entries can cause damage to some video boards.

If you have a particular video board that has special features, you can create a Device entry for that board. For example, the following entry is used for a Trident TVGA board:

```
Section "Device"
   Identifier       "Any Trident TVGA 9000"
   VendorName       "Trident"
   BoardName        "TVGA 9000"
   Chipset      "tvga9000"
   VideoRam     512
   Clocks      25 28 45 36 57 65 50 40 25 28 0 45 72 77 80 75
EndSection
```

The information in the VideoRam and Clocks lines is taken from the documentation file that accompanies XFree86, although it can be entered manually from the video card's documentation.

Some video boards require more detail, provided by additional entries in the devices sub-section. For example, the following is for an Actix GE32+ video card with 2MB of RAM on board:

```
Section "Device"
    Identifier      "Actix GE32+ 2MB"
    VendorName      "Actix"
    BoardName       "GE32+"
    Ramdac       "ATT20C490"
    Dacspeed      110
    Option       "dac_8_bit"
    Clocks       25.0  28.0  40.0   0.0  50.0  77.0  36.0  45.0
    Clocks       130.0 120.0  80.0  31.0 110.0  65.0  75.0  94.0
EndSection
```

You will see that the Ramdac and Dacspeed options, as well as an Option line, have been added to the entry. The entries that are allowed in this subsection change with each release of XFree86, so check the man pages or documentation files for more details if you want to get the most out of your video card.

The XFree86 Server

Earlier in this chapter, we looked at the XFree86 server and showed how you should choose one for your X server specifically. The server section of the Xconfig or XF86Config file is where the server specification is located. The server subsection from an XF86Config file looks like this:

```
Section "Screen"
    Driver      "svga"
    Device      "Generic SVGA"
    Monitor      "Generic Monitor"
    Subsection "Display"
        Depth           8
        Modes           "640x480"
        ViewPort        0 0
        Virtual         800 600
    EndSubsection
EndSection
```

The preceding section shows a generic SVGA driver. The card supports the VGA 640×480 and SVGA 800×600 resolutions. If you have a more powerful video card and monitor combination, you can use a specific server file if it exists, such as the driver for the Actix GE32+ card with 2MB RAM, shown as follows:

```
Section "Screen"
    Driver      "accel"
    Device      "Actix GE32+ 2MB"
    Monitor      "Generic Monitor"
    Subsection "Display"
        Depth           8
        Modes           "640x480"
        ViewPort        0 0
```

```
        Virtual         1280 1024
    EndSubsection
    SubSection "Display"
        Depth           16
        Weight          565
        Modes           "640x480"
        ViewPort    0 0
        Virtual         1024 768
    EndSubsection
EndSection
```

This card is set to use the special accelerated server file for the Actix card, supporting up to 1,280×1,024 resolutions. Check the list of servers to see whether there is one specifically designed for your video card. If you are not sure, default to a generic driver!

The options in this subsection do not apply to all cards, but you can set their values if you know them. The most important (and most often used) options are as follows:

- *Depth*: the number of color planes (the number of bits per pixel). Usually the depth is 8, although VGA16 servers have a depth of 4 and monochrome displays have a depth of 1. Accelerated video cards can have depths of 16, 24, 32, or even 64 bits per pixel, usually indicated as part of the model name (for example, the Diamond Stealth 24 card has a pixel depth of 24, although check before you assume the card's model name really is the depth!).

- *Modes*: a list of the video mode names defined in the ModeLine option in the Monitor section. This shows all the modes the card supports and that you want to use. The first mode on the list is the default value when XFree86 starts. You can then switch between the other modes when XFree86 is running.

- *Virtual*: the virtual desktop size. With extra RAM on the video card, you can have a virtual desktop larger than the screen display, and can then scroll around the virtual desktop with the mouse. You can, for example, have a virtual desktop of 1,024×768 but display only 800×600 (SVGA). The support for different virtual desktop sizes depends on the amount of RAM and the depth you use. For example, 1MB of RAM on the video card supports 1,024×768 with a depth of 8.2MB RAM supports the same size with a depth of 16 or a 1,280×1,024 desktop at a depth of 8. To use a true virtual desktop, use the fvwm window manager (usually used by default).

- *ViewPort*: used with the virtual desktop to define the coordinates of the upper-left corner of the virtual desktop when XFree86 starts.

Testing XFree86 Configurations

Now that the Xconfig or XF86Config file is completed, it's time to take the plunge and start XFree86. Use the command startx and the X startup script should load all the requisite drivers and daemons, clear the screen, then show the basic X Window session. If XFree86 can't load, it will usually display error messages as part of the termination process. Check these messages to determine whether there's any hint as to the problem. Usually, XFree86 runs into supported video mode problems. (For those used to using UNIX on other systems, startx is a front-end utility to xinit, usually used to start X.)

If you can't get XFree86 running quickly, the easiest debugging method is to step all the configuration information to the lowest denominator, such as a simple VGA system. If that works, then you can step up to more complex resolutions and configurations. This usually helps isolate the cause of the problems. If the generic VGA drivers don't work, then a configuration problem is usually the cause. Check the configuration files carefully.

The .xinitrc File

The .xinitrc is a startup file (similar to the .profile or .cshrc startup files for the shells) for X. It usually includes any local modifications to the configuration defined in the Xconfig or XF86Config files, as well as instructions for starting specific applications or window managers when XFree86 starts. If you use either the startx or runx commands to start XFree86, the .xinitrc is renamed without the period (so it would be called xinitrc).

The system's xinitrc file is usually kept as /usr/lib/X11/xinit/xinitrc or in /etc/X11/xinit/xinitrc. The latter path is more common with XFree86 and Linux, while the former is the path for X. (Linux places the file in the /etc/X11 directory structure instead of /usr/lib because some Linux installations prefer to mount the /usr directories as read-only and because sometimes they reside on a CD-ROM.)

The system's default .xinitrc file can be overridden by placing a copy in your home directory. When XFree86 starts, it first checks your home directory for the .xinitrc file, and then reads the default startup file if one isn't found. If you want to customize the behavior of the XFree86 session, copy the system file to your home directory and edit it with any editor. There are man pages for startx and xinit that explain some of the details of the startup file.

An example of a .xinitrc file is shown as follows. This is the default startup file from a straightforward XFree86 installation. The file has been cut into smaller sections so each subsection can be examined in a little more detail. The first subsection deals with setting paths:

```
userresources=$HOME/.Xresources
usermodmap=$HOME/.Xmodmap
sysresources=/usr/X11R6/lib/X11/xinit/.Xresources
sysmodmap=/usr/X11R6/lib/X11/xinit/.Xmodmap
```

These paths are usually set up in the XFree86 software, but you should check them to make sure they are valid. Remember to follow links if they exist to other directories. These variables are all that is required for XFree86.

The next subsection checks for the existence of some system resources and performs actions based on the check. Most, if not all, of these checks will not need to be modified unless you have very special requirements for your X session.

```
# merge in defaults and keymaps

if [ -f $sysresources ]; then
    xrdb -merge $sysresources
fi

if [ -f $sysmodmap ]; then
    xmodmap $sysmodmap
fi

if [ -f $userresources ]; then
    xrdb -merge $userresources
fi

if [ -f $usermodmap ]; then
    xmodmap $usermodmap
fi
```

The final subsection in the .xinitrc file runs the setroot program, if present, to set the background color (in this case, to steel blue). Finally, the fvwm window manager is executed and starts your session:

```
# start some nice programs
xsetroot -solid SteelBlue
fvwm
```

If you want to use another window manager, such as Motif's mwm manager, change the last line in this subsection. Make sure that the window manager file is in the search path, so the startup routines can find it.

22

INSTALLING AND
CONFIGURING
XFREE86

If you want to create an `xterm` session from within the `.xinitrc` file (you will need an `xterm` or other utility to start other tasks within XFree86), add the following line:

```
xterm -e /bin/bash
```

In this case, the `bash` shell is invoked within the `xterm`. You can, of course, use any shell you want.

If you create `.xinitrc` files for your own use, place them in your home directory. You can, for example, use a `.xinitrc` file like this:

```
#!/bin/sh

xterm -fn 7x13bold -geometry 80x32+10+10 &
xterm -fn 7x13bold -geometry 80x32+30+50 &
oclock -geometry 70x70-7+7 &
xsetroot -solid SteelBlue &
exec fvwm
```

This starts two `xterms` and the clock and places them on the desktop, then sets the background color to steel blue and finally starts the desktop manager. Two important notes: The last command in the script is preceded by the `exec` command and the last command is not sent to background. If you send the last command to background or forget the `exec` command, X starts up, and then immediately shuts down!

Summary

All of the previous steps will help you set up XFree86 properly, and after following them your XFree86 session should start up without a problem. The specifics of working with X are beyond the scope of this book. If you are not sure how to use X, check the documentation files that came with the release or consult a user-oriented book.

However, if you followed the steps outlined previously, your X system should now be functional and you can start working with the X system as your primary interface to Linux. After you've worked in X, it's hard to go back to character-based terminals!

From here, there are a number of chapters that you can go to that are related to this topic:

Wabi, a way to run Windows applications under Linux, is discussed in Chapter 23, "Wabi."

Ghostscript, which lets you see PostScript files onscreen and send them to the printer, is discussed in Chapter 24, "Ghostscript and Ghostview."

Programming under Linux is discussed in Part V, starting with Chapter 25, "gawk."

System administration is discussed in Part VI, starting with Chapter 32, "System Administration Basics."

Wabi

by Tim Parker

CHAPTER 23

Wabi (Windows Application Binary Interface) is a Linux and UNIX application developed to allow Microsoft Windows 3.X applications to run under X and Motif. Wabi acts as a translator between the Microsoft Windows windowing commands and their counterparts under X. By running Wabi your Linux system gets access to most Windows applications, while still retaining all the features of Linux (including its crash resistance, better performance, and window switching).

Not all Windows applications run properly under Wabi. In order to execute cleanly with Wabi, a Windows application has to be "properly behaved," meaning that the application conforms to all the standards Microsoft laid down for applications to follow. Most standard applications, such as word processors and spreadsheets, behave properly and work fine under Wabi. A few packages, notably games and some graphics tools, deviate from the Microsoft Windows standards in order to get better performance from graphics cards, and these do not run reliably (if at all) under Wabi. Also, with version 2.1 of Wabi (the current release), you cannot run Windows 95 applications.

TIP

A list of applications that have been tested and certified to run properly under Wabi is available from a number of sites, including most Linux FTP sites. One such site is:

`http://wabiapps.psgroup.com`

Don't be discouraged that all your favorite applications will not run under Wabi. Most Widows 3.x applications do, with the major exception of games. Want to run CorelDraw under Linux? No problem. Want to run Microsoft Office? Again, no sweat. Essentially, if it's an office productivity tool, it will run (as these seldom have to deviate from the Windows programming standards).

What Can Wabi Do?

As mentioned, Wabi sits in a layer between the Windows application and the X manager. When a Windows application running under Wabi issues a Windowing request, such as opening a new window, changing a title, or modifying fonts, Wabi intercepts the request and converts it to the X equivalent. When an X Windows process wants to send a message to a Windows application, Wabi converts the X message to a Windows message. As long as an application sticks to standard Windows mechanics, Wabi can handle the conversion and allow the application to run under X.

Wabi doesn't do much by itself. There's no real Wabi application you can interact with, except for some configuration tools. However, Wabi does have a ton of features that it allows to be performed under X that you will be familiar with from Windows, Windows-based, such as the following:

- Cut and paste between Windows applications
- Enhanced mode support for CPUs
- DOS format disk access
- OLE (Object Linking and Embedding) between Windows applications
- DDE (Dynamic Data Exchange) between Windows applications
- Network support
- Windows sockets programming

Wabi extends most of these features to include the X environment, too, so you can cut and paste between Windows and X applications, interact with network applications under both, and allow multiple users on the same application.

Perhaps more important to most users is what Wabi won't do. The list is short but does have some important considerations for some Windows applications. Wabi does not support

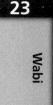

- MIDI (Musical Instrument Digital Interface)
- AVI (Audio-Visual Interface)
- IPX/SPX networking
- Shared Wabi directories
- VGA-based video drivers
- DOS-disk formatting
- (VDx) virtual device drivers

A number of these unsupported features, such as IPX/SPX and MIDI, can be provided through other Linux subsystems. Wabi is also being improved with new features all the time, so support for these items may be added in the future.

Wabi does not include Microsoft Windows 3.x due to copyright restrictions, so you need to purchase a supported copy of Windows as well as Wabi (although most users have a copy of Windows somewhere).

Installing Wabi

Wabi requires a minimum of 16MB RAM, although 32MB is recommended. At least 20MB swap space is required, although 40MB is better (and more is ideal). The Wabi directory space is about 25MB depending on the version and supported versions of Windows.

Wabi includes an installation script that takes care of all the manual steps you normally would have to do. Simply answer the installation script prompts, and the Wabi software is properly installed. If you use a tar file obtained from a source other than CD-ROM, untarring the file in an empty temporary directory will give you all the files you need, including the installation script. After Wabi has installed itself, it will prompt you for the Windows 3.x version to use. Both Windows 3.1 and Windows 3.11 are supported.

By default, Wabi installs to the /opt/wabi directory, with all binaries stored in the /opt/wabi/bin directory. You can change these defaults, but it's best to leave them there. Every time you run the Wabi system a personal directory is used, usually called wabi under your home directory. The personal directory, as the name implies, is unique to each login, and every user has one if they run Wabi. Underneath the wabi directory there will be a windows directory containing the Microsoft Windows 3.x program. This implies that each user has his own copy of Windows and that this application can't be shared. Although there are ways around this, it's best to stick to the way Wabi was intended to work. You can think of the wabi and wabi/windows directories as the same as a PC's C:\ and C:\WINDOWS directories.

TROUBLESHOOTING

If you are running Metro X 3.1.2 and try to run Wabi, your Metro X session will hang. The problem lies not with Wabis but with that version of Metro X. The more recent version of Metro X, 3.1.5 does not cause these problems. Upgrades are usually available from Metro Link, the Metro X vendor. A workaround that solves most of the problem (but does impose a performance hit) is to start Wabi with the -fs option added at the command line.

The current version of Wabi only supports 8-bit color depth (256 colors), but an unsupported interim release that handles 24-bit color depth is available. You should set your X session to use 8-bit colors for best performance.

Running Windows 3.x Applications

As mentioned earlier, Wabi supports only Windows 3.x applications. These are installed and launched on your Linux system, just as they are with a stand-alone Windows system. When you start Wabi, you will see an environment in a window that looks just like Windows 3.x. From then on, Windows behaves just as you would expect it to. Wabi takes care of mapping all devices (such as floppy disks and directories) for you.

You start Wabi in an X terminal window by typing the following command:

```
wabi &
```

You don't really need the trailing ampersand, which forces the Wabi session into the background, but it does give you a shell prompt back in your X terminal window so you can continue to use it, instead of having a locked window. When you issue the `wabi` command, the "splash screen" with a Wabi logo appears, as shown in Figure 23.1. A scroll bar at the bottom of the window shows the process of loading all the fonts Wabi needs, then the main window opens.

FIGURE 23.1.

The Wabi splash screen with status bar at the bottom.

Wabi is now loading Bitmap, Vector, and TrueType fonts

Wabi starts up a font server of its own, called wabifs, if you are running an X11 system (Metro X or XFree86 both are X11 systems).

Figure 23.2 shows the main Wabi window after the installation of Windows 3.1. As you
can see, it looks the same as the normal Windows interface with the exception of the
Motif-style windowing elements (different minimize and maximize buttons in the top
right corner of the window) and the Wabi four-pane window icon in the top-left corner. A
Wabi program group will have been created by Wabi when Windows was installed. The
Wabi program group contains release notes and some documentation.

FIGURE 23.2.

*The Wabi interface
looks like the stan-
dard Windows
interface.*

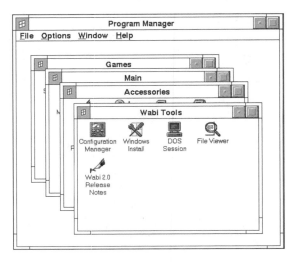

Loading new applications is as simple as with Windows: If you're using a floppy, you
select the Run command with A:SETUP or whatever the installation program name is.
Wabi behaves just like Windows in that respect. The only time you'll see a major difference between Windows and Windows under Wabi is when networking is involved, as the
two use different networking models.

Help is available on Wabi from two sources: online help (like normal Windows) and
man pages. The man pages describe command-line options, show various sample start-
up-modes, and list the environment variables Wabi uses.

Summary

Wabi is an effective way to run older Windows 3.X applications under Linux. This lets you use many of your existing applications such as word processors, spreadsheets, and utilities without having to purchase new Linux versions. From here, there are a number of chapters that may be of interest to you:

To learn more about programming in the awk language, handy for performing actions on files and working with columns of data, see Chapter 25, "gawk."

To learn more about Perl, a full-featured programming language that is easy to learn and handy for quick utilities, see Chapter 28, "Perl."

To learn more about system administration and how to keep your Linux system running smoothly, see Part VI starting with Chapter 32, "System Administration Basics."

To learn more about using your Linux system as a gateway into the Internet, see Chapter 47, "Setting up an Internet Site."

23

Wabi

Ghostscript and Ghostview

by Tim Parker

IN THIS CHAPTER

CHAPTER 24

PostScript is a popular page descriptor language (PDL) used by many application packages. One of the strengths of PostScript is that a file in the PostScript format can be printed on any printer that understands the language, regardless of operating system or printer manufacturer. This lets you generate a file using an application that prints on every PostScript-compatible printer in the world instead of having to create one file for HP LaserJet IIs, another for Epson dot matrix printers, yet another for Canon Bubblejet printers, and so on.

As far as Linux is concerned, PostScript has one major problem: It's a copyrighted name and imposes several restrictions on its use by the owner, Adobe Systems, Inc. Ghostscript was developed in an attempt to provide a utility that does the same task without those problems. As you can guess, Ghostscript is very similar to PostScript, but it has no copyright issues associated with it (and hence no licensing fees, legal worries, and so on). Actually, Ghostscript is a copyright utility, owned by the developers, but they allow it to be distributed under the GNU General Public License, making it readily available for use in Linux.

> **TIP**
>
> Ghostscript is copyrighted by Aladdin Enterprises, the utility's developer. You can contact Aladdin if you want further information about Ghostscript or to license the utility, at Aladdin Enterprises, P.O. Box 60264, Palo Alto, CA 94306 or by email at ghost@aladdin.com.

The Ghostscript page description language can be generated by most applications. A utility called Ghostview lets you see Ghostscript-formatted files on your screen, a very handy feature. Ghostscript is not a single program but a set of them. The two programs we care most about here are the interpreter for the PostScript language and a set of C functions that can be linked into applications to provide PostScript-like functionality.

Where to Obtain Ghostscript

You most likely have Ghostscript provided with your Linux distribution set (such as a CD-ROM). Ghostscript is part of the AP Disk Set (applications) with most versions of Linux. If you decided to install the AP Disk Set when you installed Linux (which most people do), you will have the files for Ghostscript already installed on your system. If you did not install the AP Disk Set, you can do so at any time and specify just the

Ghostscript utilities or the entire Disk Set, depending on your version of Linux and the installation utilities it includes.

To check whether you have Ghostscript installed on your system, you must usually search for the binaries and libraries as some versions of Linux install them in different locations. The easiest way to find out if Ghostscript is installed is to search for the binary called gs using the `find` command:

```
find / -name gs -print
```

If your system comes back with some matching entries (most likely in /usr/bin), then Ghostscript is probably installed. To verify the complete set of files is loaded you need to find out where your Linux version placed all the files. The number of files varies depending on the version of Ghostscript, but all versions include the following filenames:

```
bdftops.ps
decrypt.ps
font2c.ps
gs_dbt_e.ps
gs_dps1.ps
gs_fonts.ps
gs_init.ps
gs_lev2.ps
gs_statd.ps
gs_sym_e.ps
gs_type0.ps
gslp.ps
impath.ps
landscap.ps
level1.ps
prfont.ps
ps2ascii.ps
ps2epsi.ps
ps2image.ps
pstoppm.ps
quit.ps
showpage.ps
type1ops.ps
wrfont.ps
uglyr.gsf
Fontmap
```

24

GHOSTSCRIPT AND GHOSTVIEW

Usually, the Ghostscript files are stored in either /usr/lib/ghostscript or /usr/share/ghostscript. Often there are version numbers attached to the installation directory, which complicates the issue. Again, use the `find` command to locate one of the Ghostscript utilities:

```
find / -name gs_statd.ps -print
```

In this case we're searching for the file `gs_statd.ps`, which should be part of every Ghostscript installation. The file will be in `/usr/lib/ghostscript` on some Linux systems, while it may be placed under `/usr/share` on others. The output on a Caldera OpenLinux system looks like this:

```
[root@linux /root]# find / -name gs_statd.ps -print
/usr/share/ghostscript/3.33/gs_statd.ps
```

In this case, the Ghostscript files are in a directory called `/usr/share/ghostscript/3.33`. To check that all the files in the set are loaded, do a directory listing of the directory which contained the file you searched for. If Ghostscript is installed, you'll see a set of files like the one shown in Figure 24.1.

FIGURE 24.1.

The contents of the Ghostscript directory.

All the fonts that are required by Ghostscript are stored in one of the directories under the primary Ghostscript directory, in this case `/usr/local/ghostscript/3.33/fonts`. A lot of fonts are included with most distributions.

If your version of Linux did not include a copy of the Ghostscript utilities, you can download the set from any of the standard distribution points for Linux. See Chapter 2, "Types of Linux," to find out where to get a distribution. You can also get the Ghostscript set from Aladdin Enterprises.

Using Ghostscript

The primary program in the Ghostscript set is `gs`, which is the Ghostscript interpreter. The `gs` utility reads in any files you tell it to and interprets them for you, displaying a properly formatted document in an X window. Running `gs` from a character terminal doesn't accomplish much since a graphics window is required to show the results of its operation.

To display one or more files in X windows with Ghostscript, issue the following command, where `file1.ps` is the filename (with `.ps` extension, usually, to show it's a PostScript format file):

```
gs file1.ps …
```

You can specify more than one filename, and each file is displayed in sequence. When you issue the `gs` command you'll see a message such as "Initializing…" and a bunch of messages from the Ghostscript interpreter, and then a window will open with the contents of the file displayed. The exact messages and appearance of the X window differ depending on your version of Ghostscript. Figure 24.2 shows the output in an Xterm when you issue the `gs` command, and Figure 24.3 shows the window that Ghostscript displays with the contents of the selected file formatted properly.

FIGURE 24.2.

When you issue a gs *command Ghostscript displays status messages.*

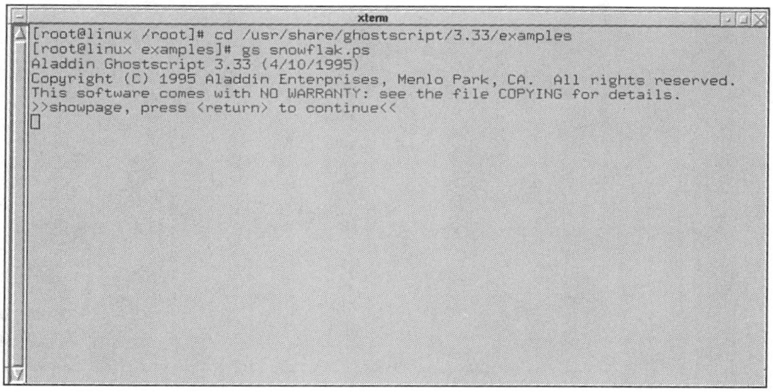

If you want to suppress all the messages Ghostscript generates (shown in Figure 24.2), use the `-q` (quiet) option, which suppresses all but major messages.

You can get help about the `gs` command through the man pages, which are often difficult to read, or from the command line by using either the `-h` or the `-?` option. When you use either option (both display the same screen output) you will see all the available options and command usage for the `gs` command. Since the output of the help screens take up more than one page, you should pipe the output to the `more` command, like this:

```
gs -h ¦ more
```

You'll see a screen like that in Figure 24.4. To move to the next page of help, press the space key. To quit the more utility, use the q command or Ctrl+C.

24

GHOSTSCRIPT AND GHOSTVIEW

FIGURE 24.3.

Ghostscript displays PostScript files in a window for you to view directly.

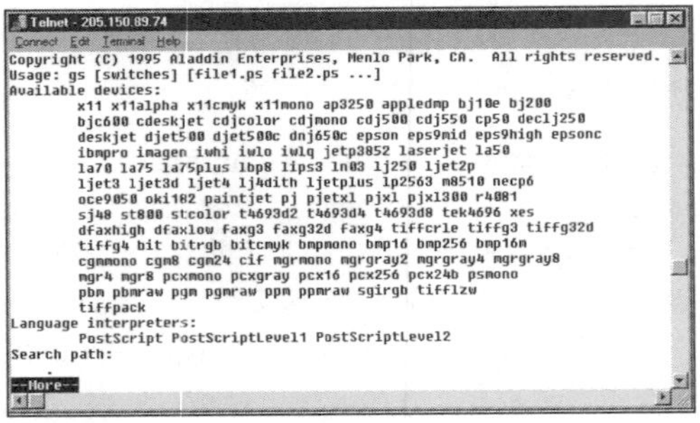

FIGURE 24.4.

Using the more *command to display the help screen for the* gs *command.*

Configuring Ghostscript for X

Some versions of Linux come with the X system premodified to handle Ghostscript output, but most do not. Ghostscript uses a set of X resources that are usually stored under the program name ghostscript and class name Ghostscript in the .Xdefaults file. Your .Xdefaults file should have three entries at a minimum in it, like this:

Ghostscript*geometry: -0+0

Ghostscript*xResolution: 72

Ghostscript*yResolution: 72

If these entries are missing from your .Xdefaults file, enter them using an editor and reload the defaults either by restarting the server or by issuing the following command, assuming you are in your home directory:

```
xrdb -merge ./.Xdefaults
```

If not, specify the path to your .Xdefaults file.

Ghostscript can make use of a number of resources in the .Xdefaults file, although most are of little use to you since defaults work just fine. The resources you can set in Ghostscript are shown in Table 24.1.

TABLE 24.1. X RESOURCES SUPPORTED BY GHOSTSCRIPT.

Resource name	Class of resource	Default value
background	Background	white
foreground	Foreground	black
borderColor	BorderColor	black
borderWidth	BorderWidth	1
geometry	Geometry	NULL
xResolution	Resolution	calculated
yResolution	Resolution	calculated
useExternalFonts	UseExternalFonts	true
useScalableFonts	UseScalableFonts	true
logExternalFonts	LogExternalFonts	false
externalFontTolerance	ExternalFontTolerance	10.0
palette	Palette	Color
maxGrayRamp	MaxGrayRamp	128
maxRGBRamp	MaxRGBRamp	5
useBackingPixmap	UseBackingPixmap	true
useXPutImage	UseXPutImage	true

24

GHOSTSCRIPT AND
GHOSTVIEW

continues

TABLE **24.1.** CONTINUED

Resource Name	Class of Resource	Default Value
useXSetTile	UseXSetTile	true
regularFonts	RegularFonts	none
symbolFonts	SymbolFonts	none
dingbatFonts	DingbatFonts	none

Redirecting Ghostscript Output

Ghostscript allows you considerable flexibility in redirecting output to other devices. On the command line you can specify a device such as a printer with the -sDEVICE option. For example, if you have a device called HPLaser, you could redirect the output of the gs command to that printer with the command:

```
gs -sDEVICE=HPLaser filename.ps
```

If you issue this command, you won't see any output in windows because the output has been redirected. If you specified multiple files on the command line, such as the following, all the files would have been sent to HPLaser:

```
gs -sDEVICE=HPLaser file1.ps file2.ps file3.ps
```

The redirection is in effect until the command terminates. Of course the device you are redirecting to must exist, or gs will return an "unknown device" message. You can see a list of all known devices with the command:

```
gs -h
```

A good chunk of the screen (shown in Figure 24.4) lists the devices that Ghostscript knows about.

You can use the order of the arguments to play with Ghostscript a little. Since the order in which arguments are given matters to Ghostscript, you can issue a command like the following, which displays file1.ps and file2.ps on your X session, and then sends file3.ps to the device HPLaser:

```
gs file1.ps file2.ps -sDEVICE=HPLaser file3.ps
```

You can change the device on the command line multiple times if you want, so that this next command will send file1.ps to the device HPLaser and file2.ps to the device CanonBJet:

```
gs -sDEVICE=HPLaser file1.ps -sDEVICE=CanonBJet file2.ps
```

In some cases it's easier just to issue separate commands; otherwise the gs command line gets pretty complicated.

Several other features are built into Ghostscript for modifying output devices. If you have an older dot matrix printer with several resolutions (such as draft and final), you can define different options for Ghostscript to trigger each device. For example, the following command tells Ghostscript to print on the device Epson using the highest resolution (24 pin) available:

```
gs -sDEVICE=Epson -r360x180
```

Since these older devices are disappearing, these command options are fading from general use.

If for some reason you don't want to use a printer or screen as output, you can redirect Ghostscript output with the option -sOutputFile, like this:

```
gs -sOutputFile out1.ps file1.ps file2.ps
```

Although Linux lets you use pipes and redirection, which are much more capable, this capability was included for those operating systems that are not as powerful as Linux!

Changing Paper Size

By default Ghostscript uses the paper sizes specified in the file gs_statd.ps, which is a configuration file for the printing utility. This file has a couple of dozen paper styles predefined for you, such as all the European and U.S. sizes. To use a size other than the default, use the -sPAPERSIZE option, followed by the gs_statd.ps name that indicates the size you want to use. For example, to use European A4 size, use the command:

```
gs -sPAPERSIZE=a4 -sDEVICE=HPLaser file1.ps
```

If the paper size you want to use is not defined already in the gs_stats.ps file, you can modify one of the existing entries or create your own.

24

> **TIP**
>
> Sometimes you'll change the paper size with the -sPAPERSIZE option only to find Ghostscript has used another paper size. That's because PostScript (and hence Ghostscript) allows a particular paper size to be embedded in the contents of a PostScript file. Even though you specify a paper size on the command line, the file's contents overrule this setting. The only way to correct this problem is to manually edit the PostScript file.

Ghostscript Environment Variables

Ghostscript uses a set of environment variables that can alter its behavior. The environment variables used by Ghostscript and their functions are shown in Table 24.2.

TABLE **24.2.** GHOSTSCRIPT VARIABLES AND THEIR MEANINGS.

Variable	What it does
GS_DEVICE	Defines the default output device.
GS_FONTPATH	Specifies a list of directories that should be scanned for fonts.
GS_LIB	Provides a search path for initialization files and fonts. Directories in the search path are separated by colons.
GS_OPTIONS	Defines a list of command line arguments to be processed before the ones actually specified on the command line.
TEMP	Defines a directory name for temporary files.

The GS_OPTIONS variable can be used to change the way Ghostscript behaves. For example, the option GS_DEVICE can be used to set the device to some value without requiring you to specify it on each command line. GS_OPTIONS can contain both arguments and options.

The TEMP variable usually points to the /tmp directory on Linux systems, but you can change this. When Ghostscript creates a temporary file it starts the filename with gs_. Unfortunately, Ghostscript doesn't always delete these files properly so you may occasionally have to go to your /tmp directly and erase any files starting with gs_. If you use Ghostscript a lot, the size of this directory can increase dramatically in short order, so keep an eye on it.

Ghostview

Ghostview is a utility to display PostScript files on the screen. Ghostview was written by Tim Theisen, not by Aladdin Enterprises, and is freely available on the Internet and through CD-ROM collections. Ghostview uses Ghostscript to display the contents, but doesn't require Ghostscript to be installed first.

The Ghostview utility is easy to run. To display the contents of the file chapter1.ps on your X screen, you would issue the command:

```
ghostview chapter1.ps
```

Most users learn to rename or alias the `ghostview` command to something a lot shorter, such as gv, to make using it easier and faster to type. To alias the command `ghostview` to gv in the `tcsh` shell, for example, simply enter:

```
alias gv ghostview
```

Ghostview's main window is a little more involved than the simple output window Ghostscript displays. The Ghostview main window is shown in Figure 24.5.

FIGURE 24.5.

The Ghostview main window shows the file being displayed by navigation shortcuts.

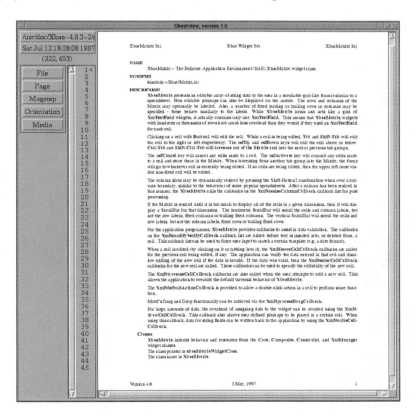

The Ghostview Panel

As you can see, the file you're displaying is in the right-hand page of the window just as it would appear using Ghostscript (which is actually what happens as Ghostview calls Ghostscript for this part of the routine). The scroll bar in the right margin lets you move through the file quickly, or you can use the page numbers on the left to move quickly to any page.

There are five buttons in the left-hand panel:

- **File.** Lets you open, reopen, or print a file, as well as display copyright information and exit Ghostview.
- **Page.** Controls which page is shown in the view panel. There are a number of options that are straightforward: Next moves to the next page, Previous moves to the previous page, Redisplay redraws the screen, Mark marks a page in the Table of Contents, and Unmark removes a mark.
- **Magstep.** Changes the magnification of the panel in the right portion of the Ghostview window.
- **Orientation.** Lets you move between landscape and portrait modes, as well as flip an image upside down or rotate 90 degrees.
- **Media.** Lets you change page sizes.

You'll find Ghostview quick and easy to work with after using it a couple of times. The top of the Ghostview window shows the version number, and the top of the left panel shows the title (if any) of the document you are displaying (PostScript allows document titles to be embedded in the page descriptor language). If no title is found, the file name is shown instead. The date underneath the title is either a date embedded in the PostScript file or the file's modification date.

TIP

One feature of Ghostview that may have you puzzled for a moment is the way pages are displayed after being minimized and expanded. When you shrink a Ghostview window to its icon, Ghostview retains all the images of the files in memory. However, when you expand the window, Ghostview first checks to see whether the file has been changed since the minimization. This can cause a slight delay in the window appearing again, especially with very large documents. Despite the delay, this is a very useful feature—it means you always have the most recent version of the document displayed.

Despite the simple look of the Ghostview window, there are a huge number of options the command supports. They tend to replace either X resources or environment variable options explained in the Ghostview documentation.

Ghostview Fonts

By default Ghostview comes with a set of PostScript type 1 and 3 fonts, which should cover every document you're likely to run into. However, you can add your own fonts to

Ghostview's arsenal. The fonts need to be placed in the Ghostscript fonts subdirectory, such as `/usr/share/ghostscript/3.33/fonts`.

You also have to edit the file Fontmap to tell Ghostview and Ghostscript about the new fonts. The format of each entry in Fontmap is simple, showing the name of the font and the file that contains it, such as the following, where `funnyfont` is the name of the font and `fun_fnt.pfb` is the PostScript definition file:

```
funnyfont (fun_fnt.pfb);
```

Ghostview X Resources

As with most applications that use X, Ghostview has a set of X resources it can use. The X resources are not the same as those used by Ghostscript. Table 24.3 lists the X resources recognized by Ghostview.

TABLE 24.3. GHOSTVIEW X RESOURCES.

Resource Name	Class of Resource	Default Value
showTitle - displays the title	Labels	true
showDate - displays the date	Labels	true
showLocator - displays the locator	Labels	true
autoCenter - centers the page in the viewport whenever the page size changes	AutoCenter	true
horizontalMargin - how many pixels should be reserved for horizontal window decorations	Margin	20
verticalMargin - how many pixels should be reserved for vertical window decorations	Margin	44
minimumMagstep - the smallest magstep to display	Magstep	-5
maximumMagstep - the largest magstep to display	Magstep	5
magstep - the default magstep	Magstep	0
orientation - the default orientation	Orientation	Portrait
page - the initial page to display	Page	

continues

24

GHOSTSCRIPT AND GHOSTVIEW

TABLE 24.3. CONTINUED

Resource Name	Class of Resource	Default Value
pageMedia - the default page media	PageMedia	Letter
forceOrientation -forces the orientation	Force	false
forcePageMedia - forces the page media	Force	false
swapLandscape - swaps the meaning of Landscape and Seascape	SwapLandscape	false
printCommand - the command used for printing	PrintCommand	
printerVariable - the name of the printer environment variable	PrinterVariable	PRINTER
busyCursor - the cursor shown when drawing to the window	Cursor	
cursor - the cursor shown when idle	Cursor	cross hair
safer - whether to run in safer mode	Safer	true

Summary

In this chapter we've looked at the Ghostview and Ghostscript utilities, two very handy related programs for working with PostScript-format files. It is useful to be able to browse through a file quickly using Ghostview instead of having to print it, so Ghostview has become one of the most-used utilities on many UNIX systems (including Linux). From here, take a look at a number of chapters that are related.

To learn about configuring printers under Linux, see Chapter 20, "Printing."

To learn about programming under Linux, see Part V starting with Chapter 25, "gawk."

To learn about setting up devices, including printers, see Chapter 33, "Devices."

Linux for Programmers

PART

V

gawk

by Tim Parker

IN THIS CHAPTER

CHAPTER 25

The awk programming language was created by the three people who gave their last-name initials to the language: Alfred Aho, Peter Weinberger, and Brian Kernighan. The gawk program included with Linux is the GNU implementation of that programming language.

The gawk language is more than just a programming language; it is an almost indispensable tool for many system administrators and UNIX programmers. The language itself is easy to learn, easy to master, and amazingly flexible. After you get the hang of using gawk, you'll be surprised how often you can use it for routine tasks on your system.

To help you understand gawk, we will follow a simple order of introducing the elements of the programming language, as well as showing good examples. You are encouraged, or course, to experiment as the chapter progresses. It's not possible to cover all the different aspects and features of gawk in this chapter, but we will look at the basics of the language and show you enough, hopefully, to get your curiosity working.

What Is the gawk Language?

gawk is designed to be an easy-to-use programming language that lets you work with information either stored in files or piped to them. The main strengths of gawk are its capabilities to do the following:

- Display some or all the contents of a file, selecting rows, columns, or fields as necessary.
- Analyze text for frequency of words, occurrences, and so on.
- Prepare formatted output reports based on information in a file.
- Filter text in a very powerful manner.
- Perform calculations with numeric information from a file.

gawk isn't difficult to learn. In many ways, gawk is the ideal first programming language because of its simple rules, basic formatting, and standard usage. Experienced programmers will find gawk refreshingly easy to use.

Files, Records, and Fields

Usually, gawk works with data stored in files. Often this is numeric data, but gawk can work with character information, too. If data is not stored in a file, it is supplied to gawk through a pipe or other form of redirection. Only ASCII files (text files) can be properly handled with gawk. Although it does have the capability to work with binary files, the results are often unpredictable. Because most information on a Linux system is stored in ASCII, this isn't a problem.

As a simple example of a file that gawk works with, consider a telephone directory. It is composed of many entries, all with the same format: last name, first name, address, telephone number. The entire telephone directory is a database of sorts, although without a sophisticated search routine. Indeed, the telephone directory relies on a pure alphabetical order to enable users to search for the data they need.

Each line in the telephone directory is a complete set of data on its own and is called a *record*. For example, the entry in the telephone directory for "Smith, John," which includes his address and telephone number, is a record.

Each piece of information in the record—the last name, the first name, the address, and the telephone number—is called a *field*. For the gawk language, the field is a single piece of information. A record, then, is a number of fields that pertain to a single item. A set of records makes up a *file*.

In most cases, fields are separated (delineated) by a character that is used only to separate fields, such as a space, a tab, a colon, or some other special symbol. This character is called a *field separator*. A good example is the file /etc/passwd, which looks like this:

```
tparker:t36s62hsh:501:101:Tim Parker:/home/tparker:/bin/bash
etreijs:2ys639dj3h:502:101:Ed Treijs:/home/etreijs:/bin/tcsh
ychow:1h27sj:503:101:Yvonne Chow:/home/ychow:/bin/bash
```

If you look carefully at the file, you can see that it uses a colon as the field separator. Each line in the /etc/passwd file has seven fields: the username, the password, the user ID, the group ID, a comment field, the home directory, and the startup shell. Each field is separated by a colon. Colons exist only to separate fields. A program looking for the sixth field in any line needs only count five colons across (because the first field doesn't have a colon before it).

That's where we find a problem with the gawk definition of fields as they pertain to the telephone directory example. Consider the following lines from a telephone directory:

```
Smith, John    13 Wilson St.             555-1283
Smith, John    2736 Artside Dr, Apt 123  555-2736
Smith, John    125 Westmount Cr          555-1728
```

We "know" there are four fields here: the last name, the first name, the address, and the telephone number. But gawk doesn't see it that way. The telephone book uses the space character as a field separator, so on the first line it sees "Smith" as the first field, "John" as the second, "13" as the third, "Wilson" as the fourth, and so on. As far as gawk is concerned, the first line when using a space character as a field separator has six fields. The second line has eight fields. Whitespace (spaces and tabs) in the preceding example are ignored by gawk as being just more characters with no special meanings. Unless you change the field separator to a space or tab character, whitespace has no meaning to gawk.

> **TIP**
>
> When working with a programming language, you must consider data the way the language will see it. Remember that programming languages take things literally.

To make sense of the telephone directory the way we want to handle it, we have to find another way of structuring the data so that there is a field separator between the sections. For example, the following uses the slash character as the field separator:

```
Smith/John/13 Wilson St./555-1283
Smith/John/2736 Artside Dr, Apt 123/555-2736
Smith/John/125 Westmount Cr/555-1728
```

By default, gawk uses blank characters (spaces or tabs) as field separators unless instructed to use another character. If gawk is using spaces, it doesn't matter how many are in a row; they are treated as a single block for purposes of finding fields. Naturally, there is a way to override this behavior, too.

Pattern-Action Pairs

The gawk language has a particular format for almost all instructions. Each command is composed of two parts: a pattern and a corresponding action. Whenever the pattern is matched, gawk executes the action that matches that pattern.

Pattern-action pairs can be thought of in more common terms to show how they work. Consider instructing someone how to get to the post office. You might say, "Go to the end of the street and turn right. At the stop sign, turn left. At the end of the street, go right." You have created three pattern-action pairs with these instructions:

```
end of street: turn right
stop sign: turn left
end of street: turn right
```

When these patterns are met, the corresponding action is taken. You wouldn't turn right before you reached the end of the street, and you don't turn right until you get to the end of the street, so the pattern must be matched precisely for the action to be performed. This is a bit simplistic, but it gives you the basic idea.

With gawk, the patterns to be matched are enclosed in a pair of slashes, and the actions are in a pair of braces:

```
/pattern1/{action1}
/pattern2/{action2}
/pattern3/{action3}
```

This format makes it quite easy to tell where the pattern starts and ends, and when the action starts and ends. All gawk programs are sets of these pattern-action pairs, one after the other. Remember these pattern-action pairs are working on text files, so a typical set of patterns might be matching a set of strings, and the actions might be to print out parts of the line that matched.

Suppose there isn't a pattern? In that case, the pattern matches every time and the action is executed every time. If there is no action, gawk copies the entire line that matched without change.

Consider the following example:

```
gawk '/tparker/' /etc/passwd
```

The gawk command looks for each line in the /etc/passwd file that contains the pattern tparker and displays it (there is no action, only a pattern). The output from the command is the one line in the /etc/passwd file that contains the string tparker. If there is more than one line in the file with that pattern, they all are displayed. In this case, gawk is acting exactly like the grep utility!

This example shows you two important things about gawk: It can be invoked from the command line by giving it the pattern-action pair to work with and a filename, and it likes to have single quotes around the pattern-action pair in order to differentiate them from the filename.

The gawk language is literal in its matching. The string cat will match any lines with cat in them, whether the word "cat" is by itself or part of another word such as "concatenate." To be exact, insert spaces on each side of the word. Also, case is important. We'll see how to expand the matching in the section "Metacharacters" a little later in the chapter.

Jumping ahead slightly, we can introduce a gawk command:

```
gawk '{print $3}' file2.data
```

The preceding command has only one action, so it performs that action on every line in the file file2.data. The action is print $3, which tells gawk to print the third field of every line. The default field separator, a space, is used to tell where fields begin and end. If we try the same command on the /etc/passwd file, nothing displays because the field separator used in that file is the colon.

We can combine the two commands to show a complete pattern-action pair:

```
gawk '/UNIX/{print $2}' file2.data
```

This command searches file2.data line by line, looking for the string UNIX. If it finds UNIX, it prints the second column of that line (record).

> **TIP**
>
> The quotation marks around the entire pattern-action pair are very important and should not be left off. Without them, the command might not execute properly. Make sure the quotation marks match (don't use a single quotation mark at the beginning and a double quotation mark at the end).

You can combine more than one pattern-action pair in a command. For example, the command

```
gawk '/scandal/{print $1} /rumor/{print $2}' gossip_file
```

scans gossip_file for all occurrences of the pattern "scandal" and prints the first column, and then starts at the top again and searches for the pattern "rumor" and prints the second column. The scan starts at the top of the file each time there is a new pattern-action pair.

Simple Patterns

As you might have figured out, gawk numbers all of the fields in a record. The first field is $1, the second is $2, and so on. The entire record is called $0. As a short form, gawk allows you to ignore the $0 in simple commands, so each of the following instructions results in the same output (the latter one because no action causes the entire line to be printed):

```
gawk '/tparker/{print $0}' /etc/passwd
```

```
gawk '/tparker/{print}' /etc/passwd
```

```
gawk '/tparker/' /etcpasswd
```

Suppose you want to do more than match a simple character string. The gawk language has many powerful features, but we'll introduce just a few. We can, for example, make a comparison of a field with a value:

```
gawk '$2 == "foo" {print $3}' testfile
```

The preceding command instructs gawk to compare the second string ($2) of each record in testfile and check to see if it is equal to the string foo. If it is, gawk prints the third column ($3).

This command demonstrates a few important points. First, there are no slashes around the pattern because we are not matching a pattern but are evaluating something. Slashes are used only for character matches. Second, the == sign means "is equal to." We must use two equal signs, because the single equal sign is used for assignment of values, as you will see shortly. Finally, we put double quotation marks around foo because we want gawk to interpret it literally. Only strings of characters that are to be literally interpreted must be quoted in this manner.

> **NOTE**
>
> Don't confuse the quotation marks used for literal characters with those used to surround the pattern-action pair on the command line. If you use the same quotation marks for both, gawk is unable to process the command properly.

Comparisons and Arithmetic

An essential component of any programming language is the ability to compare two strings or numbers and evaluate whether they are equal or different. The gawk program has several comparisons, including ==, which you just saw in an example. Table 25.1 shows the important comparisons.

TABLE 25.1. THE IMPORTANT COMPARISONS.

Comparison	Description
==	Equal to
!=	Not equal to
>	Greater than
<	Less than
>=	Greater than or equal to
<=	Less than or equal to

25

gawk

These are probably familiar to you from arithmetic and other programming languages you may have seen. From this, you can surmise that the following command will display every line in `testfile` in which the value in the fourth column is greater than 100:

```
gawk '$4 > 100' testfile
```

All of the normal arithmetic commands are available, including add, subtract, multiply, and divide. There are also more advanced functions such as exponentials and remainders (also called *moduli*). Table 25.2 shows the basic arithmetic operations that `gawk` supports.

TABLE 25.2. BASIC ARITHMETIC OPERATORS.

Operator	Description	Example
+	Addition	2+6
-	Subtraction	6-3
*	Multiplication	2*5
/	Division	8/4
^	Exponentiation	3^2 (=9)
%	Remainder	9%4 (=1)

You can combine column numbers and math, too:

```
{print $3/2}
```

This action divides the number in the third column by 2.

There is also a set of arithmetic functions for trigonometry and generating random numbers (see Table 25.3).

TABLE 25.3. RANDOM-NUMBER AND TRIGONOMETRIC FUNCTIONS.

Function	Description
sqrt(x)	Square root of x
sin(x)	Sine of x (in radians)
cos(x)	Cosine of x (in radians)
atan2(x,y)	Arctangent of x/y
log(x)	Natural logarithm of x
exp(x)	The constant e to the power x

Function	Description
`int(x)`	Integer part of *x*
`rand()`	Random number between 0 and 1
`srand(x)`	Set *x* as seed for `rand()`

The order of operations is important to gawk, as it is to regular arithmetic. The rules gawk follows are the same as with arithmetic: All multiplications, divisions, and remainders are performed before additions and subtractions:

```
{print $1+$2*$3}
```

The preceding command multiplies column two by column three and then adds the result to column one. If you wanted to force the addition first, use parentheses:

```
{print ($1+$2)*$3}
```

Because these are the same rules you have known about since grade school, they should not cause you any confusion. Remember, if in doubt, put parentheses in the proper places to force the operations.

Strings and Numbers

If you've used any other programming language, these concepts will be familiar to you. If you are new to programming, you will probably find them obvious, but it's surprising how many people get things hopelessly muddled by using strings when they should have used numbers.

A *string* is a set of characters that are to be interpreted literally by gawk. Strings are surrounded by quotation marks. Numbers are not surrounded by quotation marks and are treated as real values:

```
gawk '$1 != "Tim" {print}' testfile
```

This command prints any line in `testfile` that doesn't have the word `Tim` in the first column. If we had left out the quotation marks around `Tim`, gawk wouldn't have processed the command properly. The following command displays any line that has the string `50` in it:

```
gawk '$1 == "50" {print}' testfile
```

It does not attempt to see if the value stored in the first column is different than 50; it just does a character check. The string `50` is not equal to the number 50 as far as gawk is concerned.

Formatting Output

We've seen how to do simple actions in the commands we've already discussed, but you can do several things in an action:

```
gawk '$1 != "Tim" {print $1, $5, $6, $2}' testfile
```

The preceding command prints the first, fifth, sixth, and second columns of testfile for every line that doesn't have the first column equal to "Tim". You can place as many of these columns as you want in a print command.

Indeed, you can place strings in a print command, too:

```
gawk '$1 != "Tim" {print "The entry for ", $1, "is not Tim. ", $2}'
testfile
```

This command prints the strings and the columns as shown. Each section of the print command is separated by a comma. There are also spaces at the ends of the strings to ensure there is a space between the string and the value of the column that is printed.

You can use additional formatting instructions to make gawk format the output properly. These instructions are borrowed from the C language, and they use the command printf (print formatted) instead of print.

The printf command uses a placeholder scheme, but the gawk language knows how to format the entry because of the placeholder and looks later in the command line to find out what to insert there. An example helps clarify this :

```
{printf "%5s likes this language\n", $2}
```

The %5s part of the line instructs gawk how to format the string, in this case using five string characters. The value to place in this position is given at the end of the line as the second column. The \n at the end of the quoted section is a newline character. If the second column of a four-line file holds names, printf formats the output like this:

```
 Tim likes this language
Geoff likes this language
Mike likes this language
 Joe likes this language
```

Notice that the "%5s" format means to right-justify the column entry. This prevents awkward spacing.

The gawk language supports several format placeholders. They are shown in Table 25.4.

TABLE 25.4. FORMAT PLACEHOLDERS.

Placeholder	Description
c	If a string, the first character of the string; if an integer, the character that matches the first value
d	An integer
e	A floating-point number in scientific notation
f	A floating-point number in conventional notation
g	A floating-point number in either scientific or conventional notation, whichever is shorter
o	An unsigned integer in octal format
s	A string
x	An unsigned integer in hexadecimal format

Whenever you use one of the format characters, you can place a number before the character to show how many digits or characters are to be used. Therefore, the format "6d" would have six digits of an integer. Many formats can be on a line, but each must have a value at the end of the line, as in this example:

```
{printf "%5s works for %5s and earns %2d an hour", $1, $2, $3}
```

Here, the first string is the first column, the second string is the second column, and the third set of digits is from the third column in a file. The output looks something like this:

```
Joe works for Mike and earns 12 an hour
```

A few little tricks are useful. Consider the following command:

```
{printf "%5s likes this language\n", $2}
```

As shown in an earlier example, strings are right-justified, so this command results in the following output:

```
 Tim likes this language
Geoff likes this language
 Mike likes this language
  Joe likes this language
```

To left-justify the names, place a minus sign in the format statement:

```
{printf "%-5s likes this language\n", $2}
```

This results in the following output:

```
Tim   likes this language
Geoff likes this language
```

```
Mike   likes this language
Joe    likes this language
```

Notice that the name is justified on the left instead of on the right.

When dealing with numbers, you can specify the precision to be used:

```
{printf "%5s earns $%.2f an hour", $3, $6}
```

The preceding command uses the string in column three and puts five characters from it in the first placeholder, and then takes the value in the sixth column and places it in the second placeholder with two digits after the decimal point. The output of the command looks like this:

```
Joe earns $12.17 an hour
```

The dollar sign is inside the quotation marks in the printf command and is not generated by the system. It has no special meaning inside the quotation marks. If you want to limit the number of digits to the right of the period, you can do that, too:

```
{printf "%5s earns $%6.2f an hour", $3, $6}
```

This command puts six digits before the period and two after.

Finally, we can impose some formatting on the output lines themselves. In an earlier example, you saw the use of "\n" to add a newline character. These are called *escape codes,* because the backslash is interpreted by gawk to mean something different than a backslash. Table 25.5 shows the important escape codes that gawk supports.

TABLE 25.5. ESCAPE CODES.

Code	Description
\a	Bell
\b	Backspace
\f	Formfeed
\n	Newline
\r	Carriage return
\t	Tab
\v	Vertical tab
\ooo	Octal character ooo
\xdd	Hexadecimal character dd
\c	Any character c

You can, for example, escape a quotation mark by using the sequence \", which places a quotation mark in the string without interpreting it to mean something special:

```
{printf "I said \"Hello\" and he said "\Hello\"."
```

Awkward-looking, perhaps, but necessary to avoid problems. You'll see lots more escape characters used in examples later in this chapter.

Changing Field Separators

As I mentioned earlier, the default field separator is always a whitespace character (spaces or tabs). This is often not convenient, as we found with the /etc/passwd file. You can change the field separator on the gawk command line by using the -F option followed by the separator you want to use:

```
gawk -F":" '/tparker/{print}' /etc/passwd
```

This command changes the field separator to a colon and searches the etc/passwd file for the lines containing the string tparker. The new field separator is put in quotation marks to avoid any confusion. Also, the -F option (it must be a capital F) is before the first quotation mark enclosing the pattern-action pair. If it comes after, it won't be applied.

Metacharacters

Earlier I mentioned that gawk is particular about its pattern-matching habits. The string cat matches anything with the three letters on the line. Sometimes you want to be more exact in the matching. If you only want to match the word "cat" but not "concatenate," put spaces on each side of the pattern:

```
/ cat / {print}
```

What about matching different cases? That's where the or instruction, represented by a vertical bar, comes in.

```
/ cat ¦ CAT / {print}
```

The preceding pattern will match "cat" or "CAT" on a line. However, what about "Cat"? That's where we also need to specify options within a pattern. With gawk, we use square brackets for this. To match any combination of "cat" in upper- or lowercase, write the pattern like this:

```
/ [Cc][Aa][Tt] / {print}
```

This can get pretty awkward, but it's seldom necessary. To match just "Cat" and "cat," for example, use the following pattern:

```
/ [Cc]at / {print}
```

A useful matching operator is the tilde (~). This is used when you want to look for a match in a particular field in a record. Consider the following example:

```
$5 ~ /tparker/
```

This pattern matches any records where the fifth field is `tparker`. It is similar to the `==` operator. The matching operator can be negated, so

```
$5 !~ /tparker/
```

This pattern finds any record where the fifth field is not equal to `tparker`.

A few characters (called *metacharacters*) have special meaning to gawk. Many of these metacharacters are familiar to shell users because they are carried over from UNIX shells. The metacharacters shown in Table 25.6 can be used in gawk patterns.

TABLE 25.6. METACHARACTERS.

Metacharacter	Meaning	Example	Meaning of Example
~	The beginning of the field	`$3 ~ /^b/`	Matches if the third field starts with b
$	The end of the field	`$3 ~ /b$/`	Matches if the third field ends with b
.	Matches any single character	`$3 ~ /i.m/`	Matches any record that has a third field value of i, another character, and then m
¦	Or.	`/cat¦CAT/`	Matches cat or CAT
*	Zero or more repetitions of a character	`/UNI*X/`	Matches UNX, UNIX, UNIIX, UNIIIX, and so on
+	One or more repetitions of a character	`/UNI+X/`	Matches UNIX, UNIIX, and so on, but not UNX
\{a,b\}	The number of repetitions between a and b (both integers)	`/UNI\{1,3\}X`	Matches only UNIX, UNIIX, and UNIIIX

Metacharacter	Meaning	Example	Meaning of Example
?	Zero or one repetition of a string	/UNI?X/	Matches UNX and UNIX only
[ ]	Range of characters	/I[BDG]M/	Matches IBM, IDM, and IGM
[^]	Not in the set	/I[^DE]M/	Matches all three character sets starting with I and ending in M, except IDM and IEM

Some of these metacharacters are used frequently. You will see some examples later in this chapter.

Calling gawk Programs

Running pattern-action pairs one or two at a time from the command line would be pretty difficult (and time-consuming), so gawk allows you to store pattern-action pairs in a file. A gawk program (called a *script*) is a set of pattern-action pairs stored in an ASCII file. For example, this could be the contents of a valid gawk script:

```
/tparker/{print $6}
$2 != "foo" {print}
```

The first line looks for tparker and prints the sixth column, and the second line starts at the top of the file again and looks for second columns that don't match the string "foo," then displays the entire line. When you are writing a script, you don't need to worry about the quotation marks around the pattern-action pairs as you did on the command line, because the new command to execute this script makes it obvious where the pattern-action pairs start and end.

After you have saved all of the pattern-action pairs in a program, they are called by gawk with the -f option on the command line:

```
gawk -f script filename
```

This command causes gawk to read all of the pattern-action pairs from the file *script* and process them against the file called *filename*. This is how most gawk programs are written. Don't confuse the -f and -F options!

If you want to specify a different field separator on the command line (they can be specified in the script, but use a special format you'll see later), the -F option must follow the -f option:

```
gawk -f script -F":" filename
```

If you want to process more than one file using the script, just append the names of the files:

```
gawk -f script filename1 filename2 filename3 ...
```

By default, all output from the gawk command is displayed on the screen. You can redirect it to a file with the usual Linux redirection commands:

```
gawk -f script filename > save_file
```

There is another way of specifying the output file from within the script, but we'll come back to that in a moment.

BEGIN and END

Two special patterns supported by gawk are useful when writing scripts. The BEGIN pattern is used to indicate any actions that should take place before gawk starts processing a file. This is typically used to initialize values, set parameters such as field separators, and so on. The END pattern is used to execute any instructions after the file has been completely processed. Typically, this can be for summaries or completion notices.

Any instructions following the BEGIN and END patterns are enclosed in curly braces to identify which instructions are part of both patterns. Both BEGIN and END must appear in capitals. Here's a simple example of a gawk script that uses BEGIN and END, albeit only for sending a message to the terminal:

```
BEGIN { print "Starting the process the file" }
$1 == "UNIX" {print}
$2 > 10 {printf "This line has a value of %d", $2}
END { print "Finished processing the file.  Bye!"}
```

In this script, a message is initially printed out, and each line that has the word UNIX in the first column is echoed to the screen. Next, the file is processed again to look for any line with the second column greater than 10, and the message is generated with its current value. Finally, the END pattern prints out a message that the program is finished.

Variables

If you have used any programming language before, you know that a *variable* is a storage location for a value. Each variable has a name and an associated value, which may change.

With gawk, you assign a variable a value using the assignment operator (=):

```
var1 = 10
```

This assigns the value 10 (numeric, not string) to the variable var1. With gawk, you don't have to declare variable types before you use them as you must with most other languages. This makes it easy to work with variables in gawk.

> **NOTE**
>
> Don't confuse the assignment operator, =, which assigns a value, with the comparison operator, ==, which compares two values. This is a common error that takes a little practice to overcome.

The gawk language lets you use variables within actions:

```
$1 == "Plastic" { count = count + 1 }
```

This pattern-action pair checks to see if the first column is equal to the string "Plastic," and if it is, increments the value of count by one. Somewhere above this line we should set a preliminary value for the variable count (usually in the BEGIN section), or we will be adding one to something that isn't a recognizable number.

> **NOTE**
>
> Actually, gawk assigns all variables a value of zero when they are first used, so you don't really have to define the value before you use it. It is, however, good programming practice to initialize the variable anyway.

Here's a more complete example:

```
BEGIN { count = 0 }
$5 == "UNIX" { count = count + 1 }
END { printf "%d occurrences of UNIX were found", count }
```

In the BEGIN section, the variable count is set to zero. Then, the gawk pattern-action pair is processed, with every occurrence of "UNIX" adding one to the value of count. After the entire file has been processed, the END statement displays the total number.

Variables can be used in combination with columns and values, so all of the following statements are legal:

```
count = count + $6

count = $5 - 8

count = $5 + var1
```

Variables can also be part of a pattern. The following are both valid as pattern-action pairs:

```
$2 > max_value {print "Max value exceeded by ", $2 - max_value}

$4 - var1 < min_value {print "Illegal value of ", $4}
```

Two special operators are used with variables to increment and decrement by one, because these are common operations. Both of these special operators are borrowed from the C language:

count++	Increments count by one
count--	Decrements count by one

Built-In Variables

The gawk language has a few built-in variables that are used to represent things such as the total number of records processed. These are useful when you want to get totals. Table 25.7 shows the important built-in variables.

TABLE 25.7. THE IMPORTANT BUILT-IN VARIABLES.

Variable	Description
NR	The number of records read so far
FNR	The number of records read from the current file
FILENAME	The name of the input file
FS	Field separator (default is whitespace)
RS	Record separator (default is newline)
OFMT	Output format for numbers (default is %g)
OFS	Output field separator
ORS	Output record separator
NF	The number of fields in the current record

The NR and FNR values are the same if you are processing only one file, but if you are doing more than one file, NR is a running total of all files, while FNR is the total for the current file only.

The FS variable is useful because it controls the input file's field separator. To use the colon for the /etc/passwd file, for example, use the following command in the script, usually as part of the BEGIN pattern:

```
FS=":"
```

You can use these built-in variables as you would any other. For example, the following command gives you a way to check the number of fields in the file you are processing and generates an error message if the values are incorrect:

```
NF <= 5 {print "Not enough fields in the record"}
```

Control Structures

Enough of the details have been covered to allow us to start doing some real gawk programming. Although we have not covered all of gawk's pattern and action considerations, we have seen all the important material. Now we can look at writing control structures.

If you have any programming experience at all or have tried some shell script writing, many of these control structures will appear familiar. If you haven't done any programming, common sense should help, as gawk is cleanly laid out without weird syntax. Follow the examples and try a few test programs of your own.

Incidentally, gawk enables you to place comments anywhere in your scripts, as long as the comment starts with a # sign. You should use comments to indicate what is going on in your scripts if it is not immediately obvious.

The if Statement

The if statement is used to allow gawk to test some condition and, if it is true, execute a set of commands. The general syntax for the if statement is as follows:

```
if (expression) {commands} else {commands}
```

The expression is always evaluated to see if it is true or false. No other value is calculated for the if expression. Here's a simple if script:

```
# a simple if loop
(if ($1 == 0){
      print "This cell has a value of zero"
      }
else {
      printf "The value is %d\n", $1
      })
```

Notice that the curly braces were used to lay out the program in a readable manner. Of course, this could all have been entered on one line and gawk would have understood it, but writing in a nicely formatted manner makes it easier to understand what is going on and to debug the program if the need arises.

In this simple script, we test the first column to see if the value is zero. If it is, a message to that effect is printed. If not, the `printf` statement prints the value of the column.

The flow of the `if` statement is quite simple to follow. There can be several commands in each part, as long as the curly braces mark the start and end. There is no need to have an `else` section. It can be left out entirely, if desired. For example, this is a complete and valid gawk script:

```
(if ($1 == 0){
      print "This cell has a value of zero"
      })
```

The gawk language, to be compatible with other programming languages, allows a special format of the `if` statement when a simple comparison is being conducted. This quick-and-dirty `if` structure is harder to read for novices, and I don't recommend it if you are new to the language. For example, here's the `if` statement written the proper way:

```
# a nicely formatted if loop
(if ($1 > $2){
      print "The first column is larger"
      }
else {
      print "The second column is larger"
      })
```

Here's the quick-and-dirty method:

```
# if syntax from hell
$1 > $2{
      print "The first column is larger"
      }
{print "The second column is larger")
```

You may notice that the keywords `if` and `else` are left off. The general structure is retained: expression, true commands, and false commands. However, this is much less readable if you don't know that it is an `if` statement! Not all versions of gawk allow this method of using `if`, so don't be too surprised if it doesn't work. Besides, you should be using the more verbose method of writing `if` statements for readability's sake.

The while Loop

The while statement allows a set of commands to be repeated as long as some condition is true. The condition is evaluated each time the program loops. The general format of the gawk while loop is as follows:

```
while (expression){
    commands
    }
```

For example, the while loop can be used in a program that calculates the value of an investment over several years (the formula for the calculation is value=amount(1+interest_rate)^years):

```
# interest calculation computes compound interest
# inputs from a file are the amount, interest_rate, and years
{var = 1
while (var <= $3) {
    printf("%f\n", $1*(1+$2)^var)
    var++
    }
}
```

You can see in this script that we initialize the variable var to 1 before entering the while loop. If we don't do this, gawk assigns a value of zero. The values for the three variables we use are read from the input file. The autoincrement command is used to add one to var each time the line is executed.

The for Loop

The for loop is commonly used when you want to initialize a value and then ignore it. The syntax of the gawk for loop is

```
for (initialization; expression; increment) {
    command
    }
```

The initialization is executed only once and then ignored, the expression is evaluated each time the loop executes, and the increment is executed each time the loop is executed. Usually the increment is a counter of some type, but it can be any collection of valid commands. Here's an example of a for loop, which is the same basic program as shown for the while loop:

```
# interest calculation computes compound interest
# inputs from a file are the amount, interest_rate, and years
{for (var=1; var <= $3; var++) {
    printf("%f\n", $1*(1+$2)^var)
    }
}
```

In this case, `var` is initialized when the `for` loop starts. The expression is evaluated, and if true, the loop runs. Then the value of `var` is incremented and the expression is tested again.

The format of the `for` loop may look strange if you haven't encountered programming languages before, but it is the same as the `for` loop used in C, for example.

next and exit

The `next` instruction tells `gawk` to process the next record in the file, regardless of what it is doing. For example, consider this script:

```
{ command1
        command2
        command3
        next
        command4
}
```

As soon as the `next` statement is read, `gawk` moves to the next record in the file and starts at the top of the current script block (given by the curly brace). In this example, `command4` will never be executed because the `next` statement moves back up to `command1` each time.

The `next` statement is usually used inside an `if` loop, where you may want execution to return to the start of the script if some condition is met.

The `exit` statement makes `gawk` behave as though it has reached the end of the file, and it then executes any `END` patterns (if any exist). This is a useful method of aborting processing if there is an error in the file.

Arrays

The `gawk` language supports arrays and enables you to access any element in the array easily. No special initialization is necessary with an array, because `gawk` treats it like any other variable. The general format for declaring arrays is as follows:

```
var[num]=value
```

As an example, consider the following script, which reads an input file and generates an output file with the lines reversed in order:

```
# reverse lines in a file
{line[NR] = $0 }  # remember each line
END {var=NR                # output lines in reverse order
```

```
        while (var > 0){
        print line[var]
        var--
        }
}
```

In this simple program (try and do the same task in any other programming language to see how efficient gawk is!), we use the NR (number of records) built-in variable. After reading each line into the array line[], we simply start at the last record and print them again, stepping down through the array each time. We don't have to declare the array or do anything special with it, which is one of the powerful features of gawk.

Summary

We've only scratched the surface of gawk's abilities, but you may have noticed that it is a relatively easy language to work with and places no special demands on the programmer. That's one of the reasons gawk is so often used for quick programs. It is ideal, for example, for writing a quick script to count the total size of all the files in a directory. In the C language, this would take many lines, but it can be done in less than a dozen lines in gawk.

If you are a system administrator or simply a power user, you will find that gawk is a great complement to all the other tools you have available, especially because it can accept input from a pipe or redirection. For more information on gawk, check the man pages or one of the few gawk books that are available.

See the following chapters for information on programming:

C under Linux is discussed in Chapter 26, "Programming in C."

Perl, another handy utility included with Linux, is discussed in Chapter 28, "Perl."

Tcl and Tk, yet another programming language with extra features for X and Motif, is discussed in Chapter 29, "Introduction to Tcl and Tk."

25

gawk

Programming in C

by Rick McMullin

IN THIS CHAPTER

CHAPTER 26

Linux is distributed with a wide range of software-development tools. Many of these tools support the development of C and C++ applications. This chapter describes the tools that can be used to develop and debug C applications under Linux. It is not intended to be a tutorial on the C programming language, but rather to describe how to use the C compiler and some of the other C programming tools that are included with Linux.

We will look at some of the useful C tools that are included with the Linux distribution. These tools include pretty print programs, additional debugging tools, and automatic function prototypers.

> **TIP**
>
> Pretty print programs are programs that automatically reformat code so that it has consistent indenting.

What Is C?

C is a general-purpose programming language that has been around since the early days of the UNIX operating system. It was originally created by Dennis Ritchie at Bell Laboratories to aid in the development of UNIX. The first versions of UNIX were written using assembly language and a language called B. C was developed to overcome some of the shortcomings of B. Since that time, C has become one of the most widely used computer languages in the world.

Why did C gain so much support in the programming world? Some of the reasons that C is so commonly used include the following:

- It is a very portable language. Almost any computer that you can think of has at least one C compiler available for it, and the language syntax and function libraries are standardized across platforms. This is a very attractive feature for developers.
- Executable programs written in C are fast.
- C is the system language of all versions of UNIX.

C has evolved quite a bit over the last 20 years. In the late 1980s, the American National Standards Institute published a standard for the C language known as ANSI C. This further helped to secure C's future by making it even more consistent between platforms. The 1980s also saw an object-oriented extension to C called C++. C++ will be described in the next chapter, "Programming in C++."

The C compiler that is available for Linux is the GNU C compiler, abbreviated GCC. This compiler was created under the Free Software Foundation's programming license and is therefore freely distributable. You will find it on the book's companion CD-ROM.

The GNU C Compiler

The GNU C Compiler (GCC) that is packaged with the Slackware Linux distribution is a fully functional, ANSI C–compatible compiler. If you are familiar with a C compiler on a different operating system or hardware platform, you will be able to learn GCC very quickly. This section describes how to invoke GCC and introduces many of the commonly used GCC compiler options.

Invoking GCC

The GCC compiler is invoked by passing it a number of options and a number of filenames. The basic syntax for invoking gcc is this:

```
gcc [options] [filenames]
```

The operations specified by the command-line options are performed on each of the files that are specified on the command line. The next section describes the options that you will use most often.

GCC Options

There are more than 100 compiler options that can be passed to GCC. You will probably never use many of these options, but you will use some of them on a regular basis. Many of the GCC options consist of more than one character. For this reason you must specify each option with its own hyphen, and you cannot group options after a single hyphen as you can with most Linux commands. For example, the following two commands are not the same:

```
gcc -p -g test.c
gcc -pg test.c
```

The first command tells GCC to compile test.c with profile information for the prof command and also to store debugging information within the executable. The second command simply tells GCC to compile `test.c` with profile information for the `gprof` command.

When you compile a program using `gcc` without any command-line options, it creates an executable file (assuming that the compile was successful) and calls it `a.out`. For example, the following command creates a file named `a.out` in the current directory:

```
gcc test.c
```

To specify a name other than `a.out` for the executable file, you can use the `-o` compiler option. For example, to compile a C program file named `count.c` into an executable file named `count`, type the following command:

```
gcc -o count count.c
```

> **TIP**
>
> When you are using the `-o` option, the executable filename must occur directly after the `-o` on the command line.

There are also compiler options that allow you to specify how far you want the compile to proceed. The `-c` option tells GCC to compile the code into object code and to skip the assembly and linking stages of the compile. This option is used quite often because it makes the compilation of multifile C programs faster and easier to manage. Object code files that are created by GCC have a `.o` extension by default.

The `-S` compiler option tells GCC to stop the compile after it has generated the assembler files for the C code. Assembler files that are generated by GCC have a `.s` extension by default. The `-E` option instructs the compiler to perform only the preprocessing compiler stage on the input files. When this option is used, the output from the preprocessor is sent to the standard output rather than being stored in a file.

Optimization Options

When you compile C code with GCC, it tries to compile the code in the least amount of time and also tries to create compiled code that is easy to debug. Making the code easy to debug means that the sequence of the compiled code is the same as the sequence of the source code, and no code gets optimized out of the compile. There are many options that you can use to tell GCC to create smaller, faster executable programs at the cost of compile time and ease of debugging. Of these options, the two that you typically use are the `-O` and the `-O2` options.

The -0 option tells GCC to perform basic optimizations on the source code. In most cases these optimizations make the code run faster. The -02 option tells GCC to make the code as fast and small as it can. The -02 option causes the compilation speed to be slower than when using the -0 option, but typically results in code that executes more quickly.

In addition to the -0 and -02 optimization options, there are a number of lower-level options that can be used to make the code faster. These options are very specific and should be used only if you fully understand the consequences that these options will have on the compiled code. For a detailed description of these options, refer to the GCC man page by typing man gcc on the command line.

Debugging and Profiling Options

GCC supports several debugging and profiling options. Of these options, the two that you are most likely to use are the -g option and the -pg option.

The -g option tells GCC to produce debugging information that the GNU debugger (gdb) can use to help you to debug your program. GCC provides a feature that many other C compilers do not have. With GCC you can use the -g option in conjunction with the -0 option (which generates optimized code). This can be very useful if you are trying to debug code that is as close as possible to what will exist in the final product. When you are using these two options together, you should be aware that some of the code that you have written will probably be changed by GCC when it optimizes it. For more information on debugging your C programs, see the "Debugging GCC Applications with gdb" section in this chapter.

The -pg option tells GCC to add extra code to your program that will, when executed, generate profile information that can be used by the gprof program to display timing information about your program. For more information on gprof, see the "gprof" section in this chapter.

Debugging GCC Programs with gdb

Linux includes the GNU debugging program called gdb. gdb is a very powerful debugger that can be used to debug C and C++ programs. It enables you to see the internal structure or the memory that is being used by a program while it is executing. Some of the functions that gdb provides for you are these:

- It enables you to monitor the value of variables that are contained in your program.

- It enables you to set breakpoints that will stop the program at a specific line of code.

- It enables you to step through the code, line by line.

You can run gdb by typing gdb on the command line and pressing Enter. If your system is configured properly, gdb will start and you will see a screen that resembles the following:

```
GDB is free software and you are welcome to distribute copies of it
under certain conditions; type "show copying" to see the conditions.
There is absolutely no warranty for GDB; type "show warranty" for details.
GDB 4.12 (i486-unknown-linux), Copyright 1994 Free Software Foundation,
Inc.
(gdb)
```

When you start gdb, there are a number of options that you can specify on the command line. You will probably run gdb in the following way:

```
gdb <fname>
```

When you invoke gdb in this way, you are specifying the executable file that you want to debug. This tells gdb to load the executable file with the name fname. There are also ways of starting gdb that tell it to inspect a core file that was created by the executable file being examined, or to attach gdb to a currently running process. To get a listing and brief description of each of these other options, you can refer to the gdb man page or type gdb -h at the command line.

Compiling Code for Debugging

To get gdb to work properly, you must compile your programs so that debugging information is generated by the compiler. The debugging information that is generated contains the types for each of the variables in your program as well as the mapping between the addresses in the executable program and the line numbers in the source code. gdb uses this information to relate the executable code to the source code.

To compile a program with the debugging information turned on, use the -g compiler option.

gdb Basic Commands

The gdb supports many commands that enable you to perform different debugging operations. These commands range in complexity from very simple file-loading commands to complicated commands that allow you to examine the contents of the call stack.

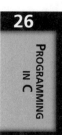

Table 26.1 describes the commands that you need to get up and debugging with gdb. To get a description of all of the gdb commands, refer to the gdb manual page.

TABLE 26.1. BASIC gdb COMMANDS.

Command	Description
file	Loads the executable file that is to be debugged.
kill	Terminates the program that you are currently debugging.
list	Lists sections of the source code used to generate the executable file.
next	Advances one line of source code in the current function, without stepping into other functions.
step	Advances one line of source code in the current function and does step into other functions.
run	Executes the program that is currently being debugged.
quit	Terminates gdb.
watch	Enables you to examine the value of a program variable whenever the value changes.
break	Sets a breakpoint in the code; this causes the execution of the program to be suspended whenever this point is reached.
make	Enables you to remake the executable program without quitting gdb or using another window.
shell	Enables you to execute UNIX shell commands without leaving gdb.

The gdb environment supports many of the same command-editing features as do the UNIX shell programs. You can tell gdb to complete unique commands by pressing the Tab key just as you do when you are using bash or tcsh. If what you type is not unique, you can make gdb print a list of all the commands that match what you have entered so far by pressing the Tab key again. You can also scroll up and down through the commands that you have entered previously by pressing the up- and down-arrow keys.

Sample gdb Session

This section goes step by step through a sample gdb session. The sample program that is being debugged is quite simple, but it is sufficient to illustrate how gdb is typically used.

We will start by showing a listing of the program that is to be debugged. The program is called greeting and is supposed to display a simple greeting followed by the greeting printed in reverse order.

```
#include   <stdio.h>

main ()
{
  char my_string[] = "hello there";

  my_print (my_string);
  my_print2 (my_string);
}

void my_print (char *string)
{
  printf ("The string is %s\n", string);
}

void my_print2 (char *string)
{
  char *string2;
  int size, i;

  size = strlen (string);
  string2 = (char *) malloc (size + 1);
  for (i = 0; i < size; i++)
    string2[size - i] = string[i];
  string2[size+1] = '\0';
  printf ("The string printed backward is %s\n", string2);
}
```

To compile the preceding program, use the gcc command followed by the filename. To rename the generated binary (instead of using the default a.out filename), use the -o option followed by the binary name, such as

```
gcc -o test test.c
```

The program, when executed, displays the following output:

```
The string is hello there
The string printed backward is
```

The first line of output displays correctly, but the second line prints something that is unexpected. The second line of output was supposed to be

```
The string printed backward is ereht olleh
```

For some reason the my_print2 function is not working properly. Let's take a look at the problem using gdb. First we need to start gdb, specifying the greeting program as the one to debug. Do this by entering the following command:

```
gdb greeting
```

TIP

Remember that you must compile the greeting program with the compiler debug options turned on.

If you forget to pass the program to debug as a parameter to gdb, load it in after gdb is started by using the file command at the gdb prompt:

```
(gdb) file greeting
```

This command loads the greeting executable just as if you had told gdb to load it on the command line.

Next, let's run greeting by entering the gdb run command. When the program is executed from within gdb, the result should resemble the following:

```
(gdb) run
Starting program: /root/greeting
The string is hello there
The string printed backward is
Program exited with code 041
```

The output of the greeting program is the same as when we executed the program outside of gdb. The question is, why is the backward print not working? To find the problem, let's set a breakpoint at the line after the for statement in the my_print2 function. To do this, list the source file by entering the list command three times at the gdb prompt:

```
(gdb) list
(gdb) list
```

TIP

Pressing Enter by itself at the gdb prompt will repeat the last command that was entered.

```
(gdb) list
```

Enter the list command for the first time and the output resembles the following:

```
1       #include   <stdio.h>
2
3       main ()
4       {
5         char my_string[] = "hello there";
6
```

```
7           my_print (my_string);
8           my_print2 (my_string);
9      }
10
```

Press Enter and gdb executes the list command again, displaying the following output:

```
11     my_print (char *string)
12     {
13        printf ("The string is %s\n", string);
14     }
15
16     my_print2 (char *string)
17     {
18        char *string2;
19        int size, i;
20
```

Pressing Enter one more time lists the rest of the greeting program:

```
21        size = strlen (string);
22        string2 = (char *) malloc (size + 1);
23        for (i = 0; i < size; i++)
24           string2[size - i] = string[i];
25        string2[size+1] = '\0';
26        printf ("The string printed backward is %s\n", string2);
26     }
```

By listing the file, we can see that the place where we want to set the breakpoint is line 24. Now, to set the breakpoint, enter the following command at the gdb command prompt:

```
(gdb) break 24
```

gdb should now print a response resembling the following:

```
Breakpoint 1 at 0x139: file greeting.c, line 24
(gdb)
```

Now let's run the program again by typing the run command. This command generates the following output:

```
Starting program: /root/greeting
The string is hello there

Breakpoint 1, my_print2 (string = 0xbfffdc4 "hello there") at greeting.c
➥:24
24    string2[size-i]=string[i]
```

We can see what is actually going wrong with the program by setting a watch which tells the value of the string2[size - i] variable expression.

To do this, type

```
(gdb) watch string2[size - i]
```

gdb returns the following acknowledgment:

```
Watchpoint 2: string2[size - i]
```

The version of gdb included on the CD-ROM accompanying this book changes the prompt to Hardware Watchpoint, but this is simply a change in the naming convention used by gdb. Now we can step through the execution of the for loop using the next command:

```
(gdb) next
```

After the first time through the loop, gdb tells us that string2[size - i] is 'h' by displaying the following message on the screen:

```
Watchpoint 2, string2[size - i]
Old value = 0 '\000'
New value = 104 'h'
my_print2(string = 0xbfffdc4 "hello there") at greeting.c:23
23 for (i=0; i<size; i++)
```

This is the value that we expected. Stepping through the loop several more times reveals similar results. Everything appears to be functioning normally. When we get to the point where i=10, the value of the string2[size - i] expression is equal to 'e,' the value of the size - i expression is equal to 1, and the program is at the last character that is to be copied over into the new string.

Step through the loop one more time and it's clear that there is no value assigned to string2[0], which is the first character of the string. Because the malloc function initializes the memory it assigns to null, the first character in string2 is the null character. This explains why nothing is printed when we tried to print string2.

Now that we've found the problem, it should be quite easy to fix. We must write the code so that the first character going into string2 is being put into string2 at offset size - 1 instead of string2 at offset size. This is because the size of string2 is 12, but it starts numbering at offset zero. The characters in the string should start at offset 0 and go to offset 10, with offset 11 being reserved for the null character.

There are many ways to modify this code so that it will work. One way is to keep a separate size variable that is one smaller than the real size of the original string. This solution is shown in the following code:

```
#include <stdio.h>

main ()
```

```
{
  char my_string[] = "hello there";

  my_print (my_string);
  my_print2 (my_string);
}

my_print (char *string)
{
  printf ("The string is %s\n", string);
}

my_print2 (char *string)
{
  char *string2;
  int size, size2, i;

  size = strlen (string);
  size2 = size -1;
  string2 = (char *) malloc (size + 1);
  for (i = 0; i < size; i++)
    string2[size2 - i] = string[i];
  string2[size] = '\0';
  printf ("The string printed backward is %s\n", string2);
}
```

Additional C Programming Tools

The Slackware Linux distribution includes a number of C development tools that have not yet been described. This section describes many of these additional tools and their typical uses.

xxgdb

xxgdb is an X Window system-based graphical user interface to gdb. All of the features that exist in the command-line version of gdb are present in xxgdb. xxgdb enables you to perform many of the most commonly used gdb commands by pressing buttons instead of typing in commands. It also graphically represents where breakpoints have been placed.

Start xxgdb by typing the following into an Xterm window.

xxgdb

When we initiate xxgdb, we can specify any of the command-line options that were available with gdb. xxgdb also has some of its own command-line options. These are described in Table 26.2.

TABLE 26.2. THE xxgdb COMMAND-LINE OPTIONS.

Option	Description
db_name	Specifies the name of the debugger to be used. The default is gdb.
db_prompt	Specifies the debugger prompt. The default is gdb.
gdbinit	Specifies the filename of the initial gdb command file. The default is .gdbinit.
nx	Tells xxgdb not to execute the .gdbinit file.
bigicon	Uses a large icon size for the xxgdb icon.

When you start xxgdb, a window opens on your screen. This window is shown in Figure 26.1.

FIGURE 26.1.

The xxgdb *main window.*

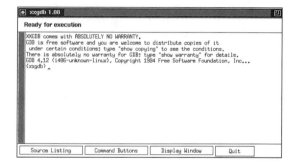

The xxgdb main window contains a message that is similar to the one displayed on the screen when the command line version of gdb is started. Near the bottom of the xxgdb main window there are four buttons. The Source Listing, Command Buttons, and Display Window buttons each bring up an additional window when they are activated. The Quit button terminates the xxgdb program.

The Source Listing button brings up a window that displays the source code for the program that is being debugged. This window is shown in Figure 26.2.

FIGURE 26.2.

The xxgdb *source listing window.*

The Command Buttons button brings up a window that contains 26 other buttons. These buttons each execute a gdb command. The gdb command-button window is illustrated in Figure 26.3.

FIGURE 26.3.
The xxgdb *command-button window.*

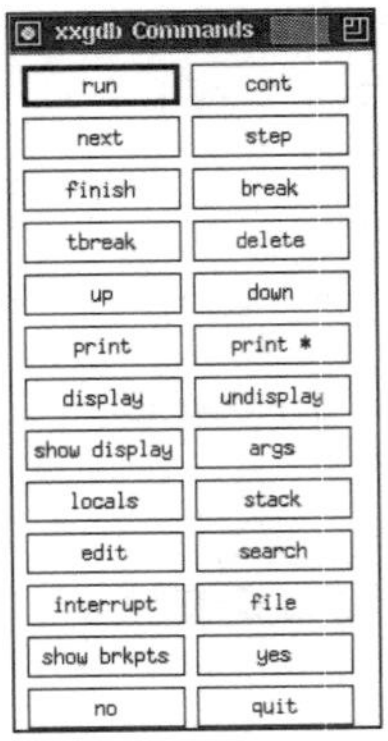
xxgdb Commands
run
cont
next
step
finish
break
tbreak
delete
up
down
print
print *
display
undisplay
show display
args
locals
stack
edit
search
interrupt
file
show brkpts
yes
no
quit

The Display Window button brings up a window that is used to display the results of any display command. You can tell xxgdb which variable or expression to display by selecting it from the source listing and then clicking on the Display button in the command-button window. The display window is illustrated in Figure 26.4.

FIGURE 26.4.
The xxgdb *display window.*

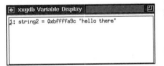

xxgdb Variable Display
1: string2 = 0xbffffa9c "hello there"

For more information on using xxgdb, refer to the xxgdb man page and the gdb man page.

calls

calls is a program that is not included on the Linux CD-ROM accompanying this book, but you can obtain a copy from the sunsite FTP site under the directory /pub/Linux/devel/lang/c/calls.tar.Z. Some older CD-ROM distributions of Linux include this file. Because it is a useful tool, we will cover it here. If you think it will be of use to you, obtain a copy from an FTP or BBS site or another CD-ROM. calls runs the GCC preprocessor on the files that are passed to it on the command line and displays a function call tree for the functions that are in those files.

TIP

To install `calls` on your system, perform the following steps while you are logged in as `root`:

1. Uncompress and `untar` the file.
2. `cd` into the `calls` subdirectory that was created by the `untar` command.
3. Move the file named `calls` to the `/usr/bin` directory.
4. Move the file named `calls.1` to the `/usr/man/man1` directory.
5. Remove the `/tmp/calls` directory.

This will install the `calls` program and man page on your system.

When `calls` prints out the call trace, it includes the filename in which the function is found in brackets after the function name.

```
main [test.c]
```

If the function is not in one of the files passed to `calls`, it does not know where that function lives and only prints the function name.

```
printf
```

`calls` also makes note of recursive and static functions in its output. Recursive functions are represented in the following way:

```
fact <<< recursive in factorial.c >>>
```

Static functions are represented as follows:

```
total [static in calculate.c]
```

As an example, assume that calls were executed with the following program as input:

```
##include <stdio.h>

main ()
{
char my_string[] = "hello there";
my_print (my_string);
my_print2(my_string);
}

my_print (char *string)
{
printf ("The string is %s\n", string);
}

my_print2 (char *string)
{
```

```
        char *string2;
        int size, size2, i;

        size = strlen (string);
        size2 = size -1;
        string2 = (char *) malloc (size + 1);
        for (i = 0; i < size; i++)
          string2[size2 - i] = string[i];
        string2[size] = '\0';
        printf ("The string printed backward is %s\n", string2);
}
```

This generates the following output:

```
1 main [test.c]
2        my_print [test.c]
3               printf
4        my_print2 [test.c]
5               strlen
6               malloc
7               printf
```

`calls` recognizes a number of command-line options that enable you to specify the appearance of the output and which function calls get displayed. For more information on these command-line options, refer to the `calls` man page or enter `calls -h` at the command line.

cproto

cproto is another program that is not included on this Linux CD-ROM but is readily available from FTP and BBS sites. cproto reads in C source files and automatically generates function prototypes for all of the functions. Using cproto saves you from having to type in a function definition for all of the functions that you have written in your programs.

TIP

To install cproto on your system, perform the following steps while you are logged in as root:

1. Uncompress and untar the file.
2. cd into the cproto subdirectory created as a result of the untar command.
3. Move the file named cproto to the /usr/bin directory.
4. Move the file named cproto.1 to the /usr/man/man1 directory.
5. Remove the /tmp/cproto directory.

This installs the cproto program and man page on your system.

Run the following code through the cproto program:

```c
#include  <stdio.h>

main ()
{
  char my_string[] = "hello there";
  my_print (my_string);
  my_print2(my_string);
}

my_print (char *string)
{
  printf ("The string is %s\n", *string);
}

my_print2 (char *string)
{
  char *string2;
  int size, size2, i;

  size = strlen (string);
  size2 = size -1;
  string2 = (char *) malloc (size + 1);
  for (i = 0; i < size; i++)
    string2[size2 - i] = string[i];
  string2[size] = '\0';
  printf ("The string printed backward is %s\n", string2);
}
```

The following output displays:

```c
/* test.c */
int main(void);
int my_print(char *string);
int my_print2(char *string);
```

This output could be redirected to an include file and used to define the prototypes for all of the functions.

indent

The indent utility is another programming utility that is included with Linux. This program, in its simplest form, reformats or pretty prints your C code so that it is consistently indented and all opening and closing braces are represented consistently. There are numerous options that enable you to specify how you want indent to format your code. For information on these options, refer to the indent man page or type indent -h at the command line.

The following example shows the default output of the indent program.

C code before running indent:

```c
#include   <stdio.h>

main () {
      char my_string[] = "hello there";
  my_print (my_string);
     my_print2(my_string); }

my_print (char *string)
{
  printf    ("The string is %s\n", *string);
}

my_print2           (char *string) {
    char *string2;
      int size, size2, i;

      size = strlen (string);
      size2 = size -1;
      string2 = (char *) malloc (size + 1);
  for (i = 0; i < size; i++)
            string2[size2 - i] = string[i];
      string2[size] = '\0';
      printf ("The string printed backward is %s\n", string2);
}
```

C code after running indent:

```c
#include   <stdio.h>

main ()
{
  char my_string[] = "hello there";
  my_print (my_string);
  my_print2 (my_string);
}

my_print (char *string)
{
  printf ("The string is %s\n", *string);
}

my_print2 (char *string)
{
  char *string2;
  int size, size2, i;

  size = strlen (string);
```

```
    size2 = size -1;
    string2 = (char *) malloc (size + 1);
    for (i = 0; i < size; i++)
      string2[size2 - i] = string[i];
    string2[size] = '\0';
    printf ("The string printed backward is %s\n", string2);
}
```

Indent does not change how the code compiles; it just changes how the source code looks. It makes the code more readable, which is always a good thing.

gprof

gprof is a program that is installed in the /usr/bin directory on your Linux system. It allows you to profile programs that you write to determine where most of the execution time is being spent.

gprof will tell you how many times each function that your program uses is called and also the percentage of the total execution time the program spent in each function. This information can be very useful if you are trying to improve the performance of a program.

To use gprof on one of your programs, you must compile the program using the -pg gcc option. This causes the program to create a file called gmon.out each time it is executed. gprof uses the gmon.out file to generate the profile information.

After you run your program and it has created the gmon.out file, you can get its profile by entering the following command:

```
gprof <program_name>
```

The program_name parameter is the name of the program that created the gmon.out file.

> ### TIP
>
> The profile data that gprof displays to the screen is quite large. If you want to examine this data, you should redirect gprof's output to a file.

f2c and p2c

f2c and p2c are two source code conversion programs. f2c converts FORTRAN code into C code, and p2c converts Pascal code into C code. Both are included in the Linux installation when you install GCC.

If you have some code that has been written using either FORTRAN or Pascal that you want to rewrite in C, f2c and p2c can prove to be very useful programs. Both programs produce C code that can typically be compiled directly by GCC without any human intervention.

If you are converting small, straightforward FORTRAN or Pascal programs, you should be able to get away with using f2c or p2c without any options. If you are converting very large programs consisting of many files, you will probably have to use some of the command-line options which are provided by the conversion program that you are using.

To invoke f2c on a FORTRAN program, enter the following command:

```
f2c my_fortranprog.f
```

TIP

f2c requires that the program being converted has either a .f or a .F extension.

To convert a Pascal program to C, enter the following command:

```
p2c my_pascalprogram.pas
```

Both of these commands create C source code files that have the same name as the original file, except with a .c extension instead of .f or .pas.

For more information on the specific conversion options that are available with f2c or p2c, refer to their respective man pages.

Summary

This chapter introduces the GNU C compiler and many of the options that you will typically use when you compile C code. It also introduces the concepts behind debugging code with the GNU debugger and illustrates the usefulness of some of the other C utility programs that are included on the Linux CD-ROM.

TIP

If you will be writing C code, the time that you spend learning how to use gdb and some of the other tools mentioned in this chapter will be more than worth the eventual time-saving that you will gain.

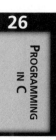

The next chapter will discuss many of the same topics, but with a focus on C++ development rather than C development. Instead of moving to C++, you can go to other chapters:

- Perl, a handy scripting language is discussed in Chapter 28, "Perl."

- Tcl and Tk, useful for macros, is discussed in Chapter 29, "Introduction to Tcl and Tk."

- The compilers available for Linux is discussed in Chapter 30, "Other Compilers."

- Smalltalk is discussed in Chapter 31, "Smalltalk/X."

Programming in C++

by Rick McMullin

In This Chapter

## CHAPTER 27

What Is C++?

C++ is an object-oriented extension to the C programming language. It was developed at Bell Labs in the early 1980s and is quickly becoming the language of choice in the computer industry. Dozens of C++ compilers are available on the market today. The most common of these for PC-based systems are Borland C++, Microsoft's Visual C++, Zortech C++, and Watcom C++. These compilers compile MS-DOS and MS Windows applications, and some of them compile code to run on OS/2 and Windows NT, as well. In addition to the number of C++ compilers that are available on DOS-based machines, a great number are also based on other hardware architectures.

Most UNIX systems have C++ compilers available from the system vendor. Linux also comes with a C++ compiler. This is the GNU C++ compiler. The GNU C++ compiler is very closely related to the GNU C compiler (GCC). In fact, since Release 2.0 of GCC, the GNU C++ compiler has been integrated with GCC. Previous to Release 2.0 of GCC, the GNU C++ compiler was a separate program known as g++. One of the major enhancements in Release 2.0 of GCC was merging these two compilers.

GCC now incorporates a C compiler, a C++ compiler, and an Objective C compiler. You will still find the g++ executable on your system, but it is now a script file that calls GCC with all the standard C++ options.

Why C++?

C++ and object-oriented programming (OOP) did not just happen. There were many fundamental reasons for the shift from structured programming to OOP. In the early days of computer programming, back when PDP-8s still roamed the earth in great numbers, there was a shift from machine language coding to assembler language coding. This was done because the computers of the day were a little more powerful than their predecessors. Programmers wanted to make their lives easier by moving some of the burden of programming onto the computer.

As the years went by and computers got even more powerful, new, higher-level languages started to appear. Examples of these languages are FORTRAN, COBOL, Pascal, and C. With these languages came a programming methodology known as structured programming. Structured programming helped to simplify the systems being designed by allowing programmers to break the problem into small pieces and then implement these pieces as functions or procedures in whatever language was being used.

The structured programming approach worked well for small to medium-sized software applications, but it started to fall apart as systems reached a certain size. OOP tried to solve some of the problems that structured programming was causing. It did this by extending some of the structured programming concepts and by introducing some of its own.

The main concepts that OOP focuses on are the following:

- Data encapsulation
- Inheritance
- Polymorphism

Data Encapsulation

In structured programming, problems often arose wherever there was a data structure that was common to several different pieces of code. One piece of code could access that data without the other piece of code being aware that anything was happening.

Data encapsulation is a process of grouping common data together, storing it into a data type, and providing a consistent interface to that data. This ensures that no one can access that data without going through the user interface that has been defined for that data.

The biggest benefit that this kind of mechanism provides is that it protects code outside the code that is directly managing this data from being affected if the structure of the data changes. This greatly reduces the complexity of large software systems.

C++ implements data encapsulation through the use of classes.

Inheritance

Inheritance is a form of code reuse in which you can inherit or use the data and behavior of other pieces of code. Inheritance is typically used only when a piece of software logically has many of the same characteristics as another piece of software, such as when one object is a specialization of another object.

Inheritance is implemented in C++ by allowing objects to be subclassed by other objects.

Polymorphism

Polymorphism occurs when a language allows you to define functions that perform different operations on objects depending on their type. The true power of this lies in the fact that you can send a message to a base class and that message can be passed down to each of its subclasses and mean different things to each of them.

Polymorphism is implemented in C++ using virtual functions.

Classes of Objects and Methods

In C++, classes can be thought of as C structures that contain not only the data fields but also operations that can be performed on those data fields. A simple example of this concept is a geometric shape. A geometric shape can be many things, such as a rectangle, a triangle, or a circle. All geometric shapes have certain attributes in common, including area and volume. You could define a structure in C called shape in the following way:

```
struct shape{
        float area;
        float volume;
}
```

If you add some common behavior to this structure, you have the equivalent of a C++ class. This would be written as follows:

```
class shape {
public:
                float area;
                float volume;
                float calc_area();
                float calc_volume():
};
```

You have now defined a C++ class. The calc_area and calc_volume items are known as methods of the class (instead of functions, as in C). Suppose you were to define a variable that was of type shape:

```
shape circle;
```

You would have created a circle object. An object is an instance of a class or a variable that is defined to be of the type of a class.

GCC Options

This section describes some of the GCC options that are most commonly used. First we'll talk about some of the options that can be used both with C and C++ and then talk about C++ specific options. Any of the compiler options that you use with C you can use with C++ as well, but some of them may not make any sense in the context of a C++ compile. If you specify options that don't make sense, the compiler just ignores them.

> **TIP**
>
> When you are compiling C++ programs, it is easiest to use the g++ script. This sets all the default C++ options so you don't have to.

A great number of compiler options can be passed to GCC. Many of these options are specific to a certain hardware platform or are for making fine-tuning adjustments to the code that is produced. You will probably never use any of these kinds of options. The options covered in this chapter are those that you will use on a regular basis.

Many of the GCC options consist of more than one character. For this reason, you must specify each option with its own hyphen and not group options after a single hyphen as you can with most Linux commands.

When you compile a program using GCC without any command-line options, it creates an executable file (assuming that the compile is successful) and calls it a.out. For example, the following command creates a file named a.out in the current directory:

```
gcc test.C
```

To specify a name other than a.out for the executable file, you can use the -o compiler option. For example, to compile a C++ program file named count.C (the capital C is used to show C++ code, as opposed to a small c for C code) into an executable file named count, type the following command:

```
gcc -o count count.C
```

> **WARNING**
>
> Don't put a space after the -o option!
>
> When you are using the -o option, the executable filename must occur directly after the -o on the command line.

Other compiler options allow you to specify how far you want the compile to proceed. The -c option tells GCC to compile the code into object code and skip the assembly and linking stages of the compile. This option is used quite often because it makes the compilation of multifile C++ programs faster and easier to manage. Object code files created by GCC have an .o extension by default.

The -S compiler option tells GCC to stop the compile after it has generated the assembler files for the C code. Assembler files generated by GCC have an .s extension by default. The -E option instructs the compiler to perform only the preprocessing compiler stage on the input files. When this option is used, the output from the preprocessor is sent to the standard output rather than being stored in a file.

Debugging and Profiling Options

GCC supports several debugging and profiling options. Of these options, the two that you are most likely to use for C++ programs are the `-gstabs+` option and the `-pg` option.

The `-gstabs+` option tells GCC to produce stabs format debugging information that the GNU debugger (gdb) can use to help you debug your program. For more information on debugging your C++ programs, see the "Debugging C++ Applications" section later in this chapter.

The `-pg` option tells GCC to add extra code to your program that will, when executed, generate profile information that can be used by the gprof program to display timing information about your program. For more information on gprof, refer to the "gprof" section in Chapter 26, "Programming in C."

GCC C++ Specific Options

The GCC options that control how a C++ program is compiled are listed in Table 27.1.

TABLE 27.1. GCC OPTIONS.

Option	Meaning
-fall-virtual	Treats all possible member functions as virtual. This applies to all functions except for constructor functions and new or delete member functions.
-fdollars-in-identifiers	Accepts $ in identifiers. You can also prohibit the use of $ in identifiers by using the -fno-dollars-in-identifiers option.
-felide-constructors	Tells the compiler to leave out constructors whenever possible.
-fenum-int-equiv	Permits implicit conversion of int to enumeration types.
-fexternal-templates	Produces smaller code for template declarations. This is done by having the compiler generate only a single copy of each template function where it is defined.
-fmemorize-lookups	Uses heuristics to compile faster. These heuristics are not enabled by default because they are effective only for certain input files.
-fno-strict-prototype	Treats a function declaration with no arguments the same way that C would treat it. This means that the compiler treats a function prototype that has no arguments as a function that will accept an unknown number of arguments.

Option	Meaning
-fno-null-objects	Assumes that objects reached through references are not null.
-fsave-memorized	Same as -fmemorize-lookups.
-fthis-is-variable	Permits assignment to "this."
-nostdinc++	Does not search for header files in the standard directories specific to C++.
-traditional	This option has the same effect as -fthis-is-variable.
-fno-default-inline	Does not assume that functions defined within a class scope are inline functions.
-wenum-clash	Warns about conversion between different enumeration types.
-woverloaded-virtual	Warns when derived class function declaration may be an error in defining a virtual function. When you define a virtual function in a derived class, it must have the same signature as the function in the base class. This option tells the compiler to warn you if you have defined a function that has the same name and a different signature as a function that is defined in one of the base classes.
-wtemplate-debugging	If you are using templates, this option warns you if debugging is not yet available.
+eN	Controls how virtual function definitions are used.
-gstabs+	Tells the compiler to generate debugging information in stabs format, using GNU extensions understood only by the GNU debugger. The extra information produced by this option is necessary to ensure that gdb handles C++ programs properly.

Debugging C++ Applications

A very important part of developing C++ programs is being able to debug them efficiently. The GNU debug application that was introduced in Chapter 26 can also be used to debug C++ applications. This section describes some of the differences between debugging C applications and debugging C++ applications.

The basic gdb commands that were introduced in Chapter 26 are listed again for your convenience in Table 27.2.

27

PROGRAMMING IN C++

TABLE 27.2. BASIC gdb COMMANDS.

Command	Description
file	Loads the executable file that is to be debugged.
kill	Terminates the program you are currently debugging.
list	Lists sections of the source code used to generate the executable file.
next	Advances one line of source code in the current function, without stepping into other functions.
step	Advances one line of source code in the current function, and does step into other functions.
run	Executes the program that is currently being debugged.
quit	Terminates gdb.
watch	Enables you to examine the value of a program variable whenever the value changes.
break	Sets a breakpoint in the code; this causes the execution of the program to be suspended whenever this point is reached.
make	This command enables you to remake the executable program without quitting gdb or using another window.
shell	Enables you to execute UNIX shell commands without leaving gdb.

From the programmer's perspective, you have more details to be aware of when debugging C++ code than when you are debugging C code. This is because of the C++ features such as virtual functions and exception handling. gdb has added features to support debugging both of these C++ specific features.

Debugging Virtual Functions

As described in the "Polymorphism" section of this chapter, virtual functions are C++'s way of implementing polymorphism. This means that there may be more than one function in a program with the same name. The only way to tell these functions apart is by their signatures. The signature of a function is composed of the types of all the arguments to the function. For example, a function with the following prototype has a signature of int,real:

```
void func(int, real);
```

You can see how this could cause the gdb a few problems. For example, if you define a class that has a virtual function called calculate, and two objects with different definitions for this function are created, how do you set a breakpoint to trigger on this function? You set breakpoints in C by specifying the function name as an argument to the gdb break command, as follows:

```
(gdb) break calculate
```

This does not work in the case of a virtual function because the debugger is not able to tell which calculate you want the breakpoint to be set on. gdb was extended in a few ways so that it could handle virtual functions. The first way to solve the problem is to enter the function name by specifying its prototype, as well. This is done in the following way:

```
break 'calculate (float)'
```

This gives gdb enough information to determine which function the breakpoint was meant for. A second solution that gdb supports is using a breakpoint menu. Breakpoint menus allow you to specify the function name of a function. If there is more than one function definition for that function, it gives you a menu of choices. The first choice in the menu is to abort the break command. The second choice is to set a breakpoint on all the functions that the break command matches. The remaining choices correspond to each function that matches the break command. The following code shows an example of a breakpoint menu:

```
(gdb) break shape::calculate
[0] cancel
[1] all
[2] file: shapes.C: line number: 153
[3] file: shapes.C: line number: 207
[4] file: shapes.C: line number: 247
> 2 3
Breakpoint 1 at 0xb234: file shapes.C, line 153
Breakpoint 2 at 0xa435: file shapes.C, line 207
Multiple breakpoints were set
Use the "delete" command to delete unwanted breakpoints
(gdb)
```

Debugging Exception Handlers

Exceptions are errors that occur within your program. Exception handlers are pieces of code that are written to handle errors and potential errors. For example, if you were writing a C program and calling the malloc function to get a block of memory, you would typically check `malloc`'s return code to make sure the memory allocation was successful. If C supported exception handling, you could specify a function that would receive or catch exceptions, and the `malloc` function would send or throw an exception to your function if one occurred.

The gdb added two new commands to support C++ exception handling: the `catch` command and the `catch info` command. The `catch` command is used to set a breakpoint in active exception handlers. The syntax of this command is as follows:

```
catch exceptions
```

`exceptions` is a list of the exceptions to catch.

The `catch info` command is used to display all the active exception handlers.

Summary of gdb C++ Specific Commands

In addition to the gdb commands that have been added to support some of the new language features contained in C++, there are also some new `set` and `show` options. These options are listed in Table 27.3.

TABLE 27.3. gdb's C++ SET AND SHOW OPTIONS.

Command	Description
set print demangle	Prints C++ names in their source form rather than in the encoded or mangled form that is passed to the assembler.
show print demangle	Shows whether print demangle is on or off.
set demangle-style	Sets the style of demangled output. The options are auto, gnu, lucid, and arm.
show demangle-style	Shows which demangle style is being used.
set print object	When displaying a pointer to an object, identifies the actual type of the object.
show print object	Shows whether print object is turned on or off.
set print vtbl	Prints C++ virtual function tables.
show print vtbl	Shows whether print vtbl is turned on or off.

GNU C++ Class Libraries

GNU C++ comes packaged with an extensive class library. A class library is a reusable set of classes that can be used to perform a specified set of functions. Some typical examples of class libraries are class libraries that handle database access, class libraries that handle graphical user interface programming, and class libraries that implement data structures.

Other examples of graphical user interface class libraries are the Microsoft Foundation Classes and Borland's Object Windows Library, both of which are class libraries used for developing Windows applications.

This section introduces several of the features that are offered by the GNU C++ class library.

Streams

The GNU iostream library, called `libio`, implements GNU C++'s standard input and output facilities. This library is similar to the I/O libraries that are supplied by other C++ compilers. The main parts of the iostream library are the input, output, and error streams. These correspond to the standard input, output, and error streams that are found in C and are called `cin`, `cout`, and `cerr`, respectively. The streams can be written to and read from using the << operator for output and the >> operator for input.

The following program uses the iostream library to perform its input and output:

```
#include <iostream.h>
int maim ()
{
        char name[10];
        cout << "Please enter your name.\n";
        cin >> name;
        cout << "Hello " << name << " how is it going?\n";
}
```

Strings

The GNU string class extends GNU C++'s string manipulation capabilities. The string class essentially replaces the character array definitions that existed in C and all the string functions that go along with the character arrays.

27

PROGRAMMING
IN C++

The string class adds UNIX shell type string operators to the C++ language, as well as a large number of additional operators. Table 27.4 lists many of the operators that are available with the string class.

TABLE 27.4. STRING CLASS OPERATORS.

Operator	Meaning
str1 == str2	Returns TRUE if str1 is equal to str2
str1 != str2	Returns TRUE if str1 is not equal to str2
str1 < str2	Returns TRUE if str1 is less than str2
str1 <= str2	Returns TRUE if str1 is less than or equal to str2
str1 > str2	Returns TRUE if str1 is greater than str2
str1 >= str2	Returns TRUE if str1 is greater than or equal to str2
compare(str1,str2)	Compares str1 to str2 without considering the case of the characters
str3 = str1 + str2	Stores the result of str1 concatenated with str2 into str3

A number of other operators are available in the string class for performing different types of string comparisons, concatenations, and substring extraction and manipulation.

Random Numbers

Classes are provided in the GCC C++ class library that allow you to generate several different kinds of random numbers. The classes used to generate these numbers are the Random class and the RNG class.

Data Collection

The class library provides two different classes that perform data collection and analysis functions. The two classes are SampleStatistic and SampleHistogram. The SampleStatistic class provides a way of collecting samples and also provides numerous statistical functions that can perform calculations on the collected data. Some of the calculations that can be performed are mean, variance, standard deviation, minimum, and maximum.

The SampleHistogram class is derived from the SampleStatistic class and supports the collection and display of samples in bucketed intervals.

Linked Lists

The GNU C++ library supports two kinds of linked lists: single linked lists implemented by the SLList class, and doubly linked lists implemented by the DLList class. Both of these types of lists support all the standard linked list operations. A summary of the operations that these classes support is shown in Table 27.5.

TABLE 27.5. LIST OPERATORS.

Operator	*Description*
list.empty()	Returns TRUE if list is empty
list.length()	Returns the number of elements in list
list.prepend(a)	Places a at the front of list
list.append(a)	Places a at the end of list
list.join(list2)	Appends list2 to list, destroying list2 in the process
a = list.front()	Returns a pointer to the element that is stored at the head of the list
a = list.rear()	Returns a pointer to the element that is stored at the end of the list
a = list.remove_front()	Deletes and returns the element that is stored at the front of the list
list.del_front()	Deletes the first element without returning it
list.clear()	Deletes all items from list
list.ins_after(i, a)	Inserts a after position i in the list
list.del_after(i)	Deletes the element following position i in the list

Doubly linked lists also support the operations listed in Table 27.6.

TABLE 27.6. DOUBLY LINKED LIST OPERATORS.

Operator	*Description*
a = list.remove_rear()	Deletes and returns the element stored at the end of the list
list.del_real()	Deletes the last element, without returning it
list.ins_before(i, a)	Inserts a before position i in the list
list.del(i, dir)	Deletes the element at the current position and then moves forward one position if dir is positive and backward one position if dir is 0 or negative

27

PROGRAMMING
IN C++

Plex Classes

Plex classes are classes that behave like arrays but are much more powerful. Plex classes have the following properties:

- They have arbitrary upper and lower index bounds.
- They can dynamically expand in both the lower and upper bound directions.
- Elements may be accessed by indices. Unlike typical arrays, bounds checking is performed at runtime.
- Only elements that have been specifically initialized or added can be accessed.

Four different types of Plexes are defined: the FPlex, the XPlex, the RPlex, and the MPlex. The FPlex is a Plex that can grow or shrink only within declared bounds. An XPlex can dynamically grow in any direction without any restrictions. An RPlex is almost identical to an XPlex, but it has better indexing capabilities. Finally, the MPlex is the same as an RPlex except that it allows elements to be logically deleted and restored.

Table 27.7 lists some of the operations that are valid on all four of the Plexes.

TABLE 27.7. OPERATIONS DEFINED FOR PlexES.

Operation	Description
Plex b(a)	Assigns a copy of Plex a to Plex b
b = a	Copies Plex a into b
a.length()	Returns the number of elements in a
a.empty()	Returns TRUE if a has no elements
a.full()	Returns TRUE if a is full
a.clear()	Removes all the elements from a
a.append(b)	Appends Plex b to the high part of a
a.prepend(b)	Prepends Plex b to the low part of a
a.fill(z)	Sets all elements of a equal to z
a.valid(i)	Returns TRUE if i is a valid index into a
a.low_element()	Returns a pointer to the element in the lowest position in a
a.high_element()	Returns a pointer to the element in the highest position in a

Plexes are a very useful class on which many of the other classes in the GNU C++ class library are based. Some of the Stack, Queue, and Linked list types are built on top of the Plex class.

Stacks

The Stacks class implements the standard version of a last-in-first-out (LIFO) stack. Three different implementations of stacks are offered by the GNU C++ class library: the VStack, the XPStack, and the SLStack. The VStack is a fixed-size stack, meaning that you must specify an upper bound on the size of the stack when you first create it. The XPStack and the SLStack are both dynamically sized stacks that are implemented in a slightly different way.

Table 27.8 lists the operations that can be performed on the Stacks classes.

TABLE 27.8. Stack CLASS OPERATORS.

Operator	Description
Stack st	Declares st to be a stack
Stack st(sz)	Declares st to be a stack of size sz
st.empty()	Returns TRUE if stack is empty
st.full()	Returns TRUE if stack is full
st.length()	Returns the number of elements in stack
st.push(x)	Puts element x onto the top of the stack
x = st.pop()	Removes and returns the top element from the stack
st.top()	Returns a pointer to the top element in the stack
st.del_top()	Deletes the top element from the stack without returning it
st.clear()	Deletes all elements from stack

Queues

The Queue class implements a standard version of a first-in-first-out (FIFO) queue. Three different kinds of queue are provided by the GNU C++ class library: the VQueue, the XPQueue, and the SLQueue. The VQueue is a fixed-size queue, so you must specify an upper bound on the size of this kind of queue when you first create it. The XPQueue and the SLQueue are both dynamically sized queues, so no upper bound is required. The operations supported by the Queue classes are listed in Table 27.9.

TABLE 27.9. Queue CLASS OPERATORS.

Operator	Description
Queue q	Declares q to be a queue
Queue q(*sz*)	Declares q to be a queue of size *sz*
q.empty()	Returns TRUE if q is empty
q.full()	Returns TRUE if q is full
q.length()	Returns the number of elements in q
q.enq(*x*)	Adds the *x* element to q
x = q.deq()	Removes and returns an element from q
q.front()	Returns a pointer to the front of q
q.del_front()	Removes an element from q and does not return the result
q.clear	Removes all elements from the queue

In addition to the normal kind of queue that is discussed in this section, the GNU C++ class library also supports double-ended queues and priority queues. Both of these types of queues have similar behavior to the regular queue. The double-ended queue adds operators for returning a pointer to the rear of the queue and deleting elements from the rear of the queue. The priority queues are arranged so that a user has fast access to the least element in the queue. They support additional operators that allow for searching for elements in the queue.

Sets

The Set class is used to store groups of information. The only restriction on this information is that no duplicate elements are allowed. The class library supports several different implementations of sets. All of the implementations support the same operators. These operators are shown in Table 27.10.

TABLE 27.10. Set OPERATORS.

Operator	Description
Set s	Declares a set named s that is initially empty
Set s(sz)	Declares a set named s that is initially empty and has a set maximum size of sz
s.empty()	Returns TRUE if s is empty
s.length()	Returns the number of elements in s

Operator	Description
`i = s.add(z)`	Adds `z` to `s`, returning its index value
`s.del(z)`	Deletes `z` from `s`
`s.clear()`	Removes all elements from `s`
`s.contains(z)`	Returns TRUE if `z` is in `s`
`s.(i)`	Returns a pointer to the element indexed by `i`
`i = a.first()`	Returns the index of the first item in the set
`s.next(i)`	Makes `i` equal to the index of the next element in `s`
`i = s.seek(z)`	Sets `i` to the index of `z` if `z` is in `s`, and 0 otherwise
`set1 == set2`	Returns TRUE if `set1` contains all the same elements as `set2`
`set1 != set2`	Returns TRUE if `set1` does not contain all the same elements as `set2`
`set1 <= set2`	Returns TRUE if `set1` is a subset of `set2`
`set1 ¦= set2`	Adds all elements of `set2` to `set1`
`set1 -= set2`	Deletes all the elements that are contained in `set2` from `set1`
`set1 &= set2`	Deletes all elements from `set1` that occur in `set1` and not in `set2`

The class library contains another class that is similar to sets. This class is known as the bag. A bag is a group of elements that can be in any order (just as is the case with sets) but in which there can also be duplicates. Bags use all the operators that sets use except for the ==, !=, ¦=, <=, ¦=, -=, and &= operators. In addition, bags add two new operators for dealing with elements that are in the bag more than once. These new operators are shown in Table 27.11.

TABLE 27.11. ADDITIONAL OPERATORS FOR BAGS.

Operator	Description
`b.remove(z)`	Deletes all occurrences of `z` from `b`
`b.nof(z)`	Returns the number of occurrences of `z` that are in `b`

Many other classes available in the GNU C++ class library provide functions other than those listed here. In addition to what comes with the compiler, many other freely available class libraries can be useful, as well.

Summary

C++ offers many advantages over C. Some of these advantages come from the concepts of object-oriented programming, and others come from the highly flexible class libraries that are available to C++ programmers. This chapter gives a brief introduction to object-oriented programming and also talks about the C++ features that exist in the GNU C compiler and the GNU debugger.

One problem that has existed with C++ for quite some time is the lack of freely available C++ development tools. You may notice that the number of free tools available for C++ programming is much smaller than the number available for C, but the tide is turning. As more and more people choose C++ over C, the number of tools and class libraries available keeps increasing. The tool support has reached the stage where learning C++ in the Linux environment is something that you can enjoy rather than avoid. See the following chapters for related information:

Programming C under Linux is discussed in Chapter 26, "Programming in C."

Perl, a handle language for quick programming tasks, is discussed in Chapter 28, "Perl."

The compilers available for Linux are discussed in Chapter 30, "Other Compilers."

Perl

by Tim Parker

CHAPTER

28

Perl, which stands for Practical Extraction and Report Language, is an interpreted programming language that was developed by Larry Wall. Perl was initially designed to make scanning and manipulating text files easier than it is in languages such as awk. This chapter includes the following topics:

- What Perl is
- Creating and executing Perl programs
- Data, variables, and arrays
- Perl programming constructs
- Perl functions

After reading this chapter, you should be familiar with some of the advantages that Perl offers over other programming languages. You should also be able to write simple Perl programs to help you in your day-to-day interactions with Linux.

What Is Perl?

As stated, Perl was originally created to make scanning and manipulating text files easier. People who are familiar with the awk programming language (see Chapter 25, "gawk") will not be surprised to learn that Perl borrowed many of its features from awk. Perl also includes some of the best features of C, sed, and the UNIX shell languages such as bash and tcsh.

Perl is very similar to the shell programming languages both in syntax and in function. There are, however, a few differences worth mentioning. One of the biggest differences between how Perl works and how shell programs work is that Perl is not purely an interpreted language. Perl programs are actually read in full and stored in an intermediate form before they are executed. Shell programs are read and executed one command at a time. This offers two advantages for Perl over shell programs. First, Perl programs execute much faster than shell programs. This is because the Perl interpreter does all the syntax checking and stripping of comments before the code execution is started. Second, you don't have to worry about a large shell program stopping halfway through its execution as a result of a syntax error because all the code is parsed before it starts executing.

The fact that Perl is not a pure interpreted language also has one disadvantage. For small programs whose execution time is not that large, the extra compile time involved in using Perl actually makes it slower than using a shell language. This is a relatively small problem and one that few people actually notice.

Creating and Executing Perl Programs

The steps you take to create and execute a Perl program are very similar to those used in creating and executing a Linux shell program. Perl programs consist of one or more Perl commands that are placed into a text file. The first thing you must do to create a Perl program is create a file in which to put Perl commands. You can do this using your text editor of choice. Let's start with a very simple example of a Perl program. The following Perl program, called `hello`, prints a greeting on the screen.

```
#!/usr/bin/perl
print "Hi there!\n";
```

There are several things worth mentioning about this example. The first is the strange-looking first line of the program. This line tells the shell program what program to run to execute the code contained in the file.

The second line of the program prints `Hi there!`, followed by a new line on the screen. C programmers will notice how much this line looks like C code.

You have one more step to take before the program will actually work, and that is to change the permissions on the file so it is executable. This is done by entering the following command:

```
chmod +x hello
```

You can now run the program by typing the following on the command line:

```
hello
```

Running this program causes the Perl interpreter to be invoked. The Perl interpreter parses the whole program and then executes the compiled code.

This is the standard way of running a Perl program. You can also run the `hello` program by invoking Perl on the command line and passing the `hello` code to it as a command-line parameter. This is done by entering the following command:

```
perl hello
```

Handling Data in Perl

At the simplest level, Perl deals with two different kinds of data: numbers and strings. This section describes how Perl handles these two forms of data and also how each can be used in Perl programs. Let's start things off with a description of how variables are used in Perl programs.

Variables

Variables in Perl are similar in function and syntax to variables found in the shell programming languages. The biggest difference is that in the shell languages you get the value of a variable by preceding it with a dollar sign, and you assign a value to a variable by using the variable name without a dollar sign in front of it.

In Perl, you *always* use a dollar sign in front of the variable name no matter whether you are assigning a value to the variable or getting the value of the variable. The following command assigns the value hello to the variable named greeting.

```
$greeting="hello";
```

In the shell languages, this command is written as follows:

```
greeting="hello"
```

or

```
set greeting = "hello" (when using tcsh)
```

Spaces on either side of the equal sign don't matter to Perl (unlike the shell programming language) so you can use whichever method is most comfortable and familiar to you. Another difference is that you can perform integer operations directly on a variable without using another command like expr. For example, the command

```
$a = 1 + 2;
```

assigns the value of 3 to the variable $a. If you enter the following two commands

```
$a = 1 + 2;
$b = 3 * $a;
```

the $b variable is assigned a value of 9.

This is the expected result, but how does Perl know that $a is a numeric value and not a string? The answer is that it does not know. Whenever a variable or literal is used as an argument to a numeric operator, it is converted to a number. In this case, there is no problem because the value stored in $a is a number. There would be a problem, however, if the value stored in $a was a string that contained a character such as b because this type of string cannot be converted to a numeric value. Perl handles this situation in a not so elegant way. If the value is not convertible to a number, it simply makes it equal to 0. By default, Perl does not even warn you about this conversion. If you invoke Perl with a -w command-line option, though, it will warn you when this type of conversion takes place.

Numbers

Perl stores all numeric data as floating-point values. You can use integers in your Perl programs, but Perl treats them all as floating-point numbers.

Perl provides a set of operators that can be used to perform comparisons between two numeric values and for performing the standard mathematical operations on numbers. Table 28.1 lists some of the operators that Perl provides for numeric data.

TABLE 28.1. NUMERIC OPERATORS.

Operator	Description
$a = op1 + op2	Stores the value of op1 plus op2 into $a
$a = op1 - op2	Stores the value of op1 minus op2 into $a
$a = op1 * op2	Stores the value of op1 times op2 into $a
$a = op1 / op2	Stores the value of op1 divided by op2 into $a
$a = op1 ** op2	Stores the value of op1 to the power of op2 into $a
$a = op1 % op2	Stores the value of op1 modulus op2 into $a
op1 == op2	Returns True if op1 is equal to op2
op1 != op2	Returns True if op1 is not equal to op2
op1 < op2	Returns True if op1 is less than op2
op1 > op2	Returns True if op1 is greater than op2
op1 <= op2	Returns True if op1 is less than or equal to op2
op1 >= op2	Returns True if op1 is greater than or equal to op2

28

PERL

Strings

Strings are sequences of one or more characters . Usually strings contain alphanumeric characters (such as the numbers from 0 to 9), the upper- and lowercase alphabet, and a handful of punctuation characters. Perl does not distinguish between these characters and nonprintable characters. This means that you can actually use Perl to scan binary files.

Strings are represented in a Perl program in one of two ways: You can enclose a string in double quotation marks or you can enclose a string in single quotation marks. When a string is enclosed in double quotation marks, it behaves in a similar way to strings that are in double quotation marks in C. A backslash can be used in a double quoted string to represent special control characters. A list of the backslash special control characters is shown in Table 28.2.

TABLE 28.2. PERL'S SPECIAL CONTROL CHARACTERS.

Character	Description
\a	Causes an audible beep
\b	Inserts a backspace
\cD	Allows you to put control characters in a string (in this case Ctrl+D)
\f	Inserts a formfeed
\e	Inserts an escape character
\E	Terminates an \L or \U special control character
\l	Causes the next letter to be lowercase
\L	Causes all characters following it until the next \E to be lowercase
\n	Inserts a newline character
\r	Inserts a return character
\t	Inserts a tab character
\\	Inserts a backslash character
\"	Inserts a double quote character
\u	Causes the next letter to be uppercase
\U	Causes all characters following it until the next \E to be uppercase

Variable substitution can occur within a string that is enclosed in double quotation marks as well. For example, if you define a variable as

```
$name="Doreen";
```

that variable can be substituted into a greeting displayed on the screen by typing the following Perl command:

```
print "Hello $name, how are you?\n";
```

This command results in the following output to be displayed on the screen:

```
Hello Doreen, how are you?
```

Strings enclosed in single quotation marks differ from strings enclosed in double quotation marks because the single quotation marks hide most special characters from the Perl interpreter. The only special characters that single quotes do not hide completely are the single quote character (') and the backslash character (\). When Perl encounters a single quote character within a string that is enclosed in single quotation marks, it assumes that it is the end of the string. This means that if you want to put a single quote in a string that is enclosed in single quotes, you must precede it with a backslash. The same rule applies if you want to put a backslash into a string enclosed in single quotes.

For example, if you want to print the string Don't do that! to the screen by enclosing it in single quotes, enter the following command:

```
print 'Don\'t do that!',"\n";
```

> **NOTE**
>
> Remember that if you put a newline character into a single quoted string, it just prints \n and doesn't insert a newline character.

Just as is the case with numbers, Perl provides several operators that can be used to manipulate and compare strings. Table 28.3 lists Perl's string operators.

TABLE 28.3. PERL'S STRING OPERATORS.

Operator	Description
op1 . op2	Concatenates op1 and op2
op1 x op2	Repeats op1, op2 times
op1 eq op2	Returns True if op1 equals op2
op1 ge op2	Returns True if op1 is greater than or equal to op2
op1 gt op2	Returns True if op1 is greater than op2
op1 le op2	Returns True if op1 is less than or equal to op2
op1 lt op2	Returns True if op1 is less than op2
op1 ne op2	Returns True if op1 is not equal to op2

File Operators

Just like the shell programming languages, Perl has a number of operators that exist only to test for certain conditions that exist in directories and files. The most useful of these operators are listed in Table 28.4.

TABLE 28.4. PERL FILE OPERATORS.

Operator	Description
-B	File is a binary file
-d	File is a directory

continues

TABLE 28.4. CONTINUED

Operator	Description
-e	File exists
-f	File is an ordinary file
-r	File is readable
-s	File has a nonzero size
-T	File is a text file
-w	File is writable
-x	File is executable
-z	File has zero size

These file operators can be used in any Perl expression. For example, the following code uses an `if` statement to decide if the `.profile` file exists in the current directory.

```
if (-e ".profile") {
        print ".profile is there\n";
}
```

Arrays

An array is an indexed list of data elements. Perl provides two different kinds of arrays. The first kind of array is similar to the arrays that are available in most high-level languages. This kind of array stores single data elements (numbers or strings) into a variable that can store any number of elements. You can get the elements you store in this variable by using the offset value of the element you are trying to find. This means that you can assign a number or a string value to an offset in an array and later use that offset to retrieve that value. For example, the following Perl statement assigns the strings January, 1st, 1999 to the array named date

```
@date = ("January", "1st", "1999");
```

> **NOTE**
>
> The number of elements you can have in the array is limited by the amount of memory you have on your system.

If you later want to retrieve one of the values you have placed into the date array, you can do so by stating the array name and the offset of the element you want. When you are retrieving the value of an array element, you must precede the name of the array with a $ instead of the @ that you used to define the array. This is because you are now referring to a single array element, which is really the same as a regular variable. For example, to assign the value of January, which is the first element in the array, to a variable called month, write the following command:

```
$month=$date[0];
```

> **NOTE**
>
> Like many Linux utilities and both C and C++, Perl starts its array indexes at offset 0. This means that an array of length 5 would have the elements [0], [1], [2], [3], and [4].

The second kind of array that is available in Perl is called an associative array (also called hashes with Perl 5 and later versions. Associative arrays are like normal arrays— they store data elements and have an index. Unlike normal arrays, the index or key is defined by the user and can be a number or a string.

Because you can define the key values for associative arrays as well as the data associated with each of these key values, assigning and accessing data from an associative array is somewhat different than it is with normal arrays. To assign a value to an associative array, you must also provide the key that you want that value to be associated with. Just as with normal arrays, associative arrays have a special symbol that is used whenever you are performing operations on the entire associative array. You usually assign variables only to elements of an associative array as opposed to dealing with the entire array all at once. The following command assigns the value hello to the associative array named words, with a key value of greeting:

```
$words{"greeting"} = "hello";
```

An operation that applies to the entire associative array looks like the following:

```
%words2 = %words;
```

This command assigns the entire contents of the words associative array to the words2 associative array.

28

PERL

To retrieve a value from the `words` associative array, use the following command:

```
$value=$words{"greeting"};
```

This assigns the string `hello` to the `value` variable.

In addition to the assignment operations that can be performed on normal arrays, associative arrays have four more operations: `keys`, `values`, `delete`, and `each`.

The `keys` operator returns a list of all the keys that are defined in the specified associative array. The following commands result in `keyarray` being equal to (`"greeting"`, `"greeting2"`).

```
$words("greeting") = "hello";
$words("greeting2") = "good-bye";
@keyarray = keys(%words);
```

The first two commands assign values to individual elements in the associative array `words`. The first command assigns `hello` with a key value of `greeting` to the array, and the second command assigns `good-bye` with a key value of `greeting2` to the array.

The last command assigns all the key values contained in the `words` associative array to the normal array called `keyarray`. Notice the `%` in front of the `words` variable in the `keys` operator. This means that the operation being performed applies to the entire associative array and not just one element of the array.

> **NOTE**
>
> The value of `keyarray` that is returned by the preceding commands could actually be (`"greeting2"`, `"greeting"`), because values in associative arrays are not stored in any particular order.

Another operator that exists for use with associative arrays is the `values` operator. The `values` operator returns a list of all the values contained in the specified associative array. The following commands result in `valuearray` being equal to (`123.5,105`) or (`105,123.5`).

```
$cost{"regular"} = 123.5;
$cost("sale") = 105;
@valuearray = values(%cost);
```

The first two commands again assign values to individual elements in the `cost` associative array. The last command executes the `values` operator on the `cost` associative array and assigns the results to the normal array called `valuearray`.

The delete operator enables you to delete elements from an associative array. You call the delete operator on a single associative array element, and it deletes both the value of that element and the key value for that element. The following commands illustrate how the delete operator works.

```
%coffee = ("instant",5.35,"ground",6.99);
delete $coffee{"ground"};
```

The first command assigns two elements to the associative array coffee. One of the elements has a key value of instant and a value of 5.35, and the other element has a key value of ground and a value of 6.99. The delete operator deletes both the key value and the value of the element in the coffee array that has a key value of ground.

The each operator enables you to easily iterate through each element that is stored in an associative array. When you run the each operator on an associative array, it returns the first element of the array. Successive calls of each on the same array return the next element in the array until the last element is reached. The following code goes through the steps the coffee array used in the last example and displays the price of each kind of coffee stored in the array.

```
while (($type, $cost) = each(%coffee)) {
        print "The price of $type coffee is $cost\n";
}
```

Perl Programming Constructs

Perl provides many of the same programming constructs that are found in all high-level programming languages. This section describes each of the programming constructs provided by Perl.

Statement Blocks

Perl statement blocks consist of one or more Perl statements enclosed in curly braces. The following code shows the sample syntax for a Perl statement block:

```
{
        statement1;
        statement2;
        ...
}
```

Statement blocks can be used anywhere that a single Perl statement can be used. They are most commonly used to group statements that are to be executed as part of an iteration statement, such as a for or while statement or as part of a conditional statement, such as an if statement.

if Statements

Perl's `if` statement is used to execute statement blocks conditionally. The syntax of the `if` statement is similar to the `if` statement syntax used in C. This syntax is shown by the following:

```
if (expression) {
        statements;
}
```

In this form, the `if` statement evaluates the expression, and if the result of that evaluation is True, it executes the statements contained in the statement block. If the expression evaluates to False, the statements in the statement block are not evaluated.

The `if` statement can be optionally accompanied by one or more `else if` clauses and one `else` clause. The syntax for a statement that contains two `else if` clauses and an `else` clause is shown in the following code:

```
if (expression1) {
        statements;
} elsif (expression2) (
        statements;
} elsif (expression3) {
        statements;
} else {
        statements;
}
```

In this form, the `if` statement evaluates expression1, and if the result of that evaluation is True, it executes the statements in the first statement block. If expression1 evaluates to False, expression2 is evaluated. If expression2 evaluates to True, the statements in the second statement block are executed. If expression2 evaluates to False, the process is repeated for the third expression. If expression3 evaluates to False, the statements in the last statement block are executed. The important thing to remember here is that one and only one of the statement blocks is executed.

> **NOTE**
>
> In Perl, an expression evaluates to True if it has a value other than zero and to False if it has a value of zero. This is different than utilities like test, which are the opposite. The reason for the difference is because Perl uses the C language's syntax for consistency among programming languages.

The following example illustrates the use of an if statement:

```
print "Please enter your name or \"help\" for a \n";
print "description of this program\n";
$name=<STDIN>;
chop($name);
if ( $name eq "" ) {
        print "This program cannot proceed without your name.\n";
        exit;
} elsif ( $name eq "help") {
        print "This program reads in the user's name and \n";
        print "prints a welcome message on the screen if the\n";
        print "name that was entered was not null.\n";
} else {
        print "Hello $name, welcome to Perl.\n";
}
```

This program asks for your name by displaying a prompt to the screen and waiting for you to enter your name on the command line. The third line of the program assigns whatever you type on the command line to the $name variable. The if statement then checks to make sure that you typed something when you were asked for your name. If the $name variable is empty, the program prints a statement that informs you that you must enter your name if you want to proceed. Next, the statement checks to see if you typed the name help on the command line. If you did, the program displays a description of itself to the screen. If the name you typed was not null and was not help, the program prints a welcome message.

A new command called chop is introduced in this example. The chop command removes the last character from the argument that is passed to it. You need to do this in the example because the last character of the entered name is a newline character. If you don't remove the newline character, your last print command prints the following output if you, for example, type in the name John on the command line:

```
Hello John
, welcome to Perl.
```

unless Statements

The Perl unless statement is the opposite of the Perl if statement. It evaluates an expression, and if the expression returns a value of False, it executes its statement block. The syntax of the unless statement is

```
unless (expression) {
        statements;
}
```

28

PERL

Any statement you can write with an `unless` statement can also be written as an `if` statement. The only difference is that you have to negate the expression when you rewrite it as an `if`. For this reason, the `unless` statement is not used very often. The following code illustrates a possible use of an `unless` statement.

```
print "Please enter your account number.\n"
$account = <STDIN>
unless ($account < 1000 ) {
        print "Since you are a preferred customer you will\n"
        print "get a 10% discount\n"
}
```

This program asks for your account number, and if the account number is greater than or equal to 1000, it displays the message indicating that you are entitled to a 10% discount. If your account number is less than 1000, the program continues processing after the end of the `unless` statement.

for Statements

So far, the only Perl programming constructs we've looked at have been conditional statements. The `for` statement is an example of a Perl iteration statement. It is used to iterate over a statement block a specified number of times. The syntax of the `for` statement is as follows:

```
for (initialize_expression; test_expression; increment_expression) {
        statements;
}
```

The `initialize_expression` is used to initialize the `increment` variable that is being used by the statement. This expression is evaluated only the first time the `for` statement executes. The `test_expression` evaluates a conditional expression that is used to determine whether to execute the statement block. If the `test_expression` evaluates to True, the statement block is executed; if it evaluates to False, the statement block is not executed. The `test_expression` is executed before each iteration of the `for` statement. The last expression in the `for` statement is the `increment_expression`. This expression is typically used to change the `increment` variable. This expression is executed after each execution of the statement block.

The following example illustrates the processing performed by a `for` statement:

```
for ($i = 0; $i < 20; $i = $i + 2) {
        print $i * 2, " ";
}
print "\nBedeba bedeba, That's all folks.\n"
```

This program prints the value of $i * 2 each time through the loop. Before the loop is executed the first time, $i is assigned a value of 0. Next the value of $i is compared to 20 and because it is less than 20, the statement block is executed. The statement block prints 0 followed by a space on the screen. Now the increment expression is evaluated. This results in $i being assigned the value of 2. The for statement continues executing in this manner until the test_expression evaluates to False (when $i is no longer less than 20). When this happens, the program continues executing at the statement that directly follows the for statement—in this case, the That's all folks print statement.

The output generated by running this program is as follows:

```
0 4 8 12 16 20 24 28 32 36
Bedeba bedeba, That's all folks.
```

for statements are often used in conjunction with fixed-size arrays. This is because the iterative nature of a for statement is naturally suited for printing and performing other calculations on this kind of array. For example, the following code fragment can be used to print all the values in an array of size 50 to the screen:

```
for ($i=0; $i < 50; $i = $i + 1) {
        print $array[$i], "\n"
}
```

When you do not know the size of an array (which is often the case when you are writing programs in Perl), the foreach or while statements are more useful for performing array manipulation.

foreach Statements

Another iteration statement available in Perl is the foreach statement. This statement is very similar to the for statement in the bash and pdksh languages and the foreach statement in the tcsh language. It executes its statement block for each element in the list that is specified as its second argument. The syntax for the foreach statement is

```
foreach $i (@list) {
    statements;
}
```

The @list variable can be passed to the foreach statement either as a variable or as a list of elements that you type directly as the second argument to the foreach statement. The following is an example of the foreach statement:

```
@myarray = (5,10,15,20,25);
foreach $i (@myarray) {
        print $i * 3, " ";
}
print "\n";
```

28

PERL

This program iterates through each element in @myarray and prints the result of three times that array element on the screen. The output generated by running this program is as follows:

```
15 30 45 60 75
```

Another interesting use of the foreach statement is to use it to change all the values in an array. This can be done by assigning a value to the variable that is being used by the foreach statement. For example, the following code multiplies each array element in the array by three and actually stores the result of this back into the array.

```
@myarray = (5,10,15,20,25);
foreach $i (@myarray) {
        $i = $i * 3;
}
```

After this code executes, @myarray is equal to (15,30,45,60,75).

while Statements

The while statement is another form of iteration statement that Perl provides. The while statement executes its statement block while a conditional expression is True. The syntax for the while statement is

```
while (expression) {
        statements;
}
```

When the while statement executes, it evaluates its expression. If the result is True, the statements contained in the statement block are executed. If the result of the expression is False, Perl goes to the first line after the while statement's statement block and continues there. Here is an example of the while statement:

```
$i = 0;
@temparray = (1,2,3,4,5,6,7);
while ($temparray[$i]) {
        print $temparray[$i];
        $i = $i + 1;
}
```

This example simply prints each of the array elements contained in @temparray to the screen. Notice that you do not need to know how many elements are in the array. The while statement continues executing until the value of $temparray[$i] is undefined, which occurs when it tries to access an element that is outside the bounds of the array.

until Statements

The until statement is very similar to the while statement. The difference is that the until statement executes its statement block only until its conditional expression becomes True, and the while statement executes its statement block while its conditional expression is True. The following program contains an example of the until statement:

```perl
$i = 0;
until ($i > 10) {
        print "$i ";
        $i = $i + 1;
}
```

This statement continues to execute and print the value of $i until $i is larger than 10. The output from this command is

```
0 1 2 3 4 5 6 7 8 9 10
```

Any until statement can also be written as a while statement. For this reason, the until statement is not used very often. The example shown for the until statement can be rewritten as a while statement, as shown by the following code:

```perl
$i = 0;
while ($i <= 10 ) {
        print "$i ";
        $i = $i + 1;
}
```

Functions

You have already seen some of the built-in Perl functions, such as print, but you have not seen how to create your own functions. Perl refers to functions that you create as subroutines. The syntax for creating a subroutine is

```perl
sub subroutine_name {
        statements;
}
```

The subroutine_name is a name you provide and is the name you use when calling the subroutine from your Perl code. The statements in the statement block are the statements that are executed every time you make a call to your subroutine.

To familiarize yourself with the syntax for creating a function, take a look at the following function which multiplies the values that are stored in the variables $num1 and $num2 each time it is called.

```
sub mult {
        print "The result of $num1 * $num2 is ",$num1 * $num2, "\n";
}
```

To invoke this function, you must precede the name of the function with an ampersand (&). For example, the following program assigns values to the $num1 and $num2 variables and invokes the mult function.

```
$num1 = 5;
$num2 = 10;
&mult;
```

Running this program results in the following output being displayed on the screen:

```
The result of 5 * 10 is 50
```

If this were all functions could do, they would not be incredibly useful. The real power of functions doesn't come into play until you start defining them so that they can accept arguments and return values.

Passing Arguments to Functions

Passing arguments to functions increases their usefulness a great deal. This is because you do not have to know the names of the variables used by the function if they are being passed in as arguments. If you rewrite the mult function so that it accepts arguments, you can use it to multiply any two numbers together instead of just the numbers stored in the $num1 and $num2 variables. The following is the mult function after it has been rewritten to use arguments.

```
sub mult2 {
        print "The result of $_[0] * $_[1] is ", $_[0] * $_[1], "\n";
}
```

The variables $_[0] and $_[1], which are the first and second elements of the @_ array, are used to store the values of the first two arguments passed to the function. The following line of code uses the new mult2 function to multiply two numbers together:

```
&mult2(14,20);
```

When this command is executed, the first argument passes to mult2 (14) and is put into the first element of the @_ array; the second argument (20) is put into the second element of the @_ array. The mult2 function prints the following message on the screen:

```
The result of 14 * 20 is 280
```

Using Return Values

What happens if you do not want to print the results of the `mult2` function to the screen but instead want to use the result in your program? Perl handles this problem by using a return value. Every function you write in Perl has a return value. By default, the return value is equal to the result of the last statement evaluated in the function. The `mult2` function returns the result of the Perl `print` function, which, if everything works properly, is equal to 1. You can rewrite the `mult` function once again so that it returns the result of the multiplication.

```
sub mult3 {
        $_[0] * $_[1];
}
```

The following code uses the `mult3` function to find the results of a multiplication:

```
$num1 = 5;
$num2 = 10;
$result = &mult3($num1 $num2);
print "The answer is $result\n"
```

When this program is executed, the result of the multiplication performed by the `mult3` function is returned and stored in the `result` variable. The program then prints the result to the screen.

Perl Operators

You have seen quite a few Perl operators in the examples in this chapter. The `print` command that's been used throughout this chapter is one example of a Perl operator. You also saw the Perl operators `keys`, `values`, `each`, and `delete` which are used to perform operations on associative arrays. Perl actually provides an unbelievable number of operators. To get a good idea of what operators are available or to get a complete listing of the Perl operators, refer to the Perl manual page.

Converting Programs to Perl

The Perl language is similar to other programming languages that come with Linux in the kinds of things it can do. The most significant of these languages are `gawk` and `sed`. The Perl distribution comes with two utility programs that allow you to convert `sed` and `gawk` programs into Perl programs. Because Perl is a superset of both these languages, any programs that can be written in `gawk` or `sed` can also be written in Perl. The two programs that perform these conversions are called `a2p` for converting `gawk` programs to Perl and `s2p` for converting `sed` programs to Perl.

28

PERL

> **NOTE**
>
> The reason that the gawk to Perl conversion utility is called a2p instead of g2p is that gawk is the GNU version of another program called awk.

To run the a2p program, simply enter the following command:

```
a2p gawk_program >perl_program
```

gawk_program is the gawk program you want to convert to Perl, and perl_program is the name you want to give to your new Perl program.

To run the s2p program, enter the following command:

```
s2p sed_program >perl_program
```

sed_program is the name of the sed program you want to convert to Perl, and perl_program is the name you want to give to your new Perl program.

Summary

This chapter introduces what is arguably the most powerful language available on Linux. Perl is a vast language. It contains operators that provide you with almost any function you could want to perform in the Linux environment. The size of the language makes becoming an expert Perl programmer difficult, but at the same time it isn't that hard to learn to use Perl for simpler tasks.

Although this chapter presents a fairly complete overview of the Perl language, it barely scratches the surface of the features that are available in Perl. If you want to learn more about Perl, refer to the Perl manual pages. You can also read more about other programming languages that are useful with Perl or find associated material in other chapters.

awk, a powerful pattern-action language that complements Perl, is discussed in Chapter 25, "gawk."

Tcl and Tk, both handy scripting utilities, are discussed in Chapter 29, "Introduction to Tcl and Tk."

CGI programming, which Perl is particularly well-suited for, is discussed in Chapter 52, "CGI Scripts."

Introduction to Tcl and Tk

by Tim Parker

In This Chapter

CHAPTER 29

What Is Tcl?

Tcl stands for Tool Command Language. (It is pronounced "tickle.") It is a scripting language similar to the shell scripting languages introduced in Chapter 14, "Shell Programming." Tcl can be used to quickly write text-based application programs.

Tcl was developed by John Ousterhout, then of the University of California at Berkeley. Tcl is an interpreted language and therefore has the usual advantages and disadvantages of all interpreted languages. The key disadvantage of interpreted languages is that they execute much slower than compiled languages. The biggest advantage of interpreted languages is that developing applications using them are usually much faster than using compiled languages. This is because the programmer doesn't have to wait for code to compile and can see any changes made to the code almost instantly.

Tcl has a core set of built-in functions that provide the basic features of its programming language. The true power of Tcl, however, is that it is easily extendible. Application programmers can add functions to Tcl and can even imbed the Tcl function library directly into their applications. This gives programmers the power to include an interpretive scripting language directly in their own application without having to do any of the work of developing the language. This means that you can provide users of your application with all the commands that exist within Tcl and also any that you create and add to the Tcl library.

Invoking Tcl commands is done by starting up the Tcl shell, called `tclsh` (or on some systems, `tcl`). Once `tclsh` is started, we can enter Tcl commands directly into it. Straying slightly from the "hello world" example found in almost every introductory language text, the following example shows instead how to write `Hello there` to the screen:

```
puts stdout "Hello there"
```

This command contains three separate words. The first word in the command is the actual command name, `puts`. The `puts` command is an abbreviation for put string; it simply writes something to the device that is specified in the second word of the command. In this case the second word tells `puts` to write to the standard output device, which is typically the screen. The third word in the `puts` command is `"Hello there"`. The quotation marks tell Tcl to interpret everything contained within them as a single word.

NOTE

The default output device is `stdout` (standard output, usually the screen), so if you intend to write something to `stdout` using the `puts` command, the second argument is optional.

Even though this is a very simple example, it illustrates the basic command syntax of the Tcl language. There are obviously many more commands contained within Tcl, but the basic syntax of all Tcl commands is the same:

```
command parameter1 parameter2 ...
```

The command can be any of the built-in Tcl commands, or it can be a user-defined extension to the Tcl command set in the form of a Tcl procedure. In either case, the fundamental syntax remains unchanged.

What Is Tk?

Tk, which was also developed by Ousterhout, is a graphical user interface extension to Tcl. Tk is based on the X Window system and allows application developers to develop X Window-based applications much faster than they could using other X Window toolkits, such as Motif or Open Look. In many ways, you can think of Tk as similar to the Windows-based Visual language series (Visual Basic, for example).

Like Tcl, Tk also has a shell that enables you to enter commands to be interpreted. The Tk shell is a superset of the Tcl command shell. This means that anything you can do in the Tcl command shell can also be done in the Tk command shell. The big difference between the two is that the Tk command shell is designed to enable you to build X Window front ends to your applications.

The Tk command shell is called wish, which stands for windowing shell. You must be running an X Window application when you invoke wish. This is because when wish is invoked, it brings up a window that displays the results of any of the graphical commands it interprets.

Now that we have seen what the Tk environment looks like, let's try enhancing the earlier "Hello there" example by displaying Hello there in a button in the wish window. To accomplish this, we must first ensure that wish has been started. This is easily done by typing the following command into an Xterm window:

```
wish
```

This command brings up the wish window and also executes the Tk interpreter in the Xterm window. We can now type Tcl or Tk commands directly in the Xterm window. The commands necessary to print Hello there in a button in the wish window are as follows:

```
button .b -text "Hello there." -command exit
pack .b
```

Notice how the syntax of the command on the first line is essentially the same as the syntax of the `puts` command. It contains the command name followed by a number of arguments. The first argument is the name we are giving to the new button. The rest of the arguments passed to the `button` command are slightly different from the arguments shown in the Tcl version of the "Hello there" example. These arguments each consist of two parts. The first part tells Tk what the argument name is, and the second part tells Tk the value of the argument.

The second argument has the name `text`, and the value of the argument is the string we want to display in the button. The third argument has the name `command` and is used to specify the command that we want to execute when that button is pushed. In this example, we don't want anything to happen if the button is pushed, so we simply tell `wish` to exit from the current script.

The `button` command created a button widget that we called `.b`. To make the button appear in the `wish` window, we must tell Tk to display the button. This is done by the `pack` command.

In this example, the `pack` command has only one argument: the name of the button created in the first command. When the `pack` command is executed, a button with the string `Hello there` displayed in it appears in the `wish` window.

Two things about this example are worth discussing in more detail. The first is why we call the button `.b` instead of `b`, `bob`, or `button1`. The significance is not the actual text in the button name (this could, in fact, be `bob` or `button1`) but the period (`.`) preceding the name of the button.

The period notation is used to represent the widget hierarchy. Each widget is contained in another widget. The root widget, or the highest level widget, is contained in the `wish` window and is called `.` (this is analogous to the Linux directory structure, in which each directory has an owner or a parent directory and the root or highest level directory is named `/`). Each time a new widget is created, we must tell Tk which widget the new widget should be contained in. In the "Hello there" example, the container specified for the button widget was `.`, the root widget.

The second item of interest is the resizing of the `wish` window that occurs after entering the `pack` command. The `wish` window shrinks to a size that is just large enough to hold the button we've created. Tk causes the `wish` window to default to a size just large enough to hold whatever it has in it. Many commands can be used to change this behavior and customize how things are displayed on the screen. You will see some of these commands later in this chapter.

The Tcl Language

Now that you have seen examples of both Tcl and Tk in action, it is appropriate to take a step back and look at the underlying Tcl language in more detail. Tcl contains a rich set of programming commands that supports all the features found in most high-level languages. This section discusses many of these features and gives examples that explain how to use them.

Tcl Variables and Variable Substitution

Like the UNIX shell programming languages, Tcl supports the concept of variables. Variables are temporary storage places used to hold information that will be needed by a program at some later point in time. In Tcl, variable names can consist of any combination of printable characters.

Typically, variable names are meaningful names that describe the information being stored in them. For example, a variable that is being used to hold the monthly sales of a product might have one of the following names:

```
Monthly_sales
"Monthly sales"
```

> **NOTE**
>
> Quotation marks cause Tcl to ignore the whitespace characters (spaces and tabs) in the variable name and treat it as one word. This is discussed in the "Quotes" section of this chapter.

The value that is placed into a variable can also be any combination of printable characters. Possible values for the `Monthly_sales` variable are

```
"40,000"
40000
"refer to table 3"
```

The Tcl `set` command is used to assign values to variables. The `set` command can be passed either one or two arguments. When two arguments are passed to the `set` command, the first one is treated as the variable name and the second is the value to assign to that variable.

When the `set` command is used with only one argument, Tcl expects the argument to be the name of a variable, and the `set` command returns the value of that variable. The following command assigns the value of 40000 to the variable Monthlysales and then echoes the value to the screen:

```
set Monthlysales 40000
```

To print the value of the Monthlysales variable to the screen, type

```
set Monthlysales
```

All values that are assigned to variables are stored as character strings. If we define a variable to be equal to the integer 40, as in the following command

```
set num 40
```

the value 40 is represented as the character string 40, not as an integer.

So far you have seen how to set variables and how to display their values to the screen, but not how they are used with commands other than the set command. To use the value of a variable in another command, we must precede the variable name with an unquoted dollar sign ($). This tells Tcl to expect a variable name and to substitute the value of that variable for the variable name. The following example shows a simple use of variable substitution:

```
set Monthlysales 40000
expr $Monthlysales * 12
```

The first command assigns the value of 40000 to the variable Monthlysales. The expr command is used to perform mathematical evaluations of expressions. In this case it takes the value of the variable Monthlysales and multiplies it by 12.

Tcl Command Substitution

Command substitution provides a way of substituting the result of a Tcl command (or commands) into an argument of another command. The syntax for command substitution is to include the commands that are being substituted into square brackets, as follows:

```
set Monthlysales 40000
set Yearlyforecast [ expr Monthlysales * 12 ]
```

The first command once again sets the variable Monthlysales to the value of 40000. The second command makes use of command substitution to set the value of Yearlyforecast equal to the result of the command in the square braces.

In this example the substitute consists of only one command. Tcl allows the substitute to consist of any valid Tcl script, meaning that it can contain any number of Tcl commands.

Quotes

There may be times when you'll want to use commands containing special characters that you don't want Tcl to interpret. By quoting these particular characters, you hide them from the Tcl interpreter.

Three kinds of quoting can be used in Tcl scripts. The first is quoting with double quotation marks (`""`). This kind of quoting is used to hide whitespace characters and command separators from the Tcl interpreter.

Whenever there are two or more words that you want Tcl to treat as a single word, you can do so by surrounding the words with quotation marks. A good example of this type of quoting is when you want to create variable names that contain more than one word or you want to assign a value that contains more than one word to a variable, as follows:

```
set "Monthly sales" 40000

set Heading1 "Description of item"
```

The second kind of quoting uses the backslash character (`\`). This type of quoting can hide any single character from the interpreter. This form of quoting is most commonly used to hide special characters, such as `$`, from the Tcl interpreter. The following example illustrates the need for backslash quoting:

```
set Header1 "The cost is \$3.50"
```

In this example the `Header1` variable is being assigned the value `The cost is $3.50`. The quotation marks are necessary to hide the fact that there are four separate words contained in the character string. The backslash in this command tells the Tcl interpreter to treat the `$` as a regular character instead of the variable substitution character. If the backslash had not been used in the command, the interpreter would have attempted to substitute the variable named `3.50` into the command. This would result in an error because there is no variable with that name defined.

The third type of quoting available in Tcl uses braces (`{}`). This quoting is more powerful than quoting using quotation marks or backslashes. Quoting using braces hides not only whitespace and command separators from the Tcl interpreter, but also any other kind of special character. This type of quoting can be used to eliminate the need for backslash quoting in character strings. The example used for backslash quoting can be written using brace quotation as follows:

```
set Header1 {The cost is $3.50}
```

The most important use of brace quoting is to defer the evaluation of special characters. This means that special characters are not processed immediately by the Tcl interpreter but are instead passed to a command that processes the special characters on its own. An example of when deferred evaluation is used is in the `while` command:

```
set count 0
while {$count < 3} {
    puts "count equals $count"
    set count [expr $count + 1]
}
```

The `while` command has to evaluate both of its arguments each time it iterates through the loop. It is therefore necessary for the interpreter to ignore the special characters in both of these arguments and leave the evaluation of these characters up to the `while` command.

Now that we have all the language basics out of the way, let's move on to some of the more advanced Tcl commands.

The `if` Command

The `if` command, just like in other languages, evaluates an expression and, based on the results of the expression, executes a set of commands. The syntax of the `if` command is the following:

```
if {expr} {commands}
```

The `if` command expects two arguments. The first argument is an expression that is used to determine whether to execute the commands contained in the second argument. The expression argument is typically an expression that evaluates to either True or False. For example:

```
$i < 10
$num = 2
```

> **NOTE**
>
> Tcl treats any expression that evaluates to zero to be False and any expression that evaluates to a nonzero value to be True. As with other programming languages like C and Perl, this is the opposite of Linux utilities like `test`. You simply have to familiarize yourself with each and get to know which are which.

Expressions such as the following, although valid, do not make much sense in the context of an `if` command:

```
$i + $b
10 * 3
```

The second argument to the `if` command is a Tcl script, which can contain any number of Tcl commands. This script is executed if the expression contained in the first argument evaluates to True.

The `if` commands can have one or more `elseif` commands and one `else` command associated with them. The syntax for these commands is shown here:

```
if {expr} {
     commands }
elseif {expr} {
     commands }
elseif {expr} {
     commands }
else {
     commands }
```

The commands associated with the first `if` or `elseif` whose expression evaluates to True are executed. If none of these expressions evaluate to True, the commands associated with the `else` command are executed.

> **WARNING**
>
> The open brace must occur on the same line as the word that precedes it. This is because new lines are treated as command separators. If you enter an `if` command where the `if {expr}` portion of the command appears on one line and the rest is on the next line, it is treated as two separate commands.

The `for` Command

The `for` command in Tcl provides a way of implementing `for` loops. Tcl `for` loops are very similar to `for` loops in other languages, such as C. The `for` command expects four arguments. The first argument is a script that is used to initialize the counter. The second argument is an expression that is evaluated each time through the loop to determine whether to continue. The third argument is used to define the increment to be used on the counter. The fourth argument is the set of commands to be executed each time through the loop.

```
for { set i 0} {$i < 10} {incr I 1} {
     puts [expr 2 * $i]
}
```

The preceding loop executes ten times. The counter `i` is initially set to 0. The `for` loop executes while `i` is less than 10, and the value of `i` is increased by 1 each time through the loop. The command that is executed each time through the loop is the `puts` command. This evaluates 2 * i each time through the loop and prints the result to the screen. The output that results from running this command is listed here:

```
0
2
4
6
8
10
12
14
16
18
```

The `while` Command

The `while` command is used to implement `while` loops in Tcl. `while` loops are very similar to `for` loops. The only real difference between them is that the `for` loop provides more enhanced features for controlling entrance and exit criteria for the loop. The syntax for the `while` loop is shown in the following example:

```
set I 0
while {$i < 10} {
       puts [expr 2 * $i]
       set i [expr $i + 1]
}
```

This `while` loop performs the same function as the example that was presented in the section describing the `for` loop. It calculates 2 * i each time through the loop and prints the result to the screen. Notice that in this example you have to handle incrementing the counter yourself. With the `for` loop, the counter incrementing was taken care of by the `for` command.

The `switch` Command

The `switch` command provides the same function as an `if` statement that has multiple `elseif` clauses associated with it. The `switch` command compares a value (this value is usually stored in a variable) with any number of patterns, and if it finds a match it executes the Tcl code associated with the matching pattern.

```
switch $thing {
       car {puts "thing is a car"}
       truck {puts "thing is a truck"}
       default {puts "I don't know what this thing is"}
}
```

The Tcl `switch` command is equivalent to the `case` statement found in Pascal and some other languages. This `switch` command compares the value that is stored in the `thing` variable (which must be set prior to these statements, of course) with the string `car` and the string `truck` to see if it matches either of them. If the value of the `thing` variable is equal to `car`, then `thing is a car` is displayed on the screen. If the value of the `thing` variable is equal to `truck`, then `thing is a truck` is displayed on the screen. If neither of these cases is true, the default clause is executed and `I don't know what this thing is` displays on the screen.

> **TIP**
>
> Whenever you need to check to see if a variable is equal to one of a number of values, use a `switch` command instead of an `if` command with multiple `elseif` clauses. This makes the code much easier to read and understand.

Comments

It is always a good idea to include comments in any Tcl code you write—or code you write in any other language, for that matter. This becomes especially important if any of the following situations are possible:

- Someone else needs to look at or maintain your code.
- Your programs get large.
- You won't be looking at code that you have written for long periods of time after you write it.

Chances are that at least one of these situations will come up with Tcl code you have written.

Comments cannot be placed in the middle of a command. They must occur between commands. The pound sign (#) is used to inform Tcl to expect a comment.

```
# This is a valid comment

set a 1 ;   # This is a valid comment

set a 1          # This is an invalid comment
```

The third comment shown here is invalid because it occurs in the middle of a command. Remember that Tcl interprets everything up to a newline character or a semicolon to be part of the command.

The Tk Language Extensions

Earlier in this chapter, a simple example of Tk displayed Hello there in a button in the wish window. Tk is much more powerful than that example showed. Along with the button widget are many other widgets provided by Tk. These include menus, scrollbars, and list boxes. This section gives you an overview of some of the other Tk widgets, as well as short examples explaining how these widgets can be used.

Frames

Frame widgets are containers for other widgets. They do not have any interesting behavior like the other Tk widgets. The only visible properties of frame widgets that you can set are the color and border appearance. You can give three different border appearances to a frame widget: flat, raised, and sunken. You can experiment with the different frame widgets to see how they look.

The flat border frame widget is not especially interesting. It looks exactly the same as the default wish window (because the default border appearance is flat).

Buttons

Button widgets are used to get specific input from a user. A button can be turned on or activated by the user of a Tk program by moving the mouse pointer over the button and then pressing the left mouse button. Tk provides the following three kinds of button widgets:

- Button
- Check button
- Radio button

The button widget is used to initiate some specific actions. The button usually has a name such as "Load file" that describes the action that results if you press the button.

Check button widgets are used to allow users of a program to turn program options on or off. When the check button is shaded the program option is on, and when the check button is not shaded the program option is off.

Radio buttons are similar to check buttons except that they are defined in groups, where only one member of a group of radio buttons is allowed to be on at one time. This means that if one radio button in a group of radio buttons is on, none of the other radio buttons in that group can be turned on. When the radio button is shaded it is on, and when the radio button is not shaded it is off.

Menus and Menu buttons

Menu widgets are used to implement pull-down menus, cascading menus, and pop-up menus. A menu is a top-level widget that contains a set of menu entries that have values or commands associated with them. Five kinds of entries can be used in menus:

- Cascade entries display a submenu when the mouse pointer passes over them. The cascade entry is similar in function to the menu button widget.

- Command entries invoke a Tcl script when activated. The command entry is similar to the button widget in function.

- Check button entries toggle a program option between on and off. When the check button is shaded the option is on, and when the check button is not shaded it is off. The check button entry is similar in function to the check button widget.

- Radio button entries toggle a program option. The difference between the radio button entry and the check button entry is that radio buttons are typically defined in groups, with the restriction that only one of the radio buttons in the group can be active at once. The radio button entry is similar in function to the radio button widget.

- Separator entries display a horizontal line in the menu. This is used for appearance purposes only. There is no behavior associated with a separator entry.

The main difference between the menu entries and the button widgets is that the button widgets can exist by themselves, but the menu entries must exist within the context of a menu widget.

Menu button widgets are similar to button widgets. The only real difference between the two is that when menu buttons are invoked they bring up menus instead of executing Tcl scripts as button widgets do. The menu button name usually describes the types of menu entries contained in the menu that the menu button activates. This means that you will find menu entries that perform some kind of file operations contained within the File menu.

You can activate a menu by moving the mouse pointer to the menu button widget and pressing the left mouse button. This activates the menu associated with the menu button and displays the menu entries that are contained in that menu to the screen. You can now move the mouse pointer down through the list of menu entries and select the one you want.

The File menu contains two command entries (the Open entry and Quit entry), one cascade entry (the Save As entry), and one separator entry. The menu that comes up as a result of clicking the mouse pointer on the Save As cascade entry contains three command entries: the Text entry, the Ver 1 file entry, and the Ver 2 file entry.

List Boxes

The list box widget enables users of a Tk application to select items from a list of one or more items. If the number of items to be displayed in the list box is larger than the number of lines in the list box, you can attach scrollbars to make the extra items accessible.

Scrollbars

Scrollbar widgets are used to control what is displayed in other widgets. Scrollbar widgets are attached to other widgets to allow users to scroll up and down through the information contained in the widget. You typically put scrollbars on any widget that is designed to contain an arbitrary number of lines of information (such as a list box) or on widgets that contain more lines of information than the widget can display, given its size.

Summary

This chapter starts off by introducing Tcl and the Tk tool kit and describes the uses of both. Although this chapter contains a lot of information, it barely scratches the surface of the programming tools provided by Tcl and the Tk tool kit.

Tcl has many more programming features than described in this book. Some of the most notable are arrays, lists, and procedures. Not all of the Tk widgets are described here, either. Some of the widgets we did not go into are canvasses, scales, labels, messages, and `textedit` widgets. If you are interested in learning more about Tcl and Tk, check out a book on the subject.

Tk is just one example of an extension to Tcl. There are many other extensions available that extend the behavior of Tcl in different ways. Some of these extensions are as follows:

- Ak: An audio extension for Tcl, Ak provides numerous commands for sound recording and playback.
- XF: An interactive graphical user interface developer for Tk.
- Tcl-DP: A Tcl extension that helps programmers develop distributed applications using Tcl.

To learn more about

Other compilers that are supported on Linux, see Chapter 30, "Other Compilers."

CGI programming, which Perl is particularly well suited for, see Chapter 52, "CGI Scripts."

Other Compilers

by Tim Parker

So far in this section we've looked at a number of popular programming languages and their support under Linux. Maybe you're not a big fan of C, C++, awk, Perl, or Tcl. Maybe you really want to program in Ada or FORTRAN on your Linux box. Don't give up hope. Linux has a wide variety of language compilers and support tools that have been ported to work under this operating system. This chapter takes a brief tour of the languages you can find and where to get them.

We can't possibly hope to cover every language available for Linux: there are new ports and language developments made almost weekly. However, we've taken a list of the most popular languages and gone from there.

Ada

The Ada language is in widespread use in military applications and has gained acceptance over the last decade. With the popularity of the language among defense-related application programmers, it was inevitable that several ports of Ada would appear for Linux. The most popular version of Ada for Linux is the GNAT (Gnu Ada Translator) package developed and primarily supported through New York University. For information about the GNAT project or for information on the latest releases of GNAT, send email to gnat-request@cs.nyu.edu. The current version of GNAT is available from several FTP sites and will need to be compiled on your Linux system using the GNU C compiler.

> **TIP**
>
> Several FTP sites mirror the NYU GNAT archive. You can find the most recent version of GNAT at the FTP site tsx-11.mit.edu in the directory /pub/linux/packages/ada.

GNAT covers both the Ada83 and Ada90 standards for the Ada language and is compatible with some commercial Ada compilers.

COBOL

COBOL has been around for decades and it is likely that there is more COBOL code written in the world than any other language. There are several commercial ports of COBOL compilers available for Linux, most notably the COBOL-85 port from Acucobol (see http://www.acucobol.com for more information). To date no public domain version of a COBOL compiler is available for Linux although there are several COBOL tools available from Linux FTP sites.

DSP

A DSP (Digital Signal Processing) package called ObjectProDSP is available for Linux. ObjectProDSP is an X-based object-oriented digital signal processing development tool useful for many engineering and science applications.

> **TIP**
>
> Several FTP sites offer ObjectProDSP for Linux. You can find several versions at the FTP site `tsx-11.mit.edu` in the directory `/pub/linux/packages/dsp`. If you use a Web browser for FTP access, use the URL `ftp://tsx-11.mit.edu/pub/linus/packages/dsp`.

The author of ObjectProDSP can be reached through email at `mtnmath@mtnmath.com`.

Eiffel

Eiffel is an object-oriented programming language that has a high code-reuse capability. Eiffel has developed a loyal following since its development by Bertrand Meyer in the late 1980s. Eiffel has been placed in the public domain and is managed by the Nonprofit International Consortium for Eiffel (NICE). As an OO language, Eiffel is superb with all the features you would expect.

> **TIP**
>
> Eiffel for Linux can be found at several FTP sites and through the Web at `http://www.cm.cf.ac.uk/Tower`.

FORTRAN

FORTRAN (Formula Translator) is one of the standard programming languages of the '60s and '70s, especially in the fields of science and engineering. There are several ports of the FORTRAN77 version of FORTRAN available on Linux FTP sites, and ports of FORTRAN90 other than commercial releases are starting to appear as well.

> **TIP**
>
> Several FTP sites offer versions of FORTRAN for Linux. You can find several versions at the FTP site `tsx-11.mit.edu` in the directory `/pub/linux/packages/fortran`. Several Linux FORTRAN support tools are available there, too.

Apart from the FORTRAN compilers, there are several support tools that have been converted to run under Linux. Most of these are available through the FTP site mentioned above, including converters from FORTRAN to C.

The toolpack package is useful for FORTRAN programmers. It includes a number of utilities for simplifying output formatting and printing tasks. The package `mpfun` allows for multiple-precision FORTRAN calculations with up to 16 million decimal digits (more than enough for most people!). There are also several tools available that check your FORTRAN code for compliance with the FORTRAN77 and FORTRAN90 standards, as well as portability.

LISP

LISP is the quintessential artificial intelligence language, developed in the late 1950s to research the AI field. A LISP compiler called `clisp` is included with most Linux CD-ROMs and can be obtained from all the standard FTP sites that offer Linux software.

Modula-3

The Modula-3 language is a development by Digital Equipment Corporation of the popular Modula-2 language (which itself is an outgrowth of Pascal). Modula-3 is an object-oriented language designed for developing multiprocess distributed applications. Modula-3 is X-based and uses an attractive GUI.

> **TIP**
>
> Several FTP sites offer versions of Modula-3 for Linux. You can find several versions at the FTP site `gatekeeper.dec.com` in the directory `/pub/DEC/Modula-3` and from the site `ftp.vlsi.polymtl.ca` in the directory `/pub/m3/binaries/LINUX/m3`. The Modula-3 home page on the Web is `http://www.research.digital.com/SRC/`.

There are new releases of Modula-3 at intervals, so check the directories mentioned above for each release's subdirectory and `tar` files.

OGI Speech Tools

OGI Speech Tools is, as the name suggests, a language for speech manipulation used for several purposes, including speech analysis and signal manipulation. The OSI tool was developed at the Center for Spoken Language Understanding. With the OGI Speech Tools you can build parsers and databases of spoken words, leading to a voice interface for Linux. A sound card is required for the OGI Speech Tools to work under Linux.

> **TIP**
>
> Several FTP sites offer OGI Speech Tools for Linux. You can find the most recent version at the FTP site `sunsite.unc.edu` in the directory `/pub/Linux/apps/sound` or at the site `tsx-11.mit.edu` in the directory `/pub/Linux/packages/ogi`.

Documentation for the OGI Speech Tools (which are fairly complex) is in the FTP directories.

Scheme

Scheme is an artificial intelligence language related to LISP but with some C thrown in. Scheme is a flexible language that is surprisingly easy to learn and work with. There are several versions of Scheme available from FTP archive sites, as well as conversion tools to other languages.

Scilab

Scilab is a mathematical package designed to allow matrix manipulation, graphing, and function design for scientists and engineers. Scilab is a public-domain package designed to compete with expensive commercial mathematics packages, although the latter tend to have better features and support. Scilab was developed at the Institut de Recherche Informatique et Automatique (INRIA) in France.

> **TIP**
>
> Scilab can be downloaded from the FTP site `ftp.inria.fr` in the directory `/INRIA/Projects/Meta2/Scilab`. There are several versions usually available and you should obtain the latest release.

Scilab is remarkably easy to learn to work with, even for those who have never used an interactive mathematics language before. It runs in an X window and has surprising flexibility and power.

Summary

These are only a few of the popular languages available for Linux. Browsing through any of the FTP sites listed in Appendix A, "Linux FTP Sites and Newsgroups," should reveal more languages for you to play with. If you are looking for a particular language, use a search engine to try and locate it. Chances are good that someone will have adapted it for you. From here, you can read the following related chapters:

The Smalltalk language and the Linux X implementation of it is discussed in Chapter 31, "Smalltalk/X."

Setting up your Linux system to allow email in and out of your site, which is especially handy for talking to other users of your favorite compiler, is described in Chapter 40, "Configuring Linux for Mail."

Downloading and reading newsgroups from Usenet, handy for keeping up with the latest happenings with each language you use, is discussed in Chapter 41, "Configuring Linux for News."

Smalltalk/X

by Rick McMullin

CHAPTER 31

This chapter describes the Smalltalk/X (ST/X) application that is included on the Linux CD-ROM. ST/X is a fairly complete implementation of the Smalltalk-80 programming environment. Anyone who has used Smalltalk-80 or any other version of Smalltalk will be impressed with this freely available implementation. This chapter also gives you an overview of the Smalltalk/X application. After reading the chapter you will be familiar with the facilities that Smalltalk/X provides and be able to navigate your way through the Smalltalk/X user interface.

What Is Smalltalk/X?

When describing Smalltalk/X, it is probably appropriate to start with a description of Smalltalk itself. Smalltalk is an object-oriented programming language that has been a continuing development project at ParcPlace Systems since the early 1970s. Although it was not the first object-oriented language, it was the first object-oriented language to gain wide use in the industry.

Smalltalk has been around for about 15 years now, but it was not until recently that it started to become popular. Many universities now teach a Smalltalk course as part of their standard computer science curriculum, and many companies have seen the value that Smalltalk adds in terms of quick development.

Smalltalk/X was developed by Claus Gittinger and was first released in 1988. It is almost identical to the behavior of the Smalltalk 80 implementation of the Smalltalk language. Smalltalk/X comes complete with an application launcher, several different browsers for browsing through the Smalltalk class hierarchy, and a very powerful debugging utility. The unique aspect of Smalltalk/X is that it can also behave as a Smalltalk-to-C translation utility. This is a very useful feature because this means that you are able to combine the speed of development that Smalltalk provides with the speed of execution that C
provides.

How to Install Smalltalk/X

Although Smalltalk/X is on the Linux CD-ROM that comes with this book, it is not installed as part of the default install scripts. The Smalltalk/X files can be found in the `devel/smalltalkx` directory on the CD-ROM. To install Smalltalk/X, perform the following steps as `root`.

1. Create a directory called `/usr/local/lib/smalltalk`.

2. Copy the following files into the `/usr/local/lib/smalltalk` directory.

   ```
   bitmaps.tar.Z
   doc.tar.Z
   exe.tar.Z
   goodies.tar.Z
   source.tar.Z
   ```

3. Uncompress and untar these files by entering the following commands:

   ```
   uncompress *.Z
   tar -xf bitmaps.tar
   tar -xf doc.tar
   tar -xf exe.tar
   tar -xf goodies.tar
   tar -xf source.tar
   ```

4. You can now delete all of the `tar` files by entering the following command:

   ```
   rm *.tar
   ```

The Smalltalk/X program should now be installed and ready to go. If you do not have write access to the `/usr/local/lib` directory, you can install Smalltalk/X in some other directory by following the same steps listed above. If you do this, you must set the `SMALLTALK_LIBDIR` variable to be equal to the new directory.

Invoking Smalltalk/X

You invoke Smalltalk/X by typing

```
smalltalk
```

in an Xterm window. When ST/X starts, it checks to see if there is an image file for it to use. If it cannot find an image file, it uses a file called `smalltalk.rc` to set up the default behavior for your environment. The image file that is loaded by default is called `st.img` and contains a snapshot of what your ST/X environment looked like the last time you exited. This allows you to resume exactly where you left off. You can save a snapshot under any name with the extension `.img`. To invoke ST/X with an image other than `st.img`, enter the following command at the prompt:

```
smalltalk -i nameofImage.img
```

Getting Around in ST/X

Once ST/X is invoked, two windows or views appear. The Transcript view and the Launcher menu. The Transcript view is shown in Figure 31.1.

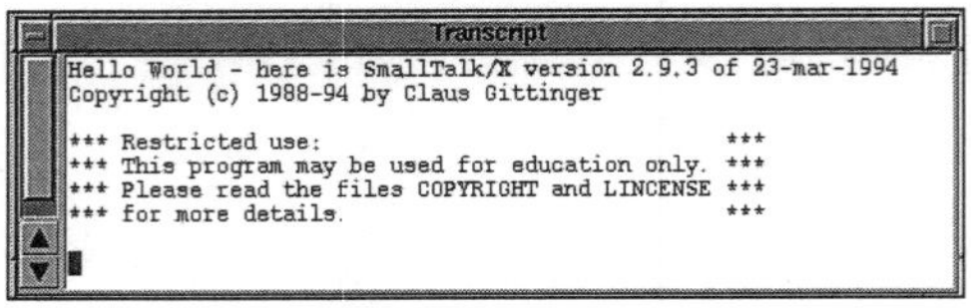

FIGURE 31.1.

The Transcript view.

The Transcript is the console where relevant systems information is shown. The Launcher menu is shown in Figure 31.2.

FIGURE 31.2.

The Launcher menu.

The Launcher allows access to the tools you will need to program your application. Table 31.1 gives the options available from the Launcher and a brief description of each.

TABLE 31.1. THE LAUNCHER MENU OPTIONS.

Option	Description
Browsers	The pull-right menu of this option gives you access to browsers, senders, and implementors.
Workspace	This option brings up a workspace view.
FileBrowser	This browser allows inspection and manipulation of files and directories.
Projects	This option allows you to choose an existing or new project.
Utilities	This contains tools specific to your programming needs.
Goodies	This contains other non-programming related tools.

Option	Description
Games & Demos	This contains some sample programs and games to play.
Info & Help	This contains topics that give you help and information on the ST/X environment and programming in Smalltalk.
Snapshot	This option takes a snapshot of your present ST/X environment and asks for the name of the image file you wish to store the snapshot in.
Exit	This option allows you to exit ST/X immediately, or exit and save a snapshot of the current environment.

The following sections describe most of these options in more detail.

The Browsers Option

The Browsers option in the Launcher menu gives you access to different browsers or editors that let you read and manipulate classes, methods, changes, senders, and implementors. The sub-options available are:

- System Browser
- Class Hierarchy Browser
- Implementors
- Senders
- Changes Browser
- Directory Browser

Each of these sub-options will be discussed in detail in this section.

The System Browser

The standard System Browser contains five subviews:

- Class category list
- Class list
- Method category list
- Method list
- Code view

The System Browser is shown in Figure 31.3.

FIGURE 31.3.

*The System
Browser.*

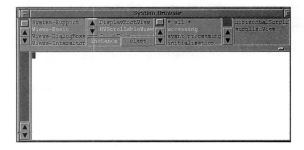

Within the ST/X system, classes are assigned to a category. A *category* is simply an attribute used for grouping classes to make them easier to handle. To select a class category, click on the name of the category in the class category list. This is the leftmost section of the top half of the System Browser. This displays, in the class list subview, all classes belonging to that category. The class list subview is the second section from the far left of the system browser. You can also select one of two special categories: * all *, which selects all classes and lists them alphabetically; and * hierarchy *, which lists all classes in a tree by inheritance.

If you select a class in the class list, all method categories for that class will be displayed in the method category list, which is the second section from the right in the top half of the System Browser. Like class categories, method categories are simply for grouping methods according to their function. When you select a method category, all methods in that category are shown in the method list view in the far right section of the browser. The special * all * category shows all methods in alphabetical order. Selecting a method from the method list shows the corresponding method's source code in the code view, which is the bottom half of the System Browser.

The browser enables you to change either a class or its metaclass. There are two toggle buttons, *class* and *instance*, in the same section of the browser as the class list view. *Instance*, which is the default, makes the changes affect the class. Selecting *class* makes the changes affect the metaclass.

A pop-up menu is available in each view by pressing the middle or menu mouse button while the pointer is in that view. The pop-up menu available in the class category view is shown in Figure 31.4 and the purpose of each function is shown in Table 31.2.

FIGURE 31.4.

*The Class
Category pop-up
menu.*

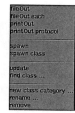

TABLE 31.2. CLASS CATEGORY POP-UP MENU FUNCTIONS.

Function	Description
fileOut	Saves all classes in the currently selected class category into one source file named `classCategory.st`.
fileOut each	Saves all classes but puts each class into a separate file called `className.st`.
printOut	Sends a printed representation of all classes selected to the printer including the method source code.
printOut protocol	Sends a protocol-only representation of all classes in the category to the printer without the method's source code.
spawn	Starts a class category browser without a class category list on the currently selected class category.
spawn class	Starts a full class browser which allows you to edit all code for the selected class in one view.
update	Re-scans all classes in the system and updates the lists shown.
find class	Pops up a dialog box to enter the name of a class you wish to search for and have displayed.
rename	Renames a category and changes the category attribute of all classes in the currently selected class category.
remove	Removes all classes and subclasses in the current class category.

The class list pop-up menu appears when you press the menu mouse button with the pointer in the class list view. The functions available from this menu are shown in Figure 31.5 and are explained in Table 31.3.

FIGURE 31.5.

The Class List pop-up menu.

TABLE 31.3. CLASS LIST POP-UP MENU FUNCTIONS.

Function	Description
fileOut	Saves the source code of the currently selected class in a file named className.st.
printOut	Sends the source code of the currently selected class to the printer.
printOut protocol	Sends a protocol description of the currently selected class to the printer. The output will contain the class description, class comment, and the class's protocol and method comments.
spawn	Starts a class browser on the currently selected class.
spawn hierarchy	Starts a browser on all subclasses of the currently selected class.
hierarchy	Shows the hierarchy of the currently selected class in the code view.
definition	Shows the class definition in the code view and allows you to change the class definition.
comment	Shows the class comment in the code view and allows you to edit it.
class instvars	Shows the class-instance-variables for the selected class and allows you to edit them.
variable search	Provides a search facility to find different variable references and all methods referencing the searched-for variable.
new class	Allows you to create a new class using the currently selected class as a template.
new subclass	Same as new class but creates a subclass of the currently selected class.
rename	Changes the name of the currently selected class.
remove	Removes the currently selected class and all of its subclasses.

The method category pop-up menu appears when you press the menu mouse button while the pointer is in the method category view. The functions available from this menu are shown in Figure 31.6 and explained in Table 31.4.

FIGURE 31.6.

The Method Category pop-up menu.

TABLE 31.4. METHOD CATEGORY POP-UP MENU FUNCTIONS.

Function	Description
fileOut	Saves the source code of the currently selected method category in a file named className-category.st.
printOut	Sends the source code of the currently selected method category to the printer.
spawn	Starts a method category browser on the currently selected method category of the currently selected class.
spawn category	Starts a browser on all methods of the class which have the same category as the currently selected one.
find method here	Searches for the method that implements a specified selector.
find method	Searches up in the class hierarchy for the first class implementing the selector you specify in the dialog box.
new category	Enables you to add a new category to the list.
copy category	Enables you to copy all methods in a class category to the currently selected class.
create access methods	Creates methods to access instance variables.
rename	Renames the currently selected method category.
remove	Removes all methods in the currently selected class that are members of the currently selected method category.

The method list pop-up menu appears when you press the menu mouse button while the pointer is in the method list view. The functions available from this menu are shown in Figure 31.7 and explained in Table 31.5.

FIGURE 31.7.

The Method List pop-up menu.

TABLE 31.5. METHOD LIST POP-UP MENU FUNCTIONS.

Function	Description
fileOut	Saves the currently selected method in a file named className-selector.st.
printOut	Sends the source code of the currently selected method to the printer.
spawn	Starts a browser for editing this method.
senders	Starts a new browser on all methods sending a specific message.
local sender	Same as senders but limits the search to the current class and its subclasses.
implementors	Starts a new browser on all methods implementing a specific message.
globals	Starts a new browser on all methods that are accessing a global that is either a global variable or a symbol, as well as all methods sending a corresponding message.
new method	Enables you to create a new method from a template in the code view.
change category	Enables you to change the category of the selected method.
remove	Removes the currently selected method.

When you add or remove instance variables to or from a system class description and *accept* (that is, save the changes), the system creates a new class instead of changing the old one. The original class still exists to give existing instances of the class a valid class even though it is no longer accessible by name. After the change, you can no longer edit the old class.

NOTE

It is recommended that you don't change the definition of system classes, only private ones. It is safer to use the copy category function to copy an

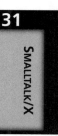

existing class and its methods to a new class and modify the new class. This is especially important for classes which are used by the system itself since changes can lead to problems in the operation of the ST/X environment.

The code view is the lower half of the System Browser. It is here that you can modify the class or instance definitions as well as methods. The pop-up menu for this area is the edit menu that appears in every text editing view in ST/X. The functions in this menu are discussed in the "Editing in Browsers" section of this chapter.

The Class Hierarchy Browser

When the Class Hierarchy Browser is selected, a dialog box appears which asks for the *name of class*. If you enter a valid class, the Class Hierarchy Browser appears for that class. This is the same as the System Browser except there is no class category list since this is for one specific class. The pop-up menus for each of the four subviews are the same as in the System Browser.

Implementors

When the Implementors option is selected, a dialog box appears which asks for a selector. A selector is the name of the type of operation a message requests of its receiver.

If you enter a valid selector, an Implementors view will be displayed. This view is similar to the one shown in Figure 31.8.

FIGURE 31.8.

The Implementors view.

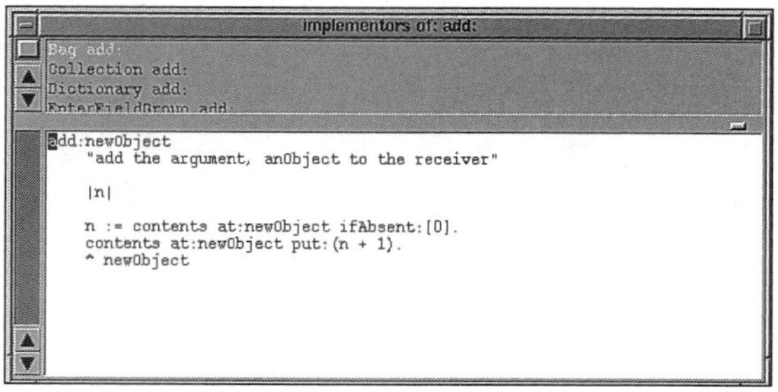

```
                    implementors of: add:
Bag add:
Collection add:
Dictionary add:
EnterFieldGroup add:

add:newObject
    "add the argument, anObject to the receiver"

    |n|

    n := contents at:newObject ifAbsent:[0].
    contents at:newObject put:(n + 1).
    ^ newObject
```

The Implementors view contains a list of the methods that implement the method specified by the selector. The pop-up menu for the top half of the Implementor view is the same as the pop-up menu for the method list subview which was discussed in the "The System Browser" section of this chapter.

Senders

When the Senders option is selected, a dialog box appears that asks for a selector. If you enter a valid selector, then a Senders view will be displayed. This view is similar to the one shown in Figure 31.9.

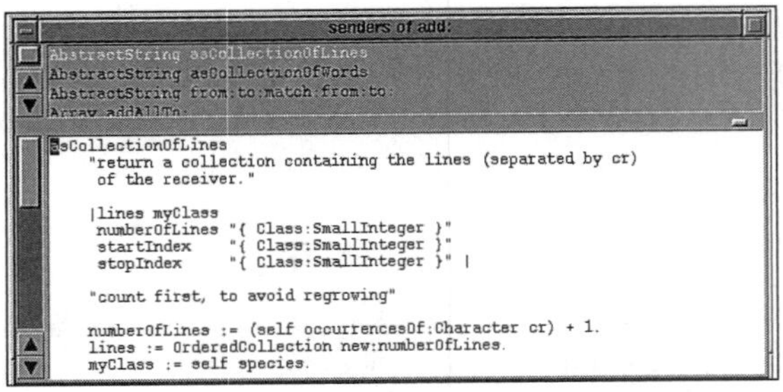

FIGURE 31.9.
Senders view.

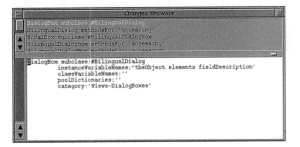

The Senders view contains a list of the methods that send the selected message. The pop-up menu for the top half of the Senders view is the same as the pop-up menu for the method list subview which was discussed in the "The System Browser" section.

The Changes Browser

Each time you make a change to either the class hierarchy or to a method, ST/X writes a record to a changes file. The Changes Browser enables you to inspect and manipulate the changes file. There are two subviews in the Changes Browser: the change list and the contents view. The change list gives a list of all changes in chronological order. An example Changes Browser is shown in Figure 31.10.

FIGURE 31.10.
The Changes Browser.

To display a change, select one of the changes from the change list. The Changes Browser then displays the contents of the change in the contents view.

The pop-up menu for the change list has the functions described in Table 31.6.

TABLE 31.6. THE CHANGE LIST POP-UP MENU.

Function	*Description*
apply change	Applies the currently selected change.
apply to end	Applies all the changes from the currently selected change to the end of the changes file.
apply all changes	Applies all the changes in the file.
delete	Deletes the currently selected change from the list.
delete to end	Deletes all changes from the currently selected change to the end of the file.
delete changes for	Deletes all changes affecting the same class.
delete all changes	Deletes all changes in the file for the same class as the currently selected change.
update	Rereads the changes file.
compress	Compresses the change list and removes multiple changes for a method leaving the most recent change compared to the current change.
version	Compares a method's source code in a change with the current version of the method and outputs a message in the Transcript view.
make a change patch	Appends the change to the end of the patches file which will be run and automatically applied at ST/X startup.
update sourcefile from change	This function is not currently implemented.
writeback	Writes the change list back to the changefile changes file. All delete/compress operations performed in the Changes Browser will not affect the changes file unless this operation is performed.

The Changes Browser can be used to recover from a system crash by reapplying all changes that were made after the last snapshot entry. To control the size of the changes file, it is a good idea to apply a compress periodically. This will remove all old changes for a method, leaving the newest one.

Directory Browser

When you select the Directory Browser option, a browser with five subviews is displayed. The top half of the browser displays the current directory and all subdirectories and files contained in it. If you select a directory, it is expanded in the next section to the right across the top half of the browser. If you select a file, the contents of the file are displayed in the lower half of the browser. The pop-up menu for the directory area has only two functions:

- up—Moves up to the directory above the one selected
- goto directory—Enables you to go to a specified directory

The content view has the same edit menu as all the other text editors and is discussed in the "Editing in Browsers" section in this chapter. A typical Directory Browser is shown in Figure 31.11.

FIGURE 31.11.

The Directory Browser.

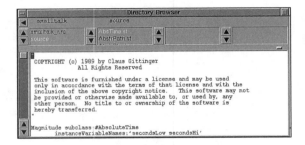

The Workspace Option

The Workspace option displays a view from which you can enter and compile Smalltalk code. The Workspace is usually used as a testing area or scratch pad when coding. You can use it to test your Smalltalk code before building it into the code library using the System Browser code view.

The File Browser Option

The File Browser gives you the ability to inspect and manipulate files and directories. The File Browser is shown in Figure 31.12.

FIGURE 31.12.

The File Browser.

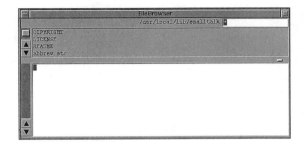

It consists of four subviews that are described in Table 31.7.

TABLE 31.7. THE FILE BROWSER SUBVIEWS.

Subview	Purpose
path-label field	Shows the name of the current directory.
file pattern field	Allows a search pattern to be entered for choosing files for the file list.
file list	Shows a list of file and directory names.
contents view	Shows the contents of a selected file.

To inspect the contents of a file, double-click the left mouse button on the name of the file in the file list. To change directories, double-click on the directory name. Directory names are always shown in the file list.

You can use the file pattern field to display the list of files matching the specified pattern. The default is *, which shows all files. The search pattern can be changed by moving the pointer to the field, editing the pattern, and then pressing enter or choosing accept from the file pattern pop-up menu.

As in the other browsers we have discussed, each subview has a pop-up menu that is activated by the menu mouse button. The path-label pop-up menu is shown in Figure 31.13.

FIGURE 31.13.

The Path-Label pop-up menu.

The functions available in this menu are described in Table 31.8.

TABLE 31.8. THE PATH-LABEL POP-UP MENU FUNCTIONS.

Function	Purpose
copy path	Copies the current pathname into the cut and paste buffer.
change directory	Opens a dialog box to enter the name of the directory you wish to change to.
change to home dir	Changes the file list to your home directory.

The file list pop-up menu is shown in Figure 31.14.

FIGURE 31.14.
The File List pop-up menu.

The functions available in this menu are described in Table 31.9.

TABLE 31.9. THE FILE LIST POP-UP MENU FUNCTIONS.

Function	Purpose
spawn	Starts another file browser on the current directory or the directory selected in the file list.
get contents	Shows the contents of the currently selected file in the contents view.
show info	Displays a view with type, size, access, and owner information for the currently selected file or directory.
show full info	Displays the same as above with more details such as the last access, last modification date, and time.
fileIn	Loads the selected file into the system by reading and evaluating Smalltalk expressions from it.
update	Rereads the directory and updates the file list.

Function	Purpose
`execute UNIX command`	Allows execution of any UNIX command through a pop-up box.
`remove`	Removes the selected file(s) or directory(s).
`rename`	Renames the selected file.
`display long list`	Shows file information in the file list. This option toggles with `display short list`, which is the default.
`show all files`	Displays all the files including hidden files. This option toggles with `hide hidden files`, which is the default.
`create directory`	Creates a new directory.
`create file`	Creates a new file.

The pop-up menu for the contents view is the same edit menu as the other text editors and is discussed in the "Editing in Browsers" section of this chapter.

The Projects Option

The Projects option of the Launcher menu enables you to create a new project or select a previously created project. When the `new project` function is selected, a new project is automatically created for you and the new project object appears on your screen. If you select the `select project` function, a dialog box appears with a list of existing projects from which to choose. Simply select a project and it is loaded into the environment.

The Utilities Option

The Utilities option provides 13 tools that assist you in programming in the ST/X environment. Table 31.10 gives you a brief description of each tool.

TABLE 31.10. THE UTILITIES OPTION.

Utility	Description
Transcript	Opens the Transcript view.
Window tree	Displays a graphical tree representation of the window hierarchy of all windows that are active or in wait state at the time it was requested.
Class tree	Displays a graphical tree representation of the class hierarchy of the system.
Event monitor	Displays a view that monitors events.

continues

TABLE 31.10. CONTINUED

Utility	Description
Process monitor	Displays a view that gives information about all currently active or waiting processes. This information changes as the state of the processes changes.
Memory monitor	Displays a graph that tells you the present memory usage and changes as the memory usage changes.
Memory usage	Displays a table of the classes and the number of instances of each, average size, bytes, and percentage of memory used by each.
collect Garbage	Runs a Generation Scavenge algorithm to collect short term objects and destroy them. If an object survives long enough, it is moved to an area of memory where it remains until the user requests its collection.
collect Garbage & compress	Same as Collect Garbage but also compresses to recover space.
fullscreen hardcopy	Takes a picture of the screen and asks for a name of a file with a `.tiff` extension in which to save the image.
screen area hardcopy	Same as fullscreen hardcopy but only for a specific area of the screen.
view hardcopy	Same as fullscreen hardcopy but for one specific view only.
ScreenSaver	Enables you to choose from one of three different screen savers to use in the ST/X environment.

The Goodies Option

The Goodies option of the Launcher menu provides a pull-right menu of six different tools that are useful at any time, not just when you program in Smalltalk. The Goodies are described in Table 31.11.

TABLE 31.11. THE GOODIES.

Goodie	Description
`Clock`	Displays an analog clock in a square with a toggle for the second hand.
`Round Clock`	Same as the clock but is round and remains visible when it is minimized.
`Directory View`	Displays a pictorial representation of files and directories. A folder represents a directory and a document is a file.

Goodie	Description
Mail Tool	A tool for managing electronic mail.
News Tool	A repository for news, information, and documents.
Draw Tool	A fairly comprehensive tool for drawing diagrams, charts, pictures, and so on.

The Games & Demos Option

Contained in the pull-right menu of this option are games for your enjoyment and example applications that may be useful. The Games & Demos option menu is shown in Figure 31.15.

FIGURE 31.15.
The Games & Demos option menu.

Editing in Browsers

All views that show text allow the usual editing functions of that text through a pop-up menu. The functions available in this menu are described in Table 31.12.

TABLE 31.12. EDITING FUNCTIONS.

Function	Description
again	Repeats the last edit.
copy	Copies the selected text.
cut	Cuts the selected text out of the file.
paste	Pastes the text that was copied or cut prior to choosing the paste option to the current position of the pointer.

continues

TABLE 31.12. CONTINUED

Function	Description
accept	Once you have completed editing, you must use this option to save the changes to the file; otherwise the changes will not be written to the file.
doIt	Evaluates the highlighted text.
printIt	Prints a representation of the result of the evaluation at the current cursor position.
inspectIt	Invokes the Inspector view on the result.
search...	Enables you to search for a specific string.
goto...	Enables you to move to a specific location in the file.
font...	Enables you to change the font of the file.
indent...	Enables you to change the indenting of the file.
save as...	Enables you to save the file under a different name.
print	Prints the file.

To select or highlight text, press the left mouse button over the first character and move the mouse (while holding the mouse button) to the end of the text you wish to select, and then release the mouse button. If you press the left mouse button again, the highlighting is removed and you can select something else.

To scroll through the text, use the scroll bars on the left of the view. By clicking the mouse below or above the thumb, the text scrolls one page for every click. If you press the Shift key at the same time as you click, the text scrolls to the position of the pointer in the scroll bar. This is useful for scrolling rapidly through long documents.

Using the Inspector

The Inspector enables you to inspect an object. It consists of two subviews, one showing the names of the object's instance variables and the other showing the value of the selected instance variable. You can start an inspector by using the inspectIt function on the edit menu or by sending one of the following messages to an object:

anObject inspect

or

anObject basicInspect

The `basicInspect` command will open a general inspector that shows instance variables as they are physically present in the object. The `inspect` command is redefined in some classes to open an inspector showing the logical contents of the object.

Using the Debugger

The Debugger is displayed whenever an error occurs in your Smalltalk code. It shows you where the error occurred and how the system got there. The Debugger runs in one of three modes; `normal`, `modal`, and `inspecting`.

When in normal mode and an error occurs in a process, which is not the event handler process, the debugger starts up on top of the erroneous process. This blocks all interaction with the affected process and its views. Other views are still active and respond as usual.

When an error occurs in the Smalltalk event handler process, the debugger starts in modal mode. While a modal debugger is active, you can not interact with any other view.

The inspecting mode can be entered from the ProcessMonitor by the pop-up menu and allows inspection of the state of other processes. But because the debugged process may continue to run, it is only possible to inspect a snapshot of the affected process.

The Debugger contains four subviews:

- The Context Walkback List shows the context chain which lead to the error.
- The Method Source View shows the method that caused the error.
- The Receiver Inspector allows inspection of the receiver of the selected message.
- The Context Inspector provides information about the arguments and local variables of this context.

The Debugger is shown in Figure 31.16.

FIGURE 31.16.

The Debugger.

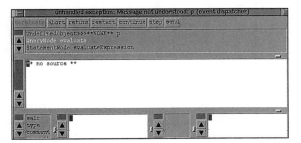

The functions that are common to each view appear as a set of buttons below the context walkback list. These functions are described in Table 31.13.

TABLE 31.13. THE DEBUGGER FUNCTION BUTTONS.

Button	Description
continue	Continues execution.
terminate	Terminates the erroneous process.
abort	Abort the current activity if possible.
step (single step)	Lets the process continue execution until the next send is executed in the currently selected context.
send (single send)	Lets the process continue execution for one message send.
return	Continues execution as if the selected context returned.
restart	Continues execution by restarting the selected context.

The walkback subview has a pop-up menu with the functions described in Table 31.14.

TABLE 31.14. WALKBACK SUBVIEW POP-UP MENU FUNCTION.

Function	Description
exit smalltalk	Leaves ST/X without saving an image.
show more	Shows 50 more contexts of the walk-back.
breakpoints	Not yet available.
trace on/off	Not yet available.
trace step	Not yet available.

A miniDebugger is entered if an error occurs within the Debugger itself. This is a line-by-line debugger that allows limited debugging without the use of a graphical user interface. It is controlled by entering commands in the Xterm window where ST/X was started. If you type ? at the miniDebugger prompt, you will get a list of commands that are available for use in this stripped-down debugger.

Summary

This chapter introduces you to the Smalltalk environment that is provided by the Smalltalk/X application. If you are interested in learning how to program using Smalltalk and don't have access to one of the commercial versions of Smalltalk, then Smalltalk/X is perfect for you. Not only does Smalltalk/X come with all the tools and programming aids that are talked about in this chapter, but it also comes with many examples and some fairly complete documentation that will make learning Smalltalk easier for you.

It is worth mentioning that Linux also comes with the GNU version of Smalltalk called `mst`. This chapter was devoted to talking about Smalltalk/X because it is much more complete than GNU Smalltalk. From here, you can learn:

> About the Perl programming language, which is used for many quick-and-dirty programming tasks, in Chapter 28, "Perl."
>
> How to back up your system so all your Smalltalk/X programs are not lost, read Chapter 45, "Backups."
>
> How to set up your Linux system so people on the Internet can access your system, read Chapter 47, "Setting up an Internet Site."

Linux for System Administrators

PART

VI

IN THIS PART

CHAPTER 32

System Administration Basics

by Tim Parker

So far in this book, you've seen how to use Linux for many different tasks. However, there are some issues we haven't dealt with because they are used rarely or only by a single administrator (who may be the only user). This chapter looks at simple system administration tasks, including the following:

- Starting and shutting down the system properly
- Managing the disk partitions
- Making backups
- `gzip`, `compress`, and `tar`
- Message of the day
- Emergency boot floppies

Of course, we can't cover everything you need to know to run a system efficiently. Instead, we will look at the basic information and utilities and leave you to experiment. For more details, check the documentation files with your Linux operating system. Better yet, consider purchasing a good UNIX system administration book, such as *Linux System Administrator's Survival Guide* (Sams Publishing, 1995). Much of the information in a UNIX system administration book will be applicable to Linux, too.

The root Account

The `root` login, as you probably know, has no limitations at all. It can do anything anywhere, access any files it wants, and control any processes. This power has its price, though: Any mistake can be disastrous, sometimes resulting in damage to the entire operating system.

A mystique has built up in the UNIX community about the `root` login, because it holds unlimited power over the system. The tendency to want to use this superuser login is overwhelming for many. However, a simple `rm` command in the wrong place can spell many hours of trouble, if not a complete reload of your entire Linux system.

For this reason, the `root` account should be employed only for limited system use, and then only when its power is necessary (such as when rebuilding a kernel, installing new software, or setting up new file systems). As a general rule, you should not use the `root` account for routine tasks.

Naturally, many people use `root` for their daily Linux sessions, ignoring any advice because they think they won't make mistakes. In truth, everyone makes a mistake occasionally. Check with any UNIX system administrator and you'll find that accidents happen with the `root` account. (I have managed to delete entire file systems more than once while trying to do two things at the same time.) Although many people ignore the rule about using `root` only when necessary, most of them eventually find out why this rule is important!

Starting and Stopping the System

There are several ways of booting the Linux operating system, as well as a few ways to safely shut it down. Some were mentioned earlier in this book. Because Linux can be installed in many different ways, there is no single "right" method of booting the operating system, so we must look at both hard-disk–based and floppy-disk–based boot procedures.

Booting from a Floppy

A boot floppy, as its name implies, is a floppy disk that boots the Linux kernel. A boot floppy has the `root` partition installed on the floppy itself instead of the hard drive (although both may coexist). Without the `root` partition, Linux would be unable to find the hard drives for the rest of the operating system.

You can create Linux boot floppies with the setup routine included in most distributions of the operating system. Check the documentation or information files that came with your Linux distribution, if there are any. Alternatively, most Linux setup utilities have a menu-driven interface that prompts you for a boot floppy setup when you rebuild or reconfigure the kernel. You should use this procedure to make a boot floppy, which is also useful for emergencies.

In most cases, a boot floppy is used only in emergencies when your system won't start up normally. The boot floppy enables you to load Linux and then mount the hard drives that are causing the problem to check for damage. Luckily, this is not required very often. If you haven't used LILO to choose the partition to boot or set your boot sequence to Linux by default, you may need the boot floppy to start up Linux. In this case, the boot floppy is much like a DOS boot floppy.

You can create a boot floppy from scratch by copying over the kernel image from the hard drive. The kernel image is usually in the file `vmlinuz`, `vmlinux`, `Image`, or `/etc/Image`, depending on the distribution of Linux. The Slackware distribution uses `vmlinuz`, which is a compressed kernel (hence the `z` in the name). Compressed kernels uncompress themselves as they are loaded into memory at boot time. The `vmlinuz` image expands to `vmlinux`. (Compressed kernels take up less disk space; that's why they are used.)

After you have identified the kernel, you can set the `root` device in the kernel image to point to the `root` partition on either the floppy or hard drive. In this case, we want the floppy. The root partition is set with the `rdev` command, whose format is as follows:

```
rdev kernelname device
```

kernelname is the name of the kernel image, and *device* is the name of the Linux `root` partition. To set a floppy boot device with the file `vmlinuz`, for the first floppy on the system, the command would be as follows:

```
rdev vmlinuz /dev/fd0
```

You can set other parameters with `rdev` as well if you want to change system defaults during boot. Check the `rdev` man page for the `rdev` help file for complete information.

As a final step in creating the boot floppy, copy the kernel image to the floppy disk. You should use a preformatted disk (format with DOS if necessary) to allow the Linux routines to identify the type of disk and its density. To copy the `vmlinuz` kernel to the first floppy drive, use this command:

```
cp vmlinuz /dev/fd0
```

The floppy should now be ready to boot the system. You may not be able to boot the system without the floppy if you change the location of the `root` partition. You can change the `root` partition back to the hard drive with the `rdev` command after completing the boot floppy, which enables you to boot from either. This can be useful when you have disks for several different boot configurations. You can also create the boot floppy from the Linux `setup` program.

Using LILO to Boot

LILO is a program that resides in the boot sector of your hard drive and allows Linux to be booted from the hard disk either after you tell it to or after a default number of seconds has elapsed.

LILO can also be used with other operating systems such as OS/2 and DOS. If you have LILO set to autoboot Linux, you must interrupt the process by pressing the Ctrl, Alt, or Shift key when the bootup is started. This displays a boot prompt that enables you to specify another operating system. If LILO is set to allow a given time before it boots into Linux, you can use the Ctrl+Alt+Shift sequence to interrupt the boot process before the timer expires and Linux starts loading. Finally, if LILO is set to not autoboot into Linux but to wait for explicit instructions, you must press Enter to boot Linux or type the name of the other operating system.

Some Linux distributions have a configuration file in the directory /etc/lilo that can be edited to provide boot information, while other versions of Linux configure LILO during the installation process. If the latter is the case, you can change the settings with the setup utility. Some versions of Linux use the configuration file /etc/lilo.conf instead of /etc/lilo.

Shutting Down Linux

You can't just turn off the power switch! This can cause damage to the file system, sometimes irreversibly. Because Linux keeps many files open at once, as well as several processes, they must all be closed down properly before you cycle the power to the unit.

There are a few ways to shut the Linux system down, but the formal method is to use the shutdown command. The syntax for shutdown is as follows:

```
shutdown [minutes] [warning]
```

minutes is the number of minutes to wait before shutting the system down and *warning* is an optional message displayed for all users currently logged in. Some versions of shutdown allow the word now instead of a time, while others require either no argument or the number 0 to shut the system down immediately without waiting. You can have shutdown reboot the system after the shutdown by adding the argument -r (for reboot).

Using shutdown is best if you have other users on your system, because it gives them a warning that they should log out, and it prevents loss of information. It can also be used to automate a shutdown much later (such as at midnight), with messages that appear just before that time warning any users still logged in.

If you can't wait and want to shut the system down immediately, use the halt command or the "three-finger salute" of Ctrl+Alt+Delete. This immediately shuts down all the processes and halts the system as quickly as possible. Then the power can be shut off.

> **WARNING**
>
> Some Linux distributions don't support Ctrl+Alt+Delete, and a couple of older distributions use it to halt the system immediately without terminating processes properly. This can cause damage. Check the documentation or man pages for information.

Mounting File Systems

File systems are not available until they are mounted onto the Linux main file system. Even hard drives must be mounted, because only the root file system is available in the / directory until the rest are mounted. The mount command is used to mount a file system.

During the boot process, the mount command is used from the startup files (such as the /etc/rc file or files under the /etc/rc.d directory) to mount all the file systems maintained in the file /etc/fstab. You can look at the file to see the type of information maintained there. Every file system that is mounted during the boot process has an entry giving its device name, its mount directory (called the mount point), the type of file system it is, and any options that apply.

You can add a new file system from a hard disk, a CD-ROM, a floppy, or any other type of device that provides a file system supported by Linux, using the mount command. The format is as follows:

```
mount filesystem mountpoint
```

filesystem is the name of the device and *mountpoint* is where in the Linux file system it should be mounted. For example, if you want to mount a SCSI CD-ROM to the file system as /usr/cdrom, issue the following command:

```
mount /dev/cd0 /usr/cdrom
```

The directory /usr/cdrom must be created before the command is given, or the mount command generates an ambiguous error. You should replace /dev/cd0 with the name of your CD-ROM device driver (/dev/cd0 for most non-SCSI CD-ROM drives and /dev/cd0 for SCSI CD-ROM drives). When the file system is mounted properly, changing to /usr/cdrom lets you access all the files on the CD-ROM as if they were part of the normal file system.

If your /etc/fstab file doesn't have any entries in it already, you have to mount the file system with a slightly different syntax:

```
mount -t fstypefilesystem mountpoint
```

fstype is the type of file system (such as ISO9660, MSDOS, and so on). The rest of the arguments are the same as the example above. The -t option is used when the file system to be mounted doesn't already have an entry in the /etc/fstab file.

Mounting a Floppy

You can mount a floppy disk with a command similar to the one in the CD-ROM example just discussed. To mount a floppy in the first floppy drive on the directory /mnt, issue the following command:

```
mount /dev/fd0 /mnt
```

Most floppy drive device names start with fd to make it clear which kind of device they are (just like most hard disks start with hd). If the file system is not the default value used by Linux, the type of file system must be specified. For example, to mount a floppy using the ext2 file system, use the -t option of the mount command:

```
mount -t ext2 /dev/fd0 /mnt
```

Creating a New File System

To create a file system on a floppy (so it can be mounted), you should use the utility mke2fs or the command mkdev fs, depending on the version of Linux. To use mke2fs, for example, issue the following command to create a floppy file system on a 1.44MB 3.5-inch disk:

```
mke2fs /dev/fd0 1440
```

Unmounting File Systems

To detach a mounted file system from your Linux file system, use the umount command with the name of the device. For example, to unmount a floppy in /dev/fd0, issue the following command:

```
umount /dev/fd0
```

The floppy is removed from the mounted point. Be sure to type umount instead of unmount!

If you want to remove the current floppy and replace it with another, you can't simply swap them. The current floppy must be unmounted and then the new one must be mounted. Failure to follow this process can result in corruption or erroneous directory listings.

Checking File Systems

Every now and again a file might get corrupted or a file system's inode table might get out of sync with the disk's contents. For these reasons, it is a good idea to check the file system at regular intervals. Several utilities can check file systems, depending on the version of Linux. The utility fsck is available for some systems, while the utility e2fsck is designed for Linux's `ext2fs` file system. Many Linux versions include other utilities such as `xfsck` and `efsfck` for different file systems. In many cases, the `fsck` command is linked to the individual file system versions.

To use `e2fsck` to check a file system, issue the command with the device name and the options a (automatically correct errors) and v (verbose output):

```
e2fsck -av /dev/hda1
```

This command checks and repairs any problems on the `/dev/hda1` (or whatever device driver you specify) partition. If any corrections are made to a partition, you should reboot the machine as soon as possible to allow the system to resync its tables.

Whenever possible, it is a good idea to unmount the file system before checking it, because this can prevent problems with open files. Of course, you can't unmount the primary `root` partition while running from it, but you can boot from a boot floppy which contains the check utilities and start them from the floppy.

Using a File as Swap Space

When you installed Linux, your setup program probably set up a partition specifically for the swap space. You can, when the original installation is completed, set Linux to use a file instead of the partition, thus freeing up the partition's disk space.

Generally, there is a performance degradation with using a file because the file system is involved, although the effect can be negligible on fast disks and CPUs. However, this is a useful technique when you need to add more swap space, such as when you temporarily want to run a swap-space–intensive application such as a compiler.

To create a file used as the swap space, issue the following command:

```
dd if=/dev/zero of=/swap bs=1024 count=16416
```

This creates a file (called swap) for swap space that is about 16MB (in this case, 16,416 blocks). If you want a different size, replace the number after count with the correct value in bytes. Next, physically create the file swap file with the following command:

```
mkswap /swap 16416
```

The number should match the blocks determined earlier. Turn the swap space on with the following command:

```
swapon /swap
```

If you want to remove the swap file and use the swap partition, use the following command followed by a standard `rm` command to remove the file:

```
swapoff /swap
```

Swap files can't be larger than 16MB with most Linux versions, but you can have up to eight swap files and partitions on your system.

Compressing Files with `gzip` and `compress`

Files abound on a UNIX system, adding up to a large chunk of disk real estate. Instead of deleting files, an alternative is to compress them so that they take up less space. Several compression utilities are available for UNIX and Linux systems. The most commonly used are `compress` and the newer GNU `gzip`.

When run on a file, `compress` creates a smaller file with the extension `.Z`, which immediately identifies the file as being compressed. To compress a file, use the following command:

```
compress filename
```

You can also use wildcards to compress several files at once. `compress` supports a number of options, but most aren't used often. By default, when a file is compressed, the uncompressed original is deleted, although this can be changed with a command-line option.

To uncompress a compressed file, run the `uncompress` program:

```
uncompress filename
```

Alternatively, you can use a wildcard such as `*.Z` to uncompress all the compressed files. Remember to include the `.Z` suffix when specifying the filename.

The `gzip` utility is a new compression tool that uses different algorithms than `compress`. The `gzip` program has a few extra features that were added since `compress` was released, such as adjustable compression (the more compression required, the longer it takes to compress). To use `gzip`, specify the filename to be compressed and the compression type:

```
gzip -9 filename
```

The `-9` option, which tells `gzip` to use the highest compression factor, will probably be the option you use the most. Alternatively, leave this option off and let `gzip` work with its default settings. A `gzip` compressed file has the extension `.gz` appended, and the original file is deleted. To uncompress a gzipped file, use the `gunzip` utility.

Using tar

The `tar` (tape archiver) utility has been used with UNIX systems for many years. Unfortunately, it's not very friendly and can be quite temperamental at times, especially when you're unfamiliar with the syntax required to make `tar` do something useful.

The `tar` program is designed to create a single archive file, much as the ZIP utilities do for DOS. With `tar`, you can combine many files into a single larger file, which makes it easier to move the collection or back it up to tape. The general syntax used by `tar` is as follows:

```
tar [options] [file]
```

The options available are lengthy and sometimes obtuse. Files can be specified with or without wildcards. A simple example of creating a `tar` archive file is as follows:

```
tar cvf archive1.tar /usr/tparker
```

This command combines all the files in `/usr/tparker` into a `tar` archive called `archive1.tar`. The c option tells `tar` to create the archive; the v tells it to be verbose, displaying messages as it goes; and the f tells it to use the filename `archive1.tar` as the output file.

The extension `.tar` is not automatically appended by `tar`, but is a user convention that helps identify the file as an archive. This convention isn't widely used, although it should be because it helps identify the file.

The c option creates new archives. (If the file existed before, it is deleted.) The u (update) option is used to append new files to an existing archive or to create the archive if it doesn't exist. This is useful if you keep adding files. The x option is used to extract files from the archive. To extract all the files in the archive in the earlier example with the `tar` command, use the following command:

```
tar xvf archive1.tar
```

There's no need to specify a filename, because the filenames and paths are retained as the archive is unpacked. It's important to remember that the path is saved with the file. So if you archive `/usr/tparker` and then move into `/usr/tparker` and issue the `extract` command, the files are then extracted relevant to the current directory, which places them in `/usr/tparker/usr/tparker`. You must be very careful to extract files properly. If you want to force a new directory path on extracted files, a command-line option allows this.

The `tar` system does not remove the original files as they are packed into the archive nor does it remove the archive file when files are extracted. These steps must be performed manually.

You can use `tar` to copy files to tapes or floppies by specifying a device name and the `f` option as a device name. To archive files in `/usr/tparker` to a floppy disk in the first drive, you could use the following command:

```
tar cvf /dev/fd0 /usr/tparker
```

This can cause a problem if the floppy doesn't have enough capacity, however, so `tar` lets you specify the capacity with the `k` option. In this case, the command for a 1.44MB floppy is as follows:

```
tar cvfk /dev/fd0 1440 /usr/tparker
```

If the floppy is full before the entire archive has been copied, `tar` prompts you for another one. It's important to keep the arguments in the right order. You see that the `f` is before the `k`, so the device name must be before the capacity. All the argument keyletters are gathered together instead of being issued one at a time followed by their value, which is one aspect of `tar` that can be very confusing.

As a last issue in backing up to floppy, it is sometimes necessary to tell the `tar` program about the blocking used (blocking identifies how many blocks are used for each chunk of information on the device). A floppy usually has a blocking factor of 4, so the command becomes the following:

```
tar cvfkb /dev/fd0 1440 4 /usr/tparker
```

A final problem with `tar` is that it can't always handle a generic device such as `/dev/fd0` and must be specifically told the disk type.

For more complete information on all the options used by `tar`, check the man pages or, even better, a good system administration book.

You can use `tar` to archive compressed files, too, in the same manner. You can also compress a `tar` file without any problems. In these cases, you might get filenames such as the following:

```
filename.tar.gz
```

Filenames such as this show that you should run `gunzip` first to recover the `tar` file, and then run `tar` to extract the files in the archive. You can run the commands together with pipes:

```
gunzip filename.tar.gz ¦ tar xvf -
```

The hyphen representing the `tar` filename after the pipe symbol is standard UNIX terminology for taking the input from the pipe (`stdin`). The `tar` command has a lot of other options, many of which are obsolete or seldom used. We look at `tar` in more detail in Chapter 45, "Backups."

Backups

The three rules of system administration are back up, back up, and back up. This might sound silly and trite, but a backup can save you whenever you do something silly to the file system or when problems occur. With UNIX, most backups are made to a tape device using `tar`, although many Linux users don't have tape units available and have to resort to floppies.

Backups are made with the `tar` utility, as mentioned earlier. The procedure is exactly the same as shown earlier. To back up the entire system on floppy, the command is as follows:

```
tar cvfbk /dev/fd0 1440 4 /
```

To back up to a high-capacity tape device larger than the file system (and hence not needing a capacity limit), called `/dev/rct0`, the command is

```
tar cvfk /dev/rct0 20 /
```

In many cases, you won't want to back up the entire system, because it's easier to reinstall off a CD-ROM. However, you should back up your user files by either backing up the entire `/usr` directory or specifically backing up your own home directory.

To restore a backup, you use the `tar` command again:

```
tar xvf /dev/rct0
```

This recovers all files from the tape device `/dev/rct0`. You can explicitly restore specific files if you need to.

Several commercial products offer automated backups, although you can do this quite easily with the `cron` command.

Setting Up Your System

You can perform several little tasks to tweak or optimize your Linux system, although in many cases they are dependent on the version you are running and other applications coexisting. We can look at a few of the miscellaneous tasks here.

Setting the System Name

The system name is contained in a file called `/etc/HOSTNAME`. It is simply the name the system calls itself for identification, which is especially useful if you are networking your Linux machine with others. Your system name (also called a host name) is what other machines will identify your machine as, so make it a unique and descriptive name. You can call the system anything you want.

To set your system name, you can either edit the system files (which should be followed by a reboot to make the changes effective) or use the `hostname` command. The following command sets the machine's name to `hellfire`:

```
hostname hellfire
```

Using a Maintenance Disk

Every system should have a maintenance disk that enables you to check the `root` file system, recover from certain disk problems, and solve simple problems such as forgetting your `root` password. The emergency disks, also called the boot/root floppies, are created with the setup program in most distributions of Linux when the configuration is changed.

You can usually create an emergency boot disk from the CD-ROM that the system came on, as well as obtain the necessary files from FTP sites.

After you have booted your machine with the emergency disk, you can mount the disk partitions with the `mount` command.

Forgetting the `root` Password

This is an embarrassing and annoying problem, but one luckily easily fixed with Linux. (If only other UNIX systems were so easy!) To recover from a problem with the `root` password, use a boot floppy and boot the system. Mount the `root` partition, and edit the `/etc/passwd` file to remove any password for `root`; then, reboot from the hard disk.

After the system has booted, you can set a password again.

> **WARNING**
>
> This points out one major security problem with Linux: Anyone with a boot floppy can get unrestricted access to your system!

Setting the Login Message

If you have more than one user on the system, you can display information about the system, its maintenance, or changes in a file called `/etc/motd` (message of the day). The contents of this file are displayed whenever someone logs in.

To change the `/etc/motd` file, use any text editor and save the contents as ASCII. You can make the contents as long as you want, but readers usually appreciate brevity. The

`/etc/motd` file is useful for informing users of downtime, backups, or new additions. You can also use it to give a more personal feel to your system.

Summary

System administration is not a complicated subject, unless you want to get into the nitty-gritty of your operating system and its configuration. For most Linux users who use the operating system for their personal experimentation, the administration steps explained in this chapter should be sufficient for most purposes. If you want to get into more detail, check out a good UNIX system administration book. From here, you may want to learn more about the following topics:

SCSI (Small Computer Systems Interface) devices and how they add to your Linux system's flexibility are discussed in Chapter 36, "SCSI Device Support."

Setting up email on your Linux system are discussed in Chapter 40, "Configuring Linux for Mail."

The `tar` command, backups, and the importance of making backup copies of your system are discussed in Chapter 45, "Backups."

Devices

by Tim Parker

CHAPTER

33

This chapter is devoted to devices that might be attached to your Linux system, such as terminals, modems, and printers. It shows you how to add and manage the different devices, and it also looks at many of the Linux commands you will need to properly administer your system.

All of this information is necessary if you are to have a smoothly running system. Even if you don't intend to add terminals or modems, you should know about the startup process and how the configuration files are handled.

Character and Block Mode Devices

Everything attached to the computer you are using to run Linux is treated as a device by the operating system. It doesn't matter whether the device is a terminal, a hard disk, a printer, a CD-ROM drive, or a modem. Everything that accepts or sends data to the operating system is a device.

The concept of treating everything on the system as a device is one of the benefits of the UNIX architecture. Each device has a special section in the kernel, called a *device driver*, which includes all the instructions necessary for Linux to communicate with the device. When a new device is developed, it can be used with Linux by writing a device driver, which is usually a set of instructions that explains how to send and receive data.

Device drivers allow the Linux kernel to include only the operating system and support software. By having the instructions for talking to devices within a set of files, they can be loaded as needed (in the case of rarely used devices) or kept in memory all the time when the operating system boots. As refinements are made to a peripheral, small changes to the device driver file can be linked into the kernel to keep the operating system informed of the new features and capabilities.

When an application instructs a device to perform an action, the Linux kernel doesn't have to worry about the mechanism. It simply passes the request to the device driver and lets it handle the communications. Similarly, when you're typing at the keyboard, your terminal's device driver accepts the keystrokes and passes them to the shell or application, filtering out any special codes that the kernel doesn't know how to handle by translating them into something the kernel can perform.

Linux keeps device files in the /dev directory, by default and convention. It is permissible to keep device files anywhere on the file system, but keeping them all in /dev makes it obvious that they are device files.

Every type of device on the Linux system communicates in one of two ways: character by character or as a set of data in a predefined chunk or block. Terminals, printers, and asynchronous modems are character devices, using characters sent one at a time and echoed by the other end. Hard drives and most tape drives, on the other hand, use blocks of data because this is the fastest way to send large chunks of information. These peripherals are called either *character mode* or *block mode devices*, based on the way they communicate.

> **NOTE**
>
> Another way to differentiate between character and block mode devices is by how the buffering to the device is handled. Character mode devices want to do their own buffering. Block mode devices, which usually communicate in chunks of 512 or 1,024 bytes, have the kernel perform the buffering.
>
> Some devices can be both character and block mode devices. Some tape drives, for example, can handle both character and block modes, and therefore have two different device drivers. The device driver that is used depends on how the user wants to write data to the device.

The device file has all the details about whether the device is a character mode or block mode device. There is an easy way to tell which type of device a peripheral is: Look at the output of the listing command that shows file permissions (such as `ls -l`). If the first character is a `b`, the device is a block mode device; a `c` indicates a character mode device.

Device files are usually named to indicate the type of device they are. Most terminals, for example, have a device driver with the name `tty` followed by two or more letters or numbers, such as `tty1`, `tty1A`, or `tty04`. The letters `tty` identify the file as a terminal (`tty` stands for teletype), and the numbers or letters identify the specific terminal referred to. When coupled with the directory name `/dev`, the full device driver name becomes `/dev/tty01`.

Major and Minor Device Numbers

There might be more than one device of the same type on a system. For example, your Linux system might have a multiport card (multiple serial ports) with 10 Wyse 60 terminals hanging off it. Linux can use the same device driver for each of the terminals because they are all the same type of device.

However, there must be a method for the operating system to differentiate which one of the 10 terminals you want to address. That's where device numbers are used. Each device is identified by two device numbers: The major number identifies the device driver to be used, and the minor number identifies the device number. For example, the 10 Wyse 60 terminals on the multiport card can all use a device file with the same major number, but each will have a different minor number, thereby uniquely identifying it to the operating system.

Every device on the system has both major and minor device numbers assigned in such a way as to ensure that they are unique. If two devices are assigned the same number, Linux can't properly communicate with them.

Some devices use the major and minor device numbers in a strange way. Some tape drives, for example, use the minor number to identify the density of the tape and adjust its output in that manner.

Device files are created with the command `mknod` (make node) and removed with the standard `rm` command.

The `mknod` Command

The `mknod` (make node) command is used for several different purposes in Linux. It can create a FIFO (first in first out) pipe or a character or block mode device file. The format of this command is

```
mknod [options] device b¦c¦p¦u major minor
```

The options can be one of the following:

    `--help` displays help information and then exits.

    `-m [mode]` sets the mode of the file to `mode` instead of the default `0666` (only symbolic notation is allowed).

    `--version` displays version information, then exits.

The argument after the device or pathname specifies whether the file is a block mode device (b), character mode device (c), FIFO device (p), or unbuffered character mode device (u). One of these arguments must be present on the command line.

Following the type of file argument are two numbers for the major and minor device numbers assigned to the new file. Every device on a UNIX system has a unique number that identifies the type of device (the major number) and the specific device itself (the minor number). Both a major and a minor number must be specified for any new block, character, or unbuffered mode device. Device numbers are not specified for a type p device.

Examples of using the `mknod` command are shown in several sections later in this chapter, when devices are added to the system.

Printer Administration

Printers are commonly used devices that can cause a few problems for system administrators. They are quite easy to configure as long as you know something about the hardware. Managing printer queues is also quite easy, but like many things in Linux, you must know the tricks to make the system work easily for you.

Linux is based on the BSD version of UNIX, which unfortunately is not the most talented UNIX version when it comes to printer administration. However, because it's unlikely that the Linux system will be used on very large networks with many printers, administration tasks can be reduced to the basics. Be warned, though, that the BSD UNIX printer administration and maintenance commands have a reputation for quirky and inconsistent behavior!

The `lpd` Printing Daemon

All printing on the Linux system is handled by the `lpd` daemon, which is usually started when the system boots. During the startup process, the `lpd` daemon reads through the file `/etc/printcap` to identify the sections that apply to any of the printers known to be attached to the system. The `lpd` daemon uses two other processes, called *listen* and *accept*, to handle incoming requests for printing and to copy them to a spooling area.

In most cases, you won't have to modify the `lpd` daemon. However, there might be times when you have to stop it manually and restart it. The command to load `lpd` is

```
lpd [-l] [port]
```

The `-l` option invokes a logging system that notes each print request. This option can be useful when you're debugging the printer system. The port number allowed in the `lpd` command line is used to specify the Internet port number if the system configuration information is to be overridden. You will probably never have to use it.

The size of the print spool area is set by an entry in the file `minfree` in each spool directory (each printer has its own spool directory). The contents of `minfree` show the number of disk blocks to keep reserved so that spooling large requests doesn't fill up the hard drive. The contents of the file can be changed with any editor.

Access to the `lpd` daemon to allow printing of a user request must pass a quick validation routine. Two files are involved: `/etc/hosts.equiv` and `/etc/hosts.lpd`. If the machine name of the sending user is not in either file, the print requests are refused. Because the local machine is always in `hosts.equiv` (as `localhost`), users on the Linux machine should always have their print requests granted.

33

DEVICES

Following a Print Request

To understand how the print daemon works, as well as how print requests are managed by Linux, it is instructive to follow a print request. When a user requests a print job with the lpr command, lpr assembles the data to be printed and copies it into the spooling queue, where lpd can find it.

> **NOTE**
>
> The lpr program is the only one in the Linux system that can actually queue files for printing. Any other program that offers printing capabilities does so by calling lpr.

As part of its spooling task, lpr also checks for instructions on how to print the file. It can get the information from three sources: the command line (supplied as arguments), environment variables (set by the shell or the user), or the system's default values.

The lpr program knows which spool to put the print request in because of the destination printer designation. The printer destination can be specified on the lpr command line or through an environment variable. When the destination printer name has been determined, lpr checks the file /etc/printcap to look up the printer's information, including the spool directory. The spool directory is usually of the form /usr/spool/printer_name, such as /usr/spool/lp1.

Within the spool directory, lpr creates two files. The first has the letters cf (control file) followed by a print ID number. The cf file contains information about the print job, including the owner's name. The second file starts with df (data file) and has the actual contents of the file to be printed with it. When lpr has finished creating the df file, it sends a signal to lpd that informs the daemon that a print job is waiting in the spool directory.

When lpd gets the signal from lpr, it checks the file /etc/printcap to see whether the printer is for a local or remote printer. If the print job is for a remote printer (one attached to another machine on the network), lpd opens a connection to the remote machine, transfers both the control and data files, and deletes the local copies.

If the print job is for a local printer, lpd checks to make sure the printer exists and is active, and then sends the print request to the printing daemon running that queue.

The `/etc/printcap` File and Spooling Directories

The `/etc/printcap` file is consulted by both the user's print command `lpr` and the `lpd` print daemon. It contains information about every printer that is accessible from the Linux machine.

The format of `/etc/printcap` is straightforward (and similar to the `/etc/termcap` file for terminal descriptions). The following is an extract from `/etc/printcap`:

```
# HP Laserjet
lp¦hplj¦laserjet-acctng¦HP LaserJet 4M in Room 425:\
        :lp=/dev/lp0:\
        :sd=/usr/spool/lp0:\
        :lf=/usr/spool/errorlog:\
        :mx#0:\
        :of=/usr/spool/lp0/hpjlp:\
```

The first field in each entry is a list of all the allowable names for the printer. These can be used with the environment variables set by a user's shell or by the system, as well as with options on the `lpr` command line with a destination printer specified. Valid names are separated by a vertical bar.

Usually, each entry includes at least three names: a short name that is four characters or less (such as `hplj`); a more complete name with an owner, if necessary (such as `laserjet-acctng`); and a full, descriptive name with any other information necessary to identify the printer (such as `HP LaserJet 4M in Room 425`).

> **NOTE**
>
> If a print job is submitted without a destination name, and one can't be determined from environment variable values, it is routed to the printer `lp`. Therefore, one of the printers (usually the system default printer) should also have the name `lp` as part of its identifier.

A comment in the file is shown with a pound symbol (sometimes called a hash mark) as the first character. Following the printer name is a set of two-character parameters and values used by the printer. The format of these entries is always one of the following:

NN	A Boolean value
NN=string	Set equal to `string`
NN#number	Set not equal to `number`

When a Boolean value is used (no assignment follows the two-character identifier), the value is set to True (zero return code) by default. If the value of False (non-zero return code) is required, the two-character identifier will not be included in the description.

Most assignments are shown with colons beginning and ending each definition to enhance readability and make the file easier for the print utilities to parse. Null values are valid assignments employed by putting two colons together.

A few of the parameters in the /etc/printcap file are worth highlighting because they are useful for administration purposes. Not all of these parameters might be present in every printer definition in the /etc/printcap file, but most appear:

sd	The spool directory
lf	The log directory for error messages
af	Accounting log file
mx	Determines the type of files that can be printed
of	Output filter program to be used when printing

All printers should have their own spool directories, usually under the printer name in /usr/spool, such as /usr/spool/hplj. Spool directories are necessary for both remote and local printers. When a new printer is added to the system, the spool directory might have to be created manually (using mkdir). The permissions for the spool directory should be set to 775. The directory must be owned by root or daemon. The group ID should be set to root or daemon, too. In both cases, daemon theoretically is the better ID for user and group, although root will work also.

The error log file can be located anywhere on the system. It can be shared by all printers, if desired, because each log entry includes the name of the printer.

The accounting log file is used to record printouts for systems in which users are charged. If accounting records are not to be used on the system, ignore the entry entirely in the /etc/printcap file. The file can also be used for generating statistics, however. Some heavily used systems may want to have the accounting file for those purposes even when charges are not incurred by the users. An entry is written to the accounting log file after a print job has completed. Account information can be displayed with the Linux pac command. (Use the man pac command to display the man pages for more information about pac.)

The mx character enables you to identify the types of files to be printed. Usually this is set to mx#0, meaning that there are no restrictions on the types of files.

Output filters modify the format of the outgoing file to the printer to fit its requirements. For example, many laser printers can't handle 66 lines per page, so the output filter repaginates to 60 lines (or whatever the number of lines per page is set to). Sometimes, special codes must be added to force line feeds, font changes, or paper bin selections. All these items are part of the output filter. Several other types of filters are available, but the output filter is the one most commonly encountered.

Within each spool directory, there may be two status files: `status` and `lock`. Each file is one line long and can be modified with an editor. These files contain a description of the current state of the printer. They are created and managed by the `lpd` printer daemon and used by several printer commands for status information.

Adding Printer Devices with `mknod`

Linux supports both parallel and serial printer devices. Both parallel and serial printers are character mode devices. Unfortunately, most Linux distributions do not have an easy-to-use printer installation and configuration utilities like many UNIX versions. Instead, the printer devices must be created and set up manually.

Parallel printers are referred to as devices `lp0`, `lp1`, or `lp2`, depending on the address of the parallel port they are used with. (The most common is the single parallel port on a PC, which is `/dev/lp0`.) Valid parallel port devices, their addresses, and their usual equivalents under MS-DOS are as follows:

`/dev/lp0`	`0x03bc`	LPT1
`/dev/lp1`	`0x0378`	LPT2
`/dev/lp2`	`0x0278`	LPT3

NOTE

To determine the address of a parallel port, you can use a diagnostic utility (such as DOS's `MSD.EXE`). Some BIOS versions display port addresses when the system is booting. If you are unsure, try the ports starting with `/dev/lp0` and wait to see whether a printout is possible. The first parallel port on a PC is typically set to address `0x03bc`.

Linux uses the `mknod` (make node) command to create a parallel printer device file. After the device is made, the ownership of the device driver file must be altered to `root` or `daemon`.

The following is a command to make a parallel printer device on the first parallel port (`/dev/lp0`):

```
mknod -m 620 /dev/lp0 c 6 0
chown root.daemon /dev/lp0
```

In this example, the file permissions are set to mode 620, the device /dev/lp0 is created, and it is set to be a character mode device with major device number of 6 and a minor device number of 0. Usually, minor device numbers start at 0 and are incremented upward; therefore, because this is the first printer added, the minor device number is set to 0.

> **NOTE**
>
> The ownership root.daemon is a special Linux convention for the daemons run by root. The entry root.daemon does not appear in the /etc/passwd file. This uses a convention that lets the first part of the entry (before the period) indicate the user and the second part (after the period) represent the group.

If a different device is configured, the device name itself must be changed to the device number. For each possible parallel port, the mknod commands are as follows:

```
mknod -m 620 /dev/lp0 c 6 0
mknod -m 620 /dev/lp1 c 6 1
mknod -m 620 /dev/lp2 c 6 2
```

In these examples, the minor device numbers have been incremented to correspond to the port number. This is not necessary, but it can help with identification.

After the mknod and chown commands have been issued, it is advisable to manually check to ensure that the ownerships are set properly and that a spool directory has been created. If the spool directory doesn't exist, you have to create it manually. The permissions and ownership requirements of the spool directory were given earlier in the section "The /etc/printcap File and Spooling Directories."

Managing Printers with lpc

Printers are controlled through a utility called lpc. The lpc program lets you perform several important functions pertaining to the printers used on your Linux system:

- Display printer status information
- Enable or disable the printer
- Enable or disable the printer queue
- Remove all print requests from a printer's queue

- Promote a particular print request to the top of the queue
- Make changes to the `lpd` printer daemon

The `lpc` program can't be used for remote printers. It affects only those directly attached and configured on the local machine.

WARNING

Be warned that `lpc` is one of the most unpredictable and unreliable programs included with the Linux operating system! It can hang up for no obvious reason, and it can also display erroneous status messages. In some cases, the only way to fix a severely screwed-up printer system is to reset the machine completely!

When used without any arguments, `lpc` prompts you for a command. The following are several valid `lpc` commands and their arguments (a vertical bar indicates a choice of arguments):

- `abort` *printer_name* ¦ `all`   This is similar to the `stop` command except it doesn't allow any print job that is currently being printed to finish before stopping the printer. When used with the `all` argument, all printers are stopped. Any job that is abnormally terminated by the `abort` command is requeued when the printer is started again. See the `stop` command for more details about the printer daemon and lock files.

- `clean` *printer_name* ¦ `all`   This removes all print jobs that are queued, including any active print jobs. In many cases, the currently printing job proceeds normally because it has been passed to the printer daemon or the printer's buffer. All other jobs are removed, though. If the `all` argument is used, all printers have their print queues cleaned.

- `disable` *printer_name* ¦ `all`   This disables the spooling of print requests to the printer (or all printers, depending on the argument). Any jobs that are already queued are unaffected. Any user trying to send a print job to the disabled printer receives a message indicating that the printer is disabled and the print job is refused. Printers are enabled and disabled through changes in the `lock` file in the spool directory.

- `down` *printer_name message*   This is used to take a printer completely offline, usually for an extended period. If a message is included, it can be as long as you want. It is placed in the `status` file in the spool directory and displayed to users trying to queue to the printer. The down command is usually used when a printer has serious problems and must be removed from the system for more than a day.

- enable *printer_name* ¦ all   This enables the spooling of print requests to the printer or all printers.

- exit   This exits from lpc (the same as quit).

- help or ?   This shows a short list of all lpc commands. If an argument is supplied, it displays a one-line description of that command (such as help abort).

- quit   This exits from lpc (the same as exit).

- restart *printer_name* ¦ all   This restarts the printer daemon and is usually used after the printer daemon has died for an inexplicable reason (which the BSD printer daemons tend to do). If the argument all is supplied, all printer daemons are restarted.

- start *printer_name*   This starts the printer, allowing it to print requests. This command starts the printer queue daemon for that printer.

- status *printer_name*   This displays the printer name, whether it has the spool queue enabled, whether printing is enabled, the number of entries in the print queue, and the status of the daemon for that printer. If there are no entries in the queue, no printer daemon will be active. However, if there are entries in the queue and the printer daemon shows as no daemon present, the daemon has died and must be started again with the restart command.

- stop *printer_name*   This stops the printer. Print requests can still be spooled, but they are not printed until the printer is started. If a job is being printed when the stop command is issued, the job completes the print process and then stops printing. The start and stop commands alter the contents of the lock file in the print spool directories. The stop command also kills the daemon for spooling to that printer.

- topq *printer_name* *print_ID*   This moves the print request with *print_ID* to the top of the print queue.

- topq *printer_name* *username*   This moves all print requests owned by *username* to the top of the queue. (This is very handy for system administrators who don't want to wait!)

- up *printer_name*   This is used to reactivate a printer that was taken down. See the down command for more information.

The lpc utility isn't very user-friendly, but it's the only way to handle printers and their queues in Linux. Several front-end menu-driven utilities are beginning to appear that simplify this task.

Managing the Printer Queue with `lpq` and `lprm`

Several commands help you administer the printer queue specifically, instead of relying on the `lpc` command. Two tasks are commonly required by a system administrator: displaying the current queue and removing print jobs in a queue.

To display the current print queue for any printer, use the `lpq` command. It has the following syntax:

```
lpq [-l] [-Pprinter_name] [job_ID ...] [username ...]
```

With no arguments at all, `lpq` displays information about the current printer queues. The `lpq` command normally displays information about who queued the print job, where it is in the queue, the files being printed, and the total size of the files. The `-l` option displays more information about each entry in the printer queue. Usually, only one line of information is displayed.

A specific printer can be displayed with the `-P` option, followed by the printer's name. If no name is supplied, the default system printer is displayed. If one or more *job_ID*s or *username*s is provided, only information about the job or jobs queued by the user is shown.

> **NOTE**
>
> Because users can't access the Linux printer spooling directories, they can remove queued print jobs only with the `lprm` command. If you are a system administrator, you might want to let all system users know how to use this command to keep unwanted print jobs from printing.

The `lprm` command is used to remove files from a printer queue. This command is often mistyped as `lpr`, which doesn't remove the file from the queue. To use `lprm`, you must know the print job ID; or, if you are logged in as `root`, you can remove all jobs for a particular printer. The syntax of the `lprm` command is as follows:

```
lprm [-Pprinter_name] [-] [job_ID ...] [username ...]
```

If the single-hyphen argument is used, `lprm` removes all jobs owned by the user who issues the command. If you are logged in as `root`, all print jobs are removed. A particular printer's jobs can be removed by using the `-P` option. For example, the command

```
lprm -Phplj -
```

removes all print jobs queued on the printer `hplj` by the user who issues the command or all print jobs for that printer, if issued by `root`.

> **WARNING**
>
> It is easy to accidentally remove all print jobs for a printer when you use the `lprm` command as `root`. Take care to use the proper syntax, or you may get frustrated at having to requeue all the jobs!

If a print job ID or a username is supplied as an argument, `lprm` removes that job or all jobs submitted by the user. If no arguments are supplied at all, the currently active job submitted by the user is deleted.

When `lprm` removes files from the queue, it echoes a message to the display. If there are no files to remove, nothing is echoed (and you will be left wondering what, if anything, happened).

If you try to use `lprm` on a job that is currently being printed, it might not be terminated properly because the file might already reside in the printer's buffer. In some cases, terminating a job that is currently printing can cause the printer to lock because some output format files can't handle the termination instructions and freeze when the lock file in the spool directory changes. In cases such as this, the `ps` command must be used to find the output filter process ID, and then it must be killed.

> **NOTE**
>
> In cases of printer lockup that don't seem to resolve themselves with the `lpc` utility, try killing the `lpd` daemon and restarting it. If that doesn't work, you will probably have to reboot the entire system.

Terminals

Most Linux systems use only the system console that came with the PC (the PC's screen and keyboard act as the system console). You won't have to make any configuration changes to Linux to use the system console effectively.

Some system administrators want to add remote terminals to allow other users to work with Linux simultaneously (it *is* a multiuser system, after all). New terminals can be added to the system in one of two ways: through a serial port on the back of the PC or through a multiport card with many serial ports on it.

Using Multiport Cards

Multiport cards provide an easy and effective method of adding many serial ports to your system. Multiport cards are offered by dozens of vendors in different configurations. They provide from 2 to 32 additional serial ports per card (for terminals, modems, or printers), and can use several different types of connectors (such as DB25 25-pin connectors, DB9 9-pin connectors, or RJ11 wide telephone-style jacks).

If you are going to use a multiport card, make sure you can find one with software device drivers that are designed to work with Linux. You can't use any multiport card designed for other versions of UNIX (or Xenix) without modification. Because multiport card device drivers are complex binaries, modification is beyond the scope of most people's programming abilities.

Multiport cards come with complete instructions for installing the device drivers for the multiport card, as well as configuring the terminals. Because the details of the configurations change depending on the manufacturer of the multiport card, you should consult the documentation accompanying the card for more information.

Adding Serial Port Terminals

You can use the serial ports on the PC to add remote terminals. The terminal can be a dedicated terminal or another PC running terminal-emulation software. Linux doesn't really care about the identity of the remote machine, except when it comes to sending instructions for screen displays.

The wiring of cables between the remote terminal and the PC hosting the Linux operating system depends on the type of connectors at both ends. In most cases, the cable is a DTE- (Data Terminal Equipment) to-DTE type, although some terminals and PC serial ports require DCE (Data Communications Equipment) cabling. As a general rule, terminals and remote computers use DTE and modems use DCE. The difference between DTE and DCE cabling is in the way the wires run from each end connector.

When connecting a terminal, however, some of the pins must be crossed to permit signals to pass properly. The wiring of such a cable (often called a *null modem* cable or *hard wired* cable) requires several crosses or shorts to make the connection valid. Serial port connectors on a PC are either a DB9 (9-pin) or a DB25 (25-pin) connector. Not all of the wires in the 25-pin (or the 9-pin, for that matter) are required for a terminal device. A complete terminal cable can be made of only three pins (send, receive, and ground), although Linux also uses the Carrier Detect wire to tell when a terminal is attached and active.

A typical DCE cable (such as for a modem) uses straight-through wiring, meaning that pin 1 on the PC end goes to pin 1 on the modem end, pin 2 goes through to pin 2, and so on. This is called a *straight* cable (also called a *modem* cable by some). The important pins and their meanings for DTE (computer to terminal) 25-pin cables are shown in Table 33.1. The cable numbers are changed for 9-pin connectors, but the crossings are the same.

TABLE 33.1. DTE CABLES FOR A 25-PIN CONNECTOR.

Terminal Pin	Computer Pin	Meaning
1	1	Ground
2	3	Transmit data / receive data
3	2	Receive data / transmit data
4	4	Ready to send
5	5	Clear to send
6	20	Data set ready / data terminal ready
7	7	Ground
8	20	Carrier detect / data terminal ready
20	6, 8	Data terminal ready / data set ready, carrier detect

Because most users want to purchase premade cables to connect remote terminals, we won't deal with building your own cables. Instead, simply visit your local computer store and explain the equipment at both ends, as well as whether you have DB9 (9-pin) or DB25 (25-pin) connectors at each end. Also note whether the connectors at each end are male (pins sticking out) or female (no pins). Usually, the PC has male serial port connectors (requiring a female end on the cable) and a terminal has female connectors (requiring a male connector on the cable); but, if you're connecting a remote PC, you need female connectors at both ends.

NOTE

If the wiring of a cable isn't clearly indicated and the vendor doesn't know whether it's a straight-through or null modem cable, you might need to purchase a null modem device. A null modem is a short connector that has the pin crossings within it, effectively converting a straight-through cable to a null modem cable, and vice versa.

The Login Process

To understand the files involved in a terminal configuration, it is useful to look at the process that occurs whenever a login occurs.

The process begins with the /etc/init daemon executing when the Linux system is booted. The init daemon is responsible for running the /etc/getty program for each terminal that is connected to the system. The init daemon knows whether a terminal is connected because of entries in two files: /etc/ttys and /etc/inittab. The /etc/ttys file lists all ports on the system and the type of terminal that is connected. The /etc/inittab file has a complete list of all terminals and their parameters. We'll look at both files in more detail later, in the section "Terminal Files: /etc/ttys and /etc/inittab."

When the /etc/ttys and /etc/inittab files indicate that a terminal is connected and active, the init daemon runs the /etc/getty program for that terminal. The getty program sets the communications parameters for the terminal and displays the login prompt on the screen.

When a user logs in on the terminal, the getty process executes the login program to request a password. The login program then validates the username and password against the entries in the /etc/passwd file. If the login is valid, the login program displays the message of the day (stored in the file /etc/motd) and executes whatever shell the user is supposed to run (as specified in /etc/passwd). Finally, the login program sets the TERM environment variable and exits.

When the login process terminates, the shell continues to execute and reads the startup files; then, it generates the shell prompt and waits for the user to issue instructions.

As you have seen, many files are involved in the startup process, all in the /etc directory. We can look at the important files (at least for terminal characteristics) in more detail.

What Are /sbin/getty and /etc/gettydefs?

The sbin/getty (/etc/getty on some systems) program is referred to quite a lot when dealing with terminals, but people often don't clearly understand what the program does. Quite simply, /sbin/getty is a binary program that sets the communications parameters between Linux and a terminal, including the speed, protocol, and any special handling of the cable.

The /sbin/getty program is called by /etc/init when a user is logging in. When called, /sbin/getty opens the serial port or other connection to the terminal and sets the communications parameters based on information in the file /etc/gettydefs (getty definitions). The getty process then generates the login prompt on the remote terminal.

Many special handling and command options are available with the getty process, but most of them are of little interest to users and casual system administrators. If you want complete information on the getty command, consult the man pages that accompany Linux.

The /etc/gettydefs file is used to supply the settings getty uses for communications. The format of each line in the gettydefs file is as follows:

```
label:initial flags: final flags: login prompt: next label
```

The *label* is used to identify each line, so that when /sbin/getty is started with an argument (as it usually is, transparent to the user), the argument is used to match the *label* and provide the configuration information. The *initial* and *final* flags are used to set any behavior for the connection before and after the login program has executed.

The *login prompt:* is the prompt to be displayed on the terminal. Usually it is just login:, but it can be any string. Finally, the *next label* is used to send getty to another line, in case it can't use the current one. This is typically used with modem lines, which start at a high speed (such as 9600 baud) and go to 4800, 2400, and 1200 in sequence, trying to connect at each step. For terminals, the next label is usually a pointer back to the line's first *label*.

An extract from a sample /etc/gettydefs file looks like this:

```
console# B19200 OPOST ONLCR TAB3 BRKINT IGNPAR ISTRIP IXON IXANY PARENB
➥ECHO
ECHOE ECHOK ICANON ISIG CS8 CREAD # B19200 OPOST ONLCR TAB3 BRKINT IGNPAR
➥ISTRIP
IXON IXANY PARENB ECHO ECHOE ECHOK ICANON ISIG CS8 CREAD #Console Login:
➥#console

9600H# B9600 # B9600 SANE IXANY PARENB TAB3 HUPCL #login: #4800H

4800H# B4800 # B4800 SANE IXANY PARENB TAB3 HUPCL #login: #2400H

2400H# B2400 # B2400 SANE IXANY PARENB TAB3 HUPCL #login: #1200H

1200H# B1200 # B1200 SANE IXANY PARENB TAB3 HUPCL #login: #300H

300H# B300 # B300 SANE IXANY PARENB TAB3 HUPCL #login: #9600H
```

If you look at the file that accompanies your Linux system, you see that there are many more lines, but they all have the same format as the preceding examples. The easiest lines to look at are the shorter ones (the last five lines in the preceding extract), but they all have the same format as the preceding examples.

These lines are for a modem, starting at 9600 baud. The initial flag is set to B9600, which sets the baud rate at 9600 baud. The final flags, used when a connection has been established, set the characteristics of the line (such as a TAB meaning three spaces). Finally, the field at the end points to the next lower speed to provide checks for slower modems or poor lines that prevent fast logins.

The first line in the preceding extract is typical for a terminal. It sets many initial and final flags that control how the terminal behaves. The reference at the end of the line is back to the same definition, because the terminal is hard-wired to the system.

> **NOTE**
>
> You shouldn't have to change the entries in the gettydefs file, because the default file contains many different configurations. You should examine the file carefully to find an entry that works with the terminal you are using. If you do make changes to the gettydefs file, you should run the command getty -c gettydefs to make the changes effective.

Terminal Files: /etc/ttys and /etc/inittab

Terminal configuration information is stored in the files /etc/ttys and /etc/inittab. These files can be modified by any editor. Some menu-driven programs are now appearing that perform changes to the files for you.

> **WARNING**
>
> Before making any changes to the terminal configuration files, make a safe copy in case the changes aren't effective and the file can't be returned to its original state easily. Simply copy the two files to new names such as /etc/tty.original and /etc/inittab.original.

The /etc/ttys file has two columns. The first shows the type of terminal, and the second shows the device name. A typical /etc/ttys file from a new installation of Linux looks like this:

```
console tty1
console tty2
console tty3
console tty4
console tty5
```

```
console tty6
vt100 ttyp0
vt100 ttyp1
vt100 ttyp2
vt100 ttyp3
```

The terminal type in the first column is used to set the TERM environment variable when you log in, unless you override the value.

The /etc/inittab file is used to set the behavior of each terminal. The format of the /etc/inittab file follows this pattern:

ID:runlevel:action:process

The *ID* is a one- or two-character string that uniquely identifies the entry. In most cases, this corresponds to the device name, such as 1 for tty1.

The *runlevel* decides the capabilities of the terminal with the various states that the Linux operating system can be in (run levels vary from 0 to 6, and A, B, and C). If no entry is provided, all *runlevel*s are supported. Multiple *runlevel*s may be mentioned in the field.

The *action* section shows how to handle the *process* field. The *action* field has several valid entries:

boot	Runs when inittab is first read
bootwait	Runs when inittab is first read
initdefault	Sets initial run level
off	Terminates the process if it is running
once	Starts the process once
ondemand	Always keeps the process running (the same as respawn)
powerfail	Executes when init gets a power fail signal
powerwait	Executes when init gets a power wait signal
sysinit	Executes before accessing the console
respawn	Always keeps the process running
wait	Starts the process once

The *action* indicates the behavior of the terminal device when the system starts and when a getty process is terminated on it.

A simple /etc/inittab file (taken from an earlier version of Linux for clarity's sake because the latest version complicates the lines a little) looks like this:

```
# inittab for Linux
id:1:initdefault:
rc::bootwait:/etc/rc
1:1:respawn:/etc/getty 9600 tty1
2:1:respawn:/etc/getty 9600 tty2
3:1:respawn:/etc/getty 9600 tty3
4:1:respawn:/etc/getty 9600 tty4
```

The first two lines (after the comment) are used when the system boots. The second line tells the system to run /etc/rc in order to boot. The rest of the lines indicate that a getty process should be started for tty1 through tty4 at 9600 baud.

Terminal Definitions: The /etc/termcap File

The /etc/termcap file holds the instructions for communicating with different terminals. Most terminals that are supported by the operating system have an entry inside this file. The termcap (terminal capabilities) file can be quite large. If you are going to make changes, copy a version to a safe filename first.

The contents of the termcap file are similar to the printer definition file /etc/printcap. Each entry in the termcap file has a name with several variations, as well as a set of codes and values for different terminal characteristics. Because terminals use many different codes for different actions, many codes can be used with some of the more talented terminals.

An extract from a termcap file shows the definitions for two fairly simple terminals, the Wyse 30 and Wyse 85:

```
w0¦wy30-vb¦wyse30-vb¦wyse 30 Visible bell:\
        :vb=\E`8\E`\072\E`9:\
        :tc=wy30:
wc¦wy85¦wyse85¦Wyse 85 in 80 column mode, vt100 emulation:\
        :is=\E[61"p\E[13l\E>\E[?1l\E[?3l\E[?7h\E[?16l\E[?5W:\
        :co#80:li#24:am:cl=\E[;H\E[2J:bs:cm=\E[%i%d;%dH:nd=2\E[C:up=2\E[A:\
        :ce=\E[0K:cd=\E[0J:so=2\E[7m:se=2\E[m:us=2\E[4m:ue=2\E[m:\
        :ku=\E[A:kd=\E[B:kr=\E[C:kl=\E[D:\
        :kh=\E[H:xn:\
        :im=:CO=\E[?25h:CF=\E[?25l:ic=\E[1@:dc=\E[1P:\
        :dl=\E[1M:al=\E[1L:GS=\EF:GE=\EG:pt:
```

The meaning of each set of codes is not really of interest to most users and system administrators. You have to start changing or rewriting terminal entries only if you are adding a terminal type that doesn't exist in the termcap file already.

The terminal characteristics in the /etc/termcap file are used by the /etc/ttys file. The first column of the ttys file gives the default terminal type used to set the TERM environment variable. Essentially, the startup routine uses a pattern-matching utility to find a matching line in the termcap file, and then reads the codes that follow.

> **NOTE**
>
> Most terminals offer multiple emulations. If you can't find the terminal type in the termcap file, look for an emulation that is supported. It's easier to emulate a different terminal than to write a termcap entry for a new type.

Adding a Terminal

Terminals are added to Linux in much the same manner as printers—using the mknod command. To add a terminal, you must decide which port the terminal will be connected to. The serial ports on a PC are referred to by Linux as /dev/ttyS0 (for COM1 in DOS terms), /dev/ttyS1 (for COM2), and so on.

Most PC systems have one or two serial ports, although up to four can be accommodated (ttyS0 to ttyS3). Linux uses the serial ports based on their addresses in the BIOS. The usual addresses for the serial ports are as follows:

ttyS0 (COM1)	0x03f8
ttyS1 (COM2)	0x02f8
ttyS2 (COM3)	0x03e8
ttyS3 (COM4)	0x02e8

If you're not sure which serial port is which, you may have to use either a DOS-based diagnostic utility (such as MS-DOS's MSD.EXE) or start at the lowest address and work up, testing the terminal each time. If the PC has only one port, it is almost always configured as COM1.

To create a new terminal device, you must run the mknod (make node) command to create the new device driver file, and then change the permissions on the file to let it be run by root or daemon. Most Linux distributions include the terminal devices already. The mknod command was covered in detail earlier in this chapter. Check out the section "The mknod Command."

A typical command for creating a new terminal device is

```
mknod -m 660 /dev/ttyS0 c 4 64
```

The -m 660 sets the permissions on the file. /dev/ttyS0 specifies the first serial port on the machine (COM1). The c indicates that the terminal is a character device (almost all terminals, except very high-speed high-end models, are character devices). The major device number is set to 4, while the minor device number is set to 64. For the other serial ports on the PC (COM2 through COM4), the commands would be as follows:

```
mknod -m 660 /dev/ttyS1 c 4 65
mknod -m 660 /dev/ttyS2 c 4 66
mknod -m 660 /dev/ttyS3 c 4 67
```

The changes in the minor device number with the preceding different commands are not required, but there must be a unique minor device number for each terminal.

After the mknod command has been executed, the device driver must be set to the proper ownership. Issue the command

```
chown root.tty /dev/ttyS0
```

replacing the /dev/ttyS0 with whatever device the command applies to. The ownership is set to root.tty.

You also want to change the entry in the /etc/ttys file to include the terminal type and device that you have added so that the startup of the terminal can be performed properly. Because the /etc/inittab file already contains entries for the standard serial ports, you can edit the entry for your new terminal's port (if necessary) to set the baud rate and other parameters that may be required.

Using stty and tset

The stty command enables you to change and query a terminal option. The stty command is very complex, with dozens of options that modify the behavior of the terminal device driver. Luckily, only the most intense system administrators have to use the many options, so in this chapter we will ignore most of the details.

To see the current settings of a terminal, use the stty command without any arguments. It displays a set of parameters. You can use this to verify that the terminal has read the configuration information properly from the /etc/inittab and /etc/gettydefs files.

Like stty, the tset command has many options, most of which are seldom used (especially if you are not dealing with strange terminals and weird connectors). The tset command is used to initialize the terminal driver. If the tset command is given with a specific argument, it uses that. Otherwise, the value in the TERM environment variable is used.

33

DEVICES

You can use `tset` within the startup files of a user who always logs in from a remote terminal (through a modem). If you put the command

```
tset -m dialup:vt100
```

in the shell startup file (`.profile`, `.cshrc`, and so on), the terminal type will be set to `vt100` every time a connection is made through the modem. Of course, this sets the terminal type even if someone isn't using a VT100 terminal, so you can use the command

```
tset -m dialup:?vt100
```

to have the user connecting through the modem prompted for the terminal type. The prompt looks like this:

```
TERM=(vt100)?
```

If the user presses Enter, the TERM variable is set to `vt100`. If the user doesn't want to use that value, she can enter the correct string at the prompt.

So far, `tset` seems to be quite simple, but, in fact, it has a very complex structure when dealing with hard-wired terminals. To properly configure a terminal connected through a serial port, you need a command such as this:

```
eval `tset -s -Q -m dialup:?vt100 -m switch:z29`
```

The full details of this type of command are unimportant for most system administrators. If you want more information, check the man pages for `tset` and `stty` that came with your Linux system.

Resetting a Screwy Terminal

Every now and then a terminal connected through a serial port starts acting screwy, either not showing a prompt or generating garbage. There are two quick ways to try to reset the terminal. If they don't work, the terminal should be shut down and restarted. (You might have to kill the processes that were running on the terminal.)

The first approach is to issue a set of Ctrl+J characters on the screwy terminal, and then type **stty sane** followed by another Ctrl+J. The command `stty sane` should reset the terminal characteristics to normal. You probably won't see the letters you are typing, so enter them carefully.

If the terminal isn't behaving at this point, try typing **reset** and pressing Enter or Ctrl+J. If this doesn't work, the terminal is hung and should be reset manually.

Adding a Modem

The process for adding a modem is very similar to that for adding a terminal. In most cases, the procedure outlined earlier in "Adding a Terminal" can be followed.

Modems are used for several purposes on a Linux system, such as networking, connecting to remote systems, and accepting incoming calls. If the modem is to act as a conduit into the Linux system for remote terminals, the procedure given in "Adding a Terminal" is followed, except for the entries that will be selected in the /etc/inittab file. In the case of a modem, find a set of lines that move through the different baud rates the modem supports.

Modems that are to be used for networking through the UUCP utility are dealt with in Chapter 37, "Networking," and Chapter 39, "UUCP." It includes information on setting the different configuration files properly.

For modems used to call out of the system, Linux has a menu-driven configuration utility as part of the setup command, which can set the proper configuration information automatically.

Summary

This chapter has shown you the basics of devices, device management, and how to add new devices to your Linux system. The information presented applies to most distributions of Linux, although there might be some slight changes in options and arguments as the different utilities are enhanced or streamlined. If you want more information about any of the commands, refer to the man pages that came with Linux, or consult a comprehensive system administration book. From here, you can learn more about:

SCSI (Small Computer System Interface) devices and how they add to your Linux system's flexibility in Chapter 36, "SCSI Device Support."

Setting up email on your Linux system in Chapter 40, "Configuring Linux for Mail."

Setting up a news server for Usenet in Chapter 41, "Configuring Linux for News."

The tar command, backups, and the importance of making backup copies of your system in Chapter 45, "Backups."

33

DEVICES

Processes

by Tim Parker

CHAPTER 34

Everything that runs on a Linux system is a process—every user task, every system daemon—everything is a process. Knowing how to manage the processes running on your Linux system is an important (indeed even critical) aspect of system administration. This chapter looks at processes in some detail. In the course of discussing processes, we won't bother with the mechanics behind how processes are allocated or how the Linux kernel manages to time-slice all the processes to run a multitasking operating system. Instead, we'll look at the nitty-gritty aspects of process control that you need in order to keep your system running smoothly.

You may come across the terms *process* and *job* used when dealing with multitasking operating systems. For most purposes, both terms are correct. However, a *job* is usually a process started by a shell (and may involve many processes), while a *process* is a single entity that is executing. To be correct, we'll use the term process throughout.

What You Need to Know About Processes

A formal definition of a process is that it is a single program running in its own virtual address space. This means that everything running under Linux is a process. This is compared to a job, which may involve several commands executing in a series. Alternatively, a single command line issued at the shell prompt may involve more than one process, especially when pipes or redirection is involved. For example, the following command will start three processes, one for each command:

```
nroff -man ps.1 ¦ grep kill ¦ more
```

Types of Processes

There are several types of processes involved with the Linux operating system. Each has its own special features and attributes. The processes involved with Linux are as follows:

- Interactive processes: A process initiated from (and controlled by) a shell. Interactive processes may be in foreground or background.

- Batch processes: Processes that are not associated with a terminal but are submitted to a queue to be executed sequentially.

- Daemon processes: Processes usually initiated when Linux boots and that run in the background until required.

Using the ps Command

The easiest method of finding out which processes are running on your system is to use the ps (process status) command. The ps command has a number of options and arguments, although most system administrators use only a couple of common command line formats. We can start by looking at the basic usage of the ps command, and then examine some of the useful options.

The ps command is available to all system users, as well as root, although the output changes a little depending on whether you are logged in as root when you issue the command.

When you are logged in as a normal system user (in other words, any login but root) and issue the ps command on the command line by itself, it displays information about every process you are running. For example, you might see the following output when you issue the command:

```
$ ps
  PID TTY STAT   TIME COMMAND
   41 v01 S      0:00 -bash
  134 v01 R      0:00 ps
```

ps Command Output

The output of the ps command is always organized in columns. The first column is labeled PID, which means "Process ID" number. Every process on the system has to have a unique identifier so Linux can tell which processes it is working with. Linux handles processes by assigning a unique number to each process, called the process ID number (or PID). PIDs start at zero when the system is booted and increment by one for each process run, up to some system-determined number (such as 65,564) at which point it starts numbering from zero again, ignoring those that are still active. Usually, the lowest number processes are the system kernel and daemons, which start when Linux boots and remain active as long as Linux is running. When you are working with processes (such as terminating them), you must use the PID.

The TTY column in the ps command output shows you which terminal the process was started from. If you are logged in as a user, this will usually be your terminal or console window. If you are running on multiple console windows, you will see all the processes you started in every window displayed.

The STAT column in the ps command output shows you the current status of the process. The two most common entries in the status column are S for "sleeping" and R for "running." A *running* process is one that is currently executing on the CPU. A *sleeping* process is one that is not currently active. Processes may switch between sleeping and running many times every second.

The TIME column shows the total amount of system (CPU) time used by the process so far. These numbers tend to be very small for most processes because they require only a short time to complete. The numbers under the TIME column are a total of the CPU time, not the amount of time the process has been alive.

Finally, the COMMAND column contains the name of the command line you are running. This is usually the command line you used, although some commands start up other processes. These are called "child" processes, and they show up in the ps output as if you had entered them as commands.

Login Shells

As a general convention, a login shell has a hyphen placed before its name (such as -bash in the preceding output) to help you distinguish the startup shell from any shells you may have started afterward. Any other shells that appear in the output do not have the hyphen in front of the name, as the following example shows:

```
$ ps
  PID TTY STAT   TIME COMMAND
   46 v01 S      0:01 -bash
   75 v01 S      0:00 pdksh
   96 v01 R      0:00 bash
  123 v01 R      0:00 ps
```

This output shows that the user's startup shell is bash (PID 46), and that he or she started up the Korn shell (pdksh, PID 75) and another Bourne shell (bash, PID 96) afterward.

Notice in the preceding outputs that the command that actually shows you the process status, ps, appears on the output because it was running when you issued the command. The ps command always appears on the output.

For the Superuser

When normal users issue the ps command, they see only their own processes. If you issue the ps command when you are logged in as the superuser (usually root, although you can change the name), you will see all the processes on the system because the root login owns everything running. This can produce very long outputs, especially on a system with several users, so you will probably want to pipe the output from the ps command to a page filter (such as `more` or `less`) or save the output in a file for further examination. Both commands are shown here:

```
ps | more
ps > /tmp/ps_file
```

Useful ps options

A useful `ps` option for checking user processes is `-u`, which adds several columns to the output of the `ps` command. The output from a user (not `root`) command using this option looks like this:

```
$ ps -u
USER       PID %CPU %MEM SIZE  RSS TTY STAT START   TIME COMMAND
bill        41  0.1  6.8  364  472 v01 S    23:19   0:01 -bash
bill       138  0.0  3.3   72  228 v01 R    23:34   0:00 ps -u
```

The most important addition to the output is the USER column, which shows who started and owns the process. The name listed under the USER column is the user's login name, as found in the `/etc/passwd` file. (`ps` does a lookup in the `/etc/passwd` file to convert the user ID number—UID—to the proper username.)

This option also adds the column labeled %CPU which shows the percentage of CPU time that has been used by the process so far. The column %MEM shows the percentage of your system's memory currently used by the process. These numbers can be handy for finding processes that consume far too much CPU or memory, called "CPU hogs" and "memory hogs" by most administrators. If you see a user process that has very high usage, it is worth checking to make sure it is a valid process and not a runaway that will continue to grind at your system's resources.

When you issue this command logged in as `root`, you see all the processes running on the system. As before, you should consider paginating the output to make it readable. With some versions of Linux's `ps` command, you can also use the `-u` option to specify a user's processes by adding each username. For example, if you are logged in as `root` and want to see only Yvonne's processes, you could issue the following command:

```
ps -u yvonne
```

This format of the `-u` option works with System V versions of `ps`, but not the BSD-based version of `ps` included with most Linux distributions (including the one of the CD-ROM). You can obtain other versions of `ps` on FTP and BBS sites. Most users can issue this command to examine other users' processes, as well. This lets them find out who is hogging all the CPU time! It also lets the superuser see the processes that users are running when they report problems, without having to wade through all the system processes, as well.

Users can also see all the processes running on the system (instead of just the processes started by them) by using the -a option. Because the superuser sees all the processes on the system anyway, the root login doesn't have to use this option, although it is still legal to use it. This output doesn't change, though. When issued by a user (not root), the -a option produces the following output:

```
$ ps -a
  PID TTY STAT TIME COMMAND
    1 psf S    0:00 init
    6 psf S    0:00 update (sync)
   23 psf S    0:00 /usr/sbin/crond -l10
   29 psf S    0:00 /usr/sbin/syslogd
   31 psf S    0:00 /usr/sbin/klogd
   33 psf S    0:00 /usr/sbin/lpd
   40 psf S    0:00 selection -t ms
   42 v02 S    0:01 -bash
   43 v03 S    0:00 /sbin/agetty 38400 tty3
   44 v04 S    0:00 /sbin/agetty 38400 tty4
   45 v05 S    0:00 /sbin/agetty 38400 tty5
   46 v06 S    0:00 /sbin/agetty 38400 tty6
   41 v01 S    0:01 -bash
  140 v01 R    0:00 ps -a
```

This is a relatively short output showing a very lightly loaded system. Most of the entries are the Linux operating system kernel and daemons, as well as serial port getty processes. Only the last two commands were started by the user who issued the ps command. Of course, you can't tell who started each process with this output, so you can combine the -u and -a options (note that you use only one hyphen, followed by the option letters):

```
$ ps -au
USER         PID %CPU %MEM SIZE  RSS TTY STAT START   TIME COMMAND
root          64  0.0  1.5   41  224 v02 S    22:25  0:00 /sbin/agetty
➥38400 tty2
root          65  0.0  1.5   41  224 v03 S    22:25  0:00 /sbin/agetty
➥38400 tty3
root          66  0.0  1.5   41  224 v04 S    22:25  0:00 /sbin/agetty
➥38400 tty4
root          67  0.0  1.5   41  224 v05 S    22:25  0:00 /sbin/agetty
➥38400 tty5
root          68  0.0  1.5   41  224 v06 S    22:25  0:00 /sbin/agetty
➥38400 tty6
root          69  0.0  1.5   56  228 s00 S    22:25  0:00 gpm -t mman
root          71  0.3  3.6  388  532 pp0 S    22:26  0:02 -bash
root         155  0.0  1.5   77  220 pp0 R    22:37  0:00 ps -au
tparker      119  0.4  3.5  372  520 v01 S    22:32  0:01 -bash
tparker      132  0.1  2.2  189  324 v01 S    22:33  0:00 vi test
```

The -au options produce a list with all the same columns as the -u option but shows all the processes running on the system. The order in which you enter the options doesn't matter, so -au is functionally the same as -ua. When you are adding several options, this can be handy.

A few other ps command line options are occasionally useful. The -1 option adds information about which processes started each process (useful when you want to identify child processes):

```
$ ps -l
 F  UID  PID  PPID  PRI  NI  SIZE  RSS  WCHAN   STAT  TTY  TIME  COMMAND
 0  501  41   1     15   0   364   472  114d9c  S     v01  0:00  -bash
 0  501  121  41    29   0   64    208  0       R     v01  0:00  ps -l
```

The PPID (Parent Process ID) column shows which process started that particular process. You will see in the extract from the preceding output, that the ps command itself was started by a bash process because the shell is the entity that is the parent of all user commands. You also see that the PPID for the login Bourne shell is PID "1", which is the init process of the operating system. (If you think about what this means, it implies that if init ever terminates, all other processes die, too. Simply put, when init dies, the entire system is off.)

> **NOTE**
>
> The Linux version of the ps command has a few idiosyncrasies. The hyphen before any options is not strictly necessary, so ps u will work in the same manner as ps -u. However, because UNIX convention (and most UNIX versions) require a hyphen, you should use them.

For System Administrators

Most system administrators get by with three versions of the ps command (when logged in as root). To display information about the system as a whole, the following command lines show practically everything there is to know about processes:

```
ps -ax
ps -aux
ps -le
```

The meaning of the primary columns in the output from the two commands has been mentioned earlier in this section. The rest of the columns are either evident from their short form or not that important. For more information, see the ps man page (which is not entirely accurate or complete, unfortunately).

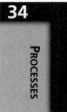

34

PROCESSES

Using `kill`

Occasionally, you will find a process that has locked up a terminal or isn't doing anything, which is generally referred to as a "hung" process. Sometimes a user will have a process that doesn't terminate properly (especially common with programmers). These are "runaway" processes. In both cases, the only way to get rid of the process and restore some normality to the system is to terminate the process entirely. This is done with the `kill` command.

> **WARNING**
>
> When you are "killing" processes and logged in as root, make sure you type the correct PID or you may inadvertently terminate another process. Check the PID carefully! Also, don't `kill` any system processes unless you know what they do and why they need to be terminated.

To use `kill`, you have to have access to another window or console where you can issue commands. If your terminal is completely locked up, you have to find another one to log in on. As a user, you can `kill` only your own processes—you cannot affect any process another user or the system is running. As `root`, you can terminate any process with the `kill` command.

In order to use the `kill` command, you need the process ID number (PID) of the process to be terminated. You have to obtain the PID with the `ps` command and note the PID. Next, use the `kill` command with the PID as an argument. For example, the following terminal session shows a user process called `bad_prog` started by Walter that has hung up and needs to be killed. The PID is obtained by displaying all of the system's processes with their usernames (we've cut the other lines from the `ps` command output for simplicity's sake):

```
$ ps -u
USER    PID %CPU %MEM SIZE RSS TTY STAT START  TIME COMMAND
walter  561 0.1 6.8 364 472 v01 S  13:19  0:01 -bash
walter  598 9.3 4.1 2736 472 v01 R  15:26  2:01 bad_prog
$ kill 598
```

When you issue the `kill` command, you don't get any return message if it works properly. The only way to verify that the process termination has been properly conducted is to issue another `ps` command and look for the PID or process name.

Killing Child Processes

Because some processes spawn child processes with different PIDs, you must be sure to check that all the child processes are terminated. The best way to do this is to watch the names of the executing processes for a few minutes to ensure the child isn't dormant, only to return later. This problem usually happens when the child processes are being generated by a parent. You should check the PPID column (use the `ps -l` option) to see which process is the parent and terminate that.

If the process doesn't terminate properly with the `kill` command, you need to use sterner measures. The `kill` command actually has several levels of operation. When issued with no arguments other than the PID, `kill` tries to gracefully terminate the process (which means any open files are closed, and generally, `kill` is polite to the process). If this doesn't work, you should use the `-9` option, which is a little more forceful in its attempt to terminate the process. For example, to forcefully terminate the process with PID 726, issue the following command:

```
kill -9 726
```

If that doesn't work, then the process may be unkillable. This does happen occasionally with Linux, and the only solution is to shut down and reboot the machine.

Killing Rights

To help prevent a user from killing another user's processes, `ps` checks for the process owner. If a user tries to `kill` another user's process, a message like this one is displayed:

```
kill: - Not owner
```

The superuser doesn't get this message because the superuser login can `kill` anything.

Summary

This chapter has shown you how to obtain listings of the processes currently executing on your Linux system and how to terminate them when they require it. Although you may not have to use this knowledge often, every operating system has occasions where something gets out of hand and you need to control it. The problems multiply as the number of users increases. Instead of rebooting the Linux system, process commands enable you to correct the problem without terminating the operating system.

See the following chapters for related information:

SCSI (Small Computer System Interface) devices and how they add to your Linux system's flexibility are discussed in Chapter 36, "SCSI Device Support."

Setting up e-mail on your Linux system is discussed in Chapter 40, "Configuring Linux for Mail."

Setting up a news server for Usenet is discussed in Chapter 41, "Configuring Linux for News."

The `tar` command, backups, and the importance of making backup copies of your system are discussed in Chapter 45, "Backups."

35

Users and Logins

by Tim Parker

IN THIS CHAPTER

CHAPTER

All access to a Linux system is through a user account. Every user must be set up by the system administrator, with the sole exception of the root account (and some system accounts that users seldom, if ever, use). While many Linux systems only have one user, that user should not use the root account for daily access. Most systems allow several users to gain access, either through multiple users on the main console, through a modem or network, or over hard-wired terminals. Knowing how to set up and manage user accounts and their associated directories and files is an important aspect of Linux system administration.

This chapter looks at the the following subjects:

- The root (superuser) account
- How to create new users
- The files a new user requires
- What is a group of users
- Managing groups

The Superuser Account

When the Linux software is installed, one master login is created automatically. This login, called root, is known as the *superuser* because there is nothing the login can't access or do. While most user accounts on a Linux system are set to prevent the user from accidentally destroying all the system files, for example, the root login can blow away the entire Linux operating system with one simple command. Essentially, the root login has no limitations.

> **WARNING**
>
> The sheer power of the root login can be addictive. When you log in as root you don't have to worry about file permissions, access rights, or software settings. You can do anything at anytime. This power is very attractive to newcomers to the operating system, who tend to do everything while logged in as root. It's only after the system has been damaged that the root login's problems become obvious: There are no safeguards! As a rule, you should only use the root login for system maintenance functions. Do not use the superuser account for daily usage!

The root login should be kept only for those purposes where you really need it. It's a good idea to change the login prompt of the root account to clearly show that you are logged in as root, and hopefully you will think twice about the commands you issue when you use that login. You can change the login prompt with the PS environment variable, discussed in Chapter 14, "Shell Programming." If you are on a standalone system and you destroy the entire file system, it's only you that is inconvenienced. If you are on a multiuser system, however, and insist on using root for common access, you will have several very angry users when you damage the operating system.

So, after all of these dire warnings, the first thing you should do on a new system is create a login for your normal daily usage. Set the root password to something that other users of the system (if there are any) will not easily guess and change the password frequently to prevent snooping.

You can also create special logins for system administration tasks that do not need wide-open access, such as tape backups. You can set a login to have root read-only access to the entire file system but without the potential for damage. This lets you back up the system properly, but not erase the kernel by accident. Similar special logins can be set up for email access, gateways to the Internet, and so on. Think carefully about which permissions each task requires and create a special login for that task—your system will be much more secure and have less chance of accidental damage.

To be precise, the superuser account doesn't have to be called root. It can have any name. The superuser account is always defined as the account with a user ID number of zero. User ID numbers are defined in the /etc/passwd file.

User Accounts: /etc/passwd

Even if you are the only user on your Linux system, you should know about user accounts and managing users. This is because you should have your own account (other than root) for your daily tasks. You therefore need to be able to create a new user. If your system lets others access the operating system, either directly or through a modem, you should create user accounts for everyone who wants access. You may also want a more generic guest account for friends who just want occasional access.

Every person using your Linux system should have his or her own unique username and password. The only exception is a guest account or perhaps an account that accesses a specific application, such as a read-only database. By keeping separate accounts for each user, your security is much tighter, and you have a better idea of who is accessing your system and what they are doing. A one-to-one correspondence between users and accounts makes tracking activities much easier.

All the information about user accounts is kept in the file /etc/passwd. The /etc/passwd file should be owned only by root and have the group ID set to zero (usually root or system group, as defined in the /etc/group file). The permissions of the /etc/passwd file should be set to allow write access only by root, but all others can have read access. (We deal with groups and permissions later in this section.) The lines in the /etc/passwd file are divided into a strict format:

username:password:user ID:group ID:comment:home directory:login command

This format can best be seen by looking at a sample /etc/passwd file. The /etc/passwd file created when a Linux system is newly installed is shown in Listing 35.1.

LISTING 35.1. THE /etc/passwd FILE CREATED WHEN LINUX IS FIRST INSTALLED.

```
root::0:0:root:/root:/bin/bash
bin:*:1:1:bin:/bin:
daemon:*:2:2:daemon:/sbin:
adm:*:3:4:adm:/var/adm:
lp:*:4:7:lp:/var/spool/lpd:
sync:*:5:0:sync:/sbin:/bin/sync
shutdown:*:6:0:shutdown:/sbin:/sbin/shutdown
halt:*:7:0:halt:/sbin:/sbin/halt
mail:*:8:12:mail:/var/spool/mail:
news:*:9:13:news:/usr/lib/news:
uucp:*:10:14:uucp:/var/spool/uucppublic:
operator:*:11:0:operator:/root:/bin/bash
games:*:12:100:games:/usr/games:
man:*:13:15:man:/usr/man:
postmaster:*:14:12:postmaster:/var/spool/mail:/bin/bash
nobody:*:-1:100:nobody:/dev/null:
ftp:*:404:1::/home/ftp:/bin/bash
```

Each line in the /etc/passwd file is composed of seven fields, separated by a full colon. If there is nothing to be entered in a field, the field is left blank, but the colons are retained to make sure each line has seven fields (which also means each line will have six colons). The seven fields (from left to right on each line) are as follows:

username	A unique identifier for the user
password	The user's password (encrypted and therefore not readable by users)
user ID (UID)	A unique number that identifies the user to the operating system

group ID (GID)	A unique number that identifies the user's group (for file permissions)
comment	Usually the user's real name, but sometimes phone numbers, departments, and so on
home directory	The directory in which the user is placed when they log in
login command	The command executed when the user logs in, normally a shell

Let's look at each field in a little more detail. You should know what each field does and how it is used by other programs on your Linux system. Note that this type of user file is used with almost every UNIX system in the world, so once you know it for Linux, you know it for most UNIX versions.

Usernames

The username is a single string, usually eight characters or less, that uniquely identifies each user. Since the username is the basis of most communications between users and other machines, the username you use (or assign to others) should be simple and obvious. Usually, this means a permutation of the user's real name. A typical username may be a combination of the user's first and last names, such as `tparker` or `timp`. The former example, composed of the first initial and last name, is fairly common in large networks.

Note that the characters in these examples are all lowercase. Case is important in Linux (as with all UNIX versions), so `tparker` and `Tparker` are two different logins. Since most Linux commands are lowercase, convention is to also keep usernames lowercase. Underscores, periods, numbers, and some special characters are allowed, but should be avoided.

Small systems, such as on a single machine, may use more familiar names, such as the user's first name only. A small system may have users with the names `tim`, `bill`, `yvonne`, and so on. If two users have the same name, then there must be some method found to differentiate between the two (such as `bill` and `billy`).

A few users like to create cryptic usernames that reflect their hobbies, nicknames, pets, lifestyle, or personality. You may find usernames such as `vader`, `grumpy`, `wizard`, and `hoops`. This type of naming is fine on small systems that are used by one or two users, but quickly becomes awkward on larger systems where other users may not know their coworkers' usernames. On the whole, if your system is used by more than a couple of people, discourage this type of username.

Passwords

The system stores the user's encrypted password in this field. (Actually, the password is encoded, not encrypted, although the convention has always been to use the term encrypted.) This field is very sensitive to changes, and any modification whatsoever can render the login useless until the system administrator performs a password change. A user's password can only be changed by the system administrator by using the passwd command when logged in as root (or by the user himself).

> **NOTE**
>
> Some versions of UNIX do not keep the passwords in the /etc/passwd file because of potential security problems. If the password fields on your system are all set to x, then another file (called a *shadow password* file) is in use. However, all versions of Linux currently available do use this field normally.
>
> Systems running either Yellow Pages or NIS (Network Information Service), both of which rely on a central file of usernames and passwords, do not use this field. However, few Linux systems use either YP or NIS, so this distinction can be ignored for the moment.

When a user logs in, the login program logically compares the password that the user types to a block of zeros and then compares that result to the entry in the password field. If they match, the user is granted access. Any deviation causes login to refuse access.

This field can be used to restrict access to the system. If you want a login to never be used for access, such as a system login like lp or sync, place an asterisk between the two colons for this field. This restricts all access. In the example /etc/passwd file shown earlier, you can see that many system logins have an asterisk as their password, effectively blocking access.

This field can also be used to allow unrestricted access by leaving it blank. If there is no password, anyone using the username is granted access immediately, with no password requested. This is a very bad habit to get into! Do not leave passwords open unless you are using your Linux system strictly for your own pleasure and have nothing of value on the file system.

Don't attempt to put a password in the password field—you cannot re-create the encryption method, and you'll end up locking the user out. At this point, only the system administrator is able to change the password and allow access.

User ID

Every username has an associated, unique user ID. The user ID, also called the UID, is used by Linux to identify everything associated with the user. The user ID is preferable to the username because numbers are easier to work with than the characters in a name, and they take up much less space. Linux tracks all processes started by a user, for example, by the user ID and *not* the username. A translation can take place in some utilities to display the username, but the utility generally examines the /etc/passwd file to match the UID to the name.

The user ID numbers are usually assigned in specific ranges. Most UNIX systems, for example, allocate the numbers from 0 to 99 for machine-specific logins, and the user ID numbers from 100 and up for users. This is a good working model and makes your system consistent with others. In the example /etc/passwd file shown earlier, you can see that root has a UID of 0, while the other system-created logins have numbers ranging upward. The login "nobody" is a special login used for NFS (Network File System) and has a UID of -1, an invalid number. When you assign user ID numbers, it is a good idea to assign them sequentially, so the first user is 100, the second 101, and so on.

Group ID

The group ID (GID) is used to track the user's startup group (in other words, the ID of the group the user belongs to when they log in). A group, as you will see later, is used for organization purposes to set file permissions, although many organizations don't bother with them. Group ID numbers range from zero on up. Linux systems assign a group called users with the group number 100 for this purpose.

The GID is used by the system when tracking file permissions, access, and file creation and modification specifications. If your system has only a single user group, then you need not worry about the GID. If you work with several groups (as might be implemented on a large system), then you need to examine the /etc/group file.

Comments

This field is used for the system administrator to add any information necessary to make the entry more self-explanatory. Typically, this area is used to enter the user's full name, although some system administrators like to add department or extension numbers for convenience. (This field is sometimes called the GECOS field, after the operating system that first used it.)

35

USERS AND LOGINS

The comment field is used by some utilities to display information about users, so make sure you don't place any sensitive information there. Electronic mail systems, for example, can access this field to show who is sending mail. While you don't have to use the field, on larger systems it can make things much easier for administrators and other users when they can discover the real name of the person the username belongs to.

Home Directory

The home directory field indicates to the login process where to place users when they log in. This is usually their home directory. Each user on the system should have her own dedicated home directory, and then the startup files will initialize the environment variable HOME to this value. The directory indicated in this field is the user's initial working directory only and places no restrictions on the user (unless file permissions have been set to restrict movement).

For the most part, user home directories are located in a common area. Linux tends to use the /home directory, so you will find home directories such as /home/tparker, /home/ychow, and so on. Other versions use /usr, /user, or /u as user home directories. In some cases where the system administrator has experience with another type of UNIX that uses an alternate directory structure, you may find the home directories changed to make life easier (and more familiar) for that administrator. As far as Linux is concerned, it doesn't care what the name of the home directory is, as long as it can be entered.

Login Command

The login command is the command to be executed when login terminates. In most cases this is a shell command that is started, such as the C Shell or Bourne Shell, to provide the user with a shell environment. In some cases, it may be a single application or front-end system that restricts what the user can do. For example, the uucp login (used for email and other simple networking tasks) executes the uucp command only. If the login command field is left empty, the operating system usually defaults to the Bourne shell (although this may change depending on the manner in which the operating system is set up).

Many versions of Linux enable users to change their login shell with the commands chsh or passwd -s. When this command is used, the file /etc/shells is searched for a match. Only those commands in the /etc/shells file are allowed as valid entries when the user tries to change his startup shell. (You can add or remove lines in the /etc/shells file using any editor.) This helps you keep tighter security on the system. The superuser account has no restrictions on the entry in this field (or any other user's field). If your system uses the /etc/shells file, make sure it has the same file permissions and ownership as the /etc/passwd file, or a user can sneak through the system security by modifying the startup command for her login.

Default System Usernames

The extract from the /etc/passwd file shown in the preceding section lists over a dozen system-dependent usernames. These all serve special purposes on the Linux system. A few of these logins are worth noting because they have specific uses for the operating system and for system administrators:

root	The superuser account (UID 0) with unrestricted access and owns many system files.
daemon	Used for system processes. This login is used only to own the processes and set their permissions properly.
bin	Owns executables.
sys	Owns executables.
adm	Owns accounting and log files.
uucp	Used for UUCP communication access and files.

The other system logins are used for specific purposes (postmaster for mail, and so on) that are usually self-explanatory. You should not change any of the system logins. In most cases, they have an asterisk in the password field preventing their use for entry purposes.

Adding Users

There are two ways to add users to your system: Manually edit the /etc/passwd file or use an automated script that prompts you for the new user's details and writes a new line to the /etc/passwd file for you. The automated approach is handy for new system administrators who are uneasy about editing a file as important as /etc/passwd or for those occasions when you have to add several users and the risk of error is thus increased. You must modify the /etc/passwd file when you are logged in as root.

WARNING

Before making changes to your /etc/passwd file, make a copy of it! If you corrupt the /etc/passwd file you will not be able to log in, even as root, and your system is effectively useless except in system administration mode. Keep a copy of the /etc/passwd file on your emergency floppy or boot floppy in case of problems.

35

USERS AND LOGINS

To add an entry to the /etc/passwd file, use any editor that saves information in ASCII. Add the new users to the end of the file, using a new line for each user. Make sure you use a unique username and user ID (UID) for each user. For example, to add a new user called "bill" to the system with a UID of 103 (remember to keep UIDs sequential for convenience) and a GID of 100 (the default group), a home directory of /home/bill, and a startup shell of the Bourne shell, add the following line to the /etc/passwd file:

```
bill::103:100:Bill Smallwood:/home/bill:/bin/sh
```

Note that we have left the password blank because you can't type in an encrypted password yourself. As soon as you have saved the changes to /etc/passwd, set a password for this account by running the following command:

```
passwd bill
```

This command prompts you for an initial password. Set the password to something that Bill will be able to use, and ask him to change the password the first time he works on the system. Many system administrators set the initial password to a generic string (such as "password" or the login name) and then force the new user to change the password the first time they log in. Using generic strings is usually acceptable if the user logs in quickly, but don't leave accounts with generic login strings sitting around too long—someone else may use the account.

After you have added the necessary line to the /etc/passwd file, you should create the user's home directory. Once created, you must set the ownership to make that user own the directory. For the preceding example, you would issue the following commands:

```
mkdir /home/bill
```

```
chown bill /home/bill
```

All users must belong to a group. If your system has only one group defined, then add the user's username to the line in the /etc/group file that represents that group. If the new user should belong to several groups, add the username to each group in the /etc/group file. The /etc/group file and groups in general are discussed in the "Groups" section later in the chapter.

Finally, the configuration files for the users' shells should be copied into their home directory and set to allow them access for customization. For example, if you copy the Bourne shell's .profile file from another user called "yvonne," you would issue the following commands:

```
cp /home/yvonne/.profile /home/bill/.profile
```

```
chown bill /home/bill/.profile
```

You should also manually check the configuration file to ensure there are no environment variables that will be incorrectly set when the user logs in. For example, there may be a line defining the HOME environment variable or the spool directories for printer and mail. Use any ASCII editor to check the configuration file. If you are using the Korn or C shell, there are other configuration files that need to be copied over and edited. Bourne shell compatibles need only a .profile, while the C Shell and compatibles need .login and .cshrc. The Korn shell and compatibles need a .profile and usually another file with environment variables embedded in it.

In general, the process for manually adding a new user to your system is as follows:

1. Add an entry for the user in the /etc/passwd file.

2. Create the user's home directory and set the ownership.

3. Copy the shell startup files and edit their settings and ownerships.

Some distributions of the Linux system have a holdover command from the Berkeley BSD UNIX version. The command vipw invokes the vi editor (or whatever the default system editor has been set to) and edits a temporary copy of the /etc/passwd file. The use of a temporary file and file lock acts as a lock mechanism to prevent two different users from editing the file at the same time. When the file is saved, vipw does a simple consistency check on the changed file, and if all appears proper, the /etc/passwd file is updated.

The automated scripts for Linux tend to have the names useradd or adduser. When run, they prompt you for all the information that is necessary in the /etc/passwd file. Both versions let you exit at any time to avoid changing the /etc/passwd file. The automated scripts also tend to ask for an initial password, which you can set to anything you want or leave blank. One advantage of the automated scripts is that they copy all the configuration files for the supported shells automatically, and in some cases, make environment variable changes for you. This can significantly simplify the process of adding users.

> **NOTE**
>
> A quick note on passwords—they are vitally important to the security of your system. Unless you are on a standalone Linux machine with no dial-in modems, every account should have a secure password. Passwords are assigned and changed with the passwd command. The superuser can change any password on the system, but a user can only change his own password.

35

USERS AND
LOGINS

Deleting Users

Just like adding new users, deleting users can be done with an automated script or manually. The automated script `deluser` or `userdel` asks which user you want to delete, and then removes the entry from the `/etc/passwd` file. Some scripts also clean out the spool and home directory files, if you want. You must make any deletions to the `/etc/passwd` file when logged in as `root`.

If you delete users manually, simply remove their entries from the `/etc/passwd` file. Then you can clean up their directories to clear disk space. You can completely delete all their files and their home directory with the following command:

```
rm -r /home/userdir
```

`/home/userdir` is the full pathname of the user's home directory. Make sure there are no files you want to keep in that directory before you blow them all away!

Next, you should remove the user's mail spool file, which is usually kept in `/usr/spool/mail/username`. For example, to remove the user `walter`'s mail file, issue the following command:

```
rm /usr/spool/mail/walter
```

The spool file is a single file, so this command cleans up the entries properly. To finish off the mail cleanup, check that the user has no entries in the mail alias files (usually `/etc/aliases`) or you can force all mail for that user to another login (such as `root`). To make any changes to the `/etc/aliases` file effective, you must run the `newaliases` command.

Finally, clean up the user's `cron` and `at` jobs. You can display the user's `crontab` file using the `crontab` command.

If you need to retain the user for some reason (such as file ownerships, a general access account, or accounting purposes), you can disable the login completely by placing an asterisk in the password field of the `/etc/passwd` file. That login can never be used once an asterisk is in the password field. If you need to reactivate the account, simply run the `passwd` command.

The process for manually deleting a user (or using an automated script that doesn't clean up directories and files) is as follows:

1. Remove the user's entry from `/etc/passwd` and `/etc/group`.
2. Remove the user's mail file and any mail aliases.

3. Remove any `cron` or `at` jobs.

4. Remove the home directory if you don't want any files it contains.

Occasionally, you may want to temporarily disable a user's account, such as when he or she goes on an extended leave or vacation. If you want to temporarily disable the login but be able to recover it at any time in the future, add an asterisk as the first character of the encrypted password. Don't alter any characters in the existing passwords, but just add the asterisk to the front. When you want to reactivate the account, remove the asterisk, and the password is back to whatever it was set at before you made the changes.

Groups

Every user on a UNIX and Linux system belongs to a group. A group is a collection of individuals lumped together for some reason. The users in a group may all work in the same department, may need access to a particular programming utility, or may all have access to use a special device, such as a scanner or color laser printer. Groups can be set up for any reason, and users can belong to any number of groups. However, a user can only be a member of one group at a time, because groups are used for determining file permissions, and Linux only allows one group ID per user at any point in time.

Groups can have their permissions set so that members of that group have access to devices, files, file systems, or entire machines that other users who do not belong to that group may be restricted from. For example, this can be useful when you have an accounting department, all members of which need access to the company's accounts. However, you wouldn't want non-accounting people to go snooping through financial statements, so creating a special group that has access to the accounting system makes sense.

Many small Linux systems have only one group, the default group, because that is the simplest way to manage a system. Then, each user's access to devices and files is controlled by the devices' or files' permissions, not the group. When you start to get several different users in logical groupings, though, groups start to make more sense. You can even use groups to control your friends' or children's access to areas on your home Linux system.

Group information is maintained in the file `/etc/group`, which is similar in layout to the `/etc/passwd` file. The default `/etc/group` file from a newly installed Linux system is shown in Listing 35.2.

LISTING 35.2. THE DEFAULT /etc/group FILE.

```
root::0:root
bin::1:root,bin,daemon
daemon::2:root,bin,daemon
sys::3:root,bin,adm
adm::4:root,adm,daemon
tty::5:
disk::6:root,adm
lp::7:lp
mem::8:
kmem::9:
wheel::10:root
floppy::11:root
mail::12:mail
news::13:news
uucp::14:uucp
man::15:man
users::100:games
nogroup::-1:
```

Each line in the file has four fields separated by colons. Two colons together mean that the field is empty and has no value specified. Each line in the file follows this format:

```
group name:group password:group ID:users
```

Each group has a line of its own in the file. The fields in the /etc/group file (from left to right) are listed as follows:

- group name—A unique name usually of eight characters or fewer (usually standard alphanumeric characters only).
- password—Usually left as an asterisk or blank, but a password can be assigned that a user must enter to join the group. Not all versions of Linux or UNIX use this field, and it is left in the file for backward-compatibility reasons.
- group ID (GID)—A unique number for each group, used by the operating system.
- users—A list of all user IDs that belong to that group.

Every Linux system has a number of default groups which belong to the operating system, usually called bin, mail, uucp, sys, and so on. You can see the system-dependent groups in the default /etc/group file as shown in Listing 35.2. In that file, all but the last two entries are system groups. You should never allow users to belong to one of these groups because it gives them access permissions that can be the same as root's. Only system logins should have access to these operating-system groups.

Default System Groups

You may have noticed in the startup /etc/group file shown in Listing 35.2 that there are several groups defined. These groups are used to set file permissions and access rights for many utilities. It's worth taking a quick look at some of the most important groups and their functions:

root/wheel/system	Usually used to enable a user to employ the su command to gain root access, it owns most system files.
daemon	Used to own spooling directories (mail, printer, and so on).
kmem	Used for programs that need to access kernel memory directly (including ps).
sys	Owns some system files; on some systems this group behaves the same as kmem.
tty	Owns all special files dealing with terminals.

The default group for the SlackWare Linux version /etc/group file, shown previously, is called users, and has a GID of 100. (Many UNIX systems have the default group called group with a group ID of 50 which is the convention.)

Adding a Group

You can edit the information in the /etc/group file manually, using any ASCII editor, or you can use a shell utility such as addgroup or groupadd which goes through the process for you. As a system administrator, you may find it easier to do the changes manually because you can see the entire group file at the time you are editing it. Not all versions of Linux have an addgroup or groupadd utility.

To manually add a group to the /etc/group file, first make a backup copy of the file. Use any ASCII editor and add one line to the file for each new group you want to create. Make sure you follow the syntax of the file carefully because incorrect entries prevent users from belonging to that group. In the following lines, two new groups have been created:

```
accounts::101:bill
scanner::102:yvonne
```

The two groups have GIDs of 101 and 102, and like user IDs, the GIDs should be assigned sequentially for convenience. The users that are in the group are appended. In these cases, only one user is in each group. You'll see how to assign multiple users to a group in the next section. The groups do not have to be in order of the GID or group name, although for convenience you usually have the file ordered by GID. You could add new lines anywhere in the file.

The /etc/group file should be checked for file permissions and ownership after you have made changes to it. The file should be owned by root and have a group owner of root (or system, depending on the group with GID 0). The file permissions should prevent anyone but root from writing the file.

Adding a User to New Groups

Users can belong to many groups, in which case their user IDs should be on each group line that they belong to in the file /etc/group. Each username on a line in the /etc/group file is separated by a comma. There is no limit to the number of users that can belong to a group, in theory, but in practice, the line length of the Linux system (255 characters) acts as an effective limiter. There are ways around this limit, but few systems will require it.

The following excerpt from a /etc/group file shows several groups with multiple members:

```
accounts::52:bill,yvonne,tim,roy,root
prgming::53:bill,tim,walter,gita,phyliss,john,root
cad::54:john,doreen,root
scanner::55:john,root,tim
```

The usernames on each line do not have to be in any particular order. Linux searches along each line to find the usernames it wants.

A user can be a member of only one group at a time while logged in, so he must use the command newgrp to change between groups they are members of. The starting group a user belongs to when he logs in is given by the GID field in the /etc/passwd file.

Deleting a Group

If you decide you don't want a particular group to exist anymore, you can simply remove the group name from the /etc/group file. You should also check the /etc/passwd file to see if any users have that group ID as their startup GID, and change it to another group they are members of. If you don't change the GIDs, the users will not be able to log in because they have no valid group membership. You should also scan the entire file system for files and directories that are owned by that group and change them to another group. Failure to make this change may prevent access to the file or directory.

Some Linux versions have shell scripts that remove group lines from the /etc/group file for you. The utility is generally called delgroup or groupdel. However, most versions of Linux don't bother with this utility.

The su Command

Sometimes you want to execute a command as another user. If you are logged in as super-user and want to create files with `bill`'s permissions and ownership set, it is easier to log in as `bill` than work as root and then reset all the parameters. Similarly, if you are logged in as a user and need to be superuser for a little while, you would have to log out and back in to make the change. An alternative is the `su` command.

The `su` command changes your effective username and grants you the permissions that username has. The `su` command takes the username you want to change to as an argument. For example, if you are logged in as a typical user and want to be root, you can issue the following command:

```
su root
```

The Linux system prompts you for the root password. If you supply it correctly, you will be root until you issue a Ctrl+D to log out of that account and back to where you started. Similarly, if you are logged in as root and want to be a user, you can issue the command with the username, such as the following:

```
su tparker
```

You won't be prompted for a password when changing from root to another user because you have superuser powers. When you Ctrl+D out of the login, you are back as root. If you are logged in as a normal user and want to switch to another non-root login, you have to supply the password, though.

Summary

In this chapter we've looked at the basics of the `/etc/passwd` and `/etc/group` files, the two files intimately connected with user access to Linux. As you have seen, these are simple files and can easily be modified by a system administrator to add users and groups at any time. Always bear in mind that these are vital files, and they should be copied to a backup filename, then edited carefully and their permissions checked after each edit. From here, you can explore the following topics:

Learn more about SCSI (Small Computer System Interface) devices and how they add to your Linux system's flexibility in Chapter 36. "SCSI Device Support."

Learn more about setting up e-mail on your Linux system in Chapter 40, "Configuring Linux for Mail."

Learn more about the `tar` command, backups, and the importance of making backup copies of your system in Chapter 45, "Backups."

35

USERS AND LOGINS

SCSI Device Support

by Tim Parker

SCSI (Small Computer System Interface), pronounced "scuzzy," is a standard method of interfacing between a computer and peripherals. It has many advantages over other interconnect systems such as IDE, albeit generally at a higher price.

SCSI uses a dedicated controller card within the computer from which a chain of devices can be connected. All the SCSI devices are coupled using a flat-ribbon cable (internally) or a shielded cable (externally). With the older SCSI standards, each SCSI chain can support seven devices. Each device has a SCSI ID number from 0 to 7. Usually, the controller card is set to use number 7 while bootable SCSI hard drives are set to use SCSI ID 0. The other numbers are available for other devices, although each ID can be used by only one device. Newer SCSI standards allow up to 15 devices and the controller card, with the devices numbered 0 through 15.

The advantages of SCSI are primarily in its high speed. Also, with most SCSI devices, all the electronics needed to control them are attached to the device, making it easier for devices to talk to one another. The other major advantage of SCSI is that you don't have to do anything special to configure the system. When you plug in a new SCSI device (such as a scanner) with a unique SCSI ID, the system controller card recognizes it because the onboard electronics identify the type of device to the card automatically.

SCSI devices must have a terminator at each end of the chain. Terminators are a set of resistors that provide an electrical indication that the chain ends at that point. There should be only two terminators on each SCSI chain, one at each end. Most SCSI controller cards have a set of switches or a block of removable resistors that terminate one end, while SCSI devices have a switch or resistors that allow that device to automatically terminate the chain. Some devices are clever enough to sense that they are the last SCSI device in a chain, and they terminate without any intervention from you.

SCSI devices can communicate with one another quickly over the chain. A scanner can send instructions straight to a hard drive, and a tape drive can dump information straight to another SCSI device without involving the operating system too much. This helps the speed and makes SCSI devices particularly flexible.

Newer SCSI Standards

A few years ago, there was only one type of SCSI system. Now, there are at least five different SCSI versions, some compatible with one another and some not. The five types of SCSI really break down into three categories, called SCSI-I, SCSI-II, and SCSI-III. SCSI-I is the traditional 8-bit wide SCSI chain supporting seven devices. The connectors on SCSI-I devices are wide 50-pin rectangular affairs. SCSI-I was limited in speed, so several faster systems have become available. It's important not to mix up the name of the SCSI system and the type of connector it uses, because the two do not always correspond. SCSI-II usually allows 15 devices on a chain and has a much smaller connector, D-shaped with 50 pins, for its devices. SCSI-II allows 15 devices, too, but has a much wider 68-pin D-shaped connector than SCSI-II.

You're likely going to hear all kinds of terms to do with SCSI, such as Fast and Wide, UltraWide, and so on. The terms relate to whether the internal SCSI connections are 50 or 68 pins, and whether the external is 40 or 68 pins. Internal and external connections can be different widths which makes this all a little confusing. Table 41.1 shows the different SCSI standards and their properties:

TABLE 41.1. SCSI STANDARDS, NAMES, AND PROPERTIES.

Name	Host Bus	Internal SCSI Connectors	External SCSI Connectors	Maximum Speed (Mbps)
SCSI (SCSI-I)	EISA/ISA/PCI	50	50 pin	10
Fast Wide (SCSI-II)	EISA	50 and 68	68	20
Fast-20 Wide (SCSI-II)	EISA	50 and 68	68	20
Fast Wide (SCSI-III)	PCI	68	68	20
Fast-20 Wide (SCSI-III)	PCI	68	68	20
Differential Fast-20 Wide (Differential SCSI)	PCI	68	68	20

There are some 40Mbps SCSI systems available, but they tend not to be compatible with too many devices at that speed. Differential SCSI, mentioned in the last row in the table, is a special kind of SCSI that handles voltages in the cables differently. This allows for longer SCSI chains and faster speeds. So far, there are only a few differential SCSI devices available, although CD-ROM and tape drives are slowly appearing. Differential SCSI tends to be more expensive than standard SCSI devices. Differential SCSI devices can't be mixed on the same chain with nondifferential devices.

We won't go into all the details of SCSI connectivity and architecture because you don't need to know these details for Linux. If you need more information, most SCSI controller cards include a good description of the theory in their accompanying documentation.

Supported SCSI Devices

You can't assume that because Linux supports SCSI, any SCSI device will work. Most versions of the operating system have a hardware compatibility file in the distribution set that lists all devices that have been tested and known to work properly with the SCSI system. Check this file carefully before you buy a new device or controller card! Some devices and cards simply don't work with Linux.

Some SCSI devices are shipped with their own kernel patches. You will have to make sure the patches correspond to the version of the Linux kernel you are using, then rebuild the kernel with the new drivers in place. If the devices don't have a Linux kernel patch, check with the manufacturer or Linux distribution sites.

SCSI Device Drivers

Every device on the Linux system must have a device file, and SCSI devices are no different. In many cases, Linux is distributed with a complete set of SCSI device files that need only to be configured properly. You should know a little about device drivers, device files, and major and minor device numbers. See Chapter 33, "Devices," for more information.

Hard Drives

SCSI disk drives are always block devices and should always use major device number 8. No "raw" SCSI devices are usually supported by Linux despite its similarity to BSD UNIX, which does support raw SCSI devices.

Sixteen minor device numbers are allocated to each SCSI disk device. Minor device number 0 represents the whole disk drive, minor numbers 1 through 4 are the four primary partitions, and minor numbers 5 through 15 are used for any extended partitions.

With Linux, SCSI disk minor device numbers are assigned dynamically, starting with the lowest SCSI ID numbers. The standard naming convention for SCSI hard drives is `/dev/sd{letter}` for the entire disk device (such as `/dev/sda` or `/dev/sdb`), and `/dev/sd{letter}{partition}` for the partitions on that device (such as `/dev/sda1` or `/dev/sda2`).

Linux presents a few problems when partitioning SCSI disks, because Linux talks directly to the SCSI interface. Each disk drive is viewed as the SCSI host sees it, with block numbers from 0 up to the highest block number. They are all assumed to be error-free. This means there is an easy way to get at the disk geometry. (For comparison, DOS requires head-cylinder-sector mapping, which is not as efficient but does allow direct manipulation.)

To partition the drive, you will either have to use the entire disk for Linux (in which case the installation takes care of it), or you can use DOS or Linux's fdisk program to create partitions for other operating systems first. Also, with systems that support both SCSI hard drives and IDE hard drives, you may have to reconfigure the system in the machine's BIOS to recognize the SCSI drive as the primary (boot) device.

CD-ROM Devices

SCSI CD-ROM drives with a block size of 512 or 2,048 bytes will work with Linux, but any other block size will not. Because most CD-ROM drives and CD-ROM disks have either 512- or 2,048-byte blocks, this shouldn't cause a problem unless the drive is from a source where other block sizes are the norm.

CD-ROM disks are offered in several different formats, not all of which are readable on a Linux system. The international standard is called ISO 9660, but not all CD-ROMs conform to this standard because it was adopted long after CD-ROMs became popular.

SCSI CD-ROMs use the major device number 11, and minor device numbers are allocated dynamically. The first CD-ROM drive found is minor 0, the second is minor 1, and so on. The naming convention used with Linux is /dev/sr{*digit*}, such as /dev/sr0 and /dev/sr1 for the first and second CD-ROM drives installed. Alternatively, some Linux distributions name the devices /dev/scd0, /dev/scd1, and so on.

After you set the CD-ROM SCSI address properly (the system should recognize the device when the SCSI card boots), the CD-ROM device must be mounted. This can be done manually or embedded in the startup sequence so that the drive is always available.

To mount a CD-ROM device, the general command is as follows:

```
mount /dev/sr0 /mount_point
```

mount_point is a directory that can be used. You must create the directory beforehand in order for the mount to work. For convenience, most systems that use CD-ROMs should create a directory called /cdrom, which is always the mount point.

If your CD-ROM doesn't mount properly with this command, the reason may be the disk type or the lack of an entry in the file /etc/fstab which identifies the CD as an ISO 9660 device. The correct syntax to mount an ISO 9660 CD-ROM (also called High-Sierra) is as follows:

```
mount -t iso9660 /dev/sr0 /mount_point
```

For this to work correctly, you must have the kernel set to support the ISO 9660 file system. If this hasn't been done, rebuild the kernel with this option added.

Linux attempts to lock the CD-ROM drive door when a disk is mounted. This is done to prevent file system confusion from a media change. Not all CD-ROM drives support door locking, but if you find yourself unable to eject a CD-ROM, it is probably because the disk is mounted (it doesn't have to be in use).

Tape Drives

Linux supports several SCSI tape drives. You should check the hardware configuration guide before purchasing one, though, to ensure compatibility. The most popular SCSI tape models, including the Archive Viper QIC drives, Exabyte 8mm drives, and Wangtek 5150S and DAT tape drives, are all known to work well.

SCSI tapes use character device major number 9 and the minor numbers are assigned dynamically. Usually, rewinding tape devices are numbered from 0, so the first tape drive is /dev/rst0 (character mode, major number 9, minor number 0), the second device is /dev/rst1 (character mode, major number 9, minor number 1), and so on. Nonrewinding devices have the high bit set in the minor number so that the first non-rewinding tape drive is /dev/nrst0 (character mode, major device 9, minor device 128).

The standard naming convention for SCSI tape drives is /dev/nrst{digit} for non-rewinding devices (such as /dev/nrst0, /dev/nrst1, and so on), and /dev/rst{digit} for rewinding devices (such as /dev/rst0 and /dev/rst1).

Generally, Linux supports tape devices that use either fixed- or variable-length blocks, as long as the block length is smaller than the driver buffer length, which is set to 32K in most Linux distribution sources (although this can be changed). Tape drive parameters such as block size, buffering process, and tape density are set with ioctls, which can be issued by the mt program.

Other Devices

Many other SCSI devices are available, such as scanners, printers, removable cartridge drives, and so on. These are handled by the Linux generic SCSI device driver. The generic SCSI driver provides an interface for sending commands to all SCSI devices.

SCSI generic devices use character mode and major number 21. The minor device numbers are assigned dynamically from 0 for the first device, and so on. The generic devices have the names /dev/sg0, /dev/sg1, /dev/sg2, and so on.

Troubleshooting SCSI Devices

Many common problems with SCSI devices are quite easy to solve. Finding the cause of the problem is often the most difficult step. It's usually helpful to read the diagnostic message that the operating system displays when it boots or attempts to use a SCSI device.

The following are the most common problems encountered with SCSI devices, their probable causes, and possible solutions:

SCSI devices show up at all possible SCSI IDs—You have configured the device with the same SCSI address as the controller, which is typically set at SCSI ID 7. Change the jumper settings to another SCSI ID.

A SCSI device shows up with all possible LUNs—The device probably has bad firmware. The file `/usr/src/linux/drivers/scsi/scsi.c` contains a list of bad devices under the variable `blacklist`. You can try adding the device to this list and see if it affects the behavior. If not, contact the device manufacturer.

Your SCSI system times out—Make sure the controller card's interrupts are enabled correctly and that there are no IRQ, DMA, or address conflicts with other boards in your system.

You get "sense errors" from error-free devices—This is usually caused by either bad cables or improper termination on the chain. Make sure the SCSI chain is terminated at both ends using external or onboard terminators. Don't terminate in the middle of the chain because this can also cause problems. You can probably use passive termination, but for long chains with several devices, try active termination for better behavior.

The tape drive is not recognized at boot time—Try booting with a tape in the drive.

A networking kernel does not work with new SCSI devices—The `autoprobe` routines for many network drivers are not passive and can interfere with some SCSI drivers. Try to disable the network portions to identify the guilty program, and then reconfigure it.

A SCSI device is detected, but the system is unable to access it—You probably don't have a device file for the device. Device drivers should be in `/dev` and configured with the proper type (block or character) and unique major and minor device numbers. Run `mkdev` for the device.

The SCSI controller card fails when it uses memory-mapped I/O—This problem is common with Trantor T128 and Seagate boards and is caused when the memory-mapped I/O ports are incorrectly cached. You should have the board's address space marked as uncacheable in the XCMOS settings. If you can't mark them as such, disable the cache and see whether the board functions properly.

Your system fails to find the SCSI devices and you get messages such as `scsi : 0 hosts` *or* `scsi%d : type:` *when the system boots*—The `autoprobe` routines on the controller cards rely on the system BIOS autoprobe and can't boot properly. This is particularly prevalent with these SCSI adapters: Adaptec 152x, Adaptec 151x, Adaptec AIC-6260, Adaptec AIC-6360, Future Domain 1680, Future Domain TMC-950, Future Domain TMC-8xx, Trantor T128, Trantor T128F, Trantor T228F, Seagate ST01, Seagate ST02, and Western Digital 7000. Check that your BIOS is enabled and not conflicting with any other peripheral BIOSs (such as on some adapter cards). If the BIOS is properly enabled, find the board's "signature" by running DOS' `DEBUG` command to check whether the board is responding. For example, use the `DEBUG` command `d=c800:0` to see whether the board replies with an acknowledgment (assuming you have set the controller card to use address 0xc8000; if not, replace the `DEBUG` command with the proper address). If the card doesn't respond, check the address settings.

Sometimes the SCSI system locks up completely—There are many possible reasons, including a problem with the host adapter. Check the host adapter with any diagnostics that came with the board. Try a different SCSI cable to see whether that is the problem. If the lockups seem to occur when multiple devices are in use at the same time, there is probably a firmware problem. Contact the manufacturer to see whether upgrades are available that would correct the problem. Finally, check the disk drives to ensure that there are no bad blocks that could affect the device files, buffers, or swap space.

Summary

SCSI has a reputation for being difficult to work with, but in fact, it is one of the easiest and most versatile systems available. After you get used to the nomenclature, SCSI offers many useful features to the Linux user. Indeed, most veteran UNIX people prefer working with SCSI because it is easy to use with the UNIX kernel and the same applies to Linux. From here, you may want to learn more about the following topics:

Shell programming and how you can use it to make your experience with bash more powerful is discussed in Chapter 14, "Shell Programming."

Setting up an Internet server with your Linux system is discussed in Chapter 47, "Setting up an Internet Site."

Using source code control systems to maintain previous versions of your files is discussed in Chapter 56, "Source Code Control."

Networking

by Tim Parker

IN THIS CHAPTER

CHAPTER 37

What Is TCP/IP?

Linux offers a complete implementation of TCP/IP (Transmission Control Protocol/Internet Protocol), the protocol used extensively on the Internet and that is commonly found in local area networks involving UNIX machines. All you need to create a network or to add your existing machine to a TCP/IP network is a network card and some modifications to files already on your Linux system.

Whether you are setting up two machines in your room to talk to each other or adding your Linux machine to an existing network of 5,000 workstations, the process is the same.

TCP/IP is an *open* networking protocol, which simply means that the technical description of all aspects of the protocol have been published. They are available for anyone to implement on their hardware and software. This open nature has helped make TCP/IP very popular. Versions of TCP/IP are now available for practically every hardware and software platform in existence, which has helped make TCP/IP the most widely used networking protocol in the world. The advantage of TCP/IP for a network operating system is simple: Interconnectivity is possible for any type of operating system and hardware platform that you might want to add.

TCP/IP is not a single protocol, but a set of over a dozen protocols. Each protocol within the TCP/IP family is dedicated to a different task. All the protocols that make up TCP/IP use the primary components of TCP/IP to send packets of data.

Transmission Control Protocol and Internet Protocol are two of the primary protocols in the TCP/IP family. The different protocols and services that make up the TCP/IP family can be grouped according to their purposes. The groups and their protocols are the following:

Transport. These protocols control the movement of data between two machines.

> TCP (Transmission Control Protocol). A connection-based service, meaning that the sending and receiving machines communicate with each other at all times.
>
> UDP (User Datagram Protocol). A connectionless service, meaning that the two machines don't communicate with each other through a constant connection.

Routing. These protocols handle the addressing of the data and determine the best routing to the destination. They also handle the way large messages are broken up and reassembled at the destination.

> IP (Internet Protocol). Handles the actual transmission of data.
>
> ICMP (Internet Control Message Protocol). Handles status messages for IP, such as errors and network changes that can affect routing.

RIP (Routing Information Protocol). One of several protocols that determine the best routing method.

OSPF (Open Shortest Path First). An alternative protocol for determining routing.

Network Addresses. These services handle the way machines are addressed, both by a unique number and a more common symbolic name.

ARP (Address Resolution Protocol). Determines the unique numeric addresses of machines on the network.

DNS (Domain Name System). Determines numeric addresses from machine names.

RARP (Reverse Address Resolution Protocol). Determines addresses of machines on the network, but in a manner opposite of ARP.

BOOTP (Boot Protocol). This starts up a network machine by reading the boot information from a server. BOOTP is commonly used for diskless workstations.

User Services. These are applications users have access to.

FTP (File Transfer Protocol). This transfers files from one machine to another without excessive overhead. FTP uses TCP as the transport.

TFTP (Trivial File Transfer Protocol). A simple file transfer method that uses UDP as the transport.

TELNET. Allows remote logins so that a user on one machine can connect to another machine and behave as though they are sitting at the remote machine's keyboard.

Gateway Protocols. These services help the network communicate routing and status information, as well as handle data for local networks.

EGP (Exterior Gateway Protocol). Transfers routing information for external networks.

GGP (Gateway-to-Gateway Protocol). Transfers routing information between Internet gateways.

IGP (Interior Gateway Protocol). Transfers routing information for internal networks.

Others. These are services that don't fall into the categories just mentioned but that provide important services over a network.

NFS (Network File System). Allows directories on one machine to be mounted on another, then accessed by users as though the directories were on the local machine.

NIS (Network Information Service). Maintains user accounts across networks, simplifying logins and password maintenance.

RPC (Remote Procedure Call). Allows remote applications to communicate with one another using function calls.

SMTP (Simple Mail Transfer Protocol). A protocol for transferring electronic mail between machines.

SNMP (Simple Network Management Protocol). Used to obtain status messages about TCP/IP configurations and software. It requires a loopback to be in place for proper operation.

If you want to connect your Linux machine to a network, you need a network card. Linux uses Ethernet, a network system that was designed to provide TCP/IP support. A term you'll see often is *packet*, which enables TCP/IP to talk to another part without leaving the machine. Essentially, you are creating a loop between software in the bundle of data and routing instructions assembled by TCP/IP and Ethernet to be sent over the network (Simple Network Management Protocol), which is an administrator's service that sends status messages about the network and devices attached to it.

All the TCP/IP protocol definitions are maintained by a standards body that is part of the Internet organization. Although changes to the protocols occasionally occur when new features or better methods of performing older functions are developed, the new versions are almost always backward-compatible.

Hardware Requirements

You can actually configure Linux to use TCP/IP without any network card or connection to a network at all, using a technique called loopback. *Loopback* is a method of instruction that enables parts of TCP/IP to talk to another part without leaving the machine. Essentially, you are creating a loop between a software exit and a software entry. Loopbacks are frequently used to test TCP/IP configurations, and some software requires a loopback to be in place for proper operation. A loopback driver always has the IP address 127.0.0.1.

If you want to connect your Linux machine to a network, you need a network card. Linux uses Ethernet, a network system that was designed to provide TCP/IP support. A term you'll see often is *packet*, which is the bundle of data and routing instructions that is assembled by TCP/IP and Ethernet to be sent over the network cables. All messages are broken into packets, and then reassembled properly at the destination.

Most Ethernet cards available today are compatible with Linux, but you should check the documentation or vendor's support operating system lists to make you don't buy a network card that won't work properly. In general, all the more popular networking cards (including Plug-and-Play models designed for Windows 95) work with Linux, although some need to be manually set to the proper IRQ and memory I/O addresses.

If you plan to do your networking over the telephone (using a serial port and a modem), you don't need a network card, but you *do* need a fast modem compatible with the service you are planning to use. For example, to use SLIP (Serial Line Interface Protocol), you generally need a modem supporting at least V.32bis speeds (14.4kbps).

Configuring Linux Files

Let's assume you have a typical PC and an Ethernet card, and you want to set up your machine to run TCP/IP over the network. In most cases, the procedure described next works. However, because there are many versions of Linux, many potential conflicts with other cards and software, and unique software requirements for some systems, this should be considered only a guide.

If your TCP/IP network doesn't work properly after following these instructions, it's time to carefully scan all the configuration files and error messages for a clue to the problem. Also, don't forget about the Linux USENET newsgroups, Linux User Groups, and other sources of information about Linux from which you can get help.

To configure the TCP/IP files, you must have installed the networking software on your system. If you haven't installed the networking portions of the distribution, you must do so before proceeding. Your kernel must also have been configured and recompiled with network support added. This is usually done during the installation process, although some users will have to force the kernel recompilation manually if they installed their software in a nonstandard manner.

First we'll deal with the use of a network card and then look at how to change the basic process to handle SLIP over a serial port and modem.

What You Need Before You Start

Before you start modifying system files, you should take a few minutes to determine a few basic pieces of information you'll need. It is advisable to write these down somewhere so that they will be handy when you need them, and also so that you won't enter two different values in two files, thereby causing major problems for the system.

IP Address

First you need an IP address, a unique number for your machine. Every machine on the network has to be identified uniquely to allow proper routing. TCP/IP-based networks use 32-bit addresses to uniquely identify networks and all the devices that reside within that network. These addresses are called *Internet addresses* or *IP addresses*.

The 32 bits of the IP address are broken into four 8-bit parts. Each 8-bit part can then have valid numbers ranging from 0 to 255. In IP addresses, the four 8-bit numbers are separated by a period, a notation called *dotted quad*. Examples of dotted quad IP addresses are 255.25.25.16 and 147.14.123.8.

For convenience, IP addresses are divided into two parts: the network number and the device number within that network. This separation into two components allows devices on different networks to have the same host number. However, since the network number is different, the devices are still uniquely identified.

For connection to the Internet, IP addresses are assigned by the Internet Network Information Center (NIC) based on the size of the network. Anyone who wants to connect to the Internet must register with the NIC to avoid duplication of network addresses. If you don't plan to connect to the Internet, you are free to create your own numbering scheme, although future expansion and integration with Internet-using networks can cause serious problems.

For maximum flexibility, IP addresses are assigned according to network size. Networks are divided into three categories: Class A, Class B, and Class C. The three network classes break the 32-bit IP addresses into different sizes for the network and host identifiers.

A Class A address uses one byte for the network address and three bytes for the device address, allowing more than 16 million different host addresses. Class B networks use two bytes for the network and two bytes for the host. Because 16 bits allows more than 65,000 hosts, only a few large companies will be limited by this type of class. Class C addresses have three bytes for the network and one for the number of hosts. This provides for a maximum of 254 hosts (the numbers 0 and 255 are reserved) but many different network IDs. The majority of networks are Class B and Class C.

You do have a limitation as to the first value. A Class A network's first number must be between 0 and 127, Class B addresses are between 128 and 191, and Class C addresses are between 192 and 223. This is because of the way the first byte is broken up, with a few of the bits at the front saved to identify the class of the network. Also, you can't use the values 0 and 255 for any part because they are reserved for special purposes.

Messages sent using TCP/IP use the IP address to identify sending and receiving devices, as well as any routing information put within the message headers. If you are going to connect to an existing network, you should find out what their IP addresses are and what numbers you can use. If you are setting up a network for your own use but plan to connect to the Internet at some point, you should contact the Network Information Center for an IP Address. On the other hand, if you are setting up a network for your own use and don't plan to have more than a telephone connection to other networks (including the Internet), you can make up your own IP addresses.

If you are only setting up a loopback driver, you don't even need an IP address. The default value for a loopback driver is 127.0.0.1.

Network Mask

Next, you need a network mask. This is pretty easy if you have picked out an IP address. The network mask is the network portion of the IP address set to the value 255, and it's used to blank out the network portion to determine routing.

If you have a Class C IP address (three bytes for network and one for devices), your network mask is 255.255.255.0. A Class B network has a network mask of 255.255.0.0, and a Class A network mask is 255.0.0.0.

If you are configuring only a loopback driver, your network mask is 255.0.0.0 (Class A).

Network Address

The network address is, strictly speaking, the IP address bitwise-ANDed to the netmask. In English, what this means is that it's the network portion of your IP address, so if your IP address is 147.120.46.7 and it's a Class B network, the network address is 147.120.0.0.

To get your own network address, just drop the device-specific part of the IP address and set it to zero. A Class C network with an IP address of 201.12.5.23 has a network address of 201.12.5.0.

If you're working with only a loopback address, you don't need a network mask.

Broadcast Address

The broadcast address is used when a machine wants to send the same packet to all devices on the network. To get your broadcast address, you set the device portion of the IP address to 255. Therefore, if you have the IP address 129.23.123.2, your broadcast address will be 129.23.123.255. Your network address will be 129.23.123.0.

If you are configuring only a loopback driver, you needn't worry about the broadcast address.

Gateway Address

The gateway address is the IP address of the machine that is the network's gateway out to other networks (such as the Internet). You need a gateway address only if you have a network that has a dedicated gateway out. If you are configuring a small network for your own use and don't have a dedicated Internet connection, you don't need a gateway address.

Normally, gateways have the same IP address as your machines, but they have the digit 1 as the device number. For example, if your IP address is 129.23.123.36, chances are that the gateway address is 129.23.123.1. This convention has been used since the early days of TCP/IP.

Loopback drivers do not require a gateway address, so if you are configuring your system only for loopback, ignore this address.

Nameserver Address

Many larger networks have a machine whose purpose is to translate IP addresses into English-like names and vice versa. It is a lot easier to call a machine bobs_pc instead of 123.23.124.23. This translation is done with a system called the Domain Name System (DNS). If your network has a name server, that's the address you need. If you want to have your own machine act as a name server (which requires some extra configuration not mentioned here), use the loopback address 127.0.0.1.

Loopback drivers don't need a name server because the machine talks only to itself. Therefore, you can ignore the nameserver address if you are configuring only a loopback driver.

Setting Up the Dummy Interface

What's a *dummy interface*? It's a bit of a trick to give your machine an IP address to work with when it uses only SLIP and PPP interfaces. A dummy interface solves the problem of a standalone machine (no network cards connecting it to other machines) whose only valid IP address to send data to is the loopback driver (127.0.0.1). While SLIP and PPP may be used for connecting your machine to the outside world, when the interface is not active, you have no internal IP address that applications can use.

The problem arises with some applications that require a valid IP address to work. Some word processors and desktop layout tools, for example, require the TCP/IP system to be operational with an IP address for the target machine. The dummy interface essentially sets an IP address for your local machine that is valid as far as TCP/IP is concerned, but doesn't really get used except to fool applications.

Creating a dummy interface is very simple. If your machine has an IP address already assigned for it in the `/etc/hosts` file, all you need to do is set up the interface and create a route. The following two commands are required:

```
ifconfig dummy machine_name
route add machine_name
```

Where *machine_name* is your local machine's name (such as `darkstar`). This creates a link to your own IP address. If you do not have an IP address for your machine in the `/etc/hosts` file, you should add one before you create the dummy interface.

Configuration Files

Configuring Linux for TCP/IP is not difficult because only a few configuration files need to have the information about IP address and such added to them. You can do this with any editor, as long as it saves the files in ASCII format. It is advisable to make copies of the configuration files before you modify them, just in case you damage the format in some way.

Many of these files are similar in every version of UNIX, including most versions of Linux, except for one or two slight naming variations. If you've ever set up a UNIX system (or snooped around one in detail), these files and steps might seem familiar. If you haven't done anything with Linux or UNIX before, just take it one step at a time and follow the instructions.

rc Files

Linux reads the `rc` (run command) files when the system boots. The `init` program initiates the reading of these files, and they usually serve to start processes such as `mail`, `printers`, `cron`, and so on. They are also used to initiate TCP/IP connections. Most Linux systems have the `rc` command files in the directory `/etc/rc.d`.

The two files of interest to TCP/IP are `rc.inet1`, which sets the network parameters, and `rc.inet2`, which starts the daemons used by TCP/IP. On some systems, these two files are combined into one larger file called either `rc.inet` or `rc.net`.

To configure the `rc.inet` files to start up the TCP/IP network, you must first make sure that the files are actually read by the `init` program. This is handled by the `/etc/inittab` and `/etc/rc.d/rc.M` files, where there are one or more lines that control the reading of the `rc.inet` files.

Some Linux versions use only the /etc/inittab file to start the TCP/IP daemons. The Slackware version, though, has a line in the /etc/inittab file that tells the init program to read the file /etc/rc.d/rc.M when running multiuser mode. The TCP/IP daemons are not started when the system is in single-user mode.

Whichever file is involved, look for a line that refers to the rc.inet1, rc.inet, or rc.net file. In some cases, this line(s) is commented out (it has a pound sign as the first character) to prevent the system from trying to run TCP/IP when there is no requirement for it. If the line is commented out, remove the comment symbol. The Slackware release of Linux, for example, has an if loop within the rc.M file that has these lines in it:

```
/bin/hostname `cat /etc/HOSTNAME | cut -f1 -d .`
/bin/sh /etc/rc.d/rc.inet1
/bin/sh /etc/rc.d/rc.inet1
```

Make sure that these lines (as well as the if loop that the lines are part of) are not commented out. You want these lines to execute each time the if condition is true. With the Slackware version, the if condition checks for the existence of the file rc.inet1.

If you can't find a reference to the rc.inet files in /etc/inittab, or a pointer to another file that has these files referenced (as with Slackware's /etc/rc.d/rc.M), you will have to add the lines to the /etc/inittab file manually. This can be scary for newcomers to Linux, so make copies of the files so you can always recover. An emergency boot floppy is also always handy to have.

Usually there is a good set of comments within the startup files to help you configure the system. There is a section for TCP/IP Ethernet support that often has a number of lines commented out. It consists of lines like this:

```
#IPADDR="127.0.0.1"
#NETMASK=""
#NETWORK="127.0.0"
#BROADCAST=""
#GATEWAY=""
```

Obviously, these correspond to the pieces of information you determined earlier. Therefore, uncomment the lines and type in the information about your machine. If you don't have one of the pieces, such as a gateway address, leave that line commented out.

In the rc.inet1 file, please note several references to the programs ifconfig and route. These programs control TCP/IP communications. ifconfig configures network device interfaces, and route configures the routing table.

Near the top of the rc.inet1 file (or whichever file is used in your version of Linux) are a couple of lines that call both ifconfig and route for the loopback driver. The lines probably look like this:

```
/sbin/ifconfig lo 127.0.0.1
/sbin/route add -net 127.0.0.0
```

Neither of these lines should be commented out. They are necessary to set the loopback driver, which must exist on the system in order for TCP/IP to function properly.

There will probably be a number of lines that are commented out below the settings for your machine's IP address with instructions to uncomment one of them. The differences between the lines is whether broadcast and netmask variables are included. To begin, try uncommenting the line that looks like this:

```
/etc/ifconfig eth0 ${IPADDR} netmask ${NETMASK} broadcast ${BROADCAST}
```

If this causes problems later during system startup, switch the uncommented line to the one that reads

```
/etc/ifconfig eth0 ${IPADDR} netmask ${NETMASK}
```

eth0 is the first device for the first Ethernet card on your system, called eth0.

Finally, if you have a gateway machine on your network, a section of the rc.inet1 file lets you enter the IP address of the gateway. Again, these lines should be uncommented. You might want to try to get the system working properly before you set up the gateway because it is easier to debug when the number of potential problems is smaller.

The rc.inet2 file starts up the daemons used by TCP/IP. In most cases, you won't have to make changes to this file because the most important daemons are usually started anyway. Look for a line that calls the inetd program, which is the most important TCP/IP daemon of all. There should be no comments on the line that starts it. It will probably look like this:

```
if [ -f ${NET}/inetd
then
        echo -n " inetd"
        ${NET}/inetd
else
        echo "no INETD found.  INET cancelled."
        exit 1
fi
```

If you read Chapter 14, "Shell Programming," or you know a little about programming in some other language, this short section might make sense. This routine checks for the existence of the inetd file and starts it if it's there. If it's not there, an error message is generated on the display (remember this is during the boot process), and the rc.inet2 file is exited.

37

NETWORKING

More commented-out daemons are probably listed below `inetd`, such as `named` (the name server daemon that converts proper names to IP address), `routed` (used for routing), and several others. Unless you know that you want one of these daemons active, leave them commented out for now.

One other daemon you might want running is `syslogd`. It usually is set to execute automatically. This is the system logging daemon, which collects log messages from other applications and stores them in log files. The log file locations, which you can change as you desire, are given in the file `/etc/syslog.conf`.

That's enough changes to the `rc` files for now. After TCP/IP is installed and tested, the rest of the daemons (`routed`, `named`, and so on) can be started one at a time to ensure they work. The first task is to get TCP/IP communicating with other machines properly. Then you tweak it!

/etc/hosts

The `/etc/hosts` file is a simple list of IP addresses and the hostnames to which they correspond. This is a good location to list all your favorite machines so that you can use the name and have the system look up the IP address. On very small networks, you can add all the machines in the network here and avoid the need to run the `named` daemon.

Every `/etc/hosts` file will have an entry for `localhost` (also called `loopback`, IP address `127.0.0.1`) and probably one for your machine if you named it when you installed the software. If you didn't supply a name and there is no line other than `localhost`, you can add it now. Use an editor and set your IP address and machine name. Don't bother adding too many other machines until you're sure the network works properly! Here's a sample `/etc/hosts` file:

```
127.0.0.1          localhost
147.12.2.42        merlin.tpci merlin
```

You will notice that the format is quite simple: an IP address in one column and the name in another column, separated by tabs. If the machine may have more than one name, supply them all. In the example, which uses random numbers for the IP address, the machine `147.12.2.42` has the name `merlin`. Because it is also part of a larger network called `tpci`, the machine can be addressed as `merlin.tpci`. Both names on the line ensure that the system can resolve either name to the same address.

You can expand the file a little if you want by adding other machines on your local network, or those you will communicate with regularly:

```
127.0.0.1          localhost
147.12.2.42        merlin.tpci merlin
147.12.2.43        wizard.tpci wizard
```

```
147.12.2.44        arthur.tpci arthur bobs_machine
147.12.2.46        lancelot.tpci lancelot
```

In this example, there are several machines from the same network (the same network address). One has three different names.

If you are using only the loopback driver, the only line that should be in the file is for the IP address 127.0.0.1 with the name localhost and your machine's name after it.

/etc/networks

The /etc/networks file lists names and IP address of your own network and other networks you connect to frequently. This file is used by the route command, started through the rc.inet1 file. One advantage of this file is that it lets you call remote networks by name, so instead of typing 149.23.24, you can type eds_net.

The /etc/networks file should have an entry for every network that will be used with the route command. If there is no entry, errors will be generated, and the network won't work properly.

A sample /etc/networks file using random IP addresses is shown next. Remember that you need only the network address and not the device portion of a remote machine's IP address, although you must fill in the rest with zeros.

```
loopback           127.0.0.0
localnet           147.13.2.0
eds_net            197.32.1.0
big_net            12.0.0.0
```

At a minimum, you must have a loopback and localnet address in the file.

/etc/host.conf

The system uses the host.conf file to resolve hostnames. It usually contains two lines that look like this:

```
order hosts, bind
multi on
```

These tell the system to first check the /etc/hosts file, and then the nameserver (if one exists) when trying to resolve a name. The multi entry lets you have multiple IP addresses for a machine in the /etc/hosts file (which happens with gateways and machines on more than one network).

If your /etc/host.conf file looks like these two lines, you don't need to make any changes at all.

resolv.conf

The `resolv.conf` file is used by the name resolver program. It gives the address of your name server (if you have one) and your domain name (if you have one). You have a domain name if you are on the Internet.

A sample `resolv.conf` file for the system `merlin.tpci.com` has an entry for the domain name, which is `tpci.com` (`merlin` is the name of an individual machine):

```
domain tpci.com
```

If a name server is used on your network, you should add a line that gives its IP address:

```
domain tpci.com
nameserver  182.23.12.4
```

If there are multiple name servers, which is not unusual on a larger network, each name server should be specified on its own line.

If you don't have a domain name for your system, you can safely ignore this file for the moment.

/etc/protocols

UNIX systems use the `/etc/protocols` file to identify all the transport protocols available on the system and their respective protocol numbers. (Each protocol supported by TCP/IP has a special number, but that's not really important at this point.) Usually, this file is not modified but is maintained by the system and updated automatically as part of the installation procedure when new software is added.

The `/etc/protocols` file contains the protocol name, its number, and any alias that may be used for that protocol. A sample `/etc/protocols` file looks like this:

```
# Internet protocols (IP)
ip      0   IP
icmp    1   ICMP
ggp     3   GGP
tcp     6   TCP
egp     8   EGP
pup     12  PUP
udp     17  UDP
hello   63  HELLO
```

If your entries don't match this, don't worry. You shouldn't have to make any changes to this file at all, but you should know what it does.

37

/etc/services

The /etc/services file identifies the existing network services. This file is maintained by software as it is installed or configured.

This file consists of the service name, a port number, and the protocol type. The port number and protocol type are separated by a slash, following the conventions mentioned in previous chapters. Any optional service alias names follow. Here's a short extract from a sample /etc/services file:

```
# network services
echo      7/tcp
echo      7/udp
discard   9/tcp    sink   null
discard   9/udp    sink   null
ftp       21/tcp
telnet    23/tcp
smtp      25/tcp     mail mailx
tftp      69/udp
# specific services
login     513/tcp
who       513/udp    whod
```

You shouldn't change this file at all, but you do need to know what it is and why it is there to help you understand TCP/IP a little better.

/etc/hostname or /etc/HOSTNAME

The file /etc/hostname or /etc/HOSTNAME is used to store the name of the system you are on. (Slackware Linux uses the uppercase version of the name.) This file should have your local machine's name in it:

```
merlin.tpci
```

That's all it needs. The hostname is used by most protocols on the system and many applications, so it is important for proper system operation. The hostname can be changed by editing the system file and rebooting the machine, although many distributions provide a utility program to ensure that this process is performed correctly.

Linux systems have a utility called hostname, which displays the current setting of the system name, as well as the uname program, which can give the node name with the command uname -n. When issued, the hostname and uname commands echo the local machine name, as the following sample session shows:

```
$ hostname
merlin.tpci.com
$ uname -n
merlin
```

Some Linux versions of hostname show only the name without the domain name attached. All the configuration files necessary for TCP/IP to function have now been set properly, so you should be able to reboot the machine and see what happens.

Testing and Troubleshooting

To try out TCP/IP, reboot your machine and carefully watch the messages displayed on-screen. If you see any error messages, they may help guide you to the faulty file or process. Otherwise, you will see the TCP/IP daemons load one after another.

The netstat Command

Probably the best approach to checking on TCP/IP is to use the netstat command, which gives you many different summaries of all network connections and their status. The netstat program provides comprehensive information. It's the program most commonly used by administrators to quickly diagnose a problem with TCP/IP.

There are many more netstat options than the ones mentioned in the next sections. For more information on netstat, start with the man page on the Linux system and then check a good UNIX networking book.

Communications End Points

The netstat command with no options shows information on all active communications end points (where data is actually being transferred or communications are established). To display all end points (active and passive), netstat uses the -a option.

The netstat output is formatted in columns that show the protocol (Proto), the amount of data in the receive and send queues (Recv-Q and Send-Q), the local and remote addresses, and the current state of the connection. Here's a truncated sample output:

```
merlin> netstat -a
Active Internet connections (including servers)
Proto Recv-Q Send-Q  Local Address          Foreign Address        (state)
ip        0      0    *.*                    *.*
tcp       0   2124    tpci.login             oscar.1034             ESTABL.
tcp       0      0    tpci.1034              prudie.login           ESTABL.
tcp   11212      0    tpci.1035              treijs.1036            ESTABL.
tcp       0      0    tpci.1021              reboc.1024
➥TIME_WAIT
tcp       0      0    *.1028                 *.*                    LISTEN
tcp       0      0    *.*                    *.*                    CLOSED
udp       0      0    localhost.1036         localhost.syslog
udp       0      0    *.1034                 *.*
udp       0      0    *.*                    *.*
udp       0      0    *.*                    *.*
```

This excerpt has three active TCP connections, as identified by the state `ESTABL.`, with one that has data being sent (as shown in the `Send-Q` column). An asterisk means that no end point is yet associated with that address.

Network Interface Statistics

The behavior of the network interface (such as the network interface card) can be shown with the `netstat -i` option. This quickly shows administrators whether there are major problems with the network connection.

The `netstat -i` command displays the name of the interface, the maximum number of characters a packet can contain (`MTU`), the number of input packets received error free (`RX-OK`), number of received packets with errors (`RX-ERR`), number of received packets dropped (RX-DRP), and the number of packets that could not be received (RX-OVR). This is followed by the same statistics for sent packets. The following is a sample output from a `netstat -i` command:

```
merlin> netstat -i
Kernel Interface table
Iface   MTU Met  RX-OK RX-ERR RX-DRP RX-OVR  TX-OK TX-ERR TX-DRP TX-OVR
➥Flags
lo     2000   0      0      0      0      0     12      0      0      0
➥BLRU
eth0   1500   0    218      0      0      0    144      0      0      0
➥BRU
```

Routing Table Information

Routing tables are continually updated to reflect connections to other machines. To obtain information about the routing tables (if there are any on your system), the `netstat -r` option is used.

Columns show the destination machine, the address of the gateway to be used, a flag to show whether the route is active (`U`) and whether it leads to a gateway (`G`) or a machine (`H` for host), a reference counter (`Refs`) that specifies how many active connections may use that route simultaneously, the number of packets that have been sent over the route (`Use`), and the interface name.

```
merlin> netstat -r
Kernel routing table
Destination     Gateway          Genmask          Flags Metric Ref Use
➥Iface
localnet        *                255.255.0.0      U     0      0    262 eth0
loopback        *                255.0.0.0        U     0      0     12 lo
default         *                0.0.0.0          U     0      0      0 eth0
```

ping

The `ping` (Packet Internet Groper) program is used to query another system and ensure a connection is active. The `ping` program operates by sending a request to the destination machine for a reply. If the destination machine's IP software receives the request, it issues a reply immediately.

The sending machine continues to send requests until the `ping` program is terminated with a break sequence. After termination, `ping` displays a set of statistics. A sample `ping` session is shown as follows:

```
prudie> ping merlin
PING merlin: 64 data bytes
64 bytes from 142.12.130.12: icmp_seq=0.  time=20.  ms
64 bytes from 142.12.130.12: icmp_seq=1.  time=10.  ms
64 bytes from 142.12.130.12: icmp_seq=2.  time=10.  ms
64 bytes from 142.12.130.12: icmp_seq=3.  time=20.  ms
64 bytes from 142.12.130.12: icmp_seq=4.  time=10.  ms
64 bytes from 142.12.130.12: icmp_seq=5.  time=10.  ms
64 bytes from 142.12.130.12: icmp_seq=6.  time=10.  ms
--- merlin PING Statistics ---
7 packets transmitted, 7 packets received, 0% packet loss
round-trip - min/avg/max = 10/12/20
```

If `ping` was unable to reach the remote machine, it displays error messages. You can also ping the `localhost`, which shows if there is an error in the loopback driver configuration files.

The `ping` program is useful because it provides four important pieces of information: whether the TCP/IP software is functioning correctly, whether a local network device can be addressed (validating its address), whether a remote machine can be accessed (again validating the address and testing the routing), and verifying the software on the remote machine.

Summary

In this chapter, you've seen how to install, configure, and test Ethernet connections to your Linux machine. The next chapter looks at the SLIP and PPP protocols used by many Linux boxes to connect to an ISP. The only other networking process usually found on a Linux box uses UUCP (UNIX-to-UNIX Copy), which is described in Chapter 44, "NIS and YP."

If you want to install a network to connect several of your machines (assuming you have more than one), you will find it quite easy and useful. If you have two machines, it is fast and efficient to connect a Linux machine and a DOS or Windows machine, as long as the other machine is running TCP/IP. There are shareware versions of TCP/IP for Windows and many commercial implementations for both DOS and Windows.

From here, you can read the next chapter which introduces SLIP and PPP or jump ahead to find out:

How to configure networks for proper security in Chapter 42, "Network Security."

How to configure NFS, NIS, and YP in Chapters 43, "NFS," and 44, "NIS and YP," respectively.

How to set up an Internet site with your Linux now-networked system in Chapter 47, "Setting up an Internet Site."

CHAPTER 38

SLIP and PPP

by Tim Parker

IN THIS CHAPTER

Most UNIX or Linux systems that want to make a connection to the Internet through an ISP or gateway do so with either Serial Line Internet Protocol (SLIP) or Point-to-Point Protocol (PPP). Both SLIP and PPP work through a dialup modem (either asynchronous, synchronous, or ISDN) to establish a link with remote systems. Linux provides both SLIP and PPP as well as an enhanced version of SLIP called CSLIP (Compressed SLIP).

You can perform SLIP and PPP configurations when you are configuring Linux TCP/IP or you can wait until you need to set them up for Internet access. Most Internet service providers prefer SLIP or PPP access from small systems as they provide fast, efficient transfers, so if you plan on using an ISP you will probably end up configuring the protocols yourself in the end.

The steps to setting up SLIP or PPP on your Linux system are not too complicated. Follow the process shown in this chapter and you'll have the SLIP or PPP setup completed in a few minutes.

Setting Up the Dummy Interface

A dummy interface (also called a loopback interface or device) is used to give your machine an IP address to work with when it uses only SLIP and PPP interfaces. A dummy interface solves the problem of a standalone machine with no network cards connecting it to other machines. Most TCP/IP services and applications need an IP address which is usually lacking in a standalone configuration. For this reason, the loopback driver is configured with a standard IP address (127.0.0.1).

Creating a dummy interface is simple. If your machine has an IP address already assigned to it in the /etc/hosts file, all you need to do is set up the interface and create a route. For Linux the two commands needed are as follows:

```
ifconfig dummy machine_name
route add machine_name
```

machine_name is your local machine's name. This creates a link to your own IP address. If you do not have an IP address for your machine in the /etc/hosts file, you should add one before you create the dummy interface by manually editing the /etc/hosts file and adding a line like this:

```
127.0.0.1    loopback
```

Some Linux systems do not use the ifconfig and route utilities, relying instead on a menu-driven user interface to set the same parameters up. In most cases with Linux, the loopback driver is added automatically for you when you install Linux. Check the

/etc/hosts file for a line with the IP address 127.0.0.1. If it doesn't exist, use whatever routine your version of Linux uses to set up new chains or simply use an editor to add it to the file, then reboot the machine to make the changes effective.

Setting Up SLIP

SLIP can be used with many dialup ISPs as well as for networking with other SLIP-equipped machines. When you are establishing a SLIP connection to another machine, the modem establishes a connection as usual, then SLIP takes over and maintains the session for you. The SLIP driver is usually configured as part of the operating system kernel, so it needs to be added if it doesn't already exist. Most Linux SLIP drivers can also handle CSLIP, a compressed SLIP version that offers higher throughput. (Not all ISPs support CSLIP, so you should check with them before configuring it for your connection.)

For many Linux operating systems that use SLIP for connections, a serial port has to be dedicated for this reason. This means that a serial port must be specifically configured to use SLIP and cannot be used for any other purpose. The kernel uses a special program usually called SLIPDISC (SLIP discipline) to control the serial port and blocks non-SLIP applications from using it even when the port is not in use by SLIP.

Configuring SLIP

For SLIP connections, two Linux programs are involved: dip and slattach. Both programs can be used to initiate the SLIP connection. You cannot dial into a SLIP line with a standard communications program because of the special system calls that SLIP uses.

dip and slattach have different purposes. The slattach program, which simply connects to the serial device, is used when there is a permanent connection to the SLIP server (no modem or setup handshaking is required). The dip program handles the initiation of the connection, the login, and connection handshaking. If you use a modem to connect to a SLIP server, you should use dip. The dip program can also be used to configure your own system as a SLIP server, allowing others to call in to it.

SLIP is a fairly simple network protocol because only two devices are involved: yours and the server's. When the connection is established, SLIP sends an IP address that will be used for that connection. Some systems use the same IP address (static), while others have a different IP address each time a connection is made (dynamic). The configuration is slightly different for each type.

The easiest way to dedicate a serial port for SLIP is the `slattach` program. This command is supported by most Linux versions. The `slattach` command takes the device name of the serial port as an argument. For example, to dedicate the second serial port (`/dev/cua1` or `/dev/tty2A`, depending on the operating system) to SLIP, issue the following command or a similar command with the proper device name instead of `/dev/cua1` (which is the Linux convention for modem serial ports):

```
slattach /dev/cua1 &
```

The `slattach` command is sent into background mode by the ampersand. Failure to send to background means the terminal or the console the command is issued from is not usable until the process is terminated. You can embed the `slattach` command in a start-up file such as the `rc` files or a session shell startup file if you want.

Once the `slattach` command has executed successfully, the serial port is set to the first SLIP device (usually `/dev/sl0`). If you are using more than one serial port for SLIP lines, you need to issue the command for each line. By default, most Linux systems set the SLIP port to use CSLIP (compressed SLIP). If you want to override this action, use the `-p` option and this device name:

```
slattach -p slip /dev/cua1 &
```

It's important to make sure that both ends of the connection use the same form of SLIP. There is `slip6` (a 6-bit version of SLIP) and adaptive SLIP (which adjusts to whatever is at the other end of the connection). For example, you cannot set your device for CSLIP and communicate with another machine running 6-bit SLIP.

After the serial port is set for SLIP usage, configure the network interface using the same procedure as normal network connections. For Linux, the commands used are `ifconfig` and `route`. For example, if your machine is called `merlin` and you are calling the remote machine `arthur`, issue the following commands:

```
ifconfig sl0 merlin-slip pointopoint arthur
route add arthur
```

The `ifconfig` command above configures the interface `merlin-slip` (the local address of the SLIP interface) to be a point-to-point connection to `arthur`. The `route` command adds the remote machine called `arthur` to the routing tables.

If you want to use the SLIP port for access to the Internet, it must have an IP address and an entry in the `/etc/hosts` file. That gives the SLIP system a valid entry on the Internet.

After the `ifconfig` and `route` commands execute, you can test and use your SLIP network. If you decide to remove the SLIP interface in the future, you must first remove the routing entry, use `ifconfig` to take down the SLIP interface, and then kill the `slattach` process. The first two steps are done with these commands:

```
route del arthur
ifconfig sl0 down
```

The termination of the `slattach` process must be done by finding the process ID (PID) of `slattach` (with the `ps` command), and then issuing a `kill` command. (See Chapter 34, "Processes," for more information on killing a process if you are unsure of the method.)

If you have a dedicated connection to the SLIP server and you want to use `slattach`, the `rc.inet1` file is modified to have the following lines in it:

```
IPADDR="123.12.3.1"        # Your machine's IP address
REMADDR="142.12.3.12"      # The SLIP server IP address

slattach -p cslip -s 19200 /dev/ttyS0     # set baud and port as needed
/etc/ifconfig sl0 $IPADDR pointopoint $REMADDR up
/etc/route add default gw $REMADDR
```

These lines, or very similar lines, appear in most `rc.inet1` or `rc.inet` files, usually commented out. Amend the information to show the proper IP addresses, ports, and baud rates. The `cslip` argument for `slattach` tells the program to use `slip` with header compression. If this causes problems, change it to `slip`.

If the SLIP server you are connecting to allocates IP addresses dynamically, you can't put an IP address in the configuration files because it changes each time. Most SLIP servers display a message with the IP address when you connect, and `dip` can capture these numbers and use them to alter the system parameters appropriately.

dip

The `dip` program greatly simplifies the connection to a SLIP server. To use it, you need a chat script that contains all the commands used to establish communications with the SLIP server during login. The chat script usually includes your login and password, too, automating the login process.

A sample `dip` chat script is included in the man pages for `dip`, so display the man page and read the contents, then save the file (by redirection or copying the man page source) and edit the script. Here's a sample chat script that you can enter by hand if necessary, making sure, of course, that you put in your own data:

```
# Connection script for SLIP
# Fetch the IP address of our target host.
```

```
main:
  # Set the desired serial port and speed.
  port /dev/cua0
  speed 38400
  # Reset the modem and terminal line.
  reset
  # Prepare for dialing.
  send ATZ1\r
  wait OK 4
  if $errlvl != 0 goto error
  dial 666-0999                          ## Change to your server's number!
  if $errlvl != 0 goto error
  wait CONNECT 60
  if $errlvl != 0 goto error
  # We are connected.  Log in to the system.
login:
  sleep 3
  send \r\n\r\n
  wait merlin> 20                ## Change to your server's prompt
  if $errlvl != 0 goto error
  send login\n
  wait name: 10                  ## Wait username: prompt
  if $errlvl != 0 goto erro
  send login_name\n                    ## Change to your own
  wait ord: 10                         ## Wait password prompt
  if $errlvl != 0 goto error
  send my_password\n                   ## Change to your own!
  wait merlin> 10
  if $errlvl != 0 goto error
  send slip\n                          ## Change to suit your server
  wait SLIP 30                         ### Wait for SLIP prompt
  if $errlvl != 0 goto error
  get $local remote 10                 ## Assumes the server sends your IP..
  if $errlvl != 0 goto error           ## address as soon as you enter slip.
  get $remote merlin                   ## slip server address from /etc/hosts
done:
  print CONNECTED to $remote with address $rmtip we are $local
  default
  mode SLIP
  goto exit
error:
  print SLIP to $host failed.
exit:
# End dip script
```

Several different variations of the chat scripts are currently available, including a few on most CD-ROM distributions. If you have access to the Internet, you can find them on some FTP sites or posted on a Linux newsgroup.

Setting Up PPP

PPP is a more powerful protocol than SLIP and is preferable for most uses. PPP functions are divided into two parts; one for the High-Level Data Link Control (HLDC) protocol, which helps define the rules for sending PPP datagrams between the two machines, and one for the PPP daemon called pppd, which handles the protocol once the HLDC system has established communications parameters.

As with SLIP, PPP establishes a modem link between two machines, then hands over the control of the line to PPP. Prior to establishing a PPP link, you must have a loopback driver established. You should also have a name resolution system in operation, even if it's the /etc/hosts file or a simple DNS cache-only name server. (See the section called "Using DNS for SLIP and PPP" later in this chapter.)

Setting Up a PPP Account

If you are letting people dial in to your system using PPP, for security reasons it is best to use PPP with a special user account called PPP. This is not necessary if you are dialing out only, and you can easily use PPP from any user account; but for more secure operation, consider creating a new user just for PPP, especially when allowing dial-ins. First, you need to add a new user to the system. You can use whatever script your operating system normally uses (such as newuser, adduser, or simple editing of the /etc/passwd file).

A sample /etc/passwd entry for the PPP account (with UID set to 201 and GID set to 51) looks like this:

```
ppp:*:201:51:PPP account:/tmp:/etc/ppp/pppscript
```

In this case, the account is set with no password (so no one can log in to the account) and because no files are created, a home directory of /tmp is used. The startup program is set to /etc/ppp/pppscript, a file you create with configuration information in it. (You can use any filename instead of pppscript.)

A sample of the pppscript file looks like this:

```
#!/bin/sh
mesg n
stty -echo
exec pppd -detach silent modem crtscts
```

The first line forces execution of the script to the Bourne (or bash) shell, regardless of which shell you're running (see Chapter 14, "Shell Programming," for more details). The second line turns off all attempts to write to the PPP account's tty. The stty command on the third line is necessary to stop everything the remote sends from being echoed to the screen again. Finally, the `exec` command on the last line runs the `pppd` daemon (which handles all PPP traffic). You will see the `pppd` daemon and its options later in this section.

Dialing Out with `chat`

PPP requires you to establish a modem connection to the remote machine before it can take over and handle the communications. There are several utilities available to do this, although the most commonly used is `chat`. The `chat` program is popular because it uses a scripting style similar to that used by UUCP.

To use `chat`, assemble a command line that looks almost the same as a UUCP `/etc/Systems` file entry. For example, to call a remote machine with a Hayes-compatible modem (using the AT command set) at the number 555-1234, use the following command. It is formatted as a `chat` script, UUCP style:

```
chat "" ATZ OK ATDT5551234 CONNECT "" login: ppp word: secret1
```

All the entries are in UUCP's send-expect format, with whatever you send to the specified remote located after what you receive from it. The `chat` script always starts with an `expect` string, which must be set to empty because the modem won't respond without any signal to it. After the empty string, first send the `ATZ` (reset) command and wait for an `OK` back from the modem, then send the `dial` command. After a `CONNECT` message is received back from the modem, the login script for the remote machine is executed and goes like this: Send a blank character first, then the `login:` (login) prompt appears, next, send the login name `ppp`, wait for the `word:` (password) prompt, and finally, send the password (substituting your login name and password, of course). After the login is complete, `chat` terminates but leaves the line open.

If the other end of the connection doesn't answer with a `login` script as soon as their modem answers, you may have to force a `BREAK` command down the line to jog the remote end. This is done with the following command:

```
chat -v "" ATZ OK ATDT5551234 CONNECT "" ogin:-BREAK-ogin: ppp word:
secret1
```

There's a security problem with this type of `chat` entry because any user doing a `ps -ef` command can see the entire command line (with its passwords). If you are the only user of your system this isn't a concern, but to save yourself any problems, you can embed the script portion of the command in a file and read the file in to `chat`. This causes the script to not appear on a `ps` output. To call a file for use with `chat`, use the `-f` option:

```
chat -f chat_file
```

The `chat_file` will contain the following line:

```
"" ATZ OK ATDT5551234 CONNECT "" login: ppp word: secret1
```

The `chat` script can help you detect common error conditions such as a busy line or no connection established. The messages from your modem (the standard Hayes command set uses the messages `BUSY` and `NO CARRIER`, respectively) are embedded in the `chat` script with the `ABORT` option, which allows you to exit from the `chat` script gracefully if one of these error conditions occurs. To handle these abort conditions, embed the `chat` keyword `ABORT` followed by the message that should trigger an abort, prior to your normal `chat` script. For example, to modify the `chat` script above to abort on a `BUSY` or `NO CARRIER` message from the modem, the script looks like this:

```
ABORT BUSY ABORT 'NO CARRIER' "" ATZ OK ATDT5551234 CONNECT "" login: ppp
➥word: secret1
```

We needed two `ABORT` commands because each takes only one argument. The rest of the `chat` script is as usual. Note the need to put quotation marks around the `NO CARRIER` message because otherwise the space in the middle will confuse the script.

Running pppd

If you have a PPP connection already established and your machine is logged in to a remote using the PPP account, you can start the `pppd` daemon to control the PPP session. If your machine is using the device `/dev/cua1` (the Linux designation for the first serial port with modem control) for its PPP connection at 38400 baud, start the `pppd` daemon with the following command:

```
pppd /dev/cua1 38400 crtscts defaultroute
```

This command tells the kernel to switch the interface on `/dev/cua1` to PPP and establish an IP link to the remote machine. The `crtscts` option, which is usually used on any PPP connection above 9600 baud, turns on handshaking.

The local system uses an IP address that is taken from the local hostname unless one is specified on the `pppd` command line (which you will seldom need to do because the local host IP address should be correct for the PPP line). If you want to force the local or remote IP addresses to be something other than the machine's default values, you can add the addresses with an option to `pppd`. The general format is to specify the local IP address, a colon, then the remote IP address:

```
147.23.43.1:36.23.1.34
```

When added to the pppd command line, the preceding option sets the local IP address as 147.23.43.1 and the remote IP address to 36.23.1.34, regardless of what the local values are. If you want to modify only one IP address, leave the other portion blank:

```
147.23.43.1:
```

This command sets the local IP address and accepts the remote IP address as whatever the machine sends.

You can use chat to establish the connection in the first place, which allows you to embed the chat command as part of the pppd command. This is best done when reading the contents of the chat script from a file (using the -f option). For example, you can issue the pppd command:

```
pppd connect "chat -f chat_file" /dev/cua1 38400 -detach crtscts modem
►defaultroute
```

chat_file holds the expect-send sequences looked at earlier. You will notice a few modifications to the pppd command other than the addition of the chat command in quotation marks. The -detach command tells pppd not to detach from the console and move to background. The modem keyword tells pppd to monitor the modem port (in case the line drops prematurely) and hang up the line when the call is finished.

The pppd daemon begins setting up the connection parameters with the remote by exchanging IP addresses, then sets communications values. After that is done, pppd sets the network layer to use the PPP link by setting the interface to /dev/ppp0 (if it's the first PPP link active on the machine). Finally, pppd establishes a kernel routing table entry to point to the machine on the other end of the PPP link.

Checking Problems

The pppd daemon echoes all warnings and error messages to the syslog facility. If you use the -v option with the chat script, chat's messages are also sent to syslog. If you have trouble with your PPP connections, you can check the syslog for details and try to isolate the problem. A word of warning about the -v option: Everything gets echoed to the logs, including usernames and passwords. This is an option you should avoid using unless necessary for debugging purposes.

Unless there is an entry in the /etc/syslog.conf file that redirects incoming error and warning messages to another file, the messages are discarded by syslog. To save the messages from pppd and chat, add this line to the /etc/syslog.conf file:

```
daemon.*    /tmp/ppp-log
```

This entry tells syslog to save any incoming messages from a daemon to the /tmp/ppp-log file. You can use any filename you want instead of /tmp/ppp-log. Many Linux versions of the syslog.conf file insist on tabs to separate the columns instead of spaces. After your script is working, remember to remove this line or the log file will grow quite large!

PPP Authentication

PPP is a wonderful protocol for modem-based communications, but it has one major problem: It has security holes large enough to drive a bus through. If even slightly incorrectly configured, anyone can use the PPP line to get into your machine or use the PPP line to get out to other systems. To help prevent this, *authentication* is often used. Authentication essentially makes sure that each end of the connection is who they say they are and is allowed to use the link.

There are two authentication schemes used by PPP: the Password Authentication Protocol (PAP) and the Challenge Handshake Authentication Protocol (CHAP). PAP is much like a login procedure. When one machine sends the login name and password to the other, the receiving machine verifies the information with a database on its end. While simple, PAP has a major flaw: Anyone can tap into the line and monitor the passwords being sent.

CHAP solves this problem, and hence, is the most favored form of authentication for PPP links. CHAP enables one machine to send a random string to the other, along with its hostname. The other end uses the hostname to look up the proper reply, combine it with the first string, encrypt it, then resend it to the first machine along with its hostname. The first machine performs the same sort of manipulation on the random string it first sent, and if the two replies match, the authentication is complete. And because CHAP doesn't authenticate only at start time but at random intervals throughout the connection, it is even more powerful.

When two machines connect, they don't use authentication unless explicitly instructed to do so. (See the auth entry in the /etc/ppp/options file discussed earlier.) When authentication is active, one end tries to use CHAP first; then, if that fails because the other end doesn't support CHAP, it will use PAP. If neither authentication scheme is supported by the other end, the connection is terminated. If you are going to use authentication for all your PPP connections, put the auth entry in the /etc/ppp/options file. If your connections don't all support authentication, then those connections will fail if auth is specified.

The information needed for both CHAP and PAP are kept in two files called /etc/ppp/chap-secrets and /etc/ppp/pap-secrets, respectively. When authentication

38

SLIP AND PPP

is active, one end checks the other for these files, trying CHAP first. If you are going to use authentication for all your connections (which is a very good idea), you can build up the chap-secrets and pap-secrets files. If you configure both chap-secrets and pap-secrets and specify the auth option in /etc/ppp/options, no unauthenticated host can connect to your machine.

The /etc/ppp/chap-secrets file consists of four columns for the client name, the server name, the secret password string, and an optional list of IP addresses. The behavior of the system is different depending on whether the local machine is being challenged to authenticate itself or is issuing a challenge to the remote. When the local machine has to authenticate itself, pppd examines the /etc/ppp/chap-secrets file for an entry in the client field that matches the local hostname and the server field equal to the remote host-name, then uses the string to build the authentication message. Such an entry in the /etc/ppp/chap-secrets file looks like this:

```
#   client            server             string        addresses
merlin.tpci.com    big_guy.big_net.com "I hate DOS"
```

This entry uses the string I hate DOS to build an authentication message back to big_guy.big_net.com. The quotations are necessary to surround the string in the file. (We'll look at the addresses column in a moment.) If you are setting up your system to connect to three different PPP remotes, you will want an entry for each server, so your file may look like this:

```
#   client            server             string        addresses
merlin.tpci.com    big_guy.big_net.com   "I hate DOS"
merlin.tpci.com    chatton.cats.com      "Meow, Meow, Meow"
merlin.tpci.com    roy.sailing.ca        "Hoist the spinnaker"
```

When your machine is sending the challenge, the process is reversed. The pppd daemon looks for the remote hostname in the client field, the local hostname in the server field, and uses the string to compare the encryption results with the string sent back by the remote. Entries in the /etc/ppp/chap-secrets file for this purpose look like this:

```
#   client            server             string        addresses
big_guy.big_net.com merlin.tpci.com      "Size isn't everything"
```

Again, you will have an entry for each remote machine you may need to authenticate. You can see that you will end up having mirror-image entries for the client and server fields for each machine you connect to (as either end may require authentication at any time). A simple /etc/ppp/chap-secrets file, however, looks like this:

```
#   client            server             string        addresses
merlin.tpci.com    big_guy.big_net.com   "I hate DOS"
big_guy.big_net.com merlin.tpci.com      "Size isn't everything"
```

```
merlin.tpci.com        chatton.cats.com      "Meow, Meow, Meow"
chatton.cats.com       merlin.tpci.com       "Here, Kitty, Kitty"
merlin.tpci.com        roy.sailing.ca        "Hoist the spinnaker"
roy.sailing.ca         merlin.tpci.com       "Man overboard"
```

The size of the file can get quite large, so CHAP allows you to use a wildcard match, usually only for your local machine:

```
#   client             server             string        addresses
merlin.tpci.com        big_guy.big_net.com  "I hate DOS"
big_guy.big_net.com merlin.tpci.com       "Size isn't everything"
merlin.tpci.com        chatton.cats.com     "Meow, Meow, Meow"
chatton.cats.com       merlin.tpci.com      "Here, Kitty, Kitty"
merlin.tpci.com        roy.sailing.ca       "Hoist the spinnaker"
*                      merlin.tpci.com      "Man overboard"
```

In this /etc/pp/chap-secrets file, the last entry allows any other machine connecting to the local host and requiring authentication to use the same string. Of course, the remote must have the same string in its chap-secrets file. This is a little less secure than a dedicated string for each remote, but can be a handy timesaver when using a number of machines only rarely.

The addresses field, which isn't used in the samples above, lets you list either symbolic names or IP addresses for the clients. This is necessary if the remote wants to use an IP address other than its normal one, which would typically cause the authentication to fail. If the address field is empty (as they all are in the samples), any IP address is allowed. A hyphen in the field disallows all IP addresses with that client.

The /etc/ppp/pap-secrets file is much the same as the chap-secrets file. The fields in the pap-secrets file are the client (called a user in the pap-secrets format) and server names, a secret string, and valid address aliases. However, the look of the file is different because the client and server names are not full domain names and the secret string is a single block of text. A sample pap-secrets file looks like this:

```
# /etc/ppp/pap-secrets
#   user    server    string      addresses
merlin      darkstar  yG55Sj29    darkstar.big_net.com
darkstar    merlin    5Srg7S      merlin.tpci.com
merlin      chatton   MeowMeow    chatton.cats.com
chatton     merlin    73wrh6s     merlin.tpci.com
```

In this example, the first two lines show a connection to the machine darkstar. The first line is how to authenticate a request from darkstar and the second how to authenticate a request from us to them. The username in the first column is the name to send to the remote, while the server field is their identification to us. This poses a problem: The pppd daemon has no way of knowing the remote host's name—all it gets is an IP address. You

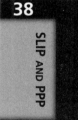

38

SLIP AND PPP

can put the IP address in the addresses column of the file or specify the remote hostname at the end of the pppd command line like this:

```
pppd ..... remotename chatton user merlin
```

This shows that the remote is called `chatton`, and our local host is `merlin`. The last portion giving the local hostname overrides the default values, if specified.

Using DNS with SLIP and PPP

If you are using SLIP or PPP to connect to the Internet for more than simple tasks (such as downloading email and news), you will probably want to use DNS. The easiest method of using DNS for your SLIP and PPP connections is to put the IP address of a name server you can access in the /etc/resolv.conf file. For example, if you can access a name server with an IP address of 145.2.12.1, make the following addition to your /etc/resolv.conf file:

```
# /etc/resolv.conf
domain        merlin.com     # the local domain
nameserver    145.2.12.1     # the Internet name server
```

After this entry has been established, SLIP or PPP sends requests for address resolution to the name server and waits for replies. The more accessible the name server is, the better the performance is. For this reason, choose a name server that is relatively close (in network terms).

Using this approach has a problem, however: All address resolution attempts must go out over the SLIP or PPP line. This can slow down applications, as well as increase the amount of network traffic over your SLIP or PPP line, sometimes to the detriment of other applications.

A way around this problem is to set up a cache-only name server on your machine. To set up a cache-only name server, you need to modify the /etc/named.boot file. To set your local machine up as a cache-only name server, your named.boot file will look like this:

```
; /etc/named.boot
directory    /var/named
cache        .db.cache               ; cache-only
primary      0.0.147.in-addr-arpa    db.cache ; loopback
```

The preceding file uses the local network name in IN-ADDR-ARPA format to specify the loopback driver, and the cache points to the file db.cache, which contains a list of root name servers.

Summary

Configuring PPP and SLIP on a Linux machine is not overly complex, although it does require proper attention to details as you modify files. After they're set up, though, PPP and SLIP can be used for Internet access, as well as access to other machines on a one-to-one basis. For more information on this subject, check out the following chapters:

General networking on Linux is discussed in Chapter 37, "Networking."

NIS and YP, which add flexibility to your Linux machine on a network are discussed in Chapter 44, "NIS and YP."

Setting up your own Internet site is discussed in Part VII starting with Chapter 47, "Setting Up an Internet Site."

38

SLIP AND PPP

UUCP

by Tim Parker

IN THIS CHAPTER

CHAPTER 39

UUCP (UNIX to UNIX CoPy) was developed to provide a simple dial-up networking protocol for UNIX systems. It is most often used today as an email transfer system, allowing non-networked machines to transfer email easily over a modem connection. It can also be used for USENET news and access to similar services that do not require a dedicated connection. UUCP is a two-machine connection between your Linux machine and another machine running UUCP. UUCP cannot be used as a remote system access system (like FTP or Telnet) nor can it be used as a standard login because the protocols do not support this type of interactive behavior. UUCP does have security features that are adequate for most purposes, but UUCP is the primary source of break-ins for many systems because most system administrators don't bother to set up the security system properly.

Linux can run any of several different versions of UUCP, most of which are compatible with one another to a reasonable extent, except when it comes to configuration and installation procedures. Many Linux versions offer you a choice between the Taylor UUCP version and the HDB (HoneyDanBer) UUCP. You can use whichever single version came with your Linux software or if you have both, you can choose between the two (or use both versions as the mood strikes you). Many Linux users prefer the Taylor UUCP implementation, while users who have worked on other UNIX systems prefer HDB because it is more recent. We'll look at both versions in this chapter. (There are even more UUCP versions, but we will ignore them because they are seldom used under Linux.) The first part of the chapter deals with configuring UUCP, and the rest of the chapter covers using it.

UUCP Configuration

Most of the configuration required for UUCP takes place under the /usr/lib/uucp directory. There are several files used by UUCP, most of which need direct administrator modification to set up properly. While the configuration process can seem awfully complex to someone who has never done it before, there are actually only a few files that need changing and only one or two entries in each file.

The configuration process for Taylor UUCP and HDB UUCP are completely different, so we will look at them separately. However, you don't have to worry about which version of UUCP is being run at the remote end of the connection because both can talk to each other (at least that's usually the case), as long as the configuration files are set up properly.

Some versions of Linux have semi-automated UUCP configuration scripts. These are more common with HDB UUCP than Taylor UUCP, but a few helpful scripts are also available for the latter. If you have one of these scripts, by all means use it, but do check the files manually afterward.

For the configuration processes discussed in the following section, we will assume that our host machine's name is `merlin`, and we want to connect via UUCP to another Linux system called `arthur`. As you go through the process, take care to enter the information in the same format as the examples, but don't mix Taylor and HDB UUCP information.

Taylor UUCP Configuration

We can begin with a quick look at the configuration files involved in the Taylor UUCP system. These are the filenames and their primary purposes:

- `/usr/lib/uucp/config`—Defines the local machine name.
- `/usr/lib/uucp/sys`—Defines the remote systems and how to call them.
- `/usr/lib/uucp/port`—Describes each port for calling out and its parameters.
- `/usr/lib/uucp/dial`—Describes the dialers for calling out.
- `/usr/lib/uucp/dialcodes`—Used to contain expansions for symbolic dialcodes but is rarely used when a straight-out telephone connection exists.
- `/usr/lib/uucp/call`—Can contain the login name and password for remote systems, but it is rarely used now.
- `/usr/lib/uucp/passwd`—Contains the login names and passwords used when remote systems connect to your local machine. Used only when `uucico` is password checking instead of using the login process.

To make the configuration process easier, we will ignore all the theory and background information and proceed with a sample configuration. You need only modify the entries to suit your own names, telephone numbers, device files, and so on, and the configuration process will be the same. It can then be repeated for as many systems as you want to connect to.

The first file to modify holds your system name and other general parameters. The file `/usr/lib/uucp/config` needs a single line entry for your system name such as this one:

```
nodename     merlin
```

The keyword `nodename` must be first on the line followed by *whitespace* (spaces or tabs), then your machine name. The information in this file may have been completed when you installed Linux, but you should manually check the contents to make sure. If your system's name isn't set correctly, the connection to the remote system won't work properly.

TIP

To use UUCP, you must have a system name. For compatibility with most versions of UUCP, keep the name to seven characters or fewer. Ideally, the UUCP name is the same name you assigned to your host during configuration. The name doesn't have to follow a convention (such as the system name used by TCP/IP for Internet access), but if you use other network protocols, keep a consistent name. If you have a domain name (for TCP/IP access) use the first component of the machine's full TCP/IP name as the UUCP name. For example, if your full domain name is `merlin.wizards.com`, use the UUCP name `merlin`.

You also need information about the remote system you want to connect to. The `/usr/lib/uucp/sys` file holds all the information about remote systems. This file usually has a few sample entries in it, which you can copy or modify. Make sure you don't leave *comment marks* (pound or hash marks) in the first column or the entries will be ignored. A `/usr/lib/uucp/sys` entry for the remote machine `merlin` looks like this:

```
# system: arthur (Bill Smallwood's Linux system)
system    arthur
time      Any
phone     555-1212
port      com1
speed     9600
chat      login: merlin password: secret1
```

The first line in the preceding extract is a comment line. Most system administrators like to put a comment line in to identify each system. The next lines identify the different aspects of the remote system, including its name (`arthur`), times at which it can be called (`Any` in this case, meaning no restrictions), the telephone number (including any area code or special digits that have to be dialed), the serial port to be used for the connection (in this case, `com1`), the speed at which to connect (9600 baud), and the chat script or login process. In this case, the chat script tells UUCP to wait until it sees the string `login:`, then to send `merlin`, wait for the prompt `password:`, and then send `secret1`.

Most login scripts require a login and password, and they must be placed in the configuration file because UUCP doesn't allow interactive sessions. This can be a bit of a problem because it allows other users on your system to see the login password for the remote machine, but because it can only be used by UUCP, this is not a major concern. Also, the file permissions on the UUCP configuration files can be set to prevent any system users (other than `root`) from looking into the file.

The port name used in the /usr/lib/uucp/sys entry does not have to match a device name on the Linux system because another file is used to match the entry to a physical device. This file is /usr/lib/uucp/port, and it requires an entry similar to this for a 9600 baud modem:

```
# com1 device port
port     com1
type      modem
device     /dev/cua0
speed     9600
dialer     Hayes
```

In the /usr/lib/uucp/port file, the name of the port used in the /usr/lib/uucp/sys file is identified on the first line. The type of connection to be used (usually modem) is on the next. The actual Linux device that corresponds to the port name is specified as a device driver (for many Linux systems this can be /dev/modem which is linked to the serial port device driver).

The modem connection speed comes next and shows the maximum speed at which the modem can be used. Finally, the name of a dialer is entered. This is a throwback to the days when modems couldn't dial themselves but used another device (called a *dialer*) to make the connection.

The dialer entry in the /usr/lib/uucp/port file is then matched to an entry in the file /usr/lib/uucp/dial which tells the modem how to dial the phone. Here's a simple entry:

```
# Hayes modem
dialer     Hayes
chat      "" ATZ OK ATDT\T CONNECT
```

This shows the script that the system uses to communicate to the Hayes modem. In this case, the \T in the command line is replaced with the telephone number to be called. Some Linux systems simplify the use of the /usr/lib/uucp/port and /usr/lib/uucp/dial files into one single entry in the /usr/lib/uucp/sys file, which names the modem file directly.

The remote end of the connection (in this case, the system `arthur`) must have corresponding entries for `merlin`. The files will be similar with only name, telephone number, and (possibly) device name and `chat` script changes. Until both ends are configured properly, you can't get a connection between the two machines.

Some Linux systems with Taylor UUCP have a utility called `uuchck` that verifies the syntax in the UUCP configuration files and printout summary information. If you don't have the `uuchck` utility, it can be downloaded from many FTP and BBS sites. Check Appendix A, "Linux FTP Sites and Newsgroups," for some of the possible sites.

By default, Taylor UUCP allows a remote system to execute only a limited number of commands when they log into your system. Typically, the remote is only allowed to execute `rmail` and `rnews`, to transfer mail and news respectively. If you want to allow extra programs to be executed, add a line to the `/usr/lib/uucp/sys` file that includes all the commands the remote system can execute. For example, the following entry specifies that the system `chatton` can execute any of the four commands given after the `commands` keyword:

```
system      chatton
....
commands      rmail rnews rsmtp rdataupdate
```

Note that all four commands must be in the usual search path used by the UUCP utilities (actually by uuxqt).

If you intend to transfer files between two machines, you must also modify the configuration files. When a remote system sends a file to your machine, the files should usually be stored in the directory `/usr/spool/uucppublic` (some systems use `/var/spool/uucppublic`) as a safety precaution. You don't want to allow a remote system to write files anywhere on your file system or they could overwrite critical system files. The convention for most UUCP systems is to use either `/usr/spool/uucppublic` or `/usr/spool/uucp/system` (in which *system* is the remote system's name) as the transfer directories.

You can specify transfer and receive directories in the `/usr/lib/uucp/sys` file. For example, the following entry for the remote system `chatton` has been modified to include specific directories for file transfers:

```
system      chatton
...
local-send      ~/send
local-receive      ~/receive
```

In this configuration, the users on your local machine can send any file that is in the `send` directory under the uucp directory (`~/send`, which means that any file to be sent to a remote system must be transferred there first), and any file incoming from a remote system is stored in the `receive` directory under the `uucp` directory. If you want to allow transfers from a user's home directory, you can specify the `/usr` directory as a starting point. Multiple entries are separated by spaces, so the following entry allows transfers from the `send` directory under the `uucp` directory or from any directory under `/usr`:

```
local-send    ~/send /usr
```

The preceding line deals only with file transfers requested or sent from your machine. If you want to enable requests for transfers from the remote machine, you need to add two more lines:

```
remote-send     /usr/lib/uucppublic
remote-request     /usr/lib/uucppublic
```

This forces the remote machine to request files and send them only to the `/usr/lib/uucppublic` directory. Again, you can offer several choices if you want, as long as they are separated by spaces.

Finally, UUCP allows machines to forward data through other machines, a process called *hopping*. In other words, if you want to send mail to the system `warlock` but can only get there through the system `wizard`, you have to instruct UUCP that your local system can get to `warlock` through `wizard`. You add a forward command to the `/usr/lib/uucp/sys` file:

```
system    wizard
...
forward    warlock
```

You should then add an entry for the `warlock` system that tells UUCP that any mail for you will be coming back through `wizard`. The matching entry is

```
system    warlock
...
forward-to    merlin
```

The `forward-to` entry is necessary so that any files returned by `warlock` are passed to `merlin`, the local host machine. Otherwise, they are discarded by UUCP as not being routable.

By default, Taylor UUCP does not allow forwarding, so system administrators should think carefully about allowing it because the potential for abuse is high.

39

UUCP

HDB UUCP Configuration

HDB UUCP is a more recent version of UUCP and its configuration files are different. In many ways, the HDB configuration is easier than Taylor UUCP's, although neither is difficult once you know the basic process.

The name of the local system is not set in the UUCP configuration files but by the Linux hostname itself. To set the system name use the `hostname` command.

The names of the remote systems are stored in the file `/usr/lib/uucp/Systems` (some older versions used the name `/usr/lib/uucp/L.sys`). There is a single line for each remote system that you will be connected to. The format of each line is as follows:

sitename   schedule   device_type   speed   phone   login_script

sitename is the name of the remote machine, *schedule* is when it can be connected, *device_type* is the type of device to use to call the remote system, *speed* is the speed (or range of speeds) that can be used to connect, *phone* is the telephone number, and *login_script* is the script used when a connection is made (such as the `chat` script in Taylor UUCP). For example, to call the remote system `arthur`, the `/usr/lib/uucp/Systems` file will have a line like this:

```
arthur Any ACU 9600 555-1212 login: uucp password: secret1
```

The `Any` entry in the schedule field tells UUCP that it can call at any time. The `ACU` entry in the device field tells UUCP to use the ACU (automatic calling unit) defined in the `/usr/lib/uucp/Devices` file.

The `/usr/lib/uucp/Devices` file (or `/usr/lib/uucp/L-devices` file in some older versions) contains information about the devices that can be used to call the remote systems. The Devices file follows this syntax:

devicetype   ttyline   dialerline   speed   dialer   [token Dialer ...]

devicetype is the name of the device (which should match the device name in the `/usr/lib/uucp/Systems` file), *ttyline* is the device driver to be used for the connecting port (usually a serial line, such as `/dev/tty2a` or `/dev/modem`), *dialerline* is an obsolete field left as a hyphen, *speed* is the speed range of the device, and *dialer* is the name of the file that tells UUCP how to use the device. A sample line for a Hayes 9600 baud modem used to connect on the second serial port of the system might have an entry in the `/usr/lib/uucp/Devices` file such as

```
ACU tty2A - 9600 dialHA96
```

This identifies the ACU entry as a 9600 baud connection through /dev/tty2A (the /dev portion of the name is not needed with HDB UUCP), and it uses a program called dialHA96 to handle the setup and dialing of the modem. There are usually programs available for most popular modems that set the modem configuration parameters automatically, leaving Linux out of that process.

If a modem program is not available to handle the modem, an entry in the file /usr/lib/uucp/Dialers can be used. The format of the Dialers entries is

```
dialer translation expect send ...
```

dialer is the name of the dialer (matching the Devices file), *translation* is the translation table to use for the phone number (converting characters when necessary to pauses, beeps, and so on), and the *expect* and *send* entries are the chat script to set up the modem. White space in the script is ignored unless it is in quotation marks. A sample line in the Dialers file looks like this:

```
hayes1200 =,-,     "" AT\r\c OK\r \EATDT\T\r\c CONNECT
```

This is the entry for a Hayes 1200 Smartmodem, identified by the name hayes1200, with translations for the = and - characters, followed by the AT commands used to set up the modem. Because these entries are usually supplied in the Dialers file for most popular modems, we won't bother going into detail about them.

Permissions for file transfers are a little more convoluted with HDB UUCP than Taylor UUCP because HDB UUCP adds many features for special handling. Instead of looking at all the file transfer permissions, you are better off consulting a specialty book on UUCP because the subject can easily consume 100 pages by itself! For this reason, we'll look at the fundamentals—just enough to get you set up properly.

Permissions for remote system access and file transfers are handled by the file /usr/lib/uucp/Permissions. The general format of the entries in this file is

```
MACHINE=remotename LOGNAME=uucp \
    COMMANDS=rmail:rnews:uucp \
    READ=/usr/spool/uucppublic:/usr/tmp \
    WRITE=/usr/spool/uucppublic:/usr/tmp \
    SENDFILES=yes REQUEST=no
```

MACHINE identifies the remote machine's name, LOGNAME is the name they use to log in (or you use to log in to their system), COMMANDS are the commands they can execute on your local system, READ is the list of directories they can read files from, WRITE is the list of directories where they can write files, SENDFILES means they can send files (yes or no), and REQUEST means they can request files from your system (yes or no). Notice the use of slashes at the end of the first four lines to indicate this is really a single long line broken up for readability. This is a typical UNIX convention.

A complete entry for the remote system `wizard` shows that it is allowed to both send and receive files but only from the `/usr/spool/uucppublic` directory, and it can only execute `mail` and `uucp` commands (the latter transfers files):

```
MACHINE=wizard LOGNAME=uucp1 \
    COMMANDS=rmail: uucp \
    READ=/usr/spool/uucppublic: \
    WRITE=/usr/spool/uucppublic: \
    SENDFILES=yes REQUEST=yes
```

To prevent the remote system from sending files, change `SENDFILES` to no. To prevent the remote system from requesting files, change `REQUEST` to no.

A UUCP Connection

When UUCP connects to a remote machine, it follows a particular series of steps. You can better understand the configuration files used by UUCP and the processes that are involved by following through a typical session. UUCP uses a process called `uucico` (UUCP Call In/Call Out) to handle the process of connecting and sending information. A UUCP connection can be started with the `uucico` command followed by the remote system name, such as

```
uucico -s arthur
```

When `uucico` starts, it examines the `/usr/lib/uucp/sys` file (Taylor UUCP) or `/usr/lib/uucp/Systems` (HDB UUCP) to see if the remote system name exists there. When it finds the proper remote system name, `uucico` reads the rest of the entries for that system, including the port to be used. From there, `uucico` uses `/usr/lib/uucp/port` and `/usr/lib/uucp/dial` (Taylor UUCP) or `/usr/lib/uucp/Devices` and `/usr/lib/uucp/Dialers` (HDB UUCP) to start the modem connection (assuming it is a modem used to establish the session, of course). When the modem is in use, `uucico` creates a lock on the device so no other application can use it (the lock is a file starting with `LCK..` and followed by the device name, such as `LCK..cua0`).

Once the `chat` scripts for setting up and dialing the modem have been executed and the remote system is connected, `uucico` uses the `chat` script in the `/usr/lib/uucp/sys` or `/usr/lib/uucp/Systems` file to log in to the remote. Once logged in, the remote machine starts its copy of `uucico`, and the two `uucico` processes establish handshaking between themselves. Finally, after the handshaking has been established, `uucico` goes ahead and handles any transfers that are queued.

When completed with the session, the local machine checks to make sure that the remote has nothing further to send and then breaks the connection. Finally, `uucico` terminates.

Direct Connections

If your two machines are directly connected through a serial port, for example (no modems involved in the connection), you can use UUCP as a simple network protocol for file transfer. The only changes to the configuration files mentioned earlier are in the port specification. Instead of using a modem device, you specify a direct connection. For example, in the `/usr/lib/uucp/sys` file (Taylor UUCP), create an entry like this:

```
port       direct1
```

Include a matching entry in the `/usr/lib/uucp/port` file that looks like this:

```
port       direct1
type       direct
speed      38400
device     /dev/cua1
```

Specify the speed of the direct connection and the port which uses it. The entries in the HDB UUCP version are similar, using the `/usr/lib/uucp/Systems` and `/usr/lib/uucp/Devices` files.

Login Scripts

The login scripts that form part of the `/usr/lib/uucp/sys` or `/usr/lib/uucp/Systems` file can be the most difficult part of a UUCP connection to set correctly. If the machine you are logging in to is a typical UNIX system, there should be only the usual login and password prompts to worry about. Other systems may require some special handling to gain access. For this reason, the login script is worth a quick look.

Generally, the layout of the login script is in a pattern-action pair, with the pattern coming from the remote machine and the action from the local. A simple login is as follows:

```
login: merlin password: secret1
```

In this case, the local system waits until it sees the string `login:` coming from the remote, sends `merlin`, waits for `password:`, then sends `secret1`. You can simplify the script a little by cutting out extra letters from the remote, because all you really need are the last couple of characters and the colon. The script could be written like this:

```
gin: merlin word: secret1
```

This type of script has a good use. Suppose the remote system sends `Login:` instead of `login:`; then the shortened form will work and the longer match won't.

39

UUCP

One useful feature of the uucico login script is the ability to wait for the remote machine to reset itself (or start a getty process, more likely). This is implemented by using a hyphen and the word BREAK in the script which tells uucico to send a break sequence if the remote site hasn't responded in a timely manner. For example, the script would be similar to this:

```
ogin:-BREAK-ogin: merlin sword: secret1
```

In this case, if the remote machine doesn't respond with a login: prompt after a short period of time, the local machine sends a break sequence and waits for the prompt again.

A few special characters can be used in the login script. The most important ones for most UUCP purposes are the following:

\c	Suppresses sending carriage return (send only)
\d	Delays one second (send only)
\p	Pauses for a fraction of a second (send only)
\t	Sends a tab (send and receive)
\r	Sends a carriage return (send and receive)
\s	Sends a space (send and receive)
\n	Sends a newline (send and receive)
\\	Sends a backslash (send and receive)

Sometimes you need to use one or more of the characters to get the remote machine to respond to a modem login. For example, the following script sends a carriage return-line feed pair before starting to match characters:

```
\n\r\p ogin: merlin word: secret1
```

This is usually enough to get the remote machine to start a getty on the port.

Changing Access Times

Both Taylor and HDB UUCP versions let you specify a time to call the remote systems. Although the examples so far show Any (meaning the system can be called at any time, day or night), you may want to restrict calls to local-cost times or to certain days of the week. The reason for limiting calls may be at your end (costs, for example) or at the remote (limited access times during the day, for example).

To specify particular days of the week to allow calls, use a two-digit abbreviation of the day (Mo, Tu, We, Th, Fr, Sa, Su), Wk for weekdays (Monday through Friday), Any (for any time), or Never (for not allowed to connect). Any combination of the days may be used, as you will see in a moment. The times for connecting are specified as a range, in 24-hour format, when a time span is required. If no time is given, it is assumed that any time during the day is allowed.

Dates and times are run together without spaces, while subsequent entries are separated by commas. Examples of restricted access times are as follows:

```
Wk1800-0730
```

```
MoWeFr
```

```
Wk2300-2400, SaSu
```

The first example allows connection only on weekdays between 6 p.m. and 7:30 a.m. The second allows connection any time on Monday, Wednesday, or Friday. The last example allows connections only between 11 p.m. and midnight on weekdays and any time on weekends. You can build up any time and date specifications you want. These apply to both Taylor and HDB UUCP versions.

UUCP Security

The permissions of the UUCP configuration files must be carefully set to allow UUCP to function properly, as well as to allow better security for the system. Simply stated, the files should all be owned by uucp, and the group should be uucp on most systems that have that group in the /etc/group file. The ownerships can be set either by making all the file changes while logged in as uucp or by setting the changes as root, and then issuing the following commands when you are in the /usr/lib/uucp directory:

```
chown uucp *
chgrp uucp *
```

As a security precaution, you should set a strong password for the uucp login if there is one on your system. Some versions of Linux do not supply a password by default, leaving the system wide open for anyone who can type uucp at the login prompt!

The file permissions should be set very tightly, preferably to read-write (and execute for directories) only for the owner (uucp). The group and other permissions should be blanked because a read access can give valuable login information, as well as passwords to someone.

When UUCP logs in to a remote system, it requires a password and login. This information is contained in the /usr/lib/uucp/sys or /usr/lib/uucp/Systems files and should be protected to prevent unauthorized snooping by setting file ownerships and permissions as mentioned.

If you have several systems connecting into yours, they can all use the same uucp login and password, or you can assign new logins and passwords as you need them. All you need to do is create a new /etc/passwd entry for each login (with a different login name from uucp, such as uucp1, uucp_arthur, and so forth) and a unique passwd. The remote system can then use that login to access your system. When you create new UUCP users in the /etc/passwd, force them to use uucico only to prevent access to other areas of your system. For example, the login uucp1, shown here, forces uucico as the startup command:

```
uucp1::123:52:UUCP Login for Arthur:/usr/spool/uucppublic:/usr/lib/uucp/
uucico
```

The home directory is set to the uucppublic directory, and uucico is the only startup program that can be run. Using different logins for remote machines also allows you to grant different access permissions for each system, preventing unwanted access.

You should also carefully control the commands that remote systems can execute on your local machine. This is done through the permissions fields of the local access file and should be monitored carefully to prevent abuse and unauthorized access. In a similar manner, if you are allowing forwarding of files through your system, you should control who is allowed to forward and where they are forwarded to.

Most important of all is to ensure that whoever accesses your system on a regular basis is someone you want access to be granted to. Don't leave your system wide open for anyone to enter because you are guaranteeing yourself disaster. Carefully watch logins and make sure file permissions and ownerships are properly set at all times.

Using UUCP

Once you have configured UUCP, you can use it to transfer files and email. In order to use UUCP, you have to know the addressing syntax which is different from what you may know from the Internet. The UUCP address syntax is

machine!target

machine is the remote machine name and *target* is the name of the user or file that you are trying to get to. For example, to send mail to the user yvonne on machine arthur, use the mail command with the following destination username

```
mail arthur!yvonne
```

UUCP lets you move through several machines to get to a target. This can help save on telephone bills or make a much wider network available to you from a small number of connections. Suppose you want to send mail to a user called `bill` on a system called `warlock`, which isn't in your configuration files but can be connected to through `arthur`. If you have permission to send mail through the system `arthur` (called a *hop*), you can send the mail with this command:

```
mail arthur!warlock!bill
```

When UUCP decodes this address, it reads the first system name (`arthur`) and sends it to that system. The UUCP processes on `arthur` then examine the rest of the address and realize the mail is to be sent on to `warlock`. If you have permission to forward through `arthur`, UUCP on `arthur` sends the mail through to `warlock` for you. You can have many hops in an address, as long as each system you are connecting to allows the pass-through and can connect to the next machine on the list. For example, the address would send data through `arthur`, `warlock`, `chatton`, and `vader` in order, and then to the user `alex`:

```
arthur!warlock!chatton!vader!alex
```

The addresses must be specified in the proper hop order or the address will fail. This multi-hop addressing can be very useful if a number of friends have local connections to other machines, allowing you to easily set up a complex network. The hard part is usually tracking the names of the systems involved. (The exclamation mark in the address is called a *bang*, so the address above is spoken as "arthur-bang-warlock-bang-chatton-bang-vader-bang-alex.")

> **TIP**
>
> Some shells don't like the bang character because it is interpreted as a special shell command. Shells, such as the C Shell, use the exclamation mark to recall previous commands so you must replace the bang with a \ to prevent the shell's interpretation. Addresses then become `arthur\!chatton\!yvonne`. This looks funny, but you get used to it.

39

UUCP

Depending on how you have your UUCP system set, it may call out to the other systems in an address whenever something is submitted to it, or if callout times are limited, the data may be spooled until a call is allowed. You have already seen how to set callout times in the `/usr/lib/uucp/sys` and `/usr/lib/uucp/Systems` files.

A quick caution about relying on UUCP for delivery of information: If the systems that are being used are not set to call immediately when there is something queued, your data can take a long time to get to its destination. For example, if one of the hops in your address only calls the next machine in the address once a day, you may have a 24-hour delay in delivery. This can be exacerbated by each machine in the network.

> **TIP**
>
> Don't rely on the contents of your data sent through UUCP to be kept confidential. Once on a remote system, any user with access privileges to the queue could snoop into your data. Ideally, the file permissions prevent anyone but the superuser accessing the data, but not all systems keep tight security. If you must send sensitive data, encrypt it and let the recipient know the decryption key through another format (not in a mail message!).

UUCP deals with all transfers as jobs, a term you'll encounter often when working with UUCP and its documentation. A *job* is a command that is to be executed on the remote system, a file that is to be transferred to or from the remote, or any other task that you want performed between the two systems.

Sending Email with UUCP

Most utilities like mail packages understand the UUCP addresses, so you don't have to worry about email not reaching the proper destination. You don't usually have to make any changes at all to applications running under Linux to get them to understand this UUCP address format. In the last section you saw how the mail package can be used with UUCP addresses.

You can use any of the usual `mail` command options to modify the behavior of the package. For example, to send the contents of the file `data_1` to yvonne on system `chatton` through the system `arthur`, and tag the mail with a subject heading, issue the following command:

```
mail -s "Data file" arthur\!chatton\!yvonne < data_1
```

Most mail packages available for Linux, including X-based mailers, work perfectly well with UUCP addresses, as well as the more common Internet addresses, but you may want to check before adopting a new mail package.

Transferring Files with UUCP

UUCP's most common use is to transfer files from one machine to another. To transfer files using UUCP, you use the `uucp` command. The syntax of the `uucp` command is

```
uucp [options] source destination
```

The options supported by uucp vary a little depending on the version and type of UUCP implementation, but most versions support the following useful options:

-c   Do not copy the file to a spool directory before sending.
            The default action is to copy to a spool directory, and uses the -C option to explicitly specify it.

-f   Don't create directories on the remote system if needed. The default action is to create directories as needed, and can be explicitly specified with the -d option.

-m   Sends mail to the person who issued the uucp command when the copy is complete.

-nuser   Sends mail to user on the remote system when the copy is complete.

The default behaviors are usually sufficient for most users, although you may want the mail options when you need confirmation of an action.

Both source and destination are the names of files or directories as appropriate, much like the cp command. However, when you are dealing with a remote system for the source or destination, you need to format the file or directory in valid UUCP address formats. For example, to send the file data_1 from your local machine's current directory to the directory /usr/spool/uucppublic on the machine arthur, use the following command:

```
uucp data_1 arthur\!/usr/spool/uucppublic
```

Notice that the remote machine name was prepended to the full target directory name. In most cases, when transferring files to remote systems you will want to use the uucppub-lic directories because most likely you will not have permission to transfer files anywhere else in the file system. Once on the remote system in the /usr/spool/uucppublic directory, it is up to the remote system's users to find the file and copy it to its intended destination directory.

If you want to send the same file to the user bill on the remote machine and store it in a subdirectory called /usr/spool/uucppublic/bill and send mail to both yourself and bill when the copy is completed, issue this command:

```
uucp -m -nbill data_1 arthur\!/usr/spool/uucppublic/bill/
```

To copy a file from a remote machine to yours, you need to specify the location of the remote. Remember, you must have access to the directory that the files reside in (as well

39

UUCP

as read permission on the file), or have the sender copy them to uucppublic. The following command will transfer the bigfile file from the directory /usr/tmp on the machine chatton to your /usr/tparker directory:

```
uucp chatton\!/usr/tmp/bigfile /usr/tparker/
```

UUCP allows wildcards to be used, although you must enclose them in quotation marks to prevent the shell from interpreting them. For example, to copy all the files starting with chap on the remote machine warlock's /usr/bill/book directory (assuming you have permission) to your own /usr/bigbook directory, issue this command:

```
uucp "warlock!/usr/bill/book/chap*" /usr/bigbook/
```

You can also specify hops in the machine transfers by adding the extra machine names to the command. This requires permissions to be set on all the machines that the hop will pass through and is seldom done. Although you probably don't want to do this either, you can transfer files from one remote system to another by specifying their names on the command line like this:

```
uucp arthur\!/usr/lib/uucppublic/bigfile warlock\!/usr/lib/uucppublic/
```

This sends the file from the arthur system to the warlock system. In most cases, the users on either of the two remote systems would issue the commands, relieving some of the file permission problems.

Checking on Transfers

You can check on the status of transfers that are scheduled but haven't taken place yet using the uustat command. When you issue the uustat command, all the UUCP transfers that are queued are listed. The format of the list is

```
jobID system user date command size
```

jobID is the ID of the UUCP job, *system* is the name of the system to transfer to (the first system in an address when multiple hops are taking place), *user* is the username who queued the job, *date* is when the job was queued, *command* is the exact command to be executed, and *size* is the size of the transfer in bytes.

If you issue the command as a user (not superuser), only your jobs are listed. The superuser lists all jobs that are queued. If you are logged in as a regular user and want to see all jobs, use the -a option:

```
uustat -a
```

To cancel a queued job, use the `-k` option of the `uustat` command along with the job ID. For example, to cancel jobID 17, issue the following command:

```
uustat -k 17
```

You can cancel only your own jobs unless you are logged in as superuser, in which case you can cancel any jobs.

Summary

UUCP is quite easy to set up, as long as you follow the rules. After the configuration files are properly set, UUCP offers an easy way to transfer email, news, and files to other systems. UUCP is also one of the easiest methods to establish a low-volume network because all you need is a modem or a direct connection. Using UUCP to transfer mail and files is as easy as using the usual `mail` and `cp` commands.

Although UUCP is less popular nowadays because of the LAN craze, it does provide a simple, very low-cost network for those who need to connect only a couple of machines. It's also great for connecting your machine to those of your friends, allowing email back and forth, and really making your Linux system act like a well-connected workstation. From here, you can learn about related topics in the following chapters:

Configuring your system for email is discussed in Chapter 40, "Configuring Linux for Mail."

Newsgroups and Linux are discussed in Chapter 41, "Configuring Linux for News."

Preventing break-in problems with your system is discussed in Chapter 42, "Network Security."

That very important subject of backups is discussed in Chapter 45, "Backups."

39

UUCP

Configuring Linux for Mail

by Tim Parker

IN THIS CHAPTER

There are two components to an email system on Linux: the mail user agent (called an MUA) that is your interface to the mail package on which you write and read mail and the underlying mail transport agent (called an MTA) that handles the sending and receiving of the mail.

There are two MTAs in common use with Linux called `sendmail` and `smail`, and literally dozens of MUAs available. There are probably more versions of email MTAs and MUAs available for Linux than any other software application, with the possible exception of editors. The most widely used email MTA system for Linux is `sendmail`, which is based on an email system developed at the University of California at Berkeley. There are several versions of `sendmail` available for Linux, each with slightly different capabilities. Another commonly used email system for Linux is `smail`, developed by Curt Noll and Ronald Karr. Again, there are several versions of `smail` currently available for Linux.

Because both `sendmail` and `smail` are supplied with most CD-ROM distributions of Linux, you may not be sure about which mail system you should use. For small installations (such as a typical Linux machine, either standalone or networked to others), either will work fine. In some ways, `smail` is slightly easier to configure and use, primarily because it is a more modern product. However, for larger systems or those with special configuration requirements, `sendmail` is more flexible and offers more configuration capabilities.

How Email Works

When you write a mail message using one of the mail user agent (MUA) user interface programs (such as Elm, Pine, or mail) on your Linux system, the application passes the message to the mail transfer agent (MTA), such as `sendmail` or `smail`. You can have several MTAs running (such as one package for LAN-based email delivery and another for UUCP delivery), although most systems use only one for convenience. The MUAs don't actually pass the message to `sendmail` or `smail` but to a generic delivery transport called `rmail`, which is usually aliased to the specific MTA you want to use.

If the mail message is for someone on the local area network (or even the same machine), the MTA should be able to figure out this information from the address. MTAs must be able to understand aliasing, as well, in case you call machines, networks, or users by different names. If the message is for a remote system user, the MTA must be able to establish a connection to a mail machine somewhere along the route to the destination and transfer the mail. The connection can be either UUCP- or TCP-based. If the latter is used, a transfer protocol called Simple Mail Transfer Protocol (SMTP) is often employed. The MTA must also be able to handle problems with the delivery of mail, such as when the destination machine is unavailable or the user doesn't exist. In this case, the mail is "bounced" or returned to the sender with an error message.

The routing of the mail messages to the destination is an important aspect of the MTA software and differs depending on which addressing scheme is used. For TCP-based addressing (usually using domain names), the default action is for an MTA to deliver messages to the destination machine based on the IP address and ignore the routing, leaving that to the IP software in the TCP/IP drivers.

Configuring `sendmail`

The most commonly used email program is `sendmail` which is supplied with most Linux versions. The `sendmail` system is extremely powerful and flexible, and because of these very attributes can, at times, be annoying and difficult to configure and administer. However, setting up `sendmail` and managing its use for most common email tasks is quite easy, as this chapter will show you. For those of you who have elected to use `sendmail` as your mail system, you will find this chapter provides enough information to satisfy all but the most complex networked system.

Because of the complexity of `sendmail`, it is often teamed with a utility called IDA, for a combined product often known as `sendmail+IDA`. IDA makes `sendmail` much easier to use and is the most common method of using `sendmail` with Linux. Indeed, with IDA in tow, `sendmail` becomes the easiest mail transport package available for Linux.

> **TIP**
>
> If your system doesn't have `sendmail+IDA` but offers only `sendmail`, you may want to consider getting `sendmail+IDA` from an FTP or BBS site. The convenience `sendmail+IDA` offers far outweighs any hassles in obtaining the files. Some current Linux releases are offering `sendmail` version 8, which is usually not supplied with IDA. Check the FTP or BBS sites for more information about `sendmail+IDA` for this (and later) releases.

The `sendmail` system by itself (without IDA) is configured primarily through a file which is usually stored as `/etc/sendmail.cf` (although some systems place the file in `/usr/lib/sendmail.cf` or other locations). The language used in the `sendmail.cf` file is completely different from other configuration files and is very complex. To see for yourself, examine the `sendmail.cf` file and try to make sense of it!

The `sendmail.cf` file handles the default actions of the `sendmail` system. There are several other files involved in the configuration, too. These are:

- `decnetxtable`: converts generic addresses to DECnet addresses
- `genericfrom`: converts internal addresses into generic ones
- `mailertable`: defines any special treatment for remote hosts and domains
- `pathtable`: defines the UUCP paths to remote machines and domains
- `uucpxtable`: forces the delivery of UUCP mail from DNS addresses
- `uucprelays`: allows shortcuts to remote hosts
- `xaliases`: converts generic addresses to internal ones

We will look at each of these tables in a little more detail in a moment. As mentioned, all the `sendmail` configuration files are difficult to edit manually. Using `sendmail+IDA` makes life much easier because IDA handles configuration through table-driven options. Each has a much simpler syntax than the `sendmail.cf` file uses.

The `sendmail+IDA` system uses a preprocessor such as m4 or dbm to generate the proper configuration files after you have specified values for many parameters. After the preprocessor, a makefile is used to create the final configuration files.

The `sendmail.cf` File

When using `sendmail+IDA`, the `sendmail.cf` file is not edited directly. Instead, a configuration process is used to generate the changes. The configuration routine is driven by a file called `sendmail.m4` which provides basic information about your system's name, the pathnames used on your system, and the default mailer used. While the `sendmail.m4` file can get pretty long, for most Linux installations that use UUCP or SMTP for mail transfers the file needs only basic information.

One important section of the `sendmail.m4` file is the definitions of directories. This area usually starts with a line defining `LIBDIR`, which look like this:

```
dnl #define(LIBDIR, /usr/local/lib/mail)
```

The `LIBDIR` directory is where `sendmail+IDA` looks for configuration files and routing tables. This is usually left alone since the default value is the general location for all Linux mail systems. If the path shown in the `sendmail.m4` file is correct, don't modify the file. This entry is usually hardcoded into the `sendmail` binary and doesn't need overwriting by the `sendmail.m4` file (or its generated `sendmail.cf` file). If you need to change this value, you will have to remove the "dnl" from the front of the line (which makes the line essentially a comment), then add the correct path and rebuild `sendmail.cf`.

The local mails used by `sendmail` is defined in the line that contains the variable `LOCAL_MAILER_DEF` and looks like this:

```
define(LOCAL_MAILER_DEF, mailers.linux)dnl
```

This line is necessary because `sendmail` doesn't actually handle mail delivery. Instead, another program takes care of this step. By default, the value used for the local mailer (which is almost always `deliver`) is contained in a file called `mailers.linux`. This file is referenced in the `LOCAL_MAILER_DEF` entry in the `sendmail.m4` file. This requires you to check the `mailers.linux` file in the same subdirectory (usually `/usr/local/lib/mail/mailers.linux`) to ensure the deliver program (or whatever delivery agent you use) is properly entered. A typical `mailers.linux` file looks like this:

```
# mailers.linux
Mlocal, P=/usr/bin/deliver, F=SlsmFDMP, S=10, R=25/10, A=deliver $u
Mprog, P=/bin/sh, F=lsDFMeuP, S=10, A=sh -c $u
```

The `deliver` mail delivery agent is also specified in the file `Sendmail.mc`, which is used to build sendmail.cf. You need to check this `Sendmail.mc` file, too, if the name of your delivery agent is not `deliver`. (If you are using `deliver`, don't worry about this file.) The `Sendmail.mc` file is important and must be read in when `sendmail.m4` is processed. There is usually a line in `sendmail.m4` that makes sure this happens. The line, which usually occurs at the top of the `sendmail.m4` file, looks like this:

```
include(Sendmail.mc)dnl
```

You may need to specify some entries in the `PSEUDODOMAINS` variable. This variable is used to handle systems that can't expand into domain names properly, usually UUCP networks. The entries in the `PSEUDODOMAINS` field tells `sendmail+IDA` not to use DNS for these networks (which will always fail). Typically, the `PSEUDODOMAINS` variable is set to the following values:

```
define(PSEUDODOMAINS, BITNET UUCP)dnl
```

You can use the `PSEUDONYMS` field to hide your machine names from the outside world. This means that whether mail was sent from `merlin.tpci.com` or `chatton.tpci.com` doesn't matter: the recipient on another network sees only the address `tpci.com`. This is called "hiding" the local machines. When used, `sendmail` accepts mail from all machines identified in the `PSEUDONYMS` variable. The `PSEUDONYMS` field is usually used as shown in the following line:

```
define(PSEUDONYMS, tpci.com)dnl
```

This entry lets any machine with the network type `tpci.com` send mail through `sendmail`.

To define the name of your local machine, you use the `DEFAULT_HOST` variable. This is usually defined as the same name as your mail server (or your basic machine's name if you are not on a network). For example, the following entry can be used to set the default mail server's name:

```
define(DEFAULT_HOST, merlin.tpci.com)dnl
```

If you do not set a valid name for the `DEFAULT_HOST` variable, no mail will be returned properly to your system.

If your system is not a mail gateway to the Internet (or other networks that are accessible from your LAN), you can set your Linux system to send mail on to another machine for processing. This is done by setting the `RELAY_HOST` and `RELAY_MAILER` variables in `sendmail.c4`. These variables set the name of the mail server that all mail should be passed on to. For example, to set your local system to route all outbound mail to a machine called `wizard`, set these two lines to look like this:

```
define(RELAY_HOST, wizard)dnl
define(RELAY_MAILER, UUCP=A)dnl
```

The `RELAY_MAILER` line specifies the mailer to use to send messages on to the `RELAY_HOST`.

Configuration Table Locations

There are several lines in the `sendmail.m4` file that define configuration tables. For the most part, these configuration files are under the directory defined by `LIBDIR`. This section of the `sendmail.m4` file has several lines that look like

```
define(ALIASES, LIBDIR/aliases)dnl
define(DOMAINTABLE, LIBDIR/domaintable)dnl
```

and so on for about seven configuration file definitions in total. You can change any of these values if you want, but be sure to move the files themselves to the specified location. On the whole, it is best to leave the files in their default location.

The file `decnetxtable` is used to translate domain names into DECnet style names. This is a holdover from earlier versions of `sendmail` and will probably never be necessary for Linux users (unless your Linux machine is on a DECnet system).

The `domaintable` file is used to force `sendmail` to perform specific instructions after using DNS. The file, which is almost never used on Linux systems, allows you to provide expansion of short-form names. For example, suppose you often send mail to the host `reallylongname.reallybignet.com` but don't want to type that entry each time. You can place an entry in the domaintable file that looks like

```
reallylongname.reallybignet.com        big.com
```

so that whenever you send mail to `bill@big.com` it is expanded by `sendmail` to `bill@reallylongname.reallybignet.com`. The `domaintable` file can also be used to correct common typographic mistakes. For example, if you find many users sending mail to `abcdef.com` instead of `abcdfe.com`, you can add a line to the `domaintable` file that corrects the domain name. Such a line looks like this:

```
abcdfe.com        abcdef.com
```

The format of the file is always correct domain followed by the incorrect (or shortened) domain name.

The `genericfrom` table is used to hide local usernames and machine addresses by converting local usernames to a generic ID that has no obvious connection to the username. It is seldom used by Linux systems because the general convention is to use real names on email and similar data. The companion file, `xaliases`, performs the generic to real conversion when mail comes back from the outside world.

The `mailertable` table is used to define any special handling for hosts or domains. Most often, `mailertable` is used to specify how certain domains or hosts are accessed and which protocol to use for them. This file doesn't have to be modified if your system only uses UUCP, but if you use SMTP or DNS, you should verify its contents.

The `mailertable` file is read from the first line down, and `sendmail` processes mail based on each line in the file. For this reason, place the most specific rules at the top of the file, with more general rules after. Rules are specified in a format that gives the method of connection, then the remote system or domain. The syntax is

```
mailer delimiter relayname     remote
```

where `mailer` is the transport to use, `delimiter` is a special character, `relayname` is the name of the system to pass the mail to, and `remote` is the remote host or domain name. The `mailer` can be one of the following values:

- TCP-A   TCP with Internet-style addresses
- TCP-U   TCP with UUCP-style addresses
- UUCP-A   UUCP with Internet-style addresses

The `delimiter` has a special meaning and must be one of the following characters:

- !   strips the hostname from the address before forwarding
- ,   doesn't modify the address at all
- :   removes the hostname only if there are intermediate hosts specified

The `mailertable` rules can be built quite easily when you are forwarding mail to a remote mail server. For example, to force `sendmail` to use UUCP through a remote mail server called `wizard` to connect to the remote system `roy.sailing.org`, add a rule like this to the mailertable file:

```
UUCP-A,wizard     roy.sailing.org
```

On a more general level, you can have a rule like this one

```
TCP-A,wizard      chatton.com
```

which forwards any mail destined for the remote network `chatton.com` to the local mail server wizard via TCP.

The `pathtable` table is used to define explicit routing to remote hosts and networks. The format of each line in the `pathtable` file uses a syntax similar to a UUCP path alias, with entries appearing alphabetically in the file. The use of the `pathtable` file is rare because most Linux systems can handle the routing without explicit instructions.

The `uucprelays` file is used to short-circuit the UUCP path to a remote site when there is a better path. For example, if your users often use the path `wizard!bignet!merlin!tpci` and you create a direct link to `tpci`, you can use `uucprelays` to redirect the mail. This file is seldom used by Linux system users.

The `uucpxtable` file is used when a UUCP-style address must be used for mail delivery. The file provides the instructions for converting a DNS format address to a UUCP format address. If you are using a mail server other than your current machine or want to use UUCP to connect to specific machines because of reliability factors, this table is necessary.

This file contains a number of entries that has a format that gives the UUCP style name followed by the domain name, such as this one:

```
chatton        chatton.com
```

This tells `sendmail` that any mail for `chatton.com` should be rerouted via UUCP to `chatton` (UUCP-style addressing). This forces mail addresses to let's say, `yvonne@chatton.com` to be rewritten as `chatton!yvonne`, which can be handled by UUCP.

Building `sendmail.cf` from `sendmail.m4`

Now that you have configured the `sendmail.m4` file and its dependent files, you can generate the `sendmail.cf` file. This is done with the m4 processor. When the `sendmail.m4` file is ready to be processed, issue the command

```
make sendmail.cf
```

or you can substitute your site name if you renamed your `sendmail.m4` file to reflect your site name (in other words, if you created a file called `tpci.m4`, you should specify `tpci.cf` in the command).

After the file has been processed, copy it to the `/etc` directory (which is where the file normally resides) and start up `sendmail` with the command

```
/usr/lib/sendmail -bd -q1h
```

or reboot your machine (because `sendmail` usually starts from the `rc` startup files). The exact paths may be different with your system, so check where these configuration files are stored.

Using `sendmail` Version 8

The latest version of `sendmail` supplied for most Linux systems is version 8. If you didn't see versions 6 or 7, don't worry: They never existed. The `sendmail` system jumped from release 5.X to 8. (One of the important additions to version 8 of `sendmail` is the anti-spam filters that lets you remove spam email. If you are getting a lot of spam, this feature alone is worth the upgrade trouble!)

For the most part, `sendmail` version 8 is similar in configuration details to the other releases of `sendmail`. One change is the inclusion of four different UUCP mail routines. Choose one of the four UUCP versions based on the following features:

- `uucp-old` (same as "uucp") Classic UUCP that uses a bang-style address and can send to only one address at a time (duplicate messages are sent when multiple recipients are specified). This version should be used only if you really need compatibility with old-style UUCP systems.
- `uucp-new` (previously know as "suucp") The same as UUCP except that it provides the `rmail` command to allow several recipients. This version is not much of an improvement over `uucp-old`.
- `uucp-dom` Allows domain name-style addressing. May not be compatible with some systems you may have to connect to.
- `uucp-uudom` A combination of `uucp-new` and `uucp-dom` to provide the best features of both. Allows bang- and DNS-style addresses with proper handling of headers.

Whichever version of UUCP you choose, it should be copied or linked to the normal UUCP binary on your Linux system.

smail

The smail mail system is similar to the sendmail system in most of its actions, although the configuration process is different. In some ways, smail is easier to work with than sendmail and can be a good choice for smaller systems. If you choose to use smail as your mailer, you will have to make some manual modifications to configuration files because there are few automated or scripted routines available.

The smail system has many options and configuration details, most of which are never used. We'll look at the primary controlling parameters that most Linux users will need, and essentially ignore those that are very seldom (if ever) used in real situations. For more information on the options and configuration controls we skip over in this chapter, see the man pages or smail documentation. We'll focus this chapter on showing you how to get smail up and running quickly and easily to handle the situations most Linux systems will find themselves working with.

Setting Up smail

The smail system requires several links to exist so smail can execute properly. The two most important links are to the files /usr/bin/rmail and /usr/lib/sendmail (sometimes located as /usr/sbin/sendmail, depending on the version of Linux). These links are necessary because most user mail applications send outgoing mail to either rmail or sendmail (depending on the mail software), and this has to be redirected to smail. Links allow this redirection to occur transparently without altering the user mail applications.

You should verify that the rmail and sendmail files are linked to smail, and if not, establish the links. Usually, the links established are symbolic and will show in a directory listing with an entry like this:

```
lrwxrwxrwx   1   root    root     6 Sep 16:35   file1 -> file2
```

The arrow (->) shows that a symbolic link exists. (For more information on links and symbolic links, see Chapter 8, "Using the File System.") Check both the rmail and sendmail binaries for these symbolic links. If the symbolic links do not exist already, create them with the following commands:

```
ln -s /usr/local/bin/smail /usr/bin/rmail
ln -s /usr/local/bin/smail /usr/lib/sendmail
```

Of course you should substitute whatever directory pathnames are valid on your system for smail, sendmail, and rmail. After you have created the links, verify that they exist by displaying the directories and look for the symbolic link notation shown earlier.

If there is the possibility of mail either entering or leaving your system through an SMTP channel, you should also establish a link between the `smail` program and the SMTP system. Use the command:

```
ln -s /usr/local/bin/smail /usr/sbin/smtpd
```

to set up the link (substituting proper paths for your system). Next, the SMTP service has to be allowed through the TCP configuration files. This is enabled by setting the `/etc/services` file to specifically allow SMTP connections. There is a line in the `/etc/services` file that looks like

```
smtp    25/tcp    # Simple Mail Transfer Protocol
```

which you should verify to be not commented out (indicated by a pound sign as the first character). This allows the SMTP link to be established as TCP port number 25 (the default value).

If you are going to leave `smail` as a daemon (started automatically with the system boot), ensure that the `smail` daemon is started in the `rc` files (such as `rc.inet2`). The usual command line for the `smail` daemon looks like this:

```
/usr/local/bin/smail -bd -q15m
```

The `-bd` option turns the daemon operation of `smail` on, which the `-q15m` tells `smail` to process messages every fifteen minutes. If you want more frequent mail delivery, change the value in the `rc` file. Alternatively, if you want mail processing less often to relieve a heavily loaded system, increase the value.

If you decide not to run `smail` as a daemon and want it spawned by `inetd` whenever mail arrives, comment out the daemon lines in the `rc` files (usually `rc.inet2`). You cannot run `smail` in both daemon and spawned mode. Next, you should modify the `/etc/inetd.conf` file to contain an entry like this:

```
smtp    stream    tcp    nowait    root    /usr/sbin/smtpd    smtpd
```

You must have the symbolic link between `smtpd` and the `smail` program for this command to function properly.

The configuration file changes necessary for `smail` depend on which connection system you use for obtaining mail. In other words, the configurations change if you are using UUCP (which is the easiest to set up) or a TCP connection on a network. We can look at each of the configuration processes separately. You can follow both, if you allow mail through both methods.

Configuring `smail` for UUCP

Configuring the `smail` system for use with UUCP incoming and outgoing mail messages is very simple. You need to edit the default `smail` configuration file, usually stored as `/usr/lib/smail/config`. Some versions of `smail` include a sample configuration file such as `config.sample` in the same directory. You can use either as a template for the UUCP modifications.

Use any ASCII editor to edit `/usr/lib/smail/config` (the path in your distribution may be different). There are four changes you need to make. The changes are for these variables:

- `visible_domain`   The domain names your site belongs to
- `visible_name`   Your site's full domain name
- `uucp_name`   Your site's UUCP-based name (usually the same as `visible_name`)
- `smart_host`   The name of the UUCP host

Each parameter in the `/usr/lib/smail/config` file uses the same format of `variable=value`. There should be no spaces on either side of the equals sign on any line. Comments in the file are preceded by a pound sign.

Setting the Local Domain Names

Begin by setting the domain name of the local machines. Locate the line in the `/usr/lib/smail/config` file that defines the variable `visible_domain`, which usually looks similar to this:

```
# Our domain name
visible_domain=tpci
```

The `visible_domain` variable sets the domain names your site belongs to and will usually be the fully qualified domain name and any aliases that may be in effect. This field is used by `smail` to find out whether the recipient of a message is local or not. The `smail` system takes the message and extracts the recipient's address, comparing it against the local machine name (from the hostname command) and all values specified on the `visible_domain` variable. If there is a match to any of these names, the message is for a local recipient. If no match occurs, the message is routed externally.

If there is more than one valid value for a local domain name, the values are separated by colons, as shown in this example:

```
visible_domain=tpci:tpci.com:tpci.UUCP
```

If your site is properly registered on UUCP maps, add the domain "uucp" to the list of valid values, as well. In this example, we belong to the domain `tpci` (from the full domain name `tpci.com`) and `uucp`:

```
visible_domain=tpci:tpci.com:uucp
```

You may have several variations of the local domain name on the `visible_domain` line to account for typographic errors, if you want.

Setting the Local Domain for Outgoing Mail

When a message is to be routed out of the local machine, the `smail` system appends the local machine's full domain name as part of the routing information. The full local machine name is defined in the `/usr/lib/smail/config` line that deals with the `visible_domain` variable. The line will look something like this:

```
# Our domain name for outgoing mail
visible_name=tpci.com
```

As a general rule, the `visible_domain` value must be a combination of the hostname and one of the domains given in the `visible_domains` variable; otherwise, the `smail` system may bounce incoming mail issued as a reply to mail sent from your site as being unrecognizable.

The `visible_name` value is usually your fully qualified domain name (if you have one) or a domain name that exists in other routing tables.

Alternate UUCP Names

The `/usr/lib/smail/config` file sometimes contains an entry for a variable called `uucp_name`. This variable is usually optional, as long as the variables `visible_domain` and `visible_name` are properly filled in. The `uucp_name` variable is used when the name of the system returned by the hostname command is not the name that is registered with the UUCP mapping tables. For example, your UUCP mapping name may be "`darkstar`" but you may have changed your machine's name to "`vader`" for any number of reasons. The `uucp_name` variable can be used to correct this change, without requiring updates to the UUCP mapping tables.

To set a value for the `uucp_name` variable, look for (or create, if one doesn't exist) the lines that define the variable. Usually, the lines look like this:

```
# UUCP mapping name
uucp_name=tpci.com
```

If your name is properly registered as set in the visible_name variable, you can simply repeat the value in the uucp_name variable with no ill effects. If your site name has changed, enter the proper value instead.

Setting a UUCP Smart Host

Some systems use another machine as a smart host, which handles the routing of messages to and from other networks. If you are using a smart host, you should put its name in the /usr/lib/smail/config file next to the variable smart_host. Look for entries in the file that resemble these lines:

```
# Smart host
smart_host=merlin
```

In this case, any mail for other networks is forwarded by smail to the machine merlin (in the fully resolved domain name merlin.tpci.com, based on the smart_host and visible_name variables). That machine can then take care of the routing out of the network. Any machine name given in the smart_host field must be reachable by UUCP, which means having a corresponding UUCP configuration entry. (See Chapter 39, "UUCP," for more information.)

Configuring smail for TCP Use

If you are going to use a network connection to transfer mail, you need to make modifications to the /usr/lib/smail/config file that specify the types of connections and host names. There are several different methods of configuring mail systems for a network, including using NFS (Network File System) to allow a single configuration file that is shared by all machines, using POP (Post Office Protocol) or IMAP (Interactive Mail Access Protocol) to handle mail on a central site, and setting up each machine as an independent mail handler. The configuration process for all these methods is much the same, the difference being whether the configuration files reside on each machine in the network or on a single machine that is then accessed by NFS or SMTP by other machines.

Start the configuration process by establishing the local domain names using the variables visible_domain and visible_name. These were discussed in detail in the previous section on configuring smail for UUCP, so we'll limit the explanation to showing final examples of these two variables. An example of these variable definitions looks like this:

```
# Our domain name
visible_domain=tpci.com
# Our domain name for outgoing mail
visible_name=tpci.com
```

This sets the local domain name and domain resolution names. The entry for `visible_domain` is used by `smail` to attach to all outgoing mail packages (instead of whatever name is generated by the hostname command). Both `visible_domain` and `visible_name` are often the same.

The next configuration step is to set the name of a smart host that handles out-of-network messages. If you are not using a smart host or your machine handles the network connections itself, you won't need to enter these values. The variables involved in setting up a smart host are `smart_path` and `smart_transport`. The `smart_path` sets the machine name of the smart host (which must be resolvable with the domain name given in `visible_domain`). The `smart_transport` specifies the type of protocol to be used to connect to the smart host. Since most smart hosts communicate (for mail purposes, at least) with SMTP, that is the most often used value, as shown in this extract from a `/usr/lib/smail/config` file:

```
# smart host routing
# smart host name
smart_host=merlin
# communications protocol to smart host
smart_transport=smtp
```

The `smart_transport` value of "smtp" (lowercase letters only) is used to identify the SMTP connection protocol.

Modifying Behavior of `smail`

The configuration files and processes previously mentioned apply to most Linux systems, and many systems require no further actions than those already covered. However, as mentioned earlier in this chapter, three components in `smail` (router, director, and transport) can each be further configured to modify their behavior. This can help you fine-tune or modify your `smail` installation to meet particular network needs. The only component we really need to examine in detail is the router because the director and transport seldom need customization for a typical Linux installation.

In most cases, the behavior of each `smail` component is handled by a file (or several files) based in the `smail` configuration directory (usually `/usr/lib/smail`). There are many sample configuration files available from Linux distribution CD-ROMs and FTP sites that show different configurations, and to obtain one of these sample files and then modify it to your host-specific details is easier than building the files from scratch. The number of options and details change with the release of `smail`, so check to see whether you have a complete version.

The router component of smail handles the resolution of destination addresses, routing to the next mail host for further forwarding, and determination of which transport should be used to send the message on. The router component performs a number of tasks, first determining whether the message is for a local or remote machine (using the variable values defined in /usr/lib/smail/config). If the message is for a local machine, the message is handed off to the director.

If the message is for a remote machine, the message's address is given to router drivers to determine to which host the message should be forwarded. The router drivers are specified in the routers file (usually /usr/lib/smail/routers). The file contains the names of the router drivers, each of which (in the order presented in the routers file) is given the message destination address to see whether they have information about the specific route required to send the message.

You don't need to specify any other routers than the default configuration in most cases. The default setup uses the following router steps, in order:

- Resolution directly by dotted quad IP address using gethostbyaddr library call
- Resolution by symbolic name using gethostbyname library calls
- Resolution using the pathalias database (given in the file /usr/lib/smail/paths— see the following)
- For UUCP addresses, resolution to see whether the destination is a UUCP neighbor
- Routing to a smart host, if one exists, when other methods to resolve the name have failed

These default routings will work for most systems, although you should comment out the UUCP router if your system is not properly configured to handle UUCP (otherwise, you will get tons of error messages). If you do not plan to use UUCP for mail, you should also comment out this router line to simplify the entire smail system.

A couple of other common situations need to be dealt with. If you are connected to the Internet, there is a problem in that smail's router doesn't recognize the MX record format. In order to properly support Internet mail, comment out the default router and enable the BIND router instead. (If your version of Linux doesn't support BIND, you can obtain and link a more recent version from FTP and BBS sites.)

If you are using both SLIP/PPP and UUCP connections, you may encounter problems with smail waiting too long for a connection. To simplify this type of installation, rearrange the order the routers are checked so that the paths file is checked before the resolver router. In many cases, since UUCP is more efficient and faster than SMTP over a SLIP/PPP line, you can disable the resolver-based router entirely.

When a router identifies the best route to the destination machine, it also gives the transport required to communicate with that machine's mail router. The actual path to the destination may be modified at this point. For example, if the remote machine chatton@bigcat.com can best be reached through a UUCP link instead of SMTP, the destination address may be modified by the router to bigcat!chatton (UUCP-style addressing). Alternatively, a destination address may become more specific. For example, the address chatton@bigcat.com may be resolved to a specific machine such as chatton@whiskers.bigcat.com if that address will get the message delivered more efficiently.

The /usr/lib/smail/paths file is used by some UUCP routers to determine a path alias. The paths file is ASCII only and contains a sorted list of entries with two columns separated by a tab: the destination site name and its UUCP bang path. No comments are allowed in the file.

Summary

This chapter looks at the configuration of both sendmail and smail mail systems for UUCP- and TCP-based mail connections. Which system you choose to use on your Linux machine is an individual choice (and a highly debated one, too). Either system works well and should provide you with trouble-free mail service. From here, there are a number of chapters you may want to read for more information. To learn about:

Setting up your Linux system to access and display Usenet newsgroups, see Chapter 41, "Configuring Linux for News."

Buttoning up your network and preventing access from the outside, read Chapter 42, "Network Security."

Backups and how to perform them (so you don't have to reinstall your mail server again!), read Chapter 45, "Backups."

Scheduling tasks to run automatically without your intervention, read Chapter 46, "cron and at."

Configuring Linux for News

by Tim Parker

IN THIS CHAPTER

CHAPTER 41

If you have an Internet connection, eventually you are going to want to access Usenet and its newsgroups. Usenet is one of the most dynamic (and often controversial) aspects of the Internet. Although you can set up, access, and work with newsgroups with access to the Internet, most Linux users are probably more interested in using Usenet specifically.

Usenet was originally developed to facilitate the provision of discussion groups (called "newsgroups" in Usenet jargon). A newsgroup lets any user with access to the system participate in a public dialog with everyone else. Usenet is supported on millions of networks, in hundreds of countries, and reaches hundreds of millions of users.

Any machine that can attach itself to the Internet either directly, through a gateway, or through a forwarding service (such as an online service provider) can become part of Usenet. All that is required to use Usenet is the software that downloads and uploads the newsgroup mail and a reader package that lets users read and write articles.

The software that implements the passing of Usenet messages over local area networks from one machine to another is the Network News Transfer Protocol (NNTP). Using NNTP, your Linux machine can interact with any others that handle the news. NNTP software is an integral part of most Linux versions, so there is no additional software to purchase or look for.

Usenet and News

There are two components to a news service for any Linux machine: actually getting the newsgroups to your machine is the responsibility of the transport software (usually CNews for UUCP connections or NNTP for TCP connection), then the newsreader assembles and presents the articles to the user. The original news system relied completely on UUCP, so much of the news software was designed for UUCP and then modified later to accommodate alternative methods. Since most of you will be using TCP/IP, we'll concentrate on NNTP in this chapter.

To transfer news from one machine to another, a technique called *flooding* is used. One machine calls another and transfers all the news articles. The machine that just received the news calls another and transfers the articles again. The news articles flow across the networks in this manner, moving from machine to machine, instead of all the machines polling a single main news source. Each machine maintains a list of other sites that it can contact to transfer mail. Each connection to another machine is called a newsfeed.

Each machine can generate new articles as the system's users interact with newsgroups. When new articles are created, the machine checks its list of newsfeeds and calls them to transfer the new mail. Since each article generated by a newsreader has a list of the machines that it has passed through (called the Path), the local machine knows whether the remote sites on its newsfeed list have already seen the article or not. As articles move from machine to machine, each machine adds its own identifier to the article's Path field, using the UUCP bang-style notation.

A restriction may be placed on the machines that can be sent an article by an entry in the Distribution field of the header. For example, if you write an article that you want to stay within your local area network, you can specify this in the distribution field of the message when you write it. Then, when a newsfeed to a machine outside the local area network is created, the Distribution field prevents the article from being sent.

To help prevent duplicates of articles moving around Usenet, each article has its own unique identifying number, called a message ID (which sits in the Message-Id field in the article header). The message ID is a combination of a unique number and the name of the machine that the article was originally posted on.

These message ID numbers are used by each machine when a connection to a newsfeed is established. A file on each system called `history` contains a list of all article ID numbers that the local system has. When the two machines communicate with each other, they can check the `history` file to find out if the message should be sent. This is involved in a news transfer protocol called `ihave/sendme`.

With the `ihave/sendme` protocol, one machine sends a list of all the message ID numbers it currently has and waits for the other machine to identify the ones it wants. These are transferred one at a time in response to "sendme" messages. Then the process can be reversed to update the other machine. This type of protocol works well but does involve a lot of overhead in the communications process. For that reason (coupled with the generally slow lines used by UUCP modem links), `ihave/sendme` protocols are not often used when a very large newsgroup transfer is to take place at regular intervals. You wouldn't want to use `ihave/sendme` to transfer 100MB of articles every day, for example, because it is so slow.

An alternative used for large transfers is *batching* of articles, wherein one machine simply sends everything it has to another. The receiving machine then performs a check of the newly arrived articles to see if it already has them. By comparing message ID numbers, the machine can discard duplicates. This tends to be a faster method for transferring, although it does have more processing overhead for the receiving machine when it crunches the newly arrived batch.

For network-based news access, there are three ways to get articles from another machine. Using NNTP, your machine can download articles you want using a technique similar to the `ihave/sendme` protocol (called *pushing* the news). Your machine can also

request specific newsgroups or articles from the remote based on the date of arrival
(called *pulling* the news). Alternatively, you can interact on an article-by-article basis
with the remote, never downloading the articles to your local machine. This is called
interactive newsreading and works only when you have a newsfeed you can log in to
(which is common these days).

NNTP

NNTP can operate in two modes: active and passive. The active mode, as mentioned earlier, is often called pushing and is much the same as CNews' `ihave/sendme` protocol in
which the sender (client) offers a particular article and waits for the receiver (server) to
accept or refuse the article. Push mode has a disadvantage for the server in that it has a
high overhead, as each article must be checked in turn.

The passive mode, or pulling, has the receiving machine requesting a list of all articles in
a particular newsgroup that have arrived since a specified date. This is done through a
`newnews` command. When the receiving machine has all the articles, it then discards any
that are duplicated or not wanted using the `article` command. This is much easier for
the sending machine because it simply sends a mass of articles, but there is a security
issue in that the server has to make sure it sends information that is allowed to pass to
the receiver.

NNTP is implemented on a Linux system with the NNTP daemon developed by Stan
Barber and Phil Lapsley, known almost universally as the "reference implementation
daemon" or `nntpd`. Usually, you only have the source code for the NNTP daemon supplied with a Linux distribution because there are several site-specific details that must be
linked into the binary.

The `nntpd` system consists of a server program and two different client programs (one for
pushing and one for pulling). In addition, most Linux `nntpd` systems include a replacement for the `inews` program.

An alternative to `nntpd` is the INN (InterNetNews) package developed by Rich Salz. This
is supplied with many Linux distribution packages, as well. INN allows both UUCP and
network-based newsfeeds but is really designed for large machines. If you anticipate a
lot of newsgroup access, INN may be a better choice than `nntpd`, although `nntpd` can
handle full newsfeeds almost as well. Because of the relative scarcity of INN and its suitability to larger networks only, we'll concentrate on `nntpd` in this chapter. If you want to
know more about INN, read the documentation files that accompany the software or
download them from an FTP or BBS site. An INN FAQ is frequently posted to the Linux
newsgroups on Usenet.

When NNTP receives an article from a remote machine, it passes it on to one of the news subsystems that must be in place. Usually, this is `rnews` or `inews`. (You can also use NNTP for batching of articles, explained earlier in this chapter, in which case the `relaynews` program handles the batch of articles.) NNTP uses the `/usr/lib/news/history` file to properly perform some protocol transfers, so this file must be configured correctly.

Installing the NNTP Server Program

The NNTP server, `nntpd`, is usually supplied as source code only, as mentioned earlier. Typically, it must be compiled on your machine to include machine-specific information. The configuration of `nntpd` is performed through a utility program usually stored as `/usr/lib/news/common/conf.h`. You can search for the program with the command:

```
find / -name conf.h -print
```

Run this program (which is a number of macros) and answer all the questions about your system.

Begin the NNTP installation process by creating a directory in which `nntpd` can store incoming articles. You should create this directory as `/usr/spool/news/.tmp` (or `/var/spool/news/.tmp`). The ownership of the directory must be set to `news`. The two commands to perform these steps are:

```
mkdir /usr/spool/news/.tmp
chown news.news /usr/spool/news/tmp
```

The NNTP server can be configured in one of two different modes. The first is as a standalone server, which starts itself from the `rc` startup files (usually `rc.inet2`) when the Linux system is booted. Alternatively, `nntpd` can be configured to be managed through `inetd`, instead of running all the time.

If you are configuring `nntpd` to run as a standalone daemon, make sure there is no line in the `/etc/inetd.conf` file that calls the daemon (this is discussed in a moment). Check the `/etc/inetd.conf` file for potential conflicts with the `nntpd` daemon started in the `rc` files.

If you want to configure `nntpd` to run through `inetd`, which can reduce the overall load on your system except when news must be processed, you need to add an entry to the `inetd` configuration file, usually stored as `/etc/inetd.conf`. The following line should be added to this file with an ASCII editor:

```
nntp    stream   tcp   nowait   news   /usr/etc/in.nntpd    nntpd
```

There may be a line like this already in the `inetd.conf` file, commented out. In this case, verify that the line reads the same as the one above and remove the comment symbol.

Whether you are configuring nntpd to run standalone or started by inetd, you also to need to verify that there is a line for the nntp service in the TCP /etc/services file. There should be a line like this

```
nntp     119/tcp          readnews          untp
```

in the /etc/services file. It will probably be commented out when you install most versions of Linux, so remove the comment symbol.

Configuring nntpd

Once the nntpd binaries have been created by running the conf.h file, you can configure the file /usr/lib/news/nntp_access to control which remote machines can use NNTP on your system. The file is organized in a set of lines, one for each remote, using this format

```
sitename       read¦xfer¦both¦no   post¦no       except
```

where sitename is the name of the remote machine that can be identified by its site name, a fully qualified domain name, or the IP address. NNTP allows for partial matches of the domain name and IP address, which are useful to providing multiple lines of information about newsgroups. If the remote machine's name or IP address matches the sitename exactly, only that one line is read (the rest of the file is ignored). If the match is only partial, that line is read, then the rest of the file is examined to find further matches. If you want to match all remote machines, you can use the sitename default.

The access permissions for the site are defined in the second field. There are four legal values, which have these meanings:

- read the remote can retrieve articles (pulling)
- xfer the remote can send articles (pushing)
- both allows both sending and receiving of articles
- no no access to articles

The third field indicates whether the remote site can post articles. If the keyword post is used, the remote can send articles and the local NNTP system will complete the header information. If the keyword no appears in the second or third field, the remote cannot post articles.

The last field identifies any newsgroups the remote is denied access to. The field is comma-separated and preceded by an exclamation mark (you will see this format frequently in C News). For example, the entry

```
chatton.bignet.com    both    post    !alt,local
```

allows the remote machine `chatton.bignet.com` to send and receive all articles except those in the `alt` and `local` newsgroup hierarchies. The remote may also post articles.

You will probably want to set up the `/usr/lib/news/nntp_access` so there is a default value for all machines, then specific entries for machines you want to work with. For example, follow this `/usr/lib/news/nntp_access` file

```
# default entry
default        xfer    no
# allow chatton full access
chatton.bignet.com    both    post
# allow brutus to read but not post
brutus.bignet.com    read    no
```

This lets any machine other than those explicitly specified transfer articles to your machine but not post them, while `chatton` and `brutus` have explicit instructions allowing them to read and post, and read-only, respectively.

Some versions of NNTP have implemented authorization systems to ensure that your machine does not get fooled into thinking another machine is at the other end of a connection. The authorization system has not been working well for most versions of `nntpd`, so it is best left alone at this point. Check future releases of `nntpd` for more information about the authorization process.

Configuring Newsreaders

A newsreader is a user interface to the newsgroups stored by a news download program such as NNTP or CNews. Newsreaders let users read, print, save, and perform many other actions on newsgroups, including replying to an article. At the newsgroup level, newsreaders let users examine a newsgroup's lists and subjects, subscribe or unsubscribe to newsgroups, and generally manage their news access.

Newsreaders vary considerably from the simple to the very complex, from character-based to graphical, and from useful to atrocious. There are many newsreaders currently available with Linux distributions, and more newsreaders are appearing as programmers convert their favorite UNIX or DOS-based newsreaders to work under Linux.

While we can't look at every newsreader currently available, we can show you the basic configuration requirements for the most commonly used newsreaders. This information, coupled with the documentation that accompanies new newsreaders, should help you set up your Linux system for optimum behavior of the news system. Since most Linux systems are supplied with `trn` and `tin` (both threaded newsreaders), they are the primary packages that we will look at in this chapter.

Configuring trn

The trn newsreader, widely used by UNIX users, is based on the classic newsreader rn (read news). The primary advantage to trn over rn is the ability to follow threads (articles that are related by subject). Most systems can run trn without any modifications to the files, unless they want to use threads.

To enable threads to be followed, trn needs to be able to construct a thread database, showing the interrelationships between articles. The trn newsreader can't do this itself, relying on a program called mthreads (usually stored as /usr/local/bin/rn/mthreads). The mthreads utility is best run in a crontab file at regular intervals (usually as often as you download full newsfeeds). Without mthreads, trn can still be used, but threads cannot be followed.

Without any arguments, mthreads generates index files for the thread databases only for newly arriving articles in all newsgroups. To index all the newsgroups from scratch, issue the command

mthreads all

This command examines the /usr/lib/news/active file and reindexes every newsgroup in that file.

If you want to index only a few newsgroups, you can supply the newsgroup names as arguments (either in the crontab file or from the shell prompt). For example, the command

mthreads rec.auto.antique

reindexes the rec.auto.antique thread database. You can reindex more than one newsgroup at a time by separating the names with a comma. You can also force entire hierarchies to be reindexed by specifying only the hierarchical name. For example, the command

mthreads alt

reindexes all the alt newsgroups. If you want to exclude certain newsgroups, preface them with an exclamation mark. For example, this command

mthreads rec.auto,rec.audio,!rec.audio.tech

reindexes all the rec.auto newsgroups, as well as all the rec.audio newsgroups except rec.audio.tech.

If your site has very heavy news traffic, you can run mthreads in daemon mode. This means mthreads doesn't have to be started at regular intervals and it immediately processes arriving articles. However, it does take system resources away. To set `mthreads` in daemon mode, use the `-d` option. By default, `mthreads` will check the newsgroups every 10 minutes. You can place this command in the `rc` startup files, if you want.

Configuring `tin`

Unlike `trn`, the `tin` newsreader doesn't need to be told to reindex the thread databases at intervals. The `tin` newsreader generates the thread indexes every time a user enters a newsgroup. The reindexing is quite fast, unless the newsgroup has more than 500 articles or so.

When `tin` reindexes a newsgroup, it stores the index file under the user's home directory as `.tin/index/newsgroup_name`. The total size of all these index files can become quite sizable if a user reads a lot of newsgroups or if there are many users on the system. The easy way to prevent this is to force `tin` to keep a single master index in one location that all users can access. To set up a single index, set the owner of `tin` to news with the command

```
chown news.news tin
```

(when you are in the `tin` directory, of course). This way, `tin` stores the index files under `/usr/spool/news/.index` (or `/var/spool/news/.index`).

You can install a daemon called `tind` that keeps the index files constantly updated. The `tind` daemon source code is supplied with some versions of Linux, but few have a compiled version, so you will need a compiler and the make utility to build a version for your system.

Summary

Once you have completed the compilation and configuration of the NNTP system, as well as your newsreaders, you're set to go. There are quite a few new newsreaders appearing for Linux, such as `nn`, which is also a threaded newsreader. The choice of a reader is a matter of personal preference. Experiment and find the one you want to use.

From here, there are a number of related chapters that may be of interest to you. To learn how to

Secure your network from hackers, read Chapter 42, "Network Security."

Back up all the configured software you've installed, read Chapter 45, "Backups."

Automate tasks like downloading news at night, read Chapter 46, "`cron` and `at`."

Network Security

by Tim Parker

IN THIS CHAPTER

CHAPTER 42

Covering everything about security would take several volumes of books, so we can only look at the basics in this chapter. We'll take a quick look at the primary defenses you need in order to protect yourself from unauthorized access through telephone lines (modems), as well as some aspects of network connections. We won't bother with complex solutions that are difficult to implement because they can require a considerable amount of knowledge and they apply only to specific configurations.

Instead, we can look at the basic methods of buttoning up your Linux system, most of which are downright simple and effective. Many system administrators either don't know what is necessary to protect a system from unauthorized access, or they have discounted the chances of a break-in happening to them. It happens with alarming frequency, so take the industry's advice: Don't take chances. Protect your system.

Weak Passwords

Believe it or not, the most common access method of breaking into a system through a network, over a modem connection, or sitting in front of a terminal is through weak passwords. Weak (which means easily guessable) passwords are very common. When these are used by system users, even the best security systems can't protect against intrusion.

If you're managing a system that has several users, you should implement a policy requiring users to set their passwords at regular intervals (usually every six to eight weeks is a good idea), and to use non-English words. The best passwords are combinations of letters and numbers that are not in the dictionary.

Sometimes, though, having a policy against weak passwords isn't enough. You may want to consider forcing stronger password usage by using public domain or commercial software that checks potential passwords for susceptibility. These packages are often available in source code, so they can be compiled for Linux without a problem.

File Security

Security begins at the file permission level and should be carried out carefully. Whether you want to protect a file from snooping by an unauthorized invader or another user, you should carefully set your umask (file creation mask) to set your files for maximum security.

Of course, this is really only important if you have more than one user on the system or have to consider hiding information from certain users. However, if you are on a system with several users, consider forcing umask settings for everyone and set read-and-write permissions only for the user, and no permissions for everyone else. This is as good as you can get with file security.

For very sensitive files (such as accounting or employee information), consider encrypting them with a simple utility. There are many such programs available. Most require only a password to trigger the encryption or decryption.

Modem Access

For most Linux users, protecting your system from access through an Internet gateway isn't important because few users have an Internet access machine directly connected to their Linux box. Instead, the concern should be about protecting yourself from break-in through the most accessible method open to system invaders: modems.

Modems are the most commonly used interface into every Linux system (unless you're running completely standalone or on a closed network). Modems are used for remote user access, as well as for network and Internet access. Securing your system's modem lines from intrusion is simple and effective enough to stop casual browsers.

Callback Modems

The safest technique to prevent unauthorized access through modems is to employ a callback modem. A *callback modem* lets users connect to the system as usual; it then hangs up and consults a list of valid users and their telephone numbers, before calling the user back to establish the call. Callback modems are quite expensive, so this is not a practical solution for many systems.

Callback modems have some problems, too, especially if users change locations frequently. Also, callback modems are vulnerable to abuse because of call-forwarding features of modern telephone switches.

42

NETWORK
SECURITY

Modem-Line Problems

The typical telephone modem can be a source of problems if it doesn't hang up the line properly after a user session has finished. Most often, this is a problem with the wiring of the modem or the configuration setup.

Wiring problems may sound trivial, but there are many systems with hand-wired modem cables that don't properly control all the pins so the system can be left with a modem session not properly closed and a logout not completed. Anyone calling that modem continues where the last user ended.

To prevent this kind of problem, make sure the cables connecting the modem to the Linux machine are complete. Replace hand-wired cables that you are unsure of with properly constructed commercial ones. Also, watch the modem when a few sessions are completed to make sure the line hangs up properly.

Configuration problems can also prevent line hangups. Check the modem documentation to make sure your Linux script can hang up the telephone line when the connection is broken. This is seldom a problem with the most commonly used modems, but off-brand modems that do not have true compatibility with a supported modem can cause problems. Again, watch the modem after a call to make sure it is hanging up properly.

One way to prevent break-ins is to remove the modem from the circuit when it's not needed. Because access through modems by unwanted intruders is usually attempted after normal business hours, you can control the serial ports that the modems are connected to by using cron to change the status of the ports or disable the ports completely after-hours.

For most systems this is not practical, but for many businesses it is a simple enough solution. If late-night access is required, one or two modem lines out of a pool can be kept active. Some larger systems keep a dedicated number for the after-hours modem line, usually different than the normal modem line numbers.

How a Modem Handles a Call

In order for a user to gain access to Linux through a modem line, the system uses the getty process. The getty process itself is spawned by the init process for each serial line. The getty program is responsible for getting user names, setting communications parameters (baud rate and terminal mode, for example), and controlling time-outs. With Linux, the serial and multiport board ports are controlled by the /etc/ttys file.

Some Linux systems allow a dialup password system to be implemented. This forces a user calling on a modem to enter a second password that validates access through the modem. If it is supported on your system, dialup passwords are usually set in a file called /etc/dialups.

The Linux system uses the file /etc/dialups to supply a list of ports that offer dialup passwords, while a second file (such as /etc/d_passwd) has the passwords for the modem lines. Access is determined by the type of shell utilized by the user. The same procedure can be applied to UUCP access.

UUCP

The UUCP program was designed with good security in mind. However, it was designed many years ago, and security requirements have changed considerably since then. A number of security problems have been found over the years with UUCP, many of which have been addressed with changes and patches to the system. Still, UUCP requires some system administration attention to ensure it is working properly and securely.

If you don't plan to use UUCP, remove the uucp user entirely from the /etc/password file or provide a strong password that can't be guessed (putting an asterisk as the first character of the password field in /etc/passwd effectively disables the login). Removing uucp from the /etc/passwd file doesn't affect anything else on the Linux system.

You should set permissions to be as restrictive as possible in all UUCP directories (usually /usr/lib/uucp, /usr/spool/uucp, and /usr/spool/uucppublic). Permissions for these directories tend to be lax with most systems, so use chown, chmod, and chgrp to restrict access only to the uucp login. The group and username for all files should be set to uucp. Check the file permissions regularly.

UUCP uses several files to control who is allowed in. These files (/usr/lib/uucp/Systems and /usr/lib/uucp/Permissions, for example) should be owned and accessible only by the uucp login. This prevents modification by an intruder with another login name.

The /usr/spool/uucppublic directory can be a common target for break-ins because it requires read-and-write access by all systems accessing it. To safeguard this directory, create two subdirectories: one for receiving files and another for sending. Further sub-directories can be created for each system that is on the valid user list, if you want to go that far.

Local Area Network Access

Most LANs are not thought of as a security problem, but they tend to be one of the easiest methods of getting into a system. If any of the machines on the network has a weak access point, all of the machines on the network can be accessed through that machine's network services. PCs and Macintoshes usually have little security, especially over call-in modems, so they can be used in a similar manner to access the network services. A basic rule about LANs is that it's impossible to have a secure machine on the same network as nonsecure machines. Therefore, any solution for one machine must be implemented for all machines on the network.

The ideal LAN security system forces proper authentication of any connection, including the machine name and the username. A few software problems contribute to authentication difficulties. The concept of a *trusted host*, which is implemented in Linux, allows a machine to connect without hassle, assuming its name is in a file on the host (Linux) machine. A password isn't even required in most cases! All an intruder has to do is determine the name of a trusted host and then connect with that name. Carefully check the `/etc/hosts.equiv`, `/etc/hosts`, and `.rhosts` files for entries that might cause problems.

One network authentication solution that is now widely used is *Kerberos*, a method originally developed at MIT. Kerberos uses a "very secure" host, which acts as an authentication server. Using encryption in the messages between machines to prevent intruders from examining headers, Kerberos authenticates all messages over the network.

Because of the nature of most networks, most Linux systems are vulnerable to a knowledgeable intruder. There are literally hundreds of known problems with utilities in the TCP/IP family. A good first step to securing a system is to disable the TCP/IP services you don't ever use because other people can use them to access your system.

Tracking Intruders

Many intruders are curious about your system but don't want to do any damage. They might get on your system with some regularity, snoop around, play a few games, and leave without changing anything. This makes it hard to know that you are being broken into, and it leaves you at the intruder's mercy should he decide to cause damage or use your system to springboard to another.

You can track users of your system quite easily by invoking *auditing*, a process that logs every time a user connects and disconnects from your system. Not all Linux versions support auditing, so consult your man pages and system documentation for more information.

If you do rely on auditing, you should scan the logs often. It might be worthwhile to write a quick summary script program that totals the amount of time each user is on the system so that you can watch for anomalies and numbers that don't mesh with your personal knowledge of the user's connect times. A simple shell script to analyze the log can be written in gawk. In addition, some audit reporting systems are available in the public domain.

Preparing for the Worst

Assuming someone does break in, what can you do? Obviously, backups of the system are helpful because they let you recover any damaged or deleted files. But beyond that, what should you do?

First, find out how the invader got in, and secure that method of access so it can't be used again. If you're not sure of the access method, close down all modems and terminals and carefully check all the configuration and setup files for holes. There has to be one, or the invader couldn't have gotten in. Also check passwords and user lists for weak or outdated material.

If you are the victim of repeated attacks, consider enabling an audit system to keep track of how intruders get in and what they do. As soon as you see an intruder log in, force him off.

Finally, if the break-ins continue, call the local authorities. Breaking into computer systems (whether in a large corporation or a home) is illegal in most countries, and the authorities usually know how to trace the users back to their calling point. They're breaking into your system and shouldn't get away with it!

Summary

Following the simple steps outlined in this chapter will give you enough security to protect your systems against all but the most determined and knowledgeable crackers. You can't do any harm with the steps mentioned, so you may as well perform them for all Linux systems that have modems or network connections. From here, you can learn about the following topics:

Setting up the Network File System is discussed in Chapter 43, "NFS."

Backups are discussed in Chapter 45, "Backups."

What's involved in setting up your Linux system as a Web server is discussed in Chapter 47, "Setting up an Internet Site."

Modifying the kernel is discussed in Chapter 57, "Working with the Kernel."

NFS

by Tim Parker

CHAPTER 43

The Network File System (NFS) was created by Sun Microsystems to share files and directories among UNIX operating systems. With NFS, when a file or directory is shared, it appears to be part of your system instead of on some remote machine. For example, if you had a Linux machine in your basement that had a filesystem full of games, NFS would let you set that games filesystem so that it appeared on your own machine as part of the standard directory structure. Every time you access the games area, you're going over the network to the other machine, but that's all transparent to you (except for time delays), thanks to NFS.

NFS can be used with different types of networks, but it was really designed to work with TCP/IP. NFS is still most often used over TCP/IP networks. Because of its popularity, implementations of NFS have been created on other operating systems so that directories can be shared across heterogeneous networks.

Under UNIX and Linux, NFS operates in peer-to-peer mode. This really means that your computer can act as a client of NFS services on another machine as well as a server to other machines on the network, or both simultaneously.

Many people love using the Network File System service at their business, but are scared to configure it themselves at home on their Linux system. They reason that the process must be convoluted, complex, and require a lot of knowledge about the operating systems. For this reason, many people don't bother with NFS, which is a shame because it is one of the most useful services TCP/IP has to offer. As you will see in this chapter, it is not difficult to implement an NFS network, either. All it takes is a little time. Of course, you should have more than one machine on your network to take advantage of the service, too.

> **NOTE**
>
> Some newer products such as VisionFS make setting up and using network-mounted drives much easier. Ports of these products are available for Linux, although they are commercial.

Configuring Linux for NFS

The NFS service makes extensive use of the Remote Procedure Call service. For this reason, the RPC server daemon must be running for NFS to be implemented. On some Linux systems you can check whether RPC is active by issuing this command at the shell prompt:

```
rpcinfo -p
```

When you do, you should see a list of all the RPC servers currently running on your machine, such as these:

```
[root@linux tparker]# rpcinfo -p
   program vers proto   port
    100000    2   tcp    111  portmapper
    100000    2   udp    111  portmapper
    300019    1   udp    737
    100001   13   udp    791  rstatd
    100001    3   udp    791  rstatd
    100001    2   udp    791  rstatd
    100001    1   udp    791  rstatd
    100001   13   tcp    796  rstatd
    100001    3   tcp    796  rstatd
    100001    2   tcp    796  rstatd
    100001    1   tcp    796  rstatd
```

If RPC is running properly, you will see at least four `rpcbind` listings (two for UDP and two for TCP) and an entry for `pcnfsd`, the NFS daemon. In the example above, there is no `pcnfsd` entry, so we know the NFS daemon is not active yet.

You must have loaded the NFS routines when Linux was installed to be able to run NFS on your system (Linux often prompts you whether you want NFS active when you run the installation script). If you didn't load it during your initial program load, add it when you need it through whatever Disk Set installation routine is supplied with your version of Linux. Some systems, such as Caldera's OpenLinux and many Slackware releases, load NFS automatically when the system boots, whether you use it or not.

Configuring Linux Servers

With most versions of Linux, NFS is started and stopped by a script called /etc/nfs. This can be linked into the startup routines to automatically load NFS when the system boots by linking the /etc/nfs file to the file /etc/rc2.d/Sname. To shut down NFS properly, you need to also link /etc/nfs to the file /etc/rc0.d/Kname. If you want to manually start and stop the NFS daemon, you can do this with the following commands:

```
/etc/nfs start
```

```
/etc/nfs stop
```

> **NOTE**
>
> Some versions of Linux use different files and directories for NFS scripts and configuration information. If the files mentioned in this chapter don't seem to exist, try using /etc/rc.d/init.d/nfs or /etc/init.d/nfs for the startup script file.

The `/etc/nfs` command starts up and shuts down the NFS server daemon when the appropriate command is issued. When you issue the `start` command, the daemons that are activated are echoed to the screen:

```
$ /etc/nfs start
Starting NFS services: exportfs mountd nfsd pcnfsd biod(x4)
Starting NLM services: statd lockd
```

With a `stop` command, you see a message that the daemons and server are shut down:

```
$ /etc/nfs stop
NFS shutdown: [NFS Shutdown Complete]
```

For a filesystem on a Linux machine to be available to NFS clients on other systems, the filesystem must be listed in the file `/etc/exports`. With some versions of Linux, the NFS daemons starts automatically if the `/etc/exports` file exists during boot time. This invokes a program called `exportfs`, which sets the filesystem as available for NFS use. If any changes are made to the `/etc/exports` file while the system is running, you can issue another `exportfs` command or simply reboot the machine to make the changes effective.

The format of the `/etc/exports` file follows:

```
directory [ -option, option ... ]
```

`directory` is the pathname of the directory or file to be shared (*exported*, in NFS terminology) by NFS, and options can be chosen from the following:

- `ro` Export the directory as read-only. (The default value is to export as read-write.)
- `rw=hostnames` Export the directory as read-mostly, which means read-only to most machines but read-write to specifically identified machines.
- `anon=uid` If an NFS request comes from an unknown user, use `uid` as the effective user ID for ownership and permissions.
- `root=hostnames` Give root access to the root users from a specified machine.
- `access=client` Give mount access to each client listed. A client can be a host name or a net group.

An example of an `/etc/exports` file helps to show the use of these options. A pound sign on a line means a comment. Here's a sample `/etc/exports` file:

```
/usr/stuff -ro          # export as read-only to anyone
/usr    -access=clients  # export to the group called clients
/usr/public             # export as read-write to anyone
```

If you make changes to the `/etc/exports` file, shut down the NFS server daemons and start them up again. Issue an exportfs command and the system should display the names of all exported filesystems. NFS is now ready for use on your server.

> **WARNING**
>
> You may notice that some versions of Linux create a new file called `/etc/xtab`, which contains the filesystem information. Do not edit this file! You should not modify the contents, or the NFS server will not function properly. The `/etc/xtab` file is generated by the `exportfs` command.

Configuring Other Linux Servers

Some versions of Linux use the `share` command to set up a directory for export. (Many versions of Linux do not support the `share` command because the functions are duplicated in the `/etc/exports` file.) The syntax of the `share` command follows:

```
share -F nfs -o options -d description path
```

Where the `-F` option indicates that the directory or files given in `path` are to be set as NFS filesystems. The options following `-o` set the type of access in the same way as the `/etc/exports` file shown above. The `-d` option can be followed by a descriptive statement used by clients to describe the export filesystem. For example, to share the directory `/usr/public` as read-write (the default), you could issue the following command:

```
share -F nfs -d "Server public directory" /usr/public
```

You can combine options, as shown in this example:

```
share -F nfs -o ro=artemis,anon=200 -d "Book material" /usr/tparker/book
```

This command shares the directory `/usr/tparker/book`, which is tagged with the description `"Book material"`, with everyone as read-write except for a machine called `artemis`, for which it is read-only. Any anonymous users accessing the system use UID 200.

The `share` command by itself usually shows you a list of all filesystems that are exported.

Setting Up a Linux Client

Linux can mount an NFS-exported filesystem from another machine with the `mount` command. The syntax for mounting an NFS filesystem follows:

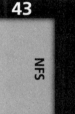

```
mount -F nfs -o options machine:filesystem mount-point
```

The -F option tells the mount command the filesystem is an NFS filesystem, machine:filesystem is the name of the remote machine and the filesystem to be mounted, and mount-point is the location in the current filesystem that the remote filesystem is to be mounted. Some versions of Linux change the syntax a little. For example, some versions use a lowercase *f* and uppercase *NFS* to indicate the type. Check the man pages for exact syntax on your version.

In use, mount is easy to work with. For example, the following command mounts the filesystem /usr/public on the remote machine called artemis on the local machine in the directory called /usr/artemis:

```
mount -F nfs artemis:usr/public /usr/artemis
```

The mount point (in this case /usr/artemis) must exist for the mount to succeed.

The -o optional component of the mount command can be used to set options from the following list:

- rw Sets the mount read-write (the default value).
- ro Sets the mount read-only.
- timeo=x Gives a timeout value in tenths of a second to attempt the mount before giving up.
- retry=x Retries *x* times before giving up.
- soft Forces the client to give up the mount attempt if an acknowledgment is not received from the remote.
- hard The client continues trying to mount the filesystem until successful.
- intr Allows the keyboard to interrupt the mount request; otherwise, the attempts go on indefinitely.

Any of these options can be combined in one mount command, as they could be for the share command. For example, the following command line tries to mount the /usr/public directory on artemis as read-only, but gives up if the mount attempt is not acknowledged by artemis:

```
mount -F nfs -o soft,ro artemis:usr/public /usr/artemis
```

The mount command by itself usually shows all mounted filesystems.

There is a simpler way to mount commonly used directories. Put the names of the directories and their mount points in the `/etc/fstab` or `/etc/vfstab` file (the file to use depends on the version of Linux). Then you can mount the files by simply issuing the mount point name. For example, this command mounts the proper filesystem as `/skunk`:

```
mount /skunk
```

Summary

As you have seen in this chapter, NFS is not very complex to set up, either as a client or server. With a few minutes work you can start sharing your directories and accessing directories on other machines. NFS is a very fast and easy way to access applications and copy files on remote machines. Although the configuration is dependent on the operating system version, a quick check of help screens or man pages will show you the proper format of the commands used in this chapter.

From here you can find related information:

> NIS and YP, which let you manage passwords network-wide, are discussed in Chapter 44, "NIS and YP."

> Automating processes on your system using the `cron` utility, very handy for system administrators, is discussed in Chapter 46, "`cron` and `at`."

> Setting up an Internet server is discussed in Chapter 47, "Setting up an Internet Site."

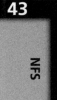

NIS and YP

by Tim Parker

IN THIS CHAPTER

Network Information Service (NIS) provides network-wide access to files that would normally be local, offering greatly improved access for users and administrators. The primary use of NIS is to keep a network-wide /etc/passwd file so you don't have to change passwords on each machine individually; instead, you can use the NIS master password files to allow global access to any machine on the network.

> **NOTE**
>
> YP stands for yellow pages and was the forerunner to NIS. Because of copyright reasons, the name had to be changed to NIS. There's a lot of old terminology from YP left in NIS. We still talk about ypmasters and ypslaves instead of the NIS equivalents, for example.

In this chapter, you'll learn how to set up NIS on a simple network. Many variations of network architecture and configurations exist, some of which get awfully complex for a network administrator. While the principles of setting up NIS and NIS domains are the same for all networks, some extra steps are required on very complex setups. For the most part, this chapter sticks with the basics since most Linux networks are straightforward.

The files normally handled by NIS are listed in Table 44.1.

TABLE 44.1. FILES HANDLED BY NIS.

File	Use
/etc/ethers	Ethernet MAC to IP address mappings
/etc/group	Group access information
/etc/hosts	IP address to host-name mappings
/etc/netmasks	IP network masks
/etc/passwd	User access information
/etc/protocols	Network protocol and number mappings
/etc/rpc	RPC numbers
/etc/services	Port number to TCP/IP protocol mappings

As you set up the NIS master and NIS slave, you will look at the most commonly used files, as well as see what has to be changed on any client machines that want to use NIS.

Setting Up the NIS Domain

NIS uses the concept of a domain to organize machines into logical groups. NIS domains have one system assigned as NIS master and one or more machines designated as NIS slaves. The NIS slaves take over the task of handling NIS requests if the NIS master is unavailable for any reason (such as a system crash or network problem). The overhead involved in setting up an NIS slave is minimal, and you should have at least one slave per network so that logins are not disabled if the master goes down. The NIS slaves can answer requests for login verification as well as the master, if so desired, to minimize the impact of NIS on the master. The master takes care of file changes and sends copies to the slaves when a change occurs.

An NIS domain doesn't have to be the same as an Internet domain, although for most networks they are identical (in other words, the entire network is the NIS domain). The NIS domain has to have a name, which can also correspond to your Internet domain name if you want. Alternatively, you can set up subsidiary domains for small logical groups in a large corporation, such as domains for accounting, research and development, and marketing.

To set up a NIS domain, you need to decide on the domain name and know the IP address of the NIS master and any NIS slaves. If you have more than one NIS domain established, you need to know which machines are handled by which NIS master. Each machine on the domain (whether one or many domains are established) must be entered into a configuration file to allow the client machine to use NIS.

To set up the NIS domain, you need to log in to each client machine on the network and set up the domain name with the following command, where `domain` is the domain name the machine will use:

```
domainname domain
```

You will need to be logged in as root or an administrative account with access to the root utilities to set these values. Because this type of command is effective only until the machine is rebooted, it is better to enter the domain name in one of the startup `rc` scripts. These differ for each version of UNIX, so you should check your `rc` commands to find out where to embed the domain name. Usually it will be in a file under the `/etc/rc.d` directory.

Some Linux systems use automated scripts to do the same sort of tasks. Caldera OpenLinux, for example, uses a tool that prompts for the NIS domain name and then the IP address of the NIS servers (masters and slaves). With this version of Linux, only three IP addresses can be entered (one master and two slaves).

NIS Daemons

NIS uses a number of daemons on the server and on all clients to enable the NIS system. On the NIS master and any NIS slaves, the daemon is usually called `ypserv`. The `ypserv` daemon waits for incoming client requests for service and handles them.

On the clients, the process `ypbind` is used. This is responsible for connecting with the YP master when the machine boots and determining any resolution steps necessary to handle logins and other network configuration information handled by NIS. The process that `ypbind` uses to connect to the NIS master and establish procedures is called a *binding* because the client is bound to the master for requests.

The binding process begins with `ypbind` sending out a broadcast message for any NIS masters on the network to respond with their IP address and the port number to send requests on. If more than one NIS master responds to the request, only the first received reply is used. If for some reason `ypbind` finds it isn't getting replies from the NIS master, it assumes the master has crashed and retransmits a request for a master.

You can find out which NIS master any client machine is bound to with the command `ypwhich`. It usually responds with the name of the NIS master, such as

```
$ ypwhich
merlin
```

Setting Up the NIS Master

Setting up an NIS master is usually straightforward. Begin by verifying the existing files on the master machine, such as `/etc/passwd` and `/etc/group`, to ensure the information is accurate and current. You should remove any expired or unwanted accounts, for example, and verify that all the login directories and commands are correct. While you are examining the `/etc/passwd` file, check to make sure that all accounts have passwords. If they don't, either assign a password or remove the account. With a network-wide NIS system in place, anyone can exploit these security holes to gain access to any machine on the network, including the NIS master and gateways machines.

After the files are ready for NIS map generation, make sure you are logged in as root, in order to set the proper ownerships and ensure full access to the filesystem. The NIS maps are generated from the standard UNIX files using the `ypinit` command with the `-m` option. The `-m` option indicates that this machine will be the NIS master. From the `root` prompt, issue the following command:

```
/usr/sbin/ypinit -m
```

The path to the ypinit program may be different on your UNIX system. Check the path if the command produces an error message when trying to execute.

When the ypinit command executes, it scans all the NIS files named in the file /var/yp and produces the NIS maps that are used by the client processes. The /var/yp file may have a different directory name on some systems, such as SCO UNIX, which uses /etc/yp as a directory for all NIS files. Check your UNIX system documentation or man pages for proper file locations. The /var/yp file contains a list of all the maps to be generated, and you will usually not have to make any changes at all to this file.

A new directory (usually called /var/yp/*domainname*, where *domainname* is the NIS domain name) is created. The maps are placed in this new domain name. If you are setting up more than one domain all handled by the same NIS master machine, the maps for each domain will be beneath the domain name's subdirectory.

As the last step in ypinit, you are asked which machines are NIS slave servers, at which point you should enter their names. The slave names are saved in a file in the domain directory.

TIP

On some versions of Linux, the NIS utilities are not in the same directories mentioned throughout this chapter. A few versions move them to other locations. To verify the proper locations, use the find command with the program name.

After the maps have been generated properly, you can start the ypserv daemon. It is best to automate the startup by editing the startup rc files to do this for you when the machine boots. There is a section in an rc file (usually the one that starts RPC) that looks like this:

```
if [ -f /etc/yp/ypserv -a -d /var/yp/`domainname` ]
then
     /etc/yp/ypserv
fi
```

This script checks for the existence of the directory /var/yp/*domainname*, where *domainname* is the domain name for your NIS domain. The entry on the first line where *domainname* is located must be in single back quotes, which means the shell should execute the domainname command and use the results. If the directory exists, the ypserv daemon is started. You should replace the directory paths with those used by your UNIX system.

44

NIS AND YP

To manually start the ypserv daemon, log in as root and issue the following command, or whatever the path to your ypserv daemon is

```
/etc/yp/ypserv
```

Next, you need to start the ypbind daemon on the server too (otherwise ypserv can't find the maps). Again, this is usually done through the rc startup scripts with an entry like this:

```
if [ -d /var/yp ]
then
   /etc/yp/ypbind
fi
```

Again, you should check that the directory path is correct. You can start the ypbind daemon manually by issuing it on the command line when logged in as root. Make sure the directory path is correct when you do so.

If you want to perform a quick test of the NIS daemons, issue a command like this one at the command line:

```
ypmatch tparker passwd
```

The ypmatch command asks NIS to use the maps to match up the next argument with the map of the third argument's name. In this example, ypmatch is instructed to look in the passwd file (passwd is the alias to passwd.byname) for the entry for tparker. You should get back the line that matches. Use any combination of map alias and entry you know exists in order to test the NIS server daemon.

Setting Up NIS Slaves

In order to set up an NIS slave, the NIS master must be configured and running. When you are sure the master is operational, log in as root to the machine to be set up as the NIS slave. The domain name of the slave must be properly set before the configuration can proceed, so check the startup rc commands for the entry that sets the domainname variable or use the domainname command to set the domain name.

To set up the NIS slave and propagate the NIS files from the master to the slave, issue the following command, substituting for whatever path is correct on your system:

```
/etc/yp/ypbind
```

Check that the binding to the master is correct by issuing the `ypwhich` command. It should return the NIS master name.

Finally, issue this command, where the path is correct and `servername` is the name of your NIS master:

```
/etc/yp/ypinit -s servername
```

The `ypbind -s` option sets the local machine up as a slave. The `ypbind` command sets up directories on the local machine and transfers all the maps from the master to the slave.

After the setup is complete, you can test the slave setup with the `ypmatch` command as shown in the previous section.

To update the maps on the slaves at regular intervals, the `ypxfer` command is used on the slave, followed by the name of the map to be transferred. For example, this command transfers the `passwd.byname` file from the master to the slave:

```
ypxfer passwd.byname
```

Most administrators either create a set of `cron` entries for transferring all the NIS files at regular intervals (such as nightly) or use a script file executed by a network administrator.

Setting Up NIS Clients

Setting up an NIS client requires that you have the domain name set properly, either with the `domainname` command or an entry in the `rc` startup files, and that the `ypbind` command has been issued properly, and the NIS client is bound to the NIS server.

When an entry in the `/etc/passwd` or `/etc/group` file must be searched for a match, the local files are examined first, and then the server is queried if no match is found. In order to instruct your client to go to the NIS master to match a login, you need to add the following entry to the bottom of the `/etc/passwd` file:

```
+:*:0:0:::
```

If you know the format of the `/etc/passwd` file entries, you will recognize this as a legal entry with no information specified. The plus sign in the username field is to instruct `ypbind` to query the NIS master. This is called a *marker entry*. The plus sign entry can be anywhere in the file. When it is reached, NIS is used, and the file is read as before if no match has been found.

44

NIS AND YP

Summary

As you can see, setting up NIS is not overly difficult. The hardest part of the process is usually getting the files that NIS uses to generate maps into proper shape, removing old entries and ensuring that security is maintained. Setting up the master and a slave can take less than half an hour, as most of the steps are automated. Often, actually finding the paths to the NIS utilities is more complex than setting up the server! From here you can read more about:

Setting up Network File System to share directories across entire networks in Chapter 43, "NFS."

Setting up cron and at to automate background processing in Chapter 46, "cron and at."

Setting up your own Internet server or WWW server in Chapter 47, "Setting up an Internet Site."

Backups

by Tim Parker

CHAPTER 45

There are three rules of system administration: 1) Backup!, 2) Backup!, and 3) Backup! Although this may sound trite, the number of people who have lost important or valuable data—not to mention all the configuration information they spend days correcting—is enormous. Even if you don't have a tape drive or other backup storage device, you should get in the habit of backing up your data. This chapter looks at how to properly do backups.

Let's begin by putting this chapter in context: if you run a system that has many users, network access, email, and so on, backups should be a very important aspect of the daily routine. If your system is used more for your own pleasure and not for any important files, then backups are not as important except as a way to recover your configuration and setup information. In either case, you should make backups—the only difference is the frequency with which you make them and how much effort you go to in order to generate backups.

Why Make Backups?

A backup is a copy of the file system or files on part of a file system stored onto another medium that can be used later to re-create the original. In most systems, the medium used for backups is tape, but floppy disks or secondary and removable hard disks can also be used.

There are so many potential sources of damage to a modern computer system, they seem to overwhelm you at times. Damage to your hard disks and their file systems and data can occur from hardware failures, power interruptions, or badly typed commands. Having a backup is sometimes your only chance of getting lost information back. While the actual process of forcing yourself to make backups can be tiresome and time-consuming, this is often outweighed by the time required to recoup any lost information in case of problems. With utilities like cron available, the task of backing up can be made much easier, too.

Part of the potential for damage (and hence the need for backups) with Linux is the nature of an operating system itself. Since Linux is a multiuser and multitasking operating system, at any moment there are many system files open. At most millisecond increments, data is being written to or read from a hard disk (even when the system has no users on it or user-started background processes).

Also, Linux maintains a lot of information in memory about its current state and the state of the file systems. This information must be written to disk frequently. When CPU processes are interrupted, system files and tables can be lost from memory. Disk files can be left in a temporary state that doesn't match the real file system status.

While damage to a file system can occur from many sources—not all of which are under the control of the system administrator—it is the administrator's task to make sure the system can be restored to a working state as quickly as possible.

This brings up one final aspect about backups: where to keep the backup media after it has been used. For most home users, the only option is to store the tapes, drives, floppies, or other media in the same place as the Linux machine. Make sure the location is away from magnetic fields (including telephones, modems, televisions, speakers, and so on). For systems that are used for more than pleasure, consider keeping copies away from the main machine, preferably away from the same physical location. This type of "off-site backup" lets you recover your data in case of a catastrophic event, such as a fire, that destroys your system and backup media library.

Backup Media

By far the most commonly used medium for backups is tape, especially tape cartridges. Tape is favored because it has a relatively low cost, easy storage requirement, and reasonable speed. The process of writing and reading data from a tape is reliable, and tapes are portable from machine to machine. All you need, of course, is a tape drive. If you don't have one, you need to find another usable medium for backups.

Possible alternative media include removable hard disks of many different types, such as the Iomega Bernoulli or ZIP drives. These are disk-platter systems, usually in a protective cartridge, that can be completely removed from the system and stored elsewhere. Several of these disks can then be cycled much like tapes are.

Another possibility is another hard disk. With the price of hard disks dropping all the time, another hard disk just for backups can be added to your system (or any other system connected by a network) and used as a full backup. The popular writable CD-ROM and WORM (write once, read many) drives makes them viable alternatives, as well.

A floppy disk drive is usually considered as a last resort backup device for large file systems, although it is very good for backing up small files. High capacity floppy drives are beginning to appear now, but the lack of Linux drivers make them unusable for most backup situations.

Setting a Backup Schedule

One of the most important aspects of making backups is to make them regularly. This is much more important for systems that support many users and have constantly changing file systems. If your Linux machine is used only for your own purpose, you can make backups when you feel there is material that should be backed up.

For most systems with only a few users, constant Internet access for email or news-groups, and similar daily changes to the file system, a daily backup schedule is important. This doesn't mean you have to make a full backup of everything on your hard drives every day; consider using incremental backups, which copy only those files that are new or have changed since the last backup.

Most UNIX system administrators prefer to perform backups during the night or early hours of the morning since there are few users logged in and no real load on the CPU, as well as the least number of open files at any one time. Because backups are easily automated using cron (see Chapter 46, "cron and at"), the exact backup time can be set to minimize impact on any other background processing tasks that may be run by the system. Since you don't have to manually start the backup process, it can be done at any time. All the system administrator has to do with this kind of backup schedule is check that the backup was completed properly, change the backup media, and log the backup.

For those with a single user or a lightly loaded Linux system, backups can be done practically anytime, although it is a good idea to have the backups performed automatically if your system is on all the time. If your Linux system is only active when you want to use it, you should get in the habit of making a backup while you do other tasks on the system.

There is a bad practice used by many DOS or Windows users when they move to UNIX backups: they keep a single tape (or other media) and continually recycle that one unit every time there is a backup. It is foolhardy to keep only one backup copy of a system as this prevents you from moving back to previous backups. For example, suppose you deleted a file a week ago and had it safely stored on a backup tape at that time. When you reuse the backup tape, the old contents are erased and you can never get the old file back.

Ideally, backup copies should be kept for days, or even weeks, before being reused. On systems with several users this is even more important because users will often remember that they need a file they deleted two months ago, after you have already recycled the tape a few times. There are methods to backup scheduling that help get around this problem, as you will see in a moment. The ideal backup routine varies depending on the system administrator's ideas about backups, but a comprehensive backup system requires at least two weeks of daily incremental backups and a full backup every week.

A full backup is a complete image of everything on the file system, including all files, and the backup media required is usually close to the total size of your file system. For example, if you have 150MB used in your file system, you will need about 150MB of tape or other media for a backup. With compression algorithms, some backup systems can get the requirements much lower, but compression is not always available. Also, you may need several volumes of media for a single full backup, depending on the capacity of the backup unit. If your tape drive can only store 80MB on a cartridge and you have to backup 150MB, you need two tapes in sequence for the one backup. Since the Linux system's cron utility can't change tapes automatically, full backups over several volumes require some operator interaction. Obviously, making a full system backup on low capacity media (like floppy disks) is a long, tedious problem as there are many volumes that must be switched.

Incremental backups (sometimes called differential backups) back up only the files that have been changed or created since the last backup. Not all operating systems have a file indicator that shows which files have been backed up (like DOS does, for example). Linux is one of these, although the modification date can be used to effectively act like a backup indicator.

Incremental backups are sometimes difficult to make with Linux, unless you restrict yourself to particular areas of the file system that are likely to have changed. For example, if your users are all in the /usr directory, you can backup only that file system area instead of the entire file system. This is often called a partial backup, as only a part of the file system is saved. (Incremental backups can be made under any operating system by using a background process that logs all changes of files to a master list, then uses the master list to create backups. The overhead of such a scheme is seldom worth the effort, though.)

How often should you backup? The usual rule is backup whenever you can't afford to lose information. For many people, this is on a daily basis. Imagine that you have been writing a document or program, and you lose all the work since the last backup: how long will it take to rewrite (if at all possible)? If the rewriting of the loss is more trouble than the time required to perform a backup, then make a backup! For the rest of this section, we'll use tapes as the backup medium, but you can substitute any other device that you want.

So how can you effectively schedule backups for your system, assuming you want to save your contents regularly? If we assume your system has several users (friends calling in by modem or family members who use it) and a reasonable volume of changes (email, newsgroups, word processing files, databases, or applications you are writing, for example), then you may want to consider daily backups. The most common backup schedule for a small, medium-volume system requires between 10 and 14 tapes, depending on whether backups are performed on weekends.

All backup tapes should be labeled with names that reflect their use. For example, label your tapes "Daily 1," "Daily 2," and so on, up to the total number of daily use tapes, such as "Daily 10." These daily use tapes are cycled through, one after another, with the cycle restarted after all the tapes have been used (so that "Daily 1" follows after "Daily 10"). With this many tapes, you have a two week supply of backups (ignoring weekend backups, in this case), enabling you to recover anything going back two weeks. If you have more tapes available, use them to extend the backup cycle. This same method is used by large corporations and organizations because it provides the best balance of speed, backup security, recoverability, and media costs.

The backups can be either full or partial, depending on your needs. A good practice is to make one full backup for every four or five partial, so that you make a full backup of your entire file system on Mondays, for example, but only back up the /usr directories on the other days of the week. You should make an exception to this process if you make changes to the Linux configuration, so that you have the changes captured with a full backup. You can keep track of the backups using a backup log, which we'll look at in a moment.

An expansion of this daily backup scheme that many administrators (including the author) prefer is the daily and weekly backup cycle. This breaks up the number of tapes into daily and weekly use. For example, if you have fourteen tapes, use ten for a daily cycle as already mentioned. These tapes can still be called "Daily 1" through "Daily 10." The other four tapes are used in a biweekly cycle and have names like "Week 1," "Week 2," and so on to "Week 4."

Using this backup system, you perform your daily backups as already mentioned, but when you get to the end of the daily cycle, you use the next weekly tape. Then you cycle through the daily tapes again, followed by the next weekly tape. (Your backup cycle is "Daily 1" through "Daily 10," "Week 1," "Daily 1" through "Daily 10," "Week 2," and so on.)

This backup cycle has one major advantage over a simple daily cycle. When the entire cycle is underway, there will be ten daily backups that cover a two week period. There are also the biweekly tapes, which extend back over four complete daily cycles or eight weeks. Recovery of a file or group of files can then be performed from the file system as it was two months ago, instead of just two weeks. This gives you a lot more flexibility in recovering information that was not noticed as missing or corrupt right away. If even more tapes are available, either the daily or biweekly cycle can be extended or monthly backups can be added.

Backup Logs

Many system administrators begin their careers by making regular backups, as they should. However, when they get to the point where they have to restore a file from a backup tape, they have no idea which tapes include the file or which tapes were used on what days. Some system administrators overcome this problem by placing a piece of paper or sticky note on each tape with the date and contents on it. This means you have to flip through the tapes to find the one you want, though, which can be awkward when there are lots of tapes. For this reason, a backup log should always be kept. (This is a good idea for all backups, Linux, DOS, and other operating systems.)

Whenever a backup is made, the backup log should be updated. A backup log doesn't have to be anything complex or elaborate. You can use the back of a notebook with a couple of vertical columns drawn in, use a form on the computer itself (which you should print out regularly, of course), or keep a loose-leaf binder with a few printed forms in it. A typical backup log needs the following information:

- the date of the backup
- the name of the backup tape (Daily 1, for example)
- the file system being backed up
- whether a full or partial backup was performed, and if partial, which directories were backed up

That's only four easy bits of information to record and can be done in a few seconds. For larger systems, a few other pieces of information can be added to complete a full backup record:

- who made the backup
- whether the backup was automatic (cron) or manual
- storage location of the tape

The dates of the backup help you keep track of when the last backup was performed and also act as an index for file recovery. If one of your system users knows they deleted a file by accident a week ago, the proper backup tape for the file restore can be determined from the backup log dates.

The backup log should be kept near the system for convenience, although some administrators prefer to keep the log in the same location as the backup media storage. Some system administrators keep a duplicate copy of the backup log in another site, just in case of catastrophic problems.

Using tar for Backups

The tar (tape archiver) program is usually the command used to save files and directories to an archive medium and recover them later. The tar command works by creating an archive file, which is a single large entity that holds many files within it (much like PKZIP does in DOS, for example). The tar command only works with archives it creates.

The format of the command is a little awkward and takes some getting used to, but fortunately, there are only a few more variations that users will need. The format of the tar command is:

```
tar switch modifiers files
```

The files section of the command indicates which files or directories you want to archive or restore. Usually this is a full file system such as /usr or in the case of recovery, a single file such as /usr/tparker/big_file.

The switch controls how tar reads or writes to the backup media. Only one switch at a time can be used with tar. The valid switches are:

- c create a new archive media
- r write to end of existing archive
- t lists names of files in an archives
- u files added if not modified or archived already
- x extract from the archive

A number of modifiers can be added to the tar command to control the archive and how tar uses it. Valid modifiers include:

- A suppress absolute filenames
- b provide a blocking factor (1-20)
- e prevent splitting files across volumes
- f specifies the archive media device name
- F specifies the name of a file for tar arguments
- k gives size of archive volume (in kilobytes)
- l displays error messages if links unresolved
- m does not restore modification times
- n indicates the archive is not a tape
- p extracts files with their original permissions
- v verbose output (lists files on the console)
- w displays archive action and waits for user confirmation

The tar command uses absolute pathnames for most actions, unless the "A" switch is specified.

A few examples will help explain the `tar` command and the use of `tar` switches. If you are using a tape drive called `/dev/tape` and the entire file system to be archived totals to less than the tape's capacity, you can create the tape archive with the command:

```
tar cf /dev/tape /
```

The "f" option is used to specify the device name, in this case `/dev/tape`. The entire root file system is archived in a new archive file (indicated by the "c"). Any existing contents on the tape are automatically overwritten when the new archive is created (it does not ask if you are sure you want to delete the existing contents of the tape, so make sure you are overwriting material you don't need). If the "v" option is included in the command, `tar` echoes the filenames and their sizes to the console as they are archived.

Now, if you need to restore the entire file system from the tape used in the above example, issue the command:

```
tar xf /dev/tape
```

This restores all files on the tape because no specific directory is indicated for recovery. The default, when no file or directory is specified, is the entire tape archive. On the other hand, if you want to restore a single file from the tape, the command is:

```
tar xf /dev/tape /usr/tparker/big_file
```

which restores only the file `/usr/tparker/big_file`.

Sometimes you may want to obtain a list of all files on a tape archive. You can do this with the command:

```
tar tvf /dev/tape
```

This uses the "v" option to display the results from `tar`. If the list is long, you may want to redirect the command to a file.

Now that you've seen the basic use of `tar`, we should look at some practical examples. Most tapes require a blocking factor when creating an archive, but with `tar`, specifying a blocking factor is not necessary when reading a tape because `tar` can figure it out automatically. The blocking factor tells `tar` how much data to write in a chunk on the tape. When archiving to a tape, the blocking factor is specified with the "b" modifier. For example, the command:

```
tar cvfb /dev/tape 20 /usr
```

creates a new archive on `/dev/tape` with a blocking factor of 20 and contains all the files in `/usr`. Most tapes can use a blocking factor of 20, and this can be assumed a default value unless your tape drive specifically won't work with this value. The only other time blocking factors are changed is for floppy disks and other hard disk volumes. Note that

45

BACKUPS

the arguments following the modifiers are in the same order as the modifier. The "f" precedes the "b" modifier so the arguments have the device before the blocking factor. The arguments must be in the same order as the modifiers, which can sometimes cause a little confusion.

Another common problem is that a tape may not be large enough to hold the entire archive, in which case more than one tape is needed. To tell `tar` the size of each tape, you need the "k" option. It uses an argument that specifies the capacity in kilobytes. For example, the command:

```
tar cvbfk 20 /dev/tape 122880 /usr
```

tells `tar` to use a blocking factor of "20" for the device `/dev/tape`. The tape capacity is 122,880 kilobytes (approx. 120MB). Again, note the order of arguments and the modifiers that match.

Floppy disks create another problem with `tar` because the blocking factor is usually different. When floppy disks are used, archives usually require more than one disk and the "k" option is used to specify the archive volumes capacity. For example, to back up the `/usr/tparker` directory to 1.2MB disks, the command is:

```
tar cnfk /dev/fd0 1200 /usr/tparker
```

where /dev/fd0 is the device name of the floppy drive and 1200 is the size of the disk in kilobytes. The "n" modifier tells `tar` that this is not a tape, and `tar` will run a little more efficiently than if the modifier had been left off.

Summary

This chapter looks at the basics of backups. You should maintain a backup log and make regular backups to protect your work. Although `tar` is a little awkward to use, once you've tried it a few times it becomes almost second nature.

A number of scripts are beginning to appear that automate the backup process or give you a menu-driven interface to the backup system. These are not in general distribution, but you may want to check FTP and BBS sites for a utility that will simplify backups for you. From here, you can go to these chapters for more information. To learn about:

Automating the backup routines on your system, see Chapter 46.

Setting up your Linux system to serve the Internet, see Chapter 47, "Setting up an Internet Site."

Applications you can run under Linux, see Chapter 62, "Adabas-D and other Databases" through Chapter 64, "Lone Star Software's Lone-Tar."

cron and at

by Tim Parker

CHAPTER 46

Automating tasks is one of the best ways to keep a system running smoothly. If you take all the repetitive system administration commands you need to run regularly and have them execute in the background without your direct involvement, system administration becomes much less onerous and bothersome. It is for this simple reason that the utilities cron and at were developed. Both allow you to execute commands at specified times automatically, without requiring any attention from you.

Using cron

The cron (short for chronograph) utility is designed to allow commands to execute at specific times without anyone directly initiating them. To do this, Linux loads cron as a clock daemon when the system starts up. (The cron utility is usually run from an rc file entry and can be disabled by commenting out the line that starts it.) When operating, cron reads the days and times it is supposed to execute a task from a file called the crontab file.

Whenever one of the crontab file's entry day and time specification matches the system's date and time, the cron daemon starts to execute the command. The cron utility doesn't just execute the task once: Whenever the day and time match, the task is re-run. This continues until the cron utility is terminated or the crontab file is modified. The automatic execution of tasks means that cron is ideal for automating regular system administration tasks, tape backups, database reorganization, and general file cleanups (such as emptying log files and queues).

On most systems, access to cron is limited to the system administrator only, although it can easily be activated for some or all users on your system. System administrators control who can send processes to be executed by cron through one of two different files, often called /usr/lib/cron/cron.allow or /usr/lib/cron/cron.deny. Many Linux systems use the names /etc/cron.d/cron.allow and /etc/cron.d/cron.deny. Both files have one username (which matches the entry in /etc/passwd) per line.

The file /usr/lib/cron/cron.allow (or /etc/cron.d/cron.allow) can contain a list of all usernames that are allowed to use cron. For example, this file allows only the logins tparker, yvonne, and bill (as well as the superuser) to submit anything to cron

```
tparker
yvonne
bill
```

Alternatively, the file /usr/lib/cron/cron.deny can contain a list of usernames that are not allowed to use cron. For example, the following file allows anyone except the logins walter and anne to use cron

```
walter
anne
```

By using one of these optional files, system administrators can control cron usage. If neither the cron.allow nor cron.deny file exists, only the superuser (root) can submit processes to cron. In order to allow all users to use cron, create an empty cron.deny file.

> **NOTE**
>
> You may be wondering why you would want to use cron when you could enter these commands at the shell prompt. That's true, but you also have to remember to do them, you need to be present to type them, and you have to wait for them to terminate. The cron system provides a way to place the most frequently used routines into a file and then forget about them. It's much easier than going through the steps of a long list of commands for backups, cleaning up directories, and so on.

Creating a crontab File

To instruct cron to process commands on particular days and at specific times, you use a utility program called crontab. The crontab program reads a file that contains the details of what you want cron to do and queues it. In addition, crontab performs several other administrative tasks, such as displaying your current cron task list, removing the list, and adding new tasks.

The file that crontab reads to determine what you want to submit to cron is usually named crontab for convenience, although it could be called anything. The crontab utility has a command option that allows you to specify the filename to be treated as instructions. Otherwise, the crontab utility reads the default filename crontab.

The crontab instruction file has a simple structure, although it takes a few minutes to get used to it. The file consists of one complete line for each process to be submitted which specifies when to run the process and what command to execute. The format of each line is as follows:

```
minute hour day-of-month month-of-year day-of-week command
```

A sample two-line extract from a `crontab` file looks like this:

```
20  1  *  *  *   /usr/bin/calendar -
0   2  *  *  *   /bin/organize_data
```

Each line in the `crontab` file has six columns separated by white space (spaces or tabs). The columns from left to right are

- The minute of the hour (0–59)
- The hour of the day (0–23)
- The day of the month (1–31)
- The month (1–12)
- The day of the week (Sun=0, Mon=1, ... Sat=6)
- The program to be executed at the specified day and time

This rather strange (at first glance) format is necessary to allow you to specify exactly when a process is to run. Without the five different categories for days and time, you can't precisely specify an event that occurs at random times during a month. As you will see in a moment, these columns are quite easy to complete.

The last column contains the command or script filename that is to be executed. A script that is to be executed can have many lines and call other scripts, or can be only a single line. The first process is initiated when the `crontab` file matches the day and time. It is important to provide an absolute pathname to the command (even if it's in your PATH), as the `cron` jobs do not inherit your environment variables and thus don't know where to look for commands. Also, you must have execute permission for the utility or script. If you are submitting `crontab` files as a user (not superuser), you must have file permissions or ownership set to allow you normal access, as `cron` executes the processes as though you owned them.

Each time and day column in the `crontab` file can contain a single number anywhere in the range of valid numbers, two numbers separated by a minus sign to show an inclusive range (such as 1–5 to show one through five), a list of numbers separated by commas to mean all of the values explicitly specified, or an asterisk meaning all legal values.

Let's look at the example of a `crontab` file again to see how this works. In the following example there are three different processes specified:

```
20        1     *  *  *   /usr/bin/calendar -
0         2     1  *  0   /bin/organize_data
10,30,50  9-18  *  *  *   /bin/setperms
```

The first command is `/usr/bin/calendar` - (the hyphen is an important part of the command). This process is executed at 20 minutes past 1 in the morning (a 24-hour clock is used), every day of the week, and each day of the year. The asterisks mean all values, hence the "each and every" meaning.

At 2:00 a.m., a script file called `/bin/organize_data` is executed on the first day of every month (the 1 in the third column) and every Sunday (the 0 in the fifth column). If the first day is a Sunday, it executes only once, of course.

The third line shows that a script called `/bin/setperms` runs at 10, 30, and 50 minutes past the hour every hour between 9:00 a.m. and 6:00 p.m. (or 18:00), every day of the week.

The entries in a `crontab` file do not have to be in any special order. As long as each entry is on a line by itself and has all six fields specified properly, `cron` organizes the information for its own use. If you have an error in the `crontab` file, `cron` mails you a notice of the problem when it processes your file. (This can be annoying if you have the entry with the error set to execute often because `cron` will mail you each time it tries to execute the entry and finds a problem. Your mailbox quickly gets filled with `cron` error messages.)

It is best to keep the `crontab` files in your home directory and name them `crontab`, unless you want to have several versions, in which case you can use any naming convention you want. Keeping the names simple, however, helps you identify which file you want `cron` to execute.

Submitting and Managing `crontab` Files

Now that you have written your `crontab` file, you can submit it for `cron` to execute. When you submit a `crontab` file, a copy of the file is made and kept in a `cron` directory, usually `/usr/spool/cron/crontabs`. The file will have the name of the submitting user (for example, a `crontab` file submitted by yvonne will have the name `/usr/spool/cron/crontabs/yvonne`. Any `crontab` files submitted by the superuser will usually have the name `root`.

To submit your `crontab` file to `cron`, use the `crontab` command followed by the name of the file with the `cron` commands in it. For example, the command submits the file called `crontab` in the current directory to `cron`:

```
crontab crontab
```

If you had previously submitted a `cron` file, it is removed and the new file is used instead.

> **TIP**
>
> Always submit a change to cron using the crontab file and an edited ASCII file. Never make changes to the file in /usr/spool/cron/crontabs.

You can see what you have submitted to cron by using the -l (list) option. This shows all the crontab entries that the cron utility knows about (essentially displaying the contents of the file with your username from /usr/spool/cron/crontabs). For example, the command shows all cron tasks for the user who submits the command:

```
crontab -l
```

If you want to remove your crontab file and not replace it, it is easily done with the -r (remove) option. This simply erases the file with your filename from the /usr/spool/cron/crontabs directory. To remove your crontab file, issue the command

```
crontab -r
```

Finally, crontab lets you call up your current cron file and start an editor (the default editor as defined by your environment variables or a system default variable) by using the -e (editor) option. When you issue the following command crontab reads your existing crontab file and loads it into the default editor (such as vi):

```
crontab -e
```

When you save the file, it is submitted to cron automatically.

Changes to the crontab file are usually effective within five minutes at most because cron reads the contents of the /usr/spool/cron/crontab file at least once every five minutes and often more frequently than that (most Linux systems have cron check the directories every minute). This also means that execution of a process you submit to cron can sometimes be delayed by a few minutes, so don't rely on cron to be exactly on time. The more heavily loaded a system is, the more delay in execution that you can expect.

On some systems, system administrators can log all cron usage by modifying an entry in the file /etc/default/cron. One line in the file should contain the variable CRONLOG. Set the value equal to YES, and cron logs every action it takes to the file /usr/lib/cron/log. Not all versions of Linux allow cron logging. If you do enable cron logging, check the log file frequently because it can grow to a large size quite quickly.

Complex cron Commands

The crontab file can contain any type of command or shell script, as long as the line is valid (in other words, it can be executed from the shell prompt). A common problem with many shell commands is the generation of output, especially error messages, which are mailed to you and can clog up your mailbox quickly. For this reason, if you antici-pate error message output (from a compiler, for example), you can redirect the output to /dev/null. For example, the following command sends the output of the date command to a file called /tmp/test1 every hour on the hour and sends any error messages to /dev/null (which essentially discards such messages):

```
0 * * * * date > /tmp/test1 2>/dev/null
```

You can do the same with the standard output, if you want, or you can redirect it else-where. For example, the cron command concatenates all the files starting with "chapt" in /usr/tparker into one large file called /usr/tparker/archive/backup:

```
30 1 * * * cat /usr/tparker/chapt* > /usr/tparker/archive/backup
```

Again, the standard error could be redirected.

You can also do piping in the crontab file. For example, if you have a list of users who are logged in to the system during the day in the file /tmp/userlist, you could have a crontab entry that looks like this:

```
0 1 * * * sort -u /tmp/userlist ¦ mail -s"users for today" root
```

This line sorts the output of /tmp/userlist so there is only one entry for each user (the -u or unique option) and mails it to root.

An important point to remember with cron is that all commands are executed, by default, in the Bourne shell (or bash, if it is the sh equivalent on your system). If you use C shell commands, the cron task will fail.

The at Program

The at program is very similar to cron except it executes a command only once at a pre-specified time (whereas cron keeps executing it). The format of the at command is

```
at time date < file
```

Most of the parameters to be used with the at command can be specified several ways, essentially to make at more versatile. The time, for example, can be specified as an absolute time (18:40 or 22:00), as two digits which are taken as hours (so 10 means ten o'clock in the morning because a 24 hour clock is the default). You can add an "a.m." or "p.m." to the time to make it clear which you mean, so 10 p.m. is unambiguously in the evening.

The at command handles a few special words instead of time designations. The command recognizes the words "noon," "midnight," "now," "next," and "zulu" for GMT conversion. (Some at versions generate an error message if you try to execute a command with the time set to "now.")

The date is an optional field and should be used when the time is not specific enough. In other words, when a date is not supplied, the next instance that the specified time occurs, the command executes whereas with a specified date, the date must match as well. The date can be given as a month's name followed by a day number (May 10) or a day of the week (either spelled out in full or abbreviated to three characters). You can specify a year, if you want, but this is seldom necessary.

As with the time, the at command recognizes two special words: "today" and "tomorrow" (although the word "today" is redundant as the command will execute today if the time is set properly).

The file to be read as input to the at command can be any file with commands in them. Alternatively, you can enter the commands at the keyboard, terminating with a Ctrl+D, although this is not recommended because of the high potential for error.

Suppose you have a file called reorg.data with the following commands in it and the file is made executable:

```
/usr/tparker/setperms
/usr/tparker/sort_database
/usr/tparker/index_database
/usr/tparker/clean_up
```

If you want to execute this file at 8:30 p.m., you can issue any one of the following commands using at:

```
at 20:30 < reorg.data
at 8:30 pm < reorg/data
at 20:30 today < reorg.data
```

There are more variations possible, but you can see the syntax. If you want the command to execute on Friday, issue the command in one of these formats:

```
at 8:30 pm Friday < reorg.data
```

```
at 20:30 Fir < reorg.data
```

Some versions of at are even more talented and handle special words. For example, this command will execute the commands next week on Monday:

```
at 0900 Monday next week < reorg.data
```

Not all versions of at can handle these complex formats.

When you submit a program to at for execution, you receive a job ID number. The job ID uniquely identifies the at command you just issued. For example, look at the output from this at command:

```
$ at 6 < do_it
job 827362.a at Wed Aug 31 06:00:00 EDT 1995
```

In this case, the job ID is 827362.a and the ID is needed to make any changes to the job.

You can list all the jobs you have queued with at using the -1 (list) option. The output usually tells you when the command is set to execute, but not what the command is:

```
$ at -l
user = tparker job 827362.a at Wed Aug 31 06:00:00 EDT 1995
user = tparker job 829283.a at Wed Aug 31 09:30:00 EDT 1995
```

Some versions of Linux may support the shorter form of the command with atq (display the at queue). If you get an error message when you issue the atq command, you have to use the at -l format.

To remove an at job from the system, you need the job ID and the at -r (remove) command. For example, the following command removes the specified job:

```
at -r 2892732.a
```

Linux does not return a message to indicate the job has been canceled, but if you list the queue, you see the job is gone. You can only remove your own jobs (except for root, which can remove any). Some Linux versions support the atrm command as well as the -r option.

All jobs that are queued into at are kept in the directory /usr/spool/cron/atjobs with the job ID number as the file name. As with cron, there is an at.allow and at.deny file in either /usr/lib/cron or /etc/cron.d directories to control who can and can't use at. As with cron, if you want all users on your system to be able to use at, create an empty cron.deny file.

When an at job is executed, all output (standard output and error messages) are mailed back to the username who submitted the job unless they have been redirected. The at command retains all the environment variables and directory settings of the user. If you look at a queued job in /usr/spool/cron/atjobs, you will see all the variables defined prior to the command about to be executed.

Summary

As you have seen, cron and at are quite easy to use. They are also a system administrator's best friend because you can automate tiresome tasks like database cleanups, disk space checking, flushing log files, and tape backups with cron or at. While cron and at can't do everything for you, they can handle repetitive tasks with ease.

Most Linux systems have a number of sample cron files supplied with the operating system. Examine those files (or list the current crontab file while logged in as root) to see what the operating system wants to execute on a regular basis. Use those commands as the starting point and add your own commands. From here there are a number of chapters you can turn to for related information:

Backing up your system is discussed in Chapter 45, "Backups."

Setting up your Linux system to serve the Internet is discussed in Chapter 47, "Setting Up an Internet Site."

Applications you can run under Linux are discussed in Chapter 62, "Adabas-D and Other Databases," through Chapter 64, "Lone Star Software's Lone-Tar."

Setting up an Internet Site

PART
VII

IN THIS PART

Setting up an Internet Site

by Tim Parker

Linux is well-suited for connecting to the Internet and for using many of the Internet services. We're not just talking about using Linux to browse the Web or using FTP to transfer files from an archive site to your machine but using Linux as your own server. You can serve up your own World Wide Web pages, provide your own FTP site, or act as a Gopher host all with a minimum amount of configuration of your Linux system. You don't need any special software, just the distribution CD-ROM or archives. This chapter looks at the ways you can connect to the Internet. The upcoming chapters show you how to set up your Linux system as a server for four popular services.

If you only want to use your Linux system to access other servers, you don't have to worry about any of the material in the next four chapters (although you may still want to read this chapter to find out how to connect to the net). On the other hand, sharing your system's resources with others—whether in a local area network, a small circle of friends, or the worldwide Internet community—can be most of the fun.

If you intend to use your Linux system to offer some Internet services (such as FTP, WWW, or Gopher) but don't want to let everyone gain access (maybe just a few friends), you may not need to worry about connecting to the Internet. You still have to set up the server software, though.

Connecting to the Internet

There are many different ways to connect to the Internet. Your choice of method depends primarily on your usage habits and the services you want access to. It may seem as though an overwhelming number of companies offer Internet access or services. Actually, there are only four ways to connect to the Internet.

Briefly, your options for connecting to the Internet are as follows:

- A direct connection to the Internet—This method uses a dedicated machine (a gateway) to connect into the Internet backbone through a high-speed telephone connection such as a T1 line (1.544Mbps) or ISDN (128kbps). This method gives you full access to all services but is expensive to set up and maintain.

- Connecting through someone else's gateway—This usually involves getting permission to use someone else's machine for full access to all Internet services.

- Using a direct service provider—This way uses a specialty company's gateway that your machine can access to offer limited or full access to Internet services. These companies are not the same as online services because all they do is act as a gateway to the Internet. Usually, this type of service provider uses modem or dedicated telephone connections with high-speed lines to provide fast service. The company you connect to becomes your Internet Service Provider (ISP).

- Using an indirect service provider—This involves using an online company (such as Delphi or CompuServe) to access some or all of the Internet's services. This is usually suitable only for low-volume usage and doesn't take advantage of Linux at all.

If you are part of a company or sharing the costs with a number of friends, online service providers are seldom able to offer the level of performance you need for support of email, FTP, and other Internet services. Another negative aspect about online services is that most do not allow you to have your own domain name.

It is rare to find a gateway that you can "borrow" for access of your own, unless you are willing to share the costs of the gateway. Most companies that have a gateway are reluctant to allow many outsiders to use their system.

This leaves only two options: a direct gateway of your own to the Internet or the use of a service provider. The choice between these two usually comes down to an issue of the connection costs. Setting up your own gateway is expensive but may be cheaper than arranging accounts with a service provider if the volume of traffic is high.

If you want access for yourself or for a very small company, it is unreasonable to have your own dedicated gateway. Setting up an account with a service provider is a possible choice for individuals, but sometimes the costs and machine overhead are too high. Service providers are typically used by small companies, and there is no reason why you can't use a service provider if you anticipate a high Internet usage.

47

SETTING UP AN INTERNET SITE

Services You Need

When deciding which method you want to use to access the Internet, one of the important items to consider is the type of services you want from the Internet. If all you need is email, then any kind of access can provide it, but some may be ridiculously expensive for what you get.

As a starting point, decide which of the following services are necessary and which are less important:

- Electronic mail—Sending mail to and from other Internet users.
- Telnet—Remote logins to other machines on the Internet.
- FTP—File transfers between machines.
- World Wide Web (WWW) access—A popular Hypertext Markup Language-based (and usually graphical) information service.

- Usenet newsgroups—A set of bulletin boards for conversations on many different subjects.
- Gopher—An information search and retrieval system.
- WAIS—A menu-based document search and retrieval system.
- Archie—A method for finding files to transfer.
- Internet Relay Chat (IRC)—A conversation system much like CB radio.

Any system that is directly connected to the Internet through a gateway (yours, a borrowed gateway, or most direct service providers) will provide complete access to all the services listed. Some direct service providers support all the services, but at a slower speed than a gateway. Slower speeds may be a limitation for the World Wide Web if you intend to use and offer graphics (instead of just text). Some service providers limit their access to email and newsgroups, so a little research is necessary.

Direct Connection Through a Gateway

A direct connection (often called a dedicated connection) is one in which you attach into the Internet backbone through a dedicated machine called a gateway or IP router. The connection is over a dedicated telephone line capable of high-speed transfers (usually at 1.44Mb per second or faster). The gateway becomes part of the Internet architecture and must remain online at all times. You can then use any other computer on the gateway's network to access the Internet services.

Typically, dedicated connections mean high volumes of traffic and require systems with an absolute minimum line speed of 9,600 baud, although high-speed fiber-optic lines with speed capabilities of 45Mbps are not unusual. It is very unlikely an individual or small company would have direct gateway access, primarily because of the high cost of installation and maintenance requirements.

To create a direct access system, you must work with the Internet Network Information Center (NIC) to set up the proper gateways on the Internet backbone for your domain. The capital expense of such a system is high, both for the initial hardware and software and for continuing support. High costs may also be involved with a dedicated telephone line capable of supporting high-speed data transfer. Common high-speed connections are T1 (1.544Mbps), T3 (4Mbps) and the much more affordable ISDN (128kbps).

Connecting Through Another Gateway

An alternative method of connecting to the Internet through a gateway relies on using a "friendly" machine or network. In such a system, a corporation or educational institution that has an Internet gateway may allow you to access the Internet through their system. Because this type of access gives you freedom on their networks, many organizations now refuse this type of piggy-back access.

If you are lucky enough to find a company or school that will let you use their network, you simply call into a communications port on the network or gateway, then route through the gateway to the Internet. In many ways, it's as though you are a machine on the provider's network. Typically, you have unlimited access to the Internet's services, although some companies do set restrictions.

Using a Service Provider

Service providers are companies that have an Internet gateway that they share, although the gateway is often transparent to the users. This type of connection is often called "dialup" and uses SLIP (serial line interface protocol) or PPP (point-to-point protocol). Some service providers offer UUCP connections for email.

Service providers usually charge a flat fee for membership with an additional charge based on the amount of time or the number of characters transferred. Joining one of these services is quite easy. Domain names can be registered through many service providers, too, allowing you to use your own domain name even though you use a provider.

The primary advantage of direct service providers is that effectively you are directly connected to the Internet. All of the interworking with the service provider's gateway is hidden inside your operating system's setup, making it transparent. A disadvantage is that you cannot always arrange full access to the Internet. Some services do not allow you to FTP through their gateway to another Internet site, for example.

If you are considering using a direct service provider, you should ask the providers in your area about the services they offer, whether special hardware or software is needed, what the fees are, and whether they are based on a flat monthly rate or based on usage, and the kind of technical support available in case you have trouble.

An alternative to using a commercial service provider is to rely on one of the command-line access systems that are springing up in major cities. Such systems provide Internet access through their own gateways as a free service (subsidized by a corporation or government) or at a minimal cost. One popular access provider of this type is FreeNet, an international organization that gives users a unique username through the FreeNet domain. FreeNet is currently only available in some cities, but it does provide an extremely inexpensive and easy access method to the Internet. All you need is an account (which is usually just a telephone call away), a modem, and communications software.

Summary

Choosing the method with which you connect to the Internet is up to you, but most individuals find a direct service provider the best balance between cost and features, as long as you plan to keep your system running most of the time. Once you have a connection to the Internet, you can set up your server, as explained in the next four chapters. From here, you can learn how to:

Set up your machine to act as an FTP server in Chapter 48, "Setting up an FTP and Anonymous FTP Site."

Set up and use Gopher in Chapter 50, "Setting up a Gopher Service."

Set up your own Web server and home page in Chapter 51, "Configuring a WWW Site."

Program your Web pages in Chapter 53, "HTML Programming Basics."

Setting Up an FTP and Anonymous FTP Site

by Tim Parker

IN THIS CHAPTER

Snap question: What is the most widely used TCP/IP and Internet service? If you answered FTP, you're right. (If you didn't choose FTP, this may come as a bit of a surprise. The fact is, FTP remains the most widely used service; although the World Wide Web is quickly catching up.) FTP's popularity is easy to figure: The FTP software is supplied with every version of UNIX and Linux; it's easy to install, configure, and use; and it gives users access to a wealth of information with very little effort. Lately, the popularity of the World Wide Web has made a different interface to FTP available: the Web browser. Most browsers such as Netscape Navigator allow you to use it for file transfers to FTP sites.

If all you want to use FTP for is connecting to another machine and transferring files, then you don't have to do much more than enable the FTP service on your system. Much more interesting to many users is turning your Linux machine into an FTP site, where others can connect and obtain files you make available. That's the primary focus of this chapter—setting up an FTP site on your Linux machine. We'll begin, though, with a quick look at using FTP and the way FTP runs on TCP. This information should help you understand how FTP works and what it does with TCP/IP.

What Is FTP?

The File Transfer Protocol (FTP) is one protocol in the TCP/IP family used to transfer files between machines running TCP/IP. (FTP-like programs are also available for some other protocols, too.) The File Transfer Protocol allows you to transfer files back and forth and manage directories. FTP is not designed to allow you access to another machine to execute programs, but it is the best utility for file manipulation. To use FTP, both ends of a connection must be running a program that provides FTP services. The end that starts the connection (the client) calls the other end (the server) and establishes the FTP protocol through a set of handshaking instructions.

Usually, when you connect to a remote system via FTP, you must log in. This means you must be a valid user, with a username and password for that remote machine. Because it is impossible to provide logins for everyone who wants to access a machine that enables anyone to gain access, many systems use "anonymous FTP" instead. Anonymous FTP enables anyone to log in to the system with the login name of "ftp" or "anonymous" with either no password or with an email address for their local system as the password.

Using FTP

Using FTP to connect to a remote site is easy. You have access to the remote machine either through the Internet (directly or through a service provider) or through a local area network if the remote machine is directly reachable. To use FTP, start the FTP client software and provide the name of the remote system you want to connect to. For example, assuming you can get to the remote machine through a LAN or the Internet (which knows about the remote machine thanks to Domain Name Service), issue the following command:

```
ftp chatton.com
```

This instructs your FTP software to try to connect to the remote machine `chatton.com` and establish an FTP session.

When the connection is completed (and assuming the remote system allows FTP logins), the remote prompts for a userID. If anonymous FTP is supported on the system, a message usually tells you exactly that. The following is for the Linux FTP archive site `sunsite.unc.edu`:

```
ftp sunsite.unc.edu
331 Guest login ok, send your complete e-mail address as password.
Enter username (default: anonymous): anonymous
Enter password [tparker@tpci.com]:
¦FTP¦ Open
230-        WELCOME to UNC and SUN's anonymous ftp server
230-              University of North Carolina
230-            Office FOR Information Technology
230-                 SunSITE.unc.edu
230 Guest login ok, access restrictions apply.
FTP>
```

After the login process is completed, you see the prompt FTP> indicating the remote system is ready to accept commands.

When you log on to some systems, you may see a short message that contains instructions for downloading files, any restrictions that are placed on you as an anonymous FTP user, or information about the location of useful files. For example, you may see messages like these (taken from the Linux FTP site):

```
To get a binary file, type: BINARY and then: GET "File.Name" newfilename
To get a text file, type:  ASCII and then: GET "File.Name" newfilename
Names MUST match upper, lower case exactly. Use the "quotes" as shown.
To get a directory, type: DIR. To change directory, type: CD "Dir.Name"
To read a short text file, type: GET "File.Name" TT
For more, type HELP or see FAQ in gopher.
To quit, type EXIT or Control-Z.

230- If you email to info@sunsite.unc.edu you will be sent help
➥information
230- about how to use the different services sunsite provides.
230- We use the Wuarchive experimental ftpd. if you "get"
```

```
➥<directory>.tar.Z
230- or <file>.Z it will compress and/or tar it on the fly. Using ".gz"
➥instead
230- of ".Z" will use the GNU zip (/pub/gnu/gzip*) instead, a superior
230- compression method.
```

After you are logged on to the remote system, you can use familiar Linux commands to display file contents and move around directories. To display the contents of a directory, for example, use the command ls (some systems support the DOS equivalent dir). To change to a subdirectory, use the cd command. To return to the parent directory (the one above the current directory), use the command cd. As you can see, these commands are the same as those you use on your local machine, except you are now navigating on the remote system.

There are no keyboard shortcuts (such as pressing the TAB key to fill in names that match) available with FTP. This means you have to type in the name of files or directories in their entirety (and correctly). If you misspell a file or directory name, you will get error messages and have to try again. Luckily, if you are performing the FTP session through X Window, you can cut and paste lines from earlier in your session.

Transferring files is the whole point of FTP, so you need to know how to retrieve a file from the remote system, as well as how to put a new file there. When you have moved through the remote system's directories and found a file you want to transfer to your local system, use the get command. This is followed by the filename. For example:

```
get "soundcard_driver"
```

transfers the file soundcard_driver from the remote machine to the current directory on your local machine. When you issue a get command, the remote system will transfer data to your local machine and display a status message when it is completed. There is no indication of progress when a large file is being transferred, so be patient. (Most versions of FTP allow you to use the hash option, which displays pound signs every time a kilobyte of information has been transferred. This can be used to show that the transfer is underway, but it doesn't offer a time to completion.)

```
FTP> get "file1.txt"
200 PORT command successful.
150 BINARY data connection for FILE1.TXT (27534 bytes)
226 BINARY Transfer complete.
27534 bytes received in 2.35 seconds (12 Kbytes/s).
```

If you want to transfer a file the other way (from your machine to the remote, assuming you are allowed to write to the remote machine's file system), use the put command in the same way. The command:

```
put "comments"
```

transfers the file comments from your current directory on the local machine (you can specify full pathnames) to the current directory on the remote machine (unless you change the path).

The commands `get` (download) and `put` (upload) are always relative to your home machine. You are telling your system to get a file from the remote and put it on your local machine or to put a file from your local machine onto the remote machine. (This is the exact opposite of `telnet`, which has everything relative to the remote machine. It is important to remember which command moves in which direction or you can overwrite files accidentally.)

The quotation marks around the filenames in the preceding examples are optional for most versions of FTP, but they do prevent shell expansion of characters, so it's best to use them. For most files, the quotation marks are not needed, but using them is a good habit to get into.

Some FTP versions provide a wildcard capability using the commands `mget` and `mput`. Both the FTP `get` and `put` commands usually transfer only one file at a time, which must be completely specified (no wildcards). The `mget` and `mput` commands enable you to use wildcards. For example, to transfer all the files with a `.doc` extension, issue the command:

```
mget *.doc
```

You will have to try the `mget` and `mput` commands to see if they work on your FTP version. (Some FTP `get` and `put` commands allow wildcards, too, so you can try wildcards in a command line to see if they work, instead.)

FTP allows file transfers in several formats, which are usually system dependent. The majority of systems (including Linux systems) have only two modes: ASCII and binary. Some mainframe installations add support for EBCDIC, while many sites have a local type that is designed for fast transfers between local network machines (the local type may use 32- or 64-bit words).

The difference between the binary and ASCII modes is simple. Text transfers use ASCII characters separated by carriage returns and new-line characters. Binary mode allows transfer of characters with no conversion or formatting. Binary mode is faster than text and also allows for the transfer of all ASCII values (necessary for non-text files). FTP cannot transfer file permissions because these are not specified as part of the protocol.

Linux' FTP provides two modes of file transfer: ASCII and binary. Some systems automatically switch between the two when they recognize a file is binary format, but you shouldn't count on the switching unless you've tested it before and know it works. To be sure, it is a good idea to manually set the mode. By default, most FTP versions start up in ASCII mode, although a few start in binary.

To set FTP in binary transfer mode (for any executable file or file with special characters embedded for spreadsheets, word processors, graphics, and so on), type the command

```
binary
```

You can toggle back to ASCII mode with the command ascii. Because you will most likely be checking remote sites for new binaries or libraries of source code, it is a good idea to use binary mode for most transfers. If you transfer a binary file in ASCII mode, it will not be usable on your system.

ASCII mode includes only the valid ASCII characters and not the 8-bit values stored in binaries. Transferring an ASCII file in binary mode does not affect the contents except in very rare instances.

To quit FTP, enter the command quit or exit. Both will close your session on the remote machine and then terminate FTP on your local machine. Users have a number of commands available within most versions of FTP. The following list outlines the ones most frequently used:

ascii	Switches to ASCII transfer mode
binary	Switches to binary transfer mode
cd	Changes directory on the server
close	Terminates the connection
del	Deletes a file on the server
dir	Displays the server directory
get	Fetches a file from the server
hash	Displays a pound character for each block transmitted
help	Displays help

lcd	Changes directory on the client
mget	Fetches several files from the server
mput	Sends several files to the server
open	Connects to a server
put	Sends a file to the server
pwd	Displays the current server directory
quote	Supplies an FTP command directly
quit	Terminates the FTP session

For most versions, FTP commands are case sensitive, and using uppercase will display error messages. Some versions perform a translation for you, so it doesn't matter which case you use. Because Linux uses lowercase as its primary character set for everything else, you should probably use lowercase with all versions of FTP, too.

How FTP Uses TCP

The File Transfer Protocol uses two TCP channels: TCP port 20 is used for data and port 21 is for commands. Both these channels must be enabled on your Linux system for FTP to function. The use of two channels makes FTP different from most other file transfer programs. By using two channels, TCP allows simultaneous transfer of FTP commands and data. FTP works in the foreground and does not use spoolers or queues.

FTP uses a server daemon that runs continuously and a separate program that is executed on the client. On Linux systems, the server daemon is called ftpd. The client program is ftp.

During the establishment of a connection between a client and server, and whenever a user issues a command to FTP, the two machines transfer a series of commands. These commands are exclusive to FTP and are known as the internal protocol. FTP's internal protocol commands are four-character ASCII sequences terminated by a new-line character, some of which require parameters. One primary advantage of using ASCII characters for commands is that users can observe the command flow and understand it easily. This helps in a debugging process. Also, the ASCII commands can be used directly by a knowledgeable user to communicate with the FTP server component without invoking the client portion (in other words, communicating with ftpd without using ftp on a local machine), although this is seldom used except when debugging (or showing off).

After logging into a remote machine using FTP, you are not actually on the remote machine. You are still logically on the client, so all instructions for file transfers and directory movement must be with respect to your local machine and not the remote one. The process followed by FTP when a connection is established is:

1. Login—Verify user ID and password
2. Define directory—Identify the starting directory
3. Define file transfer mode—Define the type of transfer
4. Start data transfer—Allow user commands
5. Stop data transfer—Close the connection

These steps are performed in sequence for each connection.

A debugging option is available from the FTP command line by adding -d to the command. This displays the command channel instructions. Instructions from the client are shown with an arrow as the first character, while instructions from the server have three digits in front of them. A PORT in the command line indicates the address of the data channel on which the client is waiting for the server's reply. If no PORT is specified, channel 20 (the default value) is used. Unfortunately, the progress of data transfers cannot be followed in the debugging mode. A sample session with the debug option enabled is shown here:

```
$ ftp -d tpci_hpws4
Connected to tpci_hpws4.
220 tpci_hpws4 FTP server (Version 1.7.109.2
➥Tue Jul 28 23:32:34 GMT 1992) ready.
Name (tpci_hpws4:tparker):
---> USER tparker
331 Password required for tparker.
Password:
---> PASS qwerty5
230 User tparker logged in.
---> SYST
215 UNIX Type: L8
Remote system type is UNIX.
---> Type I
200 Type set to I.
Using binary mode to transfer files.
ftp> ls
---> PORT 54,80,10,28,4,175
200 PORT command successful.
---> TYPE A
200 Type set to A.
---> LIST
150 Opening ASCII mode data connection for /bin/ls.
total 4
-rw-r----- 1 tparker tpci  2803 Apr 29 10:46 file1
-rw-rw-r-- 1 tparker tpci  1286 Apr 14 10:46 file5_draft
```

```
-rwxr----- 2 tparker tpci   15635 Mar 14 23:23 test_comp_1
-rw-r----- 1 tparker tpci      52 Apr 22 12:19 xyzzy
Transfer complete.
---> TYPE I
200 Type set to I.
ftp> <Ctrl-d>
$
```

You may have noticed in the preceding listing how the mode changed from binary to ASCII in order to send the directory listing, and then back to binary (the system default value).

Configuring FTP

Whether you decide to provide an anonymous FTP site or a user-login FTP system, you need to perform some basic configuration steps to get the FTP daemon active and to set the directory system and file permissions properly in order to prevent users from destroying or accessing files they shouldn't. The process can start with choosing an FTP site name. You don't really need a site name, although it can be easier for others to access your machine with one (especially anonymously). The FTP site name is of the format:

```
ftp.domain_name.domain_type
```

where *domain_name* is the domain name (or an alias) of the FTP server's domain, and *domain_type* is the usual DNS extension. For example, you could have an FTP site name of

```
ftp.tpci.com
```

showing that this is the anonymous FTP access for anyone accessing the `tpci.com` domain. It is usually a bad idea to name your FTP site with a specific machine name, such as:

```
ftp.merlin.tpci.com
```

because this makes it difficult to move the FTP server to another machine in the future. Instead, use an alias to point to the actual machine on which the FTP server sits. This is not a problem if you are a single machine connected to the Internet through a service provider, for example, but it is often necessary with a larger network. The alias is easy to set up if you use DNS. Set the alias in the DNS databases with a line like this:

```
ftp   IN   CNAME   merlin.tpci.com
```

This line points anyone accessing the machine `ftp.tpci.com` to the real machine `merlin.tpci.com`. If the machine `merlin` has to be taken out of its FTP server role for

48

SETTING UP FTP
AND ANONYMOUS
FTP SITE

any reason, a change in the machine name on this line will point the `ftp.tpci.com` access to the new server. (A change in the alias performed over DNS can take a while to become active because the change must be propagated through all the DNS databases.)

Setting Up `ftpd`

The FTP daemon, `ftpd`, must be started on the FTP server. The daemon is usually handled by `inetd` instead of the `rc` startup files, so `ftpd` is active only when someone needs it. This is the best approach for all but the most heavily loaded FTP sites. When started using `inetd`, the `inetd` daemon watches the TCP command port (channel 21) for an arriving data packet requesting a connection, and then spawns `ftpd`.

Make sure the `ftpd` daemon can be started by `inetd` by checking the `inetd` configuration file (usually `/etc/inetd.config` or `/etc/inetd.conf`) for a line that looks like this:

```
ftp    stream    tcp    nowait    root    /usr/etc/ftpd    ftpd -l
```

If the line doesn't exist, add it to the file. With most Linux systems, the line is already in the file, although it may be commented out. Remove the comment symbol if this is the case. The FTP entry essentially specifies to `inetd` that FTP is to use TCP and that it should spawn `ftpd` every time a new connection is made to the FTP port. In the preceding example, the `ftpd` daemon is started with the `-l` option, which enables logging. You can ignore this option if you want. You should replace the pathname `/usr/etc/ftpd` with the location of your FTP daemon.

There are several `ftpd` daemon options that you can add to the `/etc/inetd.config` line to control `ftpd`'s behavior. The following list contains the most commonly used options:

- `-d`   Adds debugging information to the `syslog`.
- `-l`   Activates a logging of sessions (only failed and successful logins, not debug information). If the `-l` option is specified twice, all commands are logged, too. If specified three times, the size of all `get` and `put` file transfers are added, as well.
- `-t`   Sets the timeout period before `ftpd` terminates after a session is concluded (default is 15 minutes). The value is specified in seconds after the `-t` option.
- `-T`   Sets the maximum timeout period (in seconds) that a client can request. The default is two hours. This lets a client alter the normal default timeout for some reason.
- `-u`   Sets the `umask` value for files uploaded to the local system. The default `umask` is `022`. Clients can request a different `umask` value.

FTP Logins

If you are going to set up a user-based FTP service where each person accessing your system has a valid login name and password, then you must create an account for each user in the /etc/passwd file. If you are not allowing anonymous FTP access, do not create a generic login that anyone can use.

To set up an anonymous FTP server, you must create a login for the anonymous user ID (if one doesn't already exist; many versions of Linux have the entry already completed upon installation). This is done in the normal process of adding a user to the /etc/passwd file. The login name is whatever you want people to use when they access your system, such as anonymous or ftp. You need to select a login directory for the anonymous users that can be protected from the rest of the file system. A typical /etc/passwd entry looks like this:

```
ftp:*:400:51:Anonymous FTP access:/usr/ftp:/bin/false
```

This sets up the anonymous user with a login of ftp. The asterisk password prevents anyone gaining access to the account. The user ID number (400) is, of course, unique to the entire system. For better security, it is a good idea to create a separate group just for the anonymous FTP access (edit the /etc/group file to add a new group), then set the ftp user to that group. Only the anonymous FTP user should belong to that group because it can be used to set file permissions to restrict access and make your system more secure. The login directory in the preceding example is /usr/ftp, although you can choose any directory as long as it belongs to root (for security reasons, again). The startup program shown in the preceding example is /bin/false, which helps protect your system from access to accounts and utilities that do not have a strong password protection.

Setting Up the Directories

As you will see in the next section, "Setting Permissions," you can try to make the entire anonymous FTP subdirectory structure a file system unto itself, with no allowance for the anonymous user to get anywhere other than /usr/ftp (or whatever directory you use for anonymous access). For this reason, you need to create a mini-file system just for the anonymous FTP access which holds the usual directory names and basic files anyone logging in will need.

The process for setting up the directories that your anonymous FTP login will need is simple, requiring you to create a number of directories and copy files into them. Here's the basic procedure:

1. Create the bin directory (/usr/ftp/bin, for example) and copy the directory listing command ls that users will need to view directory and file details.

2. Create the `etc` directory (`usr/ftp/etc`, for example) and copy your `passwd` file (`/etc/passwd`) and group file (`/etc/group`) into it. We'll edit these files in a moment.

3. Create the `lib` directory (`/usr/ftp/lib`, for example) and copy the files `/lib/ld.so` and `/lib/libc.so.X` (where *X* is the version number of the `libc` file) into it. These files are used by `ls`. Do this step only if your `ls` command requires these files; most versions of Linux do not have this dependency.

4. Create the `pub` directory (`/usr/ftp/pub`, for example) to hold your accessible files. We'll look at this directory in more detail in a moment.

5. Create the `dev` directory (`/usr/ftp/dev`, for example) and use the `mknod` command to copy the `/dev/zero` file. You need to retain the same major and minor device numbers as the `/dev/zero` file in `/dev`. This device file is used by `ld.so` (and hence `ls`). Do this step only if `ls` requires the `/lib` directory files mentioned earlier.

The copies of the `/etc/passwd` and `/etc/group` files are copied into the `~ftp/etc` directory. You should edit these files to remove all passwords and replace them with an asterisk. Remove all entries in both `/etc/passwd` and `/etc/group`, except those used by the anonymous FTP login (usually just `anonymous` and `bin`).

The `~ftp/pub` directory structure can be used to store the files you want to allow anonymous users to access. Copy them into this directory. You can create subdirectories as you need them for organizational purposes. It may be useful to create an upload directory somewhere in the `~ftp/pub` directory structure that has write permission, so that users can upload files to you only into this upload area.

> **NOTE**
>
> If you allow remote users to access your system, you may want to protect yourself legally by issuing a warning that their activities on your system may be recorded or logged. Unfortunately, in today's world you have to take all steps necessary to prevent getting sued!

Setting Permissions

You can use the `chroot` command to help protect your system. The `chroot` command makes the `root` directory appear to be something other than `/` on a file system. For example, since `chroot` is always set for the anonymous FTP login, any time anonymous users type a `cd` command, it can always be relative to their home directory. In other words, when they type cd /bin, they will really be changing to /usr/ftp/bin if the root has been set to /usr/ftp. This helps prevent access to any other areas of the file system than the FTP directory structure.

If you do create an upload area, you may want to set the permissions to allow execute and write, but not read (to prevent another user downloading the files someone else has uploaded).

Set all permissions for directories under ~ftp/ to prevent write access by user, group, or other. Make sure the directories and files under ~ftp are set to allow the anonymous login to read them (set their ownership and group permissions to the root login and group ID), and set only read permission. The directories will need execute and read permission to enable the anonymous users to enter them and obtain directory listings. This provides pretty good security. All directories in the ~ftp directory structure should have the permissions set with the command:

```
chmod 555 dir_name
```

which sets read-execute permission only. The exception is the upload directory, which can have write permission as noted earlier.

Test the System

Before you let anyone else onto your Linux FTP system, log into it yourself and try to access files you shouldn't be able to, move into directories out of the ~ftp structure, and write files where you shouldn't be able to. This will provide a useful test of the permissions and directory structure. Spend a few minutes trying to read and write files. Make sure your system is buttoned up: If you don't, someone else will find the holes and exploit them.

It is a useful idea to set up a mailbox for the FTP administrator so users on other systems who need help or information can send mail to you. Create a mail alias such as ftp-admin in the file /etc/aliases (and run newaliases to make it effective).

Because this is a system administration book, we won't go into much detail about how to organize your directory structure, but a few useful tips may help you. To begin, decide what you want to store in your FTP directories and organize the structure logically. For example, if you are making available programs you have written, set up separate directories for each. A README file in each directory will help show browsers what it contains. A master README or INSTRUCTIONS file in the ~ftp directory can help explain how your site is set up and what its contents are.

48

SETTING UP FTP
AND ANONYMOUS
FTP SITE

A More Secure FTP

The FTP system discussed in the preceding sections, which is the basic one supplied with practically every Linux distribution, requires a bit of work to make it secure. However, it is still vulnerable to very experienced crackers. There's a better alternative if you are paranoid about your system's security: WU FTP. Developed at Washington University, WU FTP adds some extra features to the standard FTP system:

- Better control of user and group IDs
- Better tracking of uploads and downloads
- Automatic shutdown
- Automatic compression and decompression of files

If these features sound useful, you can obtain a copy of the source code of WU FTP from several sites, although the primary site is wuarchive.wustl.edu. Check for the file /packages/wuarchive-ftpd/wu-ftpd-X.X.tar.Z (where X.X is the latest version number). You will get the source code that needs to be compiled on your Linux system.

WU FTP uses a number of environment variables to control the service, and the accompanying documentation helps you set it up properly. Setting up WU FTP is much more complex than standard FTP, and the extra security, while useful, may be unnecessary for many FTP site machines you may have set up at home or work (unless you have sensitive information).

Protecting an Anonymous FTP System

Anonymous FTP is fast, relatively easy to use, and a huge security problem if you don't carefully set up your system. The following list summarizes a few simple steps to setting up a better anonymous FTP site:

1. Create a user account called ftp. Edit the /etc/passwd file manually and replace the password with an asterisk in the second field. This prevents anyone from gaining access through the ftp account.

2. If a home directory wasn't created for the ftp user when you created the account, set up a home directory for the ftp user's sole use (such as /home/ftp).

3. Set the ftp home directory so that the root user is the owner:

        chown root /usr/ftp

4. Make the `ftp` home directory unwritable to anyone with the command:

   ```
   chmod ugo-w /usr/ftp
   ```

5. Create a `bin` directory under the `ftp` home directory:

   ```
   mkdir ~ftp/bin
   ```

6. Make the `~ftp/bin` directory owned by `root` and unwritable to anyone else:

   ```
   chown root ~ftp/bin
   chmod ugo-w ~ftp/bin
   ```

7. Place a copy of the listing commands (and any others that you want anonymous FTP users to use) in the `bin` directory:

   ```
   cp /bin/ls ~ftp/bin
   ```

8. Create an `etc` directory under the `ftp` home directory and make it owned by `root` and unwritable:

   ```
   mkdir ~ftp/etc
   chown root ~ftp/etc
   chmod ugo-w ~ftp/etc
   ```

9. Copy the `/etc/passwd` and `/etc/group` files into the `~ftp/etc` directory. Edit both files to remove all user accounts except `ftp` (and `ftp`'s group). (At the very least, remove all passwords for other accounts by placing asterisks in the password field.)

10. Create the directory `~ftp/pub/incoming`, and make it owned by `root`. Then, make the directory writable by anyone:

    ```
    mkdir ~ftp/pub/incoming
    chown root ~ftp/pub/incoming
    chmod ugo+w ~ftp/pub/incoming
    ```

11. Place any files you want accessible by anonymous FTP into the `~ftp/pub` directory. Users logging in through anonymous FTP will be able to transfer the files out. Allowing users to write files into the directory may not be desirable, so change the permissions or check the files frequently.

By following these steps (modified for your own particular needs), you can create a secure site that lets you breathe a little easier.

Summary

The information in this chapter enables you to set up your system as a full anonymous FTP site or just a site for the users you want to gain access. Although the process is simple, you have to take care to ensure the file permissions are properly set. Once your FTP site is up, you can let others on the Internet or your local area network know that you are running, as well as the type of material you store on your system. Then sit back and share!

From here, there are several other chapters you may want to read to learn more about related subjects. To learn about:

Setting ownerships and file permissions properly before and after you FTP them, read Chapter 9, "File and Directory Permissions."

Programming your Linux shell to allow you to transfer files with a single command, see Chapter 14, "Shell Programming."

Setting up your Linux system to use a local area network (so you can FTP files to other machines), read Chapter 37, "Networking."

Configuring a WAIS Site

by Tim Parker

CHAPTER 49

WAIS (Wide Area Information Service) is a menu-based tool that enables users to search for keywords in a database of documents available on your system. WAIS was developed by Thinking Machines but spun off to a separate company called WAIS Incorporated when it became immensely popular. A free version of WAIS was made available to the Clearinghouse for Networking Information Discovery and Retrieval (CNIDR) as freeWAIS, which is the version most often found on Linux systems.

WAIS lets a user enter some keywords or phrases and searches a database for those terms. A typical WAIS search screen is shown in Figure 49.1. (This screen is from the primary WAIS server at `http://www.wais.com`. This server is a good place to look for examples of how WAIS can be used.) In this example, we searched for the keywords "hubble" and "magnitude" (WAIS usually ignores case). After searching all the database indexes it knows about, WAIS shows its results, as shown in Figure 49.2.

FIGURE 49.1.

You can enter complex or simple search criteria on a WAIS search line.

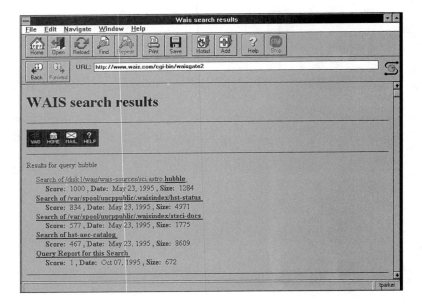

The display generated by WAIS, often displayed in a WWW browser or a WAIS browser as in these figures, lists each match along with its score from 0 to 1,000, indicating the manner in which the keywords match the index (the higher numbers are better matches). Users can then refine the list, expand it, or examine documents listed. In Figure 49.3, one of the documents listed in the search results is displayed in the WWW browser window. WAIS can handle many file formats, including text and documents, audio, JPEG and GIF files, and binaries.

FIGURE 49.2.

WAIS displays the search results with a score.

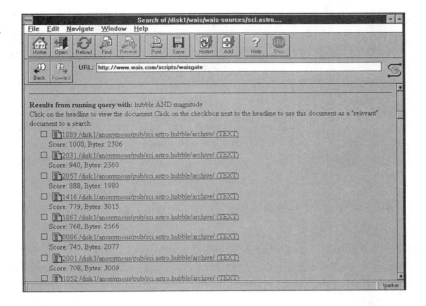

FIGURE 49.3.

Selecting any entry on the WAIS search results lets you see the file.

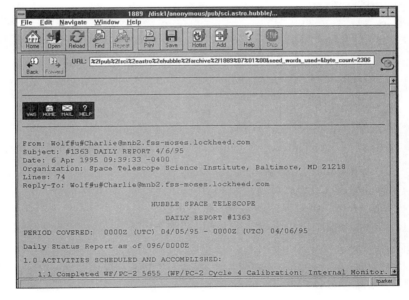

49

CONFIGURING A
WAIS SITE

The version of WAIS used commonly with Linux is called freeWAIS. This chapter looks at how you can set up a freeWAIS server on your Linux machine. WAIS is a useful service to provide if you deal with a considerable amount of information that you want to make generally available. This could be product information, details about a hobby, or practically any other type of data. All you have to want to do is make it available to others, either on your local area network or to the Internet as a whole.

The freeWAIS package has three parts to it: an indexer, a WAIS server, and a client. The indexer handles database information and generates an index that contains key words and a table indicating the word's occurrences. The server component does the matching between a user's requests and the indexed files. The client is the user's vehicle to access WAIS and is usually a WAIS or WWW browser. WWW browsers usually have an advantage over WAIS browsers in that the latter cannot display HTML documents.

A follow-up backwards-compatible WAIS system is currently available in a beta version called ZDIST. ZDIST's behavior is much like that of freeWAIS, with any changes noted in the documentation. ZDIST adds some new features and is a little smaller and faster than freeWAIS. Because of the unstable beta nature of ZDIST, we'll concentrate on freeWAIS.

Compiling and Installing freeWAIS

The freeWAIS software is often included in a complete Linux distribution CD-ROM but is also readily available from many FTP and BBS sites. Alternatively, it can be obtained by anonymous FTP from the CNIDR site as `ftp.cnidr.org`. The freeWAIS system resides in the directory `/pub/NDIR.tools/freewais/freeWAIS-X.X.tar.Z` where *X.X* is the latest version number. The CNIDR site has many binaries available for different machines, as well as generic source code which can be tailored to many different systems.

One of the files in the distribution software, which should be placed in the destination directory, is the `Makefile` used to create the program. If you are compiling the freeWAIS source yourself, examine the `Makefile` to ensure the variables are set correctly. Most are fine by default, pointing to standard Linux utilities. The following are some of the exceptions that you may have to tweak:

- `CC`   The name of the C compiler you use (usually `cc` or `gcc`).
- `CURSELIB`   Set to the current version of the `curses` library on your system.
- `TOP`   The full path to the freeWAIS source directory.

The `CFLAGS` options lets you specify compiler flags when the freeWAIS source is compiled. Many options are supported, all explained in the documentation files that accompany the source. Most of the flag settings can be left as their default values in Linux systems. A few of the specific flags you may want to alter are worth mentioning, though. The most useful are the indexer flags, two of which are potentially useful:

- -DBIO   Used to allow indexing on biological symbols and terms. Use only if your site deals with biological documents.

- -DBOOLEANS   Enables you to use Booleans as AND and NOT. This flag can be handy for extending the power of searches.

The -DBOOLEANS flag handles logical searches. For example, if you are looking for the keywords "green leaf," WAIS by default searches for the words green and leaf separately and judges matches on the two words independently. With the -DBOOLEANS flag set, the two words can be ANDed together so a match has to be with the two-word term "green leaf."

A couple of other flags that may be useful for freeWAIS sites deal with the behavior of the system as a whole:

- -DBIGINDEX   Should be set when there are many (thousands) of documents to index.

- -DLITERAL   Allows a literal search for a string, as opposed to using partial hits on the string's component words.

- -DPARTIALWORD   Allows searches with asterisks as wildcards (such as auto*).

- -DRELEVANCE_FEEDBACK   Set to ON, enables clients to use previous search results as search criteria for a new search. This is a useful option.

A number of directories are included in the distribution software, most of which are of obvious intent (bin for binaries, man for man pages, and so on). The directories used by freeWAIS in its default configuration are as follows:

- bin   Binaries
- config.c   C source code for configuration
- doc   Doc files, help files, and FAQs
- include   Header files used by the compiler
- lib   Library files
- man   Man pages
- Src   freeWAIS source code
- Wais-Sources   Directory of Internet servers
- Wais-Test   Sample indexer and service scripts

Once you have fine-tuned the configuration file information, you can compile the freeWAIS source with the `make` command:

```
make linux
```

By default, the `make` utility compiles two clients called `swais` and `waisq`. If you want to compile an X version of WAIS called `xwais` (useful if you want to allow access from X terminals or consoles), uncomment the line in the `Makefile` that ends with `makex`.

Setting Up freeWAIS

When you have the compiled freeWAIS components installed and configured properly, you can begin setting up the WAIS index files to documents available on your system. This is usually done by creating an index directory with the default name of `wsindex`. The directory usually resides just under the root of the file system (`/wsindex`) but many administrators like to keep it in a reserved area for the WAIS software (such as `/usr/wais/wsindex`). If the index files are difficult to locate, users may have problems when they try to find them.

The `wais-test` directory created when you installed freeWAIS contains a script called `test.waisindex` that creates four WAIS index files automatically for you. These are used to test the WAIS installation for proper functionality, as well as to show you how you can use the different search and index capabilities of freeWAIS. The following are the four index files:

- `test-BOOL`   Index of three example documents using the Boolean capabilities and synonyms
- `test-Comp`   Index demonstrating compressed source file handling
- `test-Docs`   Index of files in the `doc` directory showing recursive directory search
- `test-Multi`   Index of GIF images and multidocument capabilities

After graphically based (usually X-based) browsers can handle the `Multi` document formats, although any type of browser should be able to handle the other three index formats.

After you have verified that the indexing system works properly and all the components of freeWAIS are properly installed, you need to build an index file for the documents available on your system. Do this with the `waisindex` command. The `waisindex` command enables you to index files two ways using the `-t` option, followed by one of these keywords:

- `one_line`   Index each line of a document so a match can show the exact line the match occurred in.
- `text`   Index so a match shows the entire document with no indication of the exact line the match occurred in. This is the default option.

The `waisindex` command takes arguments for the name of the destination index file (`-d` followed by the filename), and the directory or files to be indexed. For example, to index a directory called `/usr/sales/sales_lit` into a destination index file called `sales`, using the `one_line` indexing approach, you would issue the command:

```
waisindex -d sales -t one_line /usr/sales/sales_lit
```

Because there is no path provided for the `sales` index file in this example, it would be stored in the current directory.

After your WAIS server is running (see the section entitled "Starting freeWAIS"), you can test the indexes by using the `waissearch` command. For example, to look for the word "WAIS" in the index files, issue the command:

```
waissearch -p 210 -d index_file WAIS
```

Where `-p` gives the port number (default value is 210), and `-d` is the path to the index file. If the search is successful (and you have something that matches) you will see messages about the number of records returned and the scores of each match. If you see error messages or nothing, check the configuration information and the index files.

A final step you can take if you want your freeWAIS system to be accessible by Internet users is to issue this command, where *Filenames* is the name of the index:

```
waisindex -export -register Filenames
```

This is registered with the Directory of Servers at `cnidr.org` and `quake.think.com`. These addresses are reached automatically with the `-register` option. Only do this step if you want all Internet users to access your WAIS service. (We will look at the `waisindex` command in much more detail shortly.)

If you want to enable clients to connect to your freeWAIS system with a WWW browser (such as Mosaic or Netscape), you must issue this command:

```
waisindex -d WWW -T HTML -contents -export /usr/resources/*html
```

Replace the `/usr/resources` path with the path to your HTML files. This line allows WAIS clients to perform keyword searches on HTML documents, as well.

If you want, you can set WAIS to only allow certain domains to connect to it. This is done in the `ir.h` file, which has a line like this:

```
#define SERVSECURITYFILE    "SERV_SEC"
```

You have to place a copy of an existing SERV_SEC file or one you create yourself in the same directory as the WAIS index files. If there is no SERV_SEC file accessible to WAIS, all domains are allowed access. (You can change the name of the file, of course, as long as the entry in ir.h matches the filename with quotation marks around it.)

Each ASCII entry in the SERV_SEC file follows a strict format for defining the domains that are granted access to WAIS. The format of each line is:

```
domain    [IP address]
```

Each line has the domain name of the host that you want to grant access to with its IP address as an optional add-on to the line. If the domain name and IP address do not match, it doesn't matter because WAIS allows access to a match of either name or address. A sample SERV_SEC file looks like this:

```
chatton.com
roy.sailing.org
bighost.bignet.com
```

Each of these three domain names can access WAIS, while any connection from a host without these domain names is refused.

The SERV_SEC file should be owned and accessible only by the user that the freeWAIS system is running as (it should not be run as root to avoid security problems), and the file should be modifiable only by root.

Similar to the SERVSECURITYFILE variable is DATASECURITYFILE, which controls access to the databases. There is a line in the ir.h file which looks like this:

```
#define DATASECURITYFILE    "DATA_SEC"
```

Where DATA_SEC is a file listing each database file and the domains that have access to it. The file should reside in the same directory as the index files. The format of the DATA_SEC file is as follows:

```
database    domain    [IP address]
```

Where database is the name of the database the permissions refer to, and domain and the optional IP address are the same as the SERV_SEC file. A sample DATA_SEC file looks like this:

```
primary    chatton.com
primary    bignet.org
primary    roy.sailing.org
sailing    roy.sailing.org
```

In this example, three domains are granted access to a database called primary (note that primary is just a filename and has no special meaning), while one domain has specific access to the database called `sailing` as well as `primary`. If you want to allow all hosts with access to the system (controlled by `SERV_SEC`) to access a particular database, you can use asterisks in the domain name and IP address fields. For example, these entries allow anyone with access to WAIS to use the `primary` database, with one domain only allowed access to the `sailing` database:

```
primary    *    *
sailing    roy.sailing.org
```

In both the `SERV_SEC` and `DATA_SEC` files, you have to be careful with the IP addresses to avoid inadvertently granting access to hosts you really don't want on your system. For example, if you specify the IP address 155.12 in your file, then any IP addresses from 155.12 through 155.120, 151.121, and so on, are also granted access because they match the IP components. Specify IP addresses explicitly to avoid this problem.

Starting freeWAIS

As with the FTP services, you can set freeWAIS to start up when the system boots by using the `rc` files from the command line at any time, or you can have the processes started by `inetd` when a service request arrives. If you want to start freeWAIS from the command line, you need to specify a number of options. A sample startup command line looks like this:

```
waisserver -u username -p 210 -l 10 -d /usr/wais/wais_index
```

The `-u` option tells `waisserver` to run as the user `username` (which has to be a valid user in `/etc/passwd`, of course), the `-p` option tells `waisserver` what port to use (the default is 210, as shown in the `/etc/services` file), and the `-d` option shows the default location of WAIS indexes. If you want to invoke logging of sessions to a file, use the `-e` option followed by the name of the logfile.

You should run `waisserver` as another user instead of root to prevent holes in the WAIS system from being exploited by a hacker. If the service is run as a standard user (such as `wais`), only the files that the user would have access to would be in jeopardy.

If the port for `waisserver` is set to 210, the service corresponds to the Internet standards for access. If you set the value to another port, you can configure the system for local area access only. If the port number is less than 1023, the WAIS service must be started and managed by root, but any port over 1023 can be handled by a normal user. If you intend to use port 210, you don't have to specify the number in the command line, although the `-p` option still must be used.

If you want to let `inetd` handle the `waisserver` startup, you need to ensure the file `/etc/services` has an entry for WAIS. The line in the `/etc/services` file looks like this, where `210` is the port number WAIS uses, and `tcp` is the protocol:

```
z3955   210/tcp   #WAIS
```

After modifying or verifying the entry in `/etc/services`, you need to add a WAIS entry to the `inetd.conf` file to start up `waisserver` whenever a request is received on port 210 (or whatever other port you are using). The entry looks like this, where the options are the same as for the command line startup mentioned above:

```
z3955   stream   tcp   nowait   root/usr/local/bin/waisserver/waisserver.d
-u   username -d /usr/wais/wais_index
```

The daemon `waisserver.d` is used when starting up in `inetd` mode, instead of `waisserver`. Again you can use the `-e` option to log activity to a file.

Building Your WAIS Indexes

After you have the freeWAIS server ready to run and everything seems to be working, it's time to provide some content for your WAIS system. Usually, documents are the primary source of information for WAIS, although you can index any type of file. The key step to providing WAIS service is to build the WAIS index using the `waisindex` command. The `waisindex` command can be a bit obtuse at times, but a little practice and some trial-and-error fiddling will help you master its somewhat awkward behavior.

The `waisindex` program works by examining all the data in the files of which you want to create an index. From its examination, `waisindex` usually generates seven different index files (depending on the content and your commands). Each file holds a list of unique words in the documents. The different index files are then combined into one large database, often called the "source" (or "WAIS source"). Whenever a client WAIS package submits a search, the search strings are compared to the source, and the results displayed with accuracy analysis (the match score).

> **TIP**
>
> The use of `waisindex` enables a client search to proceed much more quickly because the keywords in the data files have already been extracted. However, the mass of data in the index files can be sizable, so allow plenty of disk space for a WAIS server to work with. (For a typical WAIS site, assume at least double the amount of room needed for the source files.)

WAIS Index Files

The freeWAIS index files are not usually readable by a system user (although one or two files can be read with some success). Usually, `waisindex` creates seven index files, although the number may vary depending on requirements. Each index file has a specific file extension to show its purpose, based on a root name (specified on the `waisindex` command line, or defaulting to `index`). The index files and their purposes are as follows:

- `index.doc`   A document file that contains a table with the filename, a headline (title) from the file, the location of the first and last characters of an entry, the length of the document, the number of lines in the document, and the time and date the document was created.

- `index.dct`   A dictionary file that contains a list of every unique word in the files cross-indexed to the inverted file.

- `index.fn`   A filename file that contains a table with a list of the filenames, the date they were created in the index, and the type of file.

- `index.hl`   A headline file that contains a table of all headlines (titles). The headline is displayed in the search output when a match occurs.

- `index.inv`   Inverted files that contain a table associating every unique word in all the files with a pointer to the files themselves and the word's importance (determined by how close the word is to the start of the file, the number of times the word occurs in the document, and the percentage of times the word appears in the document).

- `index.src`   A source description file that contains descriptions of the information indexed, including the host name and IP address, the port watched by WAIS, the source file name, any cost information for the service, the headline of the service, a description of the source, and the email address of the administrator. The source description file is editable by ASCII editors. We will look at this file in a little more detail shortly.

- `index.status`   A status file containing user-defined information.

The source description file is a standard ASCII file that is read by `waisindex` at intervals to see whether information has changed. If the changes are significant, `waisindex` updates its internal information. A sample source file looks like this:

```
(:source
  :version 2
  :ip-address "147.120.0.10"
  :ip-name: "wizard.tpci.com"
  :tcp-port 210
```

```
:database-name "Linux stuff"
:cost 0.00
:cost-unit: free
:maintainer "wais_help@tpci.com"
:subjects "Everything you need to know about Linux"
:description "If you need to know something about Linux, it's here."
```

You should edit this file when you set up freeWAIS because the default descriptions are rather sparse and useless.

The `waisindex` Command

The `waisindex` command allows a number of options, some of which you have seen earlier in this chapter. The following list contains the primary `waisindex` options of interest to most users:

- `-a`   Appends data to an existing index file (used to update index files instead of regenerating them each time a new document is added).

- `-contents`   Indexes the file contents (default action).

- `-d`   Gives the filename root for index files (for example, `-d /usr/wais/foo` named all index files as `/usr/wais/foo.xxx`).

- `-e`   Gives the name of the log file for error information (default is `stderr`—usually the console—although you can specify `-s` for `/dev/null`).

- `-export`   Adds the host name and TCP port to descriptions for easier Internet access.

- `-l`   Gives the level of log messages. Valid values are as follows:

    0, no log

    1, log only high priority errors and warnings

    5, log medium priority errors and warnings, as well as index filename information

    10, log every event

- `-M`   Links multiple types of files.

- `-mem`   Limits memory usage during indexing (the higher the number specified, the faster the indexing process and the more memory used).

- `-nocontents`   Prevents a file from being indexed (indexes only the document header and filename).

- `-nopairs`   Instructs `waisindex` to ignore adjacent capitalized words from being indexed together.

- `-nopos`   Ignores the location of keywords in a document when determining scores.
- `-pairs`   Indexes adjacent capitalized words as a single entry.
- `-pos`   Determines scores based on locations of keywords (proximity of keywords increases scores).
- `-r`   Recursive subdirectory indexing.
- `-register`   Registers your indexes with the WAIS Directory of Services.
- `-stdin`   Uses a filename from the keyboard instead of a filename on the command line.
- `-stop`   Indicates a file containing stopwords (words too common to be indexed), usually defined in `src/ir/stoplist.c`.
- `-t`   Data file type indicator.
- `-T`   Sets the type of data to whatever follows.

The `waisindex` program has to be told the type of information in a file; otherwise it may not be able to generate an index properly. Many file types are currently defined with freeWAIS, and you can display them by entering this command with no argument:

```
waisindex
```

Although many different types are supported by freeWAIS, only a few are really in common use. The most common file types supported by freeWAIS are the following:

- `filename`   Same as text, except the filename is used as the headline.
- `first_line`   Same as text, except the first line in the file is used as the headline.
- `ftp`   Contains FTP code users can use to retrieve information from another machine.
- `GIF`   GIF images, one image per file. The filename is used as the headline.
- `mail` or `rmail`   Indexes the `mbox` mailbox contents as individual items.
- `mail_digest`   Standard email, indexed as individual messages. The subject field is the headline.
- `netnews`   Standard Usenet news, each article a separate item. The subject field is the headline.
- `one_line`   Indexes each sentence in a document separately.
- `PICT`   PICT image, one image per file. The filename is used as the headline.
- `ps`   A PostScript file with one document per file.
- `text`   Indexes the file as one document, the pathname as the heading.
- `TIFF`   TIFF image, one image per file. The filename is used as the headline.

49

CONFIGURING A
WAIS SITE

To tell `waisindex` the type of file to be examined, use the `-t` option followed by the proper type. For example, to index standard ASCII text, you could use the command:

```
waisindex -t text -r /usr/waisdata/*
```

This command indexes all the files in `/usr/waisdata` recursively, assuming they are all ASCII files.

> **TIP**
>
> When a document has been indexed, changes in the document are not reflected in the WAIS index unless a complete reindex is performed. Using the `-a` option does not update existing index entries. Instead, start the index process again. You should do this at periodic intervals as a matter of course.

Getting Fancy

You can provide some extra features for users of your freeWAIS service in a number of ways. Although this section is not exhaustive by any means, it shows you two of the easily implementable features that make a WAIS site more attractive.

To begin, suppose you want to make video, graphics, or audio available on a particular subject. Suppose, for example, your site deals with musical instruments, and you have several documents on violins. You may want to provide an audio clip of a violin being played, a video of the making of a violin, or a graphic image of a Stradivarius violin. To make these extra files available, you should have all the files with the same filename but different extensions. For example, if your primary document on violins is called `violins.txt`, you may have the following files in the WAIS directories:

- `violins.TEXT` Document describing violins
- `violins.TIFF` Image of a Stradivarius
- `violins.MPEG` Video of the making of a violin body
- `violins.MIDI` MIDI file of a violin being played

All these files should have the same root name (`violins`) but different types (recognized by `waisindex`). Then, you have to associate the multimedia files with the document file. You can do this with this command:

```
waisindex -d violin -M TEXT,TIFF,MPEG,MIDI -export /usr/waisdata/violin/*
```

This tells `waisindex` that all four types of files are to be handled. When a user searches for the keyword "violin," all four types of files are matched, and options on the browser may let them play, view, or hear the nontext components.

Another common feature is the use of synonyms to account for different methods of specifying a subject. For example, a scientist may use the keyword "feline," whereas a layperson may use "cat." You want to be able to match these two words to the same thing. This is done through a file called SOURCE.syn, which is automatically read by the search engine when it is working. The SOURCE.syn file has the following format, where *word* is the word to be used to search the databases, and *synonym* is the word(s) that should match it:

word   *synonym* [*synonym* ...]

For example, if you are dealing with domestic pets in your WAIS site, you may have the following entries in the SOURCE.syn file:

```
cat    feline
dog    canine hound pooch
bird   parrot budgie
```

The synonym file can be very useful when people use different terms to refer to the same thing. An easy way to check for the need for synonyms is to set the logging option for waisindex to 10 for a while, and see what words people are using on your site. Don't keep it on too long, however, because the logfiles can become enormous with a little traffic.

Summary

Now that WAIS is up and running on your server, you can go about the process of building your index files and letting others access your server. WAIS is quite easy to manage and offers a good way of letting other users access your system's documents. The alternative approach, for text-based systems, is Gopher, which we examine in the next chapter. From here, there are a number of chapters you can go to for more information:

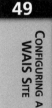

To learn how to set up a World Wide Web server on your Linux machine, see Chapter 51, "Configuring a WWW Site."

To learn how to program in HTML to set up your home pages for the Web, see Chapter 53, "HTML Programming Basics."

To learn how to use Java to provide more flexibility to your home pages, see Chapter 54, "Java and JavaScript Basics."

CHAPTER 50

Setting up a Gopher Service

by Tim Parker

IN THIS CHAPTER

Gopher is one of the most useful Internet services available because it is widely used by beginners and veterans alike. Gopher is a text-based file location system that leads you through a series of hierarchical menus to find specific files you want. Setting up a Gopher site is basically just a matter of configuring the Gopher server software and creating a number of logical directory structures with files indexed in a Gopher format.

Gopher works by having a client program (started by a user) connect to a Gopher server and retrieve information about files available on the Internet (or local area network, if the Gopher server is limited to that area). At the end of 1995, there were more than 6,000 Gopher servers on the Internet, all accessible by anyone with a Gopher client. Although the number has dropped a little since then (primarily because the World Wide Web has replaced some sites), there are still a lot of Gopher sites. Those servers contain information about more than 10 million items ranging from text files to movies, sounds, images, and many types of application binaries. Gopher enables you to display and manipulate lists of files, looking for items of interest to you.

If you or the users of your Linux system want to connect to another Gopher server, you need a Gopher client. There are several clients available with Linux distributions, on FTP and BBS sites, and through several other sources. If you don't want to allow users (or yourself) to start a Gopher client, you can use Telnet to connect to sites known as public Gopher clients. These sites allow you to log in as an anonymous user and access the Gopher system. Most Gopher client packages offer more than just Gopher programs. Typical Gopher clients enable you to access WAIS indexes, use FTP, and to some extent, interwork with the World Wide Web.

This chapter looks at how you can set up a Gopher server, allowing others to access your machine's Gopher listings. Although we won't go into detail about how you should structure your Gopher service, you will see how to configure your software.

Gopher and Linux

There are currently two versions of Gopher available for Linux systems: Gopher and Gopher+ (Gopher Plus). Gopher is freely available, but Gopher+ is a commercial product. The difference between the two is functionality. If the additional capabilities of Gopher+ are important to you and your Gopher site, you may want to consider purchasing the product. Essentially, Gopher+ adds the following features:

- Makes extended file information available
- Offers a description of a file

- Retrieves multiple versions of a file at one time (such as ASCII and PostScript simultaneously)
- Allows file retrieval based on search criteria determined by the user

Gopher+ works with Gopher, but Gopher cannot use the advanced features of Gopher+. Gopher+ and Gopher both work with WWW browsers. Gopher+ licenses tend to cost from about $100 to $500, depending on the site's conditions.

The versions of Gopher usually offered with Linux come from one of two sources: University of Minnesota Gopher and Gopher+, or GN Public License Gopher. The most recent public version of UM Gopher is version 1.3 (version 2.13 is free only to educational institutions), but the university is no longer working on the freeware Gopher product, instead concentrating on the commercial Gopher+ product. The GN Public License Gopher includes a WWW service but does not provide full functionality at present.

Gopher uses a TCP/IP family protocol known, surprisingly enough, as the Gopher protocol. This is a fairly simple request-answer protocol that is implemented for speed. When Gopher transfers information about a file it knows about (called a Gopher menu file), it follows a set format. The format used by Gopher is:

```
<type><display_name><selector string><hostname><port>
```

The fields in the Gopher menu file have the following meanings:

- *type*—A one-character description of the item (see the following bulleted list for valid codes).
- *display_name*—The menu or display name, followed by a tab character.
- *selector_string*—A unique identifier for a document on each server (usually based on the filename). The selector string is followed by a tab character.
- *hostname*—The host where the file resides, followed by a tab character.
- *port*—The port to access the host, followed by a carriage return/line feed pair (usually port 70).

The Gopher+ version of the system adds a few new attributes to each line, including the name of the system administrator responsible for the service, a simple description of the document type (text, for example), the language the file is written in, the last date the file was updated, and the size in bytes.

When a user wants to retrieve a file through the Gopher system, the hostname and port are used to create the connection to the remote server, while the selector string can be used to identify the file to be downloaded.

50

SETTING UP A GOPHER SERVICE

There are several types of files supported by Gopher, all given a unique one-character type code. The following is a list of valid codes:

- 0   Plain text file
- 1   Directory
- 2   CSO phonebook server (the hostname is the machine to connect to, the selector string is blank)
- 3   Error
- 4   BinHex Macintosh file
- 5   Binary DOS archive file
- 6   UNIX uuencoded file
- 7   Index-search server
- 8   Pointer to text-based Telnet session (hostname is the machine name to connect to and selector string is the name to log in as)
- 9   Binary file
- g   GIF file
- h   HTML document
- I   Graphic image
- i   Unselectable inline text
- M   MIME-encapsulated mail document
- P   Adobe PDF file
- s   Sound
- T   Pointer to 3270 Telnet session (hostname is machine to connect to and selector string is login name)

The Gopher system uses a number of other files on a Linux system, all of which must exist. The files necessary for Gopher are as follows:

- `tn3270` or similar 3270 emulator—Used for Telnet 3270 connections.
- `kermit` or `zmodem` communications programs—Used for downloading files. The binaries are usually called `kermit`, `sz`, `sb`, and `sx`.
- graphics utility—If you allow the display of graphics, you need a graphics utility such as `xv`.

You can modify these requirements if you have a private site (such as for your local area network), but if you are offering open access you should have all the components.

Configuring Gopher

Installing and configuring Gopher (and Gopher+) is a matter of setting a number of configuration options before compiling the system software (it is usually not precompiled for you) and configuring some standard files. Gopher+ is done in the same manner, although with some extra parameters. Because Gopher is more likely to be on a Linux site than Gopher+, we'll concentrate on that.

Throughout this section, we will use filenames without full path extensions because it really doesn't matter where you install the Gopher software, as long as the directory paths are set correctly. There is no real standard configuration for directory locations, so feel free to choose whatever works best for you.

The `gopherd.conf` File

The configuration parameters for Gopher (and Gopher+) are in a file called `gopherd.conf`, which is read by the Gopher daemon `gopherd`. The default settings generally need a little modification, although many changes are simply changing commented lines to uncommented, and vice versa.

The first step is to create an alias for the Gopher service on your machine. Perform this step with the line that defines the `hostalias`. There should be a line in the file that looks like this:

```
hostalias: tpci
```

The alias is used to find the Gopher server on your system and should not be directly tied to a real machine, so you can make changes whenever you wish. The best approach is to create an alias and tie it to a physical machine with DNS. If you are running a standalone machine, you can use either an alias tied to your machine name or your machine name directly.

You can also control the number of Gopher connections allowed at one time. This is sometimes necessary to prevent a system from bogging down due to excessive user load. The maximum number of connections Gopher allows is given in a file, usually in the directory `PIDS_Directory`. A line in the `gopherd.conf` file usually has this variable commented out because early versions didn't implement it properly or it was unstable. If you want to allow this feature, remove the comment symbol and make sure the directory it points to has the necessary files for your version of Gopher. The line usually looks like this:

```
#PIDS_Directory: /pids
```

A better way to handle the load on your system is to use the MaxConnections keyword, which sets the number of clients you support concurrently. You have to experiment to determine the best balance between system load and user service. A good starting point for a fast Linux system (80486 or Pentium CPU) is 15 to 25 users. If you are going to run a Web server at the same time, you may want to cut down this number a little, though, to spare system resources. This variable is set like this:

```
MaxConnections: 15
```

If the number of users is exceeded, an error message is generated when the connection is attempted. You can set a number of file decoders for your system. This is used when a user requests a file from Gopher and adds an extension (such as .Z, .gz, or .zip) for a compression or archive utility. The decoders recognize the extension the user supplies and invoke the proper utility to send the file properly decoded. Most gopherd.conf files have the following decoder lines already in the setup:

```
decoder: .Z /usr/ucb/zcat
decoder: .gz /usr/gnu/bin/zcat
#decoder: .adpcm /usr/openwin/bin/adpcm_dec
#decoder: .z /usr/gnu/bin/zcat
```

The last two decoders are commented out and can be uncommented if you want to offer files in these formats through Gopher. You can also add other extensions by adding new lines with the binary name (and its full path).

In addition, the amount of time a cache file stays valid should be set. This is controlled by the line using the keyword Cachetime. Set this value to a reasonable value, such as 180 seconds. You should have a line that looks like this in the gopherd.conf file:

```
Cachetime: 180
```

You can use the gopherd.conf file to restrict access to some files on your system by using the ignore keyword. Usually the gopherd.conf file has a number of defined ignores, such as these:

```
ignore: lib
ignore: bin
ignore: etc
ignore: dev
```

Any file with this type of extension is ignored. If there is a particular file extension you want to protect, add it to the list. For example, if your accounting system uses the extension .acct, you can have the Gopher clients ignore all these files by adding this line:

```
ignore: acct
```

Note that these ignore statements only work with file extensions. To be more broad, you can use wildcards and the keyword `ignore_patt` (for ignore pattern). For example, the line:

```
ignore_patt: ^usr$
```

ignores any file with the letters `usr` at the beginning of the name.

The `gopherdlocal.conf` File

In the file `gopherdlocal.conf`, you have to make two small changes to identify the system administrator, otherwise your system generates many annoying notes. The lines in the `gopherdlocal.conf` file look like this by default:

```
Admin: blank
AdminEmail: blank
```

If you do not change these entries to actual values, Gopher can generate all kinds of weird error messages. The `Admin` field usually has the administrator's name and sometimes a telephone number. For example, the file could be filled out as follows:

```
Admin: Yvonne Chow, 555-1212
AdminEmail: ychow@chatton.com
```

Another setting you should provide in the `gopherdlocal.conf` file is the `Abstract`, a short description of what your particular Gopher service provides. If you don't change the default setting, users get a message prompting them to request the `Abstract`, so you may as well do it right away. Multiple lines in an abstract value are followed by a backslash to show the continuation. A sample `Abstract` setting looks like this:

```
Abstract: This server provides sound and graphics files \
collected by the administrator on a recent trip to Outer \
Mongolia.
```

General information about your site is provided with a number of general settings for the site name, the organization that runs the site, your machine's geographic location, the latitude and longitude of your site, and a time zone setting. You can leave these blank if you want, but providing the information leads to a more complete Gopher site. The settings in a sample `gopherdlocal.conf` file look like this:

```
Site: Explore_Mongolia
Org: Mongolia Tourist Bureau
Loc: North Bay, Ontario, Canada
Geog: blank
TZ: EDT
```

The setting of `blank` for `Geog` leaves the setting with no value. Obviously, the system administrator didn't know the latitude and longitude settings.

You can set a language option used by Gopher clients to show what language most of the documents available on your site are written in. This is done like this:

```
Language: En_US
```

which refers to American English.

The setting `BummerMsg` is used to display a brief text string to a user who exceeds your maximum number of concurrent users or causes an error when accessing the system. The default value is this:

```
BummerMsg: Sorry, we have exceeded the number of permissible users
```

You can change this to whatever message you want. Be careful how you phrase it, though, because you never know who will get this message.

The last step in modifying the `gopherdlocal.conf` file is to set access procedures for users who log in to your Gopher server. Limiting the users who can get to your server is done through entries with the keyword `access`. The general format of the access line is:

```
access: hostname permissions num_users
```

where *hostname* is either the name or IP address of the host that is connecting to your server, *permissions* is the permission set for those users, and *num_users* is the maximum number of users that can be connected to the service concurrently.

The permissions are set by using any combination of the following four words, either as they are or preceded by an exclamation mark to mean "not allowed." The permission keywords are as follows:

- `browse`—Can examine directory contents. If this is forbidden, users can access entries, but they can't get directory contents.
- `ftp`—Allows server to act as gateway to FTP services.
- `read`—Can access a file. If forbidden, the user gets the `BummerMsg` when he asks for the file.
- `search`—Can access indexes (enter **7** items). If forbidden, access to the indexes is not allowed. This is used primarily with Gopher+.

For example, to set access permissions to allow up to 10 users from the network `chatton.com` to access your Gopher server with full rights, add a line like this:

```
access: chatton.com     browse ftp read search 10
```

There is at least one space between each entry, even between permissions. This access entry:

```
access: bignet.org !browse !ftp read search 3
```

allows three concurrent users from `bignet.org` to access the Gopher server and read and search, but not use FTP gateways or browse the directory listings.

If you are using IP addresses, you can use a subset of the IP address to indicate the entire network. For example, if `bignet.com`'s network address is 147.12, you can indicate the entire network with a line like this:

```
access: 147.12. !browse !ftp read search 3
```

You must follow the last quad of numbers specified in the IP address with a period, otherwise 147.120 through 147.129 will also have the same permissions (because they match the digits specified).

If you want to enable access from a particular machine, you can do that, too. For example, to allow your friend's `darkstar` machine to access your Gopher server with full permissions, add a line like this:

```
access: darkstar.domain.name browse ftp read search 1
```

Most general Gopher servers tend to allow anyone to connect, so they use a default entry to refer to anyone not explicitly defined by another access entry. The default setting is usually like this:

```
access: default !browse !ftp read search 15
```

which allows anyone to read and search Gopher directories, but not move through them or use your machine as an FTP gateway.

Setting Up the `Makefile`

Two files need modification for the compilation process to proceed properly. These two files are `Makefile.config` and `conf.h`. With many versions of Gopher available on Linux systems, the configuration parameters that these files need have already been set, but you should check the values carefully to prevent problems.

The `Makefile.config` file (used by `Makefile` to build the executables) is a lengthy file, so you should be careful while moving through it to avoid accidental changes. The important areas to examine are the directory definitions and server and client settings. These are dealt with individually in the following sections.

One setting you may wish to alter is the debugging utility, which is enabled by default in most systems. This can help you get the system running properly, but when the operation is correct, you should recompile the source with the debugging features removed to make the process faster and smaller, as well as to reduce debug information overhead. To remove debugging features, comment out the DEBUGGING line so it looks like this:

```
#DEBUGGING = -DDEBUGGING
```

By default this line is probably not commented out.

The directory definitions are usually in a block with five to seven entries, depending on the number of entries for the man pages. A typical directory definition block looks like this:

```
PREFIX = /usr/local
CLIENTDIR = $(PREFIX)/bin
CLIENTLIB = $(PREFIX)/lib
SERVERDIR = $(PREFIX)/etc

MAN1DIR = $(PREFIX)/man/man1
MAN5DIR = $(PREFIX)/man/man5
MAN8DIR = $(PREFIX)/man/man8
```

The primary change to most Makefile.config files will be the PREFIX, which is used to set the basic directory for Gopher. The default value is usually /usr/local, although you can change it to anything you want (such as /usr/gopher). The rest of the variables define subdirectories under the primary Gopher directory and are usually acceptable as they are. Each of the subdirectories can be left the way it is or you can change it to suit your own needs. You can place all the files in one directory, if you want. The meaning of each variable appears in the following list:

CLIENTDIR	Gopher client software
CLIENTLIB	Client help file (gopher.hlp)
MAN1DIR	Man pages for Gopher client
MAN8DIR	Man pages for gopherd
SERVERDIR	Gopher server (gopherd) and configuration file (gopherd.conf)

For a Gopher client to run properly on your system, you must modify the CLIENTOPTS line in the Makefile.config file. The two options for the CLIENTOPTS line to control its behavior are as follows:

-DNOMAIL	Forbids remote users from mailing files.
-DAUTOEXITONU	Allows the Gopher client to be exited with the u command as well as q command.

To use either or both of these options, add them to the CLIENTOPS line like this:

```
CLIENTOPTS = -DNOMAIL -DAUTOEXITONU
```

Four variables relating to the Gopher server must also be set. These specify the host domain name, the port Gopher should use to listen for connections, the location of the data files, and option flags.

The domain name is set with the DOMAIN variable. It should have a leading period in the name, such as:

```
DOMAIN = .tpci.com
```

You do not need to set this variable if the hostname command returns the fully qualified domain name of the server. In this case, leave the value blank.

The SERVERPORT variable defines the port Gopher uses to wait for services and is usually set for TCP port 70. This line usually looks like this:

```
SERVERPORT = 70
```

If you are not allowing general access to your Gopher site by Internet users, you can change this value. However, if you want to allow Internet users (even a very small subset) to gain access, you should leave this as port 70. If you are setting up your Gopher site for a small network only, then choose any port number you want (between 1024 and 9999) and make sure all the Gopher clients use that number, too.

The SERVERDATA variable defines the location of the data your Gopher server offers. Its default setting is usually as follows:

```
SERVERDATA = /gopher-data
```

Set the variable to point to the file location you use for your Gopher items.

The SERVEROPTS variable accepts a number of keywords that change the behavior of the Gopher service. A typical entry looks like this:

```
SERVEROPTS = -DSETPROCTITLE -DCAPFILES # -DBIO -DDL
```

Any keywords after the pound sign are ignored when Makefile runs, so you can adjust its location to set the options you want if the order of the variables allows such a simple approach. The following lists the meaning of the different keywords allowed in the SERVEROPTS entry:

-DADD_DATE_AND_TIME	Adds dates and times to titles.
-DBIO	Used only with the WAIS versions developed by Don Gilbert (wais8b5).

-DDL	Provides support for the dl database utility (requires the dl system in a directory variable called DLPATH and the DLOBJS line uncommented out to show the files getdesc.o and enddesc.o locations).
-DCAPFILES	Offers backward compatibility with the cap directory.
-DLOADRESTRICT	Restricts user access based on the number of concurrent users (see the following section).
-DSETPROCTITLE	Sets the name displayed by ps command (BSD UNIX-based systems only).

The conf.h file is used during the compilation to set other parameters about the Gopher service. The important settings, at least when setting up a Gopher service, are those that relate to the number of queries and timeout variables. These tend to occur at the end of the conf.h file.

The WAISMAXHITS variable defines the maximum number of hits a query to a WAIS database can offer, usually set to around 40. This variable is defined like this:

```
#define WAISMAXHITS 40
```

Note that the pound sign is not a comment symbol because this is written in C. The pound sign is an important part of the processor directive and should be left in place. There is no equal sign in the definition, either.

The MAXLOAD variable is used if the -DLOADRESTRICT keyword was used in the SERVEROPTS variable of Makefile.config. The MAXLOAD defines the maximum load average the Gopher service will respond to requests under (this value can be overridden on the command line). The usual definition is like this:

```
#define MAXLOAD 10.0
```

The READTIMEOUT and WRITETIMEOUT variables set the amount of time a service waits for a network read or write operation before timing out. The default settings are usually adequate. These lines look like the following:

```
#define READTIMEOUT (1*60)
#define WRITETIMEOUT (3*60)
```

The Gopher client's configuration is straightforward. Begin by defining the Gopher servers the local machine connects to with the CLIENT1_HOST and CLIENT2_HOST entries. The Gopher client chooses one of the two (if both are defined) when it is started. The entries look like this:

```
#define CLIENT1_HOST "gopher_serv.tpci.com"
#define CLIENT2_HOST "other_gopher_serv.tpci.com"
```

The ports to be used to connect to the hosts are defined with these options:

```
#define CLIENT1_PORT 70
#define CLIENT2_PORT 70
```

If you have a local service and don't want to use port 70 (to prevent access from the Internet, for example), set the proper port values. If only one Gopher server is used, set the second value to 0.

Define the language the Gopher client will use by choosing one value out of a number of options. The default is American English, set by this command:

```
#define DEFAULT_LANG "En_US"
```

Other language defines are commented out below this one. If you want to change the default language, comment the American English setting and uncomment the one you want.

When all the configuration changes are made, you can invoke the compilation process for the client and server with these commands:

```
make client
make server
```

Or you can do both client and server systems at once by using the make command with no argument. The programs and data files must be installed, too, using the command:

```
make install
```

WAIS and Gopher

Gopher clients have the ability to use WAIS indexes to search for documents, but the system must be configured to allow this. We looked at WAIS in Chapter 49, "Configuring a WAIS Site," so for the sake of providing WAIS index access to Gopher, we'll assume you have installed WAIS properly and have WAIS indexes ready for Gopher.

To provide WAIS services through Gopher, you may have to make a change in the WAIS source code. Examine the WAIS source code for a line that looks like this:

```
if (gLastAnd) printf("search_word: boolean 'and' scored/n:);
```

This line should be commented out to provide Gopher services, so if it is not, add C comment symbols before and after the line, like this:

```
/* if (gLastAnd) printf("search_word: boolean 'and' scored/n:); */
```

If the line is already commented out (or didn't exist), then you don't need to make any changes. If you change the line, though, you have to recompile WAIS by changing into the WAIS top directory and running the `makefile` (enter the command `make`).

Next, examine the Gopher `Makefile.config` file and look for the `WAISTYPE` variable. It should be defined on a line like this:

```
WAISTYPE = #-DFREEWAIS_0_4
```

Then, you have to link the Gopher and WAIS services. Suppose your Gopher source directory is `/usr/gopher/source` and the WAIS source directory is `/usr/wais/source`. You can link these services by entering the following commands:

```
cd /usr/gopher/source
ln -s /usr/wais/source/include ./ir
ln -s /usr/wais/source/client/ui .
ln -s /usr/wais/source/bin .
```

When Gopher is recompiled, it connects the links between Gopher and freeWAIS and allows the two services to interwork.

Setting Up Your Gopher Directories

Gopher directories and files are quite simple to set up and follow standard naming conventions for the most part. Before you begin, though, you should know which documents and files are to be provided through Gopher to other users, and you should be able to write a short description of each. (If you don't know the contents of a file, either read it or get the author to summarize the file for you.) For simplicity, let's assume you will use only a single directory for all your Gopher documents.

Begin by changing to the top directory you use for your Gopher directories (which you may have to create if you haven't already done so). This directory should not be where the Gopher source and configuration files are located, for convenience. Simply choose a useful name and create the directory. For example, to create the Gopher home directory `/usr/gopher/data`, issue a standard `mkdir` command:

```
mkdir /usr/gopher/data
```

Change into your Gopher directory and copy the files you want to make available into it. When you have done that, you can create a descriptive filename for each file (instead of the more obtuse filenames usually used) up to 80 characters long. For example, if you have a filename called `q1.sales`, you may want to rename it to `Company_Sales_1887_Q1` to help users identify the contents a little more easily.

The process for providing better filenames is to first create a .cap directory under your Gopher main directory (such as /usr/gopher/data/.cap). For each file in the main directory, you want to create a file in the .cap directory with the same name, but with a name and number. For example, suppose you have a file called q1.sales in /usr/gopher/data. In /usr/gopher/data/.cap you would create a file with the same name, q1.sales, which has the following contents:

```
Name=Company Sales for the First Quarter, 1887
Numb=1
```

The Name entry can have spaces or other special symbols in it because it is echoed as a complete string. The Numb entry is for the location of the entry on your Gopher menu. For example, suppose you had the preceding entry and two other files, shown by using cat to display their contents:

```
$ cat q1.sales
Name=Company Sales for the First Quarter, 1887
Numb=1

$ cat q2.sales
Name=Company Sales for the Second Quarter, 1887
Numb=2

$cat q3.sales
Name=Company Sales for the Third Quarter, 1887
Numb=3
```

When these entries are displayed in a Gopher menu they look like this:

```
1. Company Sales for the First Quarter, 1887
2. Company Sales for the Second Quarter, 1887
3. Company Sales for the Third Quarter, 1887
```

The order of filenames in the .cap directory doesn't matter, but you shouldn't have the same Numb entry more than once.

An alternative to using the .cap directory approach (which allows for easy addition of new files) is to use a single master file for each document you are making available. This file goes in your Gopher top directory and is called .names. Here's the .names file for the same three files just mentioned:

```
$ cd /usr/gopher/data
$ cat .names
# My Gopher main .names file

Path=./q1.sales
Name=Company Sales for the First Quarter, 1887
```

```
Numb=1

Path=./q2.sales
Name=Company Sales for the Second Quarter, 1887
Numb=2

Path=./q3.sales
Name=Company Sales for the Third Quarter, 1887
Numb=3
```

As you can see, this format contains the same information but adds the filename (which was not needed in .cap since the filenames were the same). One advantage to using a .names file is that you can reorder your menu entries much more easily because you only have one file to work with instead of several. Also, the .names file enables you to add an abstract describing the file. For example, you could have the following entry in a .names file:

```
Path=./gopher
Name=How to Set up A Gopher Service
Numb=16
Abstract=This document shows the steps you need to take to
set up a Gopher service.
```

You can get a little fancier with Gopher and have a menu item lead to another menu or to another machine entirely. This is done with links, controlled by a link file, which ends with .link. A .link file has five pieces of information in it, in the same format as this example:

```
Name=More Sales Info
Type=1
Port=70
Path=/usr/gopher/data/more_sales
Host=wizard.tpci.com
```

The Name entry is what a user sees on the Gopher menu and can be any type of description you want, regardless of what else is in the link file. The Type field has a number showing the type of document the file links to. The following are all valid numbers:

0	Text
1	Directory
2	CSO name server
7	Full text index
8	Telnet session
9	Binary
h	HTML file

I	Image file
M	MIME file
s	Sound file

These types are the same as the list shown earlier in this chapter for the types of files Gopher supports, although it's a little shorter here.

The `Port` field is the port for a connection to a remote system (if that's where the link leads), and the `Path` field is where the file is on the local or remote server. The `Host` field, not surprisingly, is the name of the host the file resides on. If you are setting up a link to another machine via FTP or WAIS, you need to specify the path to include the service name and any arguments. For example, if your Gopher menu leads users to a file on another machine through FTP, your link file may look like this:

```
Name=More Sales Info
Type=1
Port=+
Path=ftp:chatton.bigcat.com@/usr/gopher/cats
Host=+
```

The plus signs used in the `Port` and `Host` fields instruct the FTP service on the remote machine to return results to this machine using default ports (such as TCP port 21 for FTP). For a link to a WAIS directory, the format is:

```
Name=More Sales Info
Type=7
Port=+
Path=waisrc:/usr/wais/data
Host=+
```

Finally, you may want to have a menu item execute a program. You can do this by having the `Path` field use the `exec` command:

```
Path=exec: "args" : do_this
```

where *do_this* is the program you want to execute and *args* are any arguments to be passed to *do_this*. If you have no arguments to pass, leave the quotation marks empty. This format is a little awkward, but it does work.

Starting Gopher

A Gopher server can be started either from the `rc` startup files, from the command line, or from the `inetd` daemon. From the command line or the `rc` files, you need a command line similar to this:

```
/usr/local/etc/gopherd /usr/gopher/gopher-data 70
```

50

SETTING UP A GOPHER SERVICE

which starts the daemon with the directory the startup Gopher menus reside in and the port number for connections.

The `gopherd` command line accepts a number of optional flags to control its behavior, although most mirror entries in the configuration files. Valid flags are as follows:

`-C`	Disables directory caching.
`-c`	Runs without `chroot` restrictions.
`-D`	Enables debugging.
`-I`	`inetd` is used to invoke `gopherd`.
`-L`	Followed by a value for the maximum load average.
`-l`	Log file to record connections (filename follows the option).
`-o`	Specifies an alternate configuration file from `gopherd.conf` (filename follows the option).
`-u`	Sets the name of the owner running `gopherd` (valid username must follow the option).

To help secure your system, use `chroot` to create a separate file system structure for the Gopher area (as you did with FTP: see Chapter 48, "Setting up an FTP and Anonymous FTP Site"). The `-c` option is not as secure as running `gopherd` with `chroot` active. Also, the `-u` option should be used to make `gopherd` run as a standard user's process, instead of as `root`. This helps protect against holes in the daemon that a hacker could exploit.

If you want to run Gopher under `inetd` (started whenever a request for the service arrives), modify the `/etc/services` and `/etc/inetd.conf` file to include a line for Gopher. Normally, the entry in `/etc/services` looks like this:

```
gopher     70/tcp
```

and the entry in `/etc/inetd.conf` looks like this:

```
gopher     stream     tcp     nowait     root
    /usr/local/etc/gopherd gopherd -I -u username
```

where *username* is the name of the user to run `gopherd` as (you can set up a specific account for `gopher` in `/etc/passwd` with standard permissions).

Once the Gopher server process is up and running, you can test your Gopher installation. First, though, you will need a Gopher client. Then use the Gopher client to connect to your Gopher server (using your host name), and you should see the top directory of your Gopher resources. Another way to test your Gopher system is to use Telnet. Use Telnet to connect to the Gopher port, using a command like this:

```
telnet gopher 70
```

If the connection is properly made, you will see your Gopher system on the screen.

Yet another alternative to test your system is to use the program `gopherls`, which requires the name of the directory your Gopher source resides in. To start `gopherls`, issue a command as follows:

```
gopherls /usr/wais/gopher/data
```

specifying your Gopher data directory. You can use this technique to test new Gopher directories as you develop them.

Letting the World Know

Because you have spent a lot of time setting up your Gopher service, you can now let everyone else on the Internet know about it. (Of course, you should only do this when your Gopher service is ready, and if you want to allow general access. Don't follow these steps if you are granting access only to a few people or your local area network.)

To have your Gopher service listed in the main Gopher service directories, send an email message to the address:

```
gopher@boombox.micro.umn.edu
```

and include the Gopher service's full name as it appears on your main menu, your host's name and IP address, the port number Gopher uses (which should be TCP port 70 for general Internet access), the email account of the Gopher administrator, and a short paragraph describing your service. If you want, you can also provide a string that gives the path to the data directory, although since most Gopher systems start in the root directory, this string isn't necessary unless you have sub-menus for different purposes.

Summary

After all that, your Gopher service is ready to use. You do need to set up the Gopher file entries, but that is beyond the scope of this chapter. Consult a good Internet or Gopher book for more information on Gopher directories, files, and entries. Gopher is a handy utility if you have volumes of information you want to share, and although the configuration process can take a while, once it's completed, the Gopher system tends to work very well. To learn more about:

How to set up a World Wide Web server on your Linux machine, see Chapter 51, "Configuring a WWW Site."

How to program in HTML to set up your home pages for the Web, see Chapter 53, "HTML Programming Basics."

How to use Java to provide more flexibility to your home pages, see Chapter 54, "Java and JavaScript Basics."

`make` and the `makefile` utility, see Chapter 56, "Source Code Control."

Configuring a WWW Site

by Tim Parker

CHAPTER

51

Just about everyone on the planet knows about the World Wide Web. It's the most talked about aspect of the Internet. With the Web's popularity, more system users are getting into the game by setting up their own WWW servers and "home pages." There are now sophisticated packages that act as Web servers for many operating systems. Linux, based on UNIX, has the software necessary to provide a Web server.

You don't need fancy software to set up a Web site, only a little time and the correct configuration information. That's what this chapter is about. We'll look at how you can set up a World Wide Web server on your Linux system—whether for friends, your LAN, or the Internet as a whole.

The major aspect of the Web that attracts users and makes it so powerful, aside from its multimedia capabilities, is the use of hyperlinks. A hyperlink lets one click of the mouse move you from document to document, site to site, graphic to movie, and so on. All the instructions of the move are built into the Web code.

There are two main aspects to the World Wide Web: server and client. Client software, such as Mosaic and Netscape, is probably the most familiar. However, many different Web client packages, other than these two are also available, some specifically for X or Linux.

Web Server Software

There are three primary versions of Web server software that will run under Linux. They are from NCSA, CERN, and Plexus. The most readily available system is from NCSA, which also produces Mosaic. NCSA's Web system is fast and quite small, can run under inetd or as a standalone daemon, and provides pretty good security. For this chapter, we will use NCSA's Web software, although you can easily use either of the other two packages instead (although the configuration information will be different, of course). There are also popular versions of the Web server package Apache which are available from numerous Linux sources, too. We'll look at Apache in a section later in this chapter, after dealing with the more traditional Web server systems.

> **NOTE**
>
> The Web server software for one of the three is available via anonymous FTP or WWW sites listed here, depending on the type of server software you want:
> CERN: `ftp//ftp.w3.org/pub/httpd` (FTP)
> NCSA: `ftp.ncsa.uiuc.edu/web/httpd/unix/ncsa_httpd` (FTP)
> `http://hoohoo.ncsa.uiuc.edu` (WWW)
> Plexus: `ftp://austin.bsdi.com/plexus/2.2.1/dist/Plexus-2.2.1.tar.Z` (WWW).

The NCSA Web software is available for Linux in both compiled and source code forms. Using the compiled version is much easier because you don't have to configure and compile the source code for the Linux platform. The binaries are often provided compressed and tarred, and you have to uncompress and then extract the `tar` library. Alternatively, many CD-ROMs provide the software ready-to-go. If you do obtain the compressed form of the Web server software, follow the installation or README files to place the Web software in the proper location.

Unpacking the Web Files

If you have obtained a library of source code or binaries from an FTP or BBS site, you probably have to untar and uncompress them first. (Check with any README files, if there are any, before you do this; otherwise you may be doing this step for nothing.) Usually, you proceed by creating a directory for the Web software, and then changing it and expanding the library with a command such as this:

```
zcat httpd_X.X_XXX.tar.Z | tar xvf -
```

The software is often named by the release and target platform, such as `httpd_1.5_linux.tar.Z`. Use whatever name your `tar` file has in the preceding line. Installation instructions are sometimes in a separate `tar` file, such as `Install.tar.z`, which you have to obtain and uncompress with the command:

```
zcat Install.tar.z
```

Make sure you are in the target directory when you issue these commands, though, or you will have to move a lot of files. You can place the files anywhere; however, it is often a good idea to create a special area for the Web software that can have its permissions controlled, such as `/usr/web`, `/var/web`, or a similar name.

Once you have extracted the contents of the Web server distribution and the library files are in their proper directories, you can look at what has been created automatically. You should find the following subdirectories:

`cgi-bin`	Common gateway interface binaries and scripts
`conf`	Configuration files
`icons`	Icons for home pages
`src`	Source code and (sometimes) executables
`support`	Support applications

Compiling the Web Software

If you don't have to modify the source and recompile for Linux (because your software is the Linux version), you can skip the configuration details mentioned in the rest of this section. On the other hand, you may want to know what is happening in the source code anyway because you can better understand how Linux works with the Web server code. If you obtained a generic, untailored version of the NCSA Web server, you have to configure the software.

Begin by editing the `src/Makefile` file to specify your platform. There are several variables that you have to check for proper information:

AUX_CFLAGS	Uncomment the entry for Linux (identified by comment lines and symbols, usually).
CC	The name of the C compiler (usually `cc` or `gcc`).
EXTRA_LIBS	Add any extra libraries that need to be linked in (none are required for Linux).
FLAGS	Add any flags you need for linking (none are required for most Linux linkers).

Finally, look for the CFLAGS variable. Some of the values for CFLAGS may be set already. The following are valid values for CFLAGS:

-DSECURE_LOGS	Prevents CGI scripts from interfering with any log files written by the server software.
-DMAXIMUM_DNS	Provides a more secure resolution system at the cost of performance.
-DMINIMAL_DNS	Doesn't allow reverse name resolution, but speeds up performance.
-DNO_PASS	Prevents multiple children from being spawned.
-DPEM_AUTH	Enables PEM/PGP authentication schemes.
-DXBITHACK	Provides a service check on the execute bit of an HTML file.
-O2	Optimizing flag.

It is unlikely that you will need to change any of the flags in the CFLAGS section, but at least you now know what they do. Once you have checked the `src/Makefile` for its contents, you can compile the server software. Issue the command:

```
make linux
```

If you see error messages, check the configuration file carefully. The most common problem is the wrong platform (or multiple platforms) selected in the file.

Configuring the Web Software

Once the software is in the proper directories and compiled for your platform, it's time to configure the system. Begin with the `httpd.conf-dist` file. Copy it to the filename `httpd.conf`, which is what the server software looks for. This file handles the `httpd` server daemon. Before you edit the file, you have to decide whether you will install the Web server software to run as a daemon or whether it will be started by `inetd`. If you anticipate frequent use, run the software as a daemon. For occasional use, either is acceptable.

There are several variables in `httpd.conf` that need to be checked or have values entered for them. All the variables in the configuration file follow the syntax:

variable value

with no equal sign or special symbol between the variable name and the value assigned to it. For example, a few lines would look like this:

```
FancyIndexing on
HeaderName Header
ReadmeName README
```

Where pathnames or filenames are supplied, they are usually relative to the Web server directory, unless explicitly declared as a full pathname. You need to supply the following variables in `httpd.conf`:

AccessConfig	The location of the `access.conf` configuration file. The default value is `conf/access.conf`. You can use either absolute or relative pathnames.
AgentLog	The log file to record details of the type and version of browser used to access your server. The default value is `logs/agent_log`.
ErrorLog	The name of the file to record errors. The default is `/logs/error_log`.
Group	The Group ID the server should run as (used only when server is running as a daemon). Can be either a group name or group ID number. If a number, it must be preceded by `#`. The default is `#-1`.
MaxServers	The maximum number of children allowed.
PidFile	The file where you want to record the process ID of each `httpd` copy. The default is `/logs/httpd.pid`. Used only when the server is in daemon mode.

Port	Port number `httpd` should listen to for clients. Default port is 80. If you don't want the Web server generally available, choose another number.
ResourceConfig	The path to the `srm.conf` file, usually `conf/srm.conf`.
ServerAdmin	Email address of the administrator.
ServerName	The fully qualified host name of the server.
ServerRoot	The path above which users cannot move (usually the Web server top directory or `usr/local/etc/httpd`).
ServerType	Either standalone (daemon) or `inetd`.
StartServers	The number of server processes that are started when the daemon executes.
TimeOut	The amount of time in seconds to wait for a client request, after which it is disconnected (default is 1,800, which should be reduced).
TransferLog	The path to the location of the access log. Default is `logs/access_log`.
TypesConfig	The path to the location of the MIME configuration file. Default is `conf/mime.conf`.
User	Defines the user ID the server should run as (only valid if running as a daemon). Can be name or number but must be preceded by # if a number. Default is #-1.

The next configuration file to check is `srm.conf`, which is used to handle the server resources. The variables that have to be checked or set in the `srm.conf` file are as follows:

AccessFileName	The file that gives access permissions (default is `.htaccess`).
AddDescription	Provides a description of a type of file. For example, an entry could be `AddDescription PostScript file *.ps`. Multiple entries are allowed.
AddEncoding	Indicates that files with a particular extension are encoded somehow, such as `AddEncoding compress Z`. Multiple entries are allowed.
AddIcon	Gives the name of the icon to display for each type of file.
AddIconType	Uses MIME type to determine the icon to use.

`AddType`	Overrides `MIME` definitions for extensions.
`Alias`	Substitutes one pathname for another, such as `Alias data /usr/www/data`.
`DefaultType`	The default `MIME` type, usually `text/plain`.
`DefaultIcon`	The default icon to use when `FancyIndexing` is on (default is `/icons/unknown.xbm`).
`DirectoryIndex`	Filename to return when the URL is for your service only. Default value is `index.html`.
`DocumentRoot`	Absolute path to the HTML document directory. Default is `/usr/local/etc/httpd/htdocs`.
`FancyIndexing`	Adds icons and filename information to the file list for indexing. Default is on. (This option is for backward compatibility with the first release of HTTP.)
`HeaderName`	The filename used at the top of a list of files being indexed. Default is `Header`.
`IndexOptions`	Indexing parameters (including `FancyIndexing`, `IconsAreLinks`, `ScanHTMLTitles`, `SuppressLastModified`, `SuppressSize`, and `SuppressDescription`).
`ReadmeName`	The footer file is displayed with directory indexes. Default is `README`.
`Redirect`	Maps a path to another URL.
`ScriptAlias`	Similar to `Alias` but for scripts.
`UserDir`	Directory users can use for `httpd` access. Default is `public_html`. Usually set to a user's home page directory. Can be set to `DISABLED`.

The third file to examine and modify is `access.conf-dist`, which defines the services available to WWW browsers. Usually, everything is accessible to a browser, but you may want to modify the file to tighten security or disable some services not supported on your Web site. The format of the `conf-dist` file is different than the two preceding configuration files. It uses a set of "sectioning directives" delineated by angle brackets. The general format of an entry is:

```
<Directory Dir_Name>
...
</Directory>
```

and anything between the beginning and ending delimiters (`<Directory>` and `</Directory>`, respectively) are directives. Actually, it's not quite that easy because there are several variations that can exist in the file. The best way to customize the `access.conf-dist` file is to follow these steps for a typical Web server installation:

1. Locate the Options directive and remove the Indexes option. This prevents users from browsing the `httpd` directory. Valid Options entries are discussed shortly.

2. Locate the first Directory directive and check the path to the `cgi-bin` directory. The default path is `/usr/local/etc/httpd/cgi-bin`.

3. Find the `AllowOverride` variable and set it to `None` (this prevents others from changing the settings). The default is `All`. Valid values for the `AllowOverride` variable are discussed shortly.

4. Find the Limit directive and set to whichever value you want.

The Limit directive controls access to your server. The following are valid values for the Limit directive:

`allow`	Allows specific host names following the `allow` keyword to access the service.
`deny`	Denies specific host names following the `deny` keyword from accessing the service.
`order`	Specifies the order in which `allow` and `deny` directives are evaluated (usually set to `deny,allow` but can also be `allow,deny`).
`require`	Requires authentication through a user file specified in the `AuthUserFile` entry.

The Options directive can have several entries, all of which have a different purpose. The default entry for Options is

```
Options Indexes FollowSymLinks
```

You removed the Indexes entry from the Options directive in the first step of the preceding customization procedure. These entries all apply to the directory the `Options` field appears in. The valid entries for the Options directive are:

`All`	All features enabled.
`ExecCGI`	`cgi` scripts can be executed from this directory.
`FollowSymLinks`	Allows `httpd` to follow symbolic links.
`Includes`	`Include` files for the server are enabled.
`IncludesNoExec`	`Include` files for the server are enabled but the `exec` option is disabled.

Indexes	Enables users to retrieve server-generated indexes (doesn't affect precompiled indexes).
None	No features enabled.
SymLinksIfOwnerMatch	Follows symbolic links only if the user ID of the symbolic link matches the user ID of the file.

The AllowOverride variable is set to All by default and this should be changed. There are several valid values for AllowOverride, but the recommended setting for most Linux systems is None. The valid values for AllowOverride are as follows:

All	Access controlled by a configuration file in each directory.
AuthConfig	Enables some authentication routines. Valid values: AuthName (sets authorization name of directory); AuthType (sets authorization type of the directory, although there is only one legal value: Basic); AuthUserFile (specifies a file containing usernames and passwords); and AuthGroupFile (specifies a file containing group names).
FileInfo	Enables AddType and AddEncoding directives.
Limit	Enables Limit directive.
None	No access files allowed.
Options	Enables Options directive.

After all that, the configuration files should be properly set. While the syntax is a little confusing, reading the default values shows you the proper format to use when changing entries. Next, you can start the Web server software.

Starting the Web Software

With the configuration complete, it's time to try out the Web server software. In the configuration files, you decided whether the Web software runs as a daemon (standalone) or starts from inetd. The startup procedure is a little different for each method (as you would expect), but both startup procedures can use one of the following three options on the command line:

-d	The absolute path to the root directory of the server files (used only if the default location is not valid).
-f	The configuration file to read if not the default value of httpd.conf.
-v	Displays the version number.

If you are using `inetd` to start your Web server software, you need to make a change to the `/etc/services` file to permit the Web software. Add a line similar to this to the `/etc/services` file:

```
http      port/tcp
```

where *port* is the port number used by your Web server software (usually 80).

Next, modify the `/etc/inetd.conf` file to include the startup commands for the Web server where the last entry is the path to the `httpd` binary:

```
httpd stream tcp nowait nobody /usr/web/httpd
```

Once this is done, restart `inetd` by killing and restarting the `inetd` process or by rebooting your system, and the service should be available through whatever port you specified in `/etc/services`.

If you are running the Web server software as a daemon, you can start it at any time from the command line with the command:

```
httpd &
```

Even better, add the startup commands to the proper `rc` startup files. The entry usually looks like this:

```
# start httpd
if [ -x /usr/web/httpd ]
then
 /usr/web/httpd
fi
```

substituting the proper paths for the `httpd` binary, of course. Rebooting your machine should start the Web server software on the default port number.

To test the Web server software, use any Web browser and enter the following in the URL field:

```
http://machinename
```

where *machinename* is the name of your Web server. You can do this either over the Internet through a connection or from another machine on your network (if you have one). If you see the contents of the root Web directory or the `index.html` file, all is well. Otherwise, check the log files and configuration files for clues as to the problem.

If you haven't installed a Web browser yet, check to see if the Web server is running by using `telnet`. Issue a command like this, substituting the name of your server (and your Web port number if different than 80):

```
telnet www.wizard.tpci.com 80
```

You should get a message similar to this if the Web server is responding properly:

```
Connected to wizard.tpci.com
Escape character is '^]'.
HEAD/HTTP/1.0
HTTP/1.0 200 OK
```

You'll also see some more lines showing details about the date and content. You may not be able to access anything, but this shows that the Web software is responding properly.

Apache

Apache is a Web server package that has become very popular lately. The reason for Apache's popularity is its ready availability for many platforms and its versatility. Apache was based on the Mosaic Web server mentioned earlier in this chapter, but with a considerable amount of new code added. Apache was written as public domain software and is available to anyone who wants it. There is a sizable support community on the Web and several books dedicated to the subject on your local bookshelves.

> **TIP**
>
> As this book is being written the most current version of Apache is 1.2. There are many older versions available, but version 1.2 made many important changes to the software and is worth the effort to download if you don't have it. There is a Web site devoted to Apache at http://www.apache.org, and you can get code for the Apache Web server from most of the Linux FTP sites.

Using make with Apache Software

When you obtain the Apache software, you may have it in source code form only and not compiled for your system. Some CD-ROM versions of Linux do include pre-compiled versions of Apache, so you don't have to worry about this step if that's the case. If you download from an FTP site or a Web page, though, you'll most likely have to compile the software yourself. This isn't a major problem, though, because the entire process has been automated with a utility called make. We look at the make utility in a lot more detail in Chapter 56, "Source Code Control," but you don't need to know too much detail to follow this section.

First, let's make sure the Apache software is ready to go. If you have downloaded the file, you'll have a single compressed file (most likely called apache.tar with either a .Z or .gz extension. Copy the file to a temporary directory (any directory name will do).

You can unpack the file with one of these two commands:

```
uncompress apache.tar.Z
gunzip apache.tar.gz
```

depending on the extension of your file. (We looked at the compression systems used by Linux in Part II, "Getting to Know Linux" and Part VI, "Linux for System Administrators.")

> **TIP**
>
> If you are using the GNU `tar` version (which is included with most Linux systems) you can uncompress and untar with the single command:
>
> ```
> tar zxvf apache.tar.gz
> ```

After the file has been uncompressed it will be called `apache.tar` (or the same name as the compressed file without the `.Z` or `.gz` extension; we'll use `apache.tar` as the example throughout this section but you should substitute the real filename if it differs, of course). The `tar` file contains all the files needed by Apache and has to be untarred using this command:

```
tar xvf apache.tar
```

This will unpack the `tar` file and leave a whole bunch of separate files, mostly lowercase but a few with uppercase names like README. The README file tells you how to compile Apache when you are ready. Before compiling, you have to make sure the system is properly configured for your hardware and software. This is done through the Configuration file, which must be edited with an ASCII editor.

The Configuration file is a little awkward. There's a lot of subtlety and power in the Configuration file, most of which is much too complicated to explain in a section like this. Luckily, most of it you'll likely never need. The Configuration file is used by a special script called Configure, which generates a file called Makefile used by the `make` utility to compile Apache. There are four kinds of lines in this file:

- comments—any line starting with # is a comment.
- commands for `make`—lines that start with nothing.
- modules—any bunch of lines that start with the keyword Module.
- rules—any line that starts with the word Rule.

> **TIP**
>
> Don't directly edit the `Makefile` file. Any changes you make to this file are over-written and lost when you run the Configure script. The `Makefile` is generated automatically by the Configure tool by reading all the lines in the Configuration file.

In almost all cases for Linux, all you need do with the Configuration file is remove comment symbols from some lines or add them to others. All the rules and modules can be ignored until you get into tweaking the system. If you look at the Configuration file you'll see that most of the comments lead into a Module section. These comments can be removed to trigger the inclusion of that Module during the `Makefile` generation. The standard version of Apache for Linux has all the right choices already selected for you, but you can read through the Configuration file and see what the different options are.

> **TIP**
>
> While there is little harm in uncommenting most sections in the Configuration file, there are three you should leave commented. The `cern_meta_module` is used for backward compatibility with an old CERN server. The `dld_module` is used for dynamic-link loading of code and is not supported by Linux. Finally, `msql_auth_module` is for SQL management of large user password files and is essentially useless unless you are running Minerva SQL.

To start the generation of the `Makefile` from Configuration, you need to issue the `Configure` command (note that the uppercase letters are usually specific and must be typed if they appear that way when you do a directory listing). To run `Configure`, make sure you are logged in as `root` and simply type the utility's name:

```
Configure
```

You'll see a few messages, most likely just these two:

```
Using Configuration as config file
Configured for FreeBSD platform
```

Your second line may be a little different, depending on the version of Apache you obtained. To finish the process, you need to invoke the `make` utility (which depends on you having installed the C compiler and utilities):

```
make
```

By default, make looks for a file called Makefile and runs that. You may get error messages or simple status messages from the compiler (assuming it can be found), and then you'll get your shell prompt back. The end result of all this is a single executable file called httpd, which is the HTTP daemon. If you tried to run the httpd program, you may get a message that a file is missing. The file httpd is complaining about is the Apache run-time configuration file (usually called httpd.conf).

Editing the Configuration File

Whether you compiled the Apache daemon httpd yourself or it was supplied ready-to-go with a Linux CD-ROM, you now have to set up the configuration file which is usually called httpd.conf. Under the Apache directory there should be a subdirectory called conf. Inside this directory should be three configuration files called srm.conf-dist, access.conf-dist, and httpd.conf-dist. These files have to be copied to new filenames using these commands:

```
cp srm.conf.-dist srm.conf
cp access.conf-dist access.conf
cp httpd.conf-dist httpd.conf
```

Use any ASCII editor and open httpd.conf. The httpd.conf file contains general information about your server such as which port to use, the username to run as, and so on. Most of the information will be fine the way it is, but you can customize it if you want. Next, open srm.conf which is used to set up the document tree for the home pages as well as special HTML instructions. Again, most of the settings will be fine. Finally, the access.conf file is used to set the base levels of access to the system, and you can edit that to suit your needs or leave the default values.

> **TIP**
>
> Apache supplies three configuration files by default but it doesn't need to have three. In fact, it's often easier to do just that for convenience in customizing and configuring Apache. If you do use a single file, the file httpd.conf is the one to use. To tell Apache to ignore the access.conf and srm.conf files and place these commands in the httpd.conf file:
> ```
> AccessConfig /dev/null
> ResourceConfig /dev/null
> Delete the two files access.conf and srm.conf from the directory.
> ```

To start httpd with the configuration files you've prepared, use this command:

```
httpd -f path/httpd.conf
```

The path above should be the full path to your `httpd.conf` file. The `-f` option tells `httpd` where to read the server configuration file. This will start the `httpd` server daemon, which you can verify with the `ps` command.

Apache `httpd` Command Flags

You've seen one of the `httpd` command flags above. There are only a few flags involved with the `httpd` command. These are:

- `-d` specifies the document root directory
- `-f` specifies the server configuration file
- `-h` lists directives in force (from the Configuration file)
- `-v` shows the version number
- `-X` for debugging

A few other flags are added with each new release of Apache, but most are not used except for tweaking the system's behavior or debugging. For a full list of flags, enter the command

```
httpd -?
```

Or check for a man page or the documentation available from the `apache.org` Web site under the `/docs` directory.

Setting Up Apache for a Simple Web Site

To make things simple let's assume you want to use Apache to act as the server for your local area network. Machines on your network will use a browser to log into the Apache server for Web pages. This simple example shows how to set up Apache for a straightforward network and can be modified slightly for a Web server to the Internet.

We start by setting the root directory for the Web server. Let's assume we're setting up for a network called darkstar. The convention used by Apache is to call this `site.darkstar`. The configuration files for `site.darkstar` will be in a `conf` directory under the `site.darkstar` directory (such as `/usr/web/site.darkstar/conf`).

Set the document root directory for the site with the `-d` option of the `httpd` command:

```
httpd -d /usr/web/site.darkstar
```

All of your documents for the Web site should reside in the documentation root directory and subdirectories. For this you'll need HTML coding.

There's a lot more to Apache that lets you customize the server considerably but doing so is a little time-consuming and would take a hundred pages to explain. If you want to learn all there is to know about Apache, read the documents on the apache.org site or pick up one of the Apache books on the market.

Summary

Setting up your home page requires you to either use an HTML authoring tool or write HTML code directly into an editor. The HTML language is beyond the scope of this book, but you should find several good guides to HTML at your bookstore. HTML is rather easy to learn. With the information in this chapter, you should be able to set up your Web site to enable anyone on the Internet to connect to you. Enjoy the Web!

From here you can move to a number of different chapters depending on the type of information you are looking for. To learn about:

Writing CGI scripts for your Web page, see Chapter 52, "CGI Scripts."

HTML, the language of Web home pages, see Chapter 53, "HTML Programming Basics."

Java, which can be used to enhance the appearance and functionality of your Web pages, see Chapter 54, "Java and JavaScript Basics."

CGI Scripts

by Tim Parker

IN THIS CHAPTER

CHAPTER

52

If you do any work with the World Wide Web, you will come across the term CGI (Common Gateway Interface). While we can't hope to cover all you need to know about CGI in a chapter, we can look at what CGI is and does, why you want to use it, and how to go about using it.

If you get involved in doing more than simple Web page design (we look at HTML and Java in the next couple of chapters), you will eventually end up using CGI in some manner, usually to provide extra functionality to your Web pages. For that reason and so that you will know just what the term means, we need to look at CGI in a little bit of detail.

What Is CGI?

You now know what CGI stands for—Common Gateway Interface—but that doesn't help you to understand what CGI does. The name is a little misleading. Essentially, CGI is involved in an application that takes its starting commands from a Web page. For example, you might have a button on your Web page that launches a program to display statistics about how many people have visited your Web site. When the button is clicked, an HTML command starts up a program that does the calculation for you. CGI is involved in the interface between the HTML code and the application, and allows you to send information back and forth between the HTML code and other applications that aren't necessarily part of the Web page.

CGI does more than that, but it is usually involved in applications that interface between a Web page and a non-Web program. CGI programs don't even have to be started from a Web page, but they often are because a CGI program has a special set of environment conditions that involve interactions between components that are hard to simulate otherwise.

What does that really mean? When you run a Web page written in HTML, the Web server sets up some environment variables that control how the server operates. These environmental variables are used to control and pass information to programs, as well as many other operations. When a person clicks on a button on your Web page to launch an external application, these environmental variables are used to pass parameters to the program (such as who is starting the application, what time it is, and so on). When the application sends information back to the Web server, that information is passed back through variables.

So, when we talk about CGI programming, we really mean writing programs that involve an interface between HTML and some other program. CGI deals with the interface between the Web server and the application (hence the "interface" in the name).

What's so exciting about this? In reality, the number of behaviors you can code on a Web page in HTML is somewhat limited. CGI lets you push past those barriers to code just about anything you want and have it interact properly with the Web page. So if you have custom statistics you need to run on your Web page based on a client's data, you can do it through CGI, with CGI passing the information to the number crunching application, and then passing the results back to HTML for display on the Web page, to take a simple example. In fact, there's a whole mess of things you can do on even the simplest Web page when you start using CGI, and that is why it is so popular.

The CGI is usually built in to the Web server, although there is no requirement that it exists in all Web servers. Luckily, almost every server on the market (except the very early servers and a few stripped down ones) contain the CGI code. The latest versions of the Web servers from NCSA, Netscape, CERN, and many others all have CGI built in.

CGI and HTML

In order to run a CGI application from a Web page, you make a request to the Web server to run the CGI application. This request is made through a particular method that is responsible for invoking CGI programs. (A *method* is a procedure or function.) Many methods are built into *HTTP* (*HyperText Transfer Protocol*, the protocol used by the World Wide Web), and the method used to call the CGI application depends on the type of information you want to transfer. We'll come back to methods in a moment after we look at how the CGI code is embedded in the HTML for the Web page.

As the next chapter explains, HTML involves the use of a bunch of *tags*. To call a CGI program, a tag is used that gives the name of the program and the text that appears on the Web page when the HTML code is executed. For example, the following HTML tag displays the message "Click here to display statistics" on the Web page:

```
<a href="crunch_numbers"> Click here to display statistics </a>
```

When the user clicks there, the program called `crunch_numbers` is called. (The `<a>` and `</a>` HTML tags are *anchor* tags, which indicate a link to something else. Wherever the tag is positioned in the rest of the HTML code dictates exactly how the page will look on a Web browser.)

As you will see when we look at HTML in the next chapter, you can even use hyperlinks to call a program on another machine by supplying the domain name. For example, the following HTML tag displays the message "Display Statistics" on whatever Web page the code runs on:

```
<a href="www.tpci.com/stats.cgi"> Display Statistics </a>
```

When it is selected by the user, the program `stats.cgi` on the Web server `www.tpci.com` is located and run. This might be across the country—it doesn't matter to either HTML or CGI, as long as the reference can be resolved.

Three kinds of methods are usually used to call a CGI application: the `GET`, `HEAD`, and `POST` methods (all are part of HTTP). They differ slightly in when you use them. We can look at each briefly so you know what they do and when they are used.

A `GET` method is used when the CGI application is to receive data in an environment variable called `QUERY_STRING`. The application reads this variable and decodes it, interpreting what it needs to perform its actions. The `GET` method is usually used when the CGI application has to take information but doesn't change anything.

The `HEAD` method is much the same as the `GET` method, except the server only transmits HTTP headers to the client. Any information in the body of the message is ignored. This can be useful when you need to handle only a user ID, for example.

The `POST` method is much more flexible and uses `stdin` (standard input) to receive data. A variable called `CONTENT_LENGTH` tells the application how much of the data coming into the standard input is important so it knows when all the data has arrived. The `POST` method was developed to allow changes to the server, but many programmers use `POST` for almost every task to avoid truncation of URLs that can occur with `GET`.

A number of environment variables are used by CGI, most of which are covered in much greater detail in CGI programming books. Describing all the variables here without showing you how to use them would be a bit of a waste.

CGI and Perl

If you do get into CGI programming, you will probably find that most of it is done in the Perl programming language (which we looked at in Chapter 28, "Perl"). CGI programming can be done in any language (and many Web page designers like C, C++, or Visual Basic because they are more familiar with those languages), but Perl seems to have become a favorite among UNIX Web programmers.

The reasons for Perl's popularity are easy to understand when you know the language: It's powerful, quite simple, and easy to work with. Perl is also portable, which lets you develop CGI programs on one machine and move them without change to another platform.

There are a lot of Perl CGI scripts to be found on the Web. A quick look with a search engine such as AltaVista will usually show hundreds of examples that can be downloaded and studied. For example, one of the most commonly used Perl scripts is called GuestBook. Its role is to allow users of your Web site to sign into a guest book and leave a comment about your Web pages. Usually, the guest book records the user's name and email address, location (usually a city and state or province), and any comments they want to make. Guest books are a good way to get feedback on your Web pages and also to make them a little more friendly.

When run, the GuestBook CGI program displays a form that the user can fill in and then updates your server's database for you. A number of versions of GuestBook can be found around the Web, but a sample browser display showing the GuestBook Perl CGI script is shown in Figure 52.1.

FIGURE 52.1.

A sample GuestBook program sending data to a Perl CGI script requesting information about the

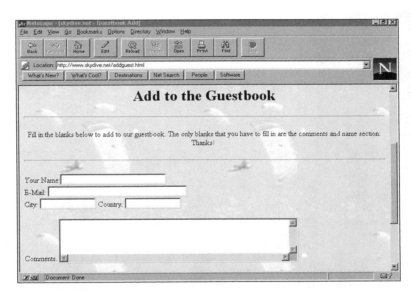

Each GuestBook Perl script looks slightly different, but the one shown in Figure 52.1 is typical. The information entered by the user is stored in the server's database for the administrator to read.

Figure 52.2 shows another Web page with a bunch of sample CGI programs launched from a menu. The selection for the domain name lookup shown in Figure 52.2 results in the CGI application doing a bunch of standard HTTP requests to the server and client, displaying the results shown in Figure 52.3. As you can see, the output shown in Figure 52.3 is in standard font and character size, and there has been no real attempt to produce fancy formatting. This is often adequate for simple CGI applications.

FIGURE 52.2.

A Web page with some sample CGI applications, a mix of Perl and C, with the domain name CGI sample ready to launch.

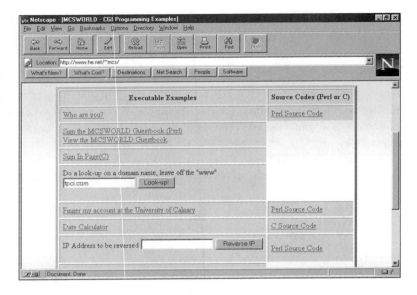

FIGURE 52.3.

The domain name lookup Perl CGI script results in this screen for the author's machine.

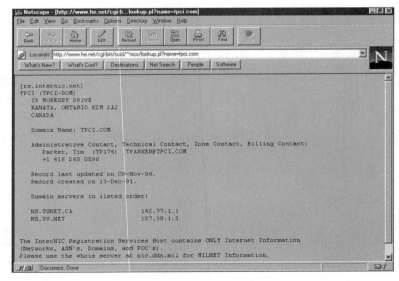

The Perl CGI scripts are not complex affairs. The example (Who Are You?) in the demonstration page shown in Figure 52.3 looks up your information through an HTTP request. The Perl code for this is shown in Figure 52.4, displayed through Netscape. As you can see, there are only a few lines of code involved. Any Perl programmer can write this type of CGI application quickly.

FIGURE **52.4.**

The Perl source code for the Who Are You? application shown in Figure 52.2.

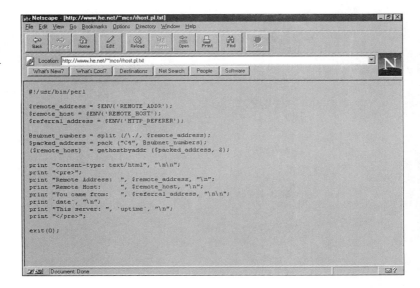

```
#!/usr/bin/perl

$remote_address = $ENV{'REMOTE_ADDR'};
$remote_host = $ENV{'REMOTE_HOST'};
$referral_address = $ENV{'HTTP_REFERER'};

@subnet_numbers = split (/\./, $remote_address);
$packed_address = pack ("C4", @subnet_numbers);
($remote_host)  = gethostbyaddr ($packed_address, 2);

print "Content-type: text/html", "\n\n";
print "<pre>";
print "Remote Address: ", $remote_address, "\n";
print "Remote Host:    ", $remote_host, "\n";
print "You came from:  ", $referral_address, "\n\n";
print `date`, "\n";
print "This server: ", `uptime`, "\n";
print "</pre>";

exit(0);
```

52

CGI SCRIPTS

Summary

CGI programming is easy to do, especially with Perl, and adds a great deal of flexibility to your applications. When you feel comfortable writing HTML code and developing your own Web pages (which we can't explain in this book because of space restrictions), you should try your hand at CGI programming and really add some zing to your Web site. We've mentioned some programming languages in this chapter that you may not have worked with or that you want more information about. Here are some useful chapters for you to read:

> To learn about the Perl programming language, which is perfect for writing CGI scripts, see Chapter 28, "Perl."
>
> To learn about using C to write CGI scripts, see Chapter 26, "Programming in C."
>
> To learn about backing up your system so you don't lose all the CGI scripts you've created, read Chapter 45, "Backups."

## CHAPTER 53

HTML Programming Basics

by Tim Parker

IN THIS CHAPTER

Having a Web server with nothing for content is useless, so you need to set up the information you will share through your Web system. This begins with Uniform Resource Locators (URLs), which are addresses to file locations. Anyone using your service only has to know the URL. You don't need to have anything fancy. If you don't have a special home page, anyone connecting to your system will get the contents of the Web root directory's `index.html` file, or failing that, a directory listing of the Web root directory. That's pretty boring, though, and most users want fancy home pages. To write a home page, you need to use HTML (HyperText Markup Language).

A home page is like a main menu. Many users may not ever see it because they can enter into any of the subdirectories on your system, or obtain files from another Web system through a hyperlink, without ever seeing your home page. However, many users want to start at the top, and that's where your home page comes in. A home page file is usually called `index.html`. It is usually at the top of your Web source directories.

Writing an HTML document is not too difficult. The language uses a set of tags to indicate how the text is to be treated (such as headlines, body text, figures, and so on). The tricky part of HTML is getting the tags in the right place, without extra material on a line. HTML is rather strict about its syntax, so errors must be avoided to prevent problems.

In the early days of the Web, all documents were written with simple text editors. As the Web expanded, dedicated Web editors that understand HTML and the use of tags began to appear. Their popularity has driven developers to produce dozens of editors, filters, and utilities—all aimed at making a Web site producer's life easier (as well as to ensure that the HTML language is properly used). HTML editors are available for many operating systems.

HTML Authoring Tools

You can write HTML documents in many ways: You can use an ASCII editor, a word processor, or a dedicated HTML tool. The choice of which method you use depends on personal preference and your confidence in HTML coding, as well as which tools you can easily obtain. Because many HTML-specific tools have checking routines or filters to verify that your documents are correctly laid out and formatted, they can be appealing. They also tend to be easier to use than non-HTML editors. On the other hand, if you are a veteran programmer or writer, you may want to stick with your favorite editor and use a filter or syntax checker afterwards.

You can use any ASCII editor to write HTML pages, including simple screen-oriented editors based on vi or emacs. They all enable you to enter tags into a page of text, but the tags are treated as words with no special meaning. There is no validity checking performed by simple editors, because they simply don't understand HTML. There are some extensions for emacs and similar full-screen editors that provide a simple template check, but they are not rigorous in enforcing HTML styles.

If you wish to use a plain editor, you should carefully check your document for the valid use of tags. One of the easiest methods of checking a document is to import it into an HTML editor that has strong HTML tag checking. Another easy method is to simply call up the document on your Web browser and carefully study its appearance.

You can obtain a dedicated HTML authoring package from some sites, although they are not as common for Linux as they are for DOS and Windows (where there are literally dozens of such tools). If you are running both operating systems, you can always develop your HTML documents in Windows, and then import them to Linux. There are several popular HTML tools for Windows, such as HTML Assistant, HTMLed, and HoTMetaL. A few of the WYSIWYG editors are also available for X, and hence run under Linux, such as HoTMetaL. Some HTML authoring tools are fully WYSIWYG, while others are character-based. Most offer strong verification systems for generated HTML code.

53

PROGRAMMING
BASICS

HTML

Developing Web Pages on Windows

As mentioned earlier there are a lot more tools available on Windows machines than Linux for developing HTML code. You can easily develop the code on your Windows system then move it across to Linux, if you run both machines. Windows- and DOS-based HTML tools come in three varieties: WYSIWYG HTML editors, non-WYSIWYG HTML editors, and add-in converters for documentation applications such as Word for Windows or WordPerfect.

Probably the most popular non-WYSIWYG HTML editor for Microsoft Windows is HTML Assistant. It is a text editor with a few additional features and a graphical interface that lets you insert the most commonly used HTML tags quickly. It allows you to open multiple windows simultaneously with cut-and-paste between them.

> **TIP**
>
> To obtain a copy of HTML Assistant through FTP, log in through anonymous FTP to `ftp.cuhk.hk` and check the directory `/pub/www/windows/util` for the file `htmlasst.zip`.

HTML Assistant has one major limitation: File sizes cannot be larger than 32KB. Large Web pages cannot be written with HTML Assistant unless you do them in sections and then combine them by using another editor. If you attempt to edit a file larger than 32KB or write enough material to exceed that limit, you can get "Out of Memory" errors and potentially lose some work.

HTML Assistant has good on-line help as well as a few useful features, like the capability to automatically instruct a Web browser to load the document you are working with so you can see how it looks properly formatted. Using this feature, you can flip between the code and the formatted screen easily, ensuring the layout is correct. This helps alleviate the problem of having a non-WYSIWYG editor.

HTML Assistant also helps you construct URLs. It maintains a list of the URLs you use, too, so jumping to any of them is quite rapid.

HTMLed is another shareware HTML editor for Microsoft Windows. It is a fast editor with full foreign character tag support and the capability to read and save in either DOS or UNIX formats. A neat feature of HTMLed is the capability to convert a URL in a MOSAIC.INI file into an HTML document while retaining the original structure. It is also relatively easy to convert ASCII documents to HTML with HTMLed, as compared to HTML Assistant.

> **TIP**
>
> To obtain a copy of HTMLed by anonymous FTP, connect to `ftp.cuhk.hk` and change to the directory `/pub/www/windows/util`. The file is `htmed10.zip` (later versions may increment to number).

HTMLed doesn't have multiple rows of buttons for tags as HTML Assistant offers. Instead, it uses a set of pull-down menus and a customizable toolbar for tags. Several toolbars can be created, with tags embedded as icons. The toolbars can "float," meaning that they can always move on top of the current document. The current version of HTMLed has no on-line help, although help is planned for a future release.

HTMLed has a clever insertion process for tags that knows the format and prevents multiple tags on a line (when illegal). This helps prevent one of the most common HTML tag errors. Like HTML Assistant, HTMLed has a button linking to a browser for rapid comparison of the code and the formatted document.

Softquad's HoTMetaL is an almost-WYSIWYG editor that is probably the preferable editor for anyone starting to write HTML pages. HoTMetaL is available for Windows and some UNIX platforms. A reduced functionality version (which is still pretty powerful) is provided as freeware, while a full-blown commercial version (HoTMetaL Pro) is also available from Softquad.

TIP

A copy of HoTMetaL can be picked up at most utility sites like NCSA and CERN. Try the Web page http://info.cren.ch/hypertext/WWW/Tools and the file HoTMetaL.html.

HoTMetaL is an integrated editor and display utility, which, while not quite WYSIWYG, provides you with a good view of what your final document format will look like. HoTMetaL almost forces you to write proper HTML code, as it checks for proper tags at the start and end of the document, and only allows tags to be inserted where legal. (This is a very useful timesaver for new HTML users.)

HoTMetaL can check your code for you and display messages about problems with tags (usually encountered when a document from another editor is imported, because HoTMetaL won't allow you to make the mistake in the first place). Unfortunately, the line in the document that HoTMetaL fingers as the guilty line is not always the one causing the problem.

HoTMetaL does have a couple of drawbacks. Any images (.GIF files) that are added to a document are not visible within the HoTMetaL window (you must load a Web viewer to see the results). Also, any document that doesn't conform to HTML code practices can't be loaded or conform to a set of rules that do not enforce proper style. This can be a problem with older HTML pages.

An alternative to using a dedicated editor for HTML documents is to enhance an existing WYSIWYG word processor to handle HTML properly. The most commonly targeted word processor for these extensions is Word for Windows, Word Perfect, and Word for DOS. Several extension products are available, of varying degrees of complexity. Most run under Windows, although a few have been ported to Linux.

The advantage to using one of these extensions is that you retain a familiar editor and make use of the near-WYSIWYG features it can provide for HTML documents. Although it can't show you the final document in Web format, it can be close enough to prevent all but the most minor problems.

CU_HTML is a template for Microsoft's Word for Windows that gives an almost WYSIWYG view of HTML documents. Graphically, CU_HTML looks much the same as Word, but with a new toolbar and pull-down menu item. CU_HTML provides a number of different styles and a toolbar of oft-used tasks. Tasks such as linking documents are easy, as are most tasks that tend to worry new HTML document writers. Dialog boxes are used for many tasks, simplifying the interface considerably.

The only major disadvantage to CU_HTML is that it can't be used to edit existing HTML documents if they are not in Word format. When CU_HTML creates an HTML document, there are two versions produced, one in HTML and the other as a Word .DOC file. Without both, the document can't be edited. An existing document can be imported, but it loses all the tags.

Like CU_HTML, ANT_HTML is an extension to Word. There are some advantages and disadvantages of ANT_HTML over CU_HTML. The documentation and help is better with ANT_HTML, and the toolbar is much better. It also has automatic insertion of opening and closing tags as needed.

HTML Development on Linux

One system that has gained popularity among Linux users is tkWWW. tkWWW is a tool for the Tcl language and its Tk extension for X. tkWWW is a combination of a Web browser and a near-WYSIWYG HTML editor. Although originally UNIX based, tkWWW has been ported to several other platforms, including Windows and Macintosh.

> **NOTE**
>
> tkWWW can be obtained through anonymous FTP to harbor.ecn.purdue.edu in the directory /pub/tcl/extensions. Copies of Tcl and Tk can be found in several sites depending on the platform required, although most distributions of Linux have Tcl and Tk included in the distribution set. As a starting point, try anonymous FTP to ftp.aud.alcatel.com in the directory tcl/extensions or check the official Tcl/Tk page at http://www.sunscript.com.

When you create a Web page with tkWWW in editor mode, you can then flip modes to browser to see the same page properly formatted. In editor mode, most of the formatting is correct, but the tags are left visible. This makes for fast development of a Web page.

Unfortunately, tkWWW must rely on Tk for its windowing, which tends to slow things down a bit on average processors. Also, the browser aspect of tkWWW is not impressive, using standard Tk frames. However, as a prototyping tool, tkWWW is very attractive, especially if you know the Tcl language.

Another option is to use an HTML filter. HTML filters are tools that let you take a document produced with any kind of editor (including ASCII text editors) and convert the document to HTML. Filters are useful when you work in an editor that has a proprietary format, such as Word.

HTML filters are attractive if you want to continue working in your favorite editor and simply want a utility to convert your document with tags to HTML. Filters tend to be fast and easy to work with, because they take a filename as input and generate an HTML output file. The degree of error checking and reporting varies with the tool.

There are filters available for most types of documents, many of which are available directly for Linux, or as source code that can be recompiled without modification under Linux. Word for Windows and Word for DOS documents can be converted to HTML with the CU_HTML and ANT_HTML extensions mentioned earlier. A few stand-alone conversion utilities have also begun to appear. The utility WPTOHTML converts Word Perfect documents to HTML. WPTOHTML is a set of macros for Word Perfect versions 5.1 and 6.0. The Word Perfect filter can also be used with other word processor formats that Word Perfect can import.

FrameMaker and FrameBuilder documents can be converted to HTML format with the tool FM2HTML. FM2HTML is a set of scripts for converting Frame documents to HTML, while preserving hypertext links and tables. It also handles GIF files without a problem. Because Frame documents are platform independent, Frame documents developed on a PC or Macintosh could be moved to the Linux platform and FM2HTML executed there.

> **NOTE**
>
> A copy of FM2HTML is available by anonymous FTP from `bang.nta.no` in the directory `/pub`. The UNIX set is called `fm2html.tar.v.0.n.m.Z`.

LaTeX and TeX files can be converted to HTML with several different utilities. There are quite a few Linux-based utilities available, including LATEXTOHTML, which can even handle inline LaTeX equations and links. For simpler documents, the utility VULCAN-IZE is faster but can't handle mathematical equations. Both LATEXTOHTML and VUL-CANIZE are Perl scripts.

> **NOTE**
>
> LATEXTOHTML is available through anonymous FTP from `ftp.tex.ac.uk` in the directory `pub/archive/support` as the file `latextohtml`. VULCANIZE can be obtained from the Web site `http://www.cis.upenn.edu/~mjd/vulcanize.html`.

RTFTOHTML is a common utility for converting RTF format documents to HTML. Many word processors handle RTF formats, so an RTF document can be saved from your favorite word processor and then RTFTOHTML run to convert the files.

> **NOTE**
>
> RTFTOHTML is available through `http://www.w3.org/hypertext/www/tools/rtftohtml-2.6.html`.

Maintaining HTML

Once you have written a Web document and it is available to the world, your job doesn't end. Unless your document is a simple text file, you will have links to other documents or Web servers embedded. These links must be verified at regular intervals. Also, the integrity of your Web pages should be checked at intervals, to ensure that the flow of the document from your home page is correct.

There are several utilities available to help you check links and also to scan the Web for other sites or documents you may want to provide a hyperlink to. These utilities tend to go by a number of names, such as robot, spider, or wanderer. They are all programs that move across the Web automatically, creating a list of Web links that you can access. (Spiders are similar to the Archie and Veronica tools for the Internet, although neither of these cover the Web.)

Although they are often thought of as utilities for users only (to get a list of sites to try), spiders and their kin are useful for document authors, too, because they show potentially useful and interesting links. One of the best known spiders is the World Wide Web Worm, or WWWW. WWWW enables you to search for keywords or create a Boolean search and can cover titles, documents, and several other search types (including a search of all known HTML pages).

A similarly useful spider is WebCrawler, which is similar to WWWW except it can scan entire documents for matches of any keywords. It displays the result in an ordered list from closest match to least likely match.

> **NOTE**
>
> A copy of World Wide Web Worm can be obtained from `http://www.cs.colorado.edu/home/mcbryan/WWWW.html`. WebCrawler is available from `http://www.biotech.washington.edu/WebCrawler/WebCrawler.html`.

A common problem with HTML documents as they age is that links that point to files or servers may no longer exist (because either the locations or the documents have changed). It is therefore good practice to validate the hyperlinks in a document on a regular basis. A popular hyperlink analyzer is HTML_ANALYZER. It examines each hyperlink and the contents of the hyperlink to ensure that they are consistent. HTML_ANALYZER functions by examining a document for all links, and then creating a text file that has a list of the links in it. HTML_ANALYZER uses the text files to compare the actual link content to what it should be.

HTML_ANALYZER actually does three tests: It validates the availability of the documents pointed to by hyperlinks (called validation); it looks for hyperlink contents that occur in the database but are not themselves hyperlinks (called completeness); and it looks for a one-to-one relation between hyperlinks and the contents of the hyperlink (called consistency). Any deviations are listed for the user.

HTML_ANALYZER users should have a good familiarity with HTML, their operating system, and the use of command-line driven analyzers. The tool must be compiled using the make utility prior to execution. There are several directories that must be created prior to running HTML_ANALYZER, and when it runs, it creates several temporary files that are not cleaned up. Therefore, HTML_ANALYZER is not a good utility for a novice.

HTML Programming Basics

HyperText Markup Language (HTML) is quite an easy language to learn and work with, and as new versions have been introduced over the last few years it has become quite powerful, too. We can't hope to teach you HTML in a single chapter in this book, but we can give you an overview of the language and how to use the basics to produce a simple Web page or two.

If you've seen a Web page before, you have seen the results of HTML. HTML is the language used to describe how the Web page will look when you access the site. The server transfers the HTML instructions to your browser, which converts those HTML lines of code into the text, images, and layouts you see on the page. A Web browser is usually used to access HTML code, but there are other tools that can do the same. There are a wide variety of browsers out there, starting with the granddaddy of them all, NCSA's Mosaic. Netscape's Navigator is the most widely used browser right now, although Microsoft is making inroads slowly with its Explorer. The browser you use doesn't matter, as they mostly do the same job—display the HTML code they receive from the server. A browser is almost always acting as a client, requesting information from the server.

The HTML language is based on another language called SGML (Standard Generalized Markup Language), which is used to describe the structure of a document and allow for better migration from one documenting tool to another. HTML does not describe how a page will look; it's not a page description language like PostScript. Instead, HTML describes the structure of a document. It will indicate which text is a heading, which is the body of the document, and where pictures should go. However, it does not give explicit instructions on how the page will look; that's up to the browser.

Why use HTML? Primarily because it is a small language, and so can transfer instructions over a network quickly. HTML does have limitations because of its size, but newer versions of the language are expanding the capabilities a little. The other major advantage ofo HTML is one most people don't think about: It is device independent. It doesn't matter what machine you run; a Web browser will take the same HTML code and translate it for the platform. The browser is the part that is device dependent. That means you can use HTML to write a Web page and not care what machine is used to read it.

What Does HTML Look Like?

HTML code is pretty straightforward, as you will see. For the most part it consists of a bunch of "tags" which describe the beginning and ending of a structure element (such as a heading, paragraph, picture, table, and so on). For each element, there should be a beginning and ending tag. A sample HTML page is shown in Figure 53.1. Don't worry about understanding it all now, as you will see this code built up in this chapter. For now, you need only see that there are beginning and ending tags around each element in the structure. (All of the screen shots used in this chapter are taken from either a Windows 95 or Windows 3.11 machine accessing the Linux server on which we are writing the HTML code through an Ethernet network. The browser is NCSA's Mosaic.)

FIGURE 53.1.

A simple example of HTML code.

A couple of important things to know about tags as we get started: They are case insensitive (so you don't have to be careful about matching case) and they are almost always paired into beginning and ending tags. The most common errors on Web pages are mismatched or unterminated tags. In many cases, the Web page will appear OK, but there may be severe formatting problems. A quick scan of your HTML code will help solve these types of problems.

> **TIP**
>
> Not all HTML tags have a beginning and ending tag. A few are single ended, meaning they usually have just a beginning. Some others are called containers, because they hold extra information. These are not always tagged at both ends.

Tags are written in angle brackets. These brackets signal to the browser that an HTML instruction is enclosed. A sample HTML code element looks like this:

```
<start_tag_name> text text text <end_tag_name>
```

where `<start_tag_name>` and `<end_tag_name>` are the starting and ending tags for the text in the middle. The type of tag describes how the text will look. For example, if they are heading tags, the text will appear larger than normal body text and may be bolded or highlighted in some way.

How do you write HTML code? There are several ways to do it. The easiest is to use any ASCII editor. Make sure you don't save HTML documents in a proprietary format like Word documents, as a Web browser can't understand anything but ASCII. Some specialized HTML editors are available which feature pull-down lists of tags and preview screens. These can be handy when you are working with very large Web pages, but for most people a simple editor is more than enough to get started with.

Starting an HTML Document

An HTML document usually begins with an instruction that identifies the document as HTML. This is a tag called <HTML> and is used by the browser to indicate the start of HTML instructions. Here's a sample chunk of code from a Web page:

```
<HTML>
<HEAD>
<TITLE> This is my Web Page! Welcome! </TITLE></HEAD>
<BODY>
<H1> This is the first heading on my page. </H1>
This is a bunch of text that is written on my home page.  I hope you like
it.
</BODY>
</HTML>
```

You can see that the first and last tags, <HTML> and </HTML>, mark the start and end of the HTML code. The slash in the second tag means the end of the structure element. These tags should be at the start and end of each HTML document you write. The <HEAD> and </HEAD> tags mark a prologue to the file and are often used for the title and key words that show up under Web search tools. There are only a few tags that are allowed inside <HEAD> tags. <TITLE> and </TITLE> give the title of the document. The <BODY> and </BODY> tags mark the start and end of the document's main body. The <H1> and </H1> tags are for a heading on the page.

This code can be read by any browser and is shown in Figure 53.2. As you can see, the title material is not displayed on the page itself, only the material between the body tags. The title is used at the top of the browser to show the page you are logged into. This acts as an identifier.

The format of the code shown above is line-by-line, but this is just for readability. You can write everything on one long line, if you want, as HTML ignores whitespace unless told otherwise. However, for debugging and rereading purposes, it is handy to keep the code cleanly organized.

FIGURE 53.2.

The sample HTML code displayed under Internet Explorer.

Here are a few more comments about the tags we've used. The `<TITLE>` tag always goes inside the header tags (`<HEAD>` and `</HEAD>`) to describe the contents of the page. You should have only a single title for your page. There can't be other tags inside the head tags. It is useful to pick a short, descriptive title for your documents so others who see it will know what they are accessing.

The `<BODY>` and `</BODY>` tags are used to enclose the main contents of your Web page, and there will probably be only one pair of them. All text and contents (links, graphics, tables, and so on) are enclosed between body tags.

There are several levels of heading tags, each of which is like a subheading of the one higher up. The heading we used in the code above is `<H1>`, which is the highest heading level. You can structure your document with many heading levels, if you want. For example, you could write this bit of code:

```
<HTML>
<HEAD>
<TITLE> This is my Web Page! Welcome! </TITLE></HEAD>
<BODY>
<H1> This is an H1. </H1>
This is a bunch of text.
<H2> This is an H2 </H2>
This is more text.
<H3> This is an H3 </H3>
This is text about the H3 heading.
<H3> This is another H3 </H3>
Here's more text about the H3 heading.
<H2> This is yet another H2 </H2>
Text to do with H2 goes here.
</BODY>
</HTML>
```

This code is shown in a browser in Figure 53.3. As you can see, the levels of heading are slightly different, with the higher headings (lower numbers) more distinctive and bolder. This lets you separate your pages into logical categories, with a heading or subheading for each. You can use these headings just as we do when writing a book: H1s can contain

H2s, H3s go below H2s, and so on. There are no rules about mixing headings (you could use only H3s, for example), but common sense usually dictates how to structure your page.

FIGURE 53.3.

Headings with different tags have different appearances.

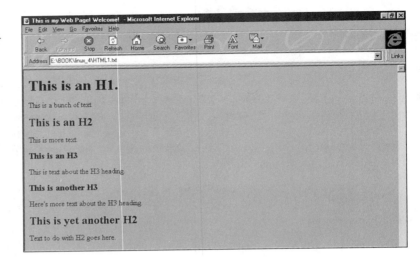

Paragraphs

What about paragraphs? There are several ways to handle paragraphs, and the rules have changed with each version of HTML. The easiest approach, though, is to use the <P> and </P> tags to mark each individual paragraphs. For example, this code has three paragraph tag pairs used:

```
<HTML>
<HEAD>
<TITLE> This is my Web Page! Welcome! </TITLE></HEAD>
<BODY>
<H1> This is an H1. </H1>
<P> This is the first paragraph.  It is a really interesting paragraph and
should be read several times because of its content. </P>
<P> Another paragraph.  It's not quite as exciting as the first, but then
it's hard to write really exciting paragraphs this late at night. </P>
<P> The closing paragraph has to be strong to make you feel good.  Oh
well, we can't always meet your expectations, can we? </P>
</BODY>
</HTML>
```

The appearance of this code in the browser is shown in Figure 53.4. Note how each paragraph is distinct and has some whitespace between it and the next paragraph. What happens if you leave out the <P> and </P> tags? Since browsers ignore whitespace including carriage returns, the text is run together as shown in Figure 53.5. So, you should use <P> and </P> tags to separate paragraphs on your page. Remember that putting lots of blank lines between paragraphs in your HTML code doesn't matter. Browsers will ignore them and run everything together.

FIGURE 53.4.

The use of paragraph tags separates text into discrete chunks with whitespace between them.

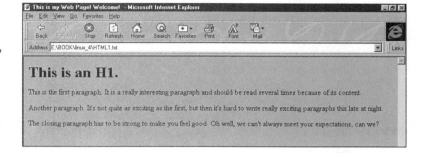

FIGURE 53.5.

Without paragraph tags, all the text is run together.

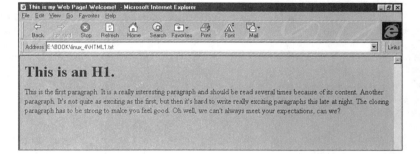

NOTE

Strictly speaking, you don't need </P> tags to indicate the end of a paragraph as another <P> would indicate the start of a new one. The <P> tag is one example of an open-ended tag, one that doesn't need a closure. However, it is good programming practice to close the pairs.

What about comments in HTML code? You might want to embed some comments to yourself about who wrote the code, what it does, when you did it, and so on. The way to write a comment into HTML code is like this:

```
<! - This is a comment ->
```

The comment has angle brackets around it, an exclamation mark as the first character, and dashes before and after the comment text. Here's an example of some HTML code with comments in it:

```
<HTML>
<!- Written 12/12/95 by TJP, v 1.23->
<HEAD>
<TITLE> This is my Web Page! Welcome! </TITLE></HEAD>
<BODY>
<H1> This is an H1. </H1>
<!- This section is about the important first para tag ->
<P> This is the first paragraph. </P>
</BODY>
</HTML>
```

Hyperlinks

Links to other places and documents are an important part of the World Wide Web. Links are quite easy to write in HTML. They begin with the link tag `<A>` and end with `</A>`. This is an example of an anchor tag, so named because it creates an anchor for links in your document.

The `<A>` tag is different from the tags we've seen so far in that it has some more text inside the angle brackets. Here's a sample link in a document:

```
<A HREF="page_2.html">Go to Page 2</A>
```

In this example, the text between the two tags is what is displayed on the screen, so the user would see the text "Go to Page 2" underlined and usually in another color to indicate it is a link. If the user clicked on it, the HREF reference in the `<A>` tag is read and the document `page_2.html` is read into the browser. HREF means Hypertext Reference, and gives the name of a file or a URL that the link points to.

You can use links either in the body of text or as a separate item on a menu, for example. This code below shows a link in a paragraph and one on a line by itself:

```
<HTML>
<HEAD>
<TITLE> This is my Web Page! Welcome! </TITLE></HEAD>
<BODY>
<H1> This is the first heading on my page. </H1>
<P>This is a bunch of text that is written on my home page.  I hope you
like it. If you would like to know more about me, choose <A
HREF="about_me".html>Tell me more about You</A> and I'll tout my virtues
for you. </P>
<P><A HREF="biblio.html">See Bibliography</A>
</BODY>
</HTML>
```

When displayed in a browser, it looks like Figure 53.6. Each link is underlined in the text to show it is a link. (Some browsers change the color of the link text; others do different things as well.)

FIGURE 53.6.

A document with two links in it.

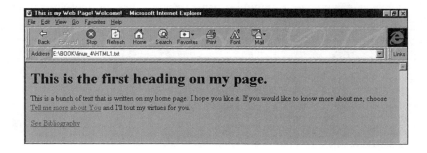

When you are specifying a link to a filename, you must be sure to specify the filename properly. There are two ways of doing this: relative and absolute. Absolute simply means you give the full path name, while relative means from the document's current location. For example, this is an absolute path name used in a link:

```
<A HREF="\usr\tparker\html_source\home.html">
```

Relative path references are from the current location and can use valid directory movement commands. These are valid examples of relative paths in a link:

```
<A HREF="..\home.htm">
<A HREF="../../html_source/home.html">
```

Links to other URLs are much the same as a link to a document, except you give the URL after HREF. For example, this is a link to the Yahoo! home page:

```
<A HREF="http://www.yahoo.com">Go to Yahoo!</A>
```

You can have as many links in your documents as you want. It helps to make the link description as useful as possible so users don't end up at pages or sites they didn't want to access. If you are linking to other sites, you should occasionally check to make sure that the link is still valid. Many home pages change location, or disappear from the Web, so links should be verified to avoid misdirection.

Lists

HTML lets you use a few different formats of lists, such as ordered, numbered, labeled, and bulleted. The lists are surrounded by tags such as <OL> and </OL> (for ordered list) or <MENU> and </MENU> (for menus). Each item in the list has its own tag <LI> or

something similar to separate it from other items. There are a few special types of list tags for glossaries and similar purposes, but we'll ignore them for the purposes of this HTML overview.

Here's an example of a simple list using the <UL> tags for unordered lists:

```
<HTML>
<HEAD>
<TITLE> This is my Web Page! Welcome! </TITLE></HEAD>
<BODY>
<H1> This is a list of some books I have written. </H1>
Here are the books I wrote on last summer's vacation.
<UL>
<LI> Mosquitos Bug me
<LI> Fun with Bears
<LI> What to eat when you have no food
<LI> Why is it raining on my vacation?
<LI> Getting lost in three easy lessons
</UL>
</BODY>
</HTML>
```

An unordered list is like a normal list, except it has bullets and is not marked by any special numbering scheme. This code is shown in a browser in Figure 53.7, where you can see the way the bullets line up and the list is presented.

FIGURE 53.7.

An unordered list in HTML.

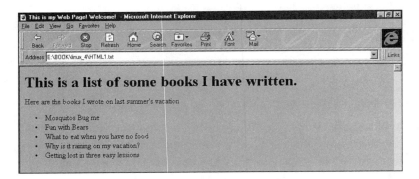

The same code could be written with <OL> and </OL> tags for an ordered list. An ordered list has numbers in front of them, as shown in Figure 53.8. This is the same code as shown above, except we changed <UL> tags to <OL> tags.

FIGURE 53.8.

An ordered list uses numbers instead of bullets.

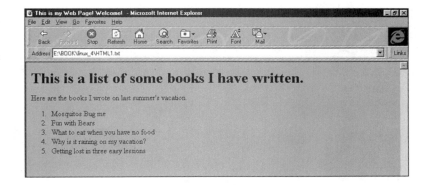

Changing Character Appearances

Character tags can be used to change the appearance of text on the screen. There are a few character tags in HTML, including styles (such as italics, boldface, and so on) and logical (which indicate emphasis, code, or other types of text). Forcing character type changes with style tags is usually not a good idea since different browsers may not present the text the way you want to. However, you can use them if you know your server will be used only with a particular type of browser, and you know how the text will look on that browser.

Logical tags are a much better choice as browsers can implement them across platforms. They let the individual browser decide how italics, for example, will look. For that reason, we'll concentrate on logical tags. There are eight logical tags in general use:

- `<CITE>` - a citation
- `<CODE>` - code sample (Courier font)
- `<DFN>` - highlights a definition
- `<EM>` - indicates emphasis, usually italics
- `<KBD>` - keyboard input to be typed by the user
- `<SAMP>` - example text, much like `<CODE>`
- `<STRONG>` - strong emphasis, usually boldface
- `<VAR>` - a variable name to be displayed as italics or underlined (usually in code)

The following code shows an example of the use of some of these styles, and the resultant Web page is shown in Figure 53.9.

```
<HTML>
<HEAD>
<TITLE> This is my Web Page! Welcome! </TITLE></HEAD>
```

```
<BODY>
<H1> This is an H1. </H1>
<P> This is a sample entry that should be <EM> emphasized using EM</EM>
and with
the <STRONG> use of Strong </STRONG> emphasis. </P>
</P>
</BODY>
</HTML>
```

FIGURE 53.9.

The use of logical character tags changes the way text appears.

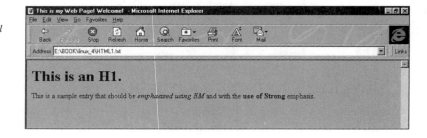

As you can see, this browser (Mosaic) interprets the <EM> tag to be emphasis and the <STRONG> tag to be bold. Most browsers do this conversion, but other tags may look different with other browsers.

If you want to force character tags, you can do so with <B> and </B> for boldface, <I> and </I> for italics, and <TT> and </TT> for typewriter mono-spaced font (code).

A Few Other Tags

A few other tags are useful in general Web page production. The first is the <PRE> tag, which means the contents between the tags are preformatted and should be left alone. Between the <PRE> and </PRE>, whitespace is important. This lets you preformat tables or other content exactly how you want it (subject to wrapping rules in the browser). For example, the code below has a PRE section in it:

```
<HTML>
<HEAD>
<TITLE> This is my Web Page! Welcome! </TITLE></HEAD>
<BODY>
<H1> This is an H1. </H1>
<P> This is a sample entry that should be <EM> emphasized using EM</EM>
and with
the <STRONG> use of Strong </STRONG> emphasis. </P>
<PRE>
This is preformatted
    text that should appear
            exactly like this in the Browser
</PRE>
```

```
</P>
</BODY>
</HTML>
```

As you can see in Figure 53.10, the spacing of the PRE material is retained, and even the text font is the same as the source (Courier).

FIGURE 53.10.

The PRE tags let you preformat text.

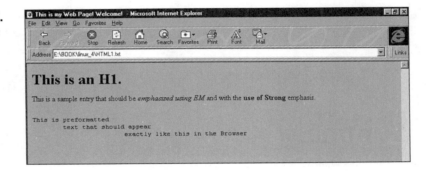

Another tag that is handy is simple. The `<HR>` tag creates a horizontal rule across the page. For example, the code above can be enhanced with a couple of HR tags like this:

```
<HTML>
<HEAD>
<TITLE> This is my Web Page! Welcome! </TITLE></HEAD>
<BODY>
<H1> This is an H1. </H1>
<P> This is a sample entry that should be <EM> emphasized using EM</EM> and
with
the <STRONG> use of Strong </STRONG> emphasis. </P>
<HR>
<PRE>
This is preformatted
    text that should appear
            exactly like this in the Browser
</PRE> <HR>
</P>
</BODY>
</HTML>
```

As you can see in Figure 53.11, two horizontal rules now appear on the page. The exact appearance of the rule may change with browsers, but the overall effect is to put a divider on the page.

53

HTML
PROGRAMMING
BASICS

FIGURE 53.11.

Use HR to draw horizontal rules across the page.

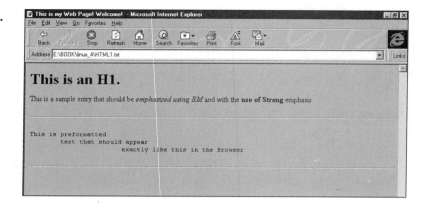

Summary

If you don't want to use a code generator or converter, you can write HTML code yourself. The programming language behind HTML is not very complicated and can be learned quickly. You don't have to have programming experience in order to learn HTML.

Setting up your home page requires that you either use an HTML authoring tool or write HTML code directly into an editor. The HTML language is beyond the scope of this book, but you should find several good guides to HTML at your bookstore. HTML is rather easy to learn. With the information in this chapter, you should be able to set up your Web site to enable anyone on the Internet to connect to you. Enjoy the Web! From here there are a number of other chapters in which you may be interested:

> To learn about the Java programming language and how it can enhance your Web pages, see Chapter 54, "Java and Javascript Basics."

> To learn about using tools to control your source code better, preventing conflicting versions and loss of code, see Chapter 56, "Source Code Control."

> To learn about some of the applications available for Linux, see Chapter 62, "Adabas-D and other Databases," through Chapter 64, "Lone Star Software's Lone-Tar."

Java and JavaScript Basics

by Tim Parker

IN THIS CHAPTER

CHAPTER 54

A quick word before we start: we're not going to teach you how to program Java in this chapter! There's far too much material to do justice in a few pages. Instead, we'll look at what Java is and does, and some of the basic programming aspects.

What is Java? Java is a programming language developed at Sun Microsystems. Sun describes Java in their press releases as "a simple, object-oriented, distributed, interpreted, robust, secure, architecture neutral, portable, high-performance, multithreaded, and dynamic language." What does all that really mean? To start with, Java was intended to be a much simpler object-oriented language to work with than C++ or SmallTalk, both of which are large and cumbersome languages to work with. By producing a small object-oriented language, Sun's developers also made Java simple and much less prone to bugs than larger languages. That's the simple and robust aspects of the language. The small size of the Java language also contributes to performance.

Java is an interpretive language, meaning that each line of source code is read by the Java interpreter and executed on that basis instead of a compiled executable. Actually, that's a bit of a simplification because Java code is pseudo-compiled to produce a binary object file, called a *class* file. This approach may be slower than a true compiled system, but by using a platform-neutral language (meaning there are no hardware or operating system-specific instructions in the language) Java source code will execute on any system with a Java interpreter. That covers the architecture-neutral and portable aspects of Sun's description. The distributed aspect comes naturally from these points, because Java source code can be easily sent from one machine to another across a network for execution. This allows a server to send Java code to clients, making a distributed system (Java runs on the client and communicates back to the server).

Because Java can run on practically any operating system, it can take advantage of the host operating system's features, such as UNIX's capability to handle multithreading. Java by itself can be thought of as multithreaded, but the operating system contributes a lot in this regard. Finally, the security aspect of Java was one of the design principles of the development group. A secure method of transferring information from client to server and vice versa was needed, and Java was designed to fill this requirement.

To provide the client and server software components, Java is designed to have the interpretive component of the language attached to other software, most commonly a Web browser. Netscape's Navigator and Microsoft's Explorer, for example, both have the client components of Java attached (or "plugged in" in Web parlance) to the browser code. When incoming Java source code is detected, the Java interpreter starts up and handles the task.

JavaScript was introduced after Java was on the market for a while. JavaScript is built into most Java-enabled Web browsers. Aside from their names, JavaScript and Java don't share very much. Many people think of JavaScript as a stripped-down Java, and that is incorrect and misleading. JavaScript is more an extension of HTML that allows users to build interactive Web pages in a client-server system.

JavaScript has a number of uses that make it attractive, including the capability to tell what a user is doing. When a user leaves a page or clicks on a certain button, the JavaScript client can communicate this information and start new routines. JavaScript is also ideal for writing little housekeeping tasks and for managing complex tasks, like string handling that is beyond HTML.

What You Need

To write Java applications you need the Java Development Kit (JDK). The JDK contains all the software necessary to write, compile, and test Java applets. Besides the JDK, all you need is a Java-enabled browser to test and display your applets. Netscape Navigator and Microsoft Explorer's latest releases all support Java, as do many other browsers. Sun developed their own Java-enabled browser called HotJava, which is available from the Sun Web site.

> **TIP**
>
> You can get the Java JDK at many sites on the Web or through FTP. The primary location is the Sun page `http://java.sun.com`, although most Linux sites (such as `www.blackdown.org`) also contain pointers to mirrors or backup sites for the JDK. For a Java-enabled Web browser, check out both Netscape and Microsoft home pages, as well as Sun's HotJava. For other browsers and Java development tools, check the Linux sites on the Web.
>
> For FTP access to the JDK, FTP to `java.sun.com` and change to the directory `/pub`, which contains the files you will need. If you expect Sun to support JDK under Linux, you'll be disappointed because they refuse to offer any kind of help.

The Sun Java section also contains a wealth of details on Java development, lots of sample code, advice, and FAQs. A white paper on Java obtained at the same site (`http://java.sun.com/tutorial/java/index.html`) is an excellent introduction to the language. The Java Development Kit is free if you are using it for personal reasons only, but if you plan to publish Java-based Web pages, you may need a license. Details are included with the JDK.

When installing the JDK make sure the path to the Java executables is in your path. Even better, link the executables to /usr/bin. The most common errors Java programmers make while learning the language are confusion about case sensitivity and class use. Java, like UNIX, is case sensitive, so developers must be careful to ensure their code is correct. Class usage follows C++ methods and must be adhered to properly. A good Java book is a must for learning the language, and there are dozens of books on Java.

For JavaScript, all you need is a JavaScript-enabled browser (such as Netscape Navigator 3.0 or higher), a standard ASCII editor or an editor that can save in ASCII, and a TCP/IP stack to communicate with other machines over the Internet or an intranet.

The Java Language

From the programmer's point of view, Java is a very stripped down object-oriented (OO) language. The principles of OO programming are suitable in most cases to client/server applications, so using OO for Java made sense. By staying with OO Java avoided the need to set up procedural language structures, all of which cause code bloat to the point that Java would not be nearly as fast. Also, by avoiding procedural language principles, Java designers can ignore many of the startup and initialization aspects of programming, again making the source code smaller and faster. Learning Java is not especially difficult. If you know an OO language such as C++, you will probably find Java easier to learn than if you've only worked in procedural languages such as C or Basic.

Java may be an OO language, but it's not strict about it. SmallTalk, for example, is considered a pure OO language because every aspect of SmallTalk is dealt with as either objects or messages, and all data are object classes. Java doesn't go quite as far, primarily to avoid an overly sizable language. Java implements all the simple C data types (integers, floating points, and characters) outside of the OO method, but everything else is object-based. This is both a benefit because it leads to smaller, faster code and a problem because it means you can't subclass Java data objects.

As mentioned earlier, Java is interpreted. When you develop Java applications, you write the Java code as you would with any other language, then pass it through a Java processor to produce the binary object file. The binary object file, called a class file in Java, is not directly human readable, but can be transmitted faster than the source code from which it was derived. When a Java-equipped browser receives the class file, it runs it through the Java interpreter which decodes the class file instructions and executes them. In one sense, Java is both a compiler and an interpreter, in much the same way many early languages that produced pseudo-code requiring a runtime module (such as many Pascal compilers were). The Java client that decodes the class file performs a conversion from generic instructions contained in the class file to machine-specific instructions for the client's hardware and operating system.

Programming in the Java language takes a little while to become comfortable with. The code often seems like a hybrid of C and C++, and experience with both is handy. However, because Java is a fairly simple language, even nonprogrammers can pick it up with a little practice. The most difficult aspects of learning Java for most people are the need to understand object-oriented design and programming, and the somewhat awkward syntax requirements (also these are familiar to C and C++ programmers). For example, here's a simple Java program:

```
// HelloWorldApp.java
class HelloWorldApp {
    public static void main (String args[]){
        System.out.println("Hello World!");
    }
}
```

This program (called HelloWorldApp) defines a single method called `main`, which returns nothing (`void`) and consists of a single Java instruction to print out the message `"Hello World!"`. The first line in the code is a comment. To compile this source code into a class file, you would invoke the Java compiler with the command line:

`javac HelloWorldApp.java`

and the compiler will grind away and produce a class file (HelloWorldApp.class) that can then be run in a Java-equipped browser, or from the command line client with the command:

`java HelloWorldApp`

which instructs Java to load the `.class` file and execute it. This applet must be run from the command line to see any results.

As you probably expect, Java is a lot more complicated than that in real life, but if you have programmed before you will see the similarities to other languages (especially C and C++). The Java language is quite rich and can take a couple of weeks to wade through, becoming familiar with its nuances as you go, but for most people Java is much more easily learned than other programming languages.

JavaScript and HTML

JavaScript commands are embedded inside HTML documents (see Chapter 53, "HTML Programming Basics," for more detail on HTML) by enclosing them with the HTML tags `<SCRIPT>` and `</SCRIPT>`. The general syntax for a JavaScript program inside an HTML document looks like this:

```
<SCRIPT language="JavaScript">
    JavaScript statements
</SCRIPTt>
```

The language option inside the `<SCRIPT>` tag is optional, but it is a good idea to use it to make sure the browser knows what script language it should use. If you want to load the JavaScript from a URL, you need to embed the URL in the `<SCRIPT>` tag like this:

```
<SCRIPT language="JavaScript" src="http://www.where.com">
```

If the JavaScript source is embedded in the HTML file, you can leave off the SRC component. For example, here's a very simple JavaScript applet in some HTML code (which has been trimmed down to the essentials):

```
<HTML>
<HEAD>
...
<SCRIPT language="JavaScript">
   alert("Welcome to my Web site!");
</SCRIPT>
</HEAD>
</HTML>
```

The `alert()` function in JavaScript displays the message in a window with an exclamation mark icon next to it. This is usually used to catch your attention when you try to do something critical, illegal, or that may cause potential problems. JavaScript's functions, as you can see, are much like C. You can define complete function within a JavaScript file, similar to in a C program.

If you are calling a file with the JavaScript source in it from your HTML code, the convention is to name the file with the .js filetype at the end (sample.js, for example). This is because several applications, including MIME, already recognize the .js filetype and can handle them properly.

We don't have the space here to go into details about JavaScript programming, but there are many good books on the subject.

Summary

We've taken a quick look at Java and JavaScript, both of which are available for Linux platforms in both server and client versions. Programming both Java and JavaScript requires a bit of past programming experience, but if you've programmed before you can use them both to add a lot of features to Web pages and HTML documents. Give them a try! After all, the software is free. Here are some useful chapters for you to read:

To learn about the Perl programming language, which is perfect for writing CGI scripts, see Chapter 28, "Perl."

To learn about using C to write CGI scripts, see Chapter 26, "Programming in C."

To learn more about HTML, see Chapter 53, "HTML Programming Basics."

To learn about backing up your system so you don't lose all the CGI scripts you've created, read Chapter 45, "Backups."

## CHAPTER 55

Creating a Solid Web Site

by Tim Parker

IN THIS CHAPTER

In this section of the book we've seen how to set up Linux to act as an Internet server, offering FTP, Gopher, WAIS, and World Wide Web services to the world. In the previous section you saw how to add mail and news to your system, too. Most people who do connect to the Internet want to use the World Wide Web, either for connecting to other sites or to make their own site available.

The Web has grown enormously in the last couple of years, inspiring many people to publish their own Web pages featuring subjects they are passionate about. One of the most common problems these Web sites run into, though, is the lack of design of a decent set of home pages and poor response from the server. In this chapter we take a brief look at some of the essentials you need to consider when you set up your own Web site using Linux. There are entire books dedicated to the proper design of Web pages, so we can only briefly look at the subject here.

It doesn't matter whether you are setting up a Web page to trumpet your own achievements in setting up Linux, or whether you are paying homage to your favorite TV show. Every Web page that is to receive visitors should follow a few simple rules for system response and page layout.

System Response

One of the most annoying aspects of using the Web is the interminable wait for some Web pages to load (or even worse, the dreaded message that the Web page can't be found!). If anything is going to discourage visitors from your site, it's waiting too long to see your home page contents. There are really two issues here: system availability and system response.

System availability is when your Web pages are available to the Internet. If you turn off your Web server machine when you are not using it, then no one will be able to access it. Anyone trying to get to your page through a search utility or directly through the URL will get the dreaded "URL not found" messages. Most users will promptly eliminate your Web site from their bookmark list, never to visit again.

The solution is simple: Keep your Web server running 24 hours a day, except when you have to take it down (briefly) for maintenance. You may not expect anyone to visit you at 4:00 a.m., but remember that the Web is worldwide and to someone many time zones away, it's early evening. A UPS (uninterruptible power supply) will help keep your server from cycling every time the power fails or varies more than your hardware's tolerance, and is a worthwhile investment.

System response really depends on two things: your machine's speed and your connection speed to the Web. If you are using a 1200 baud modem, then it doesn't matter how fast your hardware is—traffic to your site will be crippled by the slow download speed. That doesn't mean you have to have a dedicated ISDN or T1 line to your server. A normal asynchronous modem running at 28.8 kbps or faster is fine for most lightly used Web sites. If you start to get a lot of visitors and response gets slow, you'll have to invest in faster connections, but most Web sites are very low traffic anyway.

If your connection to the Internet is fast enough, chances are unlikely that your hardware will be the limiting factor. An 80486 can serve information to a standard modem much faster than the modem can transfer it, so it really doesn't matter whether you use a Pentium or not. At least not until you have a very popular site, in which case you need faster everything!

Keep Your Web Pages Clean

One of the biggest mistakes made by people setting up their first Web server is to get too complicated. You've written some really snazzy animations in Java that you want to share with the world on your Web page, and that's fine, but remember that everyone who accesses your page has to download all that code. That takes time, especially over async modems. You've designed a wonderful home page with purple lettering on a green background. It looks fine on your system, but not everyone will get the same color renditions. All they will see is a muddy color with unreadable text. All these issues are important to consider when designing a Web page. The basic rule is: Keep it simple!

Get Your Message Across at the Top of the Page

One of the most important aspects of designing your Web page is making sure whatever you are trying to convey is clear and easily understood. If you are setting up a site for your company, the company's name and purpose should be clearly understood with a quick glance at the home page. Remember that most people read from top to bottom, so important things should be toward the top of the screen. The same principle applies with advertising and newspapers: headlines and important information is right at the top where the publishers hope to catch your attention and draw you into reading the entire item. Most readers start at the top and only read down until they get distracted by something, so a clean uncluttered page design will get the reader to see all your home page.

A good example of a page design for maximum readability is if you have some Linux software you want to make available to other users. If you put the link to the software at the bottom of the page, many readers will miss it, especially if they have to scroll. Although a lot of home pages are long, not many readers bother to scroll all the way through. For this reason it's often a good idea to keep the amount of scrolling to a minimum by designing short Web pages, ideally with no scrolling required at all. Putting the demo software links at the top of the page makes them much more likely to get clicked on than something that requires scrolling or sorting through many icons at the bottom of the page.

Using Multiple Pages

If you can't fit everything that you need to say on the home page, by all means put auxiliary material on a link but make sure a reader doesn't have to traverse too many links to find out what they want to know. If you're trying to sell a product or service, for example, you don't want a reader to have to go through five or six levels of links before they find out what you are offering and how much it is. The average reader just won't last that long. A little advanced planning and some experimentation should result in a well laid out Web site. Remember to organize everything logically so that a visitor will be able to figure out your site's layout quickly.

> **TIP**
>
> There are a couple of easy ways to draw a Web visitor's attention to an item on your pages. The first is a simple horizontal rule (using the <HR> tag) across the page. Since the horizontal rule doesn't impose any overhead to download, there's no delay imposed by using it on your pages. Keep the number of horizontal lines low, though, to avoid overwhelming the reader.

Using Icons

Icons are great for letting your readers know what is important on your home page. Unfortunately, too many Web page designers go nuts and have many different kinds of icons scattered all over the page. This just doesn't work well—it distracts the reader and leads to confusion about which icons are important and which are not.

Bullets are a useful icon, as long as they are used with a short list that readers can quickly grasp. Again, go for something simple and attractive. Changing the bullet every item is confusing. The simplest icon for bulleted lists is a ball, although some browsers will add balls to bulleted lists if the list is tagged as an HTML list.

A useful icon to point out potential items of trouble for readers is the warning, caution, or stop sign. The first two are usually a yellow triangle with an exclamation mark in them. These draw the reader's attention but should be used sparingly and only where a warning is necessary.

The "new" icon, in its many forms, is handy for highlighting something new to your page for those who visit regularly. Make sure the new icon really does apply to something new. Remove such icons after a couple of weeks so your page doesn't seem stale.

Use Links Properly

Links are the key to a good site, but they have to be carefully planned. Many Web site designers make a paper flow diagram of where each page and its links lead to in order to ensure the flow is logical, clean, and doesn't cause silly loops anywhere. You should try to do this, too, if your site has more than three or four pages.

Choosing where to put the hyperlink itself is often a decision that Web page writers get mixed up with. For example, it's not good to have a line like this:

```
Click here to see the latest releases
```

when it is much more descriptive and visually drawing to have this line:

```
Click here to find out about our latest releases
```

Using HTML Tags Properly

Header tags are often misused by Web page designers. These use different size fonts to highlight titles. Keep the number of headline tags to a reasonable number and use them in order. After an <H1> tag use an <H2>, followed by <H3> and so on if applicable. Don't skip a level and jump from <H1> to <H3>, as some browsers are starting to use these elements to structure outline views of pages.

Also avoid overlapping tags, where you change fonts or emphasis within each other. For example, the series

```
<STRONG> Hello <EM> World! </EM> </STRONG>
```

may look fine on your browser but can cause problems on others. Always use tags in pairs and don't mix them.

Character tags should always be inside paragraph tags, not the other way around. For example, this is the proper way to nest character tags inside paragraph tags:

```
<A HREF="Today's news">
<UL>
  <LI>Added to the site today
  ...
</UL>
</A>
```

Avoid using the <BR> tag to force word wrapping. Instead, let HTML do the wrapping for you or you may end up with lousy looking screens. Remember that just because the format looks good on your screen with your browser doesn't mean it will look good for all your visitors.

Summary

Explaining all the principles of a solid Web page design in a few pages would be impossible. There are lots of good books on the subject. Do take care and create a clean, uncluttered site; otherwise, all your careful configuration and HTML work may be for nothing.

From here, there are a number of chapters you may want to read:

> To learn about backups so you can recover your HTML code in case of a problem, see Chapter 45, "Backups."

> And to learn how to set up your Web server properly, see Chapter 51 "Configuring a WWW Site."

> To learn about source code control so you don't have multiple copies of your HTML documents floating around your directories, see Chapter 56, "Source Code Control."

Advanced Programming Topics

PART VIII

IN THIS PART

Source Code Control

by Peter MacKinnon and Tim Parker

IN THIS CHAPTER

56

CHAPTER

A large-scale software project involving numerous files and programmers can present logistical nightmares if you happen to be the poor soul responsible for managing it:

"How do I know whether this file of input/output routines that Sue has been working on is the most current one?"

"Oh, no—I have to recompile my application, but I can't remember which of these 50 files I changed since the last compile!"

Keeping track of which file is most recent and where you put those changes yesterday (or last week) can be more of a job than actual programming.

Even small applications typically use more than one source code file. When compiling and linking C applications, you usually must deal with not only source code, but also header files and library files. Fortunately, Linux features a software development environment that, for the most part, can greatly simplify these concerns.

make

Perhaps the most important of all the software development utilities for Linux, make is a program that keeps a record of dependencies between files and only updates those files that have been changed since the last update. The term *update* usually refers to a compile or link operation, but it may also involve the removal of temporary files. This updating process can sometimes be repeated dozens of times in the course of a software project. Instead of managing these tasks manually, make can be your automatic dependency manager, giving you more time to do other important things, such as coding or watching TV.

make generates commands using a description file known as a makefile. These commands are then executed by the shell. The makefile is basically a set of rules for make to follow whenever performing an update of your program. These rules usually relate to the definition of the dependencies between files. In the case of creating a Linux executable of C code, this usually means compiling source code into object files and linking those object files together, perhaps with additional library files. make can also figure out some things for itself, such as the modification times (or timestamps) when certain files have been changed.

> **NOTE**
>
> makefile or Makefile is literally the name that the make program expects to find in the current directory. You can override the name if you want, but tradition (and who can argue with 30 years of tradition?) dictates that makefile is the name programmers should use.

make is certainly best suited for C programming, but it can also be used with other types of language compilers for Linux, such as assembler or FORTRAN.

A Sample makefile

Let's look at a simple application of make. The command

```
$ make someonehappy
```

tells Linux that you want to create a new version of someonehappy. In this case, someonehappy is an executable program; thus, there will be compiling and linking of files. someonehappy is referred to as the *target* of this make operation. The object files that are linked together to create the executable are known as someonehappy's *dependents*. The source code files that are compiled to create these object files are also indirect dependents of someonehappy.

The files that are used to build someonehappy are the following (the contents of these files are unimportant to the example):

> Two C source code files: main.c, dothis.c
>
> Three header files: yes.h, no.h, maybe.h
>
> One library file: /usr/happy/lib/likeatree.a
>
> An assembly language file: itquick.s

It appears that this is a small project, so you could choose to manually compile and link these files to build your executable. Instead, create a makefile for your someonehappy project to help automate these tedious tasks.

In your favorite editor, write the following:

```
someonehappy: main.o dothis.o itquick.o /usr/happy/lib/likeatree.a
        cc -o someonehappy main.o dothis.o itquick.o/usr/happy/lib/
►likeatree.a
main.o: main.c
        cc -c main.c
```

```
dothis.o: dothis.c
      cc -c dothis.c
itquick.o: itquick.s
      as -o itquick.o itquick.s
fresh:
      rm *.o
maybe.h: yes.h no.h
      cp yes.h no.h /users/sue/
```

Basic makefile Format

So, assuming that these files are in the same directory as the makefile, what do you have? The format of a makefile, such as the one you have made, is a series of entries. Your makefile has six entries: The first line of an entry is the dependency line, which lists the dependencies of the target denoted at the left of the colon; the second line is one or more command lines, which tells make what to do if the target is newer than its dependent (or dependents). An entry basically looks like this:

```
target: dependents
(TAB) command list
```

The space to the left of the command list is actually a tab. This is part of the makefile syntax: Each command line must be indented using a tab. A dependency line can have a series of commands associated with it. make executes each command line as if the command had its own shell. Thus, the command

```
cd somewhere
mv *.c anotherwhere
```

does not behave the way you may have intended. To remedy this kind of situation, use the following syntax whenever you need to specify more than one command:

```
dependency line
command1;command2;command3;...
```

or

```
dependency line
      command1; \
      command2; \
      command3;
```

and so on. If you use a backslash to continue a line, it must be the last character before the end-of-line character.

> **TIP**
>
> You can specify different kinds of dependencies for a target by placing the same target name on different dependency lines. Actually, make is even more powerful than described in this chapter, but unless you are working on very large projects with lots of interdependencies, you probably won't care about most of the subtleties make is capable of.

The first entry in our makefile is the key one for building our executable. It states that someonehappy is to be built if all the dependent object files and library files are present and if there are any newer files than the last version of someonehappy. Of course, if the executable is not present at all, make performs the compile command listed, but not right away. First, make checks to see which object files need to be recompiled in order to recompile someonehappy. This is a recursive operation, as make examines the dependencies of each target in the hierarchy, as defined in the makefile.

The last entry is a little goofy. It copies the header files yes.h and no.h (somehow related to maybe.h) to the home directories of the user named sue if they have been modified. This is somewhat conceivable if Sue is working on related programs that use these header files and need the most recent copies at all times. More importantly, it illustrates that make can be used to do more than compiling and linking and that make can execute several commands based on one dependency.

The fresh target is another example of a target being used to do more than just compiling. This target lacks any dependents, which is perfectly acceptable to the make program. As long as there is no file in the current directory named fresh, make executes the supplied command to remove all object files. This works because make treats any such entry as a target that must be updated.

So, if you enter the command

```
$ make someonehappy
```

make starts issuing the commands it finds in the makefile for each target that must be updated to achieve the final target. make echoes these commands to the user as it processes them. Simply entering

```
$ make
```

also works in this case because make always processes the first entry it finds in the makefile. These commands are echoed to the screen, and the make process halts if the compiler finds an error in the code.

If all of someonehappy's dependencies are up-to-date, make does nothing except inform you of the following:

```
'someonehappy' is up to date
```

You can actually supply the name (or names) of any valid target in your makefile on the command line for make. It performs updates in the order in which they appear on the command line, but still applies the dependency rules found in the makefile. If you supply the name of a fictional target (one that doesn't appear in your makefile and is not the name of a file in the current directory), make complains something like this:

```
$ make fiction
make: Don't know how to make fiction. Stop.
```

Building Different Versions of Programs

Suppose you want to have different versions of your someonehappy program that use most of the same code, but require slightly different interface routines. These routines are located in different C files (dothis.c and dothat.c), and they both use the code found in main.c. Instead of having separate makefiles for each version, you can simply add targets that do different compiles. Your makefile will look like the following one. (Note the first line that has been added. It is a comment about the makefile and is denoted by a # character followed by the comment text.)

```
# A makefile that creates two versions of the someonehappy program
someonehappy1: main.o dothis.o itquick.o /usr/happy/lib/likeatree.a
        cc -o someonehappy main.o dothis.o itquick.o/usr/happy/lib/
➥likeatree.a
someonehappy2: main.o dothat.o itquick.o /usr/happy/lib/likeatree.a
        cc -o someonehappy main.o dothat.o itquick.o/usr/happy/lib/
➥likeatree.a
main.o: main.c
        cc -c main.c
dothis.o: dothis.c
        cc -c dothis.c
dothat.o: dothat.c
        cc -c dothat.c
itquick.o: itquick.s
        as -o itquick.o itquick.s
fresh:
        rm *.o
maybe.h: yes.h no.h
        cp yes.h no.h /users/sue/
```

Thus, your makefile is now equipped to build two variations of the same program. Issue the command

```
$ make someonhappy1
```

to build the version using the interface routines found in `dothis.c`. Build your other program that uses the `dothat.c` interface routines with the following command:

```
$ make someonhappy2
```

Forcing Recompiles

It is possible to trick `make` into doing (or not doing) recompiles. An example of a situation in which you may not want `make` to recompile is when you have copied files from another directory. This operation updates the modification times of the files, though they may not need to be recompiled. You can use the `touch` utility or `make` with the `-t` option to update the modification times of all target files defined in the `makefile`.

> **TIP**
>
> Do you want to test your `makefile`? Use `make` with the `-n` option. It will echo the commands to you without actually executing them. Any coding errors written into the file generate proper error messages from the parser, but you won't have to wait for a compiler to complete its task.

Macros

`make` lets you define macros within your `makefile` which are expanded by `make` before the program executes the commands found in your `makefile`. Macros have the following format:

```
macro identifier = text
```

The text portion can be the name of a file, a directory, a program to execute, or just about anything. Text can also be a list of files or a literal text string enclosed by double quotes. The following is an example of macros that you might use in your `someonehappy` makefile:

```
LIBFILES=/usr/happy/lib/likeatree.a
objects = main.o dothis.o
CC = /usr/bin/cc
1version="This is one version of someonehappy"
OPTIONS =
```

As a matter of convention, macros are usually in uppercase, but they can be typed in lowercase as in the previous example. Notice that the `OPTIONS` macro defined in the list has no text after the equal sign. This means that you have assigned the `OPTIONS` macro to a null string. Whenever this macro is found in a command list, make generates the command as if there were no OPTIONS macro at all. By the same token, if you try to refer to an undefined macro, make will ignore it during command generation.

Macros can also include other macros, as in the following example:

```
BOOK_DIR = /users/book/
MY_CHAPTERS = ${BOOK_DIR}/pete/book
```

Macros must be defined before they are used on a dependency line, although they can refer to each other in any order.

make has internal macros that it recognizes for commonly used commands. The C compiler is defined by the CC macro, and the flags that the C compiler uses are stored in the CFLAGS macro.

Macros are referred to in the makefile by enclosing the macro name in curly brackets and preceding the first bracket with a $. If you use macros in the first someonehappy makefile, it might look like this:

```
# Time to exercise some macros
CC = /usr/bin/cc
AS = /usr/bin/as
OBJS = main.o dothis.o itquick.o
YN = yes.h no.h
# We could do the following if this part of the path might be used
→elsewhere
LIB_DIR = /usr/happy/lib
LIB_FILES = ${LIB_DIR}/likeatree.a
someonehappy:   ${OBJS} ${LIB_FILES}
        ${CC} -o someonehappy ${OBJS} ${LIB_FILES}
main.o: main.c
        cc -c main.c
dothis.o: dothis.c
        cc -c dothis.c
itquick.o: itquick.s
        ${AS} -o itquick.o itquick.s
fresh:
        rm *.o
maybe.h: ${YN}
        cp yes.h no.h /users/sue/
```

make also recognizes shell variables as macros if they are set in the same shell in which make is invoked. For example, if a C shell variable named BACKUP is defined by

```
$ setenv BACKUP /usr/happy/backup
```

you can use it as a macro in your makefile. The macro definition

```
OTHER_BACKUP = ${BACKUP}/last_week
```

is expanded by make to be

```
/usr/happy/backup/last_week
```

You can reduce the size of your makefile even further. For starters, you don't have to specify the executables for the C and assembler compilers because these are known to make. You can also use two other internal macros, referred to by the symbols $@ and $?. The $@ macro always denotes the current target; the $? macro refers to all the dependents that are newer than the current target. Both of these macros can only be used within command lines. Thus, the makefile command

```
someonehappy: ${OBJS} ${LIB_FILES}
        ${CC} -o $@ ${OBJS} ${LIB_FILES}
```

generates

```
/usr/bin/cc -o someonehappy main.o dothis.o itquick.o/usr/happy/lib/
➥likeatree.a
```

when using the following:

```
$ make someonehappy
```

The $? macro is a little trickier to use but quite powerful. Use it to copy the yes.h and no.h header files to Sue's home directory whenever they are updated. The makefile command

```
maybe.h: ${YN}
        cp $? /users/sue/
```

evaluates to

```
cp no.h /users/sue/
```

if only the no.h header file has been modified. It also evaluates to

```
cp yes.h no.h /users/sue/
```

if both header files have been updated since the last make of someonehappy.

So, with a little imagination, you can make use of some well-placed macros to shrink your makefile further and arrive at the following:

```
# Papa's got a brand new makefile
OBJS = main.o dothis.o itquick.o
YN = yes.h no.h
LIB_DIR = /usr/happy/lib
LIB_FILES = ${LIB_DIR}/likeatree.a
someonehappy:  ${OBJS} ${LIB_FILES}
        ${CC} -o $@ ${OBJS} ${LIB_FILES}
main.o: main.c
```

```
        cc -c $?
dothis.o: dothis.c
        cc -c $?
itquick.o: itquick.s
        ${AS} -o $@ $?
fresh:
        rm *.o
maybe.h: ${YN}
        cp $? /users/sue/
```

Suffix Rules

As mentioned earlier in the "Macros" section, make does not necessarily require everything to be spelled out for it in the makefile. Because make was designed to enhance software development in Linux, it knows how the compilers work, especially for C. For example, make knows that the C compiler expects to compile source code files having a .c suffix and that it generates object files having an .o suffix. This knowledge is encapsulated in a suffix rule: make examines the suffix of a target or dependent to determine what it should do next.

There are many suffix rules that are internal to make, most of which deal with the compilation of source and linking of object files. The default suffix rules that are applicable in your makefile are as follows:

```
.SUFFIXES: .o .c .s

.c.o:
        ${CC} ${CFLAGS} -c $<

.s.o:
        ${AS} ${ASFLAGS} -o $@ $<
```

The first line is a dependency line stating the suffixes for which make should try to find rules if none are explicitly written in the makefile. The second dependency line is terse: Essentially, it tells make to execute the associated C compile on any file with a .c suffix whose corresponding object file (.o) is out-of-date. The third line is a similar directive for assembler files. The new macro $< has a similar role to that of the $? directive, but can only be used in a suffix rule. It represents the dependency that the rule is currently being applied to.

These default suffix rules are powerful in that all you really have to list in your makefile are any relevant object files. make does the rest: If main.o is out-of-date, make automatically searches for a main.c file to compile. This also works for the itquick.o object file. After the object files are updated, the compile of someonehappy can execute.

You can also specify your own suffix rules in order to have `make` perform other operations. Say, for instance, that you want to copy object files to another directory after they are compiled. You can explicitly write the appropriate suffix rule in the following way:

```
.c.o:
        ${CC} ${CFLAGS} -c $<
        cp $@   backup
```

The `$@` macro, as you know, refers to the current target. Thus, on the dependency line shown, the target is a `.o` file, and the dependency is the corresponding `.c` file.

Now that you know how to exploit the suffix rule feature of `make`, you can rewrite your `someonehappy` makefile for the last time (you're probably glad to hear that news).

```
# The final kick at the can
OBJS = main.o dothis.o itquick.o
YN = yes.h no.h
LIB_FILES = /usr/happy/lib/likeatree.a
someonehappy:  ${OBJS} ${LIB_FILES}
        ${CC} -o $@ ${OBJS} ${LIB_FILES}
fresh:
        rm *.o
maybe.h: ${YN}
        cp $? /users/sue/
```

This `makefile` works as your first one did, and you can compile the entire program using the following:

```
$ make someonehappy
```

Or, just compile one component of it as follows:

```
$ make itquick.o
```

This discussion only scratches the surface of `make`. You should refer to the man page for `make` to further explore its many capabilities.

RCS

One of the other important factors involved in software development is the management of source code files as they evolve. On any type of software project, you might continuously release newer versions of a program as features are added or bugs are fixed. Larger projects usually involve several programmers, which can complicate versioning and concurrency issues even further. In the absence of a system to manage the versioning of source code on your behalf, it is very easy to lose track of the versions of files. This can lead to situations in which modifications are inadvertently wiped out or redundantly coded by different programmers. Fortunately, Linux provides just such a versioning system, called RCS (Revision Control System).

RCS is just one version control system. There are plenty of others, some public domain, some commercial. SCCS (Source Code Control System) was the first truly workable version control system developed for UNIX and is still in use. RCS is a better system than SCCS, adding many new features and abilities that the older system lacks. There are RCS systems available for most operating system platforms including all UNIX versions, DOS, Windows, and Windows NT. If you have to work on a project with many developers, there is a network-wide version of RCS available called CVS (Concurrent Versions System). CVS is included with many versions of Linux. The commands used by CVS are different than those used by RCS, and since most of you won't be jumping into network-wide version control yet, we'll focus on RCS here. The CVS man pages are included with versions of Linux than bundle CVS, if you are curious.

RCS can administer the versioning of files by controlling access to them. For anyone to update a particular file, the person must record in RCS who she is and why she is making the changes. RCS can then record this information along with the updates in an RCS file separate from the original version. Because the updates are kept independent from the original file, you can easily return to any previous version if necessary. This also has the benefit of conserving disk space because you don't have to keep copies of the entire file around. This is certainly true for situations in which versions differ only by a few lines; it is less useful if there are only a few versions, each of which is largely different from the next.

Deltas

The set of changes that RCS records for an RCS file is referred to as a *delta*. The version number has two forms. The first form contains a release number and a level number. The release number is normally used to reflect a significant change to the code in the file. When you first create an RCS file, it is given a default release of 1 and level of 1 (1.1). RCS automatically assigns incrementally higher integers for the level number within a release (for example, 1.1, 1.2, 1.3, and so on). RCS enables you to override this automatic incrementing whenever you want to upgrade the version to a new release.

The second form of the version number also has the release and level components, but adds a branch number followed by a sequence number. You might use this form if you were developing a program for a client that required bug fixes, but you don't want to place these fixes in the next "official" version. Although the next version may include these fixes anyway, you may be in the process of adding features that would delay its release. For this reason, you would add a branch to your RCS file for this other development stream, which would then progress with sequence increments. For example, imagine that you have a planned development stream of 3.1, 3.2, 3.3, 3.4, and so on. You realize that you need to introduce a bug fix stream at 3.3, which will not include the functionality proposed for 3.4. This bug fix stream would have a numbering sequence of 3.3.1.1, 3.3.1.2, 3.3.1.3, and so on.

TIP

As a matter of good development practice, each level or sequence should represent a complete set of changes. That implies that the code in each version is tested to be free of any obvious bugs. You shouldn't jump from version 2.00 to 3.00, for example, just because you fixed a few bugs in 2.00. Usually, major version increases are related to additional features, not maintenance releases.

NOTE

Is any code ever completely bug-free? This certainly isn't the case for complex programs in which bugs may become apparent only when code is integrated from different developers. Your aim is to make at least your own part of the world bug-free. While we'll never achieve bug-free programs, we can minimize the potential bugs and isolate the few that remain much more easily.

Creating an RCS file

Let's assume that you have the following file of C code, called `finest.c`:

```
/* A little something for RCS */
#include <stdio.h>
main()
{
     printf("Programming at its finest...\n");
}
```

The first step in creating an RCS file is to make an RCS directory:

```
$ mkdir RCS
```

This is where your RCS files are maintained. You can then check a file into RCS by issuing the `ci` (check-in) command. Using your trusty `finest.c` program, enter the following:

```
$ ci finest.c
```

This operation prompts for comments and then creates a file in the RCS directory called `finest.c,v`, which contains all the deltas on your file. After this, RCS transfers the contents of the original file and denotes it as revision 1.1. Anytime that you check in a file, RCS removes the working copy from the RCS directory.

Retrieving an RCS File

To retrieve a copy of your file, use the `co` (check-out) command. If you use this command without any parameters, RCS gives you a read-only version of the file, which you can't edit. You need to use the `-l` option in order to obtain a version of the file that you can edit.

```
$ co -l finest.c
```

Whenever you finish making changes to the file, you can check it back in using `ci`. RCS prompts for text that is entered as a log of the changes made. This time the `finest.c` file is deposited as revision 1.2.

RCS revision numbers consist of release, level, branch, and sequence components. RCS commands typically use the most recent version of a file, unless they are instructed otherwise. For instance, say that the most recent version of `finest.c` is 2.7. If you want to check in `finest.c` as release 3, issue the `ci` command with the `-r` option, like this:

```
$ ci -r3 finest.c
```

This creates a new release of the file as 3.1. You can also start a branch at revision 2.7 by issuing the following:

```
$ ci -r2.7.1 finest.c
```

You can remove out-of-date versions with the `rcs` command and its `-o` option.

```
$ rcs -o2.6 finest.c
```

Using Keywords

RCS lets you enter keywords as part of a file. These keywords contain specific information about such things as revision dates and creator names that can be extracted using the `ident` command. Keywords are embedded directly into the working copy of a file. When that file is checked in and checked out again, these keywords have values attached to them. The syntax is

```
$keyword$
```

which is transformed into

```
$keyword: value$
```

Some keywords used by RCS are shown in the following list:

`$Author$`	The user who checked in a revision
`$Date$`	The date and time of check-in
`$Log$`	Accumulated messages that describe the file
`Revision$`	The revision number

If your `finest.c` file used the keywords from the previous table, the command

```
$ ident finest.c
```

produces output like this:

```
$Author: pete $
$Date: 95/01/15 23:18:15 $
$Log: finest.c,v $
# Revision 1.2 95/01/15 23:18:15 pete
# Some modifications
#
# Revision 1.1 95/01/15 18:34:09 pete
# The grand opening of finest.c!
#
$Revision: 1.2 $
```

Retrieving Version Information from an RCS File

Instead of querying the contents of an RCS file based on keywords, you might be interested in obtaining summary information about the version attributes using the `rlog` command with the `-t` option. On the `finest.c` RCS file, the output from

```
$ rlog -t finest.c
```

produces output formatted like this:

```
RCS file:       finest.c,v;  Working file:    finest.c
head:           3.2
locks:          pete: 2.1;  strict
access list: rick tim
symbolic names:
comment leader:   " * "
total revisions: 10;
description:
You know...programming at its finest...
==========================================================
```

`head` refers to the version number of the highest revision in the entire stream. `locks` describes which users have versions checked out and the type of lock (strict or implicit for the RCS file owner). `access list` is a list of users who are authorized to make deltas on this RCS file. The next section illustrates how user-access privileges for an RCS file can be changed.

Administering Access

One of the most important functions of RCS is to mediate the access of users to a set of files. For each file, RCS maintain a list of users who have permission to create deltas on that file. This list is empty to begin with, so that all users have permission to make deltas. The `rcs` command is used to assign usernames or group names with delta privileges. The command

```
$ rcs -arick,tim finest.c
```

enables the users Rick and Tim to make deltas on `finest.c` and simultaneously restricts all other users (except the owner) from that privilege.

Perhaps you change your mind and decide that the user Rick is not worthy of making deltas on your wonderful `finest.c` program. You can deny him that privilege using the `-e` option:

```
& rcs -erick finest.c
```

Suddenly, in a fit of paranoia, you trust no one to make deltas on `finest.c`. Like a software Mussolini, you place a global lock (which applies to everyone, including the owner) on release 2 of `finest.c` using the `-e` and `-L` options

```
$ rcs -e -L2 finest.c
```

so that no one can make changes on any delta in the release 2 stream. Only the file owner can make changes, but this person still has to explicitly put a lock on the file for every check-out and check-in operation.

Comparing and Merging Revisions

Revisions can be compared to each other to discover what, if any, differences lie between them. This can be used as a means of safely merging together edits of a single source file by different developers. The `rcsdiff` command is used to show differences between revisions existing in an RCS file or between a checked-out version and the most current revision in the RCS file. To compare the `finest.c` 1.2 version to the 1.5 version, enter

```
$ rcsdiff -r1.2 -r1.5 finest.c
```

The output is something like

```
RCS file: finest.c,v
retrieving revision 1.1
rdiff   -r1.2 -r1.5 finest.c
6a7,8
>
> /* ...but what good is this? */
```

This output indicates that the only difference between the files is that two new lines have been added after the original line six. To just compare your current checked-out version with that of the "head" version in the RCS file, simply enter

```
$ rcsdiff finest.c
```

Once you have determined if there are any conflicts between your edits and others, you may decide to merge revisions. You can do this with the rcsmerge command. The format of this command is to take one or two filenames representing the version to be merged and a third filename indicating the working file (in the following example, this is finest.c).

The command

```
$ rcsmerge -r1.3 -r1.6 finest.c
```

produces output like this:

```
RCS file: finest.c,v
retrieving revision 1.3
retrieving revision 1.6
Merging differences between 1.3 and 1.6 into finest.c
```

If any lines between the two files overlap, rcsmerge indicates the lines that originate from a particular merged file in the working copy. You have to resolve these overlaps by explicitly editing the working copy to remove any conflicts before checking the working copy back into RCS.

NOTE

There is an implied order in which the files to be merged are placed in the rcsmerge command. If you are placing a higher version before a lower one at the -r options, this is essentially undoing the edits that have transpired from the older (lower) version to the newer (higher) version.

Tying It All Together: Working with make and RCS

The make program supports interaction with RCS, enabling you to have a largely complete software development environment. However, the whole issue of using make with RCS is a sticky one if your software project involves several people sharing source code files. Clearly, it may be problematic if someone is compiling files that need to be stable in order to do your own software testing. This may be more of a communication and scheduling issue between team members than anything else. At any rate, using make with RCS can be very convenient for a single programmer, particularly in the Linux environment.

make can handle RCS files through the application of user-defined suffix rules that recognize the ,v suffix. RCS interfaces well with make because its files use the ,v suffix, which works well within a suffix rule. You can write a set of RCS-specific suffix rules to compile C code as follows:

```
CO = co
.c,v.o:
        ${CO} $<
        ${CC} ${CFLAGS} -c $*.c
        - rm -f $*.c
```

The CO macro represents the RCS check-out command. The $*.c macro is necessary because make automatically strips off the .c suffix. The hyphen preceding the rm command instructs make to continue, even if the rm fails. For main.c stored in RCS, make generates these commands:

```
co main.c
cc -O -c main.c
rm -f main.c
```

Summary

Linux offers two key utilities for managing software development: make and RCS. make is a program that generates commands for compilation, linking, and other related development activities. make can manage dependencies between source code and object files so that an entire project can be recompiled as much as is required for it to be up-to-date. RCS is a set of source code control programs that enables several developers to work on a software project simultaneously. It manages the use of a source code file by keeping a history of editing changes that have been applied to it.

The other benefit of versioning control is that it can, in many cases, reduce disk space requirements for a project. CVS is an enhancement to the RCS programs. It automatically provides for the merging of revisions. This capability enables several developers to work on the same source code file at once, with the caveat that they are responsible for any merging conflicts that arise.

After reading about version systems, you may be more interested in getting to work programming with RCS. From here, logical chapters to read are:

Chapter 26, "Programming in C," and Chapter 27, "Programming in C++," if you want to tie your C or C++ programming with make and RCS.

Chapter 30, "Other Compilers," if you want to find out which languages are supported by Linux.

Chapter 31, "Smalltalk/X," if you want to learn about the GUI-based version of the popular object-oriented programming language Smalltalk.

## CHAPTER 57

Working with the Kernel

by Kamran Husain and Tim Parker

IN THIS CHAPTER

Usually you will want to leave the Linux kernel alone except when performing a major upgrade, installing a new networking component (such as NFS or NIS), or installing a new device driver that has special kernel requirements. The details of the process used to install the kernel drivers are usually supplied with the software. Since this isn't always the case, though, this chapter gives you a good idea of the general process for working with the kernel.

> **NOTE**
>
> First a clear warning: don't modify the kernel without knowing what you are doing. If you damage the source code or configuration information, your kernel may be unusable and in the worst cases, your file system may be affected. Take care and follow instructions carefully. There is a lot to know about kernel manipulation and we can only look at the basics in this chapter.

There are several versions of Linux in common use, with a few inconsistencies between them. For that reason, the exact instructions supplied below may not work with your version of Linux. However, the general approach is the same, and only the directory or utility names may be different. Most versions of Linux have documentation supplied that lists the recompilation process and the locations of the source code and compiled programs.

> **NOTE**
>
> Before doing anything with the kernel or utilities, make sure you have a good set of emergency boot disks, and preferably, a complete backup on tape or disk. Although the process of modifying the kernel is not difficult, it does cause problems every now and again that can leave you stranded without a working system. Boot disks are the best way to recover, so make at least one extra set.

Since the kernel is compiled with the C compiler supplied as part of Linux, we'll spend the latter part of this chapter looking at the C compiler, its flags, and how you can use it to your advantage. This isn't meant to be a complete reference to the C system, of course, but should be useful for some basic manipulations you may require when modifying the kernel (or any other source code compiled by C).

Upgrading and Installing New Kernel Software

Linux is a dynamic operating system. There are new releases of the kernel, or parts of the operating system that can be linked into the kernel, which are periodically made available to users. Whether you want to upgrade to the new releases is up to you and usually depends on the features or bug fixes that the new release offers. You will probably have to relink the kernel when new software is added, unless it is loaded as a utility or device driver.

You should avoid upgrading your system with every new release, however, for a couple of reasons. The most common problem with constant upgrades is that you may be stuck with a new software package that causes backward compatibility problems with your existing system or has a major problem with it that was not patched before the new software was released. This can cause you no end of trouble. Most new releases of software wipe out existing configuration information, so you have to reconfigure the packages that are being installed from scratch.

Also, the frequency with which new releases are made available is so high that you can spend more time simply loading and recompiling kernels and utilities than actually using the system. This becomes tiresome after a while. Since most major releases of the Linux operating system are available, the number of changes to the system are usually quite small, so you should read the release notes carefully to ensure that the release is worth the installation time and trouble

The best advice is to upgrade only once or twice a year, and only when there is a new feature or enhancement to your system that will make a significant difference to the way you use Linux. It's tempting to always have the latest and newest version of the operating system, but there is a lot to be said for having a stable, functioning operating system, too.

If you do upgrade to a new release, bear in mind that you don't have to upgrade everything. The last few Linux releases have changed only about 5 percent of the operating system with each new major package upgrade. Instead of replacing the entire system, just install those parts that will have a definite effect, such as the kernel, compilers and their libraries, and frequently used utilities. This saves time and reconfiguration.

Compiling the Kernel from Source Code

Upgrading, replacing, or adding new code to the kernel is usually a simple process. You obtain the code for the kernel, make any configuration changes, compile it, then place the code in the proper location on the file system to run the system properly. The process is often automated for you by a shell script or installation program, and some upgrades are completely automated with no need to do anything more than start the upgrade utility.

Kernel sources for new releases of Linux are available from CD-ROM distributions, FTP sites, user groups, and many other locations. Most kernel versions are numbered with a version and a patch level, so you will see kernel names like 1.12.123 where "1" is the major release, "12" is the minor version release, and "123" is the patch number. Most sites of kernel source maintain several versions simultaneously, so check through the source directories for the latest version of the kernel.

Patch releases are sometimes numbered differently and do not require the entire source of the kernel to install. In most cases, the patch will overlay a section of existing source code, and a simple recompilation is all that's necessary to install the patch. Patches are

> **NOTE**
>
> When you are installing a patch it you might want to reduce the number of open files, applications, and running processes to a minimum. This prevents problems with files being left open and corrupting the I-node table. Because patches are installed when you are logged in as root, you have the ability to kill all unnecessary applications and processes.

released quite frequently.

Most kernel source programs are maintained as a gzipped `tar` file. Unpack the files into a subdirectory of `/usr/src`, which is where most of the source code is kept for Linux. Some versions of Linux keep other directories for the kernel source, so you may want to check any documentation supplied with the system or look for a README file in the `/usr/src` directory for more instructions.

Often, unpacking the gzipped `tar` file in `/usr/src` creates a subdirectory called `/usr/src/linux`, which can overwrite your last version of the kernel source. Before starting the unpacking process, rename or copy any existing /usr/src/linux (or whatever name is used with the new kernel) so that you have a backup version in case of problems.

After the kernel source has been unpacked, you need to create two symbolic links to the /usr/include directory, if they are not created already or set by the installation procedure. Usually, the link commands required are

```
ln -sf /usr/src/linux/include/linux /usr/include/linux
ln -sf /usr/src/linux/include/asm /usr/include/asm
```

If the directory names are different on your version of Linux, substitute them for /usr/src/linux. Without these links, the upgrade or installation of a new kernel cannot proceed.

After the source code has been ungzipped and untarred and the links have been established, the compilation process can begin. You must have a version of gcc or g++ (the GNU C and C++ compilers) or some other compatible compiler available for the compilation. You may have to check with the source code documentation to make sure you have the correct versions of the compilers because occasionally new kernel features are added that are not supported by older versions of gcc or g++.

Check the file /usr/src/linux/Makefile (or whatever path the Makefile is in with your source distribution). There will be a line in the file that defines the ROOT_DEV, the device that is used as the root file system when Linux boots. Usually the line looks like this:

```
ROOT_DEV = CURRENT
```

If you have any other value, make sure it is correct for your file system configuration. If the Makefile has no value, set it as shown above.

The compilation process begins by going to the /usr/src/linux directory and issuing the command

```
make config
```

which invokes the make utility for the C compiler. The process may be slightly different for some versions of Linux, so check with the release or installation notes supplied with the source code.

Next, the config program issues a series of questions and prompts for you to answer to indicate any configuration issues that need to be completed before the actual compilation is started. These may be about the type of disk drive you are using, the CPU, any partitions, or other devices such as CD-ROMs. Answer the questions as well as you can. If

57

WORKING WITH
THE KERNEL

you are unsure, choose the default values or the one that makes the most sense. The worst case scenario is that you have to redo the process if the system doesn't run properly. (You do have an emergency boot disk ready, don't you?)

Now you have to set all the source dependencies. This is a commonly skipped step and can cause a lot of problems if not performed for each software release. Issue the command

```
make dep
```

If the software you are installing does not have a dep file, check with the release or installation notes to ensure the dependencies are correctly handled by the other steps.

After that, you can finally compile the new kernel. The command to start the process is

```
make Image
```

which compiles the source code and leaves the new kernel image file in the current directory (usually /usr/src/linux). If you want to create a compressed kernel image, use the command

```
make zImage
```

Not all release or upgrades to the kernel support compressed image compilation.

The last step in the process is to copy the new kernel image file to the boot device or a boot floppy disk. Use the command:

```
cp Image /dev/fd0
```

to place it on a floppy. Use a different device driver as necessary to place it elsewhere on the hard drive file system. Alternatively, if you plan to use LILO to boot the operating system, you can install the new kernel by running a setup program or the utility /usr/lilo/lilo. See Chapter 4, "Using LILO."

Now all that remains is to reboot the system and see if the new kernel loads properly. If there are any problems, boot from a floppy, restore the old kernel, and start the process again. Check documentation supplied with the release source code for any information about problems you may encounter or steps that may have been added to the process.

Adding Drivers to the Kernel

You may want to link in new device drivers or special software to the kernel without going through the upgrade process of the kernel itself. This is often necessary when a new device such as a multiport board or an optical drive is added to the system and should be loaded during the boot process. Alternatively, you may be adding special security software that must be linked into the kernel.

The add-in kernel software usually has installation instructions provided, but the general process is to locate the source in a directory that can be found by the kernel recompilation process (such as /usr/src). To instruct the make utility to add the new code to the kernel, modifications are often needed to the Makefile. These may be performed manually or by an installation script. Some software has its own Makefile supplied for this reason.

Then, the kernel recompilation is begun with the new software added in to the load. The process is the same as shown in the section above, with the kernel installed in the boot location or set by LILO. Typically, the entire process takes about 10 minutes and is quite trouble-free, unless the vendor of the kernel modification did a sloppy job. Make sure that the source code provided for the modification will work with your version of the Linux kernel by reading any text files that accompany the code as well as the software compatibility files included with most distributions of Linux.

Upgrading Libraries

Most of the software on a Linux system is set to use shared libraries (a set of subroutines used by many programs). When you see the message

```
Incompatible library version
```

display after you have performed an upgrade to the system and you try to execute a utility, it means that the libraries have been updated and need to be recompiled. Most libraries are backward-compatible, so existing software should work properly even after a library upgrade.

Library upgrades are less frequent than kernel upgrades, and you can find them in the same places. Usually there are documents that guide you to the latest version of a library or there may be a file explaining which libraries are necessary with new versions of the operating system kernel.

Most library upgrades are gzipped tar files, and the process for unpacking them is the same as for kernel source code except the target directories are usually /lib, /usr/lib and /usr/include. Usually, any files that have the extension .a or .aa go in the /usr/lib directory. Shared library image files, which have the format libc.so. version are installed into /lib.

You may have to change symbolic links within the file system to point to the latest version of the library. For example, if you are running library version libc.so.4.4.1 and upgraded to `libc.so.4.4.2`, you must alter the symbolic link set in `/lib` to this file. The command is

```
ln -sf /lib/libc/so/4/4/1 /lib/libc.so.4
```

where the last name in the link command is the name of the current library file in `/lib`. Your library name may be different, so check the directory and release or installation notes first.

You will also have to change the symbolic link for the file `libm.so.` version in the same manner. Do not delete the symbolic links, because all programs that depend on the shared library (including `ls`) will be unable to function.

The Linux C Compiler

Linux uses a C compiler for every compilation of the kernel (and most utilities, too). The C compiler that is available for all versions of Linux is the GNU C compiler, abbreviated `gcc`. This compiler was created under the Free Software Foundation's programming license and is therefore freely distributable.

The GNU C Compiler that is packaged with the Slackware Linux distribution is a fully functional ANSI C-compatible compiler. If you are familiar with a C compiler on a different operating system or hardware platform you will be able to learn `gcc` very quickly.

The GCC compiler is invoked by passing it a number of options and one or more filenames. The basic syntax for `gcc` is

```
gcc [options] [filenames]
```

The operations specified by the command line options will be performed on each of the files on the command line. There are well over 100 compiler options that can be passed to `gcc`. You will probably never use most of these options, but some of them you will use on a regular basis.

Many of the `gcc` options consist of more than one character. For this reason, you must specify each option with its own hyphen. You cannot group options after a single hyphen as you can with most Linux commands. For example, the following two commands are not the same:

```
gcc -p -g test.c
gcc -pg test.c
```

The first command tells `gcc` to compile `test.c` with profile information (`-p`) and also to store debugging information with the executable (`-c`). The second command simply tells `gcc` to compile `test.c` with profile information for the `gprof` command (`-pc`).

When you compile a program using gcc without any command line options, it creates an executable file (assuming that the compile was successful) and calls it a.out. To specify a name other than a.out for the executable file, use the -o compiler option. For example, to compile a C program file named count.c into an executable file named count, use the following command:

```
gcc -o count count.c
```

> **NOTE**
>
> When you are using the -o option, the executable file name must occur directly after the -o on the command line. Don't put other options between the output name and the -o signal.

There are also compiler options that allow you to specify how far you want the compile to proceed. The -c option tells gcc to compile the code into object code and to skip the assembly and linking stages of the compile. This option is used quite often because it makes the compilation of multi-file C programs faster and easier to manage. Object code files that are created by gcc have a .o extension by default.

The -S compiler option tells gcc to stop the compile after it has generated the assembler files for the C code. Assembler files that are generated by gcc have an .s extension by default. The -E option instructs the compiler to only perform the preprocessing compiler stage on the input files. When this option is used, the output from the preprocessor is sent to the standard output rather than being stored in a file.

When you compile C code with gcc, it tries to compile the code in the least amount of time and also tries to create compiled code that is easy to debug. Making the code easy to debug means that the sequence of the compiled code is the same as the sequence of the source code, and no code gets optimized out of the compile. There are many options that you can use to tell gcc to create smaller, faster executable programs at the cost of compile time and ease of debugging. Of these options the two that you will typically use are the -O and the -O2 options.

The -O option tells gcc to perform basic optimizations on the source code. In most cases, these optimizations make the code run faster. The -O2 option tells gcc to make the code as fast and small as it can. The -O2 option causes the compilation speed to be slower than it is when using the -O option but typically results in code that executes more quickly.

In addition to the -O and -O2 optimization options, there are a number of lower level options that can be used to make the code faster. These options are very specific and should only be used if you fully understand the consequences that using these options will have on the compiled code. For a detailed description of these options, refer to the gcc man page.

Debugging and Profiling Options

The gcc compiler supports several debugging and profiling options. Of these options the two that you are most likely to use are the -g option and the -pg option.

The -g option tells GCC to produce debugging information that the GNU debugger (gdb) can use to help you to debug your program. The gcc program provides a feature that many other C compilers do not. With gcc you can use the -g option in conjunction with the -O option (which generates optimized code). This can be very useful if you are trying to debug code that is as close as possible to what will exist in the final product. When you are using these two options together be aware that some of the code that you have written will probably be changed by gcc when it optimizes it.

The -pg option tells gcc to add extra code to your program that will, when executed, generate profile information that can be used by the gprof program to display timing information about your program.

Debugging gcc Programs with gdb

Linux includes the GNU debugging program called gdb. The gdb debugger is a very powerful debugger that can be used to debug C and C++ programs. It allows you to see the internal structure or the memory that is being used by a program while it is executing. Some of the functions that gdb provides are

- allows you to monitor the value of variables that are contained in your program
- allows you to set breakpoints that will stop the program at a specific line of code
- allows you to step through the code line by line

When you start gdb there are a number of options that you can specify on the command line. You will probably run gdb most often with this command:

```
gdb filename
```

When you invoke gdb in this way you are specifying the executable file that you want to debug. There are also ways of starting gdb that tell it to inspect a core file created by the executable file being examined or to attach gdb to a currently running process. To get a listing and brief description of each of these other options, you can refer to the gdb man page or type gdb‑h at the command line.

To get gdb to work properly you must compile your programs so that debugging information will be generated by the compiler. The debugging information that is generated contains the types for each of the variables in your program as well as the mapping between the addresses in the executable program and the line numbers in the source code. The gdb debugger uses this information to relate the executable code to the source code. To compile a program with the debugging information turned on use the ‑g compiler option.

Summary

Recompiling kernel source code and adding new features to the kernel proceeds smoothly as long as you know what you are doing. Don't let the process scare you, but always keep boot disks on hand. Follow instructions wherever available as most new software has special requirements for linking into the kernel or replacing existing systems. From here, there are some other subjects you may want to check out. For example, to learn about

> Using the C compiler that comes with most Linux distributions, see Chapter 26, "Programming in C."
>
> Ensuring that your system with the kernel is configured properly, see Part VI, starting with Chapter 32, "System Administration Basics."
>
> Using the source code control system to avoid too many files of slightly different contents littering your hard drive, see Chapter 56, "Source Code Control."

Writing Device Drivers

by Tim Parker

IN THIS CHAPTER

Device drivers provide an interface between the operating system and the peripherals attached to the machine. A typical device driver consists of a number of functions that accept I/O requests from the operating system and instruct the device to perform those requests. In this manner, a uniform interface between devices and the operating system kernel is provided.

We can't cover everything there is to know about device drivers in a single chapter. Indeed, several sizable books have been written on the subject. Because device drivers are not written by casual users, but mostly by talented programmers, the information supplied here is mainly an introduction to the subject.

The code snippets in this chapter are taken from a set of simple device drivers written in C. They are portable and designed for a UNIX system, but they also execute properly under Linux. Use them only as a guide, if you decide you want to write device drivers. Obtain one of the specialty books on the subject if you get serious about programming device drivers.

> **NOTE**
>
> Writing device drivers is, in theory, quite simple. However, the first time you try to write one you'll be amazed at the number of problems you encounter. Many people consider writing device drivers an art, but all it really takes is practice and experience. There's a superb sense of satisfaction in writing good device drivers.

Device Drivers

Linux uses a device driver for every device attached to the system. The basic device driver instructions are part of the kernel or loaded during the boot process. By using a device driver, the devices appear to the operating system as files that can addressed, redirected, or piped as normal files.

Each device attached to the Linux system is described in a device driver program file, and some parameters about the device are described in a *device file*, which is usually stored in the /dev directory. When you add a new peripheral to the system, either a device driver must be attached to the Linux operating system to control the device, or you must write or supply a device driver. You also need a device file in the /dev directory for each device. Otherwise, the device can't be used.

Each device file has an assigned device number that uniquely identifies the device to the operating system. Linux device numbers consist of two parts. The *major number* identifies which general type the device driver handles, while the *minor number* can specify a particular unit for that general type of device. For example, multiple hard disk drives will use the same device driver (the same major number), but each has unique minor numbers to identify the specific drives to the operating system.

There are two major types of device drivers: character mode and block mode. Any UNIX device uses one or both of the driver types. Block mode drivers are the most common type. They deal with I/O in blocks of data to and from the kernel's buffer cache (which copies to memory the data from the cache). Originally designed for use with disk drives, block mode is used with virtually all mass storage devices, such as disk drives, high-capacity tape drives, magneto-optical drives, synchronous modems, and some high-speed printers.

Character mode devices differ from block mode devices in two significant ways. I/O can be processed directly to and from the process's memory space without using the kernel's cache. In addition, I/O requests are usually passed directly to the character mode device. Terminals and printers are obvious character mode devices, as are asynchronous modems and some tape drives.

Block mode devices perform a "strategy" function that reads or writes a block of data to the device. A series of special device control functions called `ioctl()` functions are available with character mode devices. In order to use these `ioctl()` functions, block mode devices will sometimes use character mode. An example is a tape drive that can use either a character or block mode driver, depending on the type of data being written.

Regardless of the type of device driver, the driver itself performs a series of basic tasks whenever a request is made of the device. First, the device is checked to ensure that it is ready and available for use. If so, it is "opened" to allow the calling process access. `Read` or `write` commands are usually executed, and then the device is "closed" to allow other processes access to the device.

Interrupts

Interrupts are signals from the devices to the operating system to indicate that attention is required. Interrupts are generated whenever an I/O is processed and the device is ready for another process. The interrupts used by Linux are similar to those used by DOS, so if you are familiar with DOS interrupts, you know most of the story already.

Upon receipt of an interrupt, the operating system suspends whatever it is executing and processes the interrupt. In most cases, interrupts are handled by the device driver. Interrupts must be checked to ensure that they are valid and do not affect operation of a process underway, except to suspend it momentarily.

A problem with handling interrupts is that the interrupt should not suspend the Linux kernel's operation or that of the device drivers themselves, except under controlled conditions. Interrupts that are not properly handled or carefully checked can cause suspension of a device driver that was processing the I/O that the interrupt requested.

The processing of an interrupt is usually suspended during the stages when critical operation would be affected. The areas of device driver code that should not allow an interrupt to stop their processing are termed *non-stoppable* or *critical* code. Typically, interrupt suspension during critical code segments is performed by raising the CPU priority equal to or greater than the interrupt priority level. After critical code execution, the CPU priority level is lowered again.

Interrupt priority is usually manipulated with four functions: `spl5()`, `spl6()`, `spl7()`, and `splx()`. Calling one of the first three causes interrupts *not* to be acknowledged during processing. `spl5()` disables disk drives, printer, and keyboard interrupts. `spl6()` disables the system clock, while `spl7()` disables all interrupts, including serial devices. These three functions always return a code indicating the previous value of the interrupt level. `splx()` is used to restore interrupts to their previous values.

Therefore, before processing critical code, embedding the command

```
old_level = spl5();
```

in the device driver source disables interrupts until the following command is issued:

```
splx(old_level);
```

Multiple level changes are combined into device drivers as in the following example:

```
int level_a, level_b;
level_a = spl5();
/* do any code that can't be  */
/* interrupted by disk drives */
level_b = spl7();
/* do all code that can't be  */
/* interrupted by anything    */
splx(level_b);
/* any final code that's not  */
/* interrupted by disk drives */
splx(level_a);
```

This seemingly awkward method of bouncing between levels is necessary to avoid freezing the device driver and kernel, which prevents the system from operating normally. The protection mechanisms must be invoked only for as short a time as necessary.

It is usually unwise to use the `spl6()` and `spl7()` functions. `spl6()` can cause the system clock to lose time in some cases, and `spl7()` causes loss of characters in serial I/O, unless it is used for very short time spans. Even then, it is usually sufficient to use `spl5()` for all interrupts in critical code.

Anatomy of a Linux Device Driver

Device driver code is similar to normal code in its structure. In Linux, drivers are generally written in C, although assembler and C++ are still occasionally used.

Headers

A typical device driver has a header that consists of `include` statements for system functions, device register addresses, content definitions, and driver global variable definitions. Most device drivers use a standard list of `include` files, such as:

`param.h`	Kernel parameters
`dir.h`	Directory parameters
`user.h`	User area definitions
`tty.h`	Terminal and `clist` definitions
`buf.h`	Buffer header information

The `tty.h` file is used for character mode drivers, while `buf.h` is used by all block mode devices.

Device registers are defined in the device driver header and are based on the device. For a character mode device, these registers commonly refer to port addresses, such as I/O address, status bits, and control bits. Toggle commands for the device are defined as their device codes.

An example of device register's initialization is shown in the device driver for a standard screen terminal (UART) device:

```
/* define the registers */
#define RRDATA     0x01     /* receive */
#define RTDATA     0x02     /* transmit */
#define RSTATUS    0x03     /* status */
#define RCONTRL    0x04     /* control */
...etc
```

```
/* define the status registers */
#define SRRDY      0x01       /* received data ready */
#define STRDY      0x02       /* transmitter ready */
#define SPERR      0x08       /* parity error */
#define SCTS       0x40       /* clear to send status */
...etc
```

The functions the device driver must perform are dependent on the nature of the device. All devices have an open() and close() routine that allows the device to perform I/O.

Opening the Device

The open() routine must check to ensure a valid device is specified, validate the device request (permission to access the device or device not ready), then initialize the device. The open() routine is run every time a process uses the device.

The open() routine presented here is for a generic terminal device, td.

```
tdopen(device,flag)
int device,flag;
{
        /* definitions for local variables ignored */
        /* details and definitions ignored in code */

        /* check device number */
        if (UNMODEM(device) >= NTDEVS)
        {
            seterror(ENXIO);
            return;
        }

        /* check if device in use */
        /* if so, see if superuser (suser) for override */
        tp = &td_tty[UNMODEM(device)];
        address = td_address[UNMODEM(device)];
        if((tp->t_lflag & XCLUDE) && !suser())
        {
            seterror(EBBUSY);
            return;
        }

        /* if not open, initialize by calling ttinit() */
        if((tp->t_state & (ISOPEN¦WOPEN)) == 0)
        {
            ttinit(tp);
            /* initialize flags, and call tdparam() to set line */
            tdparam(device);
        }

        /* if a modem is used, check carrier status */
```

```
/* if direct, set carrier detect flags */
/* set interrupt priority to avoid overwrite */
/* wait for carrier detect signal */
/* code eliminated from example */
```

Closing the Device

The close() routine is used only after the process is finished with the device. The routine disables interrupts from the device and issues any shut-down commands. All internal references to the device are reset. close() routines are not usually required in many device drivers because the device is treated as being available throughout. Exceptions are removable media and exclusive-use devices. Some modems require closing (close()) to allow the line to be hung up.

Again, the terminal device example is used for the close() routine sample:

```
tdclose(device)
{
    register struct tty *tp;
    tp = &td_tty[UNMODEM(device)];
    (*linesw[tp->t_line].l_close)(tp);
    if(tp->t_cflag & HUPCL)
        tdmodem(device,TURNOFF);
    /* turn off exclusive flag bit */
    ip->t_lflag & =~XCLUDE
}
```

strategy Functions

strategy functions (block mode devices only) are issued with a parameter to the kernel buffer header. The buffer header contains the instructions for a read or write along with a memory location for the operation to occur to or from. The size of the buffer is usually fixed at installation and varies from 512 to 1024 bytes. It can be examined in the file param.h as the BSIZE variable. A device's block size may be smaller than the buffer block size, in which case the driver executes multiple reads or writes.

The strategy function can be illustrated in a sample device driver for a hard disk. No code is supplied, but the skeleton explains the functions of the device driver in order:

```
int hdstrategy(bp)
register struct buf *bp;
{
    /* initialize drive and partition numbers */
    /* set local variables */

    /* check for valid drive & partition */
    /* compute target cylinder */
```

58

WRITING DEVICE
DRIVERS

```
/* disable interrupts */
/* push request into the queue */
/* check controller: if not active, start it */
/* reset interrupt level */
}
```

write() Functions

Character mode devices employ a write() instruction which checks the arguments of the instruction for validity and then copies the data from the process memory to the device driver buffer. When all data is copied, or the buffer is full, I/O is initiated to the device until the buffer is empty, at which point the process is repeated. Data is read from the process memory using a simple function (cpass) that returns a -1 when end of memory is reached. The data is written to process memory using a complementary function (passc). The write() routine is illustrated for the terminal device:

```
tdwrite(device)
        {
        register struct tty *tp;
        tp=&td_tty[UNMODEM(device)];
        (*linesw[tp->t_line].l_write)(tp);
        }
```

Large amounts of data are handled by a process called copyio, which takes the addresses of source and destination, a byte count, and a status flag as arguments.

read() Functions

The read() operation for character mode devices transfers data from the device to the process memory. The operation is analogous to that of the write() procedure. For the terminal device, the read() code becomes:

```
tdread(device)
        {
        register struct tty *tp;
        tp=&td_tty[UNMODEM(device)];
        (*linesw[tp->t_line].l_read)(tp);
        }
```

A small buffer is used when several characters are to be copied at once by read() or write(), rather than continually copying single characters. clist implements a small buffer used by character mode devices as a series of linked lists that use getc and putc to move characters on and off the buffer, respectively. A header for clist maintains a count of the contents.

start and ioctl Routines

A start routine is usually used for both block and character mode devices. It takes requests or data from device queues and sends them in order to the device. Block mode devices queue data with the strategy routine, while character mode devices use clist. The start routine maintains busy flags automatically as instructions are passed to the device. When a device has finished its process, it executes an intr routine which reinitializes the device for the next process.

The character mode ioctl() routine provides a special series of instructions to drivers. These include changes in the communications method between the driver and the operating system, as well as device-dependent operations (tape load or rewind, or memory allocation, for example).

The ioctl() function can be illustrated with the terminal device example. The ioctl() routine, in this case, calls another function that sets the device parameters. No code is supplied for the called function, but the skeleton explains the process of the device driver in order:

```
tdioctl(device,cmd,arg,mode)        int device;
int cmd;
int mode;
faddr_t arg;
{
      if(ttiocom(&td_tty[UNMODEM(device)],cmd,arg,mode))
            tdparam(device)
}

tdparam(device)
{
      /* initialize variables */
      /* get address and flags for referenced line */
      addr=td_addr[UNMODEM(device)];
      cflag=td_tty[UNMODEM(device].t_cflag;

      /* check speed: if zero hang up line */
      /* set up speed change */
      /* set up line control */
      /* manage interrupts */
}
```

Using a New Device Driver

Drivers are added to Linux systems in a series of steps. First the interrupt handler is identified, and then the device driver entry points (such as open) are added to a driver entry point table. The entire driver is compiled and linked to the kernel, and then placed in the

/dev directory. (See Chapter 57, "Working with the Kernel," for more information on adding to the Linux kernel.) Finally, the system is rebooted and the device driver tested. Obviously, changes to the driver require the process to be repeated, so device driver debugging is an art that minimizes the number of machine reboots!

CAUTION

Two basic *don'ts* are important for device driver programming. Don't use sleep() or seterror() during interrupt suspensions, and don't use floating point operations.

Interrupt suspensions must be minimized, and they also must be used to avoid corruption of clist (or other buffer) data. Finally, it is important to minimize stack space.

You can simplify debugging device drivers in many cases by using judicious printf or getchar statements to another device, such as the console. Statements like printf and getchar enable you to set up code that traces the execution steps of the device driver. If you are testing the device when logged in as root, the adb debugger can be used to allow examination of the kernel's memory while the device driver executes. Careful use of adb allows direct testing of minor changes in variables or addresses, but be careful— incorrect use of adb may result in system crashes!

One of the most common problems with device drivers (other than faulty coding) is the loss of interrupts or the suspension of a device while an interrupt is pending. This causes the device to hang. A time-out routine is included in most device drivers to prevent this. Typically, if an interrupt is expected and has not been received within a specified amount of time, the device is checked directly to ensure the interrupt was not missed. If an interrupt was missed, it can be simulated by code. Using the spl functions during debugging usually helps to isolate these problems.

Block mode-based device drivers are generally written using interrupts. However, more programmers are now using *polling* for character mode devices. Polling means the device driver checks at frequent intervals to determine the device's status. The device driver doesn't wait for interrupts but this does add to the CPU overhead the process requires. Polling is not suitable for many devices, such as mass storage systems, but it can be of benefit for character mode devices. Serial devices generally are polled to save interrupt overhead.

A 19,200 baud terminal causes approximately 1,920 interrupts per second, which in turn causes the operating system to interrupt and enter the device driver that many times. By replacing the interrupt routines with polling routines, the interval between CPU demands can be hugely decreased through the use of a small device buffer to hold intermediate characters generated to or from the device. Real-time devices also benefit from polling, since the number of interrupts does not overwhelm the CPU. If you want to use polling in your device drivers, you should read one of the books dedicated to device driver design because this is a complex subject.

Summary

Most Linux users will never have to write a device driver, as most devices you can buy already have a device driver available. If you acquire brand new hardware or have an adventurous bug, you may want to try writing a driver, though. Device drivers are not really difficult to write (as long as you are comfortable coding in a high-level language like C), but drivers tend to be very difficult to debug. The device driver programmer must at all times be careful to not affect other processes or devices. However, there is a peculiar sense of accomplishment when a device driver executes properly. From here, there are some pertinent chapters to read (or re-read):

Chapter 26, "Programming in C," discusses the C programming language under Linux and how it can be used to write device drivers.

Chapter 28, "Perl," discusses the handy language Perl, which can be used with surprising ease and power for quick programming tasks.

Chapter 30, "Other Compilers," discusses other languages that are available for Linux.

58

WRITING DEVICE DRIVERS

The Wine Project

by Robert Pfister

CHAPTER 59

Wine stands for Windows Emulator. It enables MS-Windows programs to run under a UNIX X Window environment. Like DOSemu, Wine takes direct advantage of the Intel 386 architecture to actually run the MS-Windows application. Wine simply translates any MS-Windows API calls into appropriate UNIX and X Window calls. Like OS/2, MS-Windows programs running under Wine can take advantage of features of the underlying operating system. Wine is simply another user-mode Linux process that is protected from corruption by other processes. This is dubbed *crash-protection* under OS/2. Because Linux uses preemptive multitasking, Wine processes can coexist with other processes without some of the problems experienced by applications running under native MS-Windows.

Current Status of Wine

As with most of the Linux community, developers of Wine are volunteers. Wine is currently Alpha or pre-release code. Only a few of the simplest MS-Windows applications run without incident. My favorite MS-Windows Entertainment Pack game, Pipe Dream by Lucas Arts, runs acceptably under Wine.

Although Pipe Dream and other simple games are certainly playable under Wine, everything is not perfect. Some speed degradation is noticeable, as is the occasional screen glitch.

Sun Soft has implemented a similar product to Wine, called WABI, for its UNIX-based workstations. WABI has been on the market since 1994 and supports some of the more complex Windows 3.11 applications such as Microsoft Excel and Lotus Smart Suite. However, WABI cannot run Windows 95 applications. Given enough development time, it is reasonable to expect that Wine will be capable of running general MS-Windows applications as well.

Setting Up Wine

Wine is available only as source code. If you have the prerequisite software and a little patience, setting up Wine is not very difficult—even if you are not a programmer.

System Requirements

Any Linux machine suitable for running X Window can run Wine applications at a reasonable speed. In theory, Wine should have some advantages running under Linux as opposed to under MS-Windows, which is confined to the MS-DOS environment. Experiences with current versions of Wine show that an application running under Wine is slower on the same machine running MS-DOS and MS-Windows.

To make full use of Wine, you need MS-Windows 3.1 installed on a disk partition that is accessible under Linux. It is also convenient to run existing MS-Windows applications from the same directory in which they are installed under native MS-DOS and MS-Windows. The typical Linux user also has MS-DOS and MS-Windows installed on a hard drive; thus it is only a matter of making the directories available under Linux. Linux kernels as of Version 1.1.83 do not support compressed MS-DOS file systems made by MS-DOS utilities such as `stacker` and `drvspace`.

> ### TIP
>
> Some Linux installation programs will prompt you through setting up an MS-DOS partition as a Linux subdirectory. If you do not set up such a partition, add the following line to your `/etc/fstab`:
>
> `/dev/hda1 /c MSDOS defaults`
>
> `hda1` is the partition that contains MS-DOS and `/c` is the Linux subdirectory to use. In this example it is assumed that the `/c` subdirectory exists. Otherwise, use `mkdir` to create the subdirectory.

Wine is distributed as source code and must be compiled before use. It requires approximately 10MB of disk space. 3.5MB of that disk space is the source code alone. To build Wine, you need to have the following:

- GCC
- LibC
- XFree with development parts loaded
- Linux kernel newer than 99.13

Where to Get Wine Distribution

A new version of Wine is released approximately once a week. Major Linux FTP sites on the Internet contain the most recent release. On `sunsite.unc.edu`, Wine is found in the `/pub/Linux/ALPHA/Wine` directory. Wine releases are named after the date they are released. Wine-950727.tar.gz was released on 7/27/95. The most current release is the one with the latest date. For more information, check out the Web page at `http://daedalus.dra.hmg.gb/gale/wine/wine.html`.

59

THE WINE
PROJECT

How to Install Wine

Unlike DOSemu, the Wine distribution is not sensitive to where it is installed. For brevity, make a symbolic link from the actual directory (say, `/usr/src/Wine950122`) to `/usr/wine` using the `ln` command as follows:

```
bash# ln -s /usr/src/Wine950122 /usr/wine
```

A Wine distribution consists of a compressed `tar` file. To unpack the distribution, use a shell command such as

```
bash# tar -zxvf filename.tar.gz
```

How to Configure Wine Before Building

Wine must be configured before being built. The `Configure` utility prompts the user for the necessary information and automatically builds the appropriate configuration files. There are three major steps to configuring Wine:

1. Compilation configuration

2. Runtime parameters

3. Automatic system-specific configuration

The configure script begins with the following questions:

```
Build Wine as emulator or library (E/L) [E]?
Short filenames (Y/N) [N]?
Use the XPM library (Y/N) [N]?
Language [En/De/No] ?
Global configfile name  /usr/local/etc/wine.conf
```

It is safe to press Enter and accept the defaults for these questions. These parameters are added to a global configuration file, `autoconf.h`. If parameter changes are necessary, re-run `Configure`. To avoid errors, do not attempt to edit this file.

Initially Configuring Runtime Parameters with `Configure`

The questions in this section relate to lines in the global configuration file `/usr/local/etc/wine.conf`. Following each question is an explanation of its meaning.

```
Which directory do you want to use as A:
Which directory do you want to use as C:
```

Answer these questions with the Linux directory where the MS-DOS A: and C: drive are mounted. If your disk partition on which MS-Windows is mounted is `/c`, then use `/c`. If you do not plan on using a floppy disk, do not worry if A: does not point to a valid directory.

```
Where is the Windows directory 'c:\windows\'
Where is the System directory 'c:\windows\system'
Where should Windows apps store temp files 'c:\windows\temp'
Which path should be used to find progs/DLL's
➥'c:\windows;c:\windows\system'
```

These directories should match where MS-Windows is installed on your MS-DOS partition. Because the default MS-Windows installation is in c:\windows, the default answers are usually sufficient.

```
Where is sysres.dll   /usr/wine/sysres.dll'
```

The sysres.dll is a DLL that contains Wine-specific resources. These resources include bitmaps and dialog boxes for things like the About Wine menu item. The default value is sufficient here as well.

```
Where is COM1" CF_Com1 '/dev/cua0'
Where is COM2" CF_Com2 '/dev/cua1'
Where is LPT1" CF_Lpt1 '/dev/lp0'
```

As with DOSemu, the communication and printer ports under Wine can be configured as any similar port under Linux. For simplicity, it is best to map the COM and LPT ports to the same ones that appear under native MS-DOS.

```
Log messages to which file (CON = stdout) 'CON'
```

This defines where the system messages generated by Wine will go. Sending messages to CON sends them to stdout. This is the most useful place because these messages can easily be redirected elsewhere. By default, Wine generates a lot of informational messages, which slows things down a bit. A casual user will probably want to redirect these messages to /dev/null. To make this the default action, use /dev/null for the log file.

Configure displays a long list of message types and poses the following question:

```
Exclude which messages from the log  'WM_SIZE;WM_TIMER'
```

If you don't care about any status messages from Wine, leave this as the default. Individual error messages can be turned on or off as well as redirected from the command line.

At this point, Configure displays the global configuration file based on your responses to the questions. You will be asked if you want to edit the file using your default editor:

```
Do you want to edit it using vi (Y/N) [N]?
```

You can always edit this file later with your favorite text editor, so it is safe to answer no to this question.

59

THE WINE
PROJECT

Automatic System-specific Configuration

After the `wine.conf` file has been successfully built, the `Configure` utility proceeds to make changes to the source tree via the `xmkmf`. Xmkmf is a utility that creates `makefiles` for X Window and creates a `Makefile` from an `Imakefile` while taking into account the peculiarities of different X Window installations across UNIX-like platforms.

How to Build Wine

To build Wine, simply type

```
make
```

You're done with the hard part of configuring Wine. However, building Wine seems like the longest part. To build Wine from scratch takes approximately eight minutes on a 90 MHz Pentium. You will also need the `-lXext` libraries for the final link to work, so install it from your CD-ROM first.

Using Wine

Using Wine can be as simple as typing `wine` *filename*. Wine can be configured and used with a number of different options—including a debugger for tracking down internal errors in Wine itself.

Specifying Configuration Parameters

Wine's global configuration file is typically `/usr/local/etc/wine.conf`. The configuration parameters match mostly with the above questions and are organized in the format of MS-Windows `.ini` files. A sample file follows, with some comments on the usage of each section.

The following statements map MS-DOS drive letters to the matching subdirectory under Linux:

```
[drives]
A=/a
C=/c
```

These parameters tell Wine where to find Windows- and Wine-specific DLLs and directories:

```
[wine]
Windows=c:\windows
System=c:\windows\system
```

```
Temp=c:\temp
Path=c:\windows;c:\windows\system
SystemResources=/users/wine/wine950122/sysres.dll
```

The following section applies to the mapping of MS-Windows fonts to X font (note that the * is used for wildcard matching of X fonts):

```
[fonts]
system=*-helvetica
mssansserif=*-helvetica
msserif=*-times
fixedsys=*-fixed
arial=*-helvetica
helv=*-helvetica
roman=*-times
default=*-*
```

The following section maps serial ports available under Wine with corresponding Linux serial port identifiers:

```
[serialports]
Com1=/dev/cua0
Com2=/dev/cua1
```

The following section maps printer ports available under Wine with the corresponding printer port under Linux:

```
[parallelports]
Lpt1=/dev/lp0
```

These parameters determine the amount of logging and the destination:

```
[spy]
File=CON
Exclude=WM_SIZE;WM_TIMER
```

Using Command-Line Options

The Wine command line has the following format:

wine wine_*options program program_options*.

For example:

bash# /usr/wine/wine -debugmsg +all /c/windows/winmine.exe

Table 59.1 shows command-line options available with Wine.

TABLE 59.1. WINE COMMAND-LINE OPTIONS.

Option	Meaning
-depth *n*	Change the depth to use for multiple-depth screens. This configures Wine to use other than the default number of colors. (8 bitplanes is 256 colors and usually the only acceptable answer.)
-desktop geom	Run an MS-Windows application with a desktop of the size specified. For example, 850×620 would create a window of 850 by 620. Running with a desktop also eliminates the modal, or stuck-on-top, behavior of Wine applications.
-display *name*	Use an X display other than the default. This enables users to run an MS-Windows application on another X device over an attached network.
-iconic	Start application as an icon rather than full-screen. This is same functionality as run minimized from the Program Manager under native MS-Windows.
-debug	Enter debugger before starting application.
-name *name*	Set the application name. This is useful for telling the X Window manager a meaningful name for the application. The default name is wine.
-privatemap	Use a private color map. This is useful for applications that make extensive use of color. Running an application this way causes the colors of other X applications to look weird while the Wine session is the selected window.
-synchronous	Turn on synchronous display mode. This can severely slow down applications because it causes X Window to wait for the completion of each command before sending the next one. X applications can send commands to an X server that may or may not be on the same machine. Under some applications, synchronization is necessary so that graphics operations do not get optimized away by the X server.
-backingstore	This is an optimization that enables an X server to handle expose events without interrupting the client program.
-spy *file*	Turn on message spying to the specified file. This can also be done by output redirection.
-debugmsg *name*	Turn specific debugging information on or off. To get a current list of debug message types, enter the following command: wine -debugmsg help help.

The Wine Debugger

Wine has a built-in debugger that is useful for uncovering problems within the program. When an MS-Windows program exits due to a problem, the debugger starts in the xterm from which Wine was started. If you are not interested in troubleshooting Wine, simply type quit at the prompt and skip to the next section of this chapter.

The Wine debugger is similar to the GNU debugger gdb. Breakpoints can be set; examination and modification of registers as well as memory locations are possible. However, the following is a minimal debugger that includes only the commands listed in Table 59.2.

TABLE 59.2. WINE DEBUGGER COMMANDS.

Command	Meaning
break	Set a breakpoint at a specified address or symbolic value. Wine will stop before executing instructions at this address. For example, break * GDI_Ordinal_24 sets a breakpoint at the start of Windows Ellipse function known internally as GDI.24.
bt	Backtrace, or show the history of Wine calls leading to the current place. The addresses shown are the return addresses, not the calling addresses.
cont	Continue program execution until a breakpoint or error condition is reached.
define	Equates a symbol to a value. For example: define myproc 0x000001c6.
disable	Disable a specific breakpoint. Breakpoints defined by the break command are stored by breakpoint numbers. To disable a breakpoint, find the breakpoint number with the info command. To disable breakpoint number 1, simply type disable 1.
enable	Enables a breakpoint number, the opposite of disable. To enable the previously disabled breakpoint number 1, simply type enable 1.
help	Prints a help text of the available commands.
info	Provides information on the following:
	reg registers information.
	stack dumps the current stack.
	break shows the current breakpoints and whether they are enabled.
	segments shows information about memory segments in use.
mode	Switches between 16- and 32-bit modes.

59

THE WINE
PROJECT

continues

TABLE 59.2. CONTINUED

Command	Meaning
print	Prints out values of expressions given.
quit	Exits debugger and ends any MS-Windows program in progress.
set	Enables depositing of values in registers and memory.
symbolfile	Loads a symbol file containing symbolic values. The file `wine.sym` is created as part of the Wine build.
x	Examines memory values in several different formats. The format of x is x / `format address`, where `format` can be one of the following:

x	longword hexadecimal (32-bit integer)
d	longword decimal
w	word hexadecimal
b	byte
c	single character
s	null-terminated ASCII string
I	i386 instruction

A number can be specified before the `format` to indicate a repeating group. For example, listing 10 instructions after a given address would be x / 10 I 0x000001cd.

In order to benefit from using the Wine debugger, an understanding of debugging i386 assembly is essential. If you are serious about debugging Wine, an assembly language output from GCC is essential.

How Wine Works

Wine is composed of a MS-Windows program loader and a library of MS-Windows functions.

How Wine Loads Programs

Wine's first duty is to load an MS-Windows executable image into memory. This also includes any DLL files and other resources that the application needs. MS-Windows uses a different executable image type than DOS which is called NE, or new executable. DLLs and font files also use this NE format, which makes Wine's job easier.

Individual segments of the NE image must be loaded into memory, and references to other DLL and Windows calls need to be resolved. Calls to functions outside an image are referred to by the module name and function number. A call to `Ellipse` is actually stored as GDI.24.

After an executable image is loaded into memory, Wine simply jumps to the `WinMain()` function defined in the image. A call to MS-Windows graphics function `Ellipse` is stored as *GDI.24*. *GDI* is the name of the MS-Windows graphics library, and 24 is the position in that DLL where `Ellipse` starts. Wine does not need to do any instruction emulation because both Linux and MS-Windows use the i386 instruction set. When an MS-Windows primitive function is called, Wine intercepts that call and passes it to a matching library routine.

The Wine Library

Wine converts the MS-Windows API to the matching X or UNIX API calls. A call to the MS-Windows `Ellipse` function to draw an ellipse in a window has the following format:

```
Ellipse (hdc, xLeft, yTop, xRight, yBottom);
```

The definitions of xLeft, yTop, xRight, and yBottom are a bounding box for an ellipse.

The same ellipse is drawn under the X API `XDrawArc` function:

```
XDrawArc(display, d, gc, x, y, width, height, angle1, angle2);
```

Wine needs to do a little math to convert the coordinates from an `Ellipse` call to that of an `XDrawArc` call. Other parameters of the `XDrawArc` call are a bit easier to map. The *d* refers to a drawable area, which is typically a handle to a window. Under MS-Windows, this is contained in the `hdc` structure. The *gc* is a graphics context and is analogous in functionality to the *hdc* under MS-Windows. As X is capable of displaying on different machines over a network, the *display* parameter describes which display to use. The *display* parameter remains constant over the life of a Wine session. The last thing Wine has to consider is that an MS-Windows `Ellipse` call can also specify a filled ellipse. Wine checks the `hdc` and possibly uses `XFillArc` instead.

There are nearly 300 graphics primitives available under MS-Windows that need to undergo similar translations. While this might seem to be a bit of work, the graphics conversions are among the simpler things to emulate under MS-Windows.

59

THE WINE
PROJECT

Where Does Wine End and MS-Windows Begin?

Because Wine currently requires parts of MS-Windows to operate, it is a bit confusing to know where Wine ends and MS-Windows begins. Wine currently provides API calls for the following parts of a typical MS-Windows installation:

commdlg	Common Windows Dialogs
gdi	Graphics Device Interface
kernel	Kernel Interface
keyboard	Keyboard Interface
mmsystem	Multimedia System Interface
mouse	Mouse Interface
shell	Windows 3.1 Shell API Library
sound	Windows sound system
toolhelp	Debugging and tools helper calls
user	Microsoft Windows User Interface
win87em	Coprocessor/Emulator Library
winsock	Windows Socket interface (TCP/IP)

Wine requires access to some parts of MS-Windows to use features that are not implemented by Wine. One example is the MS-Windows dynamic link library OLECLI, which implements the OLE client. The Wine team has made significant headway in reducing the amount of files needed. The Wine project charter includes removing any dependency on MS-Windows files. This includes utilities and file organizations to install MS-Windows applications.

Some of the simplest MS-Windows applications run today under Wine without need of any MS-Windows code or access to any MS-Windows directories. WINMINE.EXE and SOL.EXE are examples of such applications. Although no suggested directory organization exists to support this, a quick example of doing this is the following:

1. Copy winmine.exe and win.ini to a Linux directory such as /users/windows.
2. Change the Windows path options in wine.conf to /users/windows, for example.
3. Dismount your MS-DOS partition.
4. Run Wine.

Limitations of Wine

Only a few MS-Windows software packages run correctly under Wine. Luckily, it is possible to estimate how likely a program is to run correctly without actually executing it. Unfortunately, there are some classes of applications that are unlikely to ever run under Wine.

Software That Works

The most recent versions of Wine support a good number of the MS-Windows applets and games included with the stock MS-Windows 3.1. There are considerable variations between each release of Wine. Changes that help some applications often break others. But here are some of the accessories and games that work reasonably well under Wine:

- `calc.exe`
- `clock.exe`
- `cruel.exe`
- `golf.exe`
- `notepad.exe`
- `pipe.exe`
- `pegged.exe`
- `reversi.exe`
- `winmine.exe`

Using `winestat` to Analyze Windows Programs

Part of Wine is the `winestat` utility. This is actually the same program as Wine, but instead of running an MS-Windows executable, `winestat` simply attempts to load a Windows executable and reports on how successful the load was. In loading an executable, `winestat` also loads any DLLs necessary and reports if any are missing. `winestat` looks for Windows API calls that are used by either the executable or any DLL and verifies their existence. A sample `winestat` run on the MS-Windows Paintbrush applet `pbrush` yields the following:

```
KERNEL.1 not implemented
KERNEL.54 not implemented
KERNEL.113 not implemented
KERNEL.114 not implemented
KERNEL.121 not implemented
KERNEL.154 not implemented
KERNEL.178 not implemented
```

```
KERNEL.207 not implemented
KERNEL: 52 of 66 (86.7 %)
USER: 150 of 150 (100.0 %)
GDI.151 not implemented
GDI.307 not implemented
GDI.366 not implemented
GDI.439 not implemented
GDI: 80 of 84 (95.2 %)
SHELL: 9 of 9 (100.0 %)
KEYBOARD: 2 of 2 (100.0 %)
TOTAL: 293 of 305 winapi functions implemented (96.1 %)
```

winestat calls out the individual functions by number and module that are not implemented by Wine. If you are curious as to the function name, rather than number, look at the Wine sources in the if1632 directory for the given module name's spec file. A sample kernel.spec file is as follows:

```
#1 FATALEXIT
#2 EXITKERNEL
3   pascal GetVersion() GetVersion()
...
...
...
#54 pascal16 GETINSTANCEDATA
```

Any line in a .spec file that starts with a # is considered a comment, not an implemented function. In this example, both 1 and 54 are commented, with the respective names of FATALEXIT and GETINSTANCEDATA. FATALEXIT is used for debugging MS-Windows programs under error conditions and is not important for most MS-Windows users. GETINSTANCEDATA copies configuration data from a previous instance of an application. If you are running only one instance of an application, this does not apply.

The final percentage shows which MS-Windows API calls are implemented. This is often a good measure of how much of an application could work under Wine. Unfortunately, if a single, unimplemented API call is needed to initialize your MS-Windows application, anything less than 100 percent is not good enough.

MS-Windows applications to which winestat gives an overall implementation rating over 95 percent are worth a try. Unlike DOSemu, Wine is not as prone to leaving Linux in an unusable state. However, it is not always a trivial matter to kill an errant Wine session. The easiest thing to do is to start Wine with a separate desktop: wine -desktop 800×660 *filename*. Normal methods of killing a Windows process from your window manager should work.

> **TIP**
>
> When all else fails to stop an errant Wine session, switch to a free virtual console and kill the errant Wine process. For example, Alt+Ctrl and F2 would switch to virtual console number 2. You can log in to a virtual console and use `ps -ax | grep wine` to find your Wine sessions. Use `kill -15` *pid* where *pid* is the process id returned by `ps` to stop the process.
>
> You can return to your X session by switching to the virtual console that is running X. If you don't know what console number that is, hold the Alt and Ctrl keys, and press F1 through F8 until you find it.

Major Pieces That Are Missing from Wine

Perhaps the most obvious omission from Wine is the lack of a printer interface. Because this is a complex process, work on a printer interface is little more than a few ideas. It would be a huge task to support all of the types of printers supported under MS-Windows. Wine will likely implement only a PostScript driver. Existing Linux utilities such as `GhostScript` are already capable of converting PostScript to other types of printer types, such as HP laser and inkjet printers.

The 32-bit Windows API (`win32`) is mostly unsupported. This is the executable image format for Windows NT and Windows 95, and is known as PE (portable executable). Wine currently supports the loading of resource files, such as fonts, that are in PE format, but is unable to handle executables or DLLs.

Software Unlikely to Ever Work

The Wine project has no plans to support Windows Virtual Device Drivers (VDDs). VDDs use a different image format, called LE for linear executable, that the Wine loader is unable to handle. Because VDDs do things like direct hardware manipulation, coexistence of a VDD with Linux device drivers would be a tough problem indeed. One of the uses of VDDs in commercial MS-Windows is for TCP/IP stacks. Wine supports TCP/IP through the `winsock` DLL, which uses the TCP/IP inherent in the Linux kernel.

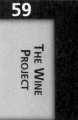

59

THE WINE
PROJECT

Summary

In this chapter you've seen how to set up and use the Wine Windows Emulator to run Windows applications. Wine is not the only way to accomplish this task; there are several other Windows emulators and binary interfaces available (such as WABI). However,

Wine is one of the oldest (at least as far as Linux is concerned) and has a good user base to support it.

From here you can explore related chapters:

Use Wabi, the Windows Application Binary Interface, which lets you run Windows applications under X, in Chapter 23, "Wabi."

Program C and C++ under Linux in Chapter 26, "Programming in C," and Chapter 27, "Programming in C++."

Use the source code control system to control multiple file versions at once in Chapter 56, "Source Code Control."

HylaFAX

by Tim Parker

One of the more useful aspects of computers is the capability to take a document you've written in your favorite word processor and fax it to someone. This saves time, paper, and effort over the old routine of printing a copy, feeding it into a fax machine, and sending it manually. Fax programs on computers allow you both to send from any application that has a print output feature and to receive incoming faxes from others.

Although the most effective fax programs available for PCs are designed for Windows, several fax utilities exist for UNIX and Linux. You can purchase a commercial fax software package for your Linux system from a number of vendors, but luckily several are free of charge. If you plan to use your Linux system regularly, you may want to consider installing one of these fax tools.

The most commonly used Linux fax utility is called HylaFAX. HylaFAX was written by Sam Leffer and is available free of charge. Rather than a poor imitation of a commercial fax package, HylaFAX is a complete fax reception and transmission system in one and rivals commercial packages in features and utility. HylaFAX depends on the Ghostscript system to handle fax images, so you may want to read up about Ghostscript (if you didn't already) in Chapter 27, "Programming in C++."

Installing HylaFAX

Most Linux distributions include HylaFAX as part of the CD-ROM set. If you didn't get a copy of HylaFAX you can download it from many FTP and Web sites. You may find a program called FlexFAX which was an earlier utility that HylaFAX is based on. If you have a choice, go for HylaFAX. For most versions of HylaFax, you're going to need a C++ compiler as well because only source code is provided. The GNU C++ compiler that comes with most Linux systems is fine.

> **TIP**
>
> HylaFAX is available from most FTP sites, but the "home" site for the tool is `ftp.sgi.com`. Check the directory listings for HylaFAX information. Documentation for HylaFAX is available through the FTP sites or on the World Wide Web at `http://www.sgi.com`.
>
> For more descriptions and history of HylaFAX, check out the site `http://www.vix.com/hylaFAX`.

If you have a gzipped, compressed, or tarred file you need to extract, the HylaFAX dumps contents from it into a temporary directory. For example, if you have the HylaFAX archive `HylaFax-v4.0-tar.gz`, you would unpack it and place it in a fax directory with these commands:

```
mkdir /usr/fax
cd /usr/fax
cp /tmp/HylaFax-v4.0-tar.gz .
gunzip HylaFax-v4.0-tar.gz
tar -xf HylaFax-v4.0-tar
```

Perform all these steps as root. Of course, you must substitute the directory in which you placed the HylaFAX archive for `/tmp` in the above commands. If you don't want to use `/usr/fax` as the HylaFAX directory, change those commands to your target directory, too.

Compiling HylaFAX

After all the files are extracted in your fax directory, you need to invoke the C++ compiler to produce an executable. There may be some important information in a file in the subdirectory `/port/linux`, usually as a file called README. To compile HylaFAX, issue the following commands (remember you must be logged in as root):

```
configure
make clean
make install
```

There are a bunch of steps that appear from the `configure` and `make` commands that we'll look at in a moment. When you issue the `configure` command, you'll see a bunch of messages about which directories HylaFAX should use:

```
HylaFAX configuration parameters are:

Directory for applications:        /usr/local/bin
Directory for lib data files:      /usr/local/lib/fax
Directory for lib executables:     /usr/local/lib/fax
Directory for servers:             /usr/local/etc
Directory for manual pages:        /usr/local/man
Directory for documentation:       /usr/local/doc/HylaFAX
Directory for spooling:            /usr/spool/fax
Type of uucp lock files:           ascii
Directory for uucp lock files:     /usr/spool/uucp
Mode for uucp lock files:          0444
Type of PostScript imager:         gs
PostScript imager program:         /usr/local/bin/gs
Default page size:                 North American Letter
```

```
Default vertical res (lpi):     98
Directory for font metrics:     /usr/local/lib/afm
Location of sendmail program:   /usr/lib/sendmail
Are these ok [yes]?
```

Don't change any of these default directory locations because they are used by many other applications in Linux. When you issue the make command, you will have to wait a few minutes while the compiler completes its task because it must pass through several stages and pull files from many locations on your system.

When the installation routine is complete, check to make sure that the directory /usr/local/bin/fax exists and has files in it. If it does, you will be able to use HylaFAX.

Adding Modems

The next step is to add modems to HylaFAX. These are added with the faxaddmodem script, which guides you through each step in configuring the modems. HylaFAX works with most Class 1 and Class 2 fax modems, which means the majority of modems that support fax capabilities available today. When you run faxaddmodem, you are asked a series of questions, most of which you should leave with the default settings (again, this routine should be run as root):

```
# faxaddmodem
Verifying your system is set up properly for fax service...

There is no entry for the fax user in the password file.
The fax software needs a name to work properly; add it [yes]?

  Added user "fax" to /etc/passwd.
  Added fax user to "/etc/passwd.sgi".

There does not appear to be an entry for the fax service in
either the yellow pages database or the /etc/services file;
should an entry be added to /etc/services [yes]?

There is no entry for the fax service in "/usr/etc/inetd.conf";
should one be added [yes]?

Poking inetd so that it rereads the configuration file.

There does not appear to be an entry for the FaxMaster in
either the yellow pages database or the /usr/lib/aliases file;
should an entry be added to /usr/lib/aliases [yes]?
Users to receive fax-related mail [root]?

Rebuilding /usr/lib/aliases database.
46 aliases, longest 81 bytes, 923 bytes total
```

Done verifying system setup.

Serial port that modem is connected to []? cua1

Ok, time to set up a configuration file for the modem. The manual
page config(4F) may be useful during this process. Also be aware
that at any time you can safely interrupt this procedure.

No existing configuration. Let's do this from scratch.

Phone number of fax modem []? +1.613.838.1234

This is the phone number associated with the modem being configured.
It is passed as an "identity"' to peer fax machines and it may
also appear on tag lines created by the fax server.
The phone number should be a complete international dialing specification
in the form +&ltcountry code> &ltarea code> &ltlocal part>.
Any other characters included for readability are automatically
removed if they might cause problems.

Area code []? 613
Country code [1]?
Long distance dialing prefix [1]?
International dialing prefix [011]?
Tracing during normal server operation [1]?
Tracing during send and receive sessions [11]?
Protection mode for received fax [0600]?
Rings to wait before answering [1]?
Modem speaker volume [off]?

The server configuration parameters are

```
    FAXNumber:              +1.613.838.1234
    AreaCode                613
    CountryCode             1
    LongDistancePrefix:     1
    InternationalPrefix:    011
    ServerTracing:          1
    SessionTracing:         11
    RecvFileMode:           0600
    RingsBeforeAnswer:      1
    SpeakerVolume:          off
```

    Are these ok [yes]?

Now we are going to probe the tty port to figure out the type
of modem that is attached. This takes a few seconds, so be patient.
Note that if you do not have the modem cabled to the port, or the
modem is turned off, this may hang (just go and cable up the modem
or turn it on, or whatever).

```
Hmm, this looks like a Class 1 modem.
Product code is "1444".
Modem manufacturer is "USRobotics".
Modem model is "Courier".

Using prototype configuration file config.usr-courier...

The modem configuration parameters are:

ModemRate:              19200
ModemFlowControl:       xonxoff
ModemFlowControlCmd:    &H2
ModemSetupDTRCmd:       S13=1&D2
ModemSetupDCDCmd:       &C1
ModemDialCmd:           DT%s@
ModemResultCodesCmd     X4

Are these ok [yes]?

Startup a fax server for this modem [yes]
/usr/etc/faxd -m /dev/cua1
```

The only prompts that need your attention are the port the modem is attached to (/dev/cua1 used above is the second serial port, since a mouse usually resides on the first) and the phone number and area code of your fax line. You will notice that HylaFAX creates a user in the /etc/passwd file called "fax" which has the same User ID number (UID) as the uucp user since the modems are often shared between these two programs. HylaFAX allows multiple modems to be configured and managed if you have several incoming lines.

The HylaFAX program uses the application called faxd.recv to allow client applications to communicate with the HylaFAX server. The faxd.recv program is usually started from inetd when the system boots into multiuser mode. The HylaFAX configuration routine will likely add the proper entries to the inetd files. If not, you can add the following line to the inetd file:

```
fax stream tcp nowait fax /usr/libexec/fax.d/faxd.recv faxd.recv
```

To start the HylaFAX daemon you need to issue the following command with the proper port that you are using for your fax modem:

```
/usr/etc/faxd -m /dev/cua1
```

If you want to start the fax daemon every time you boot your system, place this command in the /etc/rc.d file.

The same daemon, faxd, is used by HylaFAX for both sending and receiving faxes. When you are receiving a fax, there is no way to abort other than turning off the modem.

Sending a Fax

To send a fax using HylaFAX, use the `sendfax` command. Usually you will send a Postscript (or Ghostscript) file or a TIFF document using the `sendfax` command. Some other file formats (such as ASCII and troff) are converted automatically by `sendfax` before being sent. Check the documentation that accompanies your version of HylaFAX to find out which file formats are supported.

The `sendfax` Options

There are a lot of options possible with `sendfax`, as Table 60.1 shows. These options can be combined in any order in a complete command.

TABLE 60.1. HYLAFAX `sendfax` COMMAND OPTIONS.

HylaFAX option	*What it does*
-c	For comments
-d	Specifies destination
-f	From
-h	Host name
-i	Identifier to place on fax
-k	Gives the kill time
-l	Low resolution mode
-m	Medium resolution mode
-n	Suppresses cover page
-p	Specify page count to include on cover and pages
-r	Regarding text
-s	Specifies the page size name (default size is 8.5x11)
-t	Number of tries to use
-v	Echoes status messages to screen
-x	Company name to send to
-y	Location to send to
-D	Notify sender by e-mail when fax sent
-R	Notify sender by e-mail if fax must be requeued

60

HYLAFAX

A cover page is generated by default by HylaFAX whenever you send a fax. The information on the cover page is taken from command line arguments to the sendfax command. Low resolution mode (98 lines per inch) is used by default unless you override it with fine resolution (196 lines per inch), called medium resolution by HylaFAX. HylaFAX will retry sending a fax until it connects within 24 hours of the sendfax command. To override this retry time, use the -k option.

Cover Pages

If you want to override the default HylaFAX cover page, you can use the faxcover command to specify the desired contents. The faxcover command creates a Postscript sheet for the cover that is attached to the front of each of your outgoing faxes.

There are several options supported by faxcover, as shown in Table 60.2. These options can be combined in any order.

TABLE 60.2. THE faxcover COMMAND OPTIONS.

Faxcover option	*What it does*
-c	Comment
-C	Specify a template file
-f	From
-l	The destination location
-n	Sender's fax number
-p	Page count
-r	Regarding (Re) comment
-s	Pagesize name
-t	Recipient
-v	Destination voice line number
-x	Destination company name

Receiving a Fax

If you allow HylaFAX to receive faxes, they are placed in the subdirectory recvq under the HylaFAX directory. All incoming faxes are saved as TIFF files. Access to the fax receiver directory can be controlled by the system administrator.

When a fax is received, HylaFAX sends a fax to a user login set by the variable `FaxMaster`. Alternatively, you can write a shell script that checks for the user the fax is destined for and sends email to them, or spools the incoming fax automatically to a printer.

HylaFAX uses a server process called `faxrcvd` to receive faxes. The daemon is clever enough to try to determine whether the incoming call is a fax call or a voice call. This allows the same modem to be used for incoming faxes and data calls, which are answered by UUCP or a getty process.

Summary

In this chapter you've seen how to configure and use HylaFAX, probably the most powerful and effective fax application available for Linux that doesn't require you to shell out money. From here, there are a number of other chapters that you may want to read:

To learn about Ghostscript, which is useful for viewing and producing PostScript files, see Chapter 24, "Ghostscript and Ghostview."

To learn about setting up modems on your system, see Chapter 33, "Devices."

To learn about backing up your system so you don't have to reconfigure HylaFAX, read Chapter 45, "Backups."

## CHAPTER 61

Games

by Ed Treijs and Tim Parker

IN THIS CHAPTER

A variety of games come with most Linux CD-ROMs and there are a lot more available through FTP sites and CD software collections. The available games can be roughly divided between those that require X to run and those that will run in plain text mode (on a character terminal). In this chapter, you will learn about both types of games. The chapter provides a reasonably complete list of both X- and character-based games.

Which Games Have You Installed?

The games listed in this chapter come in several different installation packages, so you may not have one or more of these games on your system. For instance, the graphical versions of `tetris`, `gnuchess`, and `xfractint` are each installed separately.

If one of the listed games sounds intriguing, you may want to install it if you haven't done so already.

X Games

The following games all require X to run. You can find most of the X games in a number of directories, depending on the version of Linux you use. Typical installation directories for games are

- `/var/lib/games`
- `/usr/games`
- `/usr/lib/games`
- `/usr/local/games`
- `/usr/share/games`

In many cases, you will have all these directories installed with games in each.

Because X is a graphical, windowing environment, you might guess that X games are graphically oriented. You would be right! Almost all of the following games use color and bitmapped graphics. Often, you can specify the palette of colors the game will use.

However, you should keep in mind the following:

- Arcade games and home video game systems have dedicated hardware that is designed specifically for running games. X Window is a generic environment. Even today's powerful personal computers can't match the speed and smoothness of movement of a game machine.

- Games work your hardware and operating system software harder than any other application. For best performance, games are often programmed to run "close to the edge" and do various software and hardware tricks. You might find that one or more of these games crash your system or have strange side effects.

- The X games that come with Linux are personal efforts. The individuals who wrote the games and allow free distribution appreciate suggestions and help in further development. Don't hold these games to commercial standards—they are not commercial products.

- The Slackware version on the CD-ROM lets you install two types of games. The "Y" set contains the BSD games collection and the other set "XAP" contains the games with X Window support. Install both versions and then remove the games you don't like.

> **NOTE**
>
> It's tempting to put new games in `/usr/games`, though the most common area for user-installed games is in `/usr/local/games`. The `/usr/games` directory is usually reserved for games that come with the system.

Following is a discussion of the X games you should find on your system. Keep in mind that installation differences might mean that you have more or fewer games.

Games in the `xdm` Root Menu

If you use the X display manager `xdm`, the `xdm` Root menu (usually accessed by holding the right mouse button while the cursor is in the root screen area) has a Games submenu choice. From the Games menu, you can then choose a Demo/Gadgets submenu. If you use a different window manager, such as Motif, your menus will be correspondingly different. Games available through the menu depend on the version of Linux, too. Here's a list of some Linux X-based games and a description of them.

Spider (Small and Large)

This is double-deck solitaire. There is no difference in the play of Spider (small) and Spider (large). The difference is that the small Spider game uses smaller cards and therefore fits into a smaller window than the large Spider game.

To see this game's man page, type **man spider**.

To start this game, type **spider** in a command-line window.

This game requires a fair bit of thought, planning, and skill. The aim is to arrange cards of the same suit in descending order. You can also, however, have cards of different suits arranged in descending order. Sometimes this can help you immediately, but hinder you in the long run! Note that if you do have two or more consecutive cards of the same suit, those cards will move as a group. Spider is challenging; don't try to play it just to pass the time!

Puzzle

This is a superior version of the game—usually played at a child's party—in which you push around 15 numbered tiles on a 16×16 grid, trying to get the numbers in order.

To see this game's man page, type **man puzzle**.

To start this game, type Puzzle in a command-line window.

The reason the X version of Puzzle is superior is because the pieces move very smoothly. Let's face it, the party favor plastic versions kept jamming and sticking. This is a vast improvement.

If you click on the left box, the game gives you a random starting position. Click on the right box and watch the game solve itself! (Try clicking on the right box when the numbers are already in order.)

GNU Chess

This is a graphical version of GNU Chess that uses the xboard display system.

> **WARNING**
>
> Running GNU Chess under xboard is very resource-intensive. It may crash your system.
>
> Adding more swap space may correct an agonizingly long response time. Do not worry, it's not your system—it's GNU Chess.

Xtetris

If you've never been hooked on Tetris, here's your chance. This is a nice X implementation of a game that always seems to suffer when taken from the video arcade and placed on a home computer.

To see this game's man page, type **man xtetris**.

To start this game, type **xtetris** in a command-line window.

The colors are nicely done and the movement is relatively smooth. However, if you're used to the arcade version of Tetris, watch out for the following:

- Left- and right-arrow keys move from side to side; up- and down-arrow keys rotate clockwise and counterclockwise. Most people have a preferred direction of rotation for the pieces; experiment to find out which way is right for you.

- The spacebar, as is typical on home-computer implementation, slam-dunks the piece to the bottom rather than just hauling it down faster.

- The colors of the pieces, although attractive, are sometimes confusing. For instance, the L-shaped piece that is yellow in the arcade version is purple in Xtetris, and the L-shaped piece that is purple in the arcade version is light blue in Xtetris. Again, very confusing if you're used to the arcade version.

The purpose of the game? Arrange the pieces so they interlock without gaps. As soon as you create a (horizontal) row that's completely filled, it vaporizes. This is good, because when the pieces stack up to the top, the game is over. (Pity the Cossack doesn't come out and tap his feet when things start to get a little out of control.)

Xlander

This is an update of the old arcade game, Lunar Lander. You get a bird's-eye view from the window of your lunar lander. By operating the main and directional thruster engines, you attempt to touch down softly on the landing pad. If things go wrong, instead of a bird's-eye view, you get a meteorite's-eye view!

To see this game's man page, type **man xlander**.

To start this game, type **xlander** in a command-line window.

You may have problems getting the game to respond to your keyboard input. In that case, the moon's surface is only a short plummet away.

Xmahjongg

This is an implementation of the old Chinese game. The graphics are attractively done; the ideograms on the pieces are very nice. The game builds your castle for you, of course. This alone speeds things up considerably.

There is no man page for Xmahjongg.

Xvier

Xvier is a relative of tic-tac-toe. On a 5×5 grid, you and the computer take turns placing your pieces; the first to get four pieces in a row, horizontally, diagonally, or vertically, wins. Xvier differs from tic-tac-toe in that you can only select the column where you want to place your playing piece; your piece then falls down the column to the lowest unoccupied row.

To see this game's man page, type **man xvier**.

To start this game, type **xvier** in a command-line window.

You can change the level of the computer's play by typing a number between 0 and 9 while in the game. However, in the higher levels, the computer thinks for a *long* time. Increase the level of play only one at a time. The default level of play is 0; you may not want to exceed 3.

Ico

Ico sets a polyhedron (a solid, multisided geometric shape) bouncing around your screen. Depending on the options specified, this three-dimensional polygon can occupy its own window or use the entire root window.

To see this game's man page, type **man ico**. It can be started from the command line (within X Window) by typing **ico**. In fact, you *should* start it from the command line because of the options available. If you start it from the Demo/Gadgets menu, you will only get a wireframe polygon in its own, small window.

One interesting option you can use from the command line is `-colors`. If you specify more than one color, you get a multicolored polyhedron, with each face a different color.

With the `-colors` option, you must enter the colors to be used in the following format: `rgb:<red intensity>/<green intensity>/<blue intensity>`. The intensities have to be specified in hexadecimal notation; `000` is the lowest value and `fff` is the highest. For example, the complete command might be as follows:

```
ico -color rgb:000/888/fff rgb:e00/400/b80 rgb:123/789/def
```

This program is fairly resource-intensive and may slow down your system.

Maze

This draws a maze, and then solves it. There is no way you can solve it for yourself. Maze is a demo, not a game. On a fast system, it solves it too quickly to follow!

Xeyes

Not really a game, but cute anyway. Whenever you start Xeyes, you get a large pair of bodiless eyes that follow your cursor's movements. Running four or five copies of Xeyes at once gives your system a surreal touch.

To see this game's man page, type **man xeyes**.

To start this game, type Xeyes in a command-line window.

Xgas

This is a demo of how pure gases behave, but you don't need a degree in thermo-dynamics and statistical mechanics to find this fun to watch. You have two chambers side-by-side, with a small opening in the wall between them. The chambers can be set to different temperatures. The neat part is when you place your cursor in one of the chambers and click the left mouse button—every click launches another gas particle in a random direction!

To see this game's man page, type **man xgas**. Online help also is available.

To start this game, type **xgas** in a command-line window.

Xlogo

This displays the official X logo.

Xroach

This is halfway between a game and a demo. Don't start this up if insects give you the shivers!

If you have ever lived in a roach-infested building, this will bring back fond (or not-so-fond) memories. Every time you start another copy of Xroach, a new set of roaches goes scurrying around your screen, looking for windows to hide under. Eventually you don't see them—until you move or close some windows!

To see this game's man page, type **man xroach**.

To start this game, type **xroach** in a command-line window.

If you start Xroach from the command line, you can add -squish. You can then try to swat the insects by clicking on them. Be warned, however: they're fast. You can also specify what color the roach guts will be, should you succeed in squishing some.

Xhextris

This is a version of Tetris that uses pieces made up of hexagons. To start the game, type **xhextris** on an X Window command line. No man page is available.

Xbombs

This is an X version of Minesweeper. You are given a large grid. Some of the squares contain mines. Your job is to flag all of the mines.

This game is started by typing **xbombs** at the Linux prompt in a command-line window. No man page is available.

Starting Xbombs brings up the playing field, which is a dark gray grid, and a Score window.

You uncover a square by clicking on it with the left mouse button. If you uncover a mine, you are blown up and the game is over!

It's more likely, though, that you will either uncover a number or open up several light gray, blank squares (with no numbers or mines). The number tells you how many mines are found adjacent to that square, horizontally, vertically, or diagonally. For example, a "1" means there is only one mine adjacent to that square. If you've already determined the location of one mine adjacent to a "1" square, then it's safe to uncover all other squares next to the "1" square because they can't possibly contain a mine! In this fashion, you try to deduce the location of the mines. If you happen to uncover a square that has no number (and therefore no mines next to it), the game will automatically uncover the entire numberless area and its border.

When you think you've located a mine, you "sweep" or mark it by clicking on it with the *right* mouse button (if you click the left button accidentally and there is indeed a mine there, the game is over). The right button toggles a flag marker on and off. Note that the game does not tell you whether you have correctly placed the flag.

You will soon discover that certain patterns of numbers let you place a mine without any doubt; other times, you have to make an educated guess.

Of course, sometimes you miscalculate and blow up. To restart the game, click with either mouse button in the Score window. If you complete the game successfully, your time will be recorded.

Xpaint

This is a color drawing-and-painting program. Start it from the Linux prompt in a command-line window by typing **xpaint**. A Tool menu will appear. Start a new canvas

from the File menu. The Tool menu holds your drawing and painting implements (brushes, pencils, spray cans, and so on); the palette of colors and patterns is found underneath the canvas.

To see the man page, type `man xpaint`.

Xfractint

Xfractint is an easy way to get started with fractals. If you're not sure what a fractal is, try this program! It's almost certain that you've seen fractals before.

To see this game's man page, type `man xfractint`.

To start this game, type `xfractint` in a command-line window.

This program has an excellent setup; you can immediately generate many different fractals without getting into their detailed specifications or mathematics.

When you start Xfractint, two windows appear: one that holds the fractal image (initially empty) and another in which you enter your commands. You can go into the Type selection and choose the type of fractal to generate, or you can click on Select video mode which starts drawing a fractal in the image window. The default fractal is one of the Mandelbrot types.

When the image has been fully generated (it can take some time), you can go to the command window, type **t**, and select another type of fractal from the large list of available choices. At this point, you shouldn't have to change the defaults the program gives you. There are enough different types available.

To exit Xfractint, press the Esc key twice from the command window.

Character-based Games

There is a long history of games being written for the UNIX operating system. Many of these games were written before color, bitmapped windowing systems became common. All these games, except for Sasteroids, are character-based. This means that all graphics (if there are any!) are displayed on your screen using standard screen characters: A, *, ¦, x, and so on. In addition, all input is from the keyboard (again, Sasteroids is an exception).

An advantage of character-based games is that they do not require a graphical or windowing environment to run. A monochrome display is fine. The character-based nature of some games, such as Hangman or Bog (Boggle), takes nothing away from the play; you don't really wish for fancy color graphics when playing them. Other character-based games might strike you as interesting historical curiosities: They show you what their ingenious programmers could manage with such a simple display system, but clearly would be better served by color graphics.

TIP

Two of the more interesting (and classic) character-based games, Rogue and Hack, do not come with the Linux distribution. These games use the screen to display the rooms and corridors of a dungeon. You (and, in Hack, your trusty dog) move around the dungeon, mapping out the corridors, entering the rooms (be careful when you explore dark, unlit rooms), picking up treasure and magical items—and, last but not least, fighting monsters (or running from them!). After you have fully explored the level you're on, you can descend to a lower, more difficult level.

Every time you run Hack or Rogue, the dungeons are different. Every monster has different fighting skills, and some monsters have special talents. The magical items, which include rings, wands, scrolls, and potions, have a variety of effects. Some of the items you find, such as armor, might be enchanted or magically enhanced; but if you find a cursed item, you may have been better off not picking it up at all!

Both Rogue and Hack have their enthusiasts, but Hack is a later, more elaborate version which is generally preferred. If you come across either game on the Internet, pick it up and try it! There are also versions of Hack available for MS-DOS-based computers.

Text Adventure Games

These games follow the classic text-based formula: the system informs you that "you are in a maze of small twisty passages, all alike" or something similar; you type in your actions as **go forward**, **east**, **take sword**, and so on. If you like solving puzzles, these games will appeal to you. With text-based games, the adventure follows a defined path, and your responses are usually limited.

The following example is the start of the text-based game Battlestar, which you will learn about in the next section. Your commands are typed at the >-: prompt:

```
Version 4.2, fall 1984.
First Adventure game written by His Lordship, the honorable
Admiral D.W. Riggle


        This is a luxurious stateroom.
```

```
The floor is carpeted with a soft animal fur and the great wooden
furniture is inlaid with strips of platinum and gold.  Electronic
equipment built into the walls and ceiling is flashing wildly.  The floor
shudders and the sounds of dull explosions rumble though the room.  From a
window in the wall ahead comes a view of darkest space.  There is a small
adjoining room behind you, and a doorway right.

>-: right
        These are the executive suites of the battlestar.
Luxurious staterooms carpeted with crushed velvet and adorned with beaten
gold open onto this parlor. A wide staircase with ivory banisters leads
up or down. This parlor leads into a hallway left. The bridal suite is
right.
Other rooms lie ahead and behind you.

>-: up
        You are at the entrance to the dining hall.
A wide staircase with ebony banisters leads down here.
The dining hall is to the ahead.

>-: bye
Your rating was novice.
```

Battlestar

Type **battlestar** at the command prompt. A sample session is shown in the code in the previous section. A man page is available by typing **man battlestar.**

Dungeon

Type **dungeon** at the command prompt. Typing **help** at the game prompt gives you useful information. You start out-of-doors and must find the dungeon entrance. There is no man page for Dungeon.

Paranoia

Type **paranoia** at the command prompt. In this humorous game, you play a secret agent on a desperate mission. Unlike most text-based adventure games, Paranoia lets you choose your actions from a menu. This is useful if you hate having to find a command that the game will understand. There is no man page for **paranoia**.

Wump

Type **wump** at the command prompt. You are out hunting the Wumpus, armed with some custom arrows and relying on your wit and sense of smell. When you start the game, you are given the choice of seeing the instructions.

Type **man wumpus** to see the man page.

Word Games

The following two games are versions of popular word-finding and word-guessing games.

Boggle

Type **bog** at the command prompt. This is a version of the Parker Brothers game Boggle Deluxe. You are given a 5×5 grid of letters. In the allotted time of three minutes, you type in words made up from the given letters. By default, you must use letters that adjoin horizontally, vertically, and diagonally without reusing any letters. Plurals and different tenses count as different words—for instance, "use," "uses," "used," and "user" are all allowed in your word list. This follows the official Boggle rules. You can change these defaults, if you want.

At the end, the computer displays the list of words which it found. You can never beat the computer because it only allows you to type in real words. You will discover that the Boggle dictionary has some odd omissions; this can be annoying, but it isn't very serious.

This game works well without color graphics, although the small size of the letter grid makes your eyes blur after a while.

A man page is available by typing **man bog**.

Hangman

Type **hangman** at the command prompt. You won't miss the color graphics. The game is self-explanatory, but just in case, a man page is available; type **man hangman**. Hangman picks its words at random; sometimes the choices seem quite impossible to guess.

Card Games

Because of the lack of graphics, the following games are not as successful as the character-based word games.

Canfield

Type **canfield** at the command prompt. This is a version of solitaire. A man page is available by typing **man canfield**. This game does not have the time-wasting potential of graphics and mouse-based solitaire games.

Cribbage

Type **cribbage** at the command prompt. If you're a cribbage fan, this game is for you. A man page is available by typing **man cribbage**.

Go Fish

Type **fish** at the command prompt. It's you against the computer at Go Fish. A man page is available by typing **man fish**. One confusing aspect is that sometimes several actions are displayed all together on the screen (for instance, you have to go fish, the computer has to go fish, and it's back to you, all in one block).

Board Games

These are character-based versions of board games. The play quality is variable; backgammon is probably the best of the lot.

Backgammon

Type **backgammon** at the command prompt; or, for an easy-to-follow tutorial on how to play backgammon, type **teachgammon**. These games don't suffer from a lack of graphics, but the lack of a pointing device such as a mouse means that specifying your moves is a cumbersome task, requiring entries such as 8-12,4-5. Typing **?** at the game prompt gives you help on entering your moves.

Typing **man backgammon** gives you the manual entry for both Backgammon and Teachgammon.

Chess

Several chess and chess-related programs come in the gnuchess package. Type **gnuchess** at the prompt to play chess against the computer. There is an analysis program, gnuan. The game utility prints the chessboard position to a PostScript printer or file.

Enter your moves using standard algebraic notation—for instance, e2-4.

This is an elaborate package; you should start by reading the man page.

Mille Miglia

Type **mille** at the command prompt. This is the Linux version of a Parker Brothers racing game. You should read the man page before starting because the game's commands are not very intuitive. To see the man page, type **man mille**.

Monopoly

Type **monop** at the command prompt. This is a character-based version of the Parker Brothers game Monopoly. The computer does not actually play; it simply keeps track of who owns what and how much money each player has. You can play by yourself, but it's pretty obvious that you will, eventually, win! Unfortunately, the board is not displayed in any form, making it quite difficult to keep track of what's happening. This is an interesting effort, but the play is poor. A man page is available.

Simulations

The following games let you try your hand at being in charge. They are open-ended in that each game is different and does not follow a canned plot. They combine character graphics such as a radar display with text readouts and text-based commands.

Air Traffic Control

Type **atc** at the command prompt. Type **man atc** and read the man page first; otherwise, you will be responsible for one or more air tragedies! This game runs in real time. A good supply of caffeine will probably help you do well.

Sail

Type **sail** at the command prompt. You have a choice of over 20 scenarios, mainly historical battles involving sailing ships. You are the captain and determine what course to sail and which weapons to use. A man page is available by typing **man sail**; it's worth reading beforehand because some commands are obscure or confusing.

Trek

Type **trek** at the command prompt. You can "go where no one has gone before," hunt (and be hunted by) Klingons, and so on. A man page is available by typing **man trek**; read it before playing to avoid being a disgrace to the Federation.

"Video" Games

The following games all rely on a full-screen display, although all graphics are assembled from the standard character set.

Robots

Type **robots** at the command prompt. Robots on the screen pursue you; your only hope is to make two robots collide, at which point the robots explode. The resulting junk heap destroys any robots that run into it. You move about the screen using the hjkl keys, as used by the vi editor (diagonal movement is allowed, using yubn). Moves are simultaneous: each time you move, so do the robots. Sometimes, though, you have to teleport to get out of an impossible situation. You die if a robot touches you; otherwise, after clearing the screen, you go on to a bigger and better wave of robots. A man page is available by typing **man robots**.

Some Linux distributions may include a version of Robots that has been hacked or modified so that you can't make a misstep that brings you in contact with a robot (thus leading to your demise). This takes away from the challenge of the game.

Snake

Type **snake** at the command prompt. Use the hjkl keys to move around, picking up money (the $) while avoiding the snake (made up, appropriately, of s characters). The snake gets hungrier as you get richer. Escape the room by running to the # character or be eaten by the snake! You can also type w in an emergency to warp to a random location. A man page is available by typing **man snake**.

Tetris

Type **tetris** at the command prompt. The Tetris play screen is drawn with clever use of various characters. Ironically, although it does not look anywhere near as professional as Xtetris or other full-graphics versions, it plays very well—especially if you're used to the arcade version of Tetris. The movement keys consist of , to move left, / to move right, and . to rotate (counterclockwise!). The spacebar drops the piece. You can vary the control keys by using options with the tetris command. See the man page (type **man tetris**) for details.

Worm

Type **worm** at the command prompt. You are a worm, moving about the screen and eating numbers. As you eat the numbers, you grow in length. Do not run into yourself or into the wall! How long can you get before you (inevitably) run into something? Note that you still slowly crawl forward, even if you don't enter a move command.

A man page is available by typing **man worm**.

Math Games and Utilities

The following programs are small and interesting, although perhaps not particularly exciting.

Arithmetic

Type **arithmetic** at the command prompt. You are asked the answer to simple addition questions. This goes on until you type **Ctrl+C** to exit. A man page is available by typing **man arithmetic**.

BCD Punch Card Code, Morse Code, Paper Tape Punch Code

Type **bcd** at the command line to convert text you type to a punched card, type **morse** to see your text converted to Morse code, or type **ppt** for paper punch tape output. If the command line doesn't contain any text to encode, the programs go into interactive mode. Note that the Enter character you must use to finish each line of input gets coded as well. The bcd man page covers all three programs.

Factor

Type **factor** at the command line. This command provides you with the prime factors of any number you supply. You can type **factor <number>** to factor just the one number or **factor** without any number to go into interactive mode. Numbers can range from ×2147483648 to 2147483648. The following is a sample run of Factor:

```
darkstar:/usr/games$ factor
123
123: 3 41
36
36: 2 2 3 3
1234567
1234567: 127 9721
6378172984028367
factor: ouch
darkstar:/usr/games$
```

Primes

Type **primes** at the command prompt. If you include a range on the command line, Primes displays all prime numbers in the range. If no range is included, Primes waits for you to enter a number and then starts displaying primes greater than that number. The program is surprisingly fast! A man page is available by typing **man primes**.

Multiplayer Game: Hunt

This game requires several players. You have to hook up other terminals to your system (for instance, a character-based terminal to your serial port).

Full Graphics Game: Sasteroids

You must have a VGA or better color display for this game. Type **sasteroids** at the command prompt. The game takes over the screen, switching you to the color graphics mode. This is a relative of the arcade game Asteroids. The following keys control your ship:

Left-arrow key	Rotate counterclockwise
Right-arrow key	Rotate clockwise
Up-arrow key	Thrust
Down-arrow key	Enables the shield (one per ship)
Left Ctrl key	Fire
Left Alt key	Hyperspace

It takes a while to get the hang of the controls. The layout is very different from the standard arcade control layout. There is no man page available.

Other Thinking Games

The following programs might actually be a bit frustrating to play initially, but they can also provide hours of addictive fun!

Sokoban

Imagine yourself in charge of a warehouse containing a maze and lots of bales of cotton. Each bale is so heavy that you can only push it and not pull it. So don't push a bale into a spot where you cannot push it out. Each level in this game gets more and more challenging as you attempt to collect all the bales into a loading area where you can move to the next level. The source code is available from `sunsite.unc.edu` in the file `sokoban-src.tar.gz`.

DOOM

This exciting, though controversially gory, game is now ported to Linux as well. Complete with sound support and exquisite graphics, this Linux port does its DOS counterpart justice. One problem to keep in mind though, is that your colormaps in X may be mixed up once your cursor moves out of the X terminal you run DOOM under. Two other things to keep in mind—you have to rebuild your kernel to add the sound support and the version 1.666 of DOOM will not run external WAD files. (I recommend that you get the registered version.)

Conquest

This is an elaborate game of global conquest with equally complex instructions and display. At least the files are in an executable form, and you do not have to build them. One thing to remember is to use the `xconq` file and run `xset fp rehash` to bring up the correct fonts. A comparable game called Empire is also available in source from `tsx-11.mit.edu`, but you need a network connection to run this game.

Miscellaneous Demos and Utilities

The following programs may interest you. If you're a werewolf, Phase of the Moon will be particularly useful!

Caesar

Type `caesar` at the command line. This program attempts to decrypt encoded words. Type `man caesar` to see the man page.

Fortune

Type `fortune` at the command line for your Linux fortune-cookie message.

Number

Type `number <number>` at the command line. Converts the Arabic number given as `<number>` (for example, 41) to its equivalent in English (forty-one).

Phase of the Moon

Type `pom` at the command prompt. The program tells you the current phase of the moon. As the man page mentions, this can be useful in predicting the behavior of others and maybe yourself, too! Type `man pom` to see the man page.

Rain

Type `rain` at the command prompt. Your screen becomes rippled like a puddle in a rainstorm. On most Linux console screens, the program runs too fast to look even remotely convincing. Press Ctrl+C to exit.

Worms

Type `worms` at the command prompt (do not confuse with the `worm` program, above). This fills your screen with squirming worms. Like `rain`, the program runs much too fast on a Linux console screen. A man page is available by typing `man worms`.

Summary

You should now be able to while away the time by sitting at your machine and playing your favorite games. If you haven't installed the X system yet, maybe this is an extra incentive! This chapter leads you back to some of the previous chapters that you may not have read.

To install the X system, read Chapter 22, "Installing and Configuring XFree86."

To use several programming languages to write your own games, see Part V, starting with Chapter 25, "gawk."

To back up your system so you don't lose your high scores, see Chapter 45, "Backups."

Adabas-D and other Databases

by Tim Parker

IN THIS CHAPTER

This chapter covers some common database applications for Linux. The applications we focus on primarily in this chapter are Adabas-D, FlagShip, and dbMan V. We also look briefly at LINCKS, a free, object-oriented database management system (DBMS) for Linux.

dBASE-Compatible Databases

About a decade ago there was only one database system in wide-spread use, Ashton-Tate's dBASE. Before Windows came along, practically every database under DOS was written in dBASE, and as UNIX developed on the small platforms, ports of the dBASE system emerged there, too. Although the ownership of the dBASE package was transferred several times, a Windows-based version didn't appear fast enough (or stay stable enough) to keep the popularity of the dBASE system alive. Soon, other databases began to be used instead of dBASE.

Along with the development of faster and more powerful versions of dBASE, several companies introduced compatible products that extended the capabilities of the dBASE language. These products, written to the dBASE language set, were generically called xBase to show their ties to dBASE. A few of these xBase systems became very popular with programmers, in particular Clipper, a dBASE-compatible language compiler that accelerated the execution speed of dBASE applications enormously.

While many programmers think of dBASE as a vintage database system now, there are still thousands (if not millions) of applications that were written using that relational database package. Many of these packages are still in use today, either in the exact same format as originally developed or ported to newer xBase versions and newer operating systems. Since it is unlikely that xBase languages and applications will ever go away, it is perhaps no surprise that an xBase port for Linux was introduced.

The company that offers FlagShip, the dBASE- and Clipper-compatible database system, offers versions for many operating systems, mostly UNIX based. Their Linux version is a commercial product, selling for about $199 in the US. However, there are several demo versions available of FlagShip that expire after ten or thirty days, allowing you to see if your existing dBASE or Clipper applications will run under Linux. If they do and you want to move them over, you can then purchase a full copy of FlagShip.

What Is xBase?

xBase is a generic term for implementations of what was originally the dBASE programming language. The main players in the DOS version of this database are FoxPro (now

Adabas-D and other Databases

CHAPTER 62

987

62

ADABAS-D
AND OTHER
DATABASES

owned by Microsoft), dBASE V (now owned by Borland), and Clipper (owned by Computer Associates).

xBase is a language that has statements normally found in programming languages, such as IF, ELSE, ENDIF, and WHILE. The programming language structure is designed for accessing records in databases and not for general-purpose programming. For example, the GOTO statement in xBase refers to a record in a database, not a location in the program code. xBase has some powerful statements for processing files and getting data from forms and screens.

In addition, setting up relations between files is easy to do with xBase. The names of all fields in a file, as well as their types and lengths, are recorded in the file header. New fields can be added to a file without changing programs that use the file. The scheme allows for different, disjointed programs all accessing the database file in their own way and all using the fields in the header.

The three major manufacturers of xBase databases have largely ignored Linux as a platform for their products. What we have for Linux are FlagShip and dbMan (from Versasoft Corporation). Both of these products run on several implementations of UNIX.

Comparing the two products is like comparing apples and oranges. FlagShip is patterned after Clipper Version 5. The dbMan package resembles dBASE III+ or FoxPlus. FlagShip, like Clipper, is a compiler. dbMan is primarily an interpreter, although it is possible to "compile" dbMan programs. FlagShip is also an object-oriented language, which makes it philosophically different from dbMan, as well as from FoxPro and dBASE. Clipper and FlagShip have several C-like features. Actually, the resemblance is a plus for Linux users.

The target markets of the two are also different. dbMan is targeted primarily at individual users. If you want a program you can run on your desk to keep track of time billed to clients or that maintains a phone list of customers or your sales records, dbMan can do the job.

By contrast, FlagShip might be overkill for simple database operations, such as mailing or customer tracking lists, in other words, the casual user, not programmer. This is not to say that you cannot use it for simple applications, but you may have to learn a bit of programming to really use FlagShip's powerful features. FlagShip is more realistically aimed at people who want to develop or port software packages. Traditionally, dBASE files always have separate data (.DBF) and index files. The format of data files is pretty much uniform for all xBases. It is hard to find two products that use the same index file formats but you can use the same .DBF files with both FlagShip and dbMan.

What Is FlagShip?

FlagShip is a compiler, meaning it produces executable code with no intermediary pseudo-code. No interpretive version of FlagShip exists, so you may need an interpreter such as FoxPro or dBASE to develop complex applications. FlagShip was designed to allow existing xBase applications to run without modification (or a minimum of modification in some cases to correct filename problems) under Linux and other UNIX versions. No run-time or user royalty fees are charged, so once an application has been developed and compiled, it can be distributed anywhere without you having to pay royalties to the authors.

> **TIP**
>
> Many Web sites allow you to download the FlagShip demos, and you can find them through a search engine such as AltaVista (http://www.altavista. digital.com) or Yahoo! (http://www.yahoo.com), or direct from the vendor of FlagShip, Multisoft Datentechnik Gmbh, at http://www.fship.com. There is also an FTP server for the company at ftp://fship.com/pub/multisoft. The demo versions are quite large (about 4.5MB). Several documents are available for FlagShip from FTP and Web sites. Make sure you download the English files as most sites have both English and German documents available (Multisoft Datentechnik Gmbh is based in Germany).

FlagShip is fully compatible with dBASE and Clipper, as well as most other xBase versions, such as Fox, FoxPlus, and FoxPro, dbMan, QuickSilver, and others. It includes all the really neat features of the xBase compatibles, such as:

- Macro support
- Arrays, objects, and code blocks
- User-defined functions and user-defined commands
- Index and array sorts
- Compatibility with most xBase file formats, including .dbf, .dbt, .mem, .lbl, .frm, and .fmt
- A C API for interfacing C code and FlagShip code in one application

FlagShip has no equivalent of the dBASE dot prompt or interactive command interface found in other xBase products. However, there is a public-domain program called dbu that provides the capability to create files and indexes, add, change, or locate records, and browse files interactively.

FlagShip uses the curses toolkit for its user interface. During installation, you get a set of terminfo files specifically for FlagShip. When running a FlagShip program in an xterm, you may get hieroglyphics instead of line drawing characters. Fiddling with the acsc parameter in the fslinxterm terminfo entry may not help. Try using the vga font that comes with DOSemu package.

FlagShip doesn't have a function specifically for managing pull-down menus. What FlagShip and Clipper programmers normally do is use @PROMPT/MENU TO statements to create the horizontal menu and a function called ACHOICE() for the vertical menus. You can set hot keys with the SET KEY keyid TO statement. Normally, the statement would be a function invocation. Within this function, you can call the READVAR() function to find out which field the cursor was in when the key was pressed. An input field can be validated by adding the VALID statement parameter to the @SAY/GET statement. Again, the statement would normally be a function invocation. Within the function, the value the user typed in could be looked up in a database file.

FlagShip has functions for managing windows that work very nicely, but the functions are not part of the basic package. You have to buy the FStools library. As the name suggests, the FStools library is a clone of the Clipper Tools library. There are also windowing functions in the NanForum library (containing mathematical and statistics functions), which is public domain.

A key feature of FlagShip is the TBROWSE() object. You use this in place of the BROWSE command that exists in other languages. If you don't have any previous experience with object-oriented programming, setting up TBROWSE() for the first time is not easy. The best course of action is to use the examples and samples in the fsman pages. FlagShip is picky about reserved words. If you have a filename such as browse, you are liable to encounter problems running programs. Keep a list of all the reserved words in FlagShip and avoid using these as file or program names. Check the list of reserved words in the fsman pages.

FlagShip programs can be attached to WWW pages, making it possible for net surfers to access and update databases. This feature, plus the capability to link in your C and C++ programs, makes FlagShip a very powerful data management tool.

FlagShip has an online reference program called fsman, which contains the entire FlagShip manual of more than 1,000 pages, which means that you do not have thick manuals all over your desk. The samples of code in the manual can be saved as text files on disk. This makes it easy to incorporate programming examples in the manual into whatever program you are working on at the time. Of course, you could also use the mouse to copy text from fsman into your program by cutting and pasting between windows.

FlagShip isn't just a port of a DOS-based compiler. It has been designed to provide full functionality under UNIX. Source code will run faster under Linux than under DOS (compiler with Clipper, for example) because of the better operating system design of Linux. FlagShip also removes many of the limitations of DOS- and Windows-based xBase applications.

If you have any requirement to port dBASE or Clipper applications to Linux, or you are looking for a simple relational database system, FlagShip is an excellent choice.

Installing FlagShip

Most people obtain FlagShip from a CD-ROM collection, a Web site, or an FTP archive. In most cases, there are two versions of FlagShip available, and the choice of the correct one for your system depends on the version of Linux you are running. Typically, the files are contained in a tar archive called `fsdemo.tar` (if you are obtaining the restricted demo version). One version is optimized for more recent releases of Linux and uses ELF. An older version, usually designated with the name aout (for a.out) at the end of the filename, works on any Linux system. The ELF version is much more flexible and powerful, but in most cases the demo files are the older version.

Once you have the `fsdemo.tar` file on your Linux system in a suitable (preferably new and empty other than the `fsdemo` file) directory, you need to unpack the tar file with the command:

```
tar xvf fsdemo.tar
```

This creates a number of files, two of which are usually called `FSinstall.set` and `FSinstall`. The `FSinstall.set` file sets environment variables for the installation routine and should be run first by simply typing its name at the command line. You won't see anything when you do this. After running the `.set` file, type the `FSinstall` filename and let it install FlagShip for you.

If the installation process loads properly, you are asked if there is enough room on your filesystem, as shown in Figure 62.1.

You are then asked where you want the FlagShip program to be stored, and in most cases you should accept the default values suggested by the installation routine. If you want to change the defaults, a menu prompt lets you, and then enter the new values, as shown in Figure 62.2. Once the installation routine has finished, you are returned to the shell prompt. FlagShip is now ready to be used.

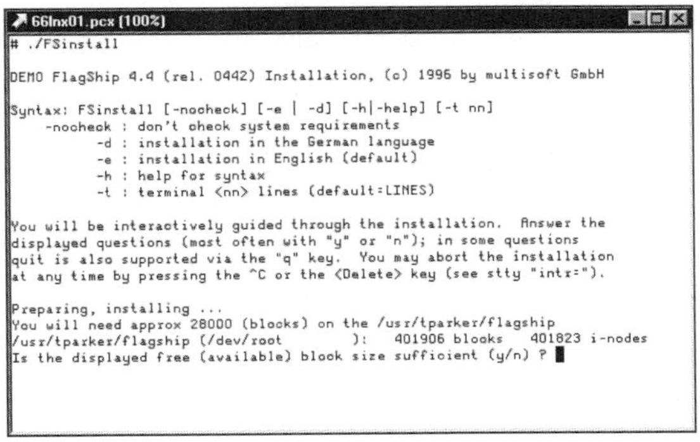

FIGURE 62.1.

The FlagShip installation routine checks that you have enough room on your hard drive.

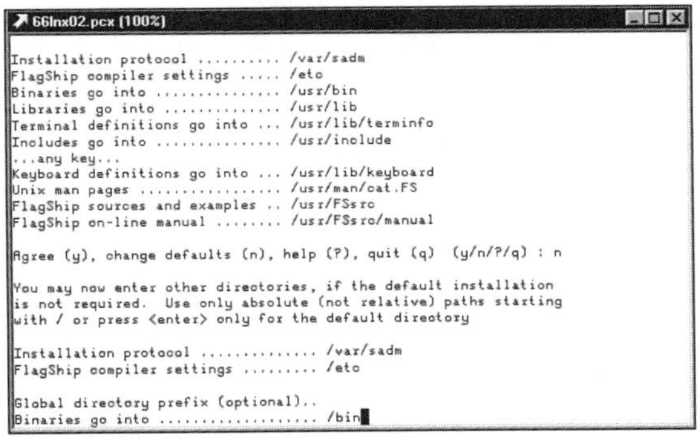

FIGURE 62.2.

You can override the default FlagShip installation settings if you want.

Using FlagShip

If you have used Clipper or one of the other xBase compilers, you will know most of the commands you need for FlagShip. A few modifications have been made because of the UNIX environment, but using FlagShip is otherwise pretty simple. Keep in mind that FlagShip is not an interactive development product: it doesn't help you design your code. FlagShip is a compiler. You can use it to develop applications if you are familiar with the dBASE language, but FlagShip is not designed to teach you dBASE or to help you develop applications.

Once you have your .prg source files ready to go, you can invoke the FlagShip compiler. In general, the command line is like this...

```
FlagShip app_name.prg -ocompiled_name -Mstart
```

...where app_name.prg is the name of the main program file (that calls all the others) and compiler_name is the name of the compiled executable (C defaults to a.out as the compiled executable name). If your main program file doesn't call all the other program files that need to be linked together, you will have to compile them separately and link them together.

Once compiled, the application runs as though it were on DOS or any other operating system. For example, Figure 62.3 shows a DOS application that has been ported to Linux and recompiled with FlagShip, and then executed. The only changes necessary to the source code were changes in path names from DOS's structure to Linux's. As you can see, even the fundamental ASCII graphics are retained and can be used on any terminal supported by Linux.

FIGURE 62.3.

A FlagShip-compiled application runs under Linux just as it would under DOS.

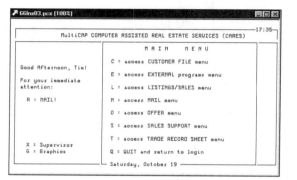

Porting Existing Applications

What do you have to worry about if you have some existing dBASE or Clipper code that you want to run under Linux? To start with, you need the .prg (program) source code. Move those files to Linux using any means you want, such as a network connection or floppy disk. FlagShip is clever enough to ignore case, which may seem trivial but isn't. Since most DOS programmers write in mixed case, converting applications to run under UNIX's case-significant environment is a major problem with other dBASE tools.

There are complete instructions on modifying code to run cleanly under FlagShip included with the software (or available through the FlagShip Web page), but essentially most application can run straight away.

FlagShip converts dBASE code into C source code and then compiles it with a C compiler. That means you will need a C compiler, which luckily is part of almost every UNIX and Linux system available. If you want to use FlagShip and haven't installed the C development system from the CD-ROM, you should do so; otherwise, you will see error messages from FlagShip. You don't need C++, only the standard C compilers that are on the CD-ROM (including the one at the end of this book). The procedure FlagShip goes through to run an application is straightforward:

1. Preprocess the code to make sure there are no syntax errors or other common errors. If there are errors, issue error messages and terminate the compilation.
2. Convert to C code.
3. Compile with the system's C compiler to produce an object file.
4. Link the object file with FlagShip's libraries and produce an executable.

The executable thus produced can be run at the Linux command line prompt.

A quick word for dBASE and Clipper veterans: you needn't bother with overlays because UNIX has no need for them. Linux uses the virtual memory on your system to enable you to load any size application (although there are limits, they can be changed). Therefore, don't bother with overlays as you would with Clipper or other xBase compilers, and instead link your code into a single, large executable. Let Linux worry about loading it.

dbMan

The dbMan program is an interpreter. When you start dbMan, you get a CMD: prompt. This is where you enter all your commands to dbMan. You can think of this as a . prompt in dBASE. For starters, you can type in ASSIST, at the CMD: prompt. ASSIST starts up a menu-driven interface similar to the ones available with FoxPro or dBASE.

The menu-driven interface is not very elaborate. ASSIST only enables one file to be open at a time, which means that it is not possible to set up relations. It is possible to start up a simple program generator from ASSIST. Again, it has a single file limitation.

You can compile programs in dbMan. Compiling a program does not produce an executable binary. It produces a .run file, which still requires dbMan to execute it. It is also possible to enter CREATE REPORT or MODIFY REPORT at the CMD: prompt. This puts you in dbMan's report writer. The report writer enables display of data by using the relational operators. dbMan provides a function called PMENU() to create pull-down menus. PMENU doesn't have any mechanism for temporarily disabling a menu choice.

dbMan handles windows differently from other xBase products. Prior to defining a window, you call PUSHWIND() to push the current window onto a stack. When a program is in its initial state, the entire screen is considered to be a window. You then call WINDOW() to create the window. When you are finished with it, you call POPWIND(), which removes the window and makes the previous window active.

dbMan enables you to define only one hot key. You do so by invoking the ONKEY() function. This has no effect until you execute the ONKEY statement. The statement will normally be DO hot-key-handler.

The BROWSE command has a long list of options. You can browse only specified fields, and you can specify the width of each field, and whether it is editable. The list of fields can include fields in other files, which is great if you have relationships set up.

dbMan does not use either termcap or terminfo. Instead, it includes a file named dbmterm.dbm. This file looks similar to termcap. There are no entries for either xterm or console. You have to create your own entries using the existing entries.

dbMan has no facility for executing functions written in C or assembler, so you have to use what they offer. There were a couple of nasty bugs in the version of dbMan I evaluated, which was version 5.32. The main bug I found was that procedure files simply didn't work if the procedure file was a .prg. If you compiled the procedure file into a .run file, it worked okay.

> **NOTE**
>
> You can get dbMan from
>
> VERASOFT Corporation
> 4340 Alamaden Expressway, #110
> San Jose, CA 95118
>
> (408) 723-9044

Adabas-D

Adabas-D is a full-featured database that offers the power of commercial database products for UNIX that sell for thousands of dollars. Supporting SQL and links to many popular database formats, Adabas-D is worth considering if you need more power than the xBase products just mentioned.

> **TIP**
>
> There are several vendors and suppliers of Adabas-D. One of the more reliable is Caldera, which offers several Linux application products, as well as their own version of Slackware Linux under the name Caldera OpenLinux. Caldera can be reached at:

Caldera Incorporated
633 South 550 East
Provo, Utah 86406

801-377-7687

knfo@caldera.com

http://www.caldera.com

Installing Adabas-D

Adabas-D is usually supplied on CD-ROM, although a few FTP sites make it available, too. Installation is quite simple. Although Caldera's version is labeled as suitable for use with their own OpenLinux, Adabas-D works on virtually all Linux implementations. Installation is simple. The following procedure works on all versions of Red Hat, Slackware, and OpenLinux we tested. We'll assume the Adabas-D software is on CD-ROM. If you have a downloaded file, it should be placed in an accessible directory and the mounting steps mentioned below skipped.

Log in as root. The installation procedure should be conducted as the root login. Mounting the CD-ROM is the first step. This is particularly easy with the command:

```
mount /mnt/cdrom
```

This version of the mount command skips one of the arguments you may have seen in earlier chapters where the mount command has both a device name and a mount point. Since both are provided with this mount command, the system loads the CD-ROM device onto the filesystem mount point /mnt/cdrom. You can use any other mount point, of course, if you want. We'll assume the default throughout this section.

After mounting the CD-ROM, change into the Adabas-D mounted directory with the command:

```
cd /mnt/cdrom
```

A directory listing at this point will show the contents of the Adabas-D. Most of the files are in subdirectories.

To make life easier for us, this version of the Adabas-D CD-ROM distribution has an installation script that takes care of the steps usually conducted manually. To execute this script, simply type the command:

```
./install
```

The preceding period and slash indicate to the shell that the install script is in the current directory. If you leave these off, Linux looks for an install program elsewhere on the filesystem before looking in the current directory. This usually results in another install routine being executed. If your version of Adabas-D does not have an installation script, there may be a list of steps you must perform manually in another file. Check the directory for instructions.

Using the installation script, you are prompted for the different packages that should be installed, as well as their directory. You should install all the packages included with the Adabas-D CD-ROM for a complete Adabas-D system, with the exception of any language you don't want (Adabas-D is usually distributed with both English and German documentation and command sets). There are usually four components to the Personal Edition system, which is the version most users will want:

- `adabas-6.1PE`. The kernel and all binary and configuration files (approximately 46MB).
- `adabas-mydb`. The sample database with a diashow of German railways (approximately 74MB).
- `adabas-docEN`. English documentation (105MB).
- `adabas-dokDE`. German documentation (79MB).

Before Adabas-D can be started, two shell variables must be set for each user account that will have access to the database package. The shell variables are

- `DBROOT`. The installation directory (/opt/adabas-d, for example).
- `PATH`. Adds DBROOT to the usual shell path (usually set as `$DBROOT/bin:$PATH`).

The `adabas-mydb` package installed earlier is a complete tutorial and sample database that details the German railway system (which is interesting by itself if you like trains!). You can run this example through an X session to see what Adabas-D is capable of. To start the demo, start X (after you have set the required shell variables) and issue the command:

```
panel
```

The user name to enter is "control," and the password is "control." The database name is "MYDB." Click the Connect button in the window and wait for the traffic light signal that appears to change to green. The database contains some pictures of the German railways. To see these pictures, start the "fotos" program in an X terminal, use the username "demo," the password "demo," and the same database name as before ("MYDB"). Adabas-D should be up and running now. If there are any problems, make sure the environment variables are set properly and that the installation didn't generate any error messages.

Documentation for the Adabas-D system is in the doc directory under the Adabas-D root directory (such as /opt/adabas-d/doc).

LINCKS

LINCKS is an object-oriented database management system. LINCKS is a good system if you intend to use it on a network and share data via RPC calls. You need to have some experience with networks, as well as an existing network to fully benefit from this package. This package is not for a single node system just because it would be an overkill for such a platform.

> **NOTE**
>
> You can get LINCKS from sunsite.unc.edu in the /pub/linux/apps/database/ lincks directory.

LINCKS is based on an append-only object-oriented structure. Objects are derived from other objects. Links can be set between objects to define relationships. You define views to an object. A view is used to specify how the data in the object is presented to a user. Multiple views can exist for the same object. Views can be inherited.

The main interface is xlincks program. Using commands similar to emacs, you can interactively browse through databases. The interface resembles the hypertext functions of a Web page. You click on a highlighted item, and the program leads to a page with more information about the topic.

Help is available in two forms: context sensitive or as a browseable database. The help file is always a button away—to access help, simply press the Help button. The contents of the help file are well organized and are a good starting place to learn about LINCKS. The manual is also available in PostScript from the sunsite archives.

LINCKS comes with a few programs in its distribution package. You can create new databases using the dbroot command. To prune databases of unreferenced objects, use the cutoff command. The main server for the application is the netserv program, which fires off a dbs process for each connected client.

Other Database Products

Of course, the xBase tools we've looked at are not the only databases available for Linux. There are a lot of non–dBASE-compatible tools out there. We can take a quick overview of some other database management systems for Linux. Most of these are free and can be found on the Internet.

- mbase v5.0 is a relational database system originally written for the Amiga and ported to other platforms. It uses a language format similar to C to do the database programming. To compile using mbase, you need ncurses and time. There are several problems with the Makefile that may require manual editing on your part. If you really want cheap, C-like access to a DBMS, you can use this package. Otherwise, get FlagShip or dbMan because they are more stable and mature.

- onyx is a database prototype program based on a language format such as C. The `make config` command starts the process and a series of questions pop up. Answering all these questions results in configuring the database properly for Linux.

- DBF is an xBase manipulation package and is a collection of utility programs that manipulate `dbf` files. Some of the utilities, such as `dbfadd`, add a record or layer of information in the database. `dbflist` lists the records in the database; `dbft` lists the structure of each database and its items.

- typhoon is yet another RDBMS. The most notable feature of this RDBMS (depending on your point of view) is that it's entirely like C. The problem is that the product still has to mature before being considered a viable RDBMS.

Summary

FlagShip and dbMan are excellent means of porting existing dBASE and dBASE-compatible programs to Linux where they run without modification in most cases and a lot faster in almost all cases. A version of FlagShip is being developed for X to run under FreeX86 or other Linux-based X versions, and that should be available in 1997. For now, though, the demo version of FlagShip lets xBase developers continue to work with their database system under Linux. The commercial product, with its hefty 1,500-page documentation, is $199 and well worth it for developers. dbMan is a logical alternative for those who don't need FlagShip's compiler features and extended capabilities.

StarOffice

by Tim Parker

StarOffice 4.0 is an X-based integrated office suite for Linux. The software is available bundled with some versions of Linux (such as Caldera OpenLinux) and is on some FTP sites and WWW pages. StarOffice 4.0, the latest version, includes three tools for office use: StarWriter is a word processor, StarCalc is a spreadsheet tool, and StarImpress is a presentation graphics package which can also generate HTML code for Web pages.

While StarOffice is not equivalent to Microsoft's Office suite for Windows or Corel's WordPerfect suite for Windows, you will be surprised at how powerful and useful StarOffice is. The tools included in the package are most of the ones that you'll need in day-to-day work, and coupled with a database package (see Chapter 62 for database packages), it makes a full-featured Linux office platform. It's also great for home use.

StarOffice is not specific to any particular Linux version. It can be installed on all the versions of Linux that are currently available, as long as an X server is running.

> **NOTE**
>
> StarOffice 4.0 is available for many platforms, including SCO UNIX. On that platform, the package sells for $550! Linux users can often get StarOffice included in a bundle or at a much lower price from companies such as Caldera. Check out `http://www.caldera.com` for more information.

Installing StarOffice

StarOffice is installed through a script, not through the Linux package management utilities. To install StarOffice, you must be logged in as `root`. StarOffice is an X application, so you should start X and open an X terminal window to conduct these steps.

To install StarOffice, which usually comes on a CD-ROM, mount the CD to whichever mount point you usually use, such as:

```
mount /dev/cdrom /usr/cdrom
```

Then open the CD-ROM directory. There will be several directories of files, one of which will be called `StarOffice4.0`. The other directories contain auxiliary files as well as license information. Next, open the `StarOffice4.0` directory, then the `bin` subdirectory. To start the installation script, type the command:

```
./setup
```

The ./ part of the command ensures the current directory's setup script is executed and not one from somewhere else in your path. After the command starts, you will see a window like that shown in Figure 63.1. In most cases, selecting the standard installation routine is the best choice unless you don't want to install one or more of the StarOffice suite components. Also, if you're short of disk space, you may want to leave off some support files.

FIGURE 63.1.
The StarOffice installation script displays this list of choices.

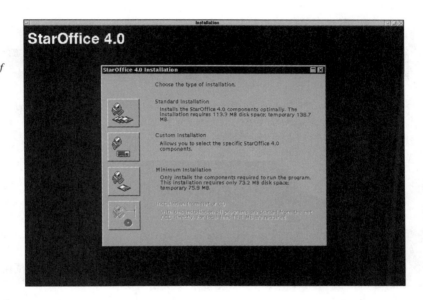

After starting the installation script, StarOffice copies all the files automatically displaying only a completion percentage line. After the installation is completed, the script exits.

Starting StarOffice

By default, StarOffice is installed in the directory /root/Office40. If you had selected the manual installation routine, you could change this path, but it tends to work well for most versions of Linux. You should include this directory and the /root/Office40/bin directory in your path if you want to execute the StarOffice suite from anywhere in the file system.

To start StarOffice, first open an X terminal window (if one is not already available). Then use cd to open the directory /root/Office40/bin (if you have not included the directory in your path) and type the command:

```
soffice&
```

If the path `/root/Office40/bin` is not in your path and the current directory (.) is missing from the path as well, you have to type:

```
./soffice&
```

The ampersand after the `soffice` command is used to force StarOffice into the background so you can continue to use the X terminal window you issued this command from. Using `soffice` is the easiest way to start StarOffice, although you can start individual applications separately if you want.

> **NOTE**
>
> StarOffice 4.0 is one of the most stable application suites available. In over a month of continual heavy-duty testing on a Slackware Linux platform, StarOffice didn't crash once. There are few applications (and even fewer operating systems) that can make this claim!

When you start StarOffice, you will see the main StarOffice window as shown in Figure 63.2. The screen is divided into a file browser on the left and a set of icons on the right for applications and help files. To examine the online help, click on one of the icons with a question mark superimposed on the book cover.

FIGURE 63.2.

The StarOffice main window lets you move around the file system or launch StarOffice applications.

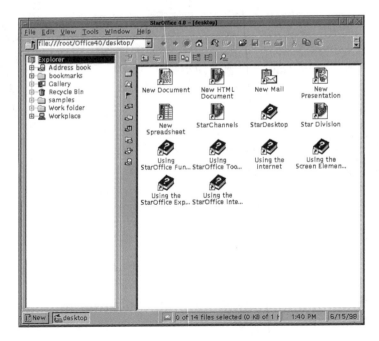

StarWriter

StarWriter is the StarOffice word processor. To open StarWriter with a blank document, double-click on the New Document icon in the StarOffice main window. This launches StarWriter, as shown in Figure 63.3. Whereas the left part of the window continues to be a file browser, the right part has changed to a word processor with icons across the top and a style window open.

FIGURE 63.3.

StarWriter is the word processor and very much resembles Microsoft's Word.

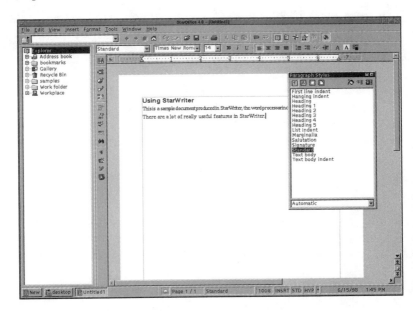

StarWriter behaves a lot like Microsoft Windows, both in the commands and shortcuts you can use and in the function of the icons across the top of the window. This makes it very easy to use StarWriter (assuming you have used Word or WordPad before).

StarWriter is full of little features that Linux users will love. A cruise through the help tools shows all kinds of little gems. For example, if you are used to sending a lot of email or using Usenet newsgroups, you're used to writing emphasis in an ASCII-based manner. For example, to bold a word or phrase in a posting on Usenet, the convention is to put asterisks before and after the word or phrase, like this: *this is important.* Similarly, if you want to underline something for emphasis, you place underscore characters before and after, like this: _underscored_. StarWriter detects these conventions and does what you want in a document, bolding or underscoring however you specify. This makes it easy to keep on using your favorite writing style in StarWriter.

StarCalc

StarCalc is the spreadsheet tool, shown in Figure 63.4. As with StarWriter, StarCalc takes a lot of its behavior from the Microsoft Office Excel tool. If you know Excel, you will feel familiar with StarCalc.

FIGURE 63.4.

StarCalc is the spreadsheet, offering Excel-like capabilities.

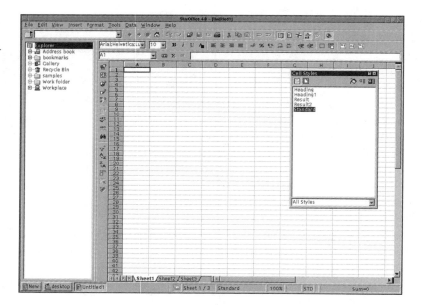

One strong feature of StarCalc that many other spreadsheet packages lack (including those running under Windows 95) is the ability to use natural language for formulas. For example, if you want to create tables with names on both the first row and column, you can do it with a single command instead of several.

StarImpress

StarImpress can be used for a number of tasks, including producing presentation graphics. As Figure 63.5 shows, StarImpress is much like PowerPoint and behaves in the same way. StarImpress includes some fancy features such as the capability to produce 3-D effects. This capability to create fast 3-D effects rivals those of dedicated UNIX-based drawing packages such as CorelDraw! for UNIX, a much more expensive software tool.

Using StarImpress with other StarOffice applications such as StarWriter makes incorporating graphics into documents really easy. You can use an OLE-like method to import graphics from StarImpress into as many locations in a StarWriter or StarCalc document as you like.

FIGURE 63.5.

StarImpress is the StarOffice presentation graphics package.

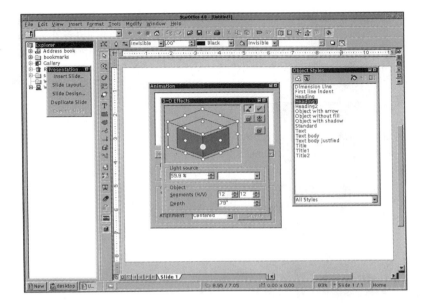

A companion utility to StarImpress is StarImage, which allows for fast image conversion from one format to another, as well as manipulation of the image contents. StarImage works with .BMP, .JPEG, .GIF, .TIFF, and .XBM images. While many of these functions can be accomplished with other Linux tools such as XV, the integration of StarImage with StarOffice makes working across tools easy.

Importing and Exporting Files

As you have seen, StarOffice looks a lot like the Microsoft Office suite of tools. This extends to file import and export capabilities. The native format that StarOffice uses to save documents, spreadsheets, and presentation graphics is not compatible with Microsoft Word, Excel, and PowerPoint, although there is the option to save StarOffice documents in several other formats. One of those formats is always the Microsoft Windows-based format, which makes moving documents from StarOffice to Windows much easier.

In addition to Office tool formats, StarOffice lets you save documents in other formats, such as ASCII, RTF (Rich Text Format), and HTML. The last is useful for creating Web pages, of course.

You can import standard Microsoft format files from Windows, after moving them over to your Linux system. They can be stored under Linux in either the same Windows format or in the native StarOffice format. The capability to move files back and forth from Windows to Linux makes StarOffice a very useful tool.

Summary

You now know how to install and are familiar with the components of StarOffice 4.0, one of the most handy X-based Linux tools available. With StarOffice, you can make use of the superior power of Linux over Windows without losing compatibility with that "other" operating system. There are several other chapters that may be of interest to you after reading this one. To learn more about:

Configuring XFree86 on your system to support StarOffice, see Chapter 22, "Installing and Configuring XFree86."

Setting up a Web page with your newly generated HTML pages from StarOffice, see Chapter 51, "Configuring a WWW Site."

Database tools, see Chapter 62, "Adabas-D and other Databases."

Lone Star Software's Lone-Tar

by Tim Parker

CHAPTER 64

As you saw in Chapter 32, "System Administration Basics," making backups on your Linux system can be a complex and often annoying procedure, especially if you don't have a high-capacity tape drive or other backup storage device available. If you have to rely on floppies for a backup, you are really in for a frustrating time, as a full backup can take dozens (if not hundreds) of disks. When floppies are all that's available, most users don't even bother.

Many users find the normal backup `tar` utility difficult and unfriendly to work with. On top of that, `tar` can error out for any number of conditions, causing you to have to restart your backup from the very beginning. In many larger UNIX environments, the use of `tar` has been replaced by custom-designed GUI-driven backup utilities, but Linux hasn't quite caught up to that point yet. However, there are a few alternatives to using straight-forward `tar`, and the best is Lone Star Software's Lone-Tar.

What Is Lone-Tar?

Lone-Tar can best be thought of as a super version of `tar`. It provides all the features of `tar`, yet adds some functionality that `tar` lacks. To be very safe, Lone-Tar does not use the standard `tar` utility, although it's behavior is similar. Lone-Tar is available for a wide variety of UNIX and non-UNIX platforms, and is compatible across them all. You could, for example, use a DOS version of Lone-Tar to back up files to a tape, and then read them into your Linux system.

Like `tar`, Lone-Tar can back up and restore entire filesystems to and from disks, tape, auxiliary hard disks, and other storage media. Lone-Tar goes beyond normal `tar` in that all special files, links (symbolic and otherwise), virtual files, and partitions can be handled as easily as standard files.

Lone-Tar can also allow backups and restores of dual drives with different capacities, which `tar` is not capable of doing easily. Most importantly, Lone-Tar has an excellent error recovery procedure built in that allows recovery of a filesystem or files on a backup medium, even when that medium has developed errors. When `tar` encounters problems with a backup medium, it terminates, effectively ruining the value of that backup set.

> ## TIP
>
> Lone-Tar sounds pretty handy so far, doesn't it? Lone-Tar is a commercial product, and Lone Star Software expects to be paid for Lone-Tar, but you can use a free version distributed on several FTP sites for a limited time to try it out. After

the trial period you can purchase a license for Lone-Tar if you find it valuable and useful. Along with the commercial version, you'll also get a well-written manual. For more information on Lone-Tar, contact Lone Star Software at

13987 W. Annapolis Ct.
Mt. Airy, MD 21765

(800) LONE-TAR

```
cowboy@cactus.com
http://www.cactus.com
ftp.cactus.com
```

Using Lone-Tar's Interface

Lone-Tar has two interfaces: command-line and menu-driven. The command-line interface is very similar to the `tar` command's syntax for compatibility's sake. This way, someone who has been using `tar` for many years and moves to Lone-Tar for the extra capabilities it offers doesn't have to relearn a whole new command set. As you may have discovered by now, `tar`'s command set is rather uninspiring, awkward, and difficult to master.

It takes years to feel comfortable with `tar`'s command line, so Lone Star Software designed a friendlier menu-driven interface, too. You can use either the command-line or the menu-driven interface to perform all Lone-Tar's functions, and they work the same. The menu-driven interface is much easier to work with, though, especially if you haven't mastered `tar`.

You can see the difference between the two interface methods by a quick look at the syntax of Lone-Tar. The syntax, very similar to `tar`'s syntax, looks like this:

```
lone-tar [MIcCrtTUxPZ] [bdefhklmnpvFEADVR] [tapefile] [block size]
[compression limit] [0-9] [floppy/tape size] files ...
```

If you are not exactly right with one of the command-line parameters, both `tar` and Lone-Tar will give you pages of error codes and options, as shown in Figure 64.1. You can display this command-line help screen at any time by simply typing this command at the command line:

```
lone-tar
```

64

LONE STAR
SOFTWARE'S
LONE-TAR

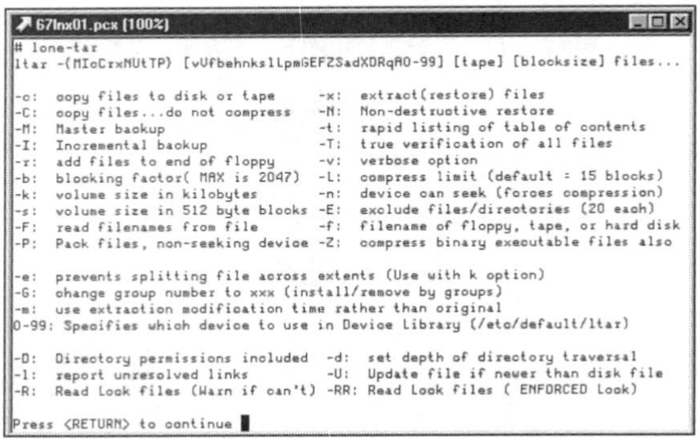

FIGURE 64.1.
The first page of command line help from Lone-Tar.

The menu-driven interface, on the other hand, is shown in Figure 64.2 and is much more friendly and easier to figure out. Each of the primary menu options leads to another menu, with mnemonic startup commands for each choice.

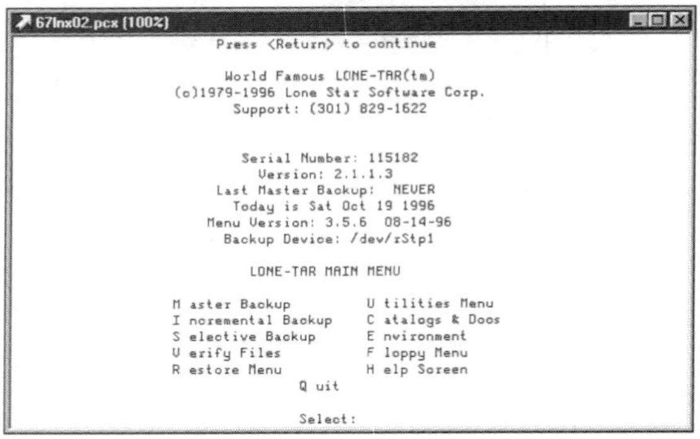

FIGURE 64.2.
The menu-drive interface from Lone-Tar is much easier and friendlier to use than the command line.

The choice of interface you use is entirely up to you, of course, but if you are not familiar with `tar`'s awkward syntax, you should stick to the menu-driven interface. UNIX veterans may want to stay with the command line interface, but the menu-driven system is much easier to work with and eliminates the chance of typing errors. For most of this chapter, we'll work with the menu-driven interface.

Installing Lone-Tar

The installation process for Lone-Tar is pretty simple. You need to log in as root and change to the `/tmp` directory. Once there, extract all the files from the CD-ROM or disk (if you have put the Lone-Tar software on the disk) with a `tar` command. For example, if you have copied the Lone-Tar files to a floppy in drive A:, you would log in to the system as root and issue the following two commands:

```
cd /tmp
tar xvf /dev/rfd0
```

The `tar` command tells Linux to extract all the files from the first floppy drive (`/dev/rfd0`) and store them in the current directory.

> **TIP**
>
> Some Linux systems don't address the first floppy as `/dev/rfd0` but prefer `/dev/fd0` instead. If you get a message about "Device unknown" when you use the command line shown above, use `/dev/fd0` as the floppy device name instead.

If you are installing from CD-ROM, you can copy the files to the `/tmp` directory directly using `cp`. For example, if the files are stored on the CD-ROM in the directory `/lone-tar`, and the CD-ROM is mounted to your Linux system in the directory `/cdrom`, you would issue the commands:

```
cd /tmp
cp /cdrom/lone-tar/* .
```

The exact command line you use depends on the location of the Lone-Tar files on the CD-ROM and the mount location on your system.

Once the files are all safely in the `/tmp` directory, you can start the installation process by issuing the command:

```
./init.ltar
```

This program was written by Lone Star Software to install all the components of Lone-Tar properly. You are asked a bunch of questions about your tape or backup drive, its capacity, and whether you want to print the online manuals. If you don't want to print the manuals during the installation process, you can print them at any time from the Lone-Tar menu.

To start the Lone-Tar system in menu-driven mode, issue the command

```
ltmenu
```

You should see a screen like the one shown in Figure 64.3. Pressing Enter takes you to the main menu shown in Figure 64.2. If you want to use your Lone-Tar system in command mode, use this command:

```
lone-tar
```

64

LONE STAR
SOFTWARE'S
LONE-TAR

Follow it by any options or by itself to display the help screen shown in Figure 64.3.

FIGURE **64.3.**

*If Lone-Tar was
installed correctly,
you should see
this welcome
screen when you
start up the menu
mode.*

Backing Up with Lone-Tar

Backups are a vital part of any Linux system, whether you use it for serious work or just for playing. The reason is simple: reloading your Linux system, reconfiguring it the way it was, and reloading all your applications can take a long time and sometimes lead to errors. Recovering from a backup tape or other backup device can take a few minutes, but requires little intervention on your part. If you have important information stored on your Linux system, then you really should have regular backups made for safety's sake because it's often impossible to reconstruct data you lost.

> **TIP**
>
> If you are forced to use floppies for your backups, you should use the Floppy choice from the main Lone-Tar menu. This option leads to the Floppy menu, which lets you back up and restore using your floppy drives instead of a tape drive.

Lone-Tar lets you make two kinds of backups: masters and incrementals. The master backup is a complete backup of your system, with every file on the filesystems backed up safely. An incremental backup is made between masters and holds the changes to the system since the last master. Incremental mode lets you make backups much quicker because there is no need to back up every file. Linux knows which files have changed because of the attributes attached to each file, and the files that have been created or modified since the last master backup are written to the backup medium. In case of a problem and a reload, the master is reloaded first, and then the incrementals made since the master. If you've lost a file or two, you can often get them from the incremental itself.

The manner in which you create master and incremental backups depends on how much you use your system, how much data you change daily, and how important your system is to you. For example, a regularly used system could get a master backup once a week to a high-capacity drive. Incrementals could be performed automatically each night.

If you don't use your system much, you can do master backups once a month and incrementals weekly, although this isn't really recommended. For heavily loaded systems, you may want to forget about incrementals all together and make a new master backup every night. One of Lone-Tar's strengths is the capability to automate backups, as you will see.

To start a master backup, choose the M option from the main menu. You are asked if you want to exclude any filesystems, as shown in Figure 64.4. By default Lone-Tar assumes it will back up everything on your system, but you may want to prevent Lone-Tar from backing up some filesystems or directories, such as a mounted CD-ROM. If you have a CD-ROM mounted under /cdrom, for example, you could use this option to tell Lone-Tar to ignore that directory (after all, there's little point in backing up a CD-ROM). You may also want to avoid backing up mounted network drives, if you have any.

FIGURE 64.4.

When creating a master backup, Lone-Tar lets you exclude directories that are not to be backed up.

You are then prompted to install a tape (or other backup media, depending on the backup device you specified during installation), and the backup process is started. You will see a few lines telling you that Lone-Tar is waiting to check the tape (in this case). After that, Lone-Tar checks the tape (or other medium) to make sure it is ready.

Lone-Tar likes to initialize each backup device itself and marks the tape or drive with a file identifying the backup as a Lone-Tar product. You don't have to mark such backups, but they do help Lone-Tar in the restoration process. An error message, such as the one shown in Figure 64.5, shows that Lone-Tar has determined that either there is no tape in the tape drive or a brand new tape has been loaded. Instructions for marking the tape are included with the Lone-Tar file, but you don't have to do this to perform a backup. Simply hitting Enter starts the backup process. Figure 64.6 shows the backup process underway. Lone-Tar echos the name of each file and its details back to you while it is backing up the system.

FIGURE 64.5.

Lone-Tar issues warnings if it detects no tape in the backup drive, or the tape is new and unmarked by Lone-Tar.

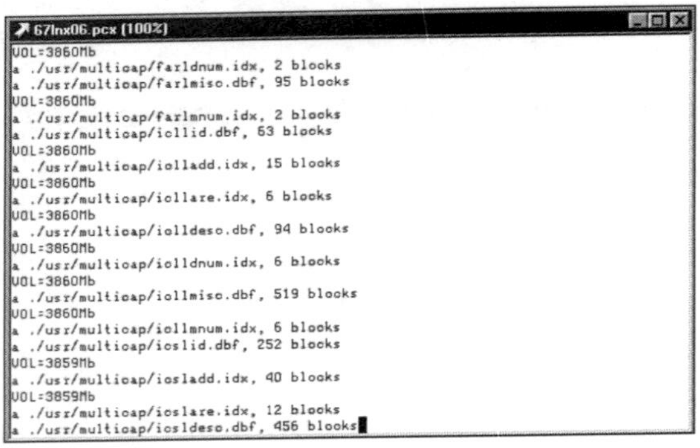

FIGURE 64.6.

During the Backup process Lone-Tar, shows you the filename and its details as it works. This lets you see Lone-Tar is working properly.

If one backup medium is not enough for the master backup, Lone-Tar prompts you to change the medium. Lone-Tar waits until you hit Enter before continuing again. After the master backup is completed, Lone-Tar returns to the Main Menu.

Lone-Tar can use compression when making backups to fit more information on a tape or removable medium. The choice of using compression is up to you, and you will probably have been asked whether you want to use it during the installation process. The advantage of compression is simple: more data in less space. The disadvantages are twofold: it takes slightly longer to make backups when using compression, and the compressed backup can only be read by Lone-Tar. A non-compressed backup can be read by tar or Lone-Tar, which is a great advantage if you are moving your backup media to another machine.

The amount of time required to make a backup depends on a number of factors, most importantly the size of the filesystem, the speed of your backup system, and the load on your system. If you have a fast system and a high-capacity fast backup device, Lone-Tar backs up your system much faster than tar itself would have. However, the speed is most limited by the backup devices themselves. A DAT SCSI drive, for example, is much faster than a QIC cartridge tape drive driven off the floppy. You will get used to the amount of time required for a master backup after a couple of backup cycles. If there's a long time required, start scheduling the backups at night while you sleep, or when you go away for a reasonable period of time. Take note that most master backups take at least an hour and often many hours, depending on the backup drives.

> **TIP**
>
> Make sure you label the tape or other medium with the date and type of backup. Write clearly! You never know when you'll have to figure out which tape was made when.

To make an incremental backup, follow the same process. Since most incremental backups are much smaller than a master backup, they also back up much faster. You really should get in the habit of making incremental backups either every day you use the Linux system, or whenever you save something you really can't afford to lose. It's better to spend ten minutes making a backup than four hours rewriting that chapter of your latest book!

A selective backup, started using the S option on the Lone-Tar menu, lets you back up only specific areas of your system. You are asked which files or directories to include or exclude, then the backup proceeds normally.

Verifying Files

The Verify option provided by Lone-Tar is a security precaution that you should make use of every time you make a backup. The Verify option scans through the backup and compares it to the original files. This makes sure that any backup errors are caught before they become serious.

It is a good habit to get into verifying each backup after it has been made. This is especially true when you have made new master backups.

Remember that some files on your system may change between the backup time and the verification time, depending on whether the system was used between the two times or not. Some automated procedures such as mail, logging, news, and automated background tasks alter files while a backup or verification is proceeding. Lone-Tar finds the files different and reports errors to you. You should carefully read the reports from the Verification process so you know which errors are important and which occurred because of these system changes.

Restoring Files

When you have to restore a file, directory, or entire filesystem, find the proper backups. If you have been using the master and incremental routine, you will need the last master and all the incrementals since that master. Alternatively, if you are just looking for a few files you accidentally deleted, you may know which tape or drive they are on and can use just that medium.

To start a restore process, select the R option from the Lone-Tar main menu. This brings up the Restore menu, shown in Figure 64.7. Most of the options on the Restore menu are self-descriptive. For example, to restore an entire tape, you would use the "Restore entire tape to hard disk" option.

FIGURE 64.7.

The Lone-Tar Restore menu.

Some of the other options on the Restore menu enable you to selectively restore directories or files, based on exact names or wildcards. You can also build a list of files or directories and have them all restored at once. Alternatively, you can decide which files or directories are not to be restored, create an exclusion list of them, and restore everything else.

After you have decided which files or directories to restore, Lone-Tar asks you to insert the tape and starts the restoration process. As with a backup, Lone-Tar echoes everything it does to the screen so you can see what it is doing.

> **TIP**
>
> When performing a restore of a few files or directories, Lone-Tar has to search through the tape or medium to find those files. This can be a slow process, depending on the speed of the backup device, so don't worry if you don't see anything happening for a few minutes. You should see the status lights on your backup device blinking to show the device is being used by Lone-Tar.

If there is more than one tape or other device involved in the backup, Lone-Tar prompts you to insert the next volume. It keeps doing so until the restore process is complete.

If you are restoring from a combination of masters and incrementals, you must repeat the restore process for each tape. For example, if you accidentally erased an entire directory, you could use the last master backup to get the main files and then go through all the incrementals made since the master was created to obtain any changes. You have to perform the updates manually by using the Restore menu.

After the restoration is completed, Lone-Tar returns to the main menu. You should verify that the backup was to the proper location and everything looks correct.

Tape-Tell is a special feature of Lone-Tar that tells you a little about when the tape was used. This hinges on the Lone-Tar file that can be put at the beginning of the medium. We discussed this file in the section above on backing up using Lone-Tar.

Utilities and Environment: Tweaking Lone-Tar

The Lone-Tar Utilities menu, shown in Figure 64.8, holds a number of useful commands and functions. Most of these options are self-explanatory, but a few are very handy for users. It is helpful to check the backup date of the last master backup occasionally as a reminder of when you should start thinking about a new master backup.

The automated use of Lone-Tar through cron is a neat feature that lets your system make backups without you being there. As you know from earlier chapters in this book, cron lets you schedule commands to be run at particular times or intervals, so you can easily set Lone-Tar to be run by cron to create incremental backups every night, twice a week, or whenever you want. You don't need to know details about cron in order to schedule backups; Lone-Tar takes care of that for you.

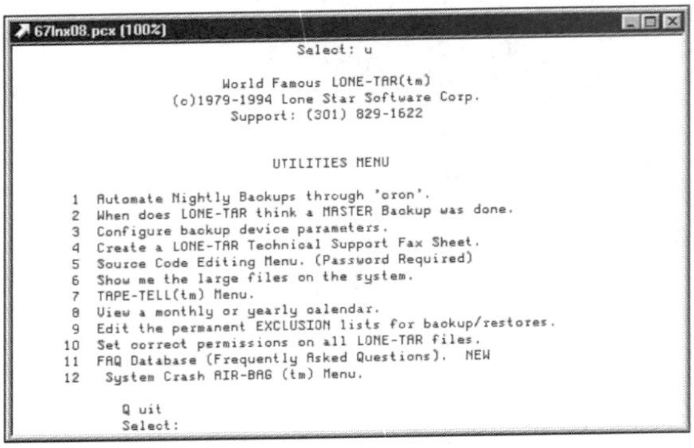

FIGURE 64.8.

The Lone-Tar Utilities menu.

```
67lnx08.pcx [100%]                                               _ □ ×
                              Select: u

                       World Famous LONE-TAR(tm)
                      (c)1979-1994 Lone Star Software Corp.
                           Support: (301) 829-1622

                            UTILITIES MENU

        1  Automate Nightly Backups through 'cron'.
        2  When does LONE-TAR think a MASTER Backup was done.
        3  Configure backup device parameters.
        4  Create a LONE-TAR Technical Support Fax Sheet.
        5  Source Code Editing Menu. (Password Required)
        6  Show me the large files on the system.
        7  TAPE-TELL(tm) Menu.
        8  View a monthly or yearly calendar.
        9  Edit the permanent EXCLUSION lists for backup/restores.
        10 Set correct permissions on all LONE-TAR files.
        11 FAQ Database (Frequently Asked Questions).  NEW
        12  System Crash AIR-BAG (tm) Menu.

            Q uit
            Select:
```

The Utilities menu also lets you change the backup device type and details, so if you have more than one backup system on your Linux system, you can change between them. This is useful if you want to make master backups to a high-capacity device but incrementals to a different device.

The Environment menu, shown in Figure 64.9, contains a list of all the settings Lone-Tar works with. Many of these were set when you installed Lone-Tar, but you can modify them as you need in order to customize your installation.

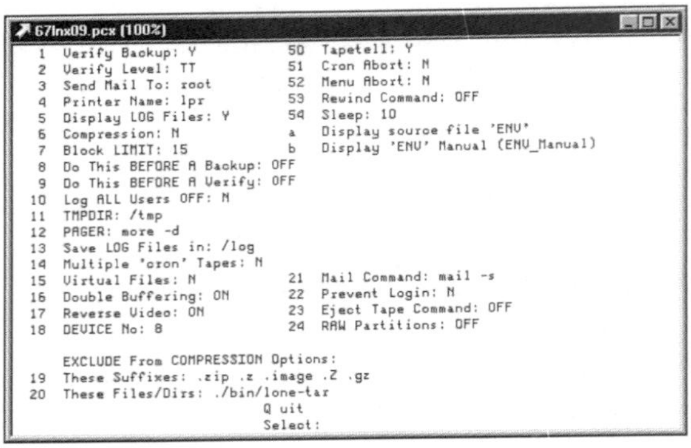

FIGURE 64.9.

The Lone-Tar Environment menu lets you alter the behavior of the backup tool.

```
67lnx09.pcx [100%]                                               _ □ ×
     1  Verify Backup: Y          50  Tapetell: Y
     2  Verify Level: TT          51  Cron Abort: N
     3  Send Mail To: root        52  Menu Abort: N
     4  Printer Name: lpr          53  Rewind Command: OFF
     5  Display LOG Files: Y       54  Sleep: 10
     6  Compression: N            a   Display source file 'ENV'
     7  Block LIMIT: 15           b   Display 'ENV' Manual (ENV_Manual)
     8  Do This BEFORE A Backup: OFF
     9  Do This BEFORE A Verify: OFF
     10 Log ALL Users OFF: N
     11 TMPDIR: /tmp
     12 PAGER: more -d
     13 Save LOG Files in: /log
     14 Multiple 'cron' Tapes: N
     15 Virtual Files: N          21  Mail Command: mail -s
     16 Double Buffering: ON       22  Prevent Login: N
     17 Reverse Video: ON         23  Eject Tape Command: OFF
     18 DEVICE No: 8              24  RAW Partitions: OFF

        EXCLUDE From COMPRESSION Options:
     19 These Suffixes: .zip .z .image .Z .gz
     20 These Files/Dirs: ./bin/lone-tar
                          Q uit
                          Select:
```

Summary

Lone-Tar has a lot of features we haven't mentioned in this chapter, but you can read the online documentation to find out more about the system. Using Lone-Tar for your backup and restore operations is fast and easy, and you'll find yourself doing them a lot more when you don't have to fumble with awkward syntax or worry about mistyping a command. You should try to use the Lone-Tar demo we've provided on the CD-ROM. You'll find it very easy to work with. From here there are a number of chapters you might be interested in:

> To learn more about mounting devices such as floppy disks and CD-ROMs, see Chapter 33, "Devices."

> To learn more about backups and making sure your system is completely covered in case of problems, see Chapter 45, "Backups."

> To learn more about automating your backups at night, see Chapter 46, "cron and at."

Appendixes

IN THIS PART

Linux FTP Sites and Newsgroups

APPENDIX A

If you have access to the Internet, either directly through an ISP (Internet Service Provider) or through an online service provider such as CompuServe, Delphi, or America Online, you can access additional sources of Linux software and information. There are two popular sources of Linux software and help available, one through FTP and the other through Linux-specific Usenet newsgroups.

If you don't have access to the Internet, you may still be able to get some of the information available through other sources, such as Bulletin Board Systems (BBSs) and CD-ROMs published by companies specializing in redistributing public domain material.

FTP Sites

FTP is a method of accessing remote systems and downloading files. It is quite easy to use and provides users that have Internet access a fast method for updating their list of binaries.

For those without FTP access but who can use electronic mail through the Internet, the utility `ftpmail` can provide access to these FTP sites.

What Is FTP?

File Transfer Protocol (FTP) is one protocol in the TCP/IP family of protocols. TCP/IP is used extensively as the communications protocol of the Internet, as well as in many Local Area Networks (LANs). UNIX systems almost always use TCP/IP as their protocol.

FTP is used to transfer files between machines running TCP/IP. FTP-like programs are also available for some other protocols.

To use FTP, both ends of a connection must be running a program that provides FTP services. To download a file from a remote system, you must start your FTP software and instruct it to connect to the FTP software running on the remote machine.

The Internet has many FTP *archive sites*. These are machines that are set up to allow anyone to connect to them and download software. In some cases, there are FTP archive sites that mirror each other. A *mirror site* is one that maintains exactly the same software as another site, so you simply connect to the one that is easier for you to access, and you have the same software available for downloading as if you had connected to the other site.

Usually, when you connect to a remote system, you must log in. This means you must be a valid user, with a username and password for that remote machine. Because it is impossible to provide logins for everyone who wants to access a public archive, many systems use anonymous FTP. *Anonymous FTP* enables anyone to log into the system with the login name of guest or anonymous and either no password or the login name for the user's local system (used for auditing purposes only).

Connecting and Downloading Files with FTP

Using FTP to connect to a remote site is quite easy. Assuming you have access to the Internet either directly or through a service provider, you must start FTP and provide the name of the remote system to which you want to connect. If you are directly connected to the Internet, the process is simple: You enter the ftp command with the name of the remote site, such as:

```
ftp sunsite.unc.edu
```

If you are using an online service, such as Delphi, you must access its Internet services menus and invoke FTP from that. Some online services allow you to enter the name of any FTP site at a prompt, whereas others have some menus that list all available sites. You may have to hunt through the online documentation for your service provider to find the correct procedure.

After you issue the FTP command, your system will attempt to connect to the remote machine. When it does (and assuming the remote system allows FTP logins), the remote will prompt you for a user ID. If anonymous FTP is supported on the system, a message usually tells you that. The login below is shown for the Linux FTP archive site sunsite.unc.edu:

```
ftp sunsite.unc.edu
331 Guest login ok, send your complete e-mail address as password.
Enter username (default: anonymous): anonymous
Enter password [tparker@tpci.com]:
¦FTP¦ Open
230-                 WELCOME to UNC and SUN's anonymous ftp server
230-                        University of North Carolina
230-                      Office FOR Information Technology
230-                             SunSITE.unc.edu
230 Guest login ok, access restrictions apply.
FTP>
```

After the login process is completed, you see the prompt FTP>, indicating the system is ready to accept commands. When you log into some systems, you see a short message that might contain instructions for downloading files, any restrictions that are placed on you as an anonymous FTP user, or information about the location of useful files. For example, you might see messages like this:

```
To get a binary file, type:  BINARY and then: GET "File.Name" newfilename
To get a text file, type:    ASCII  and then: GET "File.Name" newfilename
```

```
Names MUST match upper, lower case exactly. Use the "quotes" as shown.
To get a directory, type: DIR. To change directory, type: CD "Dir.Name"
To read a short text file, type: GET "File.Name" TT
For more, type HELP or see FAQ in gopher.
To quit, type EXIT or Control-Z.

230- If you email to info@sunsite.unc.edu you will be sent help
information
230- about how to use the different services sunsite provides.
230- We use the Wuarchive experimental ftpd. if you "get"
➥<directory>.tar.Z
230- or <file>.Z it will compress and/or tar it on the fly. Using ".gz"
➥instead
230- of ".Z" will use the GNU zip (/pub/gnu/gzip*) instead, a superior
230- compression method.
```

After you are connected to the remote system, you can use familiar Linux commands to display file contents and move around the directories. To display the contents of a directory, for example, use the command ls or the DOS equivalent dir. To change to a subdirectory, use the cd command. To return to the parent directory (the one above the current directory), use the command cdup or cd. There are no keyboard shortcuts available with FTP, so you have to type in the name of files or directories in their entirety.

When you have moved through the directories and have found a file you want to transfer to your home system, use the get command:

```
get "file1.txt"
```

The commands get (download) and put (upload) are relative to your home machine. You are telling your system to get a file from the remote location and put it on your local machine or to put a file from your local machine onto the remote machine. This is the opposite of another commonly used TCP/IP protocol, Telnet, which has everything relative to the remote machine. It is important to remember which command moves in which direction, or you could overwrite files accidentally.

The quotation marks around the filename are optional for most versions of FTP, but they do provide specific characters to the remote version (preventing shell expansion), so the quotation marks should be used to avoid mistakes. FTP provides two modes of file transfer: ASCII and binary. Some systems will automatically switch between the two, but it is a good idea to manually set the mode to ensure you don't waste time. To set FTP in binary transfer mode (for any executable file), type the command

```
binary
```

You can toggle back to ASCII mode with the command ASCII. Because you will most likely be checking remote sites for new binaries or libraries of source code, it is a good idea to use binary mode for most transfers. If you transfer a binary file in ASCII mode, it is not executable (or understandable) on your system. ASCII mode includes only the valid ASCII characters and not the Ctrl+key sequences used within binaries. Transferring an ASCII file in binary mode does not affect the contents, although spurious noise may cause a problem in rare instances.

When you issue a `get` command, the remote system transfers data to your local machine and displays a status message when it is finished. There is no indication of progress when a large file is being transferred, so be patient.

```
FTP> get "file1.txt"
200 PORT command successful.
150 BINARY data connection for FILE1.TXT (27534 bytes)
226 BINARY Transfer complete.
27534 bytes received in 2.35 seconds (12 Kbytes/s).
```

To quit FTP, type the command `quit` or `exit`. Either will close your session on the remote machine, then terminate FTP on your local machine.

Using `ftpmail`

If you don't have access to a remote site through FTP, all is not lost. If you have electronic mail, you can still get files transferred to you. Some online systems allow Internet mail to be sent and received, but do not allow direct access to FTP. Similarly, some Internet service providers offer UUCP accounts that do not allow direct connection but do provide email. To get to FTP sites and transfer files, you can use the `ftpmail` utility.

The site mentioned previously, `sunsite.unc.edu`, is a major Linux archive site that supports `ftpmail`. (All of the sites listed in this appendix as Linux FTP sites also support `ftpmail`.) To find out how to use `ftpmail`, send an email message to the login `ftpmail` at one of the sites, such as `ftpmail@sunsite.unc.edu`, and have the body of the message contain only one word: `help`.

By return mail, the `ftpmail` utility will send instructions for using the service. Essentially, you send the body of the FTP commands you want executed in a mail message, so you could get back a directory listing of the Linux directory in a mail message with this text:

```
open sunsite.unc.edu
cd /pub/Linux
ls
quit
```

You could transfer a file back through email with a similar mail message:

```
open sunsite.unc.edu
```

```
cd /pub/Linux
binary
get README
quit
```

The ftpmail system is relatively slow because you must wait for the email to make its way to the target machine and be processed by the remote, then for the return message to make its way back to you. It does provide a useful access method for those without FTP connections, though, and a relatively easy way to check the contents of the Linux directories on several machines.

Linux FTP Archive Sites

The list of Linux FTP archive sites changes slowly, but the sites listed in Table A.1 were all valid and reachable as this book went to press. Many of these sites are mirror sites, providing exactly the same contents.

To find the site nearest you, use the country identifier at the end of the site name (uk=United Kingdom, fr=France, and so on). Most versions of FTP allow either the machine name or the IP address to be used, but if the name cannot be resolved by the local Internet gateway, the IP address is the best addressing method.

TABLE A.1. LINUX FTP ARCHIVE SITES.

Site name	IP Address	Directory
tsx-11.mit.edu	18.172.1.2	/pub/linux
sunsite.unc.edu	152.2.22.81	/pub/Linux
nic.funet.fi	128.214.6.100	/pub/OS/Linux
ftp.mcc.ac.uk	130.88.200.7	/pub/linux
ftp.dfv.rwth-aachen.de	137.226.4.111	/pub/linux
ftp.informatik.rwth-aachen.de	137.226.255.3	/pub/Linux
ftp.ibp.fr	132.227.60.2	/pub/linux
ftp.uu.net	192.48.96.9	/systems/unix/linux
wuarchive.wustl.edu	128.252.135.4	/systems/linux
ftp.win.tue.nl	131.155.70.19	/pub/linux
ftp.stack.urc.tue.nl	131.155.140.128	/pub/linux
ftp.ibr.cs.tu-bs.de	134.169.34.15	/pub/linux
ftp.denet.dk	129.142.6.74	/pub/OS/linux

The primary home sites for the Linux archives are `tsx-11.mit.edu`, `sunsite.unc.edu`, and `nic.funet.fi`. *Home* sites are where most of the new software loads begin. The majority of sites in Table A.1 mirror one of these three sites.

Bulletin Boards

There are literally hundreds of Bulletin Board Systems (BBSs) across the world that offer Linux software. Some download new releases on a regular basis from the FTP home sites, whereas others rely on the users of the BBS to update the software.

A complete list of BBSs with Linux software available would be too lengthy (as well as out-of-date almost immediately) to include here. Zane Healy maintains a complete list of BBSs offering Linux material. To obtain the list, send email requesting the Linux list to `healyzh@holonet.net`.

If you don't have access to email, try posting messages on a few local bulletin board systems asking for local sites that offer Linux software or ask someone with Internet access to post email for you.

LINUX-related BBSs

Zane Healy (`healyzh@holonet.net`) maintains this list. If you know of or run a BBS that provides Linux software but isn't on this list, you should get in touch with him.

You can also get an up-to-date list on BBSs from `tsx-11.mit.edu` in the `/pub/linux/docs/bbs.list` file. The lists shown below were up-to-date at the time we went to print.

United States BBSs

Here is a list of some of the BBSs in the United States that carry Linux or information about Linux:

> 1 Zero Cybernet BBS, (301) 589-4064. MD.
>
> AVSync, 404-320-6202. Atlanta, GA.
>
> Allentown Technical, (215) 432-5699. 9600 v.32/v.42bis Allentown, PA. WWIVNet 2578
>
> Acquired Knowledge, (305) 720-3669. 14.4k v.32bis Ft. Lauderdale, FL. Internet, UUCP
>
> Atlanta Radio Club, (404) 850-0546. 9600 Atlanta, GA.
>
> Brodmann's Place, (301) 843-5732. 14.4k Waldorf, MD. RIME ->BRODMANN, Fidonet

Centre Programmers Unit, (814) 353-0566. 14.4k V.32bis/HST Bellefonte, PA.

Channel One, (617) 354-8873. Boston, MA. RIME ->CHANNEL

Citrus Grove Public Access, (916) 381-5822. ZyXEL 16.8/14.4 Sacramento, CA.

CyberVille, (817) 249-6261. 9600 TX. Fidonet 1:130/78

Digital Designs, (919) 423-4216. 14.4k, 2400 Hope Mills, NC.

Digital Underground, (812) 941-9427. 14.4k v.32bis IN. USENET

Dwight-Englewood BBS, (201) 569-3543. 9600 v.42 Englewood, NJ. USENET

EchoMania, (618) 233-1659. 14.4k HST Belleville, IL. Fidonet 1:2250/1

Enlightened, (703) 370-9528. 14.4k Alexandria, VA. Fidonet 1:109/615

Flite Line, (402) 421-2434. Lincoln, NE. RIME ->FLITE, DS modem

Georgia Peach BBS, (804) 727-0399. 14.4k Newport News, VA.

Harbor Heights BBS, (207) 663-0391. 14.4k Boothbay Harbor, ME.

Horizon Systems, (216) 899-1293. 2400 Westlake, OH.

Information Overload, (404) 471-1549. 19.2k ZyXEL Atlanta, GA. Fidonet 1:133/308

Intermittent Connection, (503) 344-9838. 14.4k HST v.32bis Eugene, OR. 1:152/35

Horizon Systems, (216) 899-1086. USR v.32 Westlake, OH.

Legend, (402) 438-2433. Lincoln, NE. DS modem

Lost City Atlantis, (904) 727-9334. 14.4k Jacksonville, FL. Fidonet

MAC's Place, (919) 891-1111. 16.8k, DS modem Dunn, NC. RIME ->MAC

MBT, (703) 953-0640. Blacksburg, VA.

Main Frame, (301) 654-2554. 9600 Gaithersburg, MD. RIME ->MAINFRAME

MegaByte Mansion, (402) 551-8681. 14.4 V,32bis Omaha, NE.

Micro Oasis, (510) 895-5985. 14.4k San Leandro, CA.

My UnKnown BBS, (703) 690-0669. 14.4k V.32bis VA. Fidonet 1:109/370

Mycroft QNX, (201) 858-3429. 14.4k NJ.

NOVA, (703) 323-3321. 9600 Annandale, VA. Fidonet 1:109/305

North Shore BBS, (713) 251-9757. Houston, TX.

PBS BBS, (309) 663-7675. 2400 Bloomington, IL.

Part-Time BBS, (612) 544-5552. 14.4k v.32bis Plymouth, MN.

Programmer's Center, (301) 596-1180. 9600 Columbia, MD. RIME

Programmer's Exchange, (818) 444-3507. El Monte, CA. Fidonet

Programmer's Exchange, (818) 579-9711. El Monte, CA.

Rebel BBS, (208) 887-3937. 9600 Boise, ID.

Rem-Jem, (703) 503-9410. 9600 Fairfax, VA.

Rocky Mountain HUB, (208) 232-3405. 38.4k Pocatello, ID. Fidonet, SLNet, CinemaNet

Ronin BBS, (214) 938-2840. 14.4 HST/DS Waxahachie (Dallas), TX.

S'Qually Holler, (206) 235-0270. 14.4k USR D/S Renton, WA.

Slut Club, (813) 975-2603. USR/DS 16.8k HST/14.4K Tampa, FL. Fidonet 1:377/42

Steve Leon's, (201) 886-8041. 14.4k Cliffside Park, NJ.

Tactical-Operations, (814) 861-7637. 14.4k V32bis/V42bis State College, PA. Fidonet 1:129/226, tac_ops.UUCP

Test Engineering, (916) 928-0504. Sacramento, CA.

The Annex, (512) 575-0667. 2400 TX. Fidonet 1:3802/216

The Annex, (512) 575-1188. 9600 HST TX. Fidonet 1:3802/217

The Computer Mechanic, (813) 544-9345. 14.4k v.32bis

The Laboratory, (212) 927-4980. 16.8k HST, 14.4k v.32bis NY. FidoNet 1:278/707

The Mothership Connection, (908) 940-1012. 38.4k Franklin Park, NJ.

The OA Southern Star, (504) 885-5928. New Orleans, LA. Fidonet 1:396/1

The Outer Rim, (805) 252-6342. Santa Clarita, CA.

The Sole Survivor, (314) 846-2702. 14.4k v.32bis St. Louis, MO. WWIVnet, WWIVlink, and so on.

Third World, (217) 356-9512. 9600 v.32 IL.

Top Hat BBS, (206) 244-9661. 14.4k WA. Fidonet 1:343/40

UNIX USER, (708) 879-8633. 14.4k Batavia, IL. USENET, Internet mail

Unix Online, (707) 765-4631. 9600 Petaluma, CA. USENET access

VTBBS, (703) 231-7498. Blacksburg, VA.

VWIS Linux Support BBS, (508) 793-1570. 9600 Worcester, MA.

Valhalla, (516) 321-6819. 14.4k HST v.32 Babylon, NY. Fidonet (1:107/25 5), USENET

Walt Fairs, (713) 947-9866. Houston, TX. Fidonet 1:106/18

WaterDeep BBS, (410) 614-2190. 9600 v.32 Baltimore, MD.

WayStar BBS, (508) 480-8371. 9600 V.32bis or 14.4k USR/HST Marlborough, MA. Fidonet 1:333/16

WayStar BBS, (508) 481-7147. 14.4k V.32bis USR/HST Marlborough, MA. Fidonet 1:333 /14

WayStar BBS, (508) 481-7293. 14.4k V.32bis USR/HST Marlborough, MA. Fidonet 1:333 /15

alaree, (512) 575-5554. 14.4k Victoria, TX.

hip-hop, (408) 773-0768. 19.2k Sunnyvale, CA. USENET access

hip-hop, (408) 773-0768. 38.4k Sunnyvale, CA.

splat-ooh, (512) 578-2720. 14.4k Victoria, TX.

splat-ooh, (512) 578-5436. 14.4k Victoria, TX.

victrola.sea.wa.us, (206) 838-7456. 19.2k Federal Way, WA. USENET

Outside of the United States

If you live outside the U.S., you can get information about Linux from these BBSs:

500cc Formula 1 BBS, +61-2-550-4317. V.32bis Sydney, NSW, Australia.

A6 BBS, +44-582-460273. 14.4k Herts, UK. Fidonet 2:440/111

Advanced Systems, +64-9-379-3365. ZyXEL 16.8k Auckland, New Zealand.

BOX/2, +49.89.601-96-77. 16.8 ZYX Muenchen, BAY, Germany.

Baboon BBS, +41-62-511726. 19.2k Switzerland.

Basil, +33-1-44670844. v.32bis Paris, Laurent Chemla, France.

BigBrother / R. Gmelch, +49.30.335-63-28. 16.8 Z16 Berlin, BLN, Germany.

Bit-Company / J. Bartz, +49.5323.2539. 16.8 ZYX MO Clausthal-Zfd., NDS, Germany.

CRYSTAL BBS, +49.7152.240-86. 14.4 HST Leonberg, BW, Germany.

CS-Port / C. Schmidt, +49.30.491-34-18. 19.2 Z19 Berlin, BLN, Germany.

Cafard Naum, +33-51701632. v.32bis Nantes, Yann Dupont, France.

DUBBS, +353-1-6789000. 19.2 ZyXEL Dublin, Ireland. Fidonet 2:263/167

DataComm1, +49.531.132-16. 14.4 HST Braunschweig, NDS, Germany. Fidonet 2:240/55

DataComm2, +49.531.132-17. 14.4 HST Braunschweig, NDS, Germany. Fidonet 2:240/55

Die Box Passau 2+1, +49.851.555-96. 14.4 V32b Passau, BAY, Germany.

Die Box Passau ISDN, +49.851.950-464. 38.4/64k V.110/X.75 Passau, BAY, Germany.

Die Box Passau Line 1, +49.851.753-789. 16.8 ZYX Passau, BAY, Germany.

Die Box Passau Line 3, +49.851.732-73. 14.4 HST Passau, BAY, Germany.

DownTown BBS Lelystad, +31-3200-48852. 14.4k Lelystad, Netherlands.

Echoblaster BBS #1, +49.7142.213-92. HST/V32b Bietigheim, BW, Germany.

Echoblaster BBS #2, +49.7142.212-35. V32b Bietigheim, BW, Germany.

FORMEL-Box, +49.4191.2846. 16.8 ZYX Kaltenkirchen, SHL, Germany.

Fiffis Inn BBS, +49-89-5701353. 14.4-19.2 Munich, Germany.

Fractal Zone BBS /Maass, +49.721.863-066. 16.8 ZYX Karlsruhe, BW, Germany.

Galaktische Archive, 0043-2228303804. 16.8 ZYX Wien, Austria. Fidonet
2:310/77 (19:00-7:00)

Galway Online, +353-91-27454. 14.4k v32b Galway, Ireland.

Gunship BBS, +46-31-693306. 14.4k HST DS Gothenburg, Sweden.

Hipposoft /M. Junius, +49.241.875-090. 14.4 HST Aachen, NRW, Germany.

Le Lien, +33-72089879. HST 14.4/V32bis Lyon, Pascal Valette, France.

Linux Server /Braukmann, +49.441.592-963. 16.8 ZYX Oldenburg, NDS,
Germany.

Linux-Support-Oz, +61-2-418-8750. v.32bis 14.4k Sydney, NSW, Australia.

LinuxServer / P. Berger, +49.711.756-275. 16.8 HST Stuttgart, BW, Germany.

Logical Solutions, 403 299-9900 through 9911. 2400 AB, Canada.

Logical Solutions, 403 299-9912, 299-9913. 14.4k AB, Canada.

Logical Solutions, 403 299-9914 through 9917. 16.8k v.32bis AB, Canada.

MM's Spielebox, +49.5323.3515. 14.4 ZYX Clausthal-Zfd., NDS, Germany.

MM's Spielebox, +49.5323.3516. 16.8 ZYX Clausthal-Zfd., NDS, Germany.

MM's Spielebox, +49.5323.3540. 9600 Clausthal-Zfd., NDS, Germany.

MUGNET Intl-Cistron BBS, +31-1720-42580. 38.4k Alphen a/d Rijn, Netherlands.

Magic BBS, 403-569-2882. 14.4k HST/Telebit/MNP Calgary, AB, Canada.
Internet/Usenet

Modula BBS, +33-1 4043 0124. HST 14.4 v.32bis Paris, France.

Modula BBS, +33-1 4530 1248. HST 14.4 V.32bis Paris, France.

Nemesis' Dungeon, +353-1-324755 or 326900. 14.4k v32bis Dublin, Ireland.

On the Beach, +444-273-600996. 14.4k/16.8k Brighton, UK. Fidonet 2:441/122

Pats System, +27-12-333-2049. 14.4k v.32bis/HST Pretoria, South Africa.

Public Domain Kiste, +49.30.686-62-50. 16.8 ZYX BLN, Germany. Fidonet
2:2403/17

Radio Free Nyongwa, 514-524-0829. v.32bis ZyXEL Montreal, QC, Canada.
USENET, Fidonet

Rising Sun BBS, +49.7147.3845. 16.8 ZYX Sachsenheim, BW, Germany. Fidonet
2:2407/4

STDIN BBS, +33-72375139. v.32bis Lyon, Laurent Cas, France.

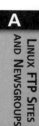

Synapse, 819-246-2344. 819-561-5268 Gatineau, QC, Canada. RIME->SYNAPSE

The Controversy, (65)560-6040. 14.4k V.32bis/HST Singapore.

The Field of Inverse Chaos, +358 0 506 1836. 14.4k v32bis/HST Helsinki, Finland.

The Purple Tentacle, +44-734-590990. HST/V32bis Reading, UK. Fidonet 2:252/305

The Windsor Download, (519)-973-9330. v32bis 14.4 ON, Canada.

Thunderball Cave, 472567018. Norway.

UB-HOFF /A. Hoffmann, +49.203.584-155. 19.2 ZYX+ Duisburg, Germany.

V.A.L.I.S., 403-478-1281. 14.4k v.32bis Edmonton, AB, Canada. USENET

bakunin.north.de, +49.421.870-532. 14.4 D 2800 Bremen, HB, Germany.

nonsolosoftware, +39 51 432904. ZyXEL 19.2k Italy. Fidonet 2:332/417

nonsolosoftware, +39 51 6140772. v.32bis, v.42bis Italy. Fidonet 2:332/407

r-node, 416-249-5366. 2400 Toronto, ON, Canada. USENET

Usenet Newsgroups

Usenet is a collection of discussion groups (called *newsgroups*) that is available to Internet users. There are more than 9,000 newsgroups with over 100MB of traffic posted every single day. Of all of these newsgroups (which cover every conceivable topic), several are dedicated to Linux.

You can access Usenet newsgroups through special software called a *newsreader* if you have access to a site that downloads the newsgroups on a regular basis. Alternatively, most online services such as CompuServe, America Online, and Delphi also offer access to Usenet. Some BBSs also are providing limited access to newsgroups.

Usenet newsgroups fall into three categories: primary newsgroups, which are readily available to all Usenet users; local newsgroups with a limited distribution; and alternate newsgroups that may not be handled by all news servers. The primary newsgroups of interest to Linux users are

comp.os.linux.admin	Installing and administering Linux systems
comp.os.linux.advocacy	Proponents of the Linux system
comp.os.linux.announce	Announcements important to the Linux community (Moderated)
comp.os.linux.answers	Questions and answers to problems
comp.os.linux.development	Ongoing work on Linux

`comp.os.linux.development.apps`	Ongoing work on Linux applications
`comp.os.linux.development.system`	Ongoing work on the Linux operating system
`comp.os.linux.hardware`	Issues with Linux and hardware
`comp.os.linux.help`	Questions and advice about Linux
`comp.os.linux.misc`	Linux-specific topics not covered by other groups
`comp.os.linux.networking`	Making the Linux system network properly
`comp.os.linux.setup`	Setup and installation problems with Linux

These newsgroups should be available at all Usenet sites unless the system administrator filters them out for some reason.

The other newsgroups tend to change frequently, primarily because they are either regional or populated with highly opinionated users who may lose interest after a while. The .alt (alternate) newsgroups are particularly bad for this. Only one .alt newsgroup was in operation when this book was written:

```
alt.uu.comp.os.linux.questions
```

There are also regional newsgroups that usually are not widely distributed or which have specific issues that may be in a language other than English. Some sample regional newsgroups carried by Usenet are

```
dc.org.linux-users
de.comp.os.linux
fr.comp.os.linux
tn.linux
```

If you do have access to Usenet newsgroups, it is advisable to regularly scan the newsgroup additions and deletions to check for new Linux newsgroups or existing groups that have folded. Most online services that provide access to Usenet maintain lists of all active newsgroups that can be searched quickly.

The traffic on most of these Linux newsgroups deals with problems and issues people have when installing, configuring, or using the operating system. Usually, there is a lot of valuable information passing through the newsgroups, so check them regularly. The most interesting messages that deal with a specific subject (called *threads*) are collected and stored for access through an FTP site.

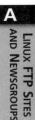

Commercial Vendors for Linux

This appendix lists all the commercial vendors that sell Linux distributions. See Appendix A, "Linux FTP Sites and Newsgroups," for a list of FTP sites that have Linux for free. The advantage of getting Linux from a commercial vendor is that you get a lot of software bundled in one package instead of having to do it for yourself. You can also get a list of these vendors from the *Linux Journal,* a monthly periodical:

> *Linux Journal*
> P.O. Box 85867
> Seattle, WA 98145-1867
> Phone: (206) 527-3385
> Fax: (206) 527-2806

The `Linux Distribution-HOWTO` file contains up-to-date information on Linux vendors that bundle packages together for sale. This list is maintained by Matt Welsh, `mdw@sunsite.unc.edu`. The `HOWTO` file can be found in `/pub/linux/docs/HOWTO/Distribution-howto` at `tsx-11.mit.edu`.

Debian Linux Distribution

> The Debian Linux Association
> Station 11
> P.O. Box 3121
> West Lafayette, IN 47906

Beta releases are available to the general public at `sunsite.unc.edu` in the directory `/pub/Linux/distributions/debian`.

Yggdrasil Plug-and-Play Linux CD-ROM and the Linux Bible

> Yggdrasil Computing, Incorporated
> 4880 Stevens Creek Blvd., Suite 205
> San Jose, CA 95129-1034
> Toll free: (800) 261-6630
> Phone: (408) 261-6630

Fax: (408) 261-6631

E-mail: info@yggdrasil.com

http://www.yggdrasil.com/linux.html

Linux from Nascent CD-ROM

Nascent Technology

Linux from Nascent CD-ROM

P.O. Box 60669

Sunnyvale, CA 94088-0669

Phone: (408) 737-9500

Fax: (408) 241-9390

E-mail: nascent@netcom.com

Unifix 1.02 CD-ROM

Unifix Software GmbH

Postfach 4918

D-38039 Braunschweig, Germany

Phone: +49 (0)531 515161

Fax: +49 (0)531 515162

Fintronic Linux Systems

Fintronic USA, Inc.

1360 Willow Rd., Suite 205

Menlo Park, CA 94025

Phone: (415) 325-4474

Fax: (415) 325-4908

E-mail: linux@fintronic.com

http://www.fintronic.com/linux/catalog.html

InfoMagic Developer's Resource CD-ROM Kit

InfoMagic, Inc.

P.O. Box 30370

Flagstaff, AZ 86003-0370

Toll free: (800) 800-6613

Phone: (602) 526-9565

Fax: (602) 526-9573

E-mail: Orders@InfoMagic.com

Linux Quarterly CD-ROM

Morse Telecommunication, Inc.

26 East Park Avenue, Suite 240

Long Beach, NY 11561

Orders: (800) 60-MORSE

Tech Support: (516) 889-8610

Fax: (516) 889-8665

E-mail: Linux@morse.net

Linux Systems Labs

Linux Systems Labs

18300 Tara Drive

Clinton Twp., MI 48036

Phone: (800) 432-0556

E-mail: dirvin@vela.acs.oakland.edu

Sequoia International Motif Development Package

Sequoia International, Inc.

600 West Hillsboro Blvd., Suite 300

Deerfield Beach, FL 33441

Phone: (305) 480-6118

Takelap Systems Ltd.

The Reddings

Court Robin Lane, Llangwm

Usk, Gwent, United Kingdom NP5 1ET

Phone: +44 (0)291 650357

E-mail: info@ddrive.demon.co.uk

Trans-Ameritech Linux Plus BSD CD-ROM

Trans-Ameritech Enterprises, Inc.

2342A Walsh Ave.

Santa Clara, CA 95051

Phone: (408) 727-3883

E-mail: roman@trans-ameritech.com

Caldera OpenLinux

Caldera Inc.

633 South 550 East

Provo, UT 84606

Phone: (801) 377-7687

E-mail: info@caldera.com

Web: http://www.caldera.com

The Linux Documentation Project

The Linux Documentation Project is a loose team of writers, proofreaders, and editors who are working on a set of definitive Linux manuals. The overall coordinator of the project is Matt Welsh, aided by Lars Wirzenius and Michael K. Johnson.

Welsh maintains a Linux home page on the World Wide Web at `http://sunsite.unc.edu/mdw/linux.html`.

They encourage anyone who wants to help to join them in developing any Linux documentation. If you have Internet email access, you can join the DOC channel of the Linux-Activists mailing list by sending mail to `linux-activists-request@ niksula.hut.fi` with the following line as the first line of the message body:

```
X-Mn-Admin: join DOC
```

Feel free to get in touch with the author and coordinator of this manual if you have questions, postcards, money, or ideas. Welsh can be reached via Internet email at `mdw@sunsite.unc.edu` or at the following address:

205 Gray Street
Wilson, NC 27893

The GNU General Public License

IN THIS APPENDIX

APPENDIX D

Linux is licensed under the GNU General Public License (the GPL or copyleft), which is reproduced here to clear up some of the confusion about Linux's copyright status.

Linux is not shareware, nor is it in the public domain. The bulk of the Linux kernel has been copyrighted since 1993 by Linus Torvalds, and other software and parts of the kernel are copyrighted by their authors. Thus, Linux is copyrighted.

However, you may redistribute it under the terms of the GPL, which follows.

GNU GENERAL PUBLIC LICENSE, Version 2, June 1991

Copyright 1989, 1991
Free Software Foundation, Inc.
675 Mass Ave,
Cambridge, MA 02139
USA

Everyone is permitted to copy and distribute verbatim copies of this license document, but changing it is not allowed.

E.1 Preamble

The licenses for most software are designed to take away your freedom to share and change it. By contrast, the GNU General Public License is intended to guarantee your freedom to share and change free software—to make sure the software is free for all its users. This General Public License applies to most of the Free Software Foundation's software and to any other program whose authors commit to using it. (Some other Free Software Foundation software is covered by the GNU Library General Public License as well.)

You can apply it to your programs, too.

When we speak of free software, we are referring to freedom, not price. Our General Public Licenses are designed to make sure that you have the freedom to distribute copies of free software (and charge for this service if you wish), that you receive source code or can get it if you want it, that you can change the software or use pieces of it in new free programs; and that you know you can do these things.

To protect your rights, we need to make restrictions that forbid anyone to deny you these rights or to ask you to surrender the rights.

These restrictions translate to certain responsibilities for you if you distribute copies of the software or if you modify it.

For example, if you distribute copies of such a program, whether gratis or for a fee, you must give the recipients all the rights that you have. You must make sure that they, too, receive or can obtain the source code. And you must show them these terms so they know their rights.

We protect your rights with two steps:

1. Copyright the software.
2. Offer you this license, which gives you legal permission to copy, distribute, and/or modify the software.

Also, for each author's protection and ours, we want to make certain that everyone understands that there is no warranty for this free software. If the software is modified by someone else and passed on, we want its recipients to know that what they have is not the original, so that any problems introduced by others will not reflect on the original authors' reputations.

Finally, any free program is threatened constantly by software patents. We wish to avoid the danger that redistributors of a free program will individually obtain patent licenses, in effect making the program proprietary. To prevent this, we have made it clear that any patent must be licensed for free use or not licensed at all.

The precise terms and conditions for copying, distribution, and modification follow.

E.2.GNU General Public License: Terms and Conditions for Copying, Distributing, and Modifying

This License applies to any program or other work which contains a notice placed by the copyright holder saying it may be distributed under the terms of this General Public License. The "Program," below, refers to any such program or work, and "a work based on the Program" means either the Program or any derivative work under copyright law: that is to say, a work containing the Program or a portion of it, either verbatim or with modifications and/or translated into another language. (Hereinafter, translation is included without limitation in the term "modification.") Each licensee is addressed as "you."

Activities other than copying, distribution, and modification are not covered by this License; they are outside its scope. The act of running the Program is not restricted, and the output from the Program is covered only if its contents constitute a work based on the Program (independent of having been made by running the Program).

Whether that is true depends on what the Program does:

1. You may copy and distribute verbatim copies of the Program's source code as you receive it, in any medium, provided that you conspicuously and appropriately publish on each copy an appropriate copyright notice and disclaimer of warranty; keep intact all the notices that refer to this License and to the absence of any warranty; and give any other recipients of the Program a copy of this License along with the Program.

   You may charge a fee for the physical act of transferring a copy, and you may at your option offer warranty protection in exchange for a fee.

2. You may modify your copy or copies of the Program or any portion of it, thus forming a work based on the Program, and copy and distribute such modifications or work under the terms of Section 1 above, provided that you also meet all of these conditions:

   a. You must cause the modified files to carry prominent notices stating that you changed the files and the date of any change.

   b. You must cause any work that you distribute or publish, that in whole or in part contains or is derived from the Program or any part thereof, to be licensed as a whole at no charge to all third parties under the terms of this License.

   c. If the modified program normally reads commands interactively when run, you must cause it, when started running for such interactive use in the most ordinary way, to print or display an announcement including an appropriate copyright notice and a notice that there is no warranty (or else saying that you provide a warranty) and that users may redistribute the program under these conditions, and telling the user how to view a copy of this License. (Exception: if the Program itself is interactive but does not normally print such an announcement, your work based on the Program is not required to print an announcement.)

These requirements apply to the modified work as a whole. If identifiable sections of that work are not derived from the Program, and can be reasonably considered independent and separate works in themselves, then this License, and its terms, do not apply to those sections when you distribute them as separate works. But when you distribute the same sections as part of a whole which is a work based on the

Program, the distribution of the whole must be on the terms of this License, whose permissions for other licensees extend to the entire whole, and thus to each and every part regardless of who wrote it.

Thus, it is not the intent of this section to claim rights or contest your rights to work written entirely by you; rather, the intent is to exercise the right to control the distribution of derivative or collective works based on the Program.

In addition, mere aggregation of another work not based on the Program with the Program (or with a work based on the Program) on a volume of a storage or distribution medium does not bring the other work under the scope of this License.

3. You may copy and distribute the Program (or a work based on it, under Section 2) in object code or executable form under the terms of Sections 1 and 2 above provided that you also do one of the following:

   a. Accompany it with the complete corresponding machine-readable source code, which must be distributed under the terms of Sections 1 and 2 above on a medium customarily used for software interchange; or,

   b. Accompany it with a written offer, valid for at least three years, to give any third party, for a charge no more than your cost of physically performing source distribution, a complete machine-readable copy of the corresponding source code, to be distributed under the terms of Sections 1 and 2 above on a medium customarily used for software interchange; or,

   c. Accompany it with the information you received as to the offer to distribute corresponding source code. (This alternative is allowed only for noncommercial distribution and only if you received the program in object code or executable form with such an offer, in accord with Subsection b above.)

The source code for a work means the preferred form of the work for making modifications to it. For an executable work, complete source code means all the source code for all modules it contains, plus any associated interface definition files, plus the scripts used to control compilation and installation of the executable. However, as a special exception, the source code distributed need not include anything that is normally distributed (in either source or binary form) with the major components (compiler, kernel, and so on) of the operating system on which the executable runs, unless that component itself accompanies the executable.

If distribution of executable or object code is made by offering access to copy from a designated place, then offering equivalent access to copy the source code from the same place counts as distribution of the source code, even though third parties are not compelled to copy the source along with the object code.

4. You may not copy, modify, sublicense, or distribute the Program except as expressly provided under this License. Any attempt otherwise to copy, modify, sublicense or distribute the Program is void, and will automatically terminate your rights under this License. However, parties who have received copies, or rights, from you under this License will not have their licenses terminated so long as such parties remain in full compliance.

5. You are not required to accept this License, since you have not signed it. However, nothing else grants you permission to modify or distribute the Program or its derivative works. These actions are prohibited by law if you do not accept this License. Therefore, by modifying or distributing the Program (or any work based on the Program), you indicate your acceptance of this License to do so, and all its terms and conditions for copying, distributing or modifying the Program or works based on it.

6. Each time you redistribute the Program (or any work based on the Program), the recipient automatically receives a license from the original licenser to copy, distribute or modify the Program subject to these terms and conditions. You may not impose any further restrictions on the recipients' exercise of the rights granted herein. You are not responsible for enforcing compliance by third parties to this License.

7. If, as a consequence of a court judgment or allegation of patent infringement or for any other reason (not limited to patent issues), conditions are imposed on you (whether by court order, agreement or otherwise) that contradict the conditions of this License, they do not excuse you from the conditions of this License. If you cannot distribute so as to satisfy simultaneously your obligations under this License and any other pertinent obligations, then as a consequence you may not distribute the Program at all. For example, if a patent license would not permit royalty-free redistribution of the Program by all those who receive copies directly or indirectly through you, then the only way you could satisfy both it and this License would be to refrain entirely from distribution of the Program.

If any portion of this section is held invalid or unenforceable under any particular circumstance, the balance of the section is intended to apply and the section as a whole is intended to apply in other circumstances.

It is not the purpose of this section to induce you to infringe any patents or other property right claims or to contest validity of any such claims; this section has the sole purpose of protecting the integrity of the free software distribution system, which is implemented by public license practices. Many people have made generous contributions to the wide range of software distributed through that system in reliance on consistent application of that system; it is up to the author/donor to decide if he or she is willing to distribute software through any other system and a licensee cannot impose that choice.

This section is intended to make thoroughly clear what is believed to be a consequence of the rest of this License.

8. If the distribution and/or use of the Program is restricted in certain countries either by patents or by copyrighted interfaces, the original copyright holder who places the Program under this License may add an explicit geographical distribution limitation excluding those countries, so that distribution is permitted only in or among countries not thus excluded. In such case, this License incorporates the limitation as if written in the body of this License.

9. The Free Software Foundation may publish revised and/or new versions of the General Public License from time to time. Such new versions will be similar in spirit to the present version, but may differ in detail to address new problems or concerns.

   Each version is given a distinguishing version number. If the Program specifies a version number of this License which applies to it and "any later version," you have the option of following the terms and conditions either of that version or of any later version published by the Free Software Foundation. If the Program does not specify a version number of this License, you may choose any version ever published by the Free Software Foundation.

10. If you wish to incorporate parts of the Program into other free programs whose distribution conditions are different, write to the author to ask for permission. For software which is copyrighted by the Free Software Foundation, write to the Free Software Foundation; we sometimes make exceptions for this. Our decision will be guided by the two goals of preserving the free status of all derivatives of our free software and of promoting the sharing and reuse of software generally.

    NO WARRANTY

11. BECAUSE THE PROGRAM IS LICENSED FREE OF CHARGE, THERE IS NO WARRANTY FOR THE PROGRAM, TO THE EXTENT PERMITTED BY APPLICABLE LAW. EXCEPT WHEN OTHERWISE STATED IN WRITING, THE COPYRIGHT HOLDERS AND/OR OTHER PARTIES PROVIDE THE PROGRAM "AS IS" WITHOUT WARRANTY OF ANY KIND, EITHER EXPRESSED OR IMPLIED, INCLUDING, BUT NOT LIMITED TO, THE IMPLIED WARRANTIES OF MERCHANTABILITY AND FITNESS FOR A PARTICULAR PURPOSE. THE ENTIRE RISK AS TO THE QUALITY AND PERFORMANCE OF THE PROGRAM IS WITH YOU. SHOULD THE PROGRAM PROVE DEFECTIVE, YOU ASSUME THE COST OF ALL NECESSARY SERVICING, REPAIR, OR CORRECTION.

12. IN NO EVENT, UNLESS REQUIRED BY APPLICABLE LAW OR AGREED TO IN WRITING, WILL ANY COPYRIGHT HOLDER, OR ANY OTHER PARTY WHO MAY MODIFY AND/OR REDISTRIBUTE THE PROGRAM AS PERMITTED ABOVE, BE LIABLE TO YOU FOR DAMAGES, INCLUDING ANY GENERAL, SPECIAL, INCIDENTAL, OR CONSEQUENTIAL DAMAGES ARISING OUT OF THE USE OR INABILITY TO USE THE PROGRAM (INCLUDING BUT NOT LIMITED TO LOSS OF DATA OR DATA BEING RENDERED INACCURATE OR LOSSES SUSTAINED BY YOU OR THIRD PARTIES OR A FAILURE OF THE PROGRAM TO OPERATE WITH ANY OTHER PROGRAMS), EVEN IF SUCH HOLDER OR OTHER PARTY HAS BEEN ADVISED OF THE POSSIBILITY OF SUCH DAMAGES.

END OF TERMS AND CONDITIONS

How to Apply These Terms to Your New Programs

If you develop a new program and you want it to be of the greatest possible use to the public, the best way to achieve this is to make it free software that everyone can redistribute and change under these terms.

To do so, attach the following notices to the program. It is safest to attach them to the start of each source file to most effectively convey the exclusion of warranty. Each file should have at least the "copyright" line and a pointer to where the full notice is found:

```
<one line to give the program's name and a brief idea of what it does.>
    Copyright (C) 19yy  <name of author>
```

```
This program is free software; you can redistribute it and/or modify it
under the terms of the GNU General Public License as published by the Free
Software Foundation; either version 2 of the License, or (at your option)
any later version.
```

```
This program is distributed in the hope that it will be useful, but
WITHOUT ANY WARRANTY; without even the implied warranty of MERCHANTABILITY
or FITNESS FOR A PARTICULAR PURPOSE. See the GNU General Public License
for more details. You should have received a copy of the GNU General
Public License along with this program; if not, write to the Free Software
Foundation, Inc., 675 Mass Ave, Cambridge, MA 02139, USA.
```

Also add information on how to contact you by electronic and paper mail.

If the program is interactive, make it output a short notice like this when it starts in an interactive mode:

```
Gnomovision version 69, Copyright (C) 19yy name of author Gnomovision
comes with ABSOLUTELY NO WARRANTY; for details type '  show w'  . This is
free software, and you are welcome to redistribute it under certain
conditions; type '  show c' for details.
```

The hypothetical commands "show w" and "show c" should show the appropriate parts of the General Public License. Of course, the commands you use may be called something other than ' "show w" and "show c"; they could even be mouse-clicks or menu items—whatever suits your program.

You should also get your employer (if you work as a programmer) or your school, if any, to sign a "copyright disclaimer" for the program, if necessary. Here is a sample; alter the names:

> *Yoyodyne, Inc., hereby disclaims all copyright interest in the program "Gnomovision" (which makes passes at compilers), written by James Hacker.*
>
> *actual signature, 1 April 1998*
>
> *Ty Coon, President of V.*

This General Public License does not permit incorporating your program into proprietary programs. If your program is a subroutine library, you may consider it more useful to permit linking proprietary applications with the library. If this is what you want to do, use the GNU Library General Public License instead of this License.

D
THE GNU
GENERAL PUBLIC
LICENSE

APPENDIX E

Copyright Information

The Linux kernel is Copyright 1991, 1992, 1993, 1994 Linus Torvalds (others hold copyrights on some of the drivers, file systems, and other parts of the kernel) and is licensed under the terms of the GNU General Public License (see COPYING in /usr/src/linux).

Many other software packages included in Slackware are licensed under the GNU General Public License, which is included in the file COPYING.

This product includes software developed by the University of California, Berkeley and its contributors:

Copyright (c) 1980, 1983, 1986, 1988, 1990, 1991 The Regents of the University of California. All rights reserved.

Redistribution and use in source and binary forms, with or without modification, are permitted, provided that the following conditions are met:

1. Redistributions of source code must retain the above copyright notice, this list of conditions, and the following disclaimer.

2. Redistributions in binary form must reproduce the above copyright notice, this list of conditions, and the following disclaimer in the documentation and/or other materials provided with the distribution.

3. All advertising materials mentioning features or use of this software must display the following acknowledgment:

   This product includes software developed by the University of California, Berkeley and its contributors.

4. Neither the name of the university nor the names of its contributors may be used to endorse or promote products derived from this software without specific prior written permission.

THIS SOFTWARE IS PROVIDED BY THE REGENTS AND CONTRIBUTORS "AS IS" AND ANY EXPRESS OR IMPLIED WARRANTIES, INCLUDING, BUT NOT LIMITED TO, THE IMPLIED WARRANTIES OF MERCHANTABILITY AND FITNESS FOR A PARTICULAR PURPOSE ARE DISCLAIMED. IN NO EVENT SHALL THE REGENTS OR CONTRIBUTORS BE LIABLE FOR ANY DIRECT, INDIRECT, INCIDENTAL, SPECIAL, EXEMPLARY, OR CONSEQUENTIAL DAMAGES (INCLUDING, BUT NOT LIMITED TO, PROCUREMENT OF SUBSTITUTE GOODS OR SERVICES; LOSS OF USE, DATA, OR PROFITS; OR BUSINESS INTERRUPTION) HOWEVER CAUSED AND ON ANY THEORY OF LIABILITY, WHETHER IN CONTRACT, STRICT LIABILITY, OR TORT (INCLUDING NEGLIGENCE OR OTHERWISE) ARISING IN ANY WAY OUT OF THE USE OF THIS SOFTWARE, EVEN IF ADVISED OF THE POSSIBILITY OF SUCH DAMAGE.

The Slackware distribution contains Info-ZIP's compression utilities. Info-ZIP's software (Zip, UnZip, and related utilities) is free and can be obtained as source code or executables from various anonymous-FTP sites, including `ftp.uu.net:/pub/archiving/zip/*`. This software is provided free—there are no extra or hidden charges resulting from the use of this compression code. Thanks Info-ZIP! :^)

Zip/Unzip source can also be found in the `slackware_source/a/base` directory.

The Slackware Installation scripts are Copyright 1993, 1994, Patrick Volkerding, Moorhead, Minnesota, USA. All rights reserved.

Redistribution and use of this software, with or without modification, is permitted provided that the following conditions are met:

1. Redistributions of this software must retain the above copyright notice, this list of conditions, and the following disclaimer.

THIS SOFTWARE IS PROVIDED BY THE AUTHOR "AS IS" AND ANY EXPRESS OR IMPLIED WARRANTIES, INCLUDING, BUT NOT LIMITED TO, THE IMPLIED WARRANTIES OF MERCHANTABILITY AND FITNESS FOR A PARTICULAR PURPOSE ARE DISCLAIMED. IN NO EVENT SHALL THE AUTHOR BE LIABLE FOR ANY DIRECT, INDIRECT, INCIDENTAL, SPECIAL, EXEMPLARY, OR CONSEQUENTIAL DAMAGES (INCLUDING, BUT NOT LIMITED TO, PROCUREMENT OF SUBSTITUTE GOODS OR SERVICES; LOSS OF USE, DATA, OR PROFITS; OR BUSINESS INTERRUPTION) HOWEVER CAUSED AND ON ANY THEORY OF LIABILITY, WHETHER IN CONTRACT, STRICT LIABILITY, OR TORT (INCLUDING NEGLIGENCE OR OTHERWISE) ARISING IN ANY WAY OUT OF THE USE OF THIS SOFTWARE, EVEN IF ADVISED OF THE POSSIBILITY OF SUCH DAMAGE.

Slackware is a trademark of Patrick Volkerding. Permission to use the Slackware trademark to refer to the Slackware distribution of Linux is hereby granted if the following conditions are met:

1. In order to be called "Slackware," the distribution may not be altered from the way it appears on the central FTP site (`ftp.cdrom.com`). This is to protect the integrity, reliability, and reputation of the Slackware distribution. Anyone wishing to distribute an altered version must have the changes approved by `volkerdi@ftp.cdrom.com` (in other words, certified to be reasonably bug-free). If the changed distribution meets the required standards for quality, then written permission to use the Slackware trademark will be provided.

2. All related source code must be included. (This is also required by the GNU General Public License.)

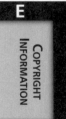

E

COPYRIGHT INFORMATION

3. Except by written permission, the Slackware trademark may not be used as (or as part of) a product name or company name. Note that you can still redistribute a distribution that doesn't meet these criteria; you just can't call it "Slackware." Personally, I hate restricting things in any way, but these restrictions are not designed to make life difficult for anyone. I just want to make sure that bugs are not added to commercial redistributions of Slackware. They have been in the past, and the resulting requests for help have flooded my mailbox! I'm just trying to make sure that I have some recourse when something like that happens.

Any questions about this policy should be directed to Patrick Volkerding <volkerdi@ftp.cdrom.com>.

Copyright notice for XView3.2-X11R6:

©Copyright 1989, 1990, 1991 Sun Microsystems, Inc. Sun design patents pending in the U.S. and foreign countries. OPEN LOOK is a trademark of USL. Used by written permission of the owners.©

©Copyright Bigelow & Holmes 1986, 1985. Lucida is a registered trademark of Bigelow & Holmes. Permission to use the Lucida trademark is hereby granted only in association with the images and fonts described in this file.

SUN MICROSYSTEMS, INC., USL, AND BIGELOW & HOLMES MAKE NO REPRESENTATIONS ABOUT THE SUITABILITY OF THIS SOURCE CODE FOR ANY PURPOSE. IT IS PROVIDED "AS IS" WITHOUT EXPRESS OR IMPLIED WARRANTY OF ANY KIND. SUN MICROSYSTEMS, INC., USL AND BIGELOW & HOLMES, SEVERALLY AND INDIVIDUALLY, DISCLAIM ALL WARRANTIES WITH REGARD TO THIS SOURCE CODE, INCLUDING ALL IMPLIED WARRANTIES OF MERCHANTABILITY AND FITNESS FOR A PARTICULAR PURPOSE. IN NO EVENT SHALL SUN MICROSYSTEMS, INC., USL OR BIGELOW & HOLMES BE LIABLE FOR ANY SPECIAL, INDIRECT, INCIDENTAL, OR CONSEQUENTIAL DAMAGES, OR ANY DAMAGES WHATSOEVER RESULTING FROM LOSS OF USE, DATA OR PROFITS, WHETHER IN AN ACTION OF CONTRACT, NEGLIGENCE OR OTHER TORTIOUS ACTION, ARISING OUT OF OR IN CONNECTION WITH THE USE OR PERFORMANCE OF THIS SOURCE CODE.

***Various other copyrights apply. See the documentation accompanying the software packages for full details.

Although every effort has been made to provide a complete source tree for this project, it's possible that something may have been forgotten. If you discover anything is missing, we will provide copies—just ask!

> **NOTE**
>
> We are required to provide any missing source to GPLed software for three years, per the following section (E.2.3.b) of the GNU General Public License.

b. *Accompany it with a written offer, valid for at least three years, to give any third party, for a charge no more than your cost of physically performing source distribution, a complete machine-readable copy of the corresponding source code, to be distributed under the terms of Sections 1 and 2 above on a medium customarily used for software interchange.*

Furthermore, if you find something is missing (even if you don't need a copy), please point it out to `volkerdi@ftp.cdrom.com` so it can be fixed.

What's on the CD-ROM?

On the *Linux Unleashed, Third Edition* CD, you will find Red Hat 5.1 Linux.

Award-Winning Operating System

Chosen by Infoworld as the Desktop Operating System product of the Year two years in a row, the Red Hat Linux Operating System continues to widen its lead over alternative OSs for users needing a reliable, secure, and high-performance computer environment on their desktop and server PCs.

Desktop Environment

With Red Hat Linux 5.1, you gain the freedom you want on your desktop. Choose from multiple window managers. Get on the Net, build some programs, and format floppy disks (all at the same time), and enjoy an extremely stable operating system that multi-tasks more smoothly than other OSs. Systems running Red Hat Linux are able to run continuously for months on end.

Internet Server

Right out of the box, Red Hat Linux can provide Internet services, including Web, email, news, DNS, and more, for multiple sites, with real virtual hosting. With RPM (Red Hat Package Manager), you can keep your systems up-to-date with the latest security releases and install new software with a single command. RPM can help system security by letting you see what files on your system have changed.

Learning Platform

With full source code (except for commercial apps), what could be a better learning platform? Learn how an operating system works from the ground up. Red Hat Linux comes complete with C, C++, F77 compilers, programming languages (python, perl, Tcl/Tk, scheme0), and tools for math- and engineering-related applications (spice, GNUplot, xfing). The Apache server provides a platform for learning CGI programming and HTML authoring.

About the Software

Please read all documentation associated with a third-party product (usually contained with files named readme.txt or license.txt) and follow all guidelines.

INDEX

SYMBOLS

T

Y-Z

By opening this package, you are agreeing to be bound by the following agreement:

Some of the programs included with this product are governed by the GNU General Public License, which allows redistribution; see the license information for each product for more information. Other programs are included on the CD-ROM by special permission from their authors.

You may not copy or redistribute the entire CD-ROM as a whole. The copying and redistribution of individual software programs on the CD-ROM is governed by terms set by individual copyright holders. The installer and code from the author(s) are copyrighted by the publisher and the author. Individual programs and other items on the CD-ROM are copyrighted by their various authors or other copyright holders. This software is sold as is without warranty of any kind, either expressed or implied, including but not limited to the implied warranties of merchantability and fitness for a particular purpose. Neither the publisher nor its dealers or distributors assumes any liability for any alleged or actual damages arising from the use of this program. (Some states do not allow for the exclusion of implied warranties, so the exclusion may not apply to you.)

NOTE

This CD-ROM uses long and mixed-case filenames requiring the use of a protected-mode CD-ROM Driver.